THIRD EDITION

FOR SALE

Economics & Consumer
DECISIONS

Michael L. Walden
Jessie X. Fan

Kendall Hunt
publishing company

Cover image © Shutterstock, Inc.

This book was previously published by Prentice-Hall, Inc.

Copyright © 2001 by Michael Walden
          2013 by Michael Walden and Jessie X. Fan

ISBN 978-1-4652-2538-2

Printed in the United States of America
10 9 8 7 6 5 4 3 2

To Michael's wife, Mary, and Jessie's husband, Randy, for your constant support, encouragement, and partnership.

CONTENTS

3 Organizing Your Financial Life 121

4 Shelter 193

5 **Buying Consumer Durables and Using Credit 283**

6 **Life Insurance 359**

ABOUT THE AUTHORS

Dr. Michael L. Walden has spent thirty-five years as an educator in the classroom, among his colleagues, and in thousands of meetings to residents of North Carolina. Walden received his Ph.D. from Cornell University and has been at North Carolina State University his entire career. He currently is a William Neal Reynolds Distinguished Professor in the Dept. of Agricultural and Resource Economics. The author of eight books and over 250 articles and reports, Walden presents daily radio programs, a monthly radio call-in program, and writes a biweekly newspaper column—in addition to his classroom teaching. Among Walden's numerous awards are the Champion-Tuck Award for quality in broadcasting, several American Council on Consumer Interests research awards, and the University of North Carolina Board of Governor's Award for Excellence in Public Service. In 2013 he was made a member of the Order of the Long Leaf Pine by North Carolina Governor Perdue.

Dr. Jessie X. Fan received her Ph.D from The Ohio State University in Family and Consumer Economics in 1993 and her Master's degree from Fudan University in China in International Economics in 1989. Since 1993 she has been at the University of Utah where she is a Professor in the Department of Family and Consumer Studies. Dr. Fan has taught many courses related to family and consumer economics, including consumer economic theory, family economic issues across the life span, family investment planning, tax planning, and families and economic policies. She served as the director of the Certified Financial Planning program at the University of Utah. Dr. Fan's research focuses on consumer expenditure behaviors, financial management, and consumer health issues. She has published many research articles in academic journals, and serves on the editorial board for four journals in the consumer and family economics field, including the Journal of Consumer Affairs and the Journal of Families and Economic Issues. She has also served on the Utah State's Child Support Guidelines Committee for many years.

ACKNOWLEDGMENTS

We would like to thank Jessie's colleagues in the Department of Family and Consumer Studies at the University of Utah and Michael's colleagues in the Department of Agricultural and Resource Economics at North Carolina State University, for their encouragement and support for us to undertake the third revision of this book.

The wonderful staff at Kendall Hunt Publishing deserve hearty thanks for their professionalism, promptness, and overall support of the project.

Last, none of this work would have been possible without the inspiration and love of Michael's wife Mary and Jessie's husband Randy and two boys: Benning and Benvin.

PREFACE TO THE THIRD EDITION

Over our lifetime we face thousands of economic decisions, from what kind of mortgage to tate, to whether to invest in a CD or a mutual fund, to whether it pays to clip coupons. These are economic decisions because they involve using our limited resources—money and time—in ways that are most beneficial to our self interest. Too often we rely on other people—realtors, insurance agents, stock brokers—who may not have our interests at heart, to make our economic decisions.

Economics—"yuk" you might say—is this a book with a lot of curves (supply and demand curves) and theoretical, yet unpractical, concepts? Unfortunately this is the reputation that economics has with many students and the general population.

Well, you're in for a surprise. Economics can be a big help in making practical financial and consumer decisions. *Economics and Consumer Decisions* brings economic theory and concepts out of the ivory tower and into the hands of everyday people. *Economics and Consumer Decisions* shows how economics can be used to help make the multitude of financial and consumer decisions we face, and it gives answers, rather than generalities, to many of the decisions. *Economics and Consumer Decisions* will equip you with the practical tools of economic analysis so that you can intelligently, and on your own, address questions such as what mortgage is best, how much life insurance do you need, and when should you buy a new car. In fact, after reading this book, you'll probably decide that economics is indispensable in making everyday decisions.

Special Features of the Text

Economics and Consumer Decisions has many special features which set it apart from other personal finance and consumer economics texts.

- *Economics and Consumer Decisions* goes beyond general and superficial coverage to provide in-depth analysis of consumer decisions. In many cases, specific answers are given for common consumer situations. For example, most books devote one or two paragraphs to the fixed vs. adjustable rate mortgage question. *Economics and Consumer Decisions* devotes seven pages and makes specific recommendations.
- Topics are in the form of questions. This is done (1) to stimulate reader interest, (2) to help the reader find responses and answers to common questions and (3) because, quite frankly, most non-experts think of financial issues in the form of questions.

- Concepts are developed from an intuitive basis rather than simply stated. For example, most texts simply give a formula or table for calculating mortgage payments. This leaves the reader able to calculate mortgage payments, but ignorant of their real meaning. *Economics and Consumer Decisions* does both. It shows readers that mortgage payments are derived from the idea that the present value sum of mortgage payments equals the mortgage loan amount. The reader is then given a formula and tables based on this idea which can be used to make payment calculations. In this way mortgage payments don't spring from some unknown financial relationship, but from a concept which the reader already intuitively understands.

- The mistakes of "pop personal finance" books are exposed. Few personal finance issues have simple, direct answers, yet many "popular" personal finance texts give simple answers. For example, many popular personal finance texts imply that everyone should own a house; that you should always pay cash rather than use credit, and that there is a way to "beat the stock market." All of these assertions are wrong. In *Economics and Consumer Decisions* there is no superficial "fluff" or "cop-outs." All decisions are developed in a logical and straightforward manner. It is shown why not everyone will make the same kind of choices.

- Several topics ignored in other texts, but which are very important to consumer decision-making, are included in *Economics and Consumer Decisions*. Concepts such as future value, discounting, and annuities, are presented in an easy-to-understand manner in Chapter 1. These concepts are introduced early because they are crucial to understanding many consumer decisions. The importance of the national economy to consumer decisions is brought home to the reader. Chapter 2 presents the national, or macro, economic concepts and issues most important to consumers. The effects of these concepts on consumer decisions are also developed throughout the text. A good example is the concept of economic cycles, and their importance to mortgage financing and investing. An entire chapter on shopping and information-gathering is included. The new edition includes an update to 2000 for all government data including inflation rates, purchasing power adjustments, and tax rules. The edition also includes several new sections devoted to decisions about personal educational and training investments, fertility, and marriage/divorce.

In short, *Economics and Consumer Decisions* finally weds economic and financial concepts to practical consumer decision-making to produce a book which will serve both as a text and a lifetime reference.

Who Can Use This Book?

Economics and Consumer Decisions is appropriate for undergraduate or graduate courses in personal finance, consumer economics, family economics, or personal decision-making. No previous knowledge of economics or finance is required. No special mathematical knowledge, other than the ability to do simple arithmetic calculations, is required. The text is self-contained and can be used by students and other interested readers.

Pedagogical Aids

Economics and Consumer Decisions is "user-friendly" and offers a number of pedagogical learning aids:

- The material is organized into eleven broad chapters, each chapter including numerous topics. Topics are titled in the form of questions. Each topic then addresses, analyzes, and answers the question.
- Each topic concludes with "THE BOTTOM LINE," a succinct summary, or lesson, of the topic.
- Keywords and key phrases are given in margins.
- Tables and figures are liberally used.
- Each chapter includes many "CONSUMER TOPICS." Each CONSUMER TOPIC addresses a consumer issue, problem, or application in more depth or presents results of relevant consumer research. CONSUMER TOPICS are set apart from the text material.
- Each chapter ends with four sections designed to reinforce the student's understanding of the text material.
  —Words and concepts you should know
  —A summary in detailed outline form for assistance in studying
  —Discussion questions
  —Problems

CHAPTER 1

Microfoundations: Concepts for Making Consumer Decisions

Introduction

You are about to plunge into the world of *practical* economics. This chapter will introduce you to (and make you an expert in!) economic concepts which are useful in making practical personal finance and consumer decisions. In fact, we will claim that you can't make wise personal finance decisions without knowledge of these concepts.

This chapter deals with economic concepts related to the individual, so-called "microeconomics." Not all microeconomic concepts are discussed. Only those concepts which are most relevant to personal decision-making are explored.

You'll learn many useful ideas in this chapter, but perhaps the most important idea is discounting. The concept of discounting simply asserts that a dollar in the future is worth less than a dollar today. Discounting will show you how to convert future dollars in such a way that they are comparable to present dollars. Discounting is critically important when analyzing any consumer decision which involves costs and/or benefits over time. Also, you must understand discounting in order to understand how any consumer loan, like a mortgage or auto loan, is set up.

And now, as they say, "away we go!"

1. Are Prices "Really" What They Seem?

Economic decisions, whether they relate to consumers or to firms, revolve around prices. For consumers, the price of a product measures the amount of resources (money) which the consumer must give up to purchase the product.

What could be easier than understanding prices? Simply look at the price posted or listed on a car, house, dress, or hammer and that's what you must pay to buy the product.

LIST PRICE   For many consumer products this is true. But for many other consumer products, especially so-called consumer durable products (cars, homes, furniture), the list price is only part of the total price. For these products, the total price is paid over a number of years, and usually includes finance costs (e.g., mortgage or loan), fuel costs, and maintenance and repair costs. As will be seen, this complicates your task in deciding whether purchasing the product is worth the price.

You must also be careful in comparing the prices of many financial products. Life insurance is a good example. The annual price paid for one type of life insurance policy, called whole life insurance, purchases both protection and an investment fund. In contrast, annual prices paid for another type of policy, called a term policy, purchases only protection. Since the price paid in each case is purchasing different things, the annual price can't be used to compare the cost of the policies.

Prices: One Time and Over Time

Time can play tricks with us, and it's no different in economics. Dealing with time in economics is a very important task.

Time can play tricks with prices. When examining and comparing prices at *one point in time*, there's no problem. You can come to conclusions about the prices of one product compared to another product very easily. For example, let's say the price of pork is $2.00 per pound today and the price of ground beef is $1.75 per pound today. These prices are **NOMINAL PRICE** nominal prices today.

In the above example you can readily say that the price of pork is *relatively* more expensive than the price of beef. In fact, you can construct the *relative* price of pork compared to beef. Here, let the price of beef be indexed at the 1.00, and then let the price of pork be $\frac{\$2.00}{\$1.75}$ or 1.14. The relative price of one product compared to another compares the prices free of any money units. Simply choose the product with the lowest price and assign it the value 1.00. Then the relative price of more expensive products show how much more expensive, on a percentage basis, the other products are compared to the lowest priced product. Table 1-1 gives you some more examples.

INCREASE/DECREASE IN RELATIVE PRICE Calculating relative prices is most helpful when looking at price changes over time. Most prices are always rising, so everything is becoming more expensive, right? Not necessarily. Prices change at different paces. Those prices increasing faster become *relatively* more expensive, while those prices increasing at a slower rate, or decreasing, become relatively less expensive. Products whose prices relatively increased are said to have had an increase in their *relative price*. Products whose prices have relatively decreased are said to have had a decrease in their relative price. Sometimes you will see the term "real price" substituted for "relative price."

Table 1-1   Calculating relative prices.

Product	Price Per Pound	Relative Price	Meaning
Pork	$2.00	$\frac{\$2.00}{\$1.75} = 1.14$	Pork is 14% more expensive per pound than beef.
Chicken	$2.20	$\frac{\$2.20}{\$1.75} = 1.26$	Chicken is 26% more expensive per pound than beef.
Ground Beef	$1.75	$\frac{\$1.75}{\$1.75} = 1.00$	Ground beef is the least expensive.

Table 1-2 gives examples of calculating changes in relative prices. A decision must first be made about what base to be used for the calculations. Two alternative bases are usually used, the Consumer Price Index (CPI) or the average hourly wage. The CPI is an index value which represents the average price of all consumer goods and services (more on the CPI later). The actual CPI index number has no meaning itself except that higher values mean average consumer prices are higher. The hourly wage, of course, does have intuitive meaning since it represents income derived from working an hour.

The left-most panel of Table 1-2 gives the nominal, or actual dollar, prices of four food products for 1990, 2000, and 2010, the CPI for each year, and the hourly wage. By just looking at these numbers, you'd conclude that all the food prices rose from 2000 to 2010, from 1990 to 2000 milk and bread became more expensive while eggs and steak became less expensive.

The second panel in Table 1-2 calculates relative prices using the CPI as the base. To get the numbers, simply divide the nominal price by the year's CPI (e.g., for eggs in 2000, 0.006 = $0.96/172.2). Look at the relative prices for steak in 1990 and 2010. Relative steak prices fell from 0.026 to 0.020. This means that, although steak price rose from $3.42/lb in 1990 to $4.30/lb in 2010, this was a *slower* increase than the increase in the average price for all consumer goods and services. Therefore, relatively speaking, steak actually became less expensive by 25 percent (the drop from 0.026 to 0.020 is a 25 percent fall). Looking at it another way, the increase in nominal steak prices from $3.42/lb to $4.30/lb was a 26 percent increase. But the increase in the CPI from 130.7 to 218.1 was a 69 percent increase. So steak increased in price less than half as much as the CPI increased.

You'll probably like the third panel of Table 1-2 better where relative prices are calculated using the average wage rate as a base. Again, divide the nominal price by the average wage rate for that year to get the relative price (e.g., for round steak in 2010, 0.231 = $4.30/$18.61). These values do have intuitive meaning because they represent the fraction of an hour necessary to work in order to buy the product. In fact, if the entries in this panel are multiplied by 60 minutes, then the result is the number of minutes that must be worked to purchase the product. These results are shown in the right-most panel of Table 1-2. Only milk became relatively more expensive between 1990 and 2010.

So What?

Why bother calculating changes in relative prices? It might be nice to know that a product hasn't increased in price as fast as other products or wages, but, big deal—if the price has increased, it still costs more.

THE "GOOD" OLD DAYS

There are two reasons why changes in relative prices are important. First, only by examining changes in relative prices can you decide how

Table 1-2 Calculating changes in relative prices.

Product	Nominal Prices			Relative Prices[a] (Using CPI as base)			Relative Prices[b] (Using wage rate base)			Minutes necessary to Work to Purchase Product[c]		
	1990	**2000**	**2010**	**1990**	**2000**	**2010**	**1990**	**2000**	**2010**	**1990**	**2000**	**2010**
Round steak, 1 lb.	$3.42	$3.28	$4.30	0.026	0.019	0.020	0.317	0.229	0.231	19	14	14
Fresh milk, 1 qt.	$1.39	$2.29	$3.32	0.011	0.013	0.015	0.129	0.160	0.178	8	10	11
Eggs, 1 doz.	$1.00	$0.96	$1.79	0.008	0.006	0.008	0.093	0.067	0.096	6	4	6
Bread, 1 loaf	$0.70	$0.99	$1.39	0.005	0.006	0.006	0.065	0.069	0.075	4	4	4
Consumer Price Index	130.7	172.2	218.1									
Average hourly wage in manufacturing	10.78	14.32	18.61									

[a]Nominal price divided by Consumer Price Index for that year.
[b]Nominal price divided by average hourly wage for that year.
[c]Relative price using wage rate as base multiplied by 60 minutes.
All nominal prices are national averages.

Data source: Statistical Abstract of the United States, various years.

your standard of living (or the standards of living of consumers in general), have changed. Think of it this way. All prices, wages, and incomes tend to increase over time. If you only looked at changes in nominal prices you'd think, "Wow, things are always getting more and more expensive—it sure was better in the good old days." This, in fact, is a false observation. Over most time periods wages and incomes have more than kept up with prices, meaning that average standards of living have increased. Another way of saving the same thing is that it has taken progressively less time for the average person to work to earn common consumer products.

But a more important reason for understanding relative prices is that it's relative prices that matter. A product has increased in price only if its relative price has increased. It's in your interest to judge the change in a product's price by the change in its *relative* price, not its nominal price. In fact, research shows that this is exactly what consumers do (see CONSUMER TOPIC: Do Consumers Respond to Relative Prices?).

DO CONSUMERS RESPOND TO RELATIVE PRICES?

C O N S U M E R T O P I C

What's important in predicting the quantity of a product which we'll buy is not how the product's nominal price has changed, but how it's changed relative to other prices.

The theory that relative prices matter has been most extensively tested for food products. A study by Eales and Unnevehr examined how consumers responded to changes in the relative prices of various meats over the period 1965–85. In this study Eales and Unnevehr examined the price change in a particular meat *relative* to changes in the average price of all foods. Here are some of their results:

An increase of 10% in the relative price of chicken results in a 2.8% *decline* in the quantity of whole chickens purchased, a 0.5% increase in the quantity of beef purchased, and a 0.1% increase in the quantity of pork purchased.

An increase of 10% in the relative price of beef results in a 5.7% *decline* in the quantity of hamburger purchased, a 2.5% increase in the quantity of chicken purchased, and a 3.1% increase in the quantity of pork purchased.

An increase of 10% in the relative price of pork results in a 7.6% *decline* in the quantity of pork purchased, a 1.7% increase in the quantity of beef purchased, and a 0.2% increase in the quantity of chicken purchased.

The results make sense. When the relative price of a meat product increases, consumers shift out of buying that product and instead buy substitute meats.

Reference: Eales, James S. and Laurian J. Unnevehr, "Demand for Beer and Chicken Products: Separability and Structural Change," *American Journal of Agricultural Economics*, Vol. 70, No. 3, August 1988, pp. 521–532.

The Bottom Line

Deciphering prices is not as easy as at first glance. The annual price of consumer durable goods, like homes and cars, includes finance, energy, and maintenance costs. Changes in relative prices should be used to judge what products have become more expensive and less expensive. Relative prices measure whether a product's price has increased faster or slower than all prices or average wages.

2. What's Your Time Worth?

You've heard the expression, "time is money." It's more than a cliche; it's an expression which has much economic meaning.

The reason that time has a value is because it is limited. There are only 24 hours in a day, 7 days in a week, and 365 days in a year, and 70 to 80 years in the average lifetime. You can't make more time or recover lost time. You use time to do everything—work, play, eat, sleep. Furthermore, when you're using time to do one activity (such as work), you can't use it to do something else (like sleep). There are always many alternative uses of time.

Pricing Your Time

Since time is a limited resource, and since time is a necessary input into any activity, time has a price. The price of your time in any activity depends on what else you could do with that time. For example, if an hour you spend watching TV could have been spent working, then the price of an hour of TV viewing is the wage rate (after taxes) less the pleasure you get from TV viewing over working. But if the hour you spend watching TV could have been used exercising, then the price of an hour of TV watching is the value you could have received from exercising less the immediate pleasure you receive from TV viewing over exercising.

The price of time therefore varies from individual to individual and activity to activity. As a rule of thumb, researchers have usually measured the value of time as a fraction of the individual's wage rate (see CONSUMER TOPIC: How Is the Value of Time Measured?). The fraction is higher the less the displeasure the individual gets from working, This means that professional workers probably value their time at VALUE OF TIME RELATED TO WAGE RATE a higher rate than other workers for two reasons. First, their wage rate is higher, and second, they probably enjoy their work more than non-professional workers.

HOW IS THE VALUE OF TIME MEASURED?

Researchers in two fields of economics have been interested in measuring the value of time. One field is transportation economics. Here the interest has been in measuring the value of time of commuters. Such studies have policy implications for efforts to encourage commuters to switch from autos to mass transit.

The transportation studies estimate commuters' value of time by observing what commuters are willing to pay for a faster mode of transportation. For example, researchers compare commuters' willingness to pay tolls in order to take a faster route, or compare the costs of a faster, yet more expensive, private auto to cheaper, yet more time-consuming, public transportation. These studies have concluded that commuters value their travel time at 20 to 70 percent of their wage rate.

Another area of interest to researchers is the value consumers place on their time spent in household chores (e.g., meal preparation, cleaning, yard work). Here researchers have used two alternative methods to estimate the value of time. One method is called the replacement cost approach. The replacement cost approach estimates the value of time in household work as the cost of hiring someone to get the work done. The other method is the opportunity cost approach. This method estimates the value of time in household work as the wage rate at which a person would just be indifferent between spending an hour in household work or spending an hour working on the job.

Zick and Bryant have estimated the value of time in household work using the opportunity cost approach.

Using a sample of 1,475 households in 11 states who completed time-use diaries, Zick and Bryant estimated the opportunity cost wage at $4.45/hr. for employed consumers and $3.95 for non-employed consumers. Inflated to 2012 the wages are $16.57 and $14.71 respectively.

References: Zick, Cathleen D. and W. Keith Bryant. "Alternative Strategies for Pricing Home Work Time," *Home Economics Research Journal*, Vol. 12, No. 2, December 1983, pp. 133–144.

Gronau, Reuben. "The Effect of Traveling Time on the Demand for Passenger Transportation," *Journal of Political Economy*, Vol. 78, No. 2, March/April 1970, pp. 377–394.

Dewees, D. N. "The Impact of Urban Transportation Investment on Land Value," *Research Report No. 11*, University of Toronto-York University Joint Program in Transportation, February 1973.

C O N S U M E R   T O P I C

Implications

SPENDING MONEY TO SAVE TIME

One major implication of the fact that time has a price is that consumers are often willing to spend money to save time. A consumer may spend $500 on a plane ride taking 3 hours rather than spend $150 to drive the same distance yet take 8 hours. A major reason for the increased sales of convenience foods that cost more per serving than home-prepared meals is that households with both parents working have a higher time price than "traditional" households with one spouse working in the marketplace.

How do you know if it's wise to spend money to save time? The answer is simple. If the money you spend to save an hour of time is less than the price of that hour of time to you, it's wise to spend money to save time. For example, a business executive might spend $300 to save an hour of travel, but if during that hour the executive can do $1000 of work for the company, then spending the money to save time is wise. An evaluation of the benefits and costs of convenience foods is given in an accompanying CONSUMER TOPIC.

Another implication of the realization that time has a price is in shopping. Frequently you hear the advice "shop around" and "comparison shop." But since shopping takes time, now you know that shopping and comparison shopping are not costless. You want to shop only up

SHOPPING AROUND   to the point where the benefits from shopping (getting lower prices and saving money) are only slightly more than the costs of shopping. (We'll talk much more about this later in Chapter 11.)

C O N S U M E R   T O P I C

ARE CONVENIENCE FOODS REALLY MORE EXPENSIVE?

Convenience foods cost more in money price, but is their total cost really more expensive? The total cost of any meal includes the money paid to buy the food plus the time cost of preparing the food for eating. Convenience foods cost more to purchase, but their preparation time is much less than for non-convenience (home-prepared) foods. Therefore, the total cost of convenience foods may actually be less than the total cost of home-prepared foods for consumers with a high value of time.

A study by Odland, Vettel, and Davis found that the total cost per serving of selected convenience foods was competitive with home-prepared foods, especially for high wage jobs. For example, they found frozen turkey and beef tip dinners were both less costly per serving for consumers with managerial and professional jobs.

The study computed the total cost per serving for three different wage levels, clerical, average, and managerial-professional. The study assumed a value of time equal to 100 percent of the wage rate for each job type. However, if managerial and professional workers enjoy their job better than clerical or average workers, then the relative advantage of convenience foods for them will be even greater (why?).

Reference: Odland, Dianne D., Ruth S. Vettel, and Carole A. Davis. "Convenience and the Cost of the 'Newer' Frozen Plate Dinners and Entrees." *Family Economics Review*, No. 1, 1986, U. S. Dept. of Agriculture.

Finally, the fact that saving time is valued by consumers means that services which do save consumers time will be more costly. Convenience food, already discussed, is an example. Another example is real estate brokers. Real estate brokers earn their commissions because they save homebuyers time in finding homes with the desired characteristics.

The Bottom Line

Time is valuable—if it weren't, why do you drive to school or work rather than walk. The price of an hour of your time is the value of what that hour could be used for in the next best alternative. _____

3. Why Isn't the Tenth Hot Dog as Good as the First?

Did you ever wonder why eating the tenth hot dog isn't as good as eating the first? Did you ever wonder why the fifth day of visiting your parents or in-laws isn't as enjoyable as the first day? Did you ever wonder why watching your third football game on Sunday isn't quite as much fun as watching the first game?

DECLINING MARGINAL VALUE

The answer to all these questions is summed-up in one phrase: *declining marginal value*. Declining marginal value simply means that we get less pleasure from additional units of a product or service than from the earlier units. The first hot dog tastes really good and gives you much eating pleasure. The second hot dog tastes almost, but not quite, as good and gives you a little less pleasure than the first. The fifth hot dog still gives you pleasure, but much less than the first or second. The tenth hot dog may in fact give you displeasure if it makes you sick! The idea of declining marginal value is shown in Figure 1-1.

The idea of declining marginal value has some important and interesting implications for consumers. First the concept is the major reason why consumers buy more of a product or service when its relative price falls. Look at Figure 1-1 again. If the price of a hot dog is equivalent to A (the value you put on the first hot dog), then you'll only buy one hot dog. You wouldn't buy the second hot dog because the value you put on the second hot dog (B) is less than the price equivalent to A. However, if the price of hot dogs fell to that equivalent to B, and if all hot dogs cost B, then you would buy two hot dogs because the value to you of

Figure 1-1. Declining marginal value.

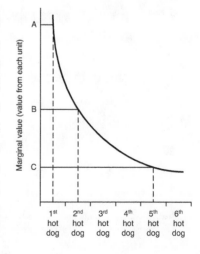

the first hot dog is greater than B, and the value to you of the second hot dog is B. So the rule is that consumers will purchase units of a good or service up to the point where the value the consumer places on the last unit bought exactly equals the price per unit of the good or service. A second implication has to do with pricing strategies of sellers. Notice in Figure 1-1 that you're willing to pay the equivalent of A for the first hot dog but only the equivalent of B for the second hot dog. If sellers charge the price equivalent of B for all hot dogs, then you'll buy two hot dogs but you'll actually get a gift on the first hot dog. The gift is that you were willing to pay the equivalent of A for the first hot dog, but you only paid the equivalent of B.

PRICING STRATEGIES Sellers recognize that these "gifts" occur if all units of a good or service are sold at the same price. Some sellers can't do anything about it. Other sellers try to do something about it by selling units of a product in a package. The package is priced in such a way as to charge the consumer the maximum value he or she would be willing to pay for each unit. For example, in Figure 1-1, if a package of two hot dogs were sold, the total price would be A + B, not B + B. In this way the seller "extracts" the maximum price the consumer is willing to pay.

The Bottom Line

As you consume more units of a product, the value you put on the last unit consumed falls from the value of earlier units. This is why consumers buy more units of a product when the price falls. This is also why sellers frequently sell products only in packages of many units.

4. Why Should You Worry about Supply and Demand?

You've probably heard the comment that the most important concepts in economics are supply and demand. Most economic situations can be broken down into supply and demand.

But why should consumers worry about supply and demand? Aren't supply and demand concepts that businessmen and women, plant managers, CEOs (chief executive officers), and government policymakers should worry about, but not consumers?

To be honest, learning about supply and demand won't help you make wise consumer decisions in the same way that learning about compound interest and discounting will. However, learning about supply and demand will help you anticipate changes in the economy which do have a profound effect on your personal economic situation. For example, understanding supply and demand will help you realize:

♦ why fuel prices will jump when unexpected cold weather hits,
♦ why orange juice prices rise when a severe freeze hits Florida,

♦ why grocery prices fall when a new supermarket enters the neighborhood, and

♦ why health care costs increase when government medical payments to consumers expand.

Demand

The concept *demand* refers to the quantity of a product which a consumer, or group of consumers, will purchase at a given price. Generally, when the price rises consumers purchase less of the product; conversely, when the price falls consumers purchase more of the product. Of course, the "prices" should be relative prices, especially when compared at different points in time. (Why?)

A *demand curve* shows the relationship between the price of a product and the quantity of that product which consumers purchase. You've already seen a demand curve. The "declining marginal value" curve in
DEMAND CURVE Figure 1-1 is really a demand curve.

As an example of an actual demand curve, look at the relationship between relative gasoline prices per gallon and average miles driven per auto in Figure 1-2. The points on the graph represent combinations of the price of driving and mileage consumption from 1980 to 2009. In general, mileage driven increased as the relative price fell. If an "average" line is drawn through the points in Figure 1-2 (note the line), the result is the so-called "downward sloping" demand curve. That is, consumption increases as relative price falls, and consumption decreases as the relative price rises.

There are two reasons why consumers buy less of a product when its relative price increases. Suppose the price of gasoline rises, with all other prices and consumer income remaining the same. Gasoline is now relatively more expensive than other consumer products. Consumers therefore have an incentive to use more of other consumer products, especially those which are sub-
SUBSTITUTION EFFECT stitutes for gasoline, and less of gasoline. For example, when the relative price of gasoline rose in the mid and late 2000s, consumers were motivated to reduce single passenger and single purpose driving trips and substitute greater use of public

Figure 1-2. The relationship between the relative price of gasoline and miles driven by consumers 1980–2009.

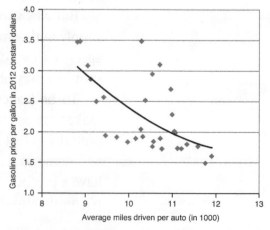

Data source: Statistical Abstract of the United States, various years.

transit, car-pooling, and multi-purpose trips. Similarly, when the relative price of oil rose during the same period, consumers bought less oil and more natural gas and wood for home heating. This is called the "substitution effect."

Of course, the availability of substitutes for a product whose price has risen and the size of other costs associated with switching from one product to another limit the degree to which consumers can reduce the consumption of a product whose relative price has risen. Consumer products that have few substitutes show less responsiveness to price changes than consumer products which have many substitutes. Compare the demand curves for medical care and beef in Figure 1-3. The demand curve for medical care is very "steep," meaning that consumption changes little as the relative price changes (notice that consumption of medical care only falls from A to B when price rises from P1 to P2). This is because there are few substitutes for medical care. In contrast, the demand curve for beef is very "flat." Consumption changes a lot when relative price changes (see the effect of price rising from P1 to P2). This is because there are many substitutes for beef.

Figure 1-3. Demand curves for medical care and beef.

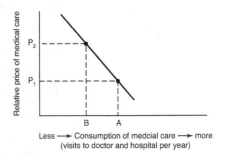

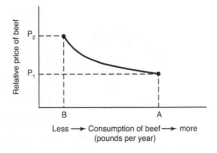

The second impact of a relative price change is on the purchasing power of a consumer's income. When the relative price of a consumer product rises and the consumer's income remains the same, it means the consumer's income will not "go as far"—that is, it falls in purchasing power. The consumer reacts by buying less of all consumer products, including the product whose price rose.

Supply

Producers of consumer products react in an opposite way to changes in the relative price of their products than do consumers. Initially, with no change in the costs of their inputs (e.g., labor, machines), producers reap higher profits when the price received for their product rises. Motivated by more profits, producers strive to manufacture a greater quantity of their products. This gives rise to a positive relationship between the relative price of a consumer product and the quantity of that product which a producer manufactures—that is, the higher the relative price the greater the quantity manufactured. Eventually, in order to produce additional amounts of a product, the producer must compete for additional inputs, such as labor and investment funds, that are being used elsewhere. This "bidding" increases the relative price of those inputs. The producer stops increasing the manufacture of additional quantities of products when the higher cost of inputs "wipes out" any extra profit made on these additional quantities.

SUPPLY CURVE

Similar to a demand curve, a "supply curve" can be drawn for producers of consumer products. The supply curve merely shows combinations of relative price of a product and quantity of that product which a producer, or group of producers, manufactures. Since producers manufacture more of the product when its relative price rises, supply curves usually slope "upward."

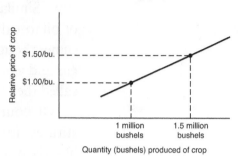

Figure 1-4. Supply curves.

Two supply curves are illustrated in Figure 1-4. The ease and cost of manufacturing additional quantities of a product determine the shape of the supply curve. For example, it is relatively easy and inexpensive for farmers to increase acreage devoted to the production of given crops in response to higher relative prices for those crops. Therefore, the supply of many crops is very responsive to changes in relative price. Such a supply curve is illustrated in the upper part of Figure 1-4. In contrast, increasing the supply of doctors requires long periods of costly education and internship. Therefore, the supply of doctors is not as responsive as crops to changes in relative price. The doctor supply curve is like that illustrated in the bottom part of Figure 1-4.

The Market

The meeting of consumers desiring to purchase a product and producers desiring to sell that product is called the market for the product. The market has two major functions. First, it establishes the price at which the product will be sold. Second, it is the place where trades take place between consumers and producers. Generally, consumers trade money to producers in return for products.

How the Market Operates

In ancient times most markets were physical locations where consumers and producers came together to make trades. Prices were established by consumers and producers arguing over the "worth" of products in an atmosphere similar to today's auctions. If producers found that their products weren't selling, they would lower the price which they'd be willing to accept from consumers. Conversely, if producers found that their products were selling rapidly, they could raise the price which they'd be willing to accept.

Today, some markets still exist in which consumers and producers come together to bid and argue over prices and to make trades. The New York Stock Exchange and tobacco markets are good examples. However, with rapid communication devices, like the Internet, available today, many markets don't require consumers (buyers) and producers (sellers) to be in the same physical location. Furthermore, many markets today are more "polite" than their ancient counterparts. Consumers and producers infrequently argue about prices. Nevertheless, consumers collectively do have an impact on prices. If a producer posts a price for a product which is higher than the price which many consumere are willing to pay, then some consumers simply won't buy the product (and instead will buy substitutes) and others will reduce their purchases of the product. The net result is that the producer finds he can't sell all of the product which he wanted to at the posted price. In order to sell more of his product, the producer lowers the relative price.

On the other hand, what if the posted price is less than the maximum price which many consumers are willing to pay for the product? In this case the available supply of the product is purchased at a rapid rate. The producer finds that he can raise the product's relative price and still sell the available supply.

The Equilibrium Price

The price of a product will ultimately settle at that price for which the quantity of the product that consumers want to buy exactly equals the quantity of the product that producers want to manufacture and sell. In economics jargon, this price is called the "equilibrium price."

The equilibrium price can be illustrated by combining the consumer demand curve for a product and the producer supply curve for the same product. In this case the demand curve is for all consumers and the supply curve is for all producers manufacturing the product. Consider the market for new cars. Given the demand and supply curves for new cars in Figure 1-5, the equilibrium price for new cars is P_e and the corresponding quantity of new cars

Figure 1-5. Equilibrium price.

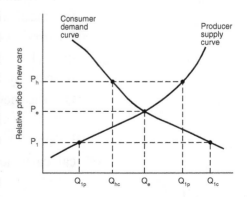

sold is Q_e. Why is P_e the equilibrium price? At prices higher than the equilibrium price, say P_h, producers desire to sell more new cars, Q_{hp}, than consumers are willing to buy, Q_{hc}. Inventories therefore increase at dealers' lots. In an effort to sell more cars prices are lowered, perhaps through gimmicks such as rebate plans and special financing. This happened in the 1990–91 recession as dealers found their cars overpriced and sales slipping.

In contrast, what if the price of new cars is below the equilibrium price at, for example, P_l. Then consumers want to buy more cars, Q_{lc}, than producers are willing to sell, Q_{lp}. Cars are being sold faster than dealers can restock them. Many consumers are willing to offer higher prices in order to be assured of purchasing a car. The higher offered prices also encourage producers to manufacture more cars. Therefore, price rises toward the equilibrium price, P_e.

How Markets Change

This is the part of this topic that you'll find most interesting and useful. Unfortunately, you had to read everything prior to this to get to this point!

Markets are rarely in equilibrium. In most cases prices and quantities are moving toward equilibrium. Markets move out of equilibrium when something happens to make either demand, supply, or both change. For example, suppose the federal government institutes a national health insurance plan which effectively reduces the price of medical care paid by consumers but does not affect the costs to doctors and hospitals of providing medical care. Medical care is therefore relatively cheaper to consumers, and consumers will therefore desire to purchase more medical care at every level of prices charged by doctors and hospitals. In essence, the demand curve for medical care has moved outward as shown in Figure 1-6. Initially, with the same price (P_1) charged by doctors and hospitals, excess demand for medical care occurs—that is, doctors' waiting rooms and hospitals become more crowded. This is seen by the difference between Q_3, the new quantity of medical care desired by consumers at price P_1, and Q_1, the quantity of medical care desired by consumers at

NATIONAL HEALTH INSURANCE

Figure 1-6. Impact of a national health insurance plan.

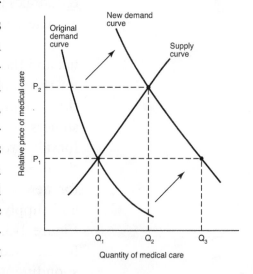

price P_1 before the institution of national health insurance. Increased competition among consumers for medical care ultimately pushes the relative price of medical care up. The higher relative price of medical care encourages more individuals to become doctors and encourages the expansion of hospitals. Ultimately, the new equilibrium price and quantity of medical care is P_2 and Q_2 respectively. The market movement from P_1,Q_1 to P_2,Q_2 may, however, take years to occur in the case of medical care. This is because of the long time it takes to train new doctors.

Figure 1-7. Impact of a damaging freeze on the orange crop.

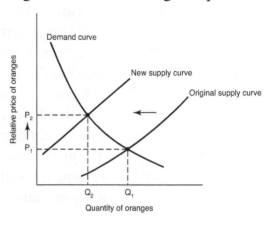

As another example of a change in market equilibrium, this time from the supply side, consider what happens if an unexpected freeze in Florida significantly damages the orange crop. Growers can now only supply a reduced number of oranges at every level of prices. This is depicted by a backward shift in the supply curve for oranges, as in Figure 1-7. Increased consumer competition for the now more limited supply of oranges means that the equilibrium price rises to P_2.

ORANGE CROP FREEZE

GAS PRICE CONTROLS

As a final example (promise!) of market changes, consider what would happen if the government reinstituted price controls on gasoline. Suppose the government said that, by law, gasoline could not be sold for more than $1.00 per gallon. This is considerably below the market price of approximately $3.60 per gallon (in 2012). What would happen?

Since $1.00 per gallon is less than the market price, gasoline is now relatively cheaper after the government decree. Consumers, collectively therefore desire to purchase more gasoline than they did at $3.60 per gallon. In Figure 1-8, consumers desire to purchase quantity Q_3 rather than quantity Q_2. But where will the extra gasoline come from? In fact, producers of gasoline will supply less gasoline (Q_1) at $1.00 per gallon

Figure 1-8. Impact of gasoline price controls.

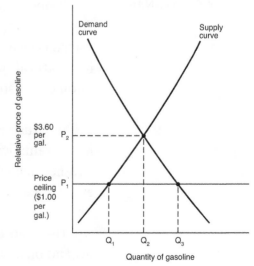

than the quantity they supplied (Q₂) at $3.60 per gallon. A shortage, the difference between Q_3 and Q_1, therefore results from the price ceiling.

TIME PRICE

How is the shortage resolved? A "black," or underground, market could develop that would sell gasoline above the ceiling. For most consumers, however, the shortage is resolved through a rise in the *time price* associated with purchasing gasoline. Fear of not being able to purchase gasoline motivates consumers to line up at gas pumps before the supply runs dry. Long lines at gas stations increase the waiting time associated with obtaining gas and hence increase the time costs of purchasing gas. The higher time cost motivates consumers to use less gasoline in order to avoid the waiting lines. The higher time cost effectively substitutes for a higher monetary cost.

So What?

Now that you know about demand curves, supply curves, markets, and equilibrium prices, what practical use are these concepts to you? Can the concepts help you in managing your personal financial affairs?

FORECASTING

The major practical usefulness of the concepts is in forecasting. You now know four things related to supply and demand:

♦ Anything that increases demand for a product without increasing supply to the same extent will result in a relative price increase;

♦ Anything that decreases demand for a product without decreasing supply to the same extent will result in a relative price decrease;

♦ Anything that increases supply of a product without increasing demand to the same extent will result in a relative price decrease; and

♦ Anything that decreases supply of a product without decreasing demand to the same extent will result in a relative price increase.

Let's see how a consumer could put these ideas to practical use with two examples:

A COLD SNAP

Suppose severe and unexpected cold weather hits in December. Average temperatures are several degrees below normal. To stay warm, consumers initially increase their consumption of fuel, including natural gas, oil, and electricity. Should consumers expect fuel prices to rise?

Figure 1-9A. Effects of severe cold weather.

Yes, fuel prices will rise, and perhaps dramatically. The unexpected cold weather increases demand for fuel at every price and shifts the demand curve outward (Figure 1-9A). Fuel prices will rise, and the extent of the rise will depend on how responsive the supply of

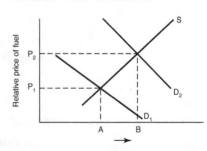

C
O
N
S
U
M
E
R

T
O
P
I
C

MORE COMPETITION LOWERS SUPERMARKET PRICES

OK, you say, economic theory implies that more firms competing for consumers' business in a given market will mean lower prices for consumers. That sounds good, but is there any evidence it actually happens in the real world?

One piece of evidence comes from a study done by Walden on supermarkets in Raleigh, North Carolina. Walden examined the impact of a new store opening in a given market area on the prices charged by six existing stores. The prices of 22 commonly purchased supermarket products were followed for 32 weeks prior to the new store opening and for 16 weeks after the opening.

The findings supported the implications of the simple model of supply and demand. Prices for half of the products were lower at the six existing stores after the opening of the new store. Furthermore, the drop in price was greater for existing stores located *closer* to the new store than for existing stores located farther from the new store. This is logical since stores located closer to each other should be stronger competitors. Prices for most of the other products showed no sensitivity to entry of the new store.

Reference: Walden, Michael L. "Testing Implications of Spatial Economics Models: Some Evidence from Food Retailing," *The Journal of Consumer Affairs,* Vol. 24, No. 1, Summer 1990, pp. 24–43.

fuel is to price changes. Over a short period of time, such as a month, the supply of fuel is probably not very responsive, so in this situation consumers should plan to budget much more money for fuel costs.

Now consider an investment example. Suppose your Uncle Ed opens the first video store in town. The store is a success and Uncle Ed makes big profits. You invest some money in Uncle Ed's store and are very

pleased with the returns on your investment. Uncle Ed's relative price and quantity of videos rented is shown as P_1 and A on Figure 1-9B.

But Uncle Ed's big profits likely won't last. Why? Observing Uncle Ed's profits, competitors will set up other video stores in town. This will shift the supply curve to the right (S_2 in Figure 1-9B) and lower prices to P_2. Uncle Ed's profits, and the return on your investment, will fall.

Figure 1-9B. Uncle Ed's large profits won't last.

The Bottom Line

One can use supply and demand curves to forecast changes in relative prices. Anything that increases demand more than supply will increase the relative

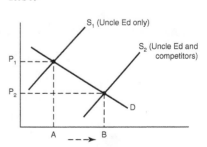

price, and anything that increases supply more than demand will decrease the relative price. An individual consumer can't have an impact on supply and demand, but understanding supply and demand will give clues about where prices are headed. _____

5. Why Should You Always Look Over Your Shoulder (Economically Speaking)?

Wouldn't life be great if each of us had all the money and time we wanted. Then we could buy and do everything we wanted, and there would be no reason for economic decision-making. In fact, there would be no reason for economics, or for this book, because economics is the science which deals with making decisions about scarce resources. If money and time are unlimited, then there's no need to worry about prioritizing purchases or deciding what is best to buy.

OPPORTUNITY COST

But consumer resources—mainly time and money—are limited, and so consumers must worry about using those resources in the best way to reach whatever goals they have. One way to keep yourself honest in this endeavor is to understand and use the concept of *opportunity cost*. Opportunity cost recognizes that when you spend time or money on any product, you're *giving up* the ability to spend that same time and money on something else. Therefore, the opportunity cost of spending money or time on any product or activity is the *value* of the next best product or activity you could obtain with that same amount of time or money. Some examples of opportunity cost are:

- the opportunity cost to John, a college student, of going to the movies for two hours is the benefit from studying for those two hours,
- the opportunity cost to Sally of buying a $35,000 Jeep Grand Cherokee is the investment she could make with that money,
- the opportunity cost to George and Jennifer of having a child is the value of making a downpayment on a new house.

IS ANYTHING "FREE"?

Opportunity cost is the economic equivalent of looking over your shoulder at other uses for your time and money. Opportunity cost forces you to recognize your missed opportunities. Opportunity cost doesn't mean that spending money or time on any product or activity is "bad" or "wrong"—that requires evaluation, which will come in later chapters. Instead, opportunity cost makes you realize that nothing is free—there's always some other use for your resources.

For example, even if someone gives you free tickets to the baseball game, the game still isn't free. There's an opportunity cost to your time spent at the game!

At this point you may say, "Come on, if I hadn't gone to the baseball game, I wouldn't have done something 'constructive'—I would have slept or watched TV." That's OK. The opportunity cost of some expenditure of time or money doesn't have to be something "constructive" or "self-improving" or "dull." The opportunity cost of any expenditure is simply the value of your next best use of that time and money, and that next best use can be anything you want. But keep yourself honest—recognize all your other opportunities. Also, you can calculate a number of opportunity costs for any number of alternative uses of your time and money.

Applications to Consumer Decision-making

The concept of opportunity cost is applicable to many consumer decisions. It will be used many times in future chapters. Here is a preview.

HOUSE
DOWN-PAYMENT

♦ Down-payment on purchase of a house: Most of us make a down-payment when buying a house. Obviously the down-payment is part of the cost of the house. But understanding the concept of opportunity cost makes you realize that the cost of the down-payment doesn't stop when the house is bought. The down-payment money could have been invested and earned interest each year. These annual interest earnings are an opportunity cost of the down-payment and should be counted as an annual cost of the house.

CASH OR CREDIT

♦ You pay cash for a new TV rather than using credit. You save hundreds of dollars in credit interest costs and are very proud of yourself for doing so. But remembering the concept of opportunity cost takes some of the luster off that pride. Using your own money isn't costless, because you could have invested that money and earned interest. These interest earnings which you give up are one opportunity cost of paying with cash. In fact, if the interest rate you earn on the cash is greater than the interest rate charged for credit, then using credit may be cheaper (more on this in Chapter 5).

SHOPPING

♦ Shopping by comparing unit prices: This is the commonly recommended method of shopping (for example, in a supermarket) and will result in the lowest money cost. But there's an opportunity cost to this shopping technique which is the extra time required as compared to other shopping methods. When the cost of time is added to the money cost of unit price shopping, it may not be the cheapest technique, especially for high income consumers.

COUPONS

♦ Clipping coupons is also recommended, as the "smart" way to shop and save money. But again, coupon clipping and organization takes time, and when the opportunity cost of that time is considered, coupon clipping may not be wise.

"But I Won't Invest—I'll Waste the Money!"

This is a common response to the recommendation that foregone interest earnings be used as an opportunity cost to spending money on some consumer product or service. You might say, "If I don't pay cash for the TV, I'll simply spend the money on something frivolous."

There are two responses to this comment. First, if you spend the money on something else (whatever that is), rather than investing, then it must be that the value of that expenditure is greater than the value you'd get from investing. No one knows better than you what you like and don't like and what gives you the most pleasure. The opportunity cost should then be measured as the value of that other expenditure. If you use the foregone interest earnings as the opportunity cost, you'll actually be underestimating the true opportunity cost!

Second, although you may not invest the money, you could, so investing is an alternative for which an opportunity cost can be easily constructed. It allows you to consider "what might have been."

The Bottom Line

Your resources of time and money are limited, so there are always many alternative uses for them. The idea of "opportunity cost" keeps you honest by forcing you to consider what else you might have done with a particular expenditure of time or money. _____

6. Why Doesn't Everyone Earn the Same Amount of Money?

Money and time are the consumer's two resources. We all have the same amount of time per week or year (although life spans vary), but wages and incomes vary quite a bit (see Table 1-3).

In a nutshell, wages and incomes vary primarily due to differences in worker skills, training, talents, and experiences, and due to differences in the amenities and characteristics of alternative jobs.

TRAINING

In general, wages are higher for jobs which require more skill and training. Highly skilled jobs are more valuable to the employer, and the employer passes these benefits on to the employee in the form of higher wages. Jobs which require more training must pay higher wages in order to entice people to undergo the training and probably put up with low pay during the training period. For example, many fewer people would be motivated to undergo the eight to ten years of medical school training at little or no pay unless they anticipated that a high-paying job would be the result. Education is one of the best predictors of earnings (see CONSUMER TOPIC).

Table 1-3   Average salaries of workers in selected occupations, 2010.

Occupation	Median pay
Dentists	$146,920
Civil engineers	$77,560
Architects	$72,550
Personal financial advisors	$64,750
Accountants	$61,690
High school teachers	$53,230
Insurance agents	$46,770
Social workers	$42,480
Travel agents	$31,870
Retail sales workers	$20,990

Data source: U.S. Bureau of Labor Statistics, Occupational Outlook Handbook: http://www.bls.gov/ooh/

C O N S U M E R   T O P I C

THE INCREASING RETURNS TO EDUCATION

Education is a major determinant of earnings. One study calculated that 42 percent of the differences in wage rates could be explained by educational differences (Fearn, Stone, and Allen).

In the 1970s college graduates could expect to earn 29 to 41 percent more than high school graduates, depending on years of experience. By the mid-1990s the average earnings premium of college graduates over high school graduates had risen to over 80 percent.

Why has a college education become more valuable. One answer is surprising, while a second answer is more well-known. The well-known answer is that the demand for college educated workers has increased as professional and technical jobs have grown at faster rates than manufacturing and other manual jobs. The surprising answer is that the relative supply of new college graduates actually fell in the 1980s. The percentage of males aged 25–34 with a college degree fell from 28½ percent in 1979 to 26.2 percent in 1987, and the percentage of females aged 25–34 with a college degree fell from 27.2 percent in 1979 to 26.7 percent in 1987. By 1996 the percentage of both genders aged 25–34 with a college degree stood

(*continued on next page*)

(*continued from previous page*)

C O N S U M E R   T O P I C

at 26.5%. Thus the rise in the earnings premium associated with a college degree seems to have resulted from the classic situation of demand increasing faster than supply.

Does this mean that everyone should get a college degree? No. Many consumers' talents are in occupations which don't require college training. These consumers would be unhappy and unproductive in a college-trained occupation. However, this doesn't deny the fact that the most assured way of earning more income is with more education.

References: Fearn, Robert M., Paul S. Stone, and Steven G. Allen. *Employment and Wage Changes in North Carolina*, Economics Information Report No. 60, North Carolina State University, January 1980.

Katz, Lawrence F. and Ana L. Revenga. "Changes in the Structure of Wages: The U. S. Versus Japan." NBER Working Paper No. 3021, National Bureau of Economic Research, Cambridge, Massachusetts, July 1989.

Mankin, N. Gregory, *Principal of Economics*, Fort Worth, Texas, The Dryden Press, 1998, p. 404.

If you have unique and extraordinary skills and talents for jobs which are in high demand, then you really have it made. There will be few or no substitutes for these types of people, so you have a "corner on the market" and can command very high wages. Sports superstars, top box office actors and actresses, and elite corporate executives are examples of such people.

Wage differentials also compensate workers for differences in the quality of the working environment. This is best explained with an example. Take the jobs of two accountants with the exact same training and experience. One accountant, Adam, takes a teaching job at the University of Santa Barbara, which is located on the coast of California in a beautiful temperate environment. The other accountant, Beth, takes a high pressure-high stress job with a New York City accounting firm. Adam teaches three classes a day, does research of his own choosing, and has the job security provided by tenure. Beth must constantly worry about keeping old accounts and getting new ones and can be fired with no notice.

WORK ENVIRONMENT

You shouldn't be surprised that Beth's initial salary is higher than Adam's. When comparing jobs with the same skill and training requirements, higher wages will be paid for those jobs which have more stress and risk or which are located in less appealing places. Lower wages will be paid for those jobs having more security and serenity and which are located in pleasant and popular places.

The Bottom Line

Jobs which require more education or training, which are riskier, or which have less desirable work environments will pay higher wages and salaries. Also, workers who have unique skills for jobs which are in high demand will earn high incomes.

7. Does Inflation Doom Us to an Existence of Poverty?

You know what inflation means—it means prices are rising and it's more expensive to buy products and services. The inflation rate simply is the percentage increase in prices.

We can talk about an inflation rate for a single product or service or for a number of products and services. Generally, the latter is more widely used. You frequently hear quoted the inflation rate for consumer products and services, the inflation rate for producer products, or the inflation rate for all products and services. In fact, when "the" inflation rate is mentioned, it always refers to one of these broad measures.

Inflation Isn't New

Inflation isn't a new phenomenon. As Figure 1-10 shows, rising prices are the rule rather than the exception. Inflation rates are highest after wars and before recessions (more on this later in the next chapter).

Inflation means the purchasing power of the dollar declines. Table 1-4 shows how the dollar's purchasing power declines over time at different average annual inflation rates. For example, with an annual inflation rate of 4 percent per year, having a dollar 15 years from now would be like having 56¢ today. However, if the annual inflation rate is 8 percent per year, having a dollar 15 years from now would be like having only 32¢ today.

Figure 1-10.   Historical inflation rates.

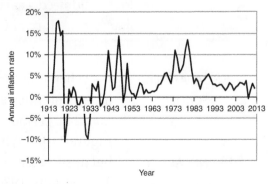

Source: U.S. Bureau of Labor Statistics, Consumer Price Index: http://www.bls.gov/cpi/home.htm

Table 1-4 Inflation rates and purchasing power of the dollar.

What a dollar will be worth after N years and annual inflation rate of:

	2%	4%	6%	8%	10%	15%
5 yrs.	91¢	82¢	75¢	68¢	62¢	50¢
10 yrs.	82	68	56	46	39	25
15 yrs.	74	56	42	32	24	12
20 yrs.	67	46	31	21	15	6
25 yrs.	61	38	23	15	9	3
30 yrs.	55	31	17	10	6	2
35 yrs.	50	25	13	7	4	1
40 yrs.	45	21	10	5	2	1/3

C O N S U M E R   T O P I C

WHERE IS IT CHEAPER TO LIVE?

We frequently talk about inflation and the cost-of-living in national terms. But the cost-of-living varies by where you live in the nation. In general, it's cheaper to live in rural areas than in urban areas, and it's cheaper to live in the Southeast and Southwest than in the East and Midwest.

An excellent source of local cost-of-living data is the Cost of Living Index by the Council for Community and Economic Research (C2ER), formerly American Chamber of Commerce Researchers Association (ACCRA). The Cost of Living Index is published quarterly for several hundred locations nationwide.

The Cost of Living Index can be used to compare salaries of alternative jobs in different locations. Suppose Joe Simpson earns $50,000 in his job in Columbia, Missouri. He is offered a similar job in Hartford, Connecticut. He finds in 2012, the cost of living index is 94.2 for Columbia, Missouri, and 124.6 for Hartford, Connecticut. Thus the cost of living in Hartford is 32.3% (124.6/94.2 - 1) higher than in Columbia. Therefore, Joe would need a salary of at least $66,150 ($50,000*1.323) in Hartford to be comparable to his salary in Columbia.

ESCALATING INFLATION When inflation rates are rising, that is, when prices are increasing at increasing rates each year, we refer to this situation as *escalating inflation*. The period 1975–1980 is a good example of escalating inflation (see Figure 1-10). When inflation rates are falling, meaning prices are rising but at successively lower rates each year, we say *disinflation* is occurring. **DISINFLATION** The periods 1980–1986 and 1990–1998 are examples of disinflation. **DEFLATION** During years when prices actually fall, we say *deflation* is occurring. Since 1929, deflation has occurred in 1933, 1939, 1949, and 1955.

Figure 1-11.   What's up, what's not (in relative price) in the 2000s.

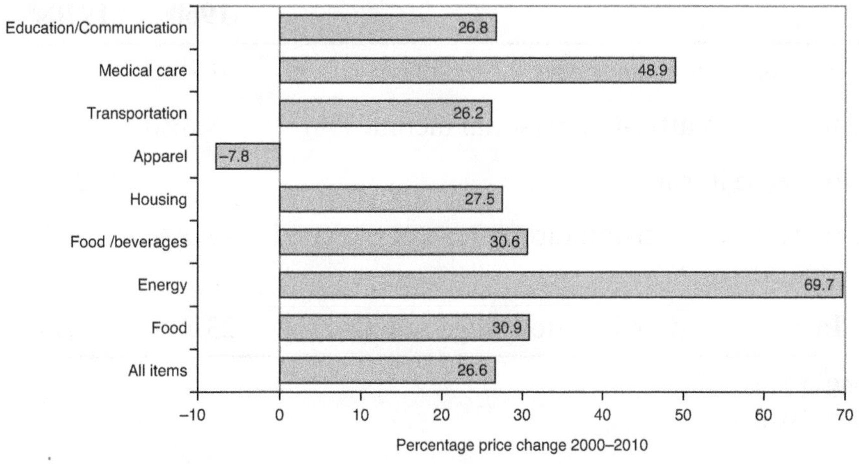

Data source: Statistical Abstract of the United States, 2012.

Not all prices change at the same rate. If a product's price rises *faster* than the inflation rate for all prices, then that product has had a *relative*, or *real*, price increase. If a product's price rises slower than the inflation rate for all prices, then that product has had a relative, or real, price decrease. You already learned about relative price changes in *Are Prices "Really" What They Seem?* Figure 1-11 shows products which have experienced relative price increases and relative price decreases in the 2000s.

**REAL PRICE
INCREASE/DECREASE**

Energy and medical care became relatively more expensive in the 2000s, apparel became less expensive both in relative and nominal prices, and the other categories had price increases very similar to the overall increase for all goods and services.

Coping with Inflation

Is inflation bad? That is, is it bad for the dollar's purchasing power to decline each year?

Most of you would say yes, but the answer is "not necessarily." As long as consumer incomes rise at the inflation rate or higher, then rising prices don't reduce consumers' standard of living. Fortunately, this has been the case in most of the recent decades (see Table 1-5). Over most years, increases in consumer income more than compensated for inflation in prices. An exception is the 1980s when wage rates didn't keep up with inflation. Personal income still rose because more people (primarily females) chose to work.

Many wage contracts are now indexed to the average inflation rate. Social Security payments are indexed to a National Wage Index, which is higher than the inflation rate for most years.

Table 1-5 Increases in prices and incomes.

	1960s[a]	1970s[b]	1980s[c]	2000s[d]	2000s[e]
1. Increase in consumer prices, (% CPI)	31.1%	112.4%	58.6%	31.8%	26.6%
2. Increase in after-tax personal income (%)	78.6%	141.8%	84.5%	61.6%	38.0%
3. Increase in wage rate	54.4%	102.3%	68.0%	52.9%	29.6%
4. Increase in after-inflation after-tax personal income (2-1)	47.5%	29.4%	25.9%	29.9%	11.4%
5. Increase in after-inflation wage rate (3-1)	23.3%	−10.1%	9.4%	21.2%	3.0%

[a]1960–1970
[b]1970–1980
[c]1980–1990
[d]1990–2000
[e]2000–2010

Data source: Consumer Price Index from the US Bureau of Labor Statistics. Per capital disposable income data from US Department of Commerce, Bureau of Economic Analysis. National wage index from the Social Security Bureau.

This doesn't mean you can ignore inflation. One reason is that your wage and income may not keep up with inflation, so inflation may reduce your standard of living. Certainly you must be concerned about keeping your income at pace with inflation. When negotiating wage or salary increases with your boss, make sure you're aware of the latest inflation statistics. If your boss doesn't give you a raise at least equal to the inflation rate, then you've really received a pay cut!

Understanding inflation and keeping track of it will also prevent you from being misled by claims of future wealth. For example, an insurance agent demonstrates how an insurance policy will provide you with $200,000 in 30 years. Yet if inflation averages 4 percent a year for the next 30 years, then $200,000 will only be worth $62,000 in purchasing power. Also, as you will see later, inflation is very important to keep in mind when making decisions about investments. Ignoring inflation can lead to disaster for your investment portfolio.

The Bottom Line

Inflation has always been with us and will always be with us. Inflation by itself is not bad or disastrous. As long as your wages and income at least keep pace with inflation, your standard of living won't suffer with inflation.

8. How Is Inflation Measured?

Inflation is an important, although not welcome, part of consumers' lives. As you will see in this book, it is very important for you to account for inflation in many consumer financial decisions.

PPI
CPI

How is inflation measured, and where do you go to get information on inflation? There are two commonly used measures of inflation, the Producer Price Index (PPI) and the Consumer Price Index (CPI). The PPI measures the average prices of inputs used by the producers of products. The PPI includes the prices of products such as corn, crude oil, copper, concrete, nails, and lumber. Approximately 70,000 industrial prices go into the calculation of the PPI. A major omission in the PPI is the price of services used in the production process.

As consumers we are most interested in the prices of consumer goods and services. Therefore the Consumer Price Index is the most relevant measure of inflation for consumers. The rest of the topic will be devoted to understanding the measurement and use of the Consumer Price Index.

Measurement of the Consumer Price Index

The Consumer Price Index, or CPI, is an index, or average, measure of prices of goods and services bought by consumers at some point in time. *Inflation* is measured by the *change* in the CPI over some time period, and the *inflation rate* is measured by the *percentage change* in the CPI over a time period.

The federal government constructs the CPI by first collecting prices for 80,000 items across the country. The prices are then averaged together to form one price. But in the averaging process, all goods and services aren't treated equally, since some are a more important part of consumer spending than others. So, before the prices are averaged, they are "weighted" by their importance in the average consumer's budget. For example, the price of electricity receives a greater weight than the price of a can of carrots.

WEIGHTING

Price information for the CPI is collected monthly. Information used to form the "weights" is collected quarterly by the Consumer Expenditure Survey, which is another U.S. government survey.

As the name implies, the Consumer Price Index is an index number. For example, in January 2013 the Consumer Price Index for all consumer items stood at 230.28 using 100 for 1982–84. No meaning can be given to this number by itself. Instead, any CPI number must be used in combination with another CPI number. For example, the all-item CPI number in January 2012 was 226.67. Therefore, from January 2012 to January 2013 the all-item CPI rose from 226.67 to 230.28. This represented a

1.6 percentage increase. Therefore, from January 2012 to January 2013 the rate of inflation, as measured by the Consumer Price Index, was 1.6 percent.

Using the Consumer Price Index

There are two beneficial uses of the CPI. One is to calculate the overall, or all-item, rate of inflation, and the second is to calculate the rate of inflation for a particular consumer item.

Table 1-6 gives the all-item CPI for December 2009 and December 2012 as well as the CPI for individual spending items. To calculate the annual rate of inflation (in percentage terms) simply perform this calculation:

$$\frac{\text{CPI this year}}{\text{CPI last year}} - 1 = \text{Annual rate of inflation}$$

For example, calculating the annual rate of inflation from December 2011 to December 2012 results in:

$$\frac{229.6}{225.7} - 1 = 1.7\%$$

INDIVIDUAL ITEM INFLATION RATES

The annual inflation rate for individual spending items is calculated in the same way. In December 2012 the CPI for "transportation" was 211.9,

Table 1-6 All-item CPI and individual item CPI: December 2009- December 2012 (1982 – 1984 = 100)

	2009	2010	2011	2012
All items	215.9	219.2	225.7	229.6
Food/beverage	218.0	221.3	231.1	235.2
Housing	215.5	216.1	220.2	224.0
Transportation	188.3	198.3	208.6	211.9
Apparel	119.4	118.1	123.5	125.7
Medical care	379.5	391.9	405.6	418.7
Recreation	113.2	112.3	113.5	114.4
Education/ communication	128.9	130.5	132.7	134.7

Data source: US Bureau of Labor Statistics.

THE CPI IN RECENT YEARS

The CPI increased modestly in the 1960s until 1968. From 1968 to 1980 the CPI grew rapidly. In fact, during this period the price level more than doubled. Since 1980, the CPI has grown much more modestly, and starting from the late 1990s the inflation rate has been in the 1 to 4 percent range with the exception of 2009 when inflation rate was negative.

Year	CPI	Annual inflation	Year	CPI	Inflation
1960	29.6	1.7%	1991	136.2	4.2%
1970	38.8	5.7%	1992	140.3	3.0%
1971	40.5	4.4%	1993	144.5	3.0%
1972	41.8	3.2%	1994	148.2	2.6%
1973	44.4	6.2%	1995	152.4	2.8%
1974	49.3	11.0%	1996	156.9	3.0%
1975	53.8	9.1%	1997	160.5	2.3%
1976	56.9	5.8%	1998	163.0	1.6%
1977	60.6	6.5%	1999	166.6	2.2%
1978	65.2	7.6%	2000	172.2	3.4%
1979	72.6	11.3%	2001	177.1	2.8%
1980	82.4	13.5%	2002	179.9	1.6%
1981	90.9	10.3%	2003	184.0	2.3%
1982	96.5	6.2%	2004	188.9	2.7%
1983	99.6	3.2%	2005	195.3	3.4%
1984	103.9	4.3%	2006	201.6	3.2%
1985	107.6	3.6%	2007	207.3	2.8%
1986	109.6	1.9%	2008	215.3	3.8%
1987	113.6	3.6%	2009	214.5	−0.4%
1988	118.3	4.1%	2010	218.1	1.6%
1989	124.0	4.8%	2011	224.9	3.2%
1990	130.7	5.4%	2012	229.6	2.1%

Data source: US Bureau of Labor Statistics.

(*continued on next page*)

C O N S U M E R   T O P I C

(continued from previous page)

The CPI values in the table (notice 1982–1984 is used as the base of 100) can be used to compare salaries at vastly different points in time. For example, suppose your father earned $15,000 in 1970. What salary would you have to earn in 2012 to be equivalent to your father's earnings? The answer is $15,000 \times \dfrac{229.6}{38.8}$, or $88,761. Or, what if your grandfather earned $8,000 in 1960. What salary would you have to earn in 2012 to be equivalent to your grandfather's earnings? The answer is $8,000 \times \dfrac{229.6}{29.6} = \$62,052$.

and in 2011 it was 208.6. Therefore, the annual rate of inflation for "transportation" from December 2011 to December 2012 was

$$\frac{211.9}{208.6} - 1 = 1.6\%$$

INFLATION RATE FOR FALLING PRICE

What if a price falls? The annual rate of iinflation is calculated in the same way. Notice from Table 1-6 that the index for apparel fell from 120.1 in 2010 to 119.5 in 2011. The annual rate of inflation for apparel from December 2009 to December 2010 was then:

$$\frac{118.1}{119.4} - 1 = -1.1\%$$

INFLATION RATE FOR OVER MANY YEARS

To compute the total rate of inflation over a number of years, do the same calculation. For example, the all-item CPI in was 215.9 in December 2009 and 229.6 for December 2012. The total rate of inflation between December 2009 and December 2012 was

$$\frac{229.6}{215.9} - 1 = 6.3\%$$

What if you have available the *annual* inflation rates for a number of years and you want to calculate a total inflation rate? You will underestimate the total inflation rate if you simply add the annual rates. Why? Because the inflation rate is a percentage increase over the previous year's cost-of-living. Adding the inflation rates implies using the first year's cost-of-living as a base for all of the increases.

Instead, the proper procedure is to multiply the annual inflation rates to compute a total inflation rate. The following example will illustrate the process.

EXAMPLE 1-1:   Compute the total inflation rate for the years 2010 to 2012 using the individual annual inflation rates:

2010	1.6%
2011	3.2%
2012	2.1%

Total inflation rate = (1.016 × 1.032 × 1.021 – 1 = 7.1%
Notice this is larger than the simple sum of 6.9%.

INDEX YEAR

The federal government periodically changes the index values. For example, in January 1988 the index values were changed from being based on 1967 = 100 to 1982–84 = 100. The government publishes the CPI before 1988 using both bases. If you want to compare current CPI to CPI before 1988, make sure you use the CPI series with 1982–1984 as the basis.

C O N S U M E R   T O P I C

YOUR INDIVIDUAL INFLATION RATE

The inflation rate calculated from the Consumer Price index is based on average consumer spending patterns. This means that if *your* spending patterns are considerably different than the average spending patterns used by the CPI, then your individual inflation rate may be different than the quoted inflation rate.

You need two sets of information in order to calculate an individual inflation rate. You need the breakdown of your after-tax spending (in percentage terms) in the categories used by the CPI, and you need the inflation rate for each of those spending categories. Multiply the inflation rate in each category by your proportional spending in the category, and add the results for all categories. The sum is your individual inflation rate.

The top of the table shows three spending patterns, that used by the CPI, the spending pattern of Judy, and the spending pattern of Joe. Judy spends relatively more on food, housing, and transportation. Joe spends relatively more on apparel, medical care, and others.

The CPI inflation rate over the December 2011 to December 2012 was 1.7%. The bottom of the table shows how the individual inflation rates for Judy and Joe are calculated. Both are somewhat higher than the "official" inflation rate.

(*continued on next page*)

	CPI Relative Importance	Judy's After-Tax Spending	Joe's After-Tax Spending
Food /beverages	14.8%	20.0%	13.0%
Housing, incl. utilities	41.5%	38.0%	13.0%
Apparel	3.6%	2.0%	20.0%
Transportation	17.3%	25.0%	13.0%
Medical care	6.6%	6.0%	25.0%
Recreation	6.3%	4.0%	1.0%
Education/ communication	6.4%	3.0%	0.0%
Others	3.5%	2.0%	15.0%
sum	100.0%	100.0%	100.0%

Judy's Inflation Rate

Food /beverages	20.0%	× 1.8%	= 0.4%
Housing, incl. utilities	38.0%	× 1.7%	= 0.7%
Apparel	2.0%	× 1.6%	= 0.0%
Transportation	25.0%	× 1.8%	= 0.4%
Medical care	6.0%	× 3.2%	= 0.2%
Recreation	4.0%	× 0.8%	= 0.0%
Education/communication	3.0%	× 1.5%	= 0.0%
Others	2.0%	× 2.1%	= 0.0%
All items			1.8%

Joe's Inflation Rate

Food /beverages	13.0%	× 1.8%	= 0.2%
Housing, incl. utilities	13.0%	× 1.7%	= 0.2%
Apparel	20.0%	× 1.6%	= 0.3%
Transportation	13.0%	× 1.8%	= 0.2%
Medical care	25.0%	× 3.2%	= 0.8%
Recreation	1.0%	× 0.8%	= 0.0%
Education/communication	0.0%	× 1.5%	= 0.0%
Others	15.0%	× 2.1%	= 0.3%
All items			2.1%

Where to Find the CPI?

The CPI is published each month by the U. S. Bureau of Labor Statistics. Data are available at the U.S. Bureau of Labor Statistics's website at http://www.bls.gov/cpi/

The Bottom Line

Calculate the inflation rate from the Consumer Price Index. Use the inflation rate to track the change in the cost-of-living and to estimate salary increases you need to stay ahead of higher prices.

9. How Can You Adjust for Inflation?

Consider this example. In the last five years yon observe that average consumer prices have risen 25 percent. Your salary has increased from $30,000 to $42,000 during the same time period. This works out to be a 40 percent salary increase. Obviously you're better off because your salary has more than kept pace with inflation.

But what if you want to express your salary *today* in terms of the purchasing power of dollars five years ago? This is the same thing as taking out of your salary increase that part that simply kept pace with inflation. How would you do this?

Think of the answer this way. Since consumer prices have increased 25 percent during the past five years, it now takes $1.25 to equal what $1.00 could buy five years ago. Therefore, to see what your income is today in terms of the *purchasing power of dollars five years ago*, simply divide your salary today by 1.25. So, your $42,000 today translates to $42,000/1.25, or $33,600 in terms of the purchasing power of dollars five years ago.

General Formulas

A general formula can be written which will allow you to convert any income, or price, in year B to an inflation-adjusted income or price in terms of purchasing power from some previous year A. The formula is:

$$\text{Income or price in a later year B in terms of purchasing power in previous year A} = \frac{\text{Income or price in a } \textit{later year } \text{B}}{1+\text{total inflation rate from year A to year B in decimal terms}}$$

The total inflation rate between year A and year B is simply the total percentage increase in prices. If inflation is measured by the change in an inflation index (e.g., the Consumer Price Index), then the total inflation rate is just the percentage change in that index. "In decimal terms" means to change the percentage number to a decimal number (e.g., 10% becomes .10). The "1" is added in the denominator of the formula to account for the fact that if there is no inflation, then the purchasing power of dollars is the same in years A and B.

Several examples will now reinforce your understanding of the use of this formula.

EXAMPLE 1-2: In 1995 the Consumer Price Index was 152.4. In 1999 the Consumer Price Index was 166.6. In 1995 John's salary was $25,000; in 1999 it was $30,000. What is John's 1999 salary in terms of 1995 dollars?

ANSWER: The total inflation rate between 1995 and 1999 is calculated as:

$\dfrac{166.6}{152.4} = 1.09$. This means the total inflation rate is 09 percent. In decimal terms this is a total inflation rate of .09.

Year A is 1995 and Year B is 1999. The calculation is:

$$\frac{\text{Salary in Year B (1999)}}{1 + \text{total inflation rate from Year A (1995) to Year B (1999)}} = \frac{\$30,000}{(1+.09)} = \$27,523$$

$27,523 is John's 1999 salary in 1995 dollars.

EXAMPLE 1-3: In 2002 a new 2000 square foot house in Salt Lake City, Utah cost $250,000. By 2012 the price had risen to $350,000. What is the house's price in 2012 in terms of 2002 dollars if the inflation rate from 2002 to 2012 was 27.6%?

ANSWER: The total inflation rate between 2002 and 2012 was 27.6%, or 0.276 in decimal terms.

The calculation is:

$$\frac{\text{House price in Year B (2012)}}{1 + \text{total inflation rate from Year A (2002) to Year B (2012)}} = \frac{\$350,000}{(1+0.276)} = \$274,295$$

$274,295 is the price of a 2000 square food house in 2012 expressed in 2002 dollars.

What if you want to express a previous year's income or price in terms of *today's dollars*. In this case, multiply the previous year's income or price by 1 plus the total inflation rate that has occurred between the two years. The general formula is:

$$\begin{array}{c}\text{Income or price in} \\ \text{previous year A in} \\ \text{terms of purchasing} \\ \text{power in a later} \\ \text{year B.}\end{array} = \begin{array}{c}\text{Income or} \\ \text{price in} \\ \text{previous} \\ \text{year A}\end{array} \times \begin{array}{c}1+\text{inflation} \\ \text{rate from} \\ \text{year A to} \\ \text{year B}\end{array}$$

EXAMPLE 1-4:   Go back to EXAMPLE 1-2 and express John's 1995 salary in terms of 1999 dollars.

ANSWER: Salary in 1995 × (1 + total inflation rate from 1995 to 1999) = $25,000 × 1.09 = $27,250.
$27,250 is John's 1995 salary in terms of 1999 dollars.

EXAMPLE 1-5:   In 2002 gasoline cost $2.00/gallon. In 2012 the price of gasoline was $3.50/gallon. The total inflation rate between 2002 and 2012 was 27.6%. What is the price of gasoline in 2002 in terms of 2012 dollars?

ANSWER: $2.00 × (1 + 0.276) = $2.55. If the price of gasoline increased at the rate of overall inflation, it would have cost $2.55/gallon in 2012 instead of $3.50/gallon. Gasoline became relatively more expensive between 2002 and 2012.

Why Bother?

Why go through these calculations? The simple answer is that it helps us compare incomes and prices between years without the complication of inflation. The calculations allow us to see if prices or incomes are relatively higher or lower between any two years.

BASE YEAR   Does it matter which year is chosen as the base? No, as long as all calculations are made using that year so that results are consistent.

Expressing incomes and prices in inflation-adjusted dollars has become common practice in news reporting and even in political campaigns. Now you know how to do it and what it means!

The Bottom Line

Adjust incomes and prices for inflation by converting dollar amounts to similar "purchasing power" dollars. Then you can determine how incomes and prices have changed *after inflation.*

10. Why Do Interest Rates Exist?

Suppose a stranger wanted to borrow $1,000 from you for a year. Also suppose that prices of all consumer products are expected to be the same a year from now as today (that is, the inflation rate is 0). Would you charge anything for loaning the money?

OPPORTUNITY COST AGAIN

Before answering, consider some of the costs to you, the lender. First, there is risk that the borrower may not repay the loan, or may not repay the loan on time. This could cause problems for you if you have plans for the use of the money. Second, there is an *opportunity cost* to you of lending money). If you keep the $1,000, you can use it in some way and derive pleasure from it. For example, $1,000 could be used as the down payment on a car, or could purchase 200 movie tickets. By lending the $1,000 for a year, you are giving up the pleasure you could derive from using the $1,000 during that year. Furthermore, your circumstances could be altered significantly during the year such that the pleasure you derive from $1,000 received a year from now is much less than the pleasure you could derive from using the $1,000 now. For example, the worst possibility is that you could die during the year and never be able to enjoy the use of the $1,000.

PRINCIPAL

For these reasons, most people must be *paid* in order to give up the use of their money for a certain period of time.[1] Individuals charge interest as the price for loaning money. Generally, the interest price is expressed as an interest rate charged for every dollar loaned per year. For example, if the interest rate is 4 percent, then the borrower of $1,000 (the 1,000 is called the *principal*) for a year must repay the original $1,000 plus the interest payment of $1,000 × .04, or $40. Or, oftentimes, repayments will be scheduled throughout the year. How these are calculated will be discussed in later chapters.

RATE OF TIME PREFERENCE

The interest rate that an individual must be paid to give up use of a dollar today, thereby reducing the pleasure that can be purchased today, is not the same for all individuals. People who have a difficult time postponing pleasure, who have a strong desire for pleasure now as compared to pleasure in the future, will only give up a dollar today if a very high interest rate is paid to them. Such individuals are said to have a *high rate of time preference,* meaning they strongly prefer having pleasure now compared to the future. Children and teenagers typically have a high rate of

---

[1]Of course, most lending is not done from individual to individual, but is conducted through a middleman, for example a bank or savings and loan association, The middleman acts as a broker who matches funds from individuals desiring to lend money to individuals desiring to borrow money. In this case the middleman must attract the money which he/she lends by paying interest to depositors. Borrowers are charged an interest cost sufficient to cover the interest paid to depositors and the cost of the middleman's operation.

time preference because they haven't learned to be forward-looking. Also, adults who have limited economic opportunities, who can't see their economic lot improving in the future, have a high rate of time preference. In comparison, individuals who have a lower desire for pleasure now as compared to pleasure in the future are said to have a low rate of time preference. Individuals with higher rates of time preference are more likely to borrow and spend, whereas individuals with low rates of time preference are more likely to save and invest. More will be said about the rate of time preference later.

REAL INTEREST RATE

The interest rate that compensates individuals for the opportunity cost of lending money and for the risk associated with those loans is called the *real interest rate*. The real interest rate can be considered as the price to borrowers of borrowing money and the reward to lenders of loaning money. The level of the real interest rate is determined by the interaction of lenders and borrowers. Historically, the real interest rate for low risk loans has averaged 3 to 5 percent annually. The real interest rate for high risk loans may be as high as 10 to 15 percent annually.

Inflation and Interest Rates

Inflation has an impact on interest rates. As already discussed (see *Does Inflation Doom Us to An Existence of Poverty?*), when inflation occurs the purchasing power of dollars declines. Inflation is of critical concern to lenders. A lender gives up dollars today, but will only be repaid with dollars in the future. Lenders will only make loans, and give up dollars today, if they are promised to be repaid more dollars in the future. But since dollars are only valuable for what they can purchase, what the lender's trade really implies is that a lender will only give up *purchasing power* today if he or she is promised to receive more *purchasing power* in the future. Since inflation decreases the purchasing power of dollars, lenders will take inflation into account in their offer to loan dollars.

To help you understand the relationship between inflation and lending, consider this example:

Suppose ABC Bank is willing to lend money at a 4 percent *real* interest rate. This means that for every $1 ABC Bank loaned for a year, it would receive back $1.04. Or, more specifically, for every $1 of purchasing power that ABC Bank loans for a year, it expects to receive back $1.04 of purchasing power. But what if during the year the inflation rate is 10 percent. Today when ABC Bank loans a $1, its purchasing power is still $1. But in a year, it will take $1.10 to buy what $1 buys today, so the purchasing power of $1 next year is only 91¢ $(\frac{\$1}{1.1})$. Therefore, when ABC Bank receives $1.04 from its borrower at the end of year, the purchasing power of this payment is only ($\frac{\$1.04}{1.10}$). Clearly, under these conditions ABC loses.

How can lenders protect themselves from this damaging effect of inflation? Quite simply. Lenders merely need to insure that the payments they receive are large enough to counteract the effects of inflation. This can be accomplished by the lender adding the expected average annual inflation rate during the term of the loan to the real interest rate. For example, if the real interest rate is 4 percent and the expected average annual inflation rate is 10 percent, then the *nominal interest rate* that lenders will charge is a combination of 10 percent and 4 percent. The nominal interest rate is the observed interest rate, and is a "combination" of the real interest rate and the expected average annual inflation rate during the loan's term.

NOMINAL INTEREST
RATE

We must pause here for a moment for a technical point. You may be tempted to "combine" the real interest rate and expected inflation rate by adding them to get the nominal interest rate. As an approximation, this is OK. Technically, however, it is wrong. If r is the real interest rate and i is the expected inflation rate, then the nominal interest rate is:

$$(1+r) \times (1+i) - 1$$

or

$$1 + r + i + r \cdot i - 1$$

or

$$r + i + r \cdot i.$$

The true nominal interest rate (r + i + r • i) is greater than the approximation (r + i) by the amount r • i. This is a minor point, but it makes a difference in financial calculations. For simplicity though, merely calculate the nominal interest rate as the real interest rate plus the expected inflation rate.

Expected Inflation Rates and Mistakes

EXPECTED INFLATION
RATE

Notice that the inflation rate which lenders add to the real interest rate is the *expected inflation* rate. Loans are made with payments scheduled in the future. As with most economic variables, the inflation rate in the future cannot be predicted exactly. Lenders therefore must guess what the average inflation rate will be during the term of their loan. If it turns out that their guess was too low, then lenders effectively lose money since the purchasing power of loan repayments will be less than expected.

You might think that lenders never underestimate future inflation rates. You're wrong, In the 1970s most lenders didn't anticipate the high inflation rates which would prevail in the late 1970s and early 1980s,

Mortgage lenders, in particular, loaned money at interest rates which turned out to be too low, and they therefore lost money on the loans. This provided a strong motivation for mortgage lenders to move to adjustable rate mortgages, which shift the risk of guessing wrong about inflation to borrower (much more about this later!).

WRONG GUESSES

Figure 1-12.   Inflation and interest rates.

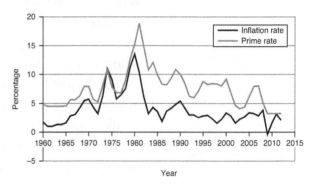

Data source: U.S. Bureau of Labor Statistics and Federal Reserve.

Making mistakes about guessing future inflation rates is not something that only lenders, like bankers, have to worry about. You as an individual investor also face the risk of guessing wrong about future inflation. This risk occurs when you purchase an investment which pays a fixed interest rate for a long period of time, like a five year CD or a 30-year bond. If the average inflation rate turns out to be higher than that implicitly assumed in the interest rate of the long term investment, then you effectively lose money.

Interest Rates and Inflation Rates Move Together

Since nominal interest rates incorporate inflation rates, it shouldn't be surprising that nominal interest rates and inflation rates move together (see Figure 1-12). When the inflation rate trends upward, interest rates trend upward, and when the inflation rate trends downward, interest rates trend downward.

Notice from Figure 1-12, however, that the inflation rate usually changes direction before interest rates change direction. This shouldn't be surprising. It takes time for lenders and investors to realize that the direction of the inflation rate has changed. During this "learning period," nominal interest rates will incorporate past inflation rates.

The Bottom Line

The interest rate charged for a loan is compensation to the lender for the opportunity cost related to giving up use of that money *and* for the expected decline in the purchasing power of money due to inflation. Interest rates and the inflation rate move together. Expect interest rates to eventually rise when the inflation rate is on the rise, and look for interest rates to fall when the inflation rate is falling._____

11. How Does Money Grow?

When you invest money, whether the investment be in a passbook savings account or bonds or something else, you are, in effect, lending money. For example, if the money is invested in a passbook savings account, those funds are loaned by the bank or savings and loan association to another consumer or to a business. If the money is invested in bonds, the funds are being loaned to a business firm or perhaps a public utility.

In most cases an investment will promise to pay you a specified interest rate each period for a specified number of periods. The period could be a day, month, quarter, or year. Often it will be useful to you to determine how this invested money will grow. The accumulated amount of your investment fund is called the *future value* of the investment.

Calculating the future value of an investment fund depends on whether interest earned from the investment is in turn also invested and earns additional interest. If so, then the future value is formed by *compounding interest*; if not, then the future value is formed by *simple interest*.

Simple Interest

Let's take simple interest first. Let P be the amount invested and let r be the periodic interest rate. Then the interest earned in one period is

$$P \times r,$$

and the accumulated amount (future value) of the investment at the end of one period is

$$P + P \times r.$$

If the investment is held for two periods, then the total interest earned for two periods is

$$P \times r + P \times r, \text{ or } 2 \times P \times r,$$

and the future value of the investment at the end of two periods is

$$P + (2 \times P \times r).$$

In general, the simple interest earned on an investment of P dollars earning a periodic interest rate of r for n periods is

$$n \times (P \times r).$$

Similarly, the future value at the end of n periods is

$$P + (n \times P \times r).$$

EXAMPLE 1-6: John James invests $100 in an investment that pays simple interest of 5 percent per year. How much interest will John earn at the end of the year and what will be the future value of his investment?

ANSWER: Here P is \$100, r is 5 percent, and n is 1.

$$\text{Interest earned } = \$100 \times .05 = \$5$$
$$\text{Future value } = \$100 + \$5 = \$105.$$

EXAMPLE 1-7:   Alternatively, John James has the opportunity of investing his \$100 in an investment that pays simple interest of 2 percent per *month*. How much interest will John earn at the end of *three* months and what will be the future value of his investment at that point?

ANSWER: Here P is \$100, r is 2 percent, and n is 3.

$$\text{Interest earned} = 3 \times (\$100 \times .02)$$
$$= 3 \times (\$2) = \$6$$
$$\text{Future value } = \$100 + \$6 = \$106.$$

The Wonderful World of Compound Interest

Figuring interest earnings and future value using compound interest is only slightly more complicated. Compound interest assumes that interest earnings are automatically reinvested at the same interest rate as is paid on the original invested amount.

To see how compound interest works, again consider an investment of P dollars in an investment paying a periodic interest rate of r. At the end of the first period the amount of interest earned is

$$P \times r,$$

and the future value of the investment is

$$P + (P \times r).$$

Notice that, algebraically, the future value amount can be rewritten as:
$$P + (P \times r) = P \times (1 + r).$$

In the second period the full amount of P × (1 + r) is invested at the interest rate r. The amount of interest earned in the second period is

$$[P \times (1 + r)] \times r,$$

and the future value of the investment at the end of the second period is

$$[P \times (1 + r)] + [P(1 + r)] \times r.$$

In simplifying this expression, notice that P × (1 + r) can be "factored out" of both terms. This gives:

$$[P \times (1 + r)] + [P \times (1 + r)] \times r = P \times (1 + r) \times (1 + r).$$

Another way of interpreting (and understanding) the result $P \times (1 + r) \times (1 + r)$ is the following. P is the original amount invested. At the end of the first period the amount P is still in the investment, hence P is multiplied by 1. But also, interest is earned on P which equals $P \times r$, hence P is also multiplied by r. Therefore, the investment accumulation, or future value, at the end of the first period is $P \times (1 + r)$. The amount $P \times (1 + r)$ now becomes the investment amount at the start of the second period. This amount is still in the investment at the end of the second period, hence

$P \times (1 + r)$ is multiplied by 1. Also, interest is earned on $P \times (1 + r)$, hence $P \times (1 + r)$ is also multiplied by r. Therefore, the future value at the end of the second period is $P \times (1 + r) \times (1 + r)$.

By the same reasoning, the future value of the investment at the end of the third period is

$$P \times (1+r) \times (1+r) \times (1+r).$$

FUTURE VALUE FORMULA

It should be evident that a general pattern has been formed. In general, the future value of an original investment of P dollars earning a compound interest rate of r per period for n periods is P multiplied by $(1 + r)$ n times, or

$$P \times (1+r)^n ,$$

where n, the number of periods that the investment is kept, is a "power function" and indicates the number of times that $(1 + r)$ is used as a multiplier. For example, $P \times (1 + r)^2$ equals $P \times (1 + r) \times (1 + r)$, and $P \times (1 + r)^4$ equals $P \times (1 + r) \times (1 + r) \times (1 + r) \times (1 + r)$. It is important to remember that the "period" of r and of n must be the same. For example, if n is years then r must be the yearly interest rate. If n is months then r must be the monthly interest rate. Also, r is in "decimal form" (e.g., 5 percent is .05).

The interest earned on an investment of P dollars earning a compound interest rate of r per period for n periods is simply

$$P \times (1+r)^n - P.$$

EXAMPLE 1-8: John James invests $100 in an investment paying 6 percent per year compounded annually. What is the future value of the investment and the interest earned after three years?

ANSWER: Here P is $100, r is 6 percent, and n is 3.

Future value = $100 \times (1 + .06)^3$

$= \$100 \times 1.06^3 = \$100 \times 1.06 \times 1.06 \times 1.06 = \$119.10$

Interest earned = $119.10 - $100 = $19.10

EXAMPLE 1-9:   Judy Davis invests $100 in an investment paying 6 percent annual interest rate compounded monthly (twelve times yearly). What is the future value of the investment after three years?

ANSWER: The period here is in months, so the interest rate must be a monthly rate. An interest rate of 6 percent annually is equivalent to an interest rate of 6/12 or .5 percent monthly. Also three years is equivalent to 36 monthly periods. Therefore, r equals .5 percent, or .005, and n equals 36 in this example.

$$\text{Future value} = 100 \times (1 + .005)^{36}$$

$$\text{Future value} = \$100 \times (1.005)^{36} = \$119.67.$$

FUTURE VALUE TABLES

Future values using compound interest can be calculated as in the above examples. One can use either a calculator with a "power function" or future value tables. A future value table gives values for $(1 + r)^n$ for given values of r and n. The values are termed *future value factors*. Three future value tables are in the Appendix. Appendix Table A-1 gives annual future value factors, that is, n is years and annual compounding is used. Appendix Table A-2 gives monthly future value factors, that is, n is months and monthly compounding is used. (Don't be confused by the fact that the interest rates in Appendix Table A-2 are stated as annual rates. The calculations did convert the annual rates to monthly rates.) Appendix Table A-3 gives sums of monthly future value factors assuming each investment is made at the end of the month (more on this later).

Given values for r and n, the future value of an initial investment of P dollars is found by:

Future value = P × (future value factor corresponding to r, interest rate, and n, periods).

Similarly, the interest earned is found by:

Interest earned = P × (future value factor corresponding to r, interest rate, and n, periods) − P.

The following examples show you how to use the future value tables.

EXAMPLE 1-10:   You invest $1,000 today in an investment that pays an annual interest rate of 12 percent compounded annually. How much will you have accumulated at the end of three years?

ANSWER: Future value = $1,000 × (future value factor for 12% annual rate and 3 years).
Look in Appendix Table A-1. Find the column headed by 12 (%) and the row headed by 3 (years). The entry is 1.405. This is the future value factor. Therefore, the future value is:

$$\$1,000 \times 1.405 = \$1,405.$$

EXAMPLE 1-11:   Yon invest $1,000 today in an investment that pays an annual interest rate of 12 percent compounded monthly. How much will you have accumulated at the end of three years?

ANSWER: Future value = $1,000 × [future value factor for 12% annual rate and 36 months (3 years × 12 months per year)]
Look in Appendix Table A-2. Find the column headed by the annual interest rate of 12 (%) and the row headed by 36 (months). The entry is 1.431. Therefore, the future value is:

$$\$1,000 \times 1.431 = \$1,431.$$

MANY EQUAL INVESTMENTS   The above examples have assumed a single investment of money at the beginning of an investment term. What happens if a number of investments of the same amount are made over an extended period? To see how to work such problems, consider the following examples.

EXAMPLE 1-12:   Doris Donaldson plans to invest $200 at the *beginning* of each year in an investment paying an annual interest rate of 8 percent compounded annually. She plans to do this for six years. How much will she have accumulated at the end of six years?

This can be worked as six separate problems, that is, $200 invested for six years at 8 percent, $200 invested for five years at 8 percent, $200 invested for four years at 8 percent, $200 invested for three years at 8 percent, $200 invested for two years at 8 percent, and $200 invested for one year at 8 percent. The total accumulation could be calculated by:

$200×(future value factor for 8% and 6 yrs.)

+$200×(future value factor for 8% and 5 yrs.)

+$200×(future value factor for 8% and 4 yrs.)

+$200×(future value factor for 8% and 3 yrs.)

+$200×(future value factor for 8% and 2 yrs.)

+$200×(future value factor for 8% and 1 yr.)

OR, using Appendix Table A-1,

$$
\begin{aligned}
\$200 \times (1,587) &= \$317.40 \\
+\$200 \times (1.469) &= 293.80 \\
+\$200 \times (1.360) &= 272.00 \\
+\$200 \times (1.260) &= 252.00 \\
+\$200 \times (1.166) &= 233.20 \\
+\$200 \times (1.080) &= \underline{216.00} \\
&\ \$1,584.40
\end{aligned}
$$

Alternatively; the future value factors can first be *summed* and then multiplied by the equal periodic investment:

$$
\$200 \times (1.587 + 1.469 + 1.360 + 1.260 + 1.166 + 1.080) =
$$
$$
\$200 \times 7.922 = \$1,584.40
$$

This shortcut can only be taken when the periodic investments are the same in dollar amount.

If Doris invested the $200 at the *end* of each of the six years, then the first $200 would be invested for five years, the second $200 would be invested for four years, the third $200 would be invested for three years, the fourth $200 would be invested for two years, the fifth $200 would be invested for one year, and the last $200 would be added at the end of the six year so no interest would be earned. Using Appendix Table A-1, the calculations are:

$$
\begin{aligned}
\$200 \times 1.469 \ (\text{FVF for 8\% and 5 yrs.}) &= \$293.80 \\
+\$200 \times 1.360 \ (\text{FW for 8\% and 4 yrs.}) &= 272.00 \\
+\$200 \times 1.260 \ (\text{FVF for 8\% and 3 yrs.}) &= 252.00 \\
+\$200 \times 1.166 \ (\text{FVF for 8\% and 2 yrs.}) &= 233.20 \\
+\$200 \times 1.080 \ (\text{FVF for 8\% and 1 yr.}) &= 216.00 \\
+\$200 \times 1.000 &= \underline{200.00} \\
&\ \$1,467.00
\end{aligned}
$$

Or, summing the future value factors first, $200 × (1.469 + 1.360 + 1.260 + 1.166 + 1.080 + 1.000) = $200 × 7.335 = $1,467.00. The future value ($1,467.00) with end of the year investing is understandably less than the future value ($1,584.40) with beginning of the year investing.

The next example looks at monthly investing.

EXAMPLE 1-13: Stan Simons plans to invest $100 at the end of each month in an investment paying an annual interest rate of 7 percent compounded monthly. Stan plans to do this for ten years. How much will he have accumulated at the end of the ten years?

You certainly want to use a shortcut with this problem since you don't want to do 120 (12 months × 10 years) multiplications or even 120 additions. One can either use a future value factor sum formula or use a table of future value factor sums such as Appendix Table A-3. Appendix Table A-3 *gives monthly future value factor sums* assuming *end* of the month investing. To solve the problem, find the 7 percent column and 120 month row in Appendix Table A-3 and read the future value factor sum (173.085). The accumulation at the end of ten years is thus:

MONTHLY FUTURE
VALUE FACTOR SUMS

$$\$100 \times 173.085 = \$17,309$$

How would beginning of the month investing change this result? Figure 1-13 gives the answer. The left side of Figure 1-13 shows investing $200 at the end of each of twelve months at an annual interest rate of 7 percent. The right side of Figure 1-13 shows investing $200 at the beginning of each of twelve months at an annual interest rate of 7 percent. The calculations differ in two ways. The future value factor sum for "beginning of month" investing includes the future value factor for the number of months in the investment term (here 1.072, the FVF for 7% and 12 months). In contrast, the future value factor sum for "end of month" investing includes 1.000, which means the final month's investment earns no interest. Therefore, to convert the future value factor sum for "end of month" investing to the future value factor sum for "beginning of month" investing, perform this operation:

$$
\begin{matrix}
\text{FVFS for} \\
\text{beginning of} \\
\text{month investing}
\end{matrix}
=
\begin{matrix}
\text{FVFS for} \\
\text{end of month} \\
\text{investing} \\
\text{(Appendix TableA-3)}
\end{matrix}
+
\begin{matrix}
\text{FVF for last} \\
\text{month in investment} \\
\text{term (Appendix} \\
\text{Table A-2)} - 1.000
\end{matrix}
$$

EXAMPLE 1-14: Re-do Stan Simons' investment plan from EXAMPLE 1-13 assuming Stan invests at the *beginning* of each month.

ANSWER: FVFS (7%, 120 mos.) from Appendix Table A-3 = 173.085.
FVFS (7%, month 120) from Appendix Table A-2 = 2.010.
FVFS for beginning of month investing = 173.085 + 2.010 − 1.000
= 174.095
Future value = $100 × 174.095 = $17,409.50.

If a problem does not state whether "end of month" or "beginning of month" investing is done, it is assumed that "end of month" investing is done.

Figure 1-13.   End of the month investing vs. beginning of the month investing ($200 per month—annual interest rate, 7%).

Month	End of Month		Beginning of Month	
1	⌐Begin		⌐Begin	$200 × 1.072 (FVF, 7%, 12mos.)
	└End	$200 ×1.066 (FVF, 7%m 11mos.)	└End	
2	⌐Begin		⌐Begin	$200 × 1.066 (FVF, 7%, 11mos.)
	└End	$200 ×1.060 (FVF, 7%, 10mos.)	└End	
3	⌐Begin		⌐Begin	$200 × 1.060 (FVF, 7%, 10mos.)
	└End	$200 ×1.054 (FVF, 7%, 9mos.)	└End	
4	⌐Begin		⌐Begin	$200 × 1.054 (FVF, 7%, 9mos.)
	└End	$200 ×1.048 (FVF, 7%, 8mos.)	└End	
5	⌐Begin		⌐Begin	$200 × 1.048 (FVF, 7%, 8mos.)
	└End	$200 ×1.042 (FVF, 7%, 7mos.)	└End	
6	⌐Begin		⌐Begin	$200 × 1.042 (FVF, 7%, 7mos.)
	└End	$200 ×1.036 (FVF, 7%, 6mos.)	└End	
7	⌐Begin		⌐Begin	$200 × 1.036 (FVF, 7%, 6mos.)
	└End	$200 ×1.030 (FVF, 7%, 5mos.)	└End	
8	⌐Begin		⌐Begin	$200 × 1.030 (FVF, 7%, 5mos.)
	└End	$200 ×1.024 (FVF, 7%, 4mos.)	└End	
9	⌐Begin		⌐Begin	$200 × 1.024 (FVF, 7%, 4mos.)
	└End	$200 ×1.012 (FVF, 7%, 3mos.)	└End	
10	⌐Begin		⌐Begin	$200 × 1.018 (FVF, 7%, 3mos.)
	└End	$200 ×1.006 (FVF, 7%, 2mos.)	└End	
11	⌐Begin		⌐Begin	$200 × 1.012 (FVF, 7%, 2mos.)
	└End	$200 ×1.006 (FVF, 7%, 1mos.)	└End	
12	⌐Begin		⌐Begin	$200 × 1.006 (FVF, 7%, 1mos.)
	└End	$200 ×1.000	└End	

Future value = $200 ×

(1.066 + 1.060 +1.054 +

1.048 + 1.042 + 1.036 +

1.030 + 1.024 + 1.018 +

1.012 + 1.006 + <u>1.000</u>) =

$200 × 12.396* = $2,479.20.

Future value = $200 × _

(1.072 + 1.066 + 1.060 +

1.054 + 1.048 + 1.042 +

1.036 + 1.030 + 1.024 +

1.018 + 1.012 + 1.006) =

$200 × 12.468* = $2,493.60

*Differs from number in Appendix Table A-3 (12.393 - FVFS, 7%, 12 mos.) due to rounding.

FUTURE VALUE FACTOR
SUM FORMULAS
Instead of using the tables, one can also apply the future value factor sum (FVFS) formulas. For beginning of the month (BOM), future value factor sum is

$$FVFS = (1+r)^n + (1+r)^{n-1} + \ldots + (1+r)^1 = \frac{(1+r)^{n+1} - 1}{r} - 1$$

For end of the month (EOM), future value factor sum is

$$FVFS = (1+r)^{n-1} + (1+r)^{n-2} \ldots + (1+r)^0 = \frac{(1+r)^n - 1}{r}$$

For monthly compounding, r is the monthly interest rate and n is the number of months. For annual compounding, r is the annual interest rate and n is the number of years.

The Bottom Line

The future value of an investment is the amount to which the investment will grow after a certain period of time. Compound interest (paying interest on interest) pays you more than simple interest. Use future value tables or a calculator with a "power" function to find the future value of an investment when compounding is used.

12. Back to the Present: What's a Future Dollar Worth?

If you could read only one topic in this book, this would be the one. (That statement should grab your attention!) The technique of converting future dollars to their current (or present) value is a technique that will be used in all consumer financial decisions. In fact, a thorough understanding of this technique is necessary in order to successfully make any consumer decision that involves spending or receiving money over a period of time.

A DOLLAR IS NOT A
DOLLAR IN TIME
A dollar today is worth more than a dollar tomorrow, for two reasons. First, the present is known and certain whereas the future is unknown and uncertain. Therefore, most consumers would rather have a dollar today than delay having it until the future. Furthermore, a dollar today can he used and pleasure purchased with it, whereas the use and pleasure derived from a dollar received in the future is delayed. Second, if inflation occurs between now and the future, the purchasing power of future dollars declines. Therefore, a dollar today is equal to a dollar of purchasing power, but a dollar in the future is equal to less than a dollar of purchasing power. For these two reasons, dollars paid and received at different points in time cannot be considered to be equal.

To reinforce this idea of the changing value of a dollar, consider these practical questions. An IRA (Individual Retirement Account) investment will accumulate for you $1,000,000 at the end of 30 years. Does that mean that you will be a millionaire in today's sense of the term? Or, an insurance policy promises you an endowment (payment) of $50,000 at the end of 20 years. Is that good? What will $50,000 buy then? Consumers have trouble making these comparisons because perceptions about the worth of a dollar are based on current prices, but prices and the value of a dollar will be different in the future.

PRESENT VALUE

DISCOUNTING

Bringing the future value of a dollar back to the present is called finding the present value of a future dollar or sum of money. Finding the *present value* of a sum of money at some future date answers the following question: What amount of money, if invested today until that future date, will yield that future sum of money? The answer is the present value of that future sum of money. Finding the present value of a future amount of money is called *discounting* that future amount. The present value of a future amount of money is the real value of the future amount of money after taking into account expected inflation *and* consumers' preferences for having money today rather than tomorrow. Finding the present value of, or discounting, a future amount of money means finding its value in today's terms.

For example, if the annual interest rate is 7 percent, then the present value of $1,000 received in 10 years is $508.39. Why? Because if $508.39 is invested and earns an annual interest rate of 7 percent compounded annually for 10 years, then its future value is $508.39 × 1.967 (future value factor, 7%, 10 yrs., Appendix Table A-1). If the 7 percent interest rate compensates you both for the opportunity cost of not having $508.39 to use today and for expected inflation, then you would consider having $508.39 today or $1,000 in ten years to be the same.

The Discount Rate

DISCOUNT RATE

The interest rate used in finding the present value of a future sum of money is called the *discount rate*. The discount rate is the rate at which future dollars are traded for present dollars. The higher the discount rate, the less valuable are future dollars compared to present (or current) dollars and the more future dollars are needed to equal one present dollar. Table 1-7 illustrates how the size of the discount rate affects the present value.

Since the discount rate is an interest rate, it is composed of two parts, a real interest rate component and a component for the expected annual inflation rate. As already discussed, the expected annual inflation rate component compensates for the reduced purchasing power of future dollars due to inflation.

The real interest rate component deserves careful discussion. The real interest rate component of the discount rate shows how the consumer,

Table 1-7 Discount rates and present values.

Future value of $1,000 in 5 years.

If discount rate is:	Present value is:
5%	$784
8%	681
10%	621
15%	497
20%	402

in the absence of inflation, would be willing to trade-off future dollars for present dollars. To emphasize, even if inflation is zero, most of us would rather have dollars now than in the future (if you didn't want to use the dollars, you could always save and invest them). Each consumer's willingness to trade-off the present for the future can be very personalized. As already mentioned, economists give the real rate component of the discount rate, which measures how the consumer values the present compared to the future, a special name, the consumer's *rate of time preference*.

RATE OF TIME PREFERENCE AGAIN

At this point you might he thinking, "This is a bunch of semantics—what practical difference does it make?" Your rate of time preference is important and can explain some important behavior. For example, suppose Joe has a higher rate of time preference than Sally. Both Joe and Sally prefer dollars now to dollars later, but Joe puts a higher value on having dollars now than does Sally. For any given expected inflation rate, Joe's discount rate is higher than Sally's, and the present value of any given future money amount will be lower for Joe than for Sally.

Consumers who have high rates of time preference (who strongly favor the present over the future) are less likely to save and invest and more likely to borrow. In contrast, consumers who have low rates of time preference are more likely to save and invest and less likely to borrow. Table 1-8 gives an example of this for Joe and Sally. Joe's rate of time preference is three times as high as Sally's, and Joe's discount rate is 14 percent compared to Sally's 8 percent rate. Joe and Sally can both borrow money and pay 12 percent interest. Joe's high discount rate makes borrowing advantageous for him, but Sally is better off not borrowing.

TEENS VS. ADULTS

With the rate of time preference concept under your belt, you can now better understand the saving and borrowing behavior of specific consumer groups, For example, teenagers tend to value the present

Table 1-8 Effects of differences in rates of time preference: An example of Joe and Sally.

	Joe	Sally
Rate of time preference	9%	3%
Expected annual inflation rate	5%	5%
Discount rate	14%	8%

Joe and Sally can both borrow $1 today and pay back $1.12 in one year (12% interest).

Joe values $1 today at $1, and values $1.12 next year at $1.12 \times \dfrac{1}{1.14} = 98¢$.

Joe will borrow values $1.12 next year at

$$\$1.12 \times \frac{1}{1.08} = \$1.04 .$$ Sally will not borrow.

relative to the future more than do adults, implying that teenagers have high rates of time preference and high discount rates. This may help explain why teenagers are more likely to borrow and less likely to save than adults.

POOR VS. NON-POOR Due to the uncertainty of their future income and economic situation, it's also thought that the poor have a higher rate of time preference and a higher discount rate than the non-poor. This may help account for the observation that the poor are more willing to borrow at higher interest rates than the non-poor.[2]

What Discount Rate Should You Use?

Selecting a discount rate in the analysis of consumer decisions is important because, as you've seen, the discount rate can significantly affect the present value result. Higher discount rates will favor options which have paybacks weighted to the present versus the future, whereas lower discount rates will favor options with paybacks weighted more to the future.

A standard discount rate used in consumer decision-making is the *interest rate earned on risk-free or low-risk investments*. Examples would be the interest rate earned on U.S. Treasury securities or on an insured CD. This will be the kind of discount rate used in this book.

---

[2]Andreasen, Alan. *The Disadvantaged Consumer*, The Free Press, 1975, p. 204.

JUNIOR GOES HOME AND TAKES A PAY CUT

C O N S U M E R   T O P I C

The baseball world was shocked and Cincinnati Reds' fans elated when superstar Ken Griffey, Jr. was traded from the Seattle Mariners to the Reds in early 2000. Griffey—nicknamed Junior—has been considered to be one of the best all-around players in the game. He signed a nine year 116.5 million dollar contract with the Reds.

Junior's salary, at $12.9 million ($116.5/9) annually, is comparable to the pay of other big league superstars. But is it really? Half of his $116.5 million total salary is deferred until after 2009. So although Junior is paid, on paper, $116.5 million for nine years of play with the Reds, he doesn't receive all that cash in nine years.

In fact, when the delayed payment of half of Junior's contract is taken into account, the present-value of his salary is calculated at between $9.2 million and $9.3 million per year. Considering that baseball experts estimate Junior could have gotten almost $20 million a year from other teams, he indeed did take a pay cut to play with his hometown team.

Source: Blum, Ronald, "Griffey Contract Slum Baseball," *The Cincinnati Enquirer,* February 12, 2000, www.enquirer.com.

However, you should recognize that if the individual for whom a particular analysis is being done has a very high rate of time preference, then a higher discount rate should be used. Also, if the analysis being done includes very risky outcomes, a high discount rate should be used.

Calculating Present Values

PRESENT VALUE
FORMULA

Finding the present value, or discounting, is actually the reverse of calculating the future value. Recall that the formula for finding the future value of an amount of money invested today (P) at compound interest rate r for n periods is:

$$\text{Future value} = P \times (1+r)^n$$

The amount invested today, P, can be considered as the present value. Therefore, this formula can be rewritten as:

$$\text{Future value} = \text{Present value} \times (1+r)^n$$

To solve for the present value, merely perform a simple set of divisions to give:

$$\text{Present value} = \text{future value} \times \frac{1}{(1+r)^n}$$

PRESENT VALUE
FACTOR

The term $\frac{1}{(1+r)^n}$ is called the *present value factor* or *discount factor.*

EXAMPLE 1-15: What is the present value of $50,000 to be received in ten years if the discount rate is 12 percent?

$$\text{Present value} = \$50,000 \times \frac{1}{(1+.12)^{10}}$$
$$= \$50,000 \times \frac{1}{3.1058}$$
$$= \$50,000 \times 3.220$$
$$= 16,100.$$

How should the answer of $16,100 be interpreted? First, $16,100 is the amount which, if invested today for ten years in an investment paying a 12 percent compound annual interest rate, will grow to the amount of $50,000. Also, $16,100 is the purchasing power of $50,000 received in ten years when it takes $1.12 next year to equal $1.00 today.

PRESENT VALUE
FACTOR TABLES

The calculation of present value (or discount) factors can be difficult and tedious, especially if a hand calculator with a power function is not available. Fortunately again, tables are available which contain present value factors for given values of r and n. Two such tables are given in the Appendix. Appendix Table A-4 gives present value factors for annual compounding, where n is in years. Appendix Table A-5 gives present value factors for monthly compounding where n is in months. The present value formula for use with Appendix Tables A-4 and A-5 is:

Present value = future value × (present value factor for interest rate r and period n).

EXAMPLE 1-16: What is the present value of $50,000 to be received in ten years if the discount rate is 12 percent, using annual compounding.

$$\text{Present value} = \$50,000 \times (\text{present value factor for interest rate}$$
$$\text{of 12 percent and 10 years from Appendix}$$
$$\text{Table A} - 4)$$
$$= \$50,000 \times .322$$
$$= \$16,100.$$

EXAMPLE 1-17: What is the present value of $1,000,000 to be received in thirty years if the discount rate is 8 percent, compounded annually?

$$\begin{aligned}
\text{Present value} &= \$1,000,000 \times (\text{present value factor for interest} \\
&\quad \text{rate of 8 percent and 30 years} \\
&\quad \text{from Appendix Table A-4}) \\
&= \$1,000,000 \times .099 \\
&= \$99,000.
\end{aligned}$$

EXAMPLE 1-18: What is the present value of $100,000 paid in two years if the discount rate is 10 percent compounded monthly?

$$\begin{aligned}
\text{Present value} &= \$100,000 \times (\text{present value factor for interest} \\
&\quad \text{rate of 10 percent and 24} \\
&\quad \text{months from Appendix Table A-5}) \\
&= \$100,000 \times .819 \\
&= \$81,900.
\end{aligned}$$

How would you find the present value of a number of payments of equal amount over some time period? You encountered a similar question with calculating a future value. One way is to find the present value of each payment individually and then add them. A shortcut is to first add the present value factors to form a present value factor sum, and then multiply the present value factor sum by the periodic payment. However, this shortcut can be done only when the periodic amounts are equal.

EXAMPLE 1-19: What is the present value of ten annual payments of $2,000 each. Each payment is made at the end of the year. Use a discount rate of 8 percent compounded annually.

ANSWER:

$$\begin{aligned}
\$2,000 \times (&\text{sum of present value factors for 7 percent} \\
&\text{and years 1 to 10, from Appendix Table A-4}). \\
&= \$2,000 \times (0.935 + 0.873 + 0.816 + 0.763 \\
&\quad + 0.713 + 0.666 + 0.623 + \\
&\quad 0.582 + 0.544 + 0.508 \\
&= \$2,000 \times 7.023 \\
&= \$14,046.
\end{aligned}$$

EXAMPLE 1-20: You make twelve monthly auto loan payments of $1.00 each. Each payment is made at the end of the month. What's the present value of all twelve payments using a discount rate of 18 percent compounded monthly?

ANSWER:

$100×(sum of present value factors for 18

percent and months 1 to 12, from Appendix Table A-5.

$100×(0.985+0.971+0.956+0.942+0.928+

0.915+0.901+0.888+0.875+0.862+

0.849+0.836)

= $100×10.899

= $1,089.90.

The above examples have all assumed payments were made at the *end* of each month or year. What happens if they're made at the beginning of a period? In this case the first payment is not discounted because it occurs now (it's present value factor is 1.000). So discounting occurs with the second payment, meaning the second payment is discounted using the present value factor associated with one period (one month or one year). Likewise, the third payment is discounted using the present value factor associated with the second period. EXAMPLE 1-21 illustrates this.

EXAMPLE 1-21: What is the present value of the twelve monthly $100 auto loan payments (from EXAMPLE 1-20) if the payments are made at the beginning of each month?

ANSWER: **Month**

1   ⌐Begin $100 × 1.000 (since payment occurs now) = $100.00
    └End

2   ⌐Begin $100 × .985 (PVF,18%,1 mo. from now) = $98.50
    └End

3   ⌐Begin $100 × .971 (PVF,18%, 2 mos. from now) = $97.10
    └End

4   ⌐Begin $100 × .956 (PVF,18%, 3 mos. from now) = $95.60
    └End

5 $\begin{bmatrix} \text{Begin} \\ \text{End} \end{bmatrix}$ $100 \times .942 \text{ (PVF,18\%, 4 mos. from now)} = \$94.20$

6 $\begin{bmatrix} \text{Begin} \\ \text{End} \end{bmatrix}$ $100 \times .928 \text{ (PVF,18\%, 5 mos. from now)} = \$92.80$

7 $\begin{bmatrix} \text{Begin} \\ \text{End} \end{bmatrix}$ $100 \times .915 \text{ (PVF,18\%, 6 mos. from now)} = \$91.50$

8 $\begin{bmatrix} \text{Begin} \\ \text{End} \end{bmatrix}$ $100 \times .901 \text{ (PVF,18\%, 7 mos. from now)} = \$90.10$

9 $\begin{bmatrix} \text{Begin} \\ \text{End} \end{bmatrix}$ $100 \times .888 \text{ (PVF,18\%, 8 mos. from now)} = \$88.80$

10 $\begin{bmatrix} \text{Begin} \\ \text{End} \end{bmatrix}$ $100 \times .875 \text{ (PVF,18\%, 9 mos. from now)} = \$87.50$

11 $\begin{bmatrix} \text{Begin} \\ \text{End} \end{bmatrix}$ $100 \times .862 \text{ (PVF,18\%, 10 mos. from now)} = \$86.20$

12 $\begin{bmatrix} \text{Begin} \\ \text{End} \end{bmatrix}$ $100 \times .849 \text{ (PVF,18\%, 11 mos. from now)} = \underline{\$84.90}$

PRESENT VALUE = $1,107.20

Notice that the first month's $100 has a present value of $100 since it occurs now. The second month's $100 is multiplied by the present value factor for month 1 since that payment occurs one month from now. The third month's $100 is multiplied by the present value factor for month 2 since that payment occurs two months from now, etc.

The next example shows what to do when the present value of a large number of future payments is to be calculated.

EXAMPLE 1-22: Tom's monthly mortgage payment for principal and interest is $600. Tom will make 360 monthly payments. Each payment is made at the end of the month. What is the present value of these payments using a discount rate of 10 percent compounded monthly?

ANSWER: To answer this question, you could first add 360 monthly present value factors, then multiply the sum by $600. This is obviously a lot of work to do!

PRESENT VALUE
FACTOR SUM TABLE

To shorten your work, *Appendix Table A-6* gives monthly present value factor *sums* for alternative combinations of interest rates and terms, assuming payments are made at the end of each month. Appendix Table A-6 shows that for an annual interest rate of 10 percent and a term of 360 months, the present value factor sum is 113.951. The present value of the 360 monthly payments of $600 each is thus:

$$\$600 \times 113.951 = \$68,370.60.$$

Do you think the $68,370.60 is related in any way to the loan amount which Tom borrowed? You'll discover the answer later.

One last point must be addressed which parallels our discussion of future value factor sums. Appendix Table A-6 has monthly present value factor sums assuming payments are made at *the* end of each month. Although end of the month payments are most common, what if payments are made at the *beginning* of each month? Two adjustments must be made to the present value factor sum from Appendix Table A-6. First, add 1.000 because the present value of the first payment is its current value. Second, subtract the present value factor for the last month of the term (from Appendix Table A-5) because the final payment occurs at the beginning of the last month rather than at the end. Thus, the calculation is:

PVFS for beginning of month payments	PVFS for end of month payments (Appendix Table A-6)		PVF for last month in payment term (from Appendix Table A-5)
		$+1.000 -$	

EXAMPLE 1-22: Redo the present value of Tom's monthly mortgage payments in EXAMPLE 1-22 assuming payments are made at the beginning of each month.

ANSWER: FVFS for beginning = 113,951 + 1.000 − PVF (10%, of month payments month 360) from Appendix Table A-5

$$= 113.951 + 1.000 - 0.050$$

$$= 114.901$$

Present value $$= \$600 \times 114,901$$

$$= \$68,940.60$$

Instead of using the tables, one can also apply the present value factor sum (PVFS) formulas. For beginning of the month (BOM), present value factor sum is

$$PVFS = \frac{1}{(1+r)^0} + \frac{1}{(1+r)^1} + \dots + \frac{1}{(1+r)^{n-1}} = 1 + \frac{1 - \frac{1}{(1+r)^{n-1}}}{r}$$

For end of the month (EOM), present value factor sum is

$$PVFS = \frac{1}{(1+r)^1} + \dots + \frac{1}{(1+r)^n} = \frac{1 - \frac{1}{(1+r)^n}}{r}$$

For monthly compounding, r is the monthly interest rate and n is the number of months. For annual compounding, r is the annual interest rate and n is the number of years.

The Bottom Line

The purchasing power of dollars paid or received at different points in time is not the same. Dollars paid or received in the future are worth less than dollars paid or received today Taking the present value of future dollars (also called discounting) is a way to adjust the value of those dollars to make their purchasing power equivalent to current dollars. In this way the value of dollars paid or received at different points in time can be compared.

13. How Do You Calculate an Average—The Economic Way?

Consider this situation. You've built up a nest egg of $100,000 which you plan to spend over 10 years. How much can you spend each year?

You might be tempted to say the answer is $10,000, since $100,000/10 is $10,000 for each of the ten years. But this is wrong. You'll actually be able to spend more than $10,000 a year. Why?

You've probably guessed the answer. It's because the $100,000 can be invested to earn interest, and the interest earnings will add to what you can spend each year. So when considering money over time, the "economic average" will produce a periodic amount greater than the normal arithmetic average. There's a name (of course) for this economic average. It's called an *annuity*.

Calculating the Annuity

The equal periodic (e.g., monthly or annual) payment which a sum of money will produce for a specific number of years, when invested at a

given interest rate, is called the *annuity*. In deriving a way to calculate

C
O
N
S
U
M
E
R

T
O
P
I
C

EQUAL PAYMENT PLANS

Equal payment plans (EPP) are frequently offered by energy companies as a way to ease the burden of fuel payments. The EPP works like this. The energy company estimates your bill for the coming year, perhaps by increasing last year's bill by some inflation rate. The estimated annual bill is divided by twelve. This payment becomes your equal monthly payment. You pay it instead of paying your actual bill (based on your actual energy consumption) each month. An important feature of the EPP is that the first EPP payment begins in the summer, typically in July.

Is the EPP a good deal for the consumer? To answer this, look at the example below for a consumer's natural gas bill. This consumer uses natural gas for heating hot water and for heating the home in the winter. Consequently, natural gas consumption is much greater in the winter than in the summer. If the consumer's monthly bill is based on actual consumption, then the monthly bill is much lower in the summer months than in the winter months. If the consumer uses the EPP, the monthly bill is $72.50 each month.

Which payment plan is cheaper? To find out, simply calculate the present value of each payment stream. In the example, an 8 percent annual discount rate is used, and monthly present value factors are taken from Appendix Table A-5.

As the calculations show, the EPP is actually slightly more expensive. The reason is simple. With the EPP, the consumer is pre-paying some of his more costly winter bills in the summer and fall months. Hence, the consumer is losing the opportunity of investing these prepayments and earning interest So the fuel company isn't giving consumers any favors.

The fuel company has an incentive to begin EPPs in an "off-season" month when energy consumption is lowest In the South, where summer energy bills for air conditioning are often higher than winter electricity bills, an EPP for electricity would more likely start in the autumn or winter.

	Jul	Aug	Sep	Oct	Nov	Dec	Jan	Feb	Mar	Apr	May	Jun
Payment based on actual consumption	$30	$30	$40	$50	$120	$130	$150	$140	$70	$50	$30	$30
EPP	$72½	$72½	$72½	$72½	$72½	$72½	$72½	$72½	$72½	$72½	$72½	$72½

Present value of payment bated on actual consumption (8% discount rate)

$$= \$30 \times 0.993 + \$30 \times 0.987 + \$40 \times 0.980 + \$50 \times 0.974$$
$$+ \$120 \times 0.967 + \$130 \times 0.961 + \$150 \times 0.955 + \$140 \times 0.948$$
$$+ \$70 \times 0.942 + \$50 \times 0.936 + \$30 \times 0.930 + \$30 \times 0.923$$
$$= \$832.57.$$

Present value of EPP
$$= \$72.50 \times 0.993 + \$72.50 \times 0.987 + \$72.50 \times 0.980$$
$$+ \$72.50 \times 0.974 + \$72.50 \times 0.967 + \$72.50 \times 0.961$$
$$+ \$72.50 \times 0.955 + \$72.50 \times 0.948 + \$72.50 \times 0.942$$
$$+ \$72.50 \times 0.936 + \$73.50 \times 0.930 + \$72.50 \times 0.923$$
$$= \$833.46.$$

the annuity, it's actually best to think of it in reverse. The string of annuity payments, when discounted by the interest rate earned by the original sum of money, will equal that original sum of money. For example, if $100,000 can be invested to earn 8 percent interest, then the annuity payment for 10 years is $14,905.35, where each payment is received at the end of each year. This means that the present value of 10 annual payments of $14,905.35, when discounted by an 8 percent annual interest rate, equals $100,000. To see this, go through the following calculations, using the present value factors from Appendix Table A-4.

$14,905.35 \times 0.926 + \$14,905.35 \times 0.857 + \$14,905.35 \times 0.794 + \$14,905.35 \times 0.735 + \$14,905.35 \times 0.681 + \$14,905.35 \times 0.630 + \$14,905.35 \times 0.583 + \$14,905.35 \times 0.540 + \$14,905.35 \times 0.500 + \$14,905.35 \times 0.463,$

which equals:

$13,802.35 + \$12,773.89 + \$11,834.85 + \$10,955.43 + \$10,150.54 + \$9,390.37 + \$8,689.82 + \$8,048.89 + \$7,452.68 + \$6,901.18 = \$100,000.$

Or, use the short-cut method:

$14,905.35 \times (0.926 + 0.857 + 0.794 + 0.735 + 0.681 + 0.630 + 0.583 + 0.540 + 0.500 + 0.463)$

or

$14,905.35 \times (6.709) = \$100,000.$

CALCULATING AN ANNUITY PAYMENT   To find an annuity payment, then, simply divide the original amount of money by the sum of the present value factors associated with the interest rate and number of annuity payments.

EXAMPLE 1-24: Melody just received an inheritance of $50,000. Melody wants an equal annual income from this money for eight years. Melody will receive the annual income at the end of each year. How much can Melody receive each year if she can invest at 6 percent compounded annually?

ANSWER: Use Appendix Table A-4. Sum the present value factors under 6 percent for years 1 to 8:

$0.943 + 0.890 + 0.840 + 0.792 + 0.747 + 0.705 + 0.665 + 0.627 = 6.209.$

Divide this sum into $50,000:

$$\frac{\$50,000}{6.209} = \$8052.83$$

Melody can receive $8052.83 each year for eight years.

Table 1-9   Spreading $50,000 over eight years.

$50,000 × 1.06 = $53,000.00;	$53,000.00 − $8,052.83 = $44,947.17
44,947.17 × 1.06 = 47,644.00;	47,644.00 − 8,052.83 = 39,591.17
39,591.17 × 1.06 = 41,966.64;	41,966.64 − 8,052.83 = 33,913.81
33,913.81 × 1.06 = 35,948.64;	35,948.64 − 8,052.83 = 27,895.81
27,895.81 × 1.06 = 29,569.56;	29,569.56 − 8,052.83 = 21,516.73
21,516.73 × 1.06 = 22,807.73;	22,807.73 − 8,052.83 = 14,754.90
14,754.90 × 1.06 = 15,640.19;	15,640.19 − 8,052.83 = 7,587.36
7,587.36 × 1.06 = 8,042.60;	8,042.60 − 8,052.83 = − 10.23
	(due to rounding)

To prove to yourself that $8052.83 can, in fact, be received each year, and at the end of eight years the $50,000 will be exhausted (used up), follow the calculations in Table 1-9.

What if, in EXAMPLE 1-24, the first payment is received immediately, and the remaining payments are received at the beginning of each year. In this case, the first present value factor is 1, so only seven additional present value factors are added from Appendix Table A-4. The annuity payment is thus:

$$\frac{\$50,000}{[1.000+0.943+0.890+0.840+0.792+0.747+0.705+0.665]}=\frac{\$50,000}{6.582}=\$7,596.48.$$

MONTHLY ANNUITY PAYMENTS

Note that this payment is less than the payment in EXAMPLE 1-24. Monthly annuity payments can also be calculated. In this case monthly present value factors are added and divided into the original sum of money.

EXAMPLE 1-25: What monthly annuity payment can Melody receive for 96 months if she earns a 10 percent annual interest rate compounded monthly on her $50,000 money? Each payment is received at the end of the month.

ANSWER: From Appendix Table A-6, find the present value factor sum for the 10 percent column and 96 month row. This is 65.901. Divide 65.901 into $50,000:

$$\frac{\$50,000}{65.901}=\$758.71 \text{ (monthly annuity payment for each of 96 months).}$$

Appendix Table A-6 helps you in this case by giving the monthly present value factor sums associated with alternative annual interest rates and monthly terms, assuming payments are received at the end of each month.

If the first monthly payment is to be received immediately and the remaining payments are received at the beginning of each month, then a different present value factor must be used. In this case, take the present value factor sum from Appendix Table A-6, add 1.000 (because the first period is received immediately) and subtract the present value factor for the final month (from Appendix Table A-5). That is:

$$
\begin{array}{l}
\text{PVFS for} \\
\text{beginning of} \\
\text{month} \\
\text{payments}
\end{array}
=
\begin{array}{l}
\text{PVFS from} \\
\text{Appendix} \\
\text{Table A-6}
\end{array}
+1.000-
\begin{array}{l}
\text{PVF for final} \\
\text{month from} \\
\text{Appendix} \\
\text{Table A-5}
\end{array}
$$

Calculating How Long an Annuity Will Last

The annuity calculation can be done in reverse to find how long a string of annuity payments will last. In this case simply divide the original money amount by the annuity payment. The result is the associated present value factor sum. If the annuity payments are annual, then go to Appendix Table A-4 and begin adding present value factors under the interest rate used until the present value factor sum is reached. Then read-off the corresponding number of years.

If the annuity payments are monthly; then go to Appendix Table A-6 and led the present value factor sum under the interest rate used. Read-off the corresponding number of months.

EXAMPLE 1-26: How long will $5,000 last if annual annuity payments of $1,000 are received and 5 percent interest is earned and payments are received at the end of each year?

ANSWER:

$$
\frac{\$5,000}{\$1,000} = 5.00.
$$

Under 5 percent in Appendix Table A4,

$$0.952 + 0.907 + 0.864 + 0.823 + 0.784 + 0.746 = 5.076,$$

which is associated with six years. The money will last approximately six years.

EXAMPLE 1-27: How long will $10,000 last if annuity payments of $100 monthly are made and 9 percent interest is earned and payments are received at the end of each month?

ANSWER:

$$\frac{\$10,000}{\$100} = 100.$$

Find 100 in Appendix Table A-6 under 9 percent interest. 100 falls between 98.594 (180 months) and 101.573 (192 months), so take halfway between and say 186 months.

The Bottom Line

An annuity is the equal periodic payment that can be generated over a period of time by a sum of money assuming the sum of money is invested. The annuity is always larger than the simple average because interest in included. You'll revisit annuities later. They're the basis for calculating loan payments!

14. When Is a Dollar in Hand Worth More Than Two Dollars in the Bush?

Consumer economics is filled with uncertainty. Will you get that new job or not? How much extra salary will you receive after earning a master's degree? Will interest rates be higher or lower next year? Will the stock market rise or fall?

Is there any way in which the various outcomes connected with a decision can be averaged when uncertainty is present? Say, for example, that there are three possibilities for your salary next year: it can stay the same at $30,000, you can get a modest raise of 5 percent to $31,500, or

EXPECTED SALARY

you can get a big raise of 10 percent to $33,000. Can you calculate, on average, what your *expected* salary will be next year?

The key word here is *expected*. To calculate your expected salary you must know one other piece of information: the *chances*, or probabilities, associated with each of the three outcomes for your salary next year. If you know the chances associated with each outcome, thee you can calculate your *expected*, or probability-weighted, salary using this formula:

$$
\begin{aligned}
\text{NEXT YEAR'S} \ = \ & \$30,000 \ \times \ (\text{CHANCE} \\
\text{EXPECTED} \ & \ \text{OF RECEIVING} \\
\text{SALARY} \ & \ \$30,000 \ \text{NEXT YEAR}) \\
+ \ & \$31,500 \ \times \ (\text{CHANCE} \\
& \ \text{OF RECEIVING} \\
& \ \$31,500 \ \text{NEXT YEAR}) \\
+ \ & \$33,000 \ \times \ (\text{CHANCE} \\
& \ \text{OF RECEIVING} \\
& \ \$33,000 \ \text{NEXT YEAR})
\end{aligned}
$$

For example, if the chance of receiving $30,000 next year is 20 percent (.20), the chance of receiving $31,500 next year is 50 percent (.50), and the chance of receiving $33,000 next year is 30 percent (.30), then next year's expected salary is:

$$\$30,000 \times (.20) + \$31,500 \times (.50) + \$33,000 \times (.30) = \$31,650.$$

The formula can be generalized for any number of outcomes for a particular situation. For example, if there are eight possible outcomes, multiply each outcome by the chance of it occurring, and then sum all the results. However, make sure the sum of chances is 100 percent.

Calculating the expected value for a number of possible outcomes is most useful in investment analysis. Here the unknown outcome is what rate of return a particular investment (like a stock) may earn. Calculating the expected value is a way to reduce all the outcomes to one number.

EXAMPLE 1-28: Susan just bought Company ABC stock. Of course Susan wants the value of the stock to rise, but there's no assurance it will. Through study and discussion with investment advisors, Susan sees four possible outcomes for the stock in the next year:

> There's a 10% chance the stock will go up 20%,
> There's a 50% chance the stock will go up 10%,
> A 20% chance the stock will not change in value,
> A 20% chance the stock will fall in value by 15%.

What's the expected change in the stock's value for next year?

ANSWER: Expected value of change in ABC stock's value:

$20\% \times (.10) + 10\% \times (.50) + 0\% \times (.20) - 15\% \times (.20) = 2\% + 5\% + 0\% - 3\% = 4\%$

The *expected* change in the stock's value is 4 percent.

Now we can answer the question heading this chapter (When is a dollar in hand worth more than two dollars in the bush?). The answer is—when the chance of the two dollars in the bush blowing away is more than 50 percent. If, for example, the chance of the two dollars blowing away is 60 percent, then the expected value of the two bush dollars is:

$$\$2 \times .40 + \$0 \times .60 = 80\text{¢}.$$

Since 80 cents is less than a dollar in hand, you'd prefer a dollar in hand!

The Bottom Line

Uncertainty exists for many economic outcomes; for example, what your salary will be next year; what return your stocks will earn, where the inflation rate will go. If chances, or probabilities, can be attached to each possible outcome, then the expected outcome (or expected value) can be calculated.

WORDS AND CONCEPTS YOU SHOULD KNOW

Nominal Price-Relative Price
Value of Time
Declining Marginal Value
Demand Curve
Supply Curve
Market
Equilibrium Price
Opportunity Cost
Wage Differences
Inflation Rate
Purchasing Power of the Dollar
Escalating Inflation
Disinflation
Deflation
Producer Price Index
Consumer Price Index

Adjusting for Inflation
Rate of Time Preference
Real Interest Rate
Expected Inflation Rate
Future Value
Simple Interest
Compound Interest
Future Value Factor
Future Value Factor Sums
Present Value
Discounting
Discount Rate
Present Value Factor
Present Value Factor Sums
Annuity
Expected Value

MICROFOUNDATIONS—A SUMMARY

1 Comparing prices.
- At same point in time: Compare nominal prices, or compute relative prices. Relative prices set one price equal to 1.00 and computes other prices relative to 1.00.

Example:	*Pork*	*Chicken*
Nominal price	$2.00/lb.	$2.20/lb.
Relative price	1.00	$\frac{\$2.20}{\$2.00} = 1.10$

- Over time: Must compare relative prices. Use a base, either Consumer Price Index or average wage rate.

Example:	*2002*	*2012*
CPI	179.0	229.6
Price of movie ticket	$8.00	$9.00
Relative price of movie ticket	$\frac{8.00}{179.9} = 0.044$	$\frac{9.00}{229.6} = 0.039$

Conclusion—Movie tickets became relatively less expensive.

2. Your time is a limited resource—therefore, it has value. The price, or value, of your time in any activity is the value of what else you could do with that time. On average, your time is worth 20 to 70 percent of your wage rate. This has implications for commuting, shopping, and household activities, to name a few.

3. Declining marginal value means you get progressively less pleasure from consumption of additional units of a product or service.

4. A demand curve shows the quantity of a product consumers buy at every price; a supply curve shows the quantity of a product firms produce at every price.
- The equilibrium price is where demand equals supply.
- If demand increases faster than supply, price rises.
- If supply increases faster than demand, price falls.

5. Every use of time or money which we make has an alternative use. The value of that alternative use is called the opportunity cost.

6. On average, jobs which require more skill, training, or experience pay higher wages. Also, jobs which are riskier, or are located in undesirable locations, pay more than the same job with less risk or located in a desirable location.

7. Inflation is a rise in the average price level of consumer goods and services. The inflation rate is the percentage increase in the average price level.
   - Inflation reduces the purchasing power of dollars.
   - A rising inflation rate is called escalating inflation.
   - Disinflation occurs when the inflation rate is falling, but is still positive.
   - Deflation occurs when the average price level falls.
   - A relative price increase occurs when a product's price rises faster than the inflation rate.
   - A relative price decrease occurs when a product's price rises slower than the inflation rate.
   - To keep ahead of inflation, your salary and investments must increase by at least the rate of inflation.

8. The average price level is measured by the Consumer Price Index (CPI). The inflation rate is measured by the percentage change in the CPI.

9. Use these formulas to adjust for inflation in order to compare incomes or prices at different points in time:

$$\text{Income or Price in a later Year B in terms of purchasing power in previous Year A} = \frac{\text{Income or Price in a later Year B}}{1 + \text{inflation rate from Year A to Year B}}$$

$$\text{Income or Price in previous Year A in terms of purchasing power in a Year B} = \text{Income or Price in Previous Year A} \times \text{1 + inflation rate from Year A to Year B}$$

10. Interest rates are charged on loans to compensate the lender for giving up use of money (real interest rate) and to compensate the lender for losses in purchasing power resulting from future inflation (inflation premium).
    - people who strongly value the present compared to the future have a high rate of time preference and are more likely to borrow.
    - The nominal, or observed, interest rate equals the real interest rate plus the expected inflation rate.

11. When compounding is used, the future value of an original investment, P, is:

$$P \times (1+r)^n, \text{ where}$$

r is the periodic interest rate and n is the number of compounding periods. The amount $(1+r)^n$ is the future value factor.

Future value factor sum is used when an equal amount of periodical investments are invested. The beginning of the month (BOM) future value factor sum formula is

$$FVFS = (1+r)^n + (1+r)^{n-1} + \ldots + (1+r)^1 = \frac{(1+r)^{n+1} - 1}{r} - 1,$$

And the end of the month (EOM) future value factor sum formula is

$$FVFS = (1+r)^{n-1} + (1+r)^{n-2} \ldots + (1+r)^0 = \frac{(1+r)^n - 1}{r}.$$

- Appendix Table A-1 gives future value factors for annual compounding.
- Appendix Table A-2 gives future value factors for monthly compounding.
- Appendix Table A-3 gives future value factor sums used when the same amount P is invested at the end of each month for a number of months; multiply the future value factor sum by P to calculate the future value.

12. Finding the present value of a future dollar amount means finding the present dollar amount which, if invested, would grow to that future dollar amount. If the investment interest rate compensates for the rate of time preference and expected inflation, then the present value and future value have the same real value.
   - The formula is:

$$\text{present value} = \text{future value} \times \frac{1}{(1+r)^n}, \text{ where}$$

$\frac{1}{(1+r)^n}$ is the present value factor.

Present value factor sum is used when a series of period payments of the same amount are discounted. The beginning of the month (BOM) present value factor sum formula is

$$PVFS = \frac{1}{(1+r)^0} + \frac{1}{(1+r)^1} + \ldots + \frac{1}{(1+r)^{n-1}} = 1 + \frac{1 - \frac{1}{(1+r)^{n-1}}}{r},$$

and the end of the month (EOM) present value factor sum formula is

$$PVFS = \frac{1}{(1+r)^1} + \ldots + \frac{1}{(1+r)^n} = \frac{1 - \frac{1}{(1+r)^n}}{r}.$$

- Appendix Table A-4 gives present value factors for annual compounding.
- Appendix Table A-5 gives present value factors for monthly compounding.
- Appendix Table A-6 gives present value factor sums used to find the present value of a series of the same monthly amounts.

13. An annuity is a series of periodic payments of the same amount derived from an original principal amount and its interest earnings. Divide the original principal amount by a present value factor sum to find the annuity amount.

14. The expected value of an outcome is the sum of each possible outcome multiplied by the probability of the outcome occurring.

DISCUSSION QUESTIONS

1. Why is it important for consumers to distinguish between nominal prices and relative prices?

2. Why is your time valuable?

3. Why do top business executives have company provided jets?

4. Do you think there's a connection between the increasing number of women working in the workplace and the growth of the convenience and prepared food industry? If you do, explain the connection.

5. When unexpected cold weather hits and fuel prices rise, most consumers think the price increase is due to greedy oil firms making big profits. What do you think, given what you know about supply and demand?

6. What is your opportunity cost of taking this course?

7. Name some reasons why doctors' salaries are high.

8. The inflation rate will probably never be reduced to zero. Does this mean we are doomed to become poorer and poorer?

9. Why would a salary contract with a "Cost-of-living" escalator be valuable?

10. Your mom says she remembers when a movie ticket cost $1.50 in the "good old days." Your mom wishes she were back in the "good old days." What's wrong with your mom's thinking?

11. Is charging interest on a loan unfair? Why or why not?

12. Why, on any loan, do you always repay more total dollars than you borrowed?

13. Why can't dollars paid or received at different points in time be treated as equal?

14. Discuss one approach that might be used to forecast next year's inflation rate.

PROBLEMS

1. The price of unleaded gasoline is \$4.00/gallon, the price of diesel is \$3.50/gallon, and the price of ethanol is \$3.75/gallon. Convert these nominal prices to relative prices using the ethanol price as the base.

2. Use the numbers below to decide if the price of a new car is relatively more expensive in 2010 than in 1990. Calculate how many hours it would take to work to afford a new car in 1990 and in 2010.

	1990	2010
Nominal price of a new car	\$15,000	\$25,000
Nominal average hourly wage	\$10.78	\$18.61

3. Joan's value of time is \$ 10/hour, and Alice's value of time is \$2/hour. Making a chicken entree at home costs \$1.50 for the inputs and 1 hour of time per serving. Buying the same pre-prepared entree costs \$4.50 in money and 10 minutes of time per serving. Calculate which is cheaper, the home prepared entree or the pre-prepared entree, for Joan and for Alice.

4. The $10,000 you use as a downpayment on a house could have been invested in a CD paying an annual interest rate of 7 percent. Therefore, what is one opportunity cost of using the $10,000 as a downpayment?

5. You're promised $1 million in 20 years. If the inflation rate averages 6 percent annually over the next 20 years, what will $1 million be worth then?

6. In 2002 Joe's salary was $50,000. In 2012 Joe's salary was $65,000. Nice increase, right? Not necessarily. In 2002 the CPI was 179.9, and in 2012 it was 229.6. Express Joe's 2012 salary in terms of 2002 dollars. Then, express Joe's 2002 salary in terms of 2012 dollars. Is Joe "really" better off in 2012 than in 2002?

7. If the CPI last year was 225, and the CPI this year (one year later) is 240, what was the inflation rate for the year?

8. Here are the annual inflation rates for the years 2009–2012:

2009: –0.4%

2010: 1.6%

2011: 3.2%

2012: 2.1%

What is the total inflation rate for 2009–2012?

9. If the real interest rate is 4 percent and the expected inflation rate is 7 percent, what is the nominal (observed) interest rate?

10. If Jack invests $1,000 today in an investment paying an annual rate of 10% compounded annually, how much will he have at the end of seven years?

11. If Jack invests $1,000 today in an investment paying an annual rate of 10% compounded monthly, how much will he have at the end of three years?

12. If Jack invests $100 at the end of every month for seven years in an investment paying an annual rate of 10% compounded monthly, how much will he have at the end of seven years? How much will he have if he invests at the beginning of each month?

13. Which is better, having $500 in two years or $750 in five years, if money can be invested at 7 percent, after-taxes, in a riskless investment?

14. What would be equivalent today to receiving $1 million in 20 years, using a discount rate of 8 percent?

15. Sally makes a $300 car payment for 36 months. Each payment is made at the end of the month. Using a 15 percent discount rate, what's the value of those total future payments today?

16. What equal monthly payment will $10,000 generate for 24 months if 6 percent interest can be earned after taxes? The payments are received at the end of each month. What equal monthly payment could be received if each payment is received at the beginning of each month?

17. Byron wants to draw $200 at the end of each month from an initial fund of $20,000. For how many months can he do this if he can earn 9 percent interest after taxes?

18. Melody wants to save $5,000 in five years. How much must she save at the end of each month if she can earn 5 percent after taxes? How much must she save at the end of each month if she can earn 10 percent after taxes?

19. Susan thinks she has a 30 percent chance of getting a GPA of 3.50 this year, a 20 percent change of getting a GPA of 3.00, a 40 percent chance of getting a GPA of 2.50, and a 10 percent chance of getting a GPA of 2.00. What is Susan's expected GPA for this year?

CHAPTER 2

Macrofoundations: What You Can't Control but Should Know About

Introduction

Like it or not, as consumers we are very much affected by the national economy, something we cannot control but have to live with. In the past three decades, consumers were hit by several economic downturns, or recessions. The 1990s started with a recession and high unemployment, but as the decade ended consumers were smiling because jobs were plentiful, inflation was low, and incomes were rising. However, in 2001 U.S. experienced another recession, possibly deepened by the attacks of September 11. Then the "Great Recession" came in late 2007 with the bursting of the U.S. housing bubble and outbreak of the financial crisis. Many consumers saw their net worth taking a hit. Some lost their jobs and faced housing foreclosures.

The problems of the national economy, such as high inflation, high interest rates, and recession, are problems which individual consumers *cannot* undo, or control. The best that consumers can do is to anticipate the problems, know their effects, and cope with them.

This is exactly what the following topics will do. The topics will address questions such as: What causes high inflation? What causes high interest rates? What causes recessions? You'll learn if inflation, high interest rates, and recessions can be easily predicted by consumers. Finally, you'll learn if the "economic roller coaster" can be ridden to your advantage.

1. How Is Your Life Affected by Economic Events?

The economy goes through irregular ups and downs. The ups and downs have tremendous influences on our economic lives.

There are four stages to each up and down cycle: peak, contraction, trough, and expansion (see Figure 2-1). The *peak* is the height of economic prosperity. Unemployment is low, inflation and interest rates are low, and the stock market is high. During a *contraction* the good times begin to fade. Jobs become progressively harder to find, inflation and interest rates begin to rise, and the stock market falls. The *trough* is the worst of times. Unemployment, inflation, and interest rates are high and the stock market is low. Prosperity returns during the *expansion,* with falling unemployment, falling

PEAK

CONTRACTION

TROUGH

EXPANSION

Figure 2-1. The economic rollercoaster.

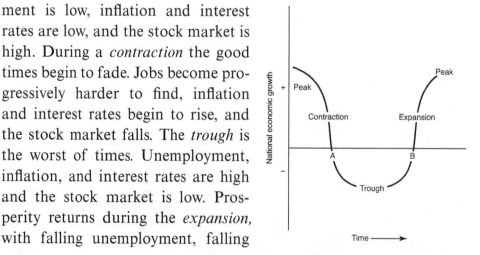

inflation and interest rates, and a rising stock market. The expansion culminates in another peak, and the roller coaster starts all over again.

RECESSION

There are two more terms to throw at you. One is called *recession.* A recession is that part of the contraction, trough, and expansion periods when national economic growth is negative, meaning the economy is actually shrinking. In Figure 2-1, the recession extends from point A to point B.

The second term is *cycle.* A cycle is one complete movement from peak to peak. Sometimes researchers also measure a cycle as a complete movement from trough to trough. The cycle is often referred to as a

CYCLE

business cycle.

How well does the model of changes in the national economy, depicted in Figure 2-1, match with reality? Figure 2-2 shows the national economic roller coaster for 1960–2012 , as measured by the unemployment rate, the prime interest rate, an index of 500 stock prices, and the inflation rate (percentage rate of change in the CPI).[1] Shaded areas are contraction periods, and unshaded areas are expansion periods.

The actual pattern fits fairly well to our model. The inflation rate and interest rate move closely together. The stock market tends to fall when inflation and interest rates rise, and the stock market rises when they fall. But the relationship between the inflation rate and unemployment rate is more complicated. Sometimes the inflation rate and unemployment rate move together and sometimes they move in opposite directions. If you study Figure 2-2 you'll see the following pattern:

♦ In the early part of an expansion, both the inflation rate and unemployment rate fall (see 1970–1971).

Figure 2-2.   The economic rollercoaster since 1960.

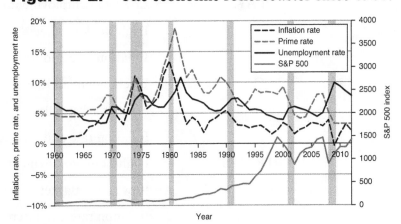

Data source: Inflation rate and unemployment rate data from the U.S. Bureau of Labor Statistics; Prime rate from the Federal Reserve System; and S&P500 from the Federal Reserve Bank of St. Louis.

---

[1]The prime interest rate is the interest rate charged by banks to their best commercial customers.

♦ In the latter part of an expansion, the inflation rate rises but the unemployment rate continues to fall (see 1972–1973).

♦ In the early part of a contraction, both the inflation rate and unemployment rate rise (see 1973).

♦ In the latter part of a contraction, the inflation rate falls, but the unemployment rate continues to rise (see 1974).

LAGGING CONSUMER EXPECTATIONS   The reason for this complex pattern between the inflation rate and unemployment rate is "lagging consumer expectations." "Lagging consumer expectations" means that it takes a while for consumers to realize that the inflation rate has changed direction. When the inflation rate begins to accelerate, consumers initially don't realize it. Consumers as workers therefore don't demand higher wages to keep up with higher inflation, so, to companies, labor becomes cheaper and the unemployment rate continues to drop. Likewise, at the other extreme when the inflation rate begins to fall, consumers initially expect the old, higher inflation rate to continue. Therefore, consumers as workers are demanding hikes in wages which are greater than the increases in prices, so, to companies, labor becomes more expensive and the unemployment rate continues to rise.

With this understanding of the somewhat complex relationship between inflation and unemployment in hand, the four components of the economic roller coaster can be modified (Table 2-1). "Peaks"

Table 2-1 "Revised" stages of the economic roller coaster (business cycle).

PEAK:	Lowest unemployment rate
	High stock market
	Inflation rate and interest rates rising
CONTRACTION:	Unemployment rate rises
	Stock market falls
	Inflation rate and interest rates rise, hit top, then fall
TROUGH:	Highest unemployment rate
	Low stock market
	Inflation rate and interest rates falling
EXPANSION:	Unemployment rate falls
	Stock market rises
	Inflation rate and interest rates fall, hit bottom, then rise.

ECONOMIC CYCLES—THE ROLLER COASTER KEEPS CHANGING

C O N S U M E R   T O P I C

Business cycles are recurrent but not regular. That is, we know that another expansion or contraction will occur, but they won't occur with any necessary regularity.

The following table shows the expansions and contractions in the economy since 1945. Fortunately, contractions tend to last a much shorter length of time than expansions. But also notice that there's no regularity to the occurrence of expansions and contractions. We can't say that every $\underline{X}$ years a contraction will occur.

In early 2000, many economists popped champagne corks, not celebrating the new millennium, but cheering the fact that the current expansion was now the longest in U.S. history.

Business Cycle Reference Dates		Duration In Months			
Peak	Trough	Contraction	Expansion	Cycle	
Quarterly dates are in parentheses		Peak to Trough	Previous Trough to this peak	Trough from Previous Trough	Peak from Previous Peak
February 1945(I)	October 1945(IV)	8	80	88	93
November 1948(IV)	October 1949(IV)	11	37	48	45
July 1953(II)	May 1954(II)	10	45	55	56
August 1957(III)	April 1958(II)	8	39	47	49
April 1960(II)	February 1961(I)	10	24	34	32
December 1969(IV)	November 1970(IV)	11	106	117	116
November 1973(IV)	March 1975(I)	16	36	52	47
January 1980(I)	July 1980(III)	6	58	64	74
July 1981(III)	November 1982(IV)	16	12	28	18
July 1990(III)	March 1991(I)	8	92	100	108
March 2001(I)	November 2001(IV)	8	120	128	128
December 2007(IV)	June 2009(II)	18	73	91	81
Average :1945–2009 (11 cycles)		11	59	73	66

Data source: National Bureau of Economic Research, Inc.

are "good times" except that rising inflation and interest rates foretell of the coming contraction. Similarly "troughs" are "bad times" except that falling inflation and interest rates are ingredients of the coming expansion.

One final point should be made. Each cycle (measured either from peak to peak or trough to trough) is not equal in length. This is why we say that economic cycles are recurrent, but not regular.

So What?

Hopefully, it should be abundantly evident how economic cycles can affect your personal financial life in many ways. If you want to borrow money and lock-in a low rate, your best bet is to do it during the early part of an expansion since here interest rates are at, or near, their low. If you're an investor in the stock market, you want to buy at a trough and sell at a peak. If you're looking for a job, you'll have the best luck at the peak of the cycle and the worst luck at the trough.

MEASURING THE SIZE AND GROWTH OF THE ECONOMY

C O N S U M E R   T O P I C

The size of the national economy is measured by a concept called Gross Domestic Product, or GDP. GDP is calculated as the sales value of all final goods and services produced in the economy in a given time period. This means, for example, that the retail value of shoes sold is included in GDP, but the cost of leather to the shoe manufacturer is not. Why? The simple reason is that the value of the leather is, of course, included in the retail price of shoes, If the cost of leather to the shoe manufacturer was also included in GDP, then leather would be double-counted.

In 2012 the U.S. GDP was $15.7 trillion. This made the U.S. economy by far the largest in the world. The concept of GDP is, however, not perfect. Unpaid activities are not included in GDP. For example, if a parent stays at home to take care of children and do household chores, then the values of these activities are not included in GDP. But if that same parent hires day care ser-

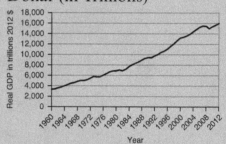

Real GDP in 2012 Constant Dollar (in Trillions)

Data source: U.S. Department of Commerce, Bureau of Economic Analysis

vices and hires a home care and cleaning service, then the values of the day care and home care activities are included in GDP.

GDP also does not include the value of illegal, or underground, activities, such as the drug trade. But, on the negative side, any harm done to the environment caused by pollution in production processes is not subtracted from GDP.

Typically, GDP grows each year simply because prices are higher. Therefore, to gauge whether the *volume* of goods and services produced has increased, economists first take out inflation (called deflating) to form *"real" GDP*. It is the change in real GDP which is used to monitor the growth of the economy. The graph shows how real GDP has changed since 1960.

The growth rate of real GDP is used to determine when a *recession* occurs. Officially, a recession occurs when the growth rate of real GDP is *negative* for at least two consecutive quarters.

But, of course, making these moves requires that you know where on the economic cycle the economy currently is and where the economic cycle is going. Here lies the "rub," because no one yet has perfected a flawless method for forecasting the economy, although there are some techniques that will get you some part of the way. But we'll save those techniques for later chapters.

The Bottom Line

The economy goes through recurrent, yet irregular ups and downs, or cycles. There are predictable patterns to movements in unemployment, interest rates, inflation, and the stock market. The economic roller coaster, or business cycle, has implications for borrowing, investing, and job hunting.

2. What Causes Inflation?

Inflation is one of the most important economic concepts that a consumer faces. Improperly accounting for inflation in your financial decisions can be disastrous. A major goal of this book is to show you how to cope with inflation in your economic decisions. But before this is done, you should know where inflation comes from. To do this, we must start with money.

The Role of Money

A modern economy is characterized by exchanges. Individuals long ago found that they could better themselves considerably if they specialized and traded. That is, rather than each individual growing his own food, making his own clothes, constructing his own house, and inventing and building his own car, individuals found that they could each reach a higher standard of living by specializing and trading. For example, Ms. Jones grows vegetables, Mr. Baker constructs houses, Ms. Thomas makes clothes, and Mr. Smith builds cars. Each individual finds that she could be more productive if she developed a skill and perfected it. Each individual satisfies her human wants by trading the products she produces to other individuals for the products they produce.

BARTER   Originally individuals traded by barter. Barter means trading on a product for product basis. For example, we teach you or your children for a year, and in exchange you provide us with food. Or, the neighbor down the street fixes your faucet and in exchange you tune-up his car.

The major disadvantage of barter is its high time cost. Not only must a barterer find someone who wants the product that the barterer has to offer, but that same person must also be someone who has a product which the barterer desires. Furthermore, such searches must be conducted for all products necessary to one's living.

EXCHANGE TICKETS

Since time spent searching for complementary barters was time that could have been spent in other endeavors, a device that would reduce bartering time was a welcome addition to a barter economy. A device that would serve as an all-purpose "exchange ticket," that would be accepted by everyone as payment for a product, would indeed reduce the costs of barter. If trade is conducted using an all-purpose exchange ticket, no longer must each individual both find a person who wants what the individual has to trade but who also has something the individual wants in exchange. With trading using the all-purpose exchange ticket, the individual can now sell his product to anyone who wants to buy it, receive exchange tickets from the buyers, and use the exchange tickets to purchase the products he wants from anyone who wants to sell those products. The use of exchange tickets expands the list of potential traders for any individual and therefore reduces the time involved in trading.[2]

Of course, the modern term for exchange tickets is *money*. Many commodities could serve as money. Desirable characteristics are that the commodity be easy to carry, universally accepted, easily identifiable, limited in supply, and not easily reproduced. Historically precious metals, such as gold and silver, served as money. In modern economies money is primarily composed of currency (paper dollars, coins) and checking accounts. Credit cards are not money. When a consumer uses a credit card he is taking out a short-term loan from a bank. Credit cards represent borrowing potential, not money.

It should be emphasized that what is used as money need not be inherently valuable. In fact, it is better if the commodity has little value in and of itself. If the commodity used as money has valuable alternative uses, individuals may be motivated to convert it to those alternative uses and not use it as money. The historical attraction of gold as money stemmed from its limited supply rather than any intrinsic value it had. In fact, gold has few practical uses.

Where Does Money Come From?—The Almighty Fed

When economies moved to a trading system based on money, the commodity used as money became valuable. Its value did not stem necessarily from its inherent worth (remember, it is better if the money commodity has few alternative uses), but from the ability of the money holder to trade money for commodities that were inherently valuable. Consequently, individuals looked for safe places to store money.

---

[2]Many modern bartering clubs have recognized the high time costs involved with bartering and have developed exchange tickets for use by members of the club. Rather than trading boats for cars or video recorders for refrigerators, sellers of products receive exchange tickets from buyers, and buyers purchase products from sellers using exchange tickets.

BANKS

PAPER MONEY

Originally, enterprising individuals offered safe havens for money in exchange for a fee. Such businesses were the first banks. The early banks were little more than a collection of safe deposit boxes. You purchased the right to deposit your money (usually coins made of precious metal) in a bank, and in return the bank issued you a paper receipt denoting the amount of money deposited. Eventually individuals found that the paper receipts could also be used as money. This was the origin of paper money.

LOANS

The originators of banks also struck upon another important idea. They found that not every depositor claimed his money at the same time. In fact, at any one time only a small fraction of the bank's total money deposits was needed on hand to meet depositors' claims. The rest of the deposits could be loaned to other individuals and interest could be earned. Furthermore, this would mean that, rather than charging individuals a fee for depositing money in the bank for safety, a fee could be paid to such depositors based on the earnings from loans. This was the birth of modern banking.

Two problems developed in the early banking system. First, each bank issued its own deposit receipts which, as mentioned above, came to be used as paper money. The lack of a uniform and universally known paper money inhibited trading between regions of the country. For example, a buyer in the South would be reluctant to accept the paper money issued from a bank in the North because the Northern bank and its financial solvency were unknown to him. In short, the prevalence of many different paper monies made each less than universally acceptable as money.

BANK FAILURES

The second problem related to the consequences of bank failures. Banks were, and still are, private enterprises which can fail. Failure occurs if the bank cannot meet the demands of its depositors. The stimulus of failure can be defaults on loans made by the bank or the bank not keeping enough deposits on hand to meet depositors' demands. A few bank failures could be handled internally by the early banking system with healthy banks loaning money to "sick" banks. Unfortunately, early bank failures tended to come in droves, so there were not enough healthy banks to bail-out the sick banks. In other words, the early banking system often totally collapsed.

THE FED

To help eliminate these problems, most modern economies ultimately instituted a "central bank," or the "banker's bank." In the United States the central bank is the Federal Reserve System, or the *Fed*. The Fed is an independent government agency whose Board of Governors is appointed by the President with the consent of the Senate.

The major goals of the Fed are to protect the financial solvency of the banking system and to promote commerce in the country. The ways the Fed tries to meet these goals are by (a) serving as the lender of last resort to the private banks, (b) issuing a common, uniform currency, (c) establishing and enforcing regulations regarding the proportion of deposits which banks must keep "on hand" to meet depositors' demands, and (d) controlling the supply of money to the economy. The latter function is of particular interest to us in understanding the reasons for inflation.

Perhaps the easiest way that the Fed could increase the supply of money in the economy would be to simply drop dollars from airplanes. Although simple, such a procedure raises a host of practical problems, such as where would the planes fly and who would get the money? Also, how would the Fed decrease the money supply if it so desired?

Instead, the Fed manipulates the money supply in a more subtle way. Recall that very early in their history banks found that they could loan part of every dollar deposited with them and still be able to meet demands for cash from their depositors. This is called *fractional reserve banking* because only a fraction of a bank's deposits (reserves) need be kept on hand—the rest can be loaned to borrowers. These loans in essence *are an increase in the money supply* because they are an expansion of the original deposits at the bank.

FRACTIONAL RESERVE BANKING

For example, assume you deposit $1 in your checking account at the bank. The $1 is obviously part of the money supply. But the $1 increases the bank's total reserves by $1. The bank knows, by experience, that it doesn't need to keep the total $1 idle in case you want to withdraw it. Instead, the bank can loan part of it, say 75¢. It makes the loan, which increases the borrower's checking account by 75¢. The original dollar deposit has therefore added another 75¢ to the money supply.

The Fed therefore can manipulate the money supply by either altering the rate at which banks create loans (and hence, new money) from a given amount of reserves, or by directly altering the amount of bank reserves. The first method involves the Fed changing the so-called *reserve requirement.*

RESERVE REQUIREMENT

The reserve requirement is the legal minimum fraction of deposits which banks must keep on hand to meet demands of depositors. An increase in the reserve requirement means that banks can now make fewer loans from a given volume of reserves—such a change results in a reduction in the money supply. Conversely, a decrease in the reserve requirement means that banks can make more loans from a given volume of reserves—such a change results in an increase in the money supply.

The second and more common way that the Fed manipulates the money supply is by directly changing

Figure 2-3. How the Federal Reserve changes the money supply.

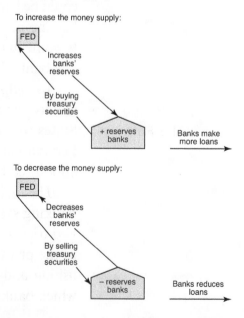

To increase the money supply:

FED — Increases banks' reserves — By buying treasury securities — + reserves banks — Banks make more loans

To decrease the money supply:

FED — Decreases banks' reserves — By selling treasury securities — − reserves banks — Banks reduces loans

**C
O
N
S
U
M
E
R

T
O
P
I
C**

WHO RUNS THE FEDERAL RESERVE?

By now you should realize that the Federal Reserve has a great deal of control over your economic life. Through its control of the money supply, the Fed can pump up the economy and create a "boom," or it can slow down the economy and create a recession. The Fed can push interest rates up or it can pull interest rates down, at least, in the short-run.

Who runs this all-powerful Federal Reserve, and are there any checks and balances on its actions?

The Federal Reserve System was established by an act of Congress in 1913, and the Fed began operations in 1914. The central governing body of the Fed is the Board of Governors. There are seven governors who are appointed by the President to terms of fourteen years. The long terms give the governors considerable political insulation. The Board of Governors is headed by a Chairman, who is also appointed by the President, and confirmed by the Senate. However, the Chairman's term is only four years. The Chairman's term does not necessarily coincide with the President's term of office.

The Fed Chairman and Board can, and frequently do, act with a great deal of independence. The President can only pressure the Fed, but cannot direct it to do anything specific. The Fed must annually report to Congress on its policies, but beyond that Congress usually leaves the Fed alone. However, Congress is the ultimate "boss" of the Fed because it can change the Fed's charter. Periodically, there are bills introduced in Congress to alter the Fed's charter.

The independence and power of the Fed make it a frequent target for criticism. When interest rates are high, when there is a recession, or when economic growth is slow, "Fed-bashing" by the President, Congress, and private citizens becomes popular. Fed-bashing means blaming the current economic situation on tight money policies of the Fed.

For a very readable account of the history, power, and operations of the Federal Reserve System, see *Secrets of the Temple: How the Federal Reserve Runs the Country* by William Greider, Touchstone Books, 1989.

OPEN MARKET
OPERATIONS

bank reserves (see Figure 2.3). In essence, when the Fed wants to expand the money supply it gives the banks more reserves, from which the banks can make more loans and create more checking accounts (money). When the Fed wants to decrease the money supply, it does the opposite—it takes reserves from the banks, forcing banks to reduce loans and their associated checking accounts. Technically, when the Fed alters banks' reserves, it doesn't simply give and take. Instead, it buys and sells U.S. Treasury securities, which are simply investments held by most banks. When the Fed increases bank reserves it does so by *buying* Treasury securities from banks in exchange for additional reserves (for example, cash which the Fed just printed). When the Fed decreases bank reserves it does so by *selling* Treasury securities to banks in exchange for part of the banks' reserves (cash). This process is called "open market operations."

Too Much of a Good Thing

To the individual consumer it probably would seem that the more money, the better. This is because each of us equates money to our individual income. We know that the more money we have the more we can buy and the better-off we are.

Such is not necessarily the case for the whole economy. First it should be recognized that money is *not* the same as income. Money is only a convenient way for consumers to *hold* some of their income. The benefit of money, as already discussed, is as a medium of exchange—it can readily be used to purchase products. If money was income, then the Fed could instantly create more income by simply printing more money.

It is useful, therefore, to think of money as merely another product in the economy, like cheese, pork chops, cars, and stocks. Consumers have a demand, or use, for money primarily related to the amount of buying they expect to do. Income which consumers do not plan to spend is usually saved and invested. Therefore, to facilitate exchanges in the economy the supply of money should grow at a rate comparable to the growth of exchanges in the economy. Since growth of exchanges in the economy is primarily related to general economic growth (in products and services), the money supply should grow at about the same rate as the economy is growing. For example, if the economy grows 3 percent annually, then a 3 percent increase in the money supply will facilitate the resulting increase in trade. The Fed can engineer this growth by altering banks' reserve requirements or reserves by enough to generate a 3 percent increase in credit.

EXCESS MONEY GROWTH EQUALS INFLATION

What happens if the Fed allows the money supply to grow faster than the economy is growing? This means that credit and consequently all spending in the economy increase by more than the increase in new products and services produced in the economy. That is, consumer demand for all products and services increases faster than the supply of products. Anytime demand increases relative to supply, the price of the product rises. (If the demand for apples increases faster than the supply, the price of apples increases.) The same happens in this case except that consumer demand increases relative to supply for *all products.* Consequently, the prices of all products rise by an amount equal to the excess of monetary growth over economic growth. This result is called *inflation.* To emphasize, inflation means a sustained increase in the prices of *all* goods and services during a given period of time. Such price increases result when the money supply grows faster than the quantity of goods and services produced in the economy. In essence, prices rise to "soak-up" the excess dollars that have been put in the economy. This process does, however, take time. A good estimate is that it takes two years for excessive money growth to lead to higher inflation.

A Rule for Predicting Inflation Rates

The above discussion suggests a simple rule for predicting the inflation rate. First, find the money growth rate for any year and express it as a percent. Second, subtract 3 percent from the money growth rate to allow for average real economic growth. The resulting number is the prediction of the inflation rate two years later. This rule can be expressed in a simple equation:

AN INFLATION
EQUATION

Money growth rate − 3% = Inflation rate 2 years later.

So, for example, if the money growth rate *last year* was 5 percent, then 5-3 or 2 percent is the inflation rate prediction for next year. Or, if the money growth rate this year is 7 percent, then 7-3 or 4 percent is the inflation rate prediction for two years in the future.

However, the money growth rate (less 3 percent) and the inflation rate don't coincide exactly. One reason is that real economic growth is not always 3 percent. For example, in 2000 real economic growth was 4.1%, whereas in 2012 it was only 2.2%. A better use of the inflation equation is to predict changes in the direction of the inflation rate. That is, calculate the inflation equation for two successive years to predict if the inflation rate will rise or fall.

Where can you get information about the money growth rate? The best source is the publication "Monetary Trends" from the Federal Reserve Bank of St. Louis.[3] Use the numbers for the money supply called "M2."[4]

EXAMPLE 2-1: Use the following money supply information to predict if the inflation rate will rise or fall between 2012 and 2013. If real economic growth was 4 percent in 2012 and 2 percent in 2013, how would your prediction change?

M2 money supply at end of:

2010: $8802.4 billion
2011: $9628.6 billion
2012: $10475.9 billion

ANSWER: Money supply growth rate for 2011:

$9628.6/$8802.4 − 1 = 9.4%

Inflation rate prediction for 2013:

9.4% − 3% = 6.4%

---

[3] Write to Federal Reserve Bank of St Louis, P.O. Box 442, St. Louis, Missouri 63166, or visit their web site at www.stls.frb.org
[4] The "M2" money supply is the value of currency, checking accounts, short term time deposits, and money market mutual funds.

Money supply growth rate for 2012:

$$\$10475.9/9628.6 - 1 = 8.8\%$$

Inflation rate prediction for 2014:

$$8.8\% - 3\% = 5.8\%$$

Conclusion: The inflation rate will be fairly stable from 2013 to 2014.

If real economic growth rate in 2013 is 4%, the inflation prediction for 2013 is: 9.4% – 4% = 5.4%. If real economic growth rate in 2014 is 2%, the inflation prediction for 2014 is: 8.8% – 2% = 6.8%.

Other (Wrong) Explanations of Inflation

Inflation has been a major economic topic of recent decades. Consequently, and to no surprise, numerous explanations have been offered for the cause of inflation. These alternative explanations are discussed and critiqued below.

1. Inflation as a "Cost-Push" Problem

One of the most frequently offered explanations of inflation is that it results when the prices of raw materials and of labor rise continually. The theory is that businessmen merely pass these higher prices on to consumers, therefore resulting in higher consumer prices, or inflation.

It is easy to understand the popularity of this explanation because it is the process which consumers and businessmen observe. Consumers and businessmen often don't follow the monetary policy of the Fed vis-a-vis the growth of the economy, but they do observe price increases posted by sellers of products.

To understand the appeal, but incorrectness, of the cost-push theory of inflation, let's try to follow the inflationary process for a single product, shoes. Start with the Fed. For whatever reason, assume the Fed increases the rate of growth of the money supply. Initially, such an action increases the supply of credit that banks can lend, lowers the price of credit (the interest rate), and consequently increases consumer borrowing and spending.

Consumers spend more on all products, including shoes. Shoe retailers observe more shoes being sold and their inventories declining, so they increase their orders of shoes from wholesalers. Increased orders to wholesalers also stimulate these merchants to place more orders with shoe manufacturers. But in order to manufacture more shoes, shoemakers must be offered a higher price, since they will have to pay a higher price to compete for more leather and to entice their workers to work extra shifts. This higher price is then "passed-on" in the form of higher costs to wholesalers, higher costs to retailers, and ultimately higher shoe prices to consumers.

So the cost-push, or "pass-through," of prices does happen, but the reason is not because the owners of raw materials, such as leather in our example, or shoemakers suddenly decide to increase their price. Rather, price increases occur due to an increase in consumer demand for products which was stimulated by an excessive supply of money to the economy.

Inflation, or an increase in the prices of all consumer products, results because the process described above for the shoe market occurs for all consumer product markets. Once inflation occurs, consumers reduce their demand for products to the levels that existed previous to the excessive monetary growth and the "excess" demand at the retail, wholesale, and manufacturing levels disappears. But does this mean that workers and owners of raw materials now reduce the wages and prices they are willing to receive to previous levels? The answer is, no. If they did, their *relative* prices and wages received would fall since consumer prices are now higher. Therefore, the result of the excessive monetary growth is simply that all production, all buying, and all selling in the economy is ultimately unaffected in *quantity* terms, but the prices of all these transactions are higher. Inflation, especially over time, results in equal percentage increases in all prices, wages, and salaries. Inflation does not change *relative* relationships in the economy. Instead, consumers and businesses' incomes and expenses are simply at higher dollars levels.

RELATIVE PRICES
UNCHANGED

2. Inflation as a Result of High Interest Rates

This is perhaps the most ridiculous of the alternative explanations of inflation. In fact, the reader who has thoroughly understood Chapter I (Micro-foundations) can probably discard this "explanation" immediately.

To say that increases in interest rates cause inflation is to reverse cause and effect. Recall from Chapter 1 that the nominal, or observed, interest rate is composed of two parts, the real interest rate and an inflation premium which protects the lender from declines in the purchasing power of future repaid dollars. An increase in inflation today generally makes lenders fear that inflation will be higher in the future. To protect themselves, lenders increase the inflation premium that is added to the real interest rate of lending. Therefore, increases in inflation cause increases in observed interest rates, and not the reverse!

3. Inflation Caused by Increases in the Price of a Major Product

This "theory" contends that higher inflation results when increases occur in the price of a major product in the economy, and other prices rise because that product is an input into the making of many other products.

Oil is the best example presented by promoters of this explanation. The price of oil increased tenfold in the 1970s. Since oil is used widely in the economy, it is only logical to expect that many, if not all, prices in the economy would also "shoot-up" as a result. Hence, higher oil prices caused higher inflation in the 1970s. Right?

Wrong! Higher oil prices, or higher prices for any product or group of products, *do not* cause permanently higher inflation. To understand why, consider what happens when the price of oil rises. Consumers must

WHY NOT USE PRICE CONTROLS TO CONTROL INFLATION?

C O N S U M E R   T O P I C

Many citizens find appealing the idea that inflation and interest rates can be controlled by law, that is, by wage and price controls. If prices are rising too quickly, simply pass a law which says that prices can only rise by a certain percentage each year.

Wage and price controls were, in fact, imposed during the Nixon Administration in the early 1970s. In general, however, economists think wage and price controls are a failure and may do more harm to the economy than good. Why?

The simple fact is that wage and price controls won't work because they ignore the economic fundamentals which are dictating that prices and wages be a certain level. If economic fundamentals dictate, workers and firms will simply change their behavior to get around the controls.

For example, suppose the economic fundamentals in the labor market indicate that a welder should earn $12/hour. However, the wage controls limit welders to only $10/hour. This means the welder effectively will take a pay cut. Certainly welders won't work as hard or as long at $10/hour than at $12/hour. So quality and quantity of welding will both be reduced.

As another example, suppose plywood prices are limited to $5/square foot by price controls, and this is below the market price. Will plywood producers grin and bear it? Probably not. One thing plywood producers may do is to "change" their product, maybe by punching holes in the plywood or adding grooves in the plywood, so they can sell it as something other than plain plywood and get around the price control. Such activities actually took place during the Nixon wage and price controls.

Wage and price controls can actually harm the economy in a couple of ways. First, controls encourage less work, as illustrated by the welder example. Second, wage and price controls require a large government bureaucracy to be established to implement and police the controls. Detailed descriptions must be written of products and job types. An army of monitors must constantly check prices and wages. All this takes resources and money. Lastly, wage and price controls deflect attention from economic fundamentals and from policymakers at the Fed and in Congress who are responsible for economic conditions.

spend more on oil products in order to consume the same amount of oil products as before the oil price increase. But where will they get the extra money? Yes, consumers can draw out of their savings in order to drive to work and heat their homes, but this can't go on forever. Eventually consumers begin to reduce their consumption and expenditures on non-oil products. But this means the demand for those products falls, and so ultimately their prices also fall.

Therefore, higher prices for oil products are ultimately counterbalanced by lower prices for non-oil products. A one-time increase in the price of oil can cause inflation to increase at a faster rate for a few months, but cannot cause a permanent increase in the long-run inflation rate. Higher oil prices do cause average prices to be higher, but they do not cause the rate of increase of prices, the inflation rate, to be permanently higher.

MONETARY ACCOMMODATION

The reason that higher prices for major products, such as oil, are often accompanied by higher inflation rates is that the Fed often correspondingly increases the growth of the money supply to try to "fool" the economy into thinking it can afford the higher oil (or other major product) price. This tactic is called *monetary accommodation*. The ultimate result, of course, is inflation, but the inflation is due to the excessive monetary growth, not to original higher product price.

4. Federal Budget Deficits as the Cause of Inflation

This argument became quite popular in the 1970s and 1980s. Supporters of this view cited increasing federal red ink during those two decades and the corresponding increasing rate of inflation. (However, supporters of the federal deficit argument ignored the fact that federal deficits climbed to new heights in the early 2010s at the same time when the inflation rate stayed low.) Since federal deficits and inflation frequently occurred together, it was easy for an observer to label one the cause and the other the effect.

But does this explanation of inflation make economic sense? Again, the answer is, no. To see why start with the federal deficit. A federal deficit occurs when the federal government spends more than it receives in revenues. To finance the deficit, the federal government borrows money. It can borrow money from two prime sources, the private market (you and me) or the Fed.

What happens if the federal government borrows from the private market? In this case the federal government sells federal debt securities, such, as Treasury bonds and Treasury bills, to you and me. Why do we buy the securities? Because usually they are excellent investments which pay top interest rates and are virtually risk-free. Therefore, in this process private citizens willingly loan money to the federal government, and the federal government uses this money to finance the deficit. No new money is created, but instead, existing money is simply willingly reallocated from private hands to the federal government.

But what if the federal government, in order to finance a budget deficit, borrows from the Fed. In this case the federal government exchanges federal debt securities for money from the Fed, which is the same type of exchange as taking place in borrowing from the private market. But unlike the private market, the Fed *creates* new money when purchasing the federal debt securities. That is, the Fed, in essence, simply prints more money and uses that money to buy the federal debt securities. Hence, the total money supply is increased, and if this increase results in monetary growth greater than the growth in the economy inflation results.

So federal deficits only stimulate inflation when the Fed finances them by printing more money. The key point is that this process requires a decision by the Fed to buy federal debt securities with new money. Congress, by creating the deficits, does not *force* the Fed to automatically finance them. Therefore, the major reason for inflation still comes back to the monetary policy of the Federal Reserve.

The Bottom Line

The inflation rate rises when the Federal Reserve System (the Fed) increases the money growth rate, and the inflation rate falls when the Fed decreases the money growth rate. To predict next year's inflation rate, take last year's money growth rate in percentage terms and subtract a forecast for next year's real economic growth rate, or subtract 3 percent. _____

3. What Pushes the Economic Roller Coaster?

We know the economy goes through ups and downs, but what or who is doing the pushing and pulling? This is a question that American economists have been trying to answer for at least one-hundred years, and there's still no definitive, complete answer. There are, however, two partial answers: "supply shocks" and Federal Reserve "fine-tuning."

Supply Shocks

A *supply shock* is an unexpected disruption in the economy which causes a significant increase in the average price level, a reduction in economic activity, and an increase in unemployment. If the reduction in economic activity and the increase in unemployment are severe enough, a *recession can result.*

BAD SUPPLY
SHOCKS

Examples of supply shocks are labor strikes, droughts, and embargoes. The best recent examples of a supply shock were the 1973 Arab oil embargo, which resulted in a fourfold increase in the price of oil, and the 1990 Iraqi invasion of Kuwait, which resulted in a doubling in the price of oil. Although we argued in the previous topic that higher oil prices don't cause a permanently higher inflation rate, they do have other impacts. Since oil is a major input to much of the U.S. economy, a tremendous oil price increase makes economic activity more expensive, which in turn means less manufacturing output, less general production, and less spending by consumers on non-oil products in order to finance the higher oil bill. In short, a recession can result. The recessions of 1973–75 and 1990–91 were in part due to these oil supply shocks.

GOOD SUPPLY
SHOCKS

There can be beneficial supply shocks. A mild winter, an unusually good growing season, and the invention of new technologies like personal computers and the Internet, which lower the cost of production are examples of supply shocks that reduce the average price level, increase economic activity, and increase income.

The practical problem with using supply shocks as causes of economic ups and downs is that supply shocks are unpredictable. It's hard to predict droughts, oil embargoes, invasions, or new cost-cutting inventions. Therefore, it's hard for you, as a consumer, to use supply shocks as a way to predict what turn the economic roller coaster will take next.

The Fed's "Fine-Tuning"

Another mover of the economic roller coaster is the Federal Reserve (Fed). In fact, the actions of the Fed in this regard are related to trying to counteract supply shocks.

STIMULATING
ECONOMY

The tool the Fed uses is the money supply. If the Fed thinks the economy is growing too slowly and unemployment is too high, the Fed "stimulates" the economy by increasing the money supply. The immediate effect of this action is to lower interest rates, stimulate investments and spending, and lower unemployment. However, you now know that more rapid growth in the money supply ultimately leads to a higher inflation rate. When consumers finally realize this, all the initial benefits of the faster money growth disappear. Interest rates go back up, and investment spending, consumer spending, and unemployment return to where they were. The result is that the faster money growth gives a temporary "boost" to the economy, which can result in a "peak" on our economic roller coaster.

What happens if the Fed wants to slow the economy? In this case the Fed decreases money growth. This action has the initial effect of raising interest rates, depressing investment and consumer spending, and increasing the unemployment rate. However, a slower rate of money growth will eventually lead to a lower inflation rate. When consumers

C
O
N
S
U
M
E
R

T
O
P
I
C

THE 1981–82 RECESSION: A RECESSION BY DESIGN

The 1981–82 recession is a classic example of a recession engineered by the Federal Reserve System. In many ways, however, the pain inflicted by the Fed in the 1981–82 recession was a response to the pleasure created by the Fed in the last half of the 1970s.

The economy grew rapidly between 1975 and 1979. Real gross domestic product increased 21 percent in that time period. The Fed was a major factor behind this economic prosperity. Between 1975 and 1979 the Fed increased the real (inflation-adjusted) money supply by 18 percent.

But by 1979 the boom was over. The growth in real GDP had ground to a halt. The Fed's "easy" money policy was now resulting in nothing more than high inflation and high interest rates. By 1979 the inflation rate had reached double-digits (13 percent), and it was to be double-digits again in both 1980 and 1981. In 1979 the prime interest rate reached 15 percent, and it would climb to over 20 percent in 1980 and 1981.

What can the Federal Reserve do to reduce inflation and interest rates? Easy, simply reverse gears from an "easy" money policy to a "tight" money policy. And the Federal Reserve certainly did reverse gears, with a vengeance. After growing 18 percent between 1973 and 1979, the Fed actually decreased the real money supply by over 10 percent between 1979 and mid-1981. This policy change was engineered by the new "get-tough" Chairman of the Fed, Paul Volcker, who took office in 1979.

There were "good news" and "bad news" effects of the Fed's tight money policy. The good news was that inflation and interest rates did fall, like a rock. The inflation rate fell from 13 percent in 1979 to 9 percent in 1981 to 4 percent in 1982. The prime interest rate fell from 21 percent in 1981 to 15 percent in 1982 to 11 percent in 1983. The bad news was that the Fed's tight money policy resulted in the recession of 1981–82. Unemployment rose to 11 percent in 1982 and industrial production dropped 13 percent from 1981–82. Unemployment rose and the economy slowed precisely because of the Fed's tight money policy.

Today Paul Volcker is viewed by many as a hero, as the man who slew the high inflation and high interest rate dragons. But those admirers may have forgotten that it took a major recession to do it.

A PLANNED RECESSION

realize the inflation rate has indeed been lowered, interest rates fall, investment and consumer spending go back up, and the unemployment rate falls back to where it was. The result is that the slower money growth initially results in a temporary downturn in the economy which, if severe enough, is a recession!

The effects of Fed monetary policy are summarized in Table 2-2. The initial effects are estimated to last about 12 months, and the long run effects occur from 12 to 24 months. So, business cycles can be caused by the Fed alternately stepping on the money supply gas pedal

Table 2-2   Effects of a change in monetary policy.

Fed policy	Initial effect 0–12 months	Long-run effect 12–24 months
Increase in money growth rate.	Lower interest rates, lower unemployment, increased economic activity and increased income ("boom").	Higher inflation rate: unemployment rate and economic activity return to original levels.
Decrease in money growth rate.	Higher interest rates, higher unemployment, decreased economic activity and decreased income ("recession").	Lower inflation rate: unemployment rate and economic activity return to original levels.

and then on the money supply brake pedal. A reduction in the money growth rate will lead to a contraction and possibly a recession, and an increase in the money growth rate will lead to an expansion and peak (see Figure 2-4).

It is ironic that actions by the Fed made in order to stimulate or cool the economy may, in fact, contribute to fluctuations in the economy. This point has been made very strongly by Professor Milton Friedman, winner of the 1977 Nobel Prize in Economics. Professor Friedman argues that if the Fed would stop trying to "fine-tune" the economy and would increase the money supply at a constant, predictable rate each year, then ups and downs in the economy would be much milder.

Figure 2-4.   The Fed and the economic rollercoaster.

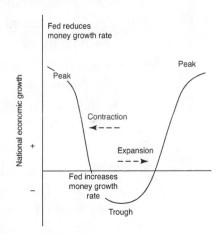

The Bottom Line

Unexpected "supply shocks," such as oil embargoes, droughts, or cost-cutting inventions, can set-off the economic roller coaster. A more common cause of economic ups and downs is the Fed's money policy. A "tightening" of money policy can lead to an economic downturn, and maybe a recession. A "loosening" of money policy can lead to an economic expansion.

4. The Long and Short of Interest Rates: What Does the Spread Tell You?

Interest rates are not all alike. In particular, economists make a distinction between two types of interest rates: long-term interest rates and short-term interest rates.

LONG-TERM INTEREST RATES

Long-term interest rates are interest rates paid on long-term financial investments, like 30 year corporate bonds and 30 year Treasury bonds. Once the long-term financial investment is bought, the

---

C O N S U M E R   T O P I C

A POLITICAL BUSINESS CYCLE

Economics and politics frequently go hand-in-hand. Nowhere is this more evident than in presidential politics and elections.

Between 1952 and 2012, in the four elections that were held during a recession or immediately after a recession (1960, 1980, 1992, 2008), the incumbent party lost. In 1960, Republican Richard Nixon tried to succeed the retiring Republican President Dwight Eisenhower, but Mr. Nixon narrowly lost to John F. Kennedy. In 1980 President Carter was running for a second term, but he lost to Ronald Reagan. The same outcome happened to President George H.W. Bush when he lost to Bill Clinton in 1992. In 2008 the economy was in a severe recession, and Republican John McCain, who was trying to succeed outgoing Republican President George W. Bush, lost to Barack Obama.

On the other hand, in the twelve elections held while the economy was expanding (1952, 1956, 1964, 1968, 1972, 1976, 1984, 1988, 1996, 2000, 2004, 2012), the incumbent party won eight of the twelve. In two of these elections in which the incumbent party lost (1952, 1968), the country was engaged in an unpopular war (Korea in 1952 and Vietnam in 1968). In 1976, the unelected President, Gerald Ford, was hurt by the fallout from the Watergate scandal which led to his predecessor's (Richard Nixon) resignation. And in 2000, the incumbent party's candidate—Al Gore—actually won the popular vote but lost in the electoral college.

What's the moral of this story for politicians, and particularly for presidents? First, if you're an incumbent President running for re-election, or the candidate of the incumbent party, a prosperous economy will do wonders for your election chances. Pressuring the Federal Reserve to pump up the money supply, or lobbying Congress to cut taxes are techniques an incumbent can use to boost the economy. Second, if you are an incumbent and a recession is needed to reduce inflation, it's better to have the recession early in the Presidential term rather than later. Richard Nixon, Ronald Reagan, and Barack Obama had recessions early in their first terms and were rewarded with re-election. Jimmy Carter, George H.W. Bush, and George W. Bush had recessions at the very end of their terms in office, and each was either not re-elected or their party's candidate did not win.

interest rate paid on it never changes. Thus, buyers of long term financial investments must be convinced that the interest rate paid on the investment will be a competitive interest rate over the long term of the investment.

SHORT-TERM INTEREST RATES

Short-term interest rates are interest rates paid on short-term financial investments, like 3 month CDs or 3 month Treasury bills. Again, once the short term financial investment is bought, the interest rate paid on it never changes. But, since the term of the investment is short, this is not as much of a concern for buyers of short-term financial investments as it is for buyers of long-term financial investments.

The Spread

Typically, the interest rate paid on a long-term investment will be higher than the interest rate paid on a short-term investment. Why? The reason is simple. The buyer of a long-term investment is committing his/her money for a much longer period of time than the buyer of a short-term investment. Over the longer term, there's more uncertainty, especially the uncertainty regarding inflation. Over the longer term, there's a greater chance that the inflation rate could charge upward, thereby reducing the purchasing power of future interest earnings. Because of this uncertainty, buyers of long-term financial investments *usually* must be compensated with a higher interest rate than buyers of short-term financial investments. The interest rate paid on long-term financial investments can be thought of as the average of future short-term interest rates expected by investors. The difference between the interest rate paid on new long-term investments and the interest rate paid on new short-term investments is called the *interest rate spread*.

INTEREST RATE SPREAD

What if investors expect future interest rates to fall? In this case, the average of expected future short-term interest rates will be less than today's short term interest rate. This means that the interest rate paid on new long-term investments will actually be lower than the interest rate paid on new short-term investments. That is, the interest rate spread in this case will be negative.

Using the Spread for Forecasting

The spread between the interest rate paid on new long-term investments and the interest rate paid on new short-term investments can tell us something about the direction that investors think future interest rates will take. If the spread is large—that is, there's a large positive difference between the long-term interest rate and the short-term interest rate—then that's an indication that investors strongly think interest rates will rise in the future (and short-term interest rates will rise much more than long-term interest rates). If the spread is negative—that is,

WHAT THE SPREAD MEANS

**C
O
N
S
U
M
E
R

T
O
P
I
C**

THE DEBATE OVER THE "RIGHT" ECONOMIC POLICY

Macroeconomic policies are those actions by the federal government designed to smooth out the economic roller coaster and to promote low inflation and low unemployment. However, there is considerable disagreement among economists as to what these policies should be.

There are at least three camps of economists in their approach to macroeconomic policy. *Keynesian* economists are in favor of active government policies to control the national economy. If the economy is in a recession or growing slowly, Keynesians recommend a government policy of more rapid money growth, lower taxes, and greater government spending in order to "pump-up" the economy. If the economy is growing too fast, Keynesians recommend the opposite policy mix— slower money growth, higher taxes, and less government spending.

Classical economists take the direct opposite view of Keynesians. Classical economists believe the economy is self-adjusting to any "shocks" that move it away from full employment. Furthermore, classical economists believe that Keynesian policy can actually contribute to economic fluctuations. This might occur if Keynesian policies are only implemented with a delay (e.g., more government spending is enacted long after the recession has ended), or if Keynesian policies are implemented on the basis of incomplete information.

Monetarists are economists who strongly believe in the power of the money policy of the Federal Reserve. Monetarists are similar in their recommendations as classical economists. Monetarists believe that much of the fluctuation in the economy is due to the Federal Reserve alternately speeding the growth of the money supply and then slowing growth. Monetarists recommend that the Fed announce and maintain a steady growth of the money supply and avoid changing the growth rate. In fact, some monetarists have gone so far as to recommend replacing the Federal Reserve Board of Governors with a computer which can be programmed to supply a steady, and unchanging, stream of money.

short-term interest rates are higher than long-term interest rates—then that's an indication that investors strongly think interest rates will fall in the future (and short-term interest rates will fall much more than long-term interest rates).

Therefore, you can use the spread between long- and short-term interest rates as an indicator of where the average investor thinks interest rates are headed. But, of course, what investors think interest rates will do in the future can be wrong. So how well has the interest rate spread performed as a predictor of future interest rate movements?

Figure 2-5 gives the answer for the period 1965–2012. In all years when the spread was negative (1969, 1973, 1974, 1979, 1980, 1981), meaning short-term rates were higher than long-term rates, interest rates fell in the following years. Furthermore, the more negative the spread, the bigger the drop in future interest rates. Conversely, large positive interest rate spreads in the mid-1980s forecasted higher interest rates in the late 1980s. However, since the 1990s the interest rate spreads have been positive but interest rates have been going down in general.

Figure 2-5. Long-term and short-term interest rates.

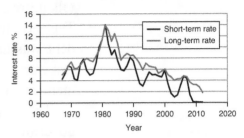

Data source: Federal Reserve Bank of St. Louis. Short-term rate is the 3-month Treasury bill secondary market rate. Long-term rate is the market yield on U.S. Treasury securities at 10-year constant maturity.

The Bottom Line

The spread between long-term and short-term interest rates is an indicator of the direction of future interest rates. When the spread is negative, meaning that short-term interest rates are higher than long-term interest rates, future interest rates should be lower. When the spread is very positive, meaning that long term interest rates are very much higher than short term interest rates, then future interest rates should be higher.

5. But What about Those Deficits?

The average American reading the newspapers or listening or watching the news would probably come to the conclusion that the twin deficits—the budget and trade deficits—are very important in determining the economic future. In the late 1990s and early 2000s the budget deficit shrunk, whereas in the late 2000s and early 2010s the deficit grew tremendously. Many crystal-ball gazers have used the deficits to forecast doom and depression for the American economy, or they have used surpluses to predict prosperity.

The practical question for you, as a consumer, is whether the budget and trade balances are useful as tools to forecast the macro-economy. The answer you'll get from this topic is "no."

Measuring the National Debt

GOVERNMENT BORROWING

A federal budget deficit occurs when the federal government's expenditures exceed its tax revenues. The federal government makes up this deficit by borrowing. The borrowing is in the form of sale of Treasury securities and U.S. savings bonds. Consumers willingly purchase the

Treasury securities and savings bonds because they're considered very safe investments and because they pay a competitive interest rate. (We'll talk more about Treasury securities and U.S. savings bonds in Chapter 9: Types of Investments). As of 2012, about a third of total U.S. public debt was held by foreign governments and international entities. The rest were held by federal governmental agencies, state and local governments, banks and corporations, and individual investors.

The budget deficit is the annual amount by which the federal government's tax revenues fall short of expenditures. In contrast, a budget surplus is the annual amount by which the federal government's tax revenues exceed expenditures. In the 84 years from 1929 to 2012 inclusive, the federal government has run a budget surplus in only 18 years.

NATIONAL DEBT

The federal, or national, debt is the current sum of all the outstanding budget deficits. On March 5, 2013, the national debt was $16.6 trillion, up from $340 billion in 1967. This represented a 4782 percent growth! How can we survive with this kind of debt and this kind of debt growth?

One thing that should give you comfort is to recognize that the 4782 percent growth in the national debt overstates its real growth, since inflation accounts for quite a bit of the increase in the dollar value of the debt. If the national debt is adjusted for inflation, then we see that the debt has grown from $340 billion in 1967 to $2.3 trillion in 2012 (in 1967 dollars), for a much more modest 616 percent increase.

Another way of looking at the national debt is to calculate the national debt to GDP ratio. This ratio indicates the country's ability to pay back its debt. Figure 2-6 shows the U.S. national debt to GDP ratio for 1967–2012. From 1967 to 1981 the percentage declined in general, while from 1982 and 1996 the percentage increased. The ratio declined again briefly in the early 2000s, only to climb drastically in the late 2000s and early 2012s. 2012 was the first year when the total amount of U.S. national debt exceeded its total GDP.

Is a High National Debt Bad?

What's the worry about the national debt? There are two worries. One is that interest rates rise as a result of the increased government borrowing. The rise in interest rates "crowds-out" private borrowing

Figure 2-6. National debt to GDP ratio.

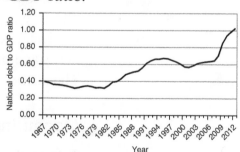

Data sources: National debt data from the U.S. Department of Treasury. GDP data from the U.S. Department of Commerce, Bureau of Economic Analysis.

and results in less private investment. A second worry is that government borrowing today merely means that more taxes have to be paid later.

Let's look at each of these worries. First, there's much evidence that higher budget deficits or a higher national debt do not cause higher interest rates.[5] For example, in the 1980s, late 2000s, and early 2010s deficits and the national debt were increasing yet interest rates were decreasing. One explanation for this may be that consumers realize that government borrowing today simply means more taxes later in order to repay the debt. Consumers therefore reduce spending and borrowing today in order

BORROWING TODAY VS. TAXING TOMORROW

to save for the future taxes. The reduced spending and increased saving counter-balances the increased government borrowing, so interest rates don't increase.

If the alternative to government borrowing is simply higher taxes today, then the worry that government borrowing will make future taxpayers poorer also doesn't hold water. To easily see this, simply pull out the present-value methodology you learned in Micro-foundations. To keep things simple, consider only a two-year period. The government has two financing options. It can tax $1 from you this year and then collect no taxes next year. Obviously the present value of this tax is $1. Or, the government can borrow $1 (say, from a foreigner) this year and not tax you, but then tax $1 + $R from you next year, where R is the interest rate paid by the government on its bonds. If R is used as the discount rate, then obviously the present value of $1 + $R paid next year is $1. So it doesn't matter if the government taxes you $1 this year or delays taxing you $1+$R next year—the two amounts are equivalent!

Is the Budget Deficit a Forecaster of Anything?

Remember that, as consumers, the macroeconomic factors we're most interested in are inflation, interest rates, and job opportunities. Do the budget deficit or national debt help us forecast any of these? No! Budget deficits and the national debt usually trail these macroeconomic factors, not precede them. In particular, the real budget deficit and real national debt usually rise after a recession has started and usually fall after an economic expansion is underway.

What is the Trade Deficit?

TRADE DEFICIT

We've also heard a lot about the U.S. trade deficit. A trade deficit simply means that U.S. consumers are buying more imported products than

TRADE SURPLUS

U.S. producers are able to sell to foreign buyers. A trade surplus means

---

[5]See Plosser, Charles, "The Effects of Government Financing Decisions on Asset Returns, *Journal of Monetary Economics,* May 1982; and Evans, Paul, "Do Large Deficits Produce High Interest Rates?" *American Economic Review,* March 1985.

the opposite—U.S. producers are selling more to foreign buyers than U.S. consumers are buying from foreign producers.

Trade deficits in the U.S. economy aren't new. From the end of World War II to 1970, the U. S. regularly ran trade surpluses. However, from 1970 to 2012, the U. S. ran a trade deficit in all but three years.

There's an easy explanation for trade deficits and surpluses. When the dollar's value rises against foreign currencies, foreign imports become less expensive and U.S. exports to foreign countries become more expensive.

EXCHANGE RATE FUNDAMENTALS

An exchange rate between two currencies is a price. Just like the price of a pound of apples shows how many dollars you must give up to get one pound of apples, the exchange rate between the U.S. dollar and the euro, for example, shows how many dollars you must give up to get one euro. If the U.S. dollar "strengthens" against the euro, this means it takes fewer U.S. dollars to equal one euro (or, said the other way around, you get more euros for one U.S. dollar). Conversely, if the U.S. dollar "weakens" against the euro, this means it takes more U.S. dollars to equal one euro (or, said the other way around, you get fewer euros for one U.S. dollar).

International economists believe that exchange rates will settle to a level where the "Law of One Price" holds. The "Law of One Price" simply means that the price of a product in, say, Germany, will be the same as the price of that same product in the U.S. when the exchange rate between currencies is taken into account and when any tariffs and transportation costs are subtracted. So, for example, if a Volkswagen costs 20,000 Euros in Germany, and if the exchange rate is $1.50 to one euro, then the same Volkswagen in the U.S. will cost $30,000, plus any shipping and tariffs involved in importing Volkswagen into the U.S. from Germany.

What will cause exchange rates to change? For example, what might cause the U.S. dollar to strengthen against the euro? The answer is based on supply and demand, but in this case, the supply and demand of currencies. Let's take a simple example. Suppose there is a 10% increase in the supply of euro (the European Central Bank prints 10% more euros), the supply of U.S. dollars does not change, and the relative demands for euros and dollars don't change. What will happen to the exchange rate? Well, if the supply of apples increases and the demand for apples doesn't change, the price of apples will fall. The same logic works here. There are now more euros relative to dollars, so the value of the euro will fall in terms of the dollars, or, saying the same thing, the dollar will strengthen against the euro. In fact, the dollar will strengthen by 10%. As such, although the price of Volkswagen in Germany is 10% higher in euros, the price of Volkswagen in U.S. dollars won't change.

Economic growth in each country can also affect the exchange rate. Faster economic growth means a greater demand for currency. If economic growth is faster in the U.S. than in Europe, then the increase in the demand for dollars will

C O N S U M E R   T O P I C

exceed the increase in the demand for euros and the dollar will strengthen relative to the euro. If economic growth is greater in Europe, the euro will strengthen against the dollar.

With these two effects (relative inflation rates and relative economic growth rates) in hand, a simple equation can be stated giving the change in the exchange rate. Continuing our example of the dollar and the euro, the equation is:

$$\begin{matrix} \text{Change in} \\ \text{exchange rate} \\ \text{of U.S. dollar} \\ \text{relative to euro} \end{matrix} = \begin{matrix} \text{Real U.S.} \\ \text{economic} \\ \text{growth} \\ \text{rate} \end{matrix} - \begin{matrix} \text{Real} \\ \text{European} \\ \text{economic} \\ \text{growth rate} \end{matrix} + \begin{matrix} \text{Euro} \\ \text{growth} \\ \text{rate} \end{matrix} - \begin{matrix} \text{U.S.} \\ \text{dollar} \\ \text{growth} \\ \text{rate} \end{matrix}$$

A positive number from the equation means the U.S. dollar strengthens against the euro and a negative number means the dollar weakens against the euro.

This creates a gap of imports over exports, or a trade deficit. On the other hand, when the dollar's value falls against foreign currencies, foreign imports become more expensive and U.S. exports to foreign countries become less expensive. This eventually reduces imports and increases exports and can result in a trade surplus. Economists have estimated that it may take up to two years for a change in the value of the dollar to affect the trade balance.

INFLATION AND THE DOLLAR'S VALUE

If changes in the trade balance are caused by changes in the dollar's value, then what are changes in the dollar's value caused by? That's a complex question, but one answer seems to be the inflation rate. When the U.S. inflation rate rises, the dollar's value falls, and when the U.S. inflation rate falls, the dollar's value rises.

This means that the trade balance, like the budget deficit, results from fundamental economic factors (e.g., inflation), and isn't of much help in predicting these factors.

The Bottom Line

Although they have received much attention in recent years, the budget and trade deficits are not very useful in forecasting fundamental economic factors such as inflation, interest rates, and unemployment.

6. Riding the Economic Roller Coaster, or How Can You Forecast the Economy?

This section is really a summary of what you've learned in this topic about forecasting. How can you use some fundamental economic factors to forecast where the economy is going, particularly with respect to inflation, interest rates, and employment opportunities?

Inflation

Use this simple equation to forecast next year's inflation rate:

$$\text{Money growth rate last year} - \text{Real economic growth rate for next year} = \text{Inflation rate next year}$$

If a forecast for next year's economic growth rate is not available, use this equation:

$$\text{Money growth rate last year} - 3\% = \text{Inflation rate next year}$$

Interest Rates

There are two indicators you can use to forecast the direction of interest rates. One is the inflation rate. The inflation rate and interest rates move together. So, if next year the inflation rate is projected to be lower, then interest rates should also be lower.

The second indicator of the direction of interest rates is the spread between long-term interest rates and short-term interest rates. When the spread is negative, meaning short term interest rates are higher than long term interest rates, then interest rates are headed down. When the spread is very positive, then interest rates are headed up.

Employment Opportunities

The Federal Reserve can "pump-up" the economy to create a "boom" period, but the Federal Reserve can also "cool down" the economy to create a recession.

If the Fed speeds-up the growth of money, look for a boom period and more job opportunities. If the Fed slows down the growth of money, look for a slower economy and fewer job opportunities. If the Fed slows money growth so much that the supply of money declines, look for a recession to occur.

Where to Find Information

Information on economic cycles, inflation, interest rates, and unemployment is available from several sources, most them are published both in paper form and online.

Survey of Current Business: Monthly; includes data on all economic variables for most recent period and for past 30 years presented in graphs and charts. Available from Superintendent of Documents, U.S. Government Printing Office, Washington, D.C. 20402. Online at http://www.bea.gov/scb/index.htm.

HOW RELIABLE IS THE INDEX
OF LEADING ECONOMIC INDICATORS?

**C
O
N
S
U
M
E
R**

**T
O
P
I
C**

The Index of Leading Economic Indicators is a weighted average of ten variables that tend to forecast changes in business activity. A fall in the Index indicates a slowdown in future business activity, and an increase in the Index indicates an increase in future business activity. The ten variables that compose the Index are:

• average weekly hours of manufacturing workers,
• average weekly initial claims for unemployment insurance,
• manufacturers' new orders,
• companies reporting slower deliveries,
• orders for plant and equipment (1982 $),
• new private housing permits,
• interest rate spread,
• an index of stock prices,
• money supply,
• index of consumer expectations.

The Index of Leading Economic Indicators does predict turning points in the economic roller coaster, but with varying degrees of forewarning. The Index began to decline 15 months before the start of the 1980 recession, but it only gave 3 months forewarning to the start of the 1981–82 recession.

Another problem with the Index is that it can give a false signal of an on-coming recession. The Index declined for six months in 1962 but no recession resulted; the Index declined for ten months in 1966 but no recession resulted; the Index declined for nine months in 1984 but no recession resulted; the Index declined for five months in 1987 but no recession resulted; and the Index declined for half a year in 1995 without a recession following.

The practical conclusion seems to be this. Recessions are always preceded by declines in the Index of Leading Economic Indicators, but the start of the decline can vary anywhere from two months to twenty months before the start of the recession. However, all declines in the Index are not followed by a recession. In other words, the Index can give a false signal for a recession.

Federal Reserve Bulletin: Monthly; includes data on all economic variables; presented in tables for recent three years. Available from Federal Reserve System, Publications Services, Mail Stop 127, Board of Governors of the Federal Reserve System, Washington, DC 20551, or go to web site http://www.federalreserve.gov/pubs/bulletin/.

National Economic Trends: Monthly; includes data on the size of the economy, sales, inflation, and many business data for most recent period and last decade; presented in graphs and charts. Available from Federal Reserve Bank of St. Louis, P.O. Box 442, St. Louis, Missouri 63166, or go to web site http://research.stlouisfed.org/publications/net/

Monetary Trends: Monthly; includes data on money supply, interest rates, budget deficit, and national debt, presented in graphs and tables for last decade. Online at http://research.stlouisfed.org/publications/mt/ Available from Federal Reserve Bank of St. Louis, P.O. Box 442, St. Louis, Missouri 63166, or go to web site www.stls.frb.org/fred.

U. S. Financial Data: Weekly; includes data on money supply and interest rates; presented in graphs. Available from Federal Reserve Bank of St. Louis, P.O. Box 66953, St. Louis, Missouri 63166, or go to web site www.stls.frb.org/fred.

The Bottom Line

Keep track of the economic roller coaster by following inflation, interest rate, and Fed policy trends in *Survey of Current Business* and similar publications.

WORDS AND CONCEPTS YOU SHOULD KNOW

Peak
Contraction
Trough
Expansion
Recession
Cycle
Lagging consumer expectations
Barter
Money
Central bank
Federal Reserve System
Fractional reserve banking
Reserve requirement
Open market operations

Equation for predicting the inflation rate
Monetary accommodation
Supply shock
Fed's fine tuning
Tight money supply policy
Loose money supply policy
Long term interest rate
Short term interest rate
Interest rate spread
Budget deficit
National debt
Treasury securities
Trade deficit
Value of the dollar

MACROFOUNDATIONS—A SUMMARY

1. The economy goes through ups and downs. The top is called a peak, the bottom is called a trough, decline is called a contraction, and growth is called an expansion. Unemployment, inflation, interest rates, and the stock market follow predictable patterns during the economy's ups and downs. Specifically:

At the peak:	Unemployment rate is low; Inflation and interest rates are rising; Stock market is high.
During a contraction:	Unemployment rate rises; Inflation and interest rates rise then fall; Stock market falls.
At the trough:	Unemployment rate is high; Inflation and interest rates are falling; Stock market is low.
During an expansion:	Unemployment rate falls; Inflation and interest rates fall, then rise; Stock market rises.

A recession occurs during the economic roller coaster when the economy is shrinking.

2. Inflation results from the money supply growing faster than the economy is growing. A change in the Federal Reserve's money policy affects the inflation rate with a time lag. Use this equation to predict the inflation rate:

$$\begin{pmatrix} \text{Money growth} \\ \text{rate last} \\ \text{year} \end{pmatrix} - \begin{pmatrix} \text{Forecast of} \\ \text{of next year's} \\ \text{real economic} \\ \text{growth rate} \\ \text{(use 3\% if not available)} \end{pmatrix} = \begin{pmatrix} \text{Inflation rate} \\ \text{next year} \end{pmatrix}$$

3. Explanations of inflation that don't include the Federal Reserve's monetary policy are incorrect.
   A. Inflation as a "Cost-Push" Problem—deals with symptom rather than cause of inflation. Sellers who increase prices in response to greater demand for their products do not cause inflation.

115

B. Inflation as a result of high interest rates—puts cart before the horse; changes in interest rates follow changes in the inflation rate.

C. Inflation caused by increases in the price of a major product—increase in the price of a major product will cause an immediate, or short-run, jump in the cost-of-living, but won't cause a change in the rate at which average prices are rising.

D. Inflation caused by budget deficits—there is a relationship between budget deficits and inflation only if the Fed increases the money supply to fund the budget deficits.

4. Long term interest rates are usually higher than short term interest rates. The greater the difference, or spread, between long and short term interest rates, the greater the chance that interest rates will rise in the future. When short term interest rates are higher than long term interest rates, meaning the spread is negative, that's a good indication that future interest rates will fall.

5. Budget and trade deficits are of little use in economic forecasting. High, or increasing, budget deficits do not signal an increase in either inflation or interest rates. Trade deficits follow from significant reductions in the inflation rate.

DISCUSSION QUESTIONS

1. Characterize the current state of the economy in terms of the unemployment rate, inflation rate, interest rates (use the prime interest rate), and the stock market (use the Standard & Poor's 500 Stock Index). Does the current economy appear to be in a contraction phase, trough, expansion phase, or peak?

2. Pete Farris is an auto worker. Times are good now, and Pete is working a lot of overtime. However, if the economy goes into a recession, there's a good chance Pete will be laid-off. Pete periodically looks at *Survey of Current Business* in the local public library. Pete notices that the real (inflation-adjusted) money supply has been falling for the past six months. What does this mean for Pete's personal economic outlook? Pete wants to purchase a new car on credit—should he do it?

3. Mary Cunningham also reads *Survey of Current Business.* Mary notices the recent decline in the real money supply. Should Mary sell her stocks now?

4. The incumbent President is nine months away from her re-election bid. Do you think she will pressure the Fed to increase the growth of the money supply or decrease the growth of the money supply. Why?

5. Why do labor unions and producers frequently get blamed for causing higher inflation?

6. If you hear a Federal Reserve Chairman say, "The Federal Reserve is committed to reducing the inflation rate," what kind of Federal Reserve policy would you expect and what would be the consequences of that policy?

7. Look up the current spread between long-term Treasury bonds and short-term Treasury bills. What does this spread tell you about the future direction of interest rates?

8. You notice that the federal budget deficit has increased from last year. Is this a good indication that the inflation rate will increase? Why or why not?

9. You notice that the U.S. inflation rate has been increasing rapidly. What should this do to the value of the U.S. dollar (against foreign currencies) and to the U.S. trade balance?

PROBLEMS

1. Last year's money growth rate was 8 percent. What is your best prediction for next year's inflation rate?

2. At the beginning of last year the money supply (M2) was $5000 billion, and at the end of last year the money supply was $5750 billion. What is your best prediction for the inflation rate next year if 3 percent real economic growth is expected next year?

3. If the 30-year Treasury bond interest rate is 7 percent, and the 90-day Treasury bill interest rate is 5 percent, what is the spread?

4. If the 30-year Treasury bond interest rate is 7 percent, and the 90-day Treasury bill interest rate is 9 percent, what is the spread? What does this spread tell you about the direction of future interest rates?

5. Use the following numbers to determine if the budget deficit has "really" increased between Year 1 and Year 2:

	Year 1	*Year 2*
Budget deficit	$ 100 billion	$ 130 billion
Gross Domestic Product	$7000 billion	$7300 billion
CPI	170	173

CHAPTER 3

Organizing Your Financial Life

Introduction

Many of you won't like this chapter (Wait, please don't leave!) because the chapter uses a lot of numbers and forms and, yes, the dreaded "b" word, "budget." Yet, years from now, you'll thank us for this chapter when you use its lessons to organize your financial life, conquer your tax fears, and save more money than you ever thought possible (well, maybe not).

This chapter has two purposes: to show you how to do a budget and a net worth statement, and to show you what's involved in calculating your tax liability. Both of these tasks involve, unfortunately, much record-keeping and number-crunching. But they're indispensable for any consumer who wants to exercise control over his or her financial life.

Although this chapter mainly deals with the organization of your finances, we won't forget economics. For example, you'll see there are some typical patterns to consumer spending and consumer net worth (what a consumer is worth) that have logical economic explanations. You'll learn that the tax rate that most matters is your *marginal* tax rate, not your average tax rate, and reducing taxes should *not* be a financial goal. Finally, the power of compound interest will be used to demonstrate that taxes are one thing that you should try to pay tomorrow rather than today (so all you procrastinators can cheer!).

1. Do You Need a Budget?

Let's face it—household budgeting has a bad reputation. Who, voluntarily, wants to subject themselves to a financial straightjacket that restricts how much can be spent on various categories?

BUDGET

You probably know what a budget is, but let's give it a formal definition anyway. A budget is a plan, or guideline, for allocating your income to expenditures and savings. You can make a weekly budget, a monthly budget, or an annual budget, but the budget time period should be long enough to include most of your expenditure categories. Most people find a monthly budget to be adequate. We'll discuss the particulars of budget-making in the next topic.

Budgeting as a Financial Lifesaver

LIVING BEYOND
MEANS

There are three types of consumers for whom a budget is a financial lifesaver. One type includes consumers who have lived beyond their means. These are consumers who chronically spend more than they earn. At the extreme they have problems meeting credit payments and they may be on the verge of personal bankruptcy. For them, financial budgeting is a must. Budgeting is the only way for them to take control of their financial problems, turn around their overspending, and prevent personal financial disaster. Budgeting will allow them to schedule payment of their debt in an orderly fashion.

CAN'T SAVE

A second type of consumer who needs budgeting is the consumer who wants and needs to save money but just doesn't seem to be able to. These consumers aren't in financial trouble like the previous group. They live within their means and are able to pay all bills. In fact, they may earn a very high income. They simply don't have anything left at the end of the month to save. A budget will help this type of consumer pinpoint "excess" expenditures and free-up money for savings.

ERRATIC INCOME

The third type of consumer who needs budgeting is the consumer who has an erratic income. An erratic income is an income which isn't constant each month of a year but fluctuates significantly from one month to the next. Consumers who work on commission or who work in industries which are very cyclical or seasonal (e.g., construction, auto manufacturing or sales, farming) have erratic incomes. In order to maintain steady consumption throughout the year, consumers with erratic incomes must save income in months when income is high and use that savings in months when income is low. Careful planning and budgeting is required in order to do this.

Budgeting as a Monitoring and Planning Device

Many consumers don't have financial problems or erratic incomes (hopefully you're one of them). They live within their income and they are able to save. Is budgeting of no use to these consumers? Can these consumers ignore the tedious task of recording expenditures and comparing total expenses to total income?

SUBCONSCIOUS BUDGET

Honestly, the answer is yes. Many of these financially secure consumers can ignore budgeting, and they do. They are able to financially "float" from month to month, paying bills as they come and still having enough left over for savings. Some of these consumers may use a "subconscious budget". This means they don't have a formal budget written down, but they intuitively keep track of spending and know whether a product or service is affordable or not. A subconscious calculator in their head tells them when to stop spending.

MONITORING

However, even these well-heeled consumers may want to use a budget for three reasons. First, a budget can be used as a monitoring device to simply keep track of where money is spent. Most of us work very hard for our money. A budget can give us the satisfaction of knowing where the money goes.

TAX PLANNING

A second use of a budget is for tax purposes. A budget can help keep track of income and of expenses which are tax-deductible (mortgage interest expenses, property taxes, medical expenses, work-related expenses). The maintenance of a budget throughout the year can significantly reduce the time needed to prepare tax returns.

Table 3-1 Uses of a budget.

Use	Used by:
A control device to reduce spending and increase savings.	Consumers who have overspent and have debt problems.
	Consumers who can't save.
	Consumers with erratic incomes.
A monitoring device to know where income goes: • useful for tax preparation, • useful to life insurance and retirement planning.	Consumers without financial problems.

LIFE INSURANCE
AND RETIREMENT
PLANNING

Finally a budget can be a big help in life insurance and retirement planning. In one form of life insurance planning, the consumer needs to know the family's spending requirement necessary to maintain the current standard of living. In retirement planning the retiree or retired couple need to estimate consumption expenditures during retirement. For both of these tasks, a current budget would be a big help.

The potential uses of a budget are summarized in Table 3-1.

We don't want to kid you. There is a time cost to budgeting. It takes time to set up a budget and to continuously collect and record the information necessary to maintain a budget. The financially secure consumer must decide if the benefits from budgeting are worth these time costs.

The Bottom Line

Budgeting is a "must" for consumers who have chronic financial problems and for consumers who need to save but can't seem to find the money for it. For financially secure consumers, budgeting does have benefits in expenditure monitoring, tax planning, and life insurance and retirement planning. Such financially secure consumers must decide if the benefits from budgeting are worth the time costs of establishing and maintaining a budget.

2. How Does the Average Consumer Spend Money?

Before we take you through the details of budget making, it's useful to look at average spending patterns and budgets by consumers. This look will do two things for you. First, it will reveal patterns of consumer spending, particularly with respect to age and income. As will be explained, these patterns make a lot of economic sense. You can use the patterns as a guideline to your own spending as you age and as your income changes.

GUIDES

Second, the budgets can be used as guideposts against which to compare your own spending. For example, you can look at the percent of income spent on food for consumers of your age or your income to judge if you are spending more than average or less than average. You may want to use this information to make changes in your own spending.

Tables 3-2 and 3-3 show average spending patterns for different age groups and income categories of consumers. The entries in the tables show the spending shares on various items.

Spending Patterns by Age

Distinct spending patterns by age can be detected by looking at Table 3-2. Here's a summary of the major patterns:

Food at home:	This share goes through ups and downs with age, and is the highest for those 75+.
Food away from home:	This share generally declines with age.
Shelter:	The share of spending on shelter declines until age 74, then rises.
Utilities:	The share spent on utilities rises with age.
Apparel:	The share generally declines with age.
Transportation:	This share generally declines with age.
Health care:	This share increases with age, and is substantially higher for consumers over age 65.
Entertainment:	This share rises with age but declines for those 75+.
Education:	This share is the largest for those under 25 years.
Cash contribution:	This share increases with age.
Personal insurance and pensions:	This share increases until middle age, then declines.

These patterns make common sense. Spending shares on most categories decline with age, with the exception of the elderly for some categories (e.g., health care). The reduction in spending allows middle-aged consumers to increase their contributions to personal insurance, pensions, and savings.

Spending Patterns by Income

The spending patterns with income (Table 3-3) also make common sense. Here's a summary:

Table 3-2 Spending patterns by age group, % of spending, 2011

Expenditure Category	All Consumer Units	Under 25 Years	25–34 Years	35–44 Years	45–54 Years	55–64 Years	65–74 Years	75 Years and Older
Average annual expenditures	$49,705	$29,912	$48,097	$57,271	$58,050	$53,616	$44,646	$32,688
Food at home	7.7	8.0	7.2	8.0	7.6	7.3	8.0	9.1
Food away from home	5.3	6.6	5.7	5.5	5.2	4.9	5.0	4.4
Alcoholic beverages	0.9	1.4	1.1	0.9	0.9	0.9	0.9	0.7
Shelter	19.8	22.5	21.8	21.1	19.1	18.2	17.8	19.1
Utilities, fuels, and public services	7.5	6.4	6.9	7.1	7.4	7.6	8.5	9.6
Household operations	2.3	1.7	2.8	2.6	1.7	1.8	2.1	3.9
Housekeeping supplies	1.2	0.9	0.9	1.2	1.2	1.3	1.6	1.7
Household furnishings and equipment	3.0	2.9	3.1	2.9	2.9	3.1	3.8	2.6
Apparel and services	3.5	4.8	3.8	3.9	3.4	3.2	2.7	3.2
Transportation	16.7	18.3	18.4	16.9	16.4	16.8	15.6	13.2
Health care	6.7	2.8	4.4	4.8	5.9	7.5	11.3	13.6
Entertainment	5.2	4.5	5.0	5.1	5.5	5.2	5.6	4.4
Personal care products and services	1.3	1.1	1.2	1.3	1.2	1.3	1.4	1.6
Reading	0.2	0.2	0.2	0.2	0.2	0.3	0.4	0.5
Education	2.1	7.5	2.2	1.4	3.2	1.6	0.6	0.7
Tobacco products and smoking supplies	0.7	0.9	0.8	0.6	0.8	0.7	0.6	0.4
Miscellaneous	1.6	1.0	1.3	1.4	1.6	1.7	1.8	2.1
Cash contributions	3.5	1.2	2.3	2.7	3.0	3.9	5.7	6.8
Personal insurance and pensions	10.9	7.4	11.1	12.3	12.8	12.6	6.6	2.5

Data source: U.S. Bureau of Labor Statistics, 2011 Consumer Expenditure Survey.

Table 3-3 Spending patterns by income group, % of spending 2011

Expenditure category	Less than $5,000	$5,000 to $9,999	$10,000 to $14,999	$15,000 to $19,999	$20,000 to $29,999	$30,000 to $39,999	$40,000 to $49,999	$50,000 to $69,999	$70,000 and more
Average annual expenditures	$22,960	$20,884	$19,959	$24,806	$30,398	$36,769	$40,306	$50,034	$81,767
Food at home	9.4	12.1	12.0	10.3	9.2	9.5	7.9	8.0	6.5
Food away from home	5.7	5.2	4.4	4.8	4.8	5.0	4.9	5.1	5.5
Alcoholic beverages	1.0	1.1	0.7	0.6	0.7	0.9	0.8	0.8	1.0
Shelter	22.5	23.7	25.4	22.0	22.3	21.1	20.9	19.2	18.6
Utilities, fuels, and public services	9.1	9.9	11.4	11.0	9.8	9.1	9.1	8.0	6.1
Household operations	2.2	1.6	1.7	2.4	2.3	2.1	2.1	1.9	2.5
Housekeeping supplies	1.2	1.4	1.5	1.8	1.3	1.3	1.3	1.3	1.1
Household furnishings and equipment	2.4	2.3	2.5	2.5	2.7	3.0	2.7	3.4	3.1
Apparel and services	4.9	4.5	3.7	3.3	3.1	4.0	2.9	3.5	3.5
Transportation	15.1	15.3	12.8	16.2	15.3	17.4	17.7	18.0	16.6
Health care	5.4	5.3	7.9	8.2	8.7	7.5	8.2	7.4	5.8
Entertainment	3.9	4.8	4.6	4.4	5.4	4.6	4.7	5.7	5.3
Personal care products and services	1.1	1.4	1.2	1.2	1.2	1.3	1.3	1.2	1.3
Reading	0.2	0.2	0.2	0.2	0.2	0.2	0.2	0.3	0.2
Education	8.3	4.5	1.7	1.4	1.7	1.2	1.3	1.3	2.4
Tobacco products and smoking supplies	1.3	1.5	1.7	1.3	1.2	1.0	1.0	0.8	0.4
Miscellaneous	2.3	1.8	1.6	1.4	2.0	1.5	1.6	1.4	1.5
Cash contributions	2.8	2.2	2.7	4.2	2.9	3.0	3.1	3.1	3.8
Personal insurance and pensions	1.4	1.4	2.1	2.7	4.9	6.4	8.2	9.7	14.8

Data source: U.S. Bureau of Labor Statistics, 2011 Consumer Expenditure Survey.

Food at home: This share declines with income, with the exception of the lowest income group.

Food away from home: This share first declines and then rises with income.

Shelter: The share of spending on shelter increases then decreases with income.

Utilities: The share spent on utilities first rises and then declines with income.

Apparel: The share generally declines with income.

Transportation: This share generally rises with income.

Health care: This share first rises and then declines with income.

Entertainment: Share of total spending is highest for the two highest income groups.

Education: This share increases with income.

Cash contribution: This share is the highest for those with income between $15,000 and $19,999.

Personal insurance and pensions: This share increases with income.

In summary, spending shares on most of the major categories decline as income rises, thereby freeing up the resources to increase the share for personal insurance and pensions and other savings.

Impact of Children on Spending

As you might expect, children have a big impact on spending patterns. Douthitt and Fedyk have carefully estimated the impact of children on family spending.[1] They found that families with children:

♦ spend a larger share of their income on home-prepared food and a smaller share of their income on food in restaurants (food away from home) than childless families,

♦ spend a larger share of their income on clothing than childless families beginning when the oldest child is 6 and peaking when the oldest child is 18,

♦ spend a larger share of their income on housing than childless families when children are young and a smaller share when children have gone,

♦ spend a larger share of their income on transportation and durable goods than childless families when the children pass age 16.

---

[1]Douthitt, Robin A. and Joanne M. Fedyk, "The Influence of Children on Family Life Cycle Spending Behavior: Theory and Applications." *Journal of Consumer Affairs*, Vol. 22, No. 2, Winter 1988, pp. 220–248.

DEFINING THE POVERTY LEVEL

C O N S U M E R   T O P I C

Frequently we talk about poverty, but what do we mean? There is, in fact, an "official" poverty level established by the Bureau of the Census. The chart shows this official poverty level for a family of four from 1967 to 2012. Families with incomes below the poverty level are considered "officially" poor and are eligible for many government programs. There's a different poverty level for each family size.

You might expect that the poverty level is derived by extensive surveys conducted by the government. Wrong! In the 1960s an economist at the Social Security Administration estimated that an average family spent one-third of their income on food. Based on this discovery, the economist speculated that a subsistence budget could be estimated by multiplying a minimally adequate food budget by three. This was

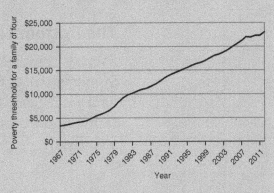

first done using estimates of minimally adequate food budgets in 1967. Each year the poverty level is updated by simply multiplying the previous year's level by the increase in the cost of living as measured by the Consumer Price Index.

There are two potential flaws with this methodology for estimating the poverty level. First, the methodology doesn't include the value of government programs like food stamps, subsidized health care, and Medicaid. The Census Bureau estimates that including these benefits would decrease the poverty level by 10 to 13 percent.

Second, there is no assurance that the multiplier of three between a minimally adequate food budget and the poverty level income is maintained each year. If, for example, the current multiplier is higher than three, then the poverty level is underestimated.

Reference: Motley Brian, "Counting the Poor," *Federal Reserve Bank of San Francisco Weekly Letter*, April 6, 1990.

What about Savings?

There is a clear pattern for saving with most households. Young households, with all the demands on their income, aren't able to save. In fact, young households are heavy borrowers. Then, as the household ages, saving does occur until retirement, when the typical household drains down on savings to meet living expenses.

Likewise, there's a direct relationship between saving and household income. As you might expect, saving rises as household income increases.

Indeed, data from the 2011 Consumer Expenditure Survey confirms the ties between saving and household age and income. The savings rate for young (under age 25) and elderly (75 and over) households is negative at –9% and –3%, respectively, indicating borrowing, while the savings rate is positive for other age groups. Similarly, the saving rate is –118% for households in the lowest 20 percentile of the income distribution but 38% for households in the highest 20% of income distribution.

CAN'T SAVE WHEN YOUNG

So if you find that you can't save when you're young, don't worry about it. But if you find you can't save when you reach your peak earning years during middle age, than you should worry about it. If you find you're in this boat, then maybe you need to take up . . . yes, that's right . . . budgeting!

The Bottom Line

Average consumer spending and saving follow predictable patterns. Spending shares fall and saving shares rise with income and with age until retirement. If you find you aren't able to save during the peak earning years of middle age, then you should have your spending habits monitored.

3. Does a Budget Have to Be a Financial Straightjacket?

Yes! This topic addresses the concepts and techniques of the dreaded "b" word—budget." Budgeting isn't a piece of cake—just ask the White House and Congress! We all have unlimited wants and desires. Most of us don't like budgeting because a budget makes us confront the economic fact of life that limited resources mean we can't have everything we want. However, the benefit of budgeting is that it helps us prioritize our wants and desires and achieve as many of them as we can.

Well, we tried to psych you up enough about budgeting. Let's get to it.

Elements of Budgeting

A budget matches your income to your expenses and savings. In setting up a budget, you must decide what to include as income, what categories of expenses and savings to use, and what time period to use.

What Income to Use

Income used in budgeting should include all regularly received income such as wages and salaries, rental income, regular investment income (bond dividends, interest from CDs), pension income, and any regularly received public assistance money. Only include income that you expect to receive.

For most consumers, income is the same each month of a year. However, as discussed earlier, consumers whose income is primarily derived from commissions or cyclical jobs have erratic income from month to month.

These consumers will have to draw down on savings during months when income is low in order to maintain the same consumption each month. In this case withdrawal from savings will periodically supplement income.

BORROWING

Should borrowing be included in income? No. As will be discussed in more detail in the credit chapter, borrowing is a claim against future income. A lender gives you money today to buy something, and in exchange you repay the loan, with interest, in the future. So borrowing doesn't increase your income in the long run. Borrowing shows up as monthly loan repayments. You purchase the product now but you pay for it in the future.

GROSS INCOME

It's recommended that gross income (total income before any deductions for taxes and Social Security) be used rather than net income (take home income). If gross income is used, then deductions for taxes, Social Security, and retirement saving should be recorded. This will allow monitoring of those taxes and savings.

Expense Categories

How many expense categories to use is one of the hardest decisions to make about budgeting. The more categories you use the more closely you can monitor your precise expenditures. But this comes at the cost of more time and paperwork devoted to budgeting.

"NICKEL AND DIME SPENDING"

Most consumers don't realize how many different products and services they buy within a year. It's very easy to "nickel and dime" yourself into not saving by making a large number of small expenditures.

You don't want to use all possible spending categories, but you do want to use enough categories to give you control over spending. A suggestion for expense categories is given in Table 3-4.

The categories should be self-explanatory. If the monthly amount withheld for federal and state income taxes is adequate (that is, you don't pay extra at tax time), then record these withholding amounts. If you have to pay extra at tax time, then divide the expected extra amount by twelve and add it to the amount withheld.

Many consumers purchase some of their personal care items in food stores, so there may be some mixing together of the food and personal care categories.

For homeowners, the mortgage payment should include the monthly amount collected for home insurance and property taxes. Renters will have little or no amounts to put in the home maintenance and repair category.

EDUCATION

Educational expenses are those expenses on top of what all consumers pay for education through their taxes. Educational expenses include tuitions, fees, and charges for private schools or private training. How are college expenses handled? The answer depends on whether the consumer has previously saved for college or if the consumer must borrow to meet college expenses. If the consumer has previously saved for college and is able to pay for college out of those savings, then record the expenditure in the education expense category and show a counterbalancing reduction in the education savings category. If borrowing must be done to finance college, then record the loan repayments in the education category.

Table 3-4 Suggested expense and savings categories for budgeting.

Expense Categories

Income taxes: includes federal, state, and local (if applicable) income taxes; sales taxes included with product expenditures.

Food, beverage, and tobacco products at home.

Personal care: drug store products.

Rent or mortgage payment.

Home maintenance and repair: maintenance and repair to structure; landscaping.

Utilities: includes home fuel, electricity, telephone.

Household furnishings and operations: furniture, linens, appliances, furniture and appliance repair, credit payments for purchase of furniture and appliances.

Child daycare.

Clothing: includes adult and child clothing, shoes, jewelry.

Vehicle fuel.

Vehicle repairs and maintenance.

Vehicle insurance.

Vehicle credit payments.

Medical: includes insurance.

Education: Direct education expenses, including job training.

Life and disability insurance.

Entertainment: includes vacations.

Miscellaneous.

Savings Categories

Social Security contributions.

Pension and retirement contributions.

Education.

Vacation.

Durable good replacement: includes replacement of vehicle, appliances, furnace/AC, roof.

Emergency savings.

Table 3-4 also includes a number of savings categories. Social Security contributions and pension contributions are generally deductions from your paycheck. Retirement contributions are other saving you do for retirement, such as IRA (Individual Retirement Account) and annuity investments. Education saving is money you put aside for your children's college education or for other kinds of education or training for you or your children.

Durable good replacement is saving you may want for future replacement of durable products which eventually wear out, such as cars, refrigerators, washers and dryers, and the roof of your house (if you're a homeowner). Saving now for these products will mean you won't have to borrow to buy them later.

Emergency savings is money set aside to handle unexpected and unplanned expenditures. Emergency savings is very important for consumers with erratic incomes.

Time Period

For the vast majority of consumers, budgeting on a monthly basis is most useful. This is because many bills are due monthly (rent, mortgage, fuel, electricity, credit payments) and because monthly paychecks are the most common type. Also, a month is a long enough time to make changes to spending behavior.

MONTHLY
BUDGET

If a monthly basis is used for budgeting, then all expenses should be recorded on a monthly basis. This is fine for expenditures which do occur monthly, but what about expenditures which may occur only a couple times a year, such as insurance premiums and home maintenance and repairs? The easiest way to handle these expenses is to first calculate their yearly amount and then allocate 1/12 of this each month. For example, suppose your auto insurance is $1,000 annually, paid in installments of $500 every six months. You should allocate $1,000/12, or $83.33, each month for auto insurance. The $83.33/month will actually be saved until the payment is due. We could get fancy and calculate what would need to be budgeted each month assuming the "saved" amounts earn interest, but for such a short period of time the interest earnings will amount to very little. In this case, we'll consider the interest earnings to be "gravy."

Remember Inflation

Spending will not remain constant because of inflation. Inflation means a rise in prices and income. The dollar entries in budgets cannot be maintained from year to year. Each year inflation will push up the cost of buying the same amount of food, fuel, or clothing.

ADJUSTING BUDGET
ENTRIES
Each year you should adjust the dollar amounts in your budget for inflation. The easiest way to do this is to put budget entries both in dollar terms and as a percent of your income. Then, as your income rises (hopefully with inflation), adjust the dollar amount up to maintain the same percentage.

Calculating Savings Goals

Many of us set up a budget because we want to save more. But how are savings requirements calculated? If, for example, you want to save $5,000 for a house down payment in two years, or if you want to save for a new furnace, how do you calculate the required monthly amount to put aside?

If you want to save $5,000 in five years (60 months), your first guess might be that you need to save $\frac{\$5,000}{60}$, or $83.33 each month. But this ignores interest earnings. Interest earnings will reduce the necessary amount to save.

There are two procedures for calculating savings goals. One procedure uses nominal amounts and nominal interest rates. The other procedure uses real amounts and real interest rates. Don't let your eyes glaze over, we will explain the differences below.

Using Nominal Amounts and Rates

If there's a certain nominal amount you want to save in the future, call it $X, and the amount to save each month is $Y in order to accumulate $X, then the future value sum of $Y, saved each month for the number of months in the term, will equal $X. That is:

$$\$Y \times \begin{bmatrix} \text{FVFS associated with} \\ \text{given nominal interest} \\ \text{rate and no. of months} \end{bmatrix} = \$X$$

So, the amount to save each month is:

$$\$Y = \frac{\$X}{(\text{FVFS, nominal}) (\text{interest rate,}) (\text{no. of months})}$$

Let's quickly go to some examples.

EXAMPLE 3-1: Betsy and Graig want to save $5,000 in three years for a house down payment. If they can invest money at a 6 percent after-tax interest rate, how much must they save each month to reach their goal?

ANSWER:

$$\text{Monthly amount to save} = \frac{\$5,000}{\text{FVFS}(6\%, 36 \text{ mos.})}$$

$$= \frac{\$5.000}{39,336 \text{ from}}$$

Appendix Table A-3

$$= \underline{\$127.11}$$

EXAMPLE 3-2: Lorraine wants to go to Hawaii for a vacation in two years. Her trip will cost $2,500. How much must she save each month to accumulate the $2,500 if she can earn 8 percent after taxes?

ANSWER:

$$\text{Monthly amount to save} = \frac{\$2,500}{\text{FVFS}(8\%, 24 \text{ mos.})}$$

$$= \frac{\$2,500}{25.933}$$

$$= \$96.40$$

Using Real Amounts and Rates

UNCERTAINTY ABOUT FUTURE PRICE

There are two problems with calculating savings goals using nominal amounts and rates, especially when the saving will occur over several years. First, the farther in the future the purchase of a product or service will occur, the more uncertain we are about the actual purchase price. This is because of our inability to perfectly predict inflation rates. Second, saving the same dollar amount each year when the savings will take place over many years means the burden of savings (the savings rate) will be higher in the early years and then fall. This is because most consumers' incomes rise over time. The same dollar amount of savings in the early years will thus be a higher percentage of income than in later years.

BURDEN OF SAVINGS

The way to handle these problems is to work with "real" amounts and "real" interest rates. Follow these six steps:

1. Use current prices or costs as the desired final amount to be saved.
2. Pick a number equal to the expected *difference* between the nominal interest rate and the inflation rate; use this as the real interest rate.

3. Calculate the annual FVFS associated with the real interest rate and the years of saving.
4. Divide the total (real) amount to be saved from Step 1 by the FVFS from Step 3; this gives the first year's amount to be saved.
5. Divide the first year's amount to be saved by 12 to get the monthly amount to save.
6. Each year increase the monthly amount to save by the product or service's inflation rate in the past year.

Let's quickly do an example.

EXAMPLE 3-3:   Ben estimates he will need to replace his car in ten years. He'd like to begin saving a monthly amount for this car purchase so he won't have to borrow money and pay high interest rates. If Ben were to make the purchase today he estimates he'd need $10,000 in cash. If Ben expects that his savings will earn an interest rate 2 percentage points higher than the inflation rate in car prices, how much should Ben be putting aside each month this year?

ANSWER:

Step (1):	$10,000 in real terms is the savings goal.
Step (2):	The real interest rate is 2 percent.
Step (3):	The annual FVFS associated with 2 percent and 10 years is:

1.020 + 1.040 + 1.061 + 1.082 + 1.104 + 1.126 + 1.149 + 1.172 + 1.195 + 1.219 = 11.168.

Step (4): $\dfrac{\$10,000}{11.168} = \$895.42 =$ First year's amount to be saved.

Step (5): $\dfrac{\$895.42}{12} = \$74.62 =$ First year's monthly amount to be saved.

Step (6):   Each year increase $74.62 by the inflation rate in auto prices.

WHEN TO USE SAVINGS APPROACHES

The "nominal" approach to savings goals should be used for short-run savings objectives (those less than 5 years away) where it is relatively easy to project the actual dollar amount needed to be saved. The "real" approach should be used for long-run savings objectives (those more than 5 years away) where it's difficult to project the actual dollar amount needed to be saved. In particular, the "real" approach should be used to calculate saving for retirement, for college education, and for replacement of durable goods (car, household appliances, furnace, roof). Later in the investment and retirement chapters, more detailed procedures will be outlined for calculating educational and retirement savings requirements.

Where to Get Data for a Budget

SALES AND CREDIT CARD RECEIPTS

Most of our financial transactions leave a paper trail. The best sources of budget information are canceled checks, sales receipts, and credit card receipts. If payments are made with cash, get a receipt. Get into the habit of filing each canceled check, sales receipt, and credit card receipt into the appropriate budget category. Take time each month to go through this information and record your expenditures in each budget category. Compare the totals of actual spending for each category to the amount you had budgeted.

What to Cut in a Budget

If, after looking at your current spending, you decide you want to cut spending and increase saving, what do you cut? This is a hard question to answer because budget cutting is difficult (just ask the White House and Congress). Cutting spending means reducing pleasure and enjoyment now. Budget cutting means some of our current wants and desires won't be met.

Since each individual puts her own value on any good or service, no other person can tell that individual what to buy and what not to buy. So simply take the following as suggestions. Ultimately, only you can decide what spending items to cut in your budget.

FIXED EXPENDITURES

1. First, recognize that some expenditures can't be changed in the short-run. Call these *fixed* expenditures. They include taxes, rent or mortgage, all insurance payments, credit payments, and a large part of utility payments.

    In the short run, you'll have to concentrate on budget cutting in discretionary expenditures. Discretionary expenditures are spending that can quickly be changed and can be postponed. Discretionary expenditures include food and beverages, especially food away from home, personal care, home maintenance, furnishings, clothing, and entertainment.

SUBSTITUTE TIME FOR MONEY

2. Reduce expenses by substituting time for money. Reduce food expenses by cutting back on restaurant spending and reducing purchases of prepared and convenience foods. Prepare cheaper foods at home and eat in. Substitute entertainment at home for more costly entertainment out of the home.

C
O
N
S
U
M
E
R

T
O
P
I
C

HOW DO WE "SPEND" OUR TIME?

For many families, time budgeting is just as important as financial budgeting. Especially in today's world of two-working parents and a multitude of activities for the children, wisely using your time is sometimes more critical than wisely using your income.

How do consumers, on average, spend their time? The American Time Use Survey, conducted by the U.S. Bureau of Labor Statistics, collects information about the activities people do during and day and how much time they spend doing them.

The table presents results from the American Time Use Survey from 2007–2011. Time spent (average hours per day) in various activities is given for married mothers and fathers with own children less than 18. Three employments combinations are given: both spouses work full time, mother employed part time and father employed full time, and mothers not employed and father employed full time.

Time budget in primary activities by married mothers and fathers with own household children under 18 by employment status of self and spouse, average for the combined years 2007–11.

| | Average hours per day | | | | | |
| Activity | Both Spouses Work Full Time | | Mother Employed Part Time and Father Employed Full Time | | Mother not Employed and Father Employed Full Time | |
	Mothers	Fathers	Mothers	Fathers	Mothers	Fathers
Total, all activities	24.00	24.00	24.00	24.00	24.00	24.00
Personal care activities, mostly sleeping	8.96	8.59	9.15	8.52	9.43	8.74
Household activities	1.95	1.34	2.62	1.21	3.51	1.07
Purchasing goods and services	0.55	0.34	0.63	0.34	0.72	0.37
Caring for and helping household members, mostly children	1.29	0.88	1.92	0.93	2.62	0.84
Working and work-related activities	5.27	6.07	2.78	6.07	0.08	6.20
Leisure and sports	2.91	3.68	3.45	3.62	4.09	3.55
Travel	1.35	1.41	1.37	1.48	1.15	1.40
Other activities, not elsewhere classified	1.73	1.70	2.08	1.83	2.40	1.82

Data source: U.S. Bureau of Labor Statistics, American Time Use Survey.

The table reveals some interesting patterns. In general, mothers spend more time on personal care activities, household activities, purchasing activities, and caring for children and other household members than fathers. Fathers spend more time on paid work and travel. When both parents are employed, fathers worked more hours but also had more hours spent on leisure and sports. Stay-at-home mothers spend much more time in household activities and in child care compared to fathers, but also spend more time in leisure and sports.

Households who have hectic days and who don't know "where the time goes," should consider doing a time budget. For an average day, simply keep track of how the time is spent on both household and work activities. Do a time budget for both spouses. If one spouse spends considerable more time working (either household work or market work) then this time budget may be used to "bargain" a more equitable work load.

SPEND ON LONG-RUN BENEFITS

3. Reduce spending on goods and services that give only temporary, immediate benefits. Consumer spending can be divided into spending on consumer durable goods and spending on consumer non-durable goods. Durable goods are products which last a long time and which provide benefits over that long period (a house and car are examples). Non-durable goods are products which are used up relatively quickly. Food is the best example of a non-durable good, but entertainment and clothing are also examples.

   The point is that a dollar spent on a non-durable good provides an immediate, yet temporary benefit, whereas a dollar spent on a durable good provides more long-lasting benefits. If funds are short, go for the long-run benefits.

REDUCE CLOTHING AND TRANSPORTATION SPENDING

4. Zero-in on reducing clothing and transportation spending. Together these categories take 20 to 25 percent of your income. Much of clothing provides immediate, or short-run, benefits. Consider selling second or third vehicles in order to save maintenance, repair, and insurance costs, and consider using public transportation or car-pooling.

A Budgeting Example—Peg and Al Can't Save

Peg and Al's personal finances are a disaster. Together they earn $50,000 annually, are 35 years old, but they can't save a dime. They do contribute to Social Security and a company pension, but beyond these they just haven't been able to put any money aside.

Peg and Al would like to save enough for a new car in 7 years (current price tag of $14,000). They'd also like to take a vacation in two years that would cost about $2,500, and the furnace will need replacing in about four years at an estimated cost of $6,500. Peg and Al would like to save enough to afford all these future expenditures. They can earn a 6 percent after-tax return on their investments. What should Peg and Al do?

CURRENT BUDGET   **Step 1:**   Do a *current budget* which identifies where Peg and Al's money is currently going. Do this on an annual basis. Peg and Al's current budget is in Table 3-5.

OBJECTIVE BUDGET   **Step 2:**   Form an annual *objective budget* by identifying spending categories to cut in order to free up money for savings. Move the reduction in spending to savings. The objective budget shows the desired amount of spending and saving.

How much more must Peg and Al save each month to meet their savings goals? Here are the calculations:

Car: Use "real" approach. Real price = $14,000. Use 2% real rate and 7 years FVFS = 1.020 + 1.040 + 1.061 + 1.082 + 1.104 + 1.126 + 1.149 = 7.582.

$$\text{Initial annual amount to save} = \frac{\$14,000}{7.582} = \$1,846.48$$

$$\text{Monthly amount to save in first yr.} = \frac{\$1,846.48}{12} = \$153.87$$

Vacation: Use nominal approach. Assume nominal interest rate of 6%. Monthly amount to save:

$$\frac{\$2,500}{\text{FVFS},6\%,24 \text{ mos.}} = \frac{\$2,500}{25.432} = \$98.30.$$

(Annual amount = $1,179.60.)

Furnace: Use nominal approach. Assume nominal interest rate of 6%. Monthly amount to save:

$$\frac{\$65,000}{\text{FVFS},6\%,48 \text{ mos.}} = \frac{\$65,000}{54.098} = \$120.15.$$

(Annual amount = $1,441.80.)

Peg and Al's current budget reveals that they're spending more than the average household with their income on food and beverages, shelter (rent or mortgage), clothing, and miscellaneous expenditures (refer to Figure 3-3). Shelter expenditures are fixed in the short-run, so Peg and Al decide to reduce food and beverage, clothing, entertainment, and miscellaneous expenditures. Their objective budget and savings are shown in Table 3-6.

Table 3-5   Peg and Al's current and objective budgets.

	Current Annual Budget		Objective Annual Budget	
	$	%	$	%
Income	50,000.00	100.0	50,000.00	100.0
Taxes	4,000.00	8.0	4,000.00	8.0
Food and beverages	8,250.00	16.5	7,250.00	14.5
Personal care	500.00	1.0	500.00	1.0
Rent or Mtg.	8,000.00	16.0	8,000.00	16.0
Home maintenance and repair	500.00	1.0	500.00	1.0
Utilities	3,000.00	6.0	3,000.00	6.0
Home furnishings and operations	500.00	1.0	500.00	1.0
Child day care	0.00	0.0	0.00	0.0
Clothing	4,000.00	8.0	1,782.12	3.6
Vehicle fuel	3,000.00	6.0	3,000.00	6.0
Vehicle repairs & maintenance	1,000.00	2.0	1,000.00	2.0
Vehicle ins.	2,000.00	4.0	2,000.00	4.0
Vehicle credit payments	4,000.00	8.0	4,000.00	8.0
Medical	1,000.00	2.0	1,000.00	2.0
Education	0.00	0.0	0.00	0.0
Life and disability insurance	1,000.00	2.0	1,000.00	2.0
Entertainment	2,000.00	4.0	1,000.00	2.0
Miscellaneous	1,000.00	2.0	750.00	1.5
Social Security	3,750.00	7.5	3,750.00	7.5
Pensions	2,500.00	5.0	2,500.00	5.0
Other savings:				
Education	0.00	0.0	0.00	0.0
Vacation	0.00	0.0	1,179.60	2.3
Car replacement	0.00	0.0	1,846.48	3.7
Furnace replacement	0.00	0.0	1,441.80	2.9
Total other savings	0.00	0.0	4,467.88	

NEGATIVE SAVINGS   **Step 3:**   Set up the monthly objective budget. The monthly objective budget is just the annual objective budget divided by 12. Record actual spending for each month. If more money is saved than budgeted, put this money in a category called "other savings." If money is withdrawn from saving in any

Table 3-6 Peg and Al's monthly objective budget and actual spending.

	Month 1		Month 2		Month 3		Quarterly Sum			
	Budgeted	Actual	Budgeted	Actual	Budgeted	Actual	Budgeted	Actual	Difference (actual-budgeted)	% (Difference/budgeted)
Income	$4,166.67	$4,166.67	$4,166.67	$4,166.67	$4,166.67	$4,166.67	$12,500.00	$12,500.00	0.00	(0.0%)
Taxes	333.33	333.33	333.33	333.33	333.33	333.33	1,000.00	1,000.00	0.00	(0.0%)
Food	604.17	700.00	604.17	685.00	604.17	680.00	1,812.50	2,065.00	252.50	(13.9%)
Personal care	41.67	50.00	41.67	35.00	41.67	44.00	125.00	129.00	4.00	(3.2%)
Rent/Mortgage	666.67	666.67	666.67	666.67	666.67	666.67	2,000.00	2,000.00	0.00	(0.0%)
Home maintenance/repair	41.67	25.00	41.67	45.00	41.67	40.00	125.00	110.00	-15.00	(-12.0%)
Utilities Home furnishings/	250.00	260.00	250.00	242.00	250.00	265.00	750.00	767.00	17.00	(2.3%)
operations	41.67	40.00	41.67	45.00	41.67	38.00	125.00	123.00	-2.00	(-1.6%)
Child day care	0.00	0.00	0.00	0.00	0.00	0.00	0.00	0.00	0.00	(0.0%)
Clothing	148.51	165.00	148.51	170.00	148.51	165.00	445.53	500.00	54.47	(12.2%)
Vehicle fuel	250.00	230.00	250.00	225.00	250.00	250.00	750.00	705.00	45.00	(-6.0%)
Vehicle repair maintenance	83.33	0.00	83.33	260.00	83.33	0.00	250.00	260.00	10.00	(4.0%)
Vehicle insurance	166.67	0.00	166.67	0.00	166.67	500.00	500.00	500.00	0.00	(0.0%)
Vehicle credit payments	333.33	333.33	333.33	333.33	333.33	333.33	1,000.00	1,000.00	0.00	(0.0%)
Medical	83.33	0.00	83.33	100.00	83.33	100.00	250.00	200.00	-50.00	(-20.0%)
Education	0.00	0.00	0.00	0.00	0.00	0.00	0.00	0.00	0.00	(0.0%)
life and disability insurance	83.33	0.00	83.33	0.00	83.33	250.00	250.00	250.00	0.00	(0.0%)
Entertainment	83.33	100.00	83.33	110.00	83.33	100.00	250.00	310.00	60.00	(19.4%)
Miscellaneous	62.50	60.00	62.50	55.00	62.50	70.00	187.50	185.00	2.50	(-1.3%)
Savings:										
Social Security	312.50	312.50	312.50	312.50	312.50	312.50	937.50	937.50	0.00	(0.0%)
Pension	208.33	208.33	208.33	208.33	208.33	208.33	625.00	625.00	0.00	(0.0%)
Education	0.00	0.00	0.00	0.00	0.00	0.00	0.00	0.00	0.00	(0.0%)
Vacation	98.30	98.30	98.30	98.30	98.30	98.30	294.90	294.90	0.00	(0.0%)
Car replacement	153.87	153.87	153.87	153.87	153.87	22.40	461.61	330.14	-131.47	(-28.5%)
Furnace replacement	120.15	120.15	120.15	120.15	120.15	0.00	60.45	240.30	-120.15	(-33.3%)
Other saving	0.00	310.19	0.00	0.00	0.00	-310.19	0.00	0.00	0.00	(0.0%)
TOTAL	**$4,166.67**	**$4,166.67**	**$4,166.67**	**$4,166.67**	**$4,166.67**	**$4,166.67**	**$12,500.00**	**$12,500.00**	**0.00**	**(0.0%)**

month, record this amount as *negative savings.* Make sure that income equals expenses plus savings each month. They must balance.

Peg and Al's monthly objective budget and actual spending are shown in Table 3-6. Actual taxes are tax withholding. Notice in Month 1 that Peg and Al save an additional $310.19. However, this is primarily due to the fact that insurance payments are not made until the end of Month 3 and no medical expenses and vehicle repair and maintenance expenses were incurred in Month 1. In Month 3 this $310.19 is needed to meet expenses. Notice that its withdrawal from "other saving" is recorded as "–$310.19." In all three months income equals expenses plus savings ($4,166.67).

COMPARISONS   **Step 4:**   At the end of a time period long enough to include payment of expenses like insurance and vehicle repairs, compare total budgeted expenses and savings to actual expenses and savings for each category and compute any differences. Define the differences as actual expenses minus budgeted expenses, so a positive difference means actual expenses were greater than budgeted expenses, and a negative difference means actual expenses were less than budgeted expenses. Also compute the percentage that the difference is of the budgeted amount.

Peg and Al's insurance payments are made quarterly, so their quarterly totals are shown in the last four columns of Table 3-6. For example, Peg and Al budgeted $1,812.50 for food, but they actually spent $2,065.00. Thus they over-spent $252.50 on food, which is 13.9 percent over the budgeted amount of $1,812.50. In contrast, Peg and Al budgeted $461.61 for car savings over the three months but could only save $240.30. They under-saved for the car by $131.47 (note that this is recorded as–$131.47), which is 28.5 percent of the budgeted amount of $461.61.

Step 5:   Identify categories with large percentage differences between budgeted and actual expenses and savings, and use this information to make decisions about changes in the budget.

For Peg and Al, the largest percentages of over-spending for the three months are entertainment (19.4 percent over budget), food (13.9 percent over budget), and clothing (12.2 percent over budget). The largest percentages of under-spending or under-savings are furnace saving (33.3 percent under budget), car saving (28.5 percent under budget), medical spending (20 percent under budget), and home maintenance and repair (12 percent under budget).

ADJUSTMENTS

It's obvious that Peg and Al have not brought their actual spending in line with their budget. Specifically, their over-spending on food, clothing, and entertainment has not allowed them to save enough for the car and furnace. They have under-spent on home maintenance/repair and on medical, but the dollar amounts are relatively small and these expenditures usually occur unexpectedly and in large amounts. Therefore, Peg and Al decide not to budget less for these two categories.

To remedy their over-spending and under-saving situation, Peg and Al decide on two changes. They will eliminate the goal of a $2,500 vacation in two years. This will release $98.30 for additional budgeted spending each month. They will take $17 of this amount and add it to entertainment, since entertainment now is a substitute for a vacation later. This brings budgeted monthly entertainment spending to $100.33, which is very close to what was actually spent each of the three months.

Peg and Al will add the remainder of the $98.30 ($98.30 − $17, or $81.30) to monthly food spending. This brings budgeted monthly food spending to $685.47, which again is very close to what was actually spent for each of the three months.

Peg and Al's big problem will be to reduce clothing spending to no more than the budgeted monthly amount of $148.51. To do this, Peg and Al decide not to take their credit cards on weekend trips to the mall and to only carry $20 in cash on these trips.

Peg and Al will continue recording monthly budgets and quarterly totals. At the end of each quarter they will review their situation. Also, at the end of a year they will review their yearly progress and make decisions about necessary changes.

The Bottom Line

If you can't seem to save money, if you have a definite savings goal, if your income is erratic, or if you just want to find out where your income goes, then you may want to set up a budget. If you want to reduce spending in order to increase savings, then reducing restaurant spending, reducing clothing spending, and (in the long run) reducing transportation spending are the best candidates. Over time spending will rise due to inflation. When comparing spending over time, compare the share (%) of income spent on each category. _____

4. How Do You Tell "How You're Doing"?

CASH FLOW

You are now a master at budgeting (see how much confidence we have in you!). You can think of budgeting as a "flow" concept. A budget shows how income which flows in to a consumer in turn flows out in the form of expenses and savings. Business analysts who do budgets call this cash-flow. A budget compares cash which flows in to cash which flows out.

ASSETS LIABILITIES

But how do we measure the financial consequences of our budget and spending decisions? This is done by taking a snapshot of our financial situation at any point in time. The snapshot is called a "net worth statement." The savings that we do in our budgets are accumulated in investments, which are more generally called *assets*. Assets show the value of the stock of things we own. The borrowing that we do is in the form of loans, which are more generally called liabilities. Liabilities show the value of what we owe. The difference between your assets and your liabilities at any point in time is called your *net worth*. The relationship between budgets and net worth is shown in Figure 3-1.

NET WORTH

POSITIVE AND NEGATIVE NET WORTH

Net worth means what it says—it tells you how much you are worth if you "cashed-in" all of your assets and paid all of your debts. In other words, net worth tells you what the "bottom line" is if you sold your home, personal property, cars, stocks, bonds, cashed-in everything else, and then paid all loan balances and debts. If the result is positive, then your net worth is positive. If the result is a negative number, then your net worth is negative.

Why would you want to construct a net worth statement? There are two reasons. First, you're frequently asked to supply a net worth statement, or at least a partial one, when you apply for a loan. Lenders are more likely to grant you a loan the more positive your net worth is.

Second, you may want to periodically construct net worth statements in order to gauge your financial progress. The typical pattern followed by a consumer's net worth is shown in Figure 3-2. Net worth is usually negative

Figure 3-1. Relationship between budgeting and net worth.

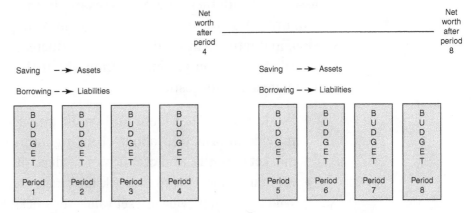

Figure 3-2. Pattern of net worth.

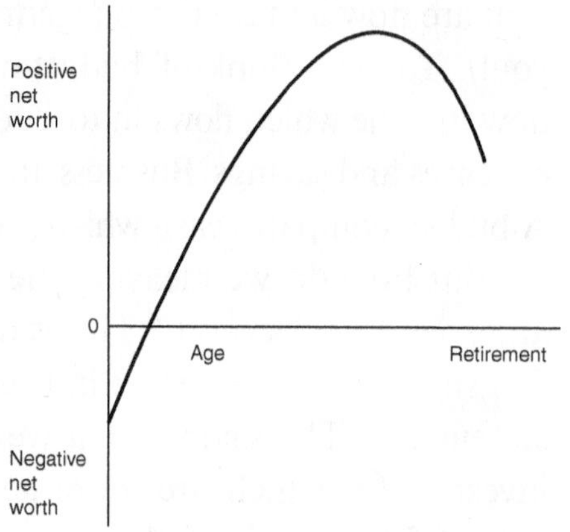

during the consumer's young adult years (20s to mid-30s). Here the consumer is just starting to save and has also borrowed much to finance purchase of durable goods (house, car, appliances, furniture). Net worth typically rises through the consumer's peak earning years until retirement. During retirement net worth falls as investments are converted to income for living expenses.

Constructing a Net Worth Statement

The concept behind construction of a net worth statement is simple. Net worth equals the value of assets minus the value of liabilities. The only tricky thing in this concept is that the value of assets must be *market value*, that is, what cash you could get for the assets if they were sold today. For example, the market value of your stocks is not what you paid for them, but what you could sell them for now.

MARKET VALUE

Table 3-7 lists items which should be included in a net worth statement. Look first at the list of assets. Remember that the value you put on the assets should be the cash you would receive if the assets were sold today. Furthermore, this cash should be less any fees, or penalties, associated with their sale. So, for example, the penalty charged for early withdrawal of money from a certificate of deposit or from IRA, pension, and retirement fund should be deducted.

Where can you get information about the market value of assets? Here are some suggestions:

◆ Bank, savings and loan, and credit union monthly statements can provide information about checking and savings accounts, money market deposits, and certificates of deposit.
◆ Monthly statements from stock brokerage firms and from mutual fund syndicates can provide market values for stocks, bonds, and mutual funds.

Table 3-7   Components of a net worth statement.

I. **Assets You Own**

    A. Liquid Assets

        Average balance in checking account.

        Savings accounts and money market deposite.

        Money market mutual funds.

    B. Other Financial Assets

        Certificates of deposit

        Stocks

        Bonds

        Other mutual funds

        Cash value of life insurance

        Company pension

        IRA, Keogh, SEP, and deferred compensation retirement funds.

    C. Real Assets

        Collectibles (coins, stamps, artwork, expensive rugs)

        Sales value of home less sales lee

        Other real estate

        Autos

        Furniture and appliances

        Personal property (clothing, furs, jewelry)

II. **Liabilities You Owe**

        Credit card balances

        Balance on personal loans

        Other unpaid loans or bills

        Balance on auto loans

        Balance on home mortgage

        Balance on home equity loan or second mortgage

        Balance on education loans

♦ Prices listed in financial newspapers or financial websites such as Yahoo Finance can give market value for gold and other precious metals accounts.

♦ Consult dealers and others experts for market values of collectibles.

♦ Your life insurance agent can tell you the cash value of your policies.

♦ Your employer can provide current information on the value of your pension fund. Also, many pension and retirement funds are handled by mutual fund or stock brokerage firms. Frequently they will send you monthly or quarterly statements.

THE AVERAGE NET WORTH STATEMENT

Table 1 shows how average net worth varies by age. As expected, net worth is very low for young families and increases by age. Data for 2010 show that while mean net worth declines for families in retirement, median net worth continues to grow for those 65 and older.

Table 2 shows what composes the asset side of family net worth, and how this distribution is different for families with different levels of income. For each of the assets, the percentage of families holding the asset increases with family income.

Table 1. Median and mean net worth by age of family head, 2010

	Net Worth	
Age	Median	Mean
All families	$ 77,300	$498,800
Less than 35	$ 9,300	$ 65,300
35–44	$ 42,100	$217,400
45–54	$117,900	$573,000
55–64	$179,400	$880,500
65–74	$206,700	$848,400
75 or more	$216,800	$677,900

Table 2. Percentage of families holdings particular assets by family income percentile, 2010

Percentile of income	Trans-action accounts	Certifi-cates of deposit	Savings bonds	Bonds	Stocks	Pooled invest-ment funds	Retire-ment accounts	Cash value life insur-ance	Other man-aged assets	Other	Any finan-cial asset
All families	92.5	12.2	12.0	1.6	15.1	8.7	50.4	19.7	5.7	8.0	94.0
Less than 20	76.2	5.7	3.6	.1	3.8	2.1	11.2	10.7	1.7	7.0	79.2
20–39.9	91.1	11.1	6.0	*	6.0	3.5	30.5	17.2	4.2	6.7	93.6
40–59.9	96.4	11.7	10.8	*	11.7	5.8	52.8	19.5	5.5	9.6	97.8
60–79.9	98.9	15.8	16.0	1.3	17.3	8.8	69.7	22.8	6.9	7.3	99.6
80–89.9	99.8	12.1	23.0	2.0	25.7	14.6	85.7	25.8	7.8	8.5	100.0
90–100	99.9	21.5	24.4	8.3	47.8	32.1	90.1	30.9	12.3	10.3	100.0

Data source for both tables: Board of the Governors of the Federal Reserve System, Survey of Consumer Finances, 2010.

♦ A real estate agent can give you a good idea of the current sales value of your home and other real estate. Subtract 6 percent of these values to account for real estate sales fees.

♦ The auto Bluebook gives the sales value of existing (used) cars. The Bluebook is available at most libraries, lenders, and on-line.

♦ The market value of furniture, appliances, and personal property is the most difficult to peg. Firms that buy and sell used furniture and appliances can give you "ballpark" figures. Check stores that sell secondhand clothing, such as Goodwill and Salvation Army stores, for ideas about the market value of clothing. If you have expensive furs and jewelry, consult with appraisers who market these items.

Obtaining information about liabilities you owe is easier. In most cases the lender who provided the loan will give you the current loan balance (you don't want the original loan amount; you want what you owe today). You may already have a sheet showing the loan balance at different dates.

Classification of Assets

LIQUID ASSETS

It is useful to distinguish different kinds of assets. "Liquid" assets are assets that can be cashed-in quickly with little risk of loss of value. The balance in your checking account is a liquid asset because the money can be quickly withdrawn with no risk of loss. Other liquid assets are savings accounts, money market deposits, and money market mutual funds.

OTHER FINANCIAL ASSETS

Other financial assets can be converted to cash with time, although some loss or penalty may be incurred. These assets include certificates of deposit, stocks, bonds, other mutual funds, the cash value of life insurance, IRA, Keogh, and SEP retirement funds, and deferred compensation retirement funds. Two values should be noted for the IRA, Keogh, SEP, and deferred compensation retirement funds. One is the current dollar value. The other is the cash value if the funds were cashed in now. Due to taxes and penalties, the cash value will be approximately 40 percent less than the dollar value. The cash value is the figure which should be used.

REAL ASSETS

Other assets are classified as "real" assets. These include collectibles, your home and other real estate, autos, furniture and appliances, and personal property. It usually takes a long time to convert these assets to cash.

Financial Ratios and Their Use

ASSET/DEBT RATIO

A net worth statement can of course be used to calculate net worth. Calculation of net worth tells you if you could cash-in all your assets, pay-off all your debts, and still have anything left over. Consumers can also calculate their asset/debt ratio. This is simply the ratio of assets to liabilities (or debt). If the ratio is greater than 1, assets are greater than liabilities. If the ratio is under 1, assets are less than liabilities.

Although net worth and asset/debt ratios are interesting figures, they're not very useful. Most consumers don't contemplate cashing in all their assets to pay their debts. In particular, most consumers wouldn't want to cash in their home, cars, personal property, and other "real" assets. Instead, four other ratios from the net worth statement are more useful. They are:

Liquid assets/total debt—tells what fraction of total liabilities (debt) could be paid off with liquid assets.

Liquid assets + other financial assets/total debt—tells what fraction of total liabilities (debt) could be paid off with liquid assets and by cashing-in other financial assets.

Liquid assets/non-mortgage debt—mortgages are considered long-run debt by most consumers, so this ratio measures the fraction of other debt which could be paid off with liquid assets.

Liquid assets + other financial assets/non-mortgage debt—tells what fraction of non-mortgage debt could be paid off with liquid assets and by cashing-in other financial assets.

If the net worth statement is combined with the consumer's budget, then four other ratios can be calculated which provide useful information. They are:

Liquid assets/budgeted monthly expenditures—if the consumer's income drops sharply and unexpectedly, this ratio tells how many months liquid assets could carry the consumer.

Liquid assets + other financial assets/budgeted monthly expenditures—tells how many months liquid assets and the cash value of other financial assets could carry the consumer.

Liquid assets/one year's debt payments—tells how many years debt payments could be met by liquid assets.

Liquid assets + other financial assets/one year's debt payments—tells how many years debt payments could be met by liquid assets and the cash value of other financial assets.

There are no "right" numbers for these eight ratios. Consumers who have more secure jobs and jobs with better promise of salary increases can afford to have lower ratios than consumers with unstable jobs and jobs with erratic incomes. However, most consumers should have liquid assets necessary to carry expenditures for three months and enough liquid and financial assets to carry expenditures for six months.

An Example

Table 3-8 shows Peg and Al's net worth statement and financial ratios.

Monthly expenditures are from Table 3-6, and yearly debt payments are from Table 3-5. Monthly expenditures do not include funds for taxes, Social Security and pension since these expenditures would not be made if the consumer wasn't working.

Table 3-8   Peg and Al's net worth statement and financial ratios.

Assets		
A. Liquid		
Checking account balance		$1,500
Savings account and money market deposits		1,000
Money market mutual funds		500
B. Other financial assets		
Certificates of deposit		2,000
Stocks		1,000
Bonds		1,000
Other mutual funds		3,000
Cash value of life insurance		500
Company pension		0
IRA, Keogh, SEPs, deferred compensation (after taxes and penalties)		3,000
C. Real Assets		
Collectibles		0
Home		80,000
Other real estate		0
Autos		8,000
Furniture and appliances		3,000
Personal property		2,000

Liabilities		
Credit card balances		1,000
Personal loans		0
Unpaid loans or bills		0
Auto loans		7,000
Home mortgage		56,000
Home equity loan or second mortgage		0
Education loans		0

Liquid assets   = $ 3,000

Other financial assets   =   10,500

Real assets   =   93,000

TOTAL ASSETS   = $106,500

TOTAL LIABILITIES   =   64,000

NET WORTH = $106,500 − $64,000 = $42,500

(continued on next page)

Table 3-8 Peg and Al's net worth statement and financial ratios. (continued)

$$\frac{\text{Assets}}{\text{Liabilities}} = \frac{\$106,500}{\$64,000} = 1.66$$

$$\frac{\text{Liquid assets}}{\text{Total debt}} = \frac{\$3,000}{\$64,000} = 0.05$$

$$\frac{\text{Liquid and financial assets}}{\text{Total debt}} = \frac{\$13,500}{\$64,000} = 0.21$$

$$\frac{\text{Liquid assets}}{\text{Non-mortg.debt}} = \frac{\$3,000}{\$8,000} = 0.38$$

$$\frac{\text{Liquid and financial assets}}{\text{Non-mortg.debt}} = \frac{\$13,500}{\$8,000} = 1.69$$

$$\frac{\text{Liquid assets}}{\text{Monthly expenditures}} = \frac{\$3,000.00}{\$2,940.19^{1}} = 1.02$$

$$\frac{\text{Liquid and financial assets}}{\text{Monthly expenditures}} = \frac{\$13,500.00}{\$2,940.19} = 4.59$$

$$\frac{\text{Liquid assets}}{\text{One year's debt payment}^{2}} = \frac{\$3,000}{\$12,000} = 0.25$$

$$\frac{\text{Liquid and financial assets}}{\text{One year's debt payments}} = \frac{\$13,500}{\$12,000} = 1.13$$

[1] From Table 3-6; equals monthly income minus taxes, Social Security, pension and savings.

[2] From Table 3-5; equals mortgage payments ($8,000) plus vehicle credit payments ($4,000).

Notice that most of Peg and Al's assets are in their home. This is typical for most consumers. One bright spot is their ratio of liquid and financial assets to monthly expenditures, which shows that these assets could carry them 4 ½ months. The main conclusion Peg and Al should reach from the financial ratios is that they should increase their liquid assets.

The Bottom Line

A net worth statement shows what you are worth if you cashed in all your assets and paid all your debts. If you're young, just starting your career and family, and have just made some major purchases, don't be surprised if your net worth is negative. As time marches on, your net worth should increase. Financial ratios allow you to see how far your liquid and other assets could carry you if your salary or wages were interrupted. _____

AN INCREASING TAX BITE?

C
O
N
S
U
M
E
R

T
O
P
I
C

Most Americans would probably say their tax bite has increased over the years. Indeed, as the graph shows, they would be mostly right. The tax burden, measured as all taxes as a percentage of Gross Domestic Product, has generally increased over time. In 1929, the tax burden was about 10%. It reached the highest in the late 1990s to 31%. In 2011, tax was about 27% of GDP.

The increased in the tax bite has not been smooth. There was a doubling of the tax bite between 1929 and 1943 as a result of the Great Depression and World War II. The tax burden then steadily increased to 29% by 1982. Between 1982 and 2007 the total tax bite has hovered around 30%. The Bush era tax cuts decreased the tax bite to about 27% in late 2000s.

Data source: The Tax Policy Center, Urban Institute and Brookings Institution.

5. How Big Is Your Tax Bite?

Consumers pay many taxes—federal income tax, state income tax, Social Security tax, sales tax, and property tax are the main ones. Table 3-9 shows a breakdown of these taxes and their relative size.

The tax system does not treat all consumer expenditures and investments equally. Interest costs on consumer home loans are allowed as deductions for tax purposes, whereas interest costs on other consumer loans aren't allowed as tax deductions. Likewise, some investment returns are taxed and some aren't. These differences make it important for you to consider tax treatment in many consumer decisions.

Your Tax Bracket

For financing and investing decisions, the tax of most concern is the federal income tax. To understand how federal taxes affect consumer decisions you must know what tax bracket you're in. Your federal income

Table 3-9. The tax bite, 2010

	Billions $	% of personal income
Personal income	$12,547.0	
Federal income taxes	$898.5	7.2%
Federal excise taxes and other taxes	$207.9	1.7%
Social Security contributions	$864.8	6.9%
State and local property taxes	$441.7	3.5%
State and local sales taxes	$431.2	3.4%
State and local income taxes	$260.3	2.1%
Other state taxes	$93.6	0.7%
Total taxes	$3,198.1	25.5%

Data Source: Personal income from the Statistical Abstract of the United States 2012. Federal, state, and local tax data from the Tax Policy Center.

tax bracket is the amount of additional federal income tax you pay on an extra dollar of taxable income. Or, saying the same thing, your federal tax bracket is the reduction in your federal income tax due to a reduction in your income by one dollar.

Social Security and Medicare Payroll Tax Bracket

There are two types of federal taxes to worry about, the Social Security and Medicare tax and the federal income tax. The Social Security and Medicare tax, also called FICA (for Federal Insurance Contributions Act) or the payroll tax, is easy. It's a flat rate on only your wage and salary earnings up to a certain limit. In 2013, if you are an employee (you work for somebody else), the rate is 7.65% of the first $113,700 of your total wage and salary income. Of the 7.65%, 1.45% is allocated for the Medicare program. On income over $113,700 only the 1.45% Medicare tax portion is levied. This means that for employees in 2013, there are two payroll tax brackets:

7.65% for additional wages and salary income under $113,700,

1.45% for additional wage and salary income over $113.700.

Social Security tax is not collected from non-wage and non-salary income, such as investment income.

For self-employed individuals, the rate doubles as they have to pay both the employer and employee portions of the FICA tax. For self-employed individuals in 2013, the FICA tax brackets are:

15.3% for additional wages and salary income under $113,700,
2.9% for additional wage and salary income over $113.700.

The maximum wage and salary income to which the tax rate applies is changed every year. The tax rate for employees changed from 1% in 1937 (only Social Security tax) to 3.85% for Social Security and 0.35% for Medicare in 1966 when Medicare tax was first introduced. The most recent rate increase was in 1986 for Medicare tax rate and 1990 for Social Security tax rate.

Federal Income Tax Brackets

The federal income tax system is very complicated (what an understatement, you might say!). We'll only hit the highlights here. In the next topic we will walk you through the completion of a federal income tax form.

There are two basic elements to the federal income tax system, tax rates and taxable income to which those rates apply. *Taxable income* is your income minus allowable adjustments, exemptions, and deductions. Adjustments are allowable reductions in income. The most important exemption is the *personal exemption.* You can take a personal exemption for each family member, including yourself. The most important deduction is the *standard deduction.* You take the standard deduction unless your allowable *itemized deductions* are bigger (more on this later). In 2013 each personal exemption is $3,900 and the standard deduction is $6,100 for singles and $12,200 for married taxpayers filing jointly. Both the personal exemption and the standard deduction are indexed for inflation, meaning they are increased each year by whatever the inflation rate has been the previous year.

Once you have reduced your income by allowable exemptions and deductions to get taxable income, taxable income is multiplied by the appropriate tax rate to get taxes owed. However, if your taxable income is high enough, it will have to be broken into segments and each segment multiplied by a different tax rate. Table 3-10 shows the 2013 federal income tax brackets and tax rates which apply to each income bracket.

Table 3-11 shows the calculation of the federal income tax for two situations. John Jones's situation is simple. His income is low so after personal exemption and standard deduction, his taxable income is $33,000, which falls in the first and second brackets (10% and 15%). The Robinson family situation is a little more complicated. Their taxable income must be broken down into the three tax brackets it spans, and each income segment is taxed at a different rate.

The federal income tax brackets are indexed. This means that each year the income ranges for each bracket are increased by the previous year's inflation rate. The inflation rate (using the CPI) is measured from August to August of the previous year. If, for example, the inflation rate for August 2013 to August 2014 was 3%, then all the taxable income numbers in Table 3–10 would be increased by 3% for 2014. As an illustration, the 25% bracket for singles would go from $36,250–$87,850 to $37,338–$90,486.

TAXABLE INCOME

PERSONAL
EXEMPTION
STANDARD
DEDUCTION
ITEMIZED
DEDUCTIONS

Table 3-10. Federal income tax brackets, 2013.

Filing Status	Taxable Income	Rate
Single	$0 to $8,925	10%
Personal exemption: $3,900 per person	$8,925 to $36,250	15%
Standard deduction: $6,100 per family	$36,250 to $87,850	25%
	$87,850 to $183,250	28%
	$183,250 to $398,350	33%
	$398,350 to $400,000	35%
	$400,000+	39.6%
Joint	$0 to $17,850	10%
Personal exemption: $3,900 per person	$17,850 to $72,500	15%
Standard deduction: $12,200 per family	$72,500 to $146,400	25%
	$146,400 to $223,050	28%
	$223,050 to $398,350	33%
	$398,350 to $450,000	35%
	$450,000+	39.6%

Table 3-11. Examples of federal income tax calculations

A. John Jones: single, earning income of $43,000

Total income		$43,000.00
Minus 1 personal exemption	–	$3,900.00
minus standard deduction	–	$6,100.00
Taxable income	=	$33,000.00
Federal income tax:		
First $8,925 taxed at 10%		$892.50
The remaining taxed at 15%	+	$3,611.25
Total federal income tax	=	$4,503.75

B. Mary and Joe Robinson: married, 2 children, total income of $180,000

Total income		$160,000.00
Minus 4 personal exemption	–	$15,600.00
minus standard deduction	–	$12,200.00
Taxable income	=	$132,200.00
Federal income tax:		
First $17,850 taxed at 10%		$1,785.00
Next ($72,500–$17,850) taxed at 15%	+	$8,197.50
Last ($132,200–$72,500) taxed at 25%	+	$14,925.00
Total federal income tax	=	$24,907.50

Frequently, consumers and commentators confuse the terms "marginal tax rate" and "average tax rate." Marginal tax rate is the same as tax bracket. The marginal tax rate shows the extra tax paid if income increases by $1. In Table 3-11, John Jones's marginal tax rate is 15%, which means if he earns one more dollar, his tax will be increased by 15 cents (15% of $1). The average tax rate is simply the tax paid divided by income. In Table 3-11, John Jones' marginal tax rate is 15%, and his average tax rate is 10.47% ($4,503.75/$43,000), and Mary and Joe Robinson's average tax rate is 15.57% ($24,907.50/$160,000). Given that marginal tax rate increases with income, which is called a progressive tax system, one's average tax rate will always be less than your marginal tax rate.

Marginal tax rates, or as we'll call them—tax brackets, are more useful in consumer decision-making because they help us calculate the consequences of changes in our income.

C O N S U M E R T O P I C

DEBATE ABOUT TAX PROCRESSIVITY AND REGRESSIVITY

A *progressive* tax system is a system in which marginal tax rates, or tax brackets, increase with income. That is, under a progressive tax system, a rich woman pays more tax on an *extra* dollar of income than a poor woman pays. This is in contrast to a *proportional tax* system where the rich woman and poor woman both pay the same tax on each extra dollar of income. (Remember, however, that even under a proportional tax the rich woman pays more total tax than the poor woman because the rich woman has more income.)

A *regressive* tax system is a system where the percentage of a household's income paid in a tax declines with income. The sales tax in most states is considered a regressive tax because lower income households spend most of their income and thus pay more sales tax, per dollar of their income, than higher income households.

There are many arguments about tax progressivity and regressivity. Some commentators and politicians argue that the progressivity of the federal income tax should be increased and the top tax bracket raised for the rich. They argue that an extra dollar of income is worth much less to a rich person than to a poor person. Therefore, to make the "burden" of taxation the same, the rich person should pay a higher tax rate on extra income than a poor person.

The argument against a progressive tax system is that it discourages additional work and additional savings. If an individual knows that 70 cents out of each extra dollar of income will be taxed away, then he will be less likely to work for that extra dollar than if only 33 cents of it would be taxed away. In fact, the supporters of a less progressive tax system argue that cutting marginal tax rates for the rich will stimulate so much extra work and extra investment that both the total taxes paid by the rich and the percentage of all taxes paid by the rich will rise.

Some politicians have recommended replacing the federal income tax with a new national sales tax. But, in older to reduce the regressivity of such a tax, they recommend rebating the tax to households with incomes under a certain level.

State, Local, and Total Income Tax Brackets

TOTAL INCOME
TAX BRACKET

Most states also have income taxes and some cities do too (local income taxes are not the same as property taxes). The income ranges for the brackets usually differ from the federal income ranges, but the rates are much lower than the federal income tax rates.

If, for example, your state has an income tax, then you can form your *total income tax* bracket as the combination of your federal and state income tax brackets. However, your total income tax bracket is not simply the sum of the two income tax brackets. The simple sum cannot be used because state and local income taxes are *deductible* for federal income tax purposes. The value of the deduction is simply the federal income tax bracket multiplied by the state or local income tax bracket. That is, each dollar of a deduction saves not a dollar in taxes, but saves that dollar multiplied by the tax bracket. So, to find your total income tax bracket, find both the federal and state income tax rates which apply to the next dollar of income you would earn, then use this formula:

TOTAL INCOME TAX BRACKET =

federal	+	state	−	(federal)	×	(state)
income		income		(income)		(income)
tax		tax		(tax)		(tax)
bracket		bracket		(bracket)		(bracket)

EXAMPLE 3-4: Mike's federal income tax bracket is 28 percent and his state income tax bracket is 7 percent. What is Mike's total income tax bracket?

ANSWER:

$$28\% + 7\% - (28\% \times 7\%)$$
$$= .28 + .07 - (.28 \times .07)$$
$$= .33 \text{ or } 33\%.$$

If your locality also has an income tax, then use this formula to find your total income tax bracket: total income tax bracket = federal income tax bracket + state income tax bracket + local income tax bracket − (federal income tax bracket) × (state + local income tax bracket).

PROPERTY AND
SALES TAXES

We've talked about Social Security taxes and income taxes. What about other taxes, like property taxes and sales taxes. We won't discuss these taxes because we're primarily concerned about taxes which affect your decisions about earning income, that is, your decisions about working and investing. Property and sales taxes are taxes that apply to particular ways of spending your income. Certainly you should recognize that the more you spend, the more sales tax you'll pay, and the more property you own, the more property tax you'll pay.

Using Tax Brackets in Consumer Decisions

Your tax brackets are very important in analyzing borrowing and investing decisions as well as decisions about work.

Some loans, such as mortgages and home equity loans, are favored by the tax laws because their interest payments are tax-deductible. How much are such deductions worth to you? Their value is equal to the income taxes they save. How is this tax saving calculated? It's calculated as your relevant *income tax bracket multiplied by the tax deduction*. The relevant tax bracket is the tax bracket of the tax for which the deduction applies.

EXAMPLE 3-5:   Elaine and Tim have bought a home and will be able to claim $6,000 in mortgage interest payments as a tax deduction for both their federal and state income tax. If their total federal and state income tax bracket is 33 percent, how much tax will this deduction save them?

ANSWER: $6,000 \times .33 = \$1,980.$

There are two amendments to this simple rule. All taxpayers get to take a standard deduction. As indicated earlier, the federal standard deduction for single taxpayers in 2013 is $6,100 and for married taxpayers (filing jointly) is $12,200. You claim the standard deduction if you don't have other deductions which exceed it. You *can't* claim both the standard deduction and other deductions. This means that if a tax deduction you are allowed does not exceed the standard deduction, then you're better-off taking the standard deduction.

EXAMPLE 3-6:   Cynthia and Phil have bought a small house which will provide them with only $3,500 in interest and property tax deductions. Should they use this tax deduction?

ANSWER: No. Since Cynthia and Phil's standard deduction ($12,200) is greater than the mortgage and property interest deduction of $3,500, they're better off with the standard deduction.

The second amendment concerns the appropriate income tax bracket to use. A large tax deduction may move you into a lower tax bracket. In this case you must split the tax deduction into two parts, that part which applies to the higher tax bracket, and that part which applies to the lower bracket, before calculating the tax savings.

EXAMPLE 3-7: Joanne and Steve's taxable income with standard deduction is $75,000. A home they purchased will give them $5000 more deduction compared to the standard deduction so their taxable income is reduced to $70,000. What is the value of this deduction for federal income tax?

ANSWER: According to the 2013 tax brackets, taxable income between $17,850 and $72,500 is taxed at 15% rate, whereas taxable income between $72,501 and $146,400 is taxed at 25% rate. An additional deduction of $5, 000 reduces Joanne and Steve's marginal tax rate from 25% to 15%. The tax saving from a reduction of taxable income from $75,000 to $72,500 is $625 [($75,000–$72,500)*25%]. The tax saving from the further reduction of taxable income from $72,500 to $70,000 is $375 [($72,500–$70,000)*15%]. The total value of this extra $5000 deduction is $1,000 ($625+$375).

ADJUSTING INTEREST RATES

Tax brackets can also be used to adjust interest rates. For interest rates which you pay as a borrower, if the interest payments are tax deductible, the after tax interest rate for borrowing equals:

after tax interest rate for borrowing = interest rate – (income (tax (bracket × interest) rate).

For example, if you pay 10 percent interest on a $1,000 loan, your interest payment is $100. But if that interest is deductible and you're in the 28 percent tax bracket, you save 28 percent of $100, or $28, in taxes. So, counting your tax savings, you've paid only $72 ($100–$28) in after-tax interest, or 7.2 percent of $1,000.

Similarly, for interest rates which you receive as an investor, if the interest earnings are taxed, then the after tax interest rate for investing also equals:

after tax interest rate for investing = interest rate – (income (tax (bracket × interest) rate)

EXAMPLE 3-8: Diane and Dave are comparing interest rates for loans. A personal loan from a bank charges 10 percent but interest payments are not tax deductible. A home equity loan charges 12 percent but interest payments are tax deductible. Which loan is cheaper, after-taxes, if Diane and Dave's income tax bracket is 33 percent?

ANSWER: after tax   = 10%.   This is the same as the

interest rate   before - tax rate since

for personal   interest payments are

loan   *not* tax - deductible

after tax   = $12\% - (33\% \times 12\%)$

interest rate = $.12 - (.33 \times .12)$

for home   = .08 or 8%.

equity loan

The home equity loan is cheaper.

EXAMPLE 3-9:   You can invest your money in a taxable corporate bond paying 10 percent interest or a tax-free municipal bond paying 7 percent interest. After taxes, which pays the higher interest rate, if your income tax bracket is 28 percent?

ANSWER: after tax   = $10\% - (28\% \times 10\%)$

interest rate   = $.10 - (.28 \times .10)$

on taxable   = .072 or 7.2%

corporate bond

after - tax   = 7%, since no taxes are due.

interest rate

on tax - free

municipal bond

The taxable corporate bond pays the higher after-tax interest rate.

The last examples show you how to calculate income you keep, after taxes, resulting from a pay increase. In this case, in addition to deducting income tax, you must also consider Social Security taxes.

EXAMPLE 3-10:   Craig received a pay increase of $5,000, which boosts his pay from $30,000 to $35,000. How much of the $5,000 raise will Craig keep if his total income tax bracket is 35 percent? Craig is a single taxpayer.

ANSWER: Income taxes paid out of the $5,000 = $5,000 \times .35 = \$1,750.00$.

S.S. taxes paid out of the $5,000 = $5,000 \times 0.0765 = \$382.50$.

Pay raise that Craig keeps = $5,000 - \$1,750 - \$382.50 = \$2,867.50$

EXAMPLE 3-11: In 2013, Tina received a pay increase of $6,000, which boosts her salary from $120,000 to $126,000. Tina's total (federal and state) income tax bracket is 38 percent, and she is a single taxpayer. How much of the $6,000 does she keep?

ANSWER: Income taxes paid out of $6,000 = $6,000 \times .38 = $2,280.

Social Security taxes paid out of the $6,000 = $6,000 \times 0.0145 (only Medicare tax) = $87.

Pay rise that Tina keeps = $6,000 - $2,280 - $87 = $3,633.

IS A SECOND JOB WORTHWHILE?

C O N S U M E R   T O P I C

You've learned about the tax bite that workers face—federal income taxes, state income taxes, Social Security taxes, and maybe local income taxes. But there are other expenses related to working. You must get to and from work, so you pay either public transportation costs or commuting costs for a private auto. There are work-related costs for clothes. Day care costs may have to be paid if you have young children.

Consideration of taxes and other work related expenses is particularly important when a spouse, who has stayed at home, is thinking of entering the labor market. The income of the spouse may be taxed at a higher income tax rate because the new income will be stacked on top of the couple's existing income. Additional costs for transportation and clothing will be faced. If the couple has young children, child care costs will have to be paid when the spouse goes to work.

It doesn't stop here. With both spouses working, less time will be available for household chores. The family will probably eat out more and make more use of costly convenience and prepared foods. A cleaning service may be hired to do the household cleaning.

All this means that before a spouse moves from the homemaker position to a position in the labor force, a careful analysis of the benefits and costs should be done. This example shows you how to do such an analysis:

Jenny and Jerry have one pre-school child. Jerry is a lawyer but Jenny has played the role of homemaker. Jenny is considering taking a $20,000 a year job. Jenny and Jerry's total income tax bracket is 32 percent. Here are the expenses that will be paid out of the $20,000 paycheck:

Income taxes (.32 × $20,000)	$ 6,400
Social Security taxes (.0765 × $20,000)	1,530
Clothing	1,000
Commuting	1,500
Child care	3,000
Home cleaning service	1,500
Extra food costs	1,500
TOTAL	$16,430

The household coffers are increased by only $20,000 − $16,402 = $3,598. To this, however, must be added any employee paid benefits, such as health insurance and pension contributions. Also, although Social Security taxes are a cost now, they provide benefits later in retirement. Further, Jenny can shelter some of her income and reduce taxes by using deferred compensation plans (more on this in the chapter on retirement).

So the net financial benefits of a spouse taking a job will always be less than the gross salary, especially if child care expenses must be paid for young children. However, the intangible benefits to working, such as improvements in self-esteem and confidence and the future returns from having a career, must also be considered.

The Bottom Line

Your income tax bracket tells you how much of an extra dollar earned goes for income taxes, and also tells you the value of tax deductions. The tax bracket can also be used to calculate after-tax interest rates for borrowing and after-tax interest rates for investing. Your income tax bracket, together with the Social Security tax rate, can be used to tell you how much of a pay increase you actually keep.

6. How Can You Cut Through the Tax Form Jungle?

Many (most?) consumers are intimidated by income tax forms. They shouldn't be. Completing income tax forms is not that hard. In this topic you'll learn the basic steps involved in completing the most important of the tax forms, the federal income tax form. Most state income tax forms are very similar.

Before we start, let us issue a warning. Although the structure of the federal income tax form has remained the same for a long time, the details are frequently changed by Congress. The information presented here is up-to-date as of 2013. However, be watchful of any major changes made by Congress.

A Six-Step Process

Figure 3-3 summarizes the six steps involved in calculating a consumer's federal income tax, and Figure 3-4 shows where these steps appear on the federal income tax form. Let's go over each step in detail.

Step 1:   Calculate Total Income

Tthe first step is to calculate total income. Here you must follow the Internal Revenue Service's rules about what is and what isn't included as income.

Figure 3-3.

1. Calculate gross income

| TOTAL $ INCOME |

2. Subtract adjustments
    to get adjusted gross
    income (AGI).

| ADJUSTED GROSS INCOME |

3. Subtract standard deduction
    or itemized deductions and
    subtract value of exemptions:
    Result is taxable income.

| TAXABLE INCOME |

4. Apply tax rates to calculate
    tax liability.

| TAX LIABILITY |

5. Subtract tax credits:
    Result is tax owed.

| TAX OWED |

6. Compare tax owed to tax withheld and
    decide if must pay more or if get refund.

| TAX OWED |

| TAX WITHHELD |

If TAX OWED minus TAX WITHHELD >0 ->PAY BALANCE.

If TAX OWED minus TAX WITHHELD <0 ->GET REFUND.

Included as income are:

♦ Wages, salaries, and other income, including bonuses and awards, tips, commissions, Christmas gifts, sick pay, and unemployment compensation.

♦ Fringe benefits provided by your employer must be included as income unless it is specifically excluded by the tax code. For example, the value of health insurance provided by employers is not taxed.

♦ Disability, pension, and annuity benefits, although there are some deductions and credits for these.

♦ Interest income from investments must be reported as income. However, some interest income is exempt from taxation, such as interest earned on municipal bonds and interest earned on retirement investments such as IRAs and annuities (more on this later).

♦ Dividends received from stock and mutual fund investments and profits (capital gains) earned from the sale of any investment, particularly stocks, bonds, and mutual funds.

♦ Rental income; for example, income you receive from renting an apartment building or house you own.

♦ Alimony benefits you receive from a spouse are considered income, but child support payments are not.

♦ The fair market value of property received from bartering, gambling winnings, and contest prizes and awards all must be included as income.

♦ Refunds from state and local income taxes of the previous year must be included.

This requirement always causes confusion to taxpayers because they think they're being taxed twice. But they're not and here's the reason why. As you'll see, you can deduct from income for federal tax purposes money that was *withheld* from your paycheck for state and local income taxes. If you receive a refund, that means too much was withheld. However, federal taxes were *not* paid on this excess withholding. Therefore, the refund must be declared as income in the next year. If, however, you deduct only state and local taxes actually *paid*, then any refunds do not have to be declared as income.

Total income includes:

♦ wages and salaries
♦ some fringe benefits
♦ disability, pension, and annuity benefits
♦ investment interest income
♦ dividends

♦ rental income
♦ alimony benefits received from spouse
♦ barter income, gambling winnings, contest prizes and awards
♦ state and local income tax refunds

Although this list is long and perhaps complicated, most consumers receive their income from only three sources: wages and salaries, interest income, and dividend income. Wage and salary income will be listed on a "W-2" form received from your employer. Interest and dividend income will be listed on forms received from the institutions holding your investments.

NON-IRS INCOME

There are some monies which you may receive and which are income to you, but which the IRS does not consider as income. The most important of these are benefits received from accident, health, and life insurance policies, gifts and inheritances, and Social Security benefits.

Step 2: Subtract Adjustments to Income

There are three categories that fall under the title "adjustments to income." You are not taxed on these monies. Subtract their sum from total income to get "adjusted gross income."

♦ Contributions to Individual Retirement Accounts (IRAs), Keogh plans, and Self-Employed Programs (SEPs): IRAs, Keoghs and SEPs are all retirement savings plans that allow the taxpayer to set aside money for his retirement. They are not the same as company pension plans. They allow taxpayers to supplement their pension plan. The details about these plans are described in the Retirement Planning chapter.

There is another set of retirement saving plans called deferred compensation plans, in which employees can set aside money each year. Contributions are deducted directly from a paycheck so a contributor never sees the money. Contributions don't even show up as part of income on the W-2 form. Therefore, deferred compensation contributions are not part of "adjustment to income."

♦ Any penalty you paid for withdrawing money from a time savings deposit at a bank, savings and loan, or credit union is an "adjustment to income" and can be subtracted from total income. A time savings deposit is a savings deposit with a specified term. A certificate of deposit is a good example. If you withdraw money from a certificate of deposit before the end of its term, you may be charged a penalty.

♦ Alimony paid to a spouse is an adjustment to income.

| Adjustments to income: | ♦ Penalties paid for withdrawing money |
| ♦ Contributions to IRAs, Keogh plans | ♦ Alimony paid to a spouse |

Step 3:   Subtract Standard Deduction or Itemized Deductions and Subtract Value of Exemptions.

Deductions are like adjustments to income. Certain expenses which you make are allowed to be taken as deductions. These deductions are subtracted from adjusted gross income. Thus, you are not taxed on the income which you spent on the deductions.

WHY DEDUCTIONS

There's no necessary and logical reason why certain expenditures are allowable as deductions and why others aren't. Congress and the President are the ultimate authorities on what are included as deductions. Frequently, Congress and the President use deduction as an incentive to motivate consumers to make certain expenditures, or to make certain expenditures more affordable. For example, to encourage homeownership and to make homeownership more affordable, mortgage interest expenses were made a deduction.

What if a taxpayer doesn't make expenditures that are classified as deductions? In this case the taxpayer takes the standard deduction and subtracts it from adjusted gross income. The standard deduction was discussed in the previous topic (see Table 3-10). It makes sense for a taxpayer to use the deductions she has only if their sum exceeds the standard deduction. That is, a taxpayer will only use whichever is larger, the standard deduction or the sum of expenditures allowable as deductions which she made.

What expenditures are allowable as deductions (so-called "itemized" deductions)? The list is long, complex, and can be variable as Congress makes changes in the tax code. We'll just hit the major deductions here which affect the majority of consumers.

♦ The interest on mortgages which are used to buy, build, or improve your home is deductible as long as the mortgages total $1 million or less.

♦ The interest on home equity loans up to $100,000 of home equity debt.

- State and local income taxes which you pay or which are withheld from your income are deductible.
- Property taxes are deductible.
- Certain medical and dental expenses which you pay (that is which aren't reimbursed by your insurance) are deductible. However, only that part of the expenses which exceed 7.5 percent of your adjusted gross income are deductible. So, for example, if your adjusted gross income is $30,000, then only unreimbursed medical and dental expenses exceeding $2,250 (.075 × $30,000) are deductible.

Medical and dental expenses which are deductible include doctor and hospital expenses, health insurance premiums, prescription medicines, nursing home expenses, and the costs of special medical equipment.

- Charitable contributions, including the market value of donated property, are deductible up to 50 percent or 30 percent of adjusted gross income depending on the type of contribution.
- Casualty and theft losses not related to a business and which aren't reimbursed by insurance are deductible. These are losses caused by natural disasters, car accidents, and robbery.
- If you are an employee and have travel, meal, and entertainment expenses related to your work, some of these expenses may be deductible. The expenses must be required and necessary for your job.
- If you are an employee and have educational expenses which are required by your employer, or which are necessary to maintain or improve your skills on the job, then some of the expenses are deductible.

Adjustments to income:

- Mortgage interest
- State and local income taxes
- Property taxes
- Unreimbursed medical and dental expenses which exceed 7.5% of adjusted gross income

- Charitable contributions
- Unreimbursed non-business casualty and theft losses
- Some work-related travel, meal, and entertainment expenses
- Educational expenses required by your job

Keep track of changes which Congress often makes in these deductions. Also keep records and receipts of deductible expenses in case of an audit.

The value of exemptions is the number of exemptions you claim multiplied by the personal exemption value (in 2013 this value is $3,900, see Table 3-10). Most taxpayers will claim an exemption for themselves, their spouses, and dependents. To be a dependent, four major tests must be passed:

Test 1: The person must be a relative or member of your household. A household member is someone who is not a relative but who has lived with you the entire year.

Test 2: The person must have total income under $3,900 unless he or she is a child under 19 or a student under 24.

Test 3: The person must be a U.S. citizen or legal resident.

Test 4: You must provide more than half of the person's "support." "Support" includes money spent on food, shelter, clothing, education, medical care, recreation, and transportation.

Subtract deductions (either itemized or standard) and the value of exemptions from adjusted gross income to get taxable income.

Step 4:   Apply Tax Rates to Calculate Tax Liability

For most households, a tax table is provided with your tax form that shows the tax owed for your taxable income. If your taxable income is very high, you may need to do some calculations on your own.

What is filing status? There are four types. If you're single, then your filing status is "single." If you're married and you and your spouse file together on one form, then your status is "married filing jointly." If you're married and you and your spouse file separate returns, your status is "married filing separately." If you are unmarried or separated from your spouse and you provide the support for children or relatives, then your status is "head of household."

Step 5:   Subtract Tax Credits to Get Tax Owed

Tax credits are much better than deductions or adjustments to income. One dollar of a deduction reduces taxable income by one dollar but reduces taxes by only the taxpayer's tax bracket. For example, if your tax bracket is 28 percent, then every dollar of deductions or adjustments to income reduce your taxes by 28 cents.

A tax credit reduces taxes dollar for dollar with the credit. That is, a $100 tax credit reduces taxes by $100. So a $1 tax credit is 3 or 4 times as good as a $1 deduction or adjustment to income.

So what are these great tax credits? The key tax credits for households in 2013 are:

♦ The Earned Income Credit is designed to help working low income taxpayers. For such households, federal income taxes are reduced, or, if the household's tax liability is already zero, cash is paid to the household equal to the amount of the credit.

♦ The child and dependent care credit is available for taxpayers who pay someone to care for their dependent child (under age 13), a disabled dependent, or a disabled spouse so that the taxpayer can work or look for work. The amount of the credit depends on qualified care expenses, number of dependents and taxable income.

♦ If you are over age 65 or if you are totally disabled, you can take a special tax credit. The amount of the credit depends on your filing status, age, and spouse's age.

♦ If you have children, you can claim a tax credit per child. However, the credit is reduced for taxpayers above certain income levels.

♦ American opportunity credit can be claimed for expenses paid for tuition, certain fees and course material for higher education for the first four years of post-secondary education. The credit amount decreases as family income increases.

♦ Adoption tax credit is for individuals who adopt a child and paid out-of-pocket expenses relating to the adoption. The amount of tax credit is directly related to how much money one spends on adoption-related expenses. If the child is a special-need child, one is entitled to claim the full amount of the adoption credit even if one's out-of-pocket expenses are less.

Tax credits:
♦ earned income credit
♦ child and dependent care credit
♦ Adoption tax credit

♦ American opportunity credit
♦ elderly and disabled credit
♦ child credit

Reduce your tax liability by any tax credits to get the tax owed.

Step 6: Compare the Tax Owed to Tax Withheld

If the tax owed is greater than the tax withheld, then you must pay the balance to the IRS. If the tax owed is less than the tax withheld, then you'll get a refund back from the IRS.

An Example

Figure 3-4 gives a sample federal income tax calculation for Joe and Alice Snively. Although the form says the year is 2012 (the latest form available at the time of this printing), information for tax year 2013 is used.

Joe and Alice's total income is $102,000, including $100,000 in wages and salaries, $1,500 in investment interest, and $500 in dividend income. The sources of interest and dividend income are listed on a supplementary from (Schedule B).

Joe and Alice have one adjustment to their income, a $5,000 IRA contribution. Their adjusted gross income (AGI) is therefore $97,000.

Joe and Alice's deductions are listed on Schedule A. Note that Joe and Alice cannot deduct their medical and dental expenses because the amount ($800) does not exceed 7.5% of their AGI ($7,275 = $97,000*7.5%). Joe and Alice can deduct their state and local income taxes, home mortgage interest, and charitable contributions, for a total itemized deduction of $15,000. Since $15,000 exceeds the standard deduction of $12,200 in 2013 for married couples filing jointly, Joe and Alice use the $15,000 itemized deduction on Line40 of the 1040 form. In 2013, each exemption is worth $3,900, so Joe and Alice's three exemptions are worth $11,700. Subtracting $15,000 and $11,700 from the AGI of $97,000 gives Joe and Alice a taxable income of $70,300. (line 42).

Joe and Alice can use either the tax table (in 1040 instruction) to find their tax based on a taxable income of $70,300, or calculate their tax by using the tax bracket and rate information given in Table 3-10. For 2013, their first $17,850 taxable income is taxed at 10% for $1,785.00. Because Joe and Alice's taxable income is less than $72,500, all their remaining income is taxed at 15% for $7,867.50 [($70,300-$17,850)*15%]. So their total tax liability is $9,652.50 ($1,785.00+7,867.50). Their $1000 child credit reduces their tax bill to $8,652.50. However, since $10,000 was withheld from their paychecks, Joe and Alice receive a refund of $1,347.50 (line 74a).

The Bottom Line

For most consumers, completing the federal tax form is not difficult. It involves a six step procedure, going from total income to adjusted gross income to taxable income to tax liability to tax owed to paying the balance or receiving a refund. A tax credit is 3 to 4 times more valuable than a tax deduction or adjustment to income. Tax credits reduce taxes dollar for dollar with the credit.

7. Should Reducing Taxes Be a Financial Goal?

This can be a short topic (yippie! you say!) because the answer to the question is no. Reducing taxes should *not* be a financial goal. Instead, increasing after tax income should be your prime financial goal.

Figure 3-4. Joe and Alice Snively's tax return.

Form **1040**	Department of the Treasury—Internal Revenue Service (99) **U.S. Individual Income Tax Return** 2013	OMB No. 1545-0074	IRS Use Only—Do not write or staple in this space.

For the year Jan. 1–Dec. 31, 2013, or other tax year beginning , 2012, ending , 20		See separate instructions.

Your first name and initial	Last name	Your social security number
Joe E.	Snively	555 55 5551

If a joint return, spouse's first name and initial	Last name	Spouse's social security number
Alice G.	Snively	555 55 5552

Home address (number and street). If you have a P.O. box, see instructions. Apt. no.
18 Elm st

▲ Make sure the SSN(s) above and on line 6c are correct.

City, town or post office, state, and ZIP code. If you have a foreign address, also complete spaces below (see instructions).
Knoxville, TN

Foreign country name | Foreign province/state/county | Foreign postal code

Presidential Election Campaign
Check here if you, or your spouse if filing jointly, want $3 to go to this fund. Checking a box below will not change your tax or refund. ☐ You ☐ Spouse

Filing Status
Check only one box.

1. ☐ Single
2. ☑ Married filing jointly (even if only one had income)
3. ☐ Married filing separately. Enter spouse's SSN above and full name here. ▶
4. ☐ Head of household (with qualifying person). (See instructions.) If the qualifying person is a child but not your dependent, enter this child's name here. ▶
5. ☐ Qualifying widow(er) with dependent child

Exemptions

6a ☑ **Yourself.** If someone can claim you as a dependent, **do not** check box 6a . . . . .
b ☑ **Spouse** . . . .

Boxes checked on 6a and 6b — **2**

c **Dependents:**	(2) Dependent's social security number	(3) Dependent's relationship to you	(4) ✓ if child under age 17 qualifying for child tax credit (see instructions)
(1) First name Last name			
Jessica Snively	555 55 5553	Daughter	☑
			☐
			☐
			☐

No. of children on 6c who:
• **lived with you** — **1**
• did not live with you due to divorce or separation (see instructions) —
Dependents on 6c not entered above —

If more than four dependents, see instructions and check here ▶ ☐

d Total number of exemptions claimed . . . .   Add numbers on lines above ▶ **3**

Income

Attach Form(s) W-2 here. Also attach Forms W-2G and 1099-R if tax was withheld.

If you did not get a W-2, see instructions.

Enclose, but do not attach, any payment. Also, please use Form 1040-V.

7	Wages, salaries, tips, etc. Attach Form(s) W-2	7	100000	00
8a	**Taxable** interest. Attach Schedule B if required	8a	1500	00
b	**Tax-exempt** interest. **Do not** include on line 8a . . . **8b** 50 00			
9a	Ordinary dividends. Attach Schedule B if required	9a	500	00
b	Qualified dividends **9b**			
10	Taxable refunds, credits, or offsets of state and local income taxes	10		
11	Alimony received	11		
12	Business income or (loss). Attach Schedule C or C-EZ	12		
13	Capital gain or (loss). Attach Schedule D if required. If not required, check here ▶ ☐	13		
14	Other gains or (losses). Attach Form 4797	14		
15a	IRA distributions . **15a**	b Taxable amount	15b	
16a	Pensions and annuities **16a**	b Taxable amount	16b	
17	Rental real estate, royalties, partnerships, S corporations, trusts, etc. Attach Schedule E	17		
18	Farm income or (loss). Attach Schedule F	18		
19	Unemployment compensation	19		
20a	Social security benefits **20a**	b Taxable amount	20b	
21	Other income. List type and amount	21		
22	Combine the amounts in the far right column for lines 7 through 21. This is your **total income** ▶	22	102000	00

Adjusted Gross Income

23	Educator expenses	23		
24	Certain business expenses of reservists, performing artists, and fee-basis government officials. Attach Form 2106 or 2106-EZ	24		
25	Health savings account deduction. Attach Form 8889 .	25		
26	Moving expenses. Attach Form 3903	26		
27	Deductible part of self-employment tax. Attach Schedule SE .	27		
28	Self-employed SEP, SIMPLE, and qualified plans	28		
29	Self-employed health insurance deduction	29		
30	Penalty on early withdrawal of savings	30		
31a	Alimony paid b Recipient's SSN ▶	31a		
32	IRA deduction	32	5000	00
33	Student loan interest deduction	33		
34	Tuition and fees. Attach Form 8917	34		
35	Domestic production activities deduction. Attach Form 8903	35		
36	Add lines 23 through 35	36	5000	00
37	Subtract line 36 from line 22. This is your **adjusted gross income** ▶	37	97000	00

For Disclosure, Privacy Act, and Paperwork Reduction Act Notice, see separate instructions.   Cat. No. 11320B   Form **1040** (2012)

Form 1040 (2012) Page **2**

Tax and Credits	38	Amount from line 37 (adjusted gross income)		38	
	39a	Check if: ☐ **You** were born before January 2, 1948, ☐ Blind. ☐ **Spouse** was born before January 2, 1948, ☐ Blind. } Total boxes checked ▶ 39a			
Standard Deduction for—	b	If your spouse itemizes on a separate return or you were a dual-status alien, check here▶ 39b☐			
• People who check any box on line 39a or 39b **or** who can be claimed as a dependent, see instructions.	40	**Itemized deductions** (from Schedule A) **or** your **standard deduction** (see left margin) . .		40	
	41	Subtract line 40 from line 38		41	
	42	**Exemptions.** Multiply $3,800 by the number on line 6d.		42	
	43	**Taxable income.** Subtract line 42 from line 41. If line 42 is more than line 41, enter -0- . .		43	
• All others:	44	**Tax** (see instructions). Check if any from: **a** ☐ Form(s) 8814 **b** ☐ Form 4972 **c** ☐ 962 election		44	
Single or Married filing separately, $5,950	45	**Alternative minimum tax** (see instructions). Attach Form 6251		45	
	46	Add lines 44 and 45 . . . . ▶		46	
Married filing jointly or Qualifying widow(er), $11,900	47	Foreign tax credit. Attach Form 1116 if required	47		
	48	Credit for child and dependent care expenses. Attach Form 2441	48		
	49	Education credits from Form 8863, line 19	49		
Head of household, $8,700	50	Retirement savings contributions credit. Attach Form 8880	50		
	51	Child tax credit. Attach Schedule 8812, if required . . .	51		
	52	Residential energy credits. Attach Form 5695	52		
	53	Other credits from Form: **a** ☐ 3800 **b** ☐ 8801 **c** ☐	53		
	54	Add lines 47 through 53. These are your **total credits**		54	
	55	Subtract line 54 from line 46. If line 54 is more than line 46, enter -0- . . . . ▶		55	
Other Taxes	56	Self-employment tax. Attach Schedule SE		56	
	57	Unreported social security and Medicare tax from Form: **a** ☐ 4137 **b** ☐ 8919 . .		57	
	58	Additional tax on IRAs, other qualified retirement plans, etc. Attach Form 5329 if required . .		58	
	59a	Household employment taxes from Schedule H		59a	
	b	First-time homebuyer credit repayment. Attach Form 5405 if required		59b	
	60	Other taxes. Enter code(s) from instructions		60	
	61	Add lines 55 through 60. This is your **total tax** . . . . ▶		61	
Payments	62	Federal income tax withheld from Forms W-2 and 1099 . .	62		
	63	2012 estimated tax payments and amount applied from 2011 return	63		
If you have a qualifying child, attach Schedule EIC.	64a	**Earned income credit (EIC)**	64a		
	b	Nontaxable combat pay election 64b			
	65	Additional child tax credit. Attach Schedule 8812	65		
	66	American opportunity credit from Form 8863, line 8 . . .	66		
	67	Reserved	67		
	68	Amount paid with request for extension to file	68		
	69	Excess social security and tier 1 RRTA tax withheld	69		
	70	Credit for federal tax on fuels. Attach Form 4136	70		
	71	Credits from Form: **a** ☐ 2439 **b** ☐ Reserved **c** ☐ 8801 **d** ☐ 8885	71		
	72	Add lines 62, 63, 64a, and 65 through 71. These are your **total payments** . . . . . ▶		72	
Refund	73	If line 72 is more than line 61, subtract line 61 from line 72. This is the amount you **overpaid**		73	
	74a	Amount of line 73 you want **refunded to you.** If Form 8888 is attached, check here . ▶☐		74a	
Direct deposit? See instructions.	▶ b	Routing number ☐☐☐☐☐☐☐☐☐ ▶ **c** Type: ☐ Checking ☐ Savings			
	▶ d	Account number ☐☐☐☐☐☐☐☐☐			
	75	Amount of line 73 you want **applied to your 2013 estimated tax** ▶	75		
Amount You Owe	76	**Amount you owe.** Subtract line 72 from line 61. For details on how to pay, see instructions ▶		76	
	77	Estimated tax penalty (see instructions)	77		
Third Party Designee		Do you want to allow another person to discuss this return with the IRS (see instructions)? ☐ **Yes.** Complete below. ☐ **No**			
		Designee's name ▶	Phone no. ▶	Personal identification number (PIN) ▶ ☐☐☐☐☐	
Sign Here Joint return? See instructions. Keep a copy for your records.		Under penalties of perjury, I declare that I have examined this return and accompanying schedules and statements, and to the best of my knowledge and belief, they are true, correct, and complete. Declaration of preparer (other than taxpayer) is based on all information of which preparer has any knowledge.			
		Your signature	Date	Your occupation	Daytime phone number
		Spouse's signature. If a joint return, **both** must sign.	Date	Spouse's occupation	If the IRS sent you an Identity Protection PIN, enter it here (see inst.) ☐☐☐☐☐☐
Paid Preparer Use Only		Print/Type preparer's name	Preparer's signature	Date	Check ☐ if self-employed	PTIN
		Firm's name ▶		Firm's EIN ▶	
		Firm's address ▶		Phone no.	

Form **1040** (2012)

Figure 3-4. Joe and Alice Snively's tax return.

SCHEDULE A (Form 1040)		Itemized Deductions		OMB No. 1545-0074

Department of the Treasury
Internal Revenue Service (99)

▶ Information about Schedule A and its separate instructions is at *www.irs.gov/form1040*.
▶ Attach to Form 1040.

2012
Attachment
Sequence No. **07**

Name(s) shown on Form 1040
Joe E and Alice G Shively

Your social security number
555555551

Medical and Dental Expenses		**Caution.** Do not include expenses reimbursed or paid by others.					
	1	Medical and dental expenses (see instructions)	**1**	800	00		
	2	Enter amount from Form 1040, line 38 **2** 97000 00					
	3	Multiply line 2 by 7.5% (.075)	**3**	7275	00		
	4	Subtract line 3 from line 1. If line 3 is more than line 1, enter -0-				**4**	0 00
Taxes You Paid	5	State and local (**check only one box**):					
		a ☑ Income taxes, **or**	**5**	4000	00		
		b ☐ General sales taxes					
	6	Real estate taxes (see instructions)	**6**	1700	00		
	7	Personal property taxes	**7**				
	8	Other taxes. List type and amount ▶ _____					
		_____	**8**				
	9	Add lines 5 through 8				**9**	5700 00
Interest You Paid	10	Home mortgage interest and points reported to you on Form 1098	**10**	9000	00		
	11	Home mortgage interest not reported to you on Form 1098. If paid to the person from whom you bought the home, see instructions and show that person's name, identifying no., and address ▶					
Note. Your mortgage interest deduction may be limited (see instructions).		_____					
		_____	**11**				
	12	Points not reported to you on Form 1098. See instructions for special rules	**12**				
	13	Mortgage insurance premiums (see instructions)	**13**				
	14	Investment interest. Attach Form 4952 if required. (See instructions.)	**14**				
	15	Add lines 10 through 14				**15**	9000 00
Gifts to Charity	16	Gifts by cash or check. If you made any gift of $250 or more, see instructions	**16**	300	00		
If you made a gift and got a benefit for it, see instructions.	17	Other than by cash or check. If any gift of $250 or more, see instructions. You **must** attach Form 8283 if over $500	**17**				
	18	Carryover from prior year	**18**				
	19	Add lines 16 through 18				**19**	300 00
Casualty and Theft Losses	20	Casualty or theft loss(es). Attach Form 4684. (See instructions.)				**20**	
Job Expenses and Certain Miscellaneous Deductions	21	Unreimbursed employee expenses—job travel, union dues, job education, etc. Attach Form 2106 or 2106-EZ if required. (See instructions.) ▶ _____	**21**				
	22	Tax preparation fees	**22**				
	23	Other expenses—investment, safe deposit box, etc. List type and amount ▶ _____					
		_____	**23**				
	24	Add lines 21 through 23	**24**				
	25	Enter amount from Form 1040, line 38 **25**					
	26	Multiply line 25 by 2% (.02)	**26**				
	27	Subtract line 26 from line 24. If line 26 is more than line 24, enter -0-				**27**	
Other Miscellaneous Deductions	28	Other—from list in instructions. List type and amount ▶ _____					
		_____				**28**	
Total Itemized Deductions	29	Add the amounts in the far right column for lines 4 through 28. Also, enter this amount on Form 1040, line 40				**29**	15000 00
	30	If you elect to itemize deductions even though they are less than your standard deduction, check here ▶ ☐					

For Paperwork Reduction Act Notice, see Form 1040 instructions.   Cat. No. 17145C   Schedule A (Form 1040) 2012

Figure 3-4.   Joe and Alice Snively's tax return.

SCHEDULE B (Form 1040A or 1040) Department of the Treasury Internal Revenue Service (99)	**Interest and Ordinary Dividends** ▶ Attach to Form 1040A or 1040. ▶ Information about Schedule B (Form 1040A or 1040) and its instructions is at *www.irs.gov/form1040.*	OMB No. 1545-0074 20**12** Attachment Sequence No. **08**

Name(s) shown on return	Your social security number
Joe E and Alice G Snively	555555551

Part I **Interest** (See instructions on back and the instructions for Form 1040A, or Form 1040, line 8a.) **Note.** If you received a Form 1099-INT, Form 1099-OID, or substitute statement from a brokerage firm, list the firm's name as the payer and enter the total interest shown on that form.	**1**	List name of payer. If any interest is from a seller-financed mortgage and the buyer used the property as a personal residence, see instructions on back and list this interest first. Also, show that buyer's social security number and address ▶		**Amount**	
		ABC Bank		1000	00
		Garden Savings & Loan		500	00
			1		
				1500	00
	2	Add the amounts on line 1	**2**		
	3	Excludable interest on series EE and I U.S. savings bonds issued after 1989. Attach Form 8815	**3**		
	4	Subtract line 3 from line 2. Enter the result here and on Form 1040A, or Form 1040, line 8a . . . . ▶	**4**	1500	00

Note. If line 4 is over $1,500, you must complete Part III.

Part II **Ordinary Dividends** (See instructions on back and the instructions for Form 1040A, or Form 1040, line 9a.) **Note.** If you received a Form 1099-DIV or substitute statement from a brokerage firm, list the firm's name as the payer and enter the ordinary dividends shown on that form.	**5**	List name of payer ▶		**Amount**	
		Super safe bond funds		500	00
			5		
	6	Add the amounts on line 5. Enter the total here and on Form 1040A, or Form 1040, line 9a . . . . ▶	**6**	500	00

Note. If line 6 is over $1,500, you must complete Part III.

Part III **Foreign Accounts and Trusts** (See instructions on back.)	You must complete this part if you **(a)** had over $1,500 of taxable interest or ordinary dividends; **(b)** had a foreign account; or **(c)** received a distribution from, or were a grantor of, or a transferor to, a foreign trust.		**Yes**	**No**
	7a	At any time during 2012, did you have a financial interest in or signature authority over a financial account (such as a bank account, securities account, or brokerage account) located in a foreign country? See instructions	☐	✓
		If "Yes," are you required to file Form TD F 90-22.1 to report that financial interest or signature authority? See Form TD F 90-22.1 and its instructions for filing requirements and exceptions to those requirements	☐	✓
	b	If you are required to file Form TD F 90-22.1, enter the name of the foreign country where the financial account is located ▶		
	8	During 2012, did you receive a distribution from, or were you the grantor of, or transferor to, a foreign trust? If "Yes," you may have to file Form 3520. See instructions on back	☐	✓

For Paperwork Reduction Act Notice, see your tax return instructions.	Cat. No. 17146N	Schedule B (Form 1040A or 1040) 2012

Unfortunately, many taxpayers get caught up in the "save taxes syndrome." They say, "I'm paying too much in taxes. How can I reduce my tax bill?" They put money in any investment which reduces their taxes without seeing if their bottom line, their after-tax income, is higher.

What taxpayers should not look at is whether a particular investment saves taxes; after all, one way for the investment to save taxes is for the investment to lose money! Instead, the taxpayer should look at the *after-tax* rate of return, or interest rate, earned by the investment. You already know how to do this (go back to the previous topic). Calculating the after-tax interest rate on an investment allows comparison of investments which do save taxes and which don't save taxes.

The Bottom Line

Don't fall into the trap of focusing on reducing taxes as a financial goal. Instead, focus on the goal of increasing after-tax income. Compare the after-tax rates of return of investments in order to determine which is best.

8. Is Postponing Taxes a Good Idea?

Your mom always said, "Do your chores today; don't put them off until tomorrow." As a child you frequently wanted to do the opposite—postpone unpleasant chores and activities until tomorrow and enjoy yourself today.

We don't want to make your mom angry at us. However, with respect to taxes, you were right and your mom was wrong. In most cases, paying taxes is one of those chores where postponing them until tomorrow is a good idea.

Why is this so? The answer is simple. If you postpone paying taxes, the money that would have gone to taxes could be invested. Hopefully, the investment will earn more money. When the time comes to pay taxes, you'll have more money to pay taxes on, your tax bill will be higher, but you'll have more after-tax money left. Only if the future tax *rate* is significantly higher compared to today might postponing taxes be a bad idea.

An Example

WAYS OF
POSTPONING TAXES

Let's look at an example to illustrate this point. You face three choices for investing $1,000 of your income. In Choice A you pay taxes on the $1,000 today and you pay taxes on any interest which the remaining money earns. In Choice B you pay taxes on the $1,000 *later*, but you pay taxes on any interest which the $1,000 earns. In Choice C you pay

Figure 3-5. To postpone or not to postpone taxes.

Choice	Now	End of Year 1	End of Year 2	End of Year 3	End of Year 4	End of Year 5
A	$1,000 Pay taxes of 25%. Leaves $750.	$750 earns $75 interest. Pay tax of 25% on $75. Leaves $750 + $56.25 = $806.25	$806.25 earns $80.63 interest. Pay tax of 25% on $80.63. Leaves $806.25 + $60.47 = $866.72	$866.72 earns $86.67 interest. Pay tax of 25% on $86.67. Leaves $866.72 + $65.00 = $931.72	$931.72 earns $93.17 interest. pay tax of 25% on $93.17. Leaves $931.72 + 69.88 = $1,001.60	$1,001.60 earns $100.16 interest. Pay tax of 25% on $100.16. Leaves $1,001.60 + $75.12 = $1,076.72
B	$1,000	$1,000 earns $100 interest. Pay tax of 25% on $100. Leaves $1000 + $75 = $1,075	$1,075 earns $107.50 interest. Pay tax of 25% on $107.50. Leaves $1075 + $80.63 = $1,155.63	$1,155.63 earns $115.56 interest.Pay tax of 25% on $115.56. Leaves $1155.63 + $86.67 = $1,242.30	$1,242.30 earns $124.23 interest. pay tax of 25% on $124.23. Leaves $1242.30 + 93.17 = $1,335.47	$1,335.47 earns $133.55 interest. Pay tax of 25% on $133.55. Leaves $1335.47 + $100.12 = $1,435.63 Pay 25% tax on original $1000. Leaves $750 + $453.63 interest = $1.185.63
C	$1,000	$1,000 earns $100 interest. Total = $1,100	$1,100 earns $110 interest. Total = $1,210	$1,210 earns $121 interest. Total = $1,331	$1,331 earns $133.10 interest. Total = $1,464.10	$1,464.10 earns $146.41 interest. Total = $1,610.51. pay 25% tax on total. Leaves $1,207.88

taxes on the $1,000 later and you pay taxes on all interest earnings later. If each of the three investments earn a before-tax interest rate of 10 percent and your tax bracket is 25 percent, which investment is better for a term of five years?

The calculations are given in Figure 3-5. Choice C (postponing taxes on everything) gives the largest after-tax result, followed by Choice B (postponing taxes on the initial $1,000), and followed by Choice A (pay taxes as money is earned). So, as we expected, postponing taxes wins. Furthermore, it shouldn't surprise you that the longer that taxes are postponed, the more money you make because you have a longer time to invest the money that would have been paid in taxes. For example, if the investment term in Figure 3-5 was ten years rather than five years, the advantages of Choices C and B over Choice A would be much greater.

We'll return to the subject of postponing taxes in the Retirement Planning chapter. There are several retirement investments which allow taxes to be postponed. As you'll see, these investments are very worthwhile.

The Bottom Line

Legally postponing taxes is usually to your benefit. Investments which allow you to postpone taxes will earn more money, even after taxes are ultimately paid, than investments which pay taxes today. However, postponing taxes illegally, which results in tax penalties, is not wise. _____

9. What Is Financial Planning?

We conclude this chapter by discussing a concept that is frequently used in connection with consumer financial decisions. The concept is financial planning.

FINANCIAL PLAN

Figure 3-6 outlines the elements of financial planning. Financial planning includes all decisions related to the spending and saving of a consumer's financial resources. In particular, a financial plan presents a consumer with spending and saving goals and tells a consumer how much to save for specific goals, such as college education and retirement. Also, financial planning will help a consumer make specific decisions about mortgages, credit, insurance, investments, and the replacement of durable goods. In short, if a consumer decision involves money, it fits into financial planning.

How does financial planning differ from consumer economics? Whereas financial planning concentrates on consumer decisions involving the spending and saving of money, consumer economics examines decisions about both consumer resources, money and *time*. This means that

Figure 3-6.   Elements of financial planning.

Spending	—	Budgeting—How much to spend?

Mortgage or rent	—	Rent or own; What kind of mortgage?
Credit payments	—	How much credit; What kind of credit?
Life, health and disability insurance	—	How much insurance; What kind of insurance?
Car and other durable goods	—	When to replace?

Saving	—	How much to save?

Investments	—	What kind of investments; Tradeoffs between risk and return.
Education saving	—	How much to save for college education?
Retirement	—	How much to save for retirement?
other saving	—	How much to save for other goals?

consumer economics examines all of the financial decisions dealt with by financial planning, but with one extra complication—time, and the cost of time are always taken into consideration. In addition, the broader scope of consumer economics means it tackles some topics not addressed by financial planning, such as shopping and information gathering.

The Bottom Line

Financial planning is making decisions about spending and saving designed to meet a consumer's financial goals. Consumer economics addresses these issues but also includes consideration of time and the cost of time.

SHOULD YOU BUY THE SERVICES OF A FINANCIAL PLANNER

C O N S U M E R

T O P I C

Financial planning is a relatively new profession. A financial planner is supposed to be a one-stop financial adviser. A financial planner will give advice on all personal financial decisions, including credit, insurance, investing, and retirement planning. The advantage of a financial planner over a stock broker, insurance agent, or banker is that the financial planner can look at your entire financial picture and see how the individual pieces fit together. The other financial advisers generally look only at one part of your personal finances.

There are two things that a financial planner can do. One is to offer advice—that is, to provide a financial plan to meet your goals. This financial plan might tell you how much insurance coverage to have, how much to save for your children's education, how much to save for your retirement, and where to invest your savings. You pay a fee to the financial planner for this advice.

The second thing that financial planners can do is to implement the financial plan. Here the financial planner will buy the insurance and buy the investments which were recommended in the financial plan. The planner is compensated by the commissions earned on the purchase of financial products.

Planners who offer only advice on financial plans are called "fee-only" planners. Planners who offer both advice and implementation of the plan are called "fee and commission" planners. Fee-only planners often claim they are more objective than "fee and commission" planners because they're not tempted to consider certain investments by high commissions and they're not tempted to make frequent trades just to generate more commissions. Fee and commission planners reply that someone must implement the plan, so why not the person who designed the plan.

In selecting a financial planner, look first at the planner's credentials. In most states, anyone can call himself a financial planner regardless of his training. So in shopping for a planner, it's "buyer beware." You'd prefer a planner who has a college degree in economics, business, finance, or accounting. Also, look for financial planner with credentials such as "certified financial planner" (CFP). The CFP Board sets rigorous standards for education, ethical, testing, and experience for such certification.

However, after grinding through this text, hopefully you won't need the services of a financial planner. You can act as your own personal financial adviser!

WORDS AND CONCEPTS YOU SHOULD KNOW

Budget
Erratic income
Subconscious budget
Spending patterns by age
Spending patterns by income
Gross income
Net income
Expense categories
Retirement savings
Durable good saving
Emergency saving
Fixed expenditures
Discretionary expenditures
Substitute time for money
Durable goods
Non-durable goods
Current budget
Objective budget
Negative savings
Net worth statement
Assets
Liabilities
Market value of assets
Liquid assets
Real assets
Financial ratios
Asset/debt ratio
Liquid + other financial assets/Total debt
Liquid assets/Non-mortgage debt

Liquid + other financial assets/Non-mortgage debt
Liquid assets/Budgeted monthly expenditures
Liquid + other financial assets/Budgeted monthly expenditures
Liquid assets/One year's debt payments
Liquid + other financial assets/One year's debt payments
Taxable income
Personal exemption
Standard deduction
Itemized deductions
Tax brackets
Total income tax bracket
Benefit of deductions
After-tax interest rate
Total income
Adjusted gross income
Tax liability
Tax credit
Tax withheld
Tax owed
Filing status
Earned income credit
Child and dependent care credit
Postponing taxes
Financial planning
Consumer economies

ORGANIZING YOUR FINANCIAL LIFE—A SUMMARY

1. A budget is a necessity for consumers who have debt problems, can't save, or have erratic incomes. For other consumers, a budget is beneficial as a way to monitor expenses and saving and is useful in tax planning and life insurance and retirement planning.

2. Average consumer spending patterns are strongly related to age and income. Savings rates typically increase with income and with age until retirement. Children have a big impact on average consumer spending. Families with children spend more on home-prepared food, clothing, housing, and transportation.

3. A budget matches your income to your expenses and savings. Most budgets are done on a monthly basis. Borrowing should not be included as income. Instead, credit payments should be listed as an expense. A current budget shows how you are currently spending your income. An objective budget shows how you want to spend your income.
   A. Expense categories should be specific enough to allow accurate monitoring of expenses, but not so detailed as to make the time costs of budgeting prohibitive. Expenses that occur on a non-monthly basis (e.g., semi-annually, annually) should still be allocated monthly.
   B. Savings categories include Social Security contributions, pension and retirement contributions, saving for specific goals (such as education, a vacation, or replacement of durable goods), and emergency savings.
      (1) For specific dollar-amount savings goals, calculate the monthly amount to save by:

$$\frac{\text{Monthly Amount to Save}}{} = \frac{\text{Dollar-amount goal}}{\text{FVFS associated with nominal interest rate and number of months.}}$$

   (2) For savings objectives which are very distant and for which it's difficult to project a dollar-amount goal, calculate the initial annual amount to save by:

$$\frac{\text{Initial Annual Amount to Save.}}{} = \frac{\text{Current dollar cost of objectives}}{\text{FVFS associated with real interest rate and number of years to save.}}$$

183

Then divide by 12 to obtain the monthly savings amount.

Each year increase the monthly amount to save by the inflation rate.

C. Expect to increase the dollar amount in budget each year due to inflation.

D. Data for a budget can come from canceled checks, sales receipts, and credit card receipts.

E. Fixed expenditures in a budget are those which can't be changed in the short-run.

(1) Short-run budget-cutting should concentrate on cutting discretionary expenditures.

(2) Also cut expenses in a budget by substituting time for money (eat at home), reducing expenses on non-durable goods, and reducing expenses on clothing.

(3) In the long-run reduce expenses in a budget by cutting transportation costs.

4. A budget is a "flow" document. It shows how income which flows in to your hands flows out as expenses and savings. A net worth statement shows the consequences of your budget. It is a snapshot at a single point in time which compares the value of your assets to the value of your debts.

A. Net worth is the difference between assets and liabilities. Net worth typically increases until retirement.

B. In constructing a net worth statement, it's important to value assets at their market value, that is, what they could be sold for today.

(1) Liquid assets are assets that can be cashed-in quickly with little risk of loss of value.

(2) Other financial assets are assets which can be converted to cash with time, although some loss or penalty may be incurred.

(3) Real assets are assets which take a long time to convert to cash.

C. Numerous financial ratios can be calculated to evaluate a net worth statement:

Liquid assets/Total debt

Liquid + other financial assets/Total debt

Liquid + other financial assets/Non-mortgage debt

The net worth statement can be combined with the budget to produce other financial ratios:

Liquid assets/Budgeted monthly expenditures

liquid + other financial assets/Budgeted monthly expenditures

Liquid assets/One year's debt payments

Liquid + other financial assets/One year's debt payments

5. Your tax bracket is the percent of an additional dollar you earn that is paid in taxes.

A. There are seven official federal income tax brackets in 2013: 10%, 15%, 25%, 28%, 33%, 35%, and 39.6%.

B. The Social Security tax for employees is 7.65% on the first $113,700 (2013) of wages and salaries.

C. Many states and localities also have income taxes.

D. Use income tax brackets to find the value of tax deductions and to convert investment interest rates to after-tax interest rates.

6. Follow a six step process to calculate the federal income tax you owe. The process for most state and local income taxes is similar.

    A.   Calculate gross income.

    B.   Subtract adjustments to income such as IRA contributions and alimony paid to a spouse.

    C.   Subtract the standard deduction or itemized deductions if they are greater. The major itemized deductions are mortgage interest, state and local income taxes, property taxes, and certain medical and dental expenses. Also, subtract the value of exemptions.

    D.   Apply tax rates to calculate tax liability.

    E.   Subtract tax credits to get tax owed. The major tax credits are the earned income credit for low income taxpayers, the child and dependent care credit, and the elderly and disabled credit.

    F   Compare the tax owed to the tax withheld to calculate the refund or balance due.

7. Reducing taxes should not be a financial goal. Instead, increasing after-tax income should be your prime financial goal. Compare the after-tax rate of return of investments to judge their benefit to your financial health.

8. In most cases, postponing taxes is a good idea. Money which would have been paid in taxes can be invested, and more money will be left even after taxes are ultimately paid.

9. Financial planning includes all decisions related to the spending and saving of a consumer's financial resources. Consumer economics is broader than financial planning. Consumer economics includes all decisions related to the allocation of the consumer's financial and time resources.

DISCUSSION QUESTIONS

1. Bob's finances are great. His debts are manageable, he is able to save, and he doesn't have difficulty buying what he wants. Why might Bob still want to construct a budget?

2. Sarah and Stan are both age 28, have two young children, and have debts for their home, cars, and furniture. They can't save. Should they worry?

3. Wilma and Fred are both age 50. Their children are grown and gone. Their mortgage is almost totally paid. Wilma and Fred can't seem to save. Should they worry?

4. Should you expect the dollar amounts in your budget to remain the same each year? Why or why not?

5. What are the two methods for calculating monthly savings requirements necessary to meet savings goals? When is each method used?

6. What's the difference between fixed expenditures and discretionary expenditures? Why is the distinction important?

7. If you must cut spending, what items in your budget would you cut?

8. What is the relationship between your annual budgets and your net worth statement at a given point in time?

9. What are liquid assets and why are they important?

10. Identify three financial ratios. How are they used?

11. Why is your income tax bracket important?

12. Would a flat tax of, say 15 percent, applied to your gross income necessarily result in a smaller amount of tax owed than under the current tax system?

13. Why shouldn't reducing taxes be your financial goal?

14. Why is postponing taxes usually a good idea?

PROBLEMS

1. Joe wants to have $3,000 for a house down payment in three years. How much must he save each month if he can earn 5 percent, after taxes, on his investments?

2. Joe also wants to buy a new car in eight years. The car he wants to buy costs $15,000 today. If Joe expects to earn an interest rate 4 percentage points higher than the auto inflation rate, how much should Joe save each month in the first year? How should this savings change in subsequent years?

3. Construct your current budget. If you are dissatisfied with it, construct an objective budget.

4. A simple budget for George and Gracie for three months is shown below. Do a quarterly analysis of the budget showing dollar and percentage differences between budgeted and actual expenses and savings. What parts of their budget should George and Gracie reconsider?

| | ----------Month 1--------- | | ----------Month 2----------- | | ----------Month 3-------- | |
Income	Budgeted $2,000	Actual $2,000	Budgeted $2,000	Actual $2,000	Budgeted $2,000	Actual $2,000
Taxes	$200	$200	$200	$200	$200	$200
Food	320	360	320	350	320	370
House[1]	800	820	800	770	800	830
Transp.[2]	300	280	300	290	300	300
Medical	40	0	40	0	40	120
Entertainment	50	120	50	90	50	30
Soc. Sec.	150	150	150	150	150	150
Savings	140	70	140	150	140	0
TOTAL	$2,000	$2,000	$2,000	$2,000	$2,000	$2,000

[1] Includes $650/month mortgage payment.
[2] Includes $100/month car payment.

5. George and Gracie's net worth statement is shown below. Use this statement in combination with George and Gracie's budget (from question 4) to calculate the following:

Net worth
Assets/Liabilities
Liquid assets/Total debt
Liquid + financial assets/Total debt
Liquid assets/Non-mortgage debt
Liquid + financial assets/Non-mortgage debt
Liquid assets/Monthly expenditures
Liquid + financial assets/Monthly expenditures
Liquid assets/One year's debt payments
Liquid + financial assets/One year's debt payments

Use this information to determine how George and Gracie are doing.

Assets

Checking account	$3,000
Savings accounts	6,000
CDs	5,000
Stocks	0
Bonds	0

IRAs	4,000
Home	50,000
Autos	3,000
Furniture and appliances	2,000
Personal property	2,000

Liabilities

Credit card balances	$2,000
Personal loans	5,000
Auto loans	1,000
Home mortgage	40,000

6. Byron's federal income tax bracket is 15 percent and his state income tax bracket is 5 percent. What is Byron's total income tax bracket?

7. Pete spends $9,000 on home mortgage interest. If his tax bracket is 28 percent and he has other deductions which exceed the standard deduction, how much does he save in taxes with this deduction?

8. Which is better, a fully taxable investment paying 15 percent or a tax free investment paying 12½ percent if the investor's tax bracket is 35 percent?

9. Use the following information for George and Gracie to calculate the federal taxes they owe:

Filing status: married filing joint return.

Exemptions: four, including two children under age 10.

Wages, salaries, tips:	$84,000
Interest income:	2,500
Tax refund from last year:	300
IRA contribution:	1,000
Unreimbursed medical and dental expenses:	500
State and local income taxes:	1,500
Real estate taxes:	1,000
Home mortgage interest:	3,500
Charitable contributions:	200

If George and Gracie had $8,400 withheld for federal taxes, will they receive a refund or will they pay more to the federal government?

CHAPTER 4

Shelter

Introduction

For most consumers, expenditures on housing take the biggest bite out of the paycheck. In 2011 the average American consumer spent 20 cents out of each dollar of total expenditure on shelter.[1] If fuel costs are added, the total rises to 27¢ of each dollar! There are a number of decisions related to shelter, such as whether to own or rent, where to live, how large of a dwelling to choose, and how to finance a home purchase.

The rapid value appreciation of houses in the decades before the financial crisis of 2007 made one form of shelter—homeownership—extremely popular. In fact, for many consumers a certain aura was attached to homeownership in that it was considered an instant road to wealth. At that same time many consumers considered renting to be money wasted "down the drain." Many personal finance advisors therefore recommended, with few qualifications, buying over renting. Such simplistic advice is dangerous and often misleading because housing is a risky investment, as the sharp housing market downturn during the 2007–2010 financial crisis would show. A major goal of this chapter is to develop a framework for evaluating the own versus rent decision free of cliches and oversimplifications.

As any consumer who has recently purchased a house knows, financing a home is a complex and often confusing task. The conventional fixed rate, fixed payment mortgage is no longer the only mortgage "on the block." Instead, it has been joined by the adjustable rate mortgage, the graduated payment mortgage, the growing-equity mortgage, the shared equity mortgage, the shared appreciation mortgage, the 15-year mortgage, the bi-weekly mortgage, and seller-financing. Quite a choice to say the least! Another goal of this chapter is to show you how to understand and evaluate this apparent maze of home financing options.

As will be the case in other chapters, this chapter applies a few simple and, hopefully, intuitive economic concepts to practical consumer decisions. The major focus is on the buy versus rent decision and the home finance decision. The "roadmap" for the chapter is as follows. First, considerations involved in where to live (for example, rural area vs. small town vs. large city) are discussed. Second, the determinants of housing price are examined. The elements and meaning of home-ownership costs are then tackled, and within this context is discussed why homeownership is often so popular despite high housing prices and sometimes high mortgage interest rates. Third, the meaning and calculation of the major homeownership cost, mortgage payments, are presented. Mortgage payments are related to the idea of present value discussed in Chapter 1. Next, a framework for making the rent versus

---

[1] U.S. Bureau of Labor Statistics, *Consumer Expenditure Survey*, 2011.

buy decision and for evaluating home-ownership as an investment is recommended. This is followed by a discussion and comparison of alternative mortgage designs. The chapter concludes with a discussion of an assortment of other shelter topics, such as prepaying a mortgage, second mortgages, and the size of the downpayment.

1. Where to Live

Most consumers choose to live near their place of work. Since transportation costs to and from work are a major expense, locating near the place of work cuts down on commuting costs.

As most consumers know, choosing to live and work in a rural area, small town, or large city presents different lifestyles, opportunities, and costs. Since rural areas, by their nature, are less dense, housing costs tend to be lower than in towns and cities. Consumers in rural areas also find it cheaper to visit open spaces and forests and their associated recreational activities. However, hospitals, supermarkets, shopping centers, and theaters aren't as plentiful and accessible in rural areas as in towns and cities. Therefore, products and services provided by these establishments are more costly to rural consumers, especially in terms of transportation costs.

Large cities present the opposite set of opportunities and costs to consumers than do rural areas. Since cities have larger populations, demand for hospitals, museums, shopping centers, supermarkets, and specialized services, products, and activities will be greater than in rural areas.[2] These products and services will therefore be more plentiful in cities and easier to access by consumers than in rural areas. In contrast, with greater density, housing available in cities will be more expensive (this will be discussed in greater detail in the next section) and visiting open spaces and outdoor recreational activities will be more expensive than in rural areas. Towns present opportunities and costs in between those found in rural areas and large cities.

Choosing where to live therefore depends, in part, on your preferences for open space and outdoor recreational activities versus hospitals, supermarkets, shopping centers, and specialized products, services, and activities. Consumers preferring open space and outdoor activities will be more apt to choose rural areas, whereas consumers preferring hospitals, supermarkets, shopping centers, etc. will be more likely to choose cities.

---

[2]For example, specialized products, services, and activities, such as foreign auto mechanics, ethnic restaurants, and community theaters are more often found in large cities than in towns and rural areas because of the "critical mass" of people needed to support these activities. There are exceptions to this generalization with college towns being the best example.

Where to Live in the Country

Many times each year popular magazines and other organizations will publish lists of "the best places to live in America." The rankings are based on a composite score involving many factors, but most notably including environmental amenities, school quality and housing costs.

These lists ignore one crucial point, which is that there's no free lunch when it comes to environmental amenities, school quality, or other locational factors which we desire. Because demand for living in cities with cleaner air or better schools will be greater than demand in cities without these qualities, cities with a better "quality of life" will be able to "charge" for their amenities through higher shelter prices (housing prices and rents) and lower wages and salaries. That is, consumers who value the amenities will either be willing to pay higher prices for shelter or accept lower wages in order to live in a city with a higher quality of life. Conversely, cities with a lower quality of life will only be able to attract consumers with lower shelter prices and/or higher wages and salaries.

A study by Blomquist, Berger, and Hoehn recognized this tradeoff when they ranked cities by quality of life.[3] Their quality of life composite included seven "climate" factors (precipitation, humidity, heating degree days, cooling degree days, wind speed, sunshine, and proximity to a coast), six "environmental factors" (visibility, total suspended particulates, effluent dischargers, landfill waste, proximity to superfund sites, and proximity to hazardous waste sites), and three "urban conditions" factors (central city location, violent crimes, and teacher-pupil ratios). The researchers used 1980 Census data for 46,000 individuals and 34,000 housing units in 253 locations to calculate the impact of each of the factors on shelter prices and wages. As expected, they found that factors which consumers like, such as higher teacher-pupil ratios, were associated with higher housing prices and lower wages, whereas factors which consumers disliked, such as humidity, were associated with lower housing prices and higher wages. In other words, the housing and labor markets adjusted for amenities.

Why would anyone choose to live in a city with poor amenities or working conditions? The answer is simple. These consumers value the reduction in shelter prices or increase in wages they receive by living there more than they value the reduction in amenities.

---

[3] Blomquist, Glenn C, Mark G. Berger, and John P. Hoehn. "New Estimates of Quality of Life in Urban Areas," *The American Economic Review,* Vol. 78, No. 1, March 1988, pp. 89-107.

The Bottom Line

There's no "free lunch" in choosing where to live. Cities with a better "quality of life" will have higher shelter costs and lower wages, and cities with a poorer "quality of life" will have lower shelter costs and higher wages. Consumers who place a low value on "quality of life" factors are better-off living in cities with low quality of life rankings. _____

2. What Determines the Prices of Shelter?

Let's first consider houses. Some of the factors that determine the price of homes are obvious to everyone. Bigger homes cost more, homes with more bathrooms and bedrooms and homes with garages cost more, and homes with ceramic tubs and hardwood floors cost more. Table 4-1 shows the additional cost for some of these factors for homes in Raleigh, North Carolina.

VALUE OF SCHOOLS

But there are some other "not-so-obvious" factors which affect the price of homes. We've already discussed some of these in the previous topic. When you buy a house, you're also "buying" the surrounding neighborhood. Homes cannot be moved (at least usually), so the attractiveness of a particular house is influenced by such things as the quality of the neighborhood schools, the crime rate in the neighborhood, the neatness of yards and landscaping, the local air quality, and the demographic composition of the neighborhood. For example, Table 4-1 shows that homes in Raleigh, North Carolina, that are in school districts where standardized test scores are higher sell for more. Neighborhood associations, subdivision covenants, and zoning are often used to maintain neighborhood standards in order to enhance property values.

"LOCATION PREMIUM"

Lastly, you have probably heard about the three factors important to real estate: location, location, and location. Well, location also matters for homes. Homes that are located closer to major centers of employment and shopping will cost more (see Figure 4-1). Why is this? It's because proximity saves money; for example, if you're closer to your job, you will save money in commuting. People will prefer to live closer to their jobs and schools and shopping, so the same house closer to centers of employment and shopping will generally be more valuable (everything else equal). For example, in Raleigh, NC, for every mile that a home is closer to the center of Raleigh, it's price increases by $700. This is called a "location premium." Furthermore, the location premium is bigger the bigger and more important the city. Home prices are so high in Washington, D.C., and New York City not because homes are any better built there, but because many people want to live near the centers of political power and finance.

Table 4-1 Additional price associated with selected house, neighborhood, and locational characteristics, Raleigh, NC, 1988.

Characteristic	Price Premium
Full bath	$8200
Half bath	4000
Single car garage	4500
Double car garage	9700
Square foot of space	43
Ceramic bathtub	3800
Hardwood floor in dining room	4200
Deck	7700
Outside storage building	5000
Middle school test performance[a]	300
High school SAT scores[b]	50
1 mile closer to center of Raleigh	700

[a]Increase in house price related to each percentile increase in average California Achievement Test score at school.
[b]Increase in house price related to each increase of one point in Scholastic Achievement Test total score.

Source: Michael L. Walden, Magnet Schools and the Differential Impact of School Quality on Residential Property Values, The Journal of Real Estate Research, Summer 1990 5(2), 221–230.

The prices of homes are determined by how the *average* buyer judges their worth. But as an individual buyer, you should compare your personal valuation to the average valuation. For example, if you don't work in the center of town, then there's no reason for you to pay a premium for a house located close to the center of town. You'll save money on the house price, and you won't spend any more on commuting, if you buy a house located further out. Likewise, if neat and well-landscaped yards don't give you pleasure, don't buy a house in a neighborhood where all the yards are immaculate!

Figure 4-1. Relationship between house price and location.

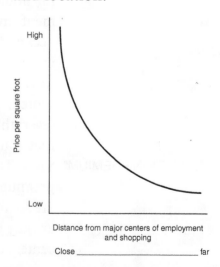

FACTORS AFFECTING RENTS

The same principles that influence the price of owner-occupied houses also influence the rent of rental units, such as apartments. Rent is the price paid for the use of shelter owned by someone else. Thus it makes sense that rents should be related to the amount of shelter services received. Larger apartments, apartments in better condition, and apartments with more amenities should rent for more.

Table 4-2 shows the relationship between rent and selected apartment characteristics for a sample of apartments in the Phoenix metropolitan area. Characteristics both of the apartment (condition, fireplace, dishwasher, patio, etc.) and of the apartment complex (swimming pool, exercise room) affect rents.

Location of the apartment also matters. Apartments which are closer to centers of employment or major roads will save the renter commuting time and money, and as a result, the renter would be willing to pay more rent. Table 4-2 shows that in Phoenix, every mile closer to an expressway results in a $7.57 increase in monthly rent.

The Bottom Line

You can reduce shelter costs by living in a house or apartment farther away from city centers and from centers of employment. However, your driving costs will be higher as a result.

Table 4-2   Effect of selected characteristics on apartment rents in Phoenix, Arizona.

Characteristic	Additional Monthly Rent
Above average condition	$11.00
Additional square footage	0.19 per square foot
Additional bathroom	9.29
Fireplace	24.42
Dishwasher	26.83
Patio	14.79
Landlord pays electric	62.26
Swimming pool	26.83
Exercise room	14.45
1 mile closer to expressway	7.57

Source: From research reported in Karl L Guntermann and Stefan Norrbin, "Explaining the Variability of Apartment Rents," Journal of the American Real Estate and Urban Economics Association, *Volume 15, No. 4, Winter 1987, pp. 321–340.*

3. What Are the Costs of Owning a Home?

The cost of renting is simple—it's merely the rental payment made for use of the dwelling. Rent is *not* "money down the drain" because it is payment for services received. The landlord provides the consumer with a place to live, and in exchange the consumer makes payments to the landlord. The negative perception of renting is due to the superior investment performance achieved by home-ownership during some recent years. The investment aspects of homeownership are discussed later. If homeowners began losing money when homes were sold (as some did in the first half of the 1980 and in the late 2000s), then the attitude toward renting would change.

Homeownership costs differ from the price of the house. The price of the house is only one component of homeownership costs. The house price is primarily reflected in financing costs carried by the buyer.

One-Time Costs

CLOSING COSTS, DOWN PAYMENT, SELLING COSTS

It is useful to consider homeownership costs in two categories. One category is one-time costs. These costs include *closing costs* paid at the time of purchase, the *downpayment,* and *selling costs* paid when the house is sold. Closing costs include such expenditures as loan origination fees, survey fees, lawyer fees, and advance tax and insurance payments. Closing costs are generally in the neighborhood of 3–4 percent of the mortgage loan amount. The downpayment is the buyer's initial cash payment toward the purchase price of the house. Selling costs are primarily realtor commissions which the homeowner pays when the house is sold.

Periodic Costs

The second category of homeownership costs are periodic costs. These costs are paid periodically, such as monthly. Each is considered individually below.

OPPORTUNITY COST

♦ *Lost Investment Returns on Closing Costs and Downpayment.* This is usually an overlooked and misunderstood cost. The point is simply that the homeowner could have used the closing costs and downpayment funds for some other purpose. By spending those funds on housing the homeowner is giving up the benefits he or she could have received by using those funds in another way. Therefore, there is an opportunity cost to the closing costs and downpayment. Although those funds could have been used in any way the homeowner chose, one alternative is investing them. Thus, one measure of the opportunity cost related to closing costs and the downpayment is the periodic return (that is, interest) that could have been earned by investing those funds. For example, if closing costs and the downpayment are $5,000, and if the homeowner can earn 10 percent annually from an investment, then the foregone return on the closing costs and downpayment is $500 annually ($5,000 × .10) or approximately $41.67 monthly ($5,000 × .10 × 1/12).

MORTGAGE PAYMENT

- *Principal and Interest Payment.* In most cases the homeowner borrows money to purchase the house and repays the loan by making periodic payments over time. The payments are called *mortgage payments.* Part of each mortgage payment goes toward reducing the loan amount and is called the principal payment. The rest of each mortgage payment is interest due on the outstanding loan and is called the interest payment. The meaning and calculation of these payments are examined in detail in a later section.

- *Property Taxes.* The homeowner usually must pay property taxes on the value of the house and land. In most cases periodic (e.g., monthly) payments earmarked for property taxes are made to the homeowner's mortgage lender.

- *Hazard Insurance.* Similarly in most cases the homeowner's mortgage lender requires that the buyer purchase hazard insurance for the house to protect it from specified disasters. Again, the mortgage lender generally collects monthly payments from the homeowner and earmarks them for hazard insurance.

- *Operating and Maintenance Costs.* The homeowner faces periodic costs for heating and cooling, electricity, repairs, and maintenance on the house.

Factors Reducing the Cost of Homeownership

Homeownership enjoys tax benefits and investment characteristics which effectively reduce the "out-of-pocket" costs of owning a house. In essence, these are "negative costs;" that is, they should be subtracted each period from the total of the periodic costs outlined above.

Tax Deductions

The homeowner benefits from substantial tax deductions by being able to deduct from federal and state taxable income property taxes and the interest paid on the mortgage loan. To the extent that such deductions reduce taxes paid by the homeowner, the deductions reduce the cost of homeownership.

In Chapter 3 you learned that the value of tax deductions is the amount by which the deductions reduce taxes paid. To review, the reduction in taxes is dependent on two factors: the taxpayer's marginal tax rate and the amount by which the new deductions increase the taxpayer's total deductions. The (annual) value of the homeownership deductions is:

> Homeowner's marginal tax rate × (annual
> interest paid on mortgage loan + annual
> property taxes – standard deduction).

Notice that this calculation can result in a negative number. This occurs if the homeownership tax deductions are less than the standard deduction. In this case the homeownership tax deductions are worth nothing to the homeowner, and the homeowner is better off taking the standard deduction. Notice that the bigger the standard deduction, the smaller the tax benefits of homeowning.

If the homeowner has other tax deductions which total more than the standard deduction, then the annual value of the homeownership deductions is simply:

> Homeowner's marginal tax rate × (annual
> interest paid on mortgage loan + annual
> property taxes).

The marginal tax rate used is the combined federal and state marginal tax rates, *not* including the Social Security tax rate. (Why?)

EXAMPLE 4-1: Jim and Sherry Smith just bought a house for which they will pay $8000 in interest on their mortgage loan and $2000 in property taxes the first year. Their marginal tax rates are 28 percent for the federal government and 7 percent for their state government. The standard deduction for both the federal and state income taxes is $7350. What is the approximate value of their homeownership tax deductions in the first year?

ANSWER:

> Federal taxes saved equal:
> $.28 \times (\$8000 + \$2000 - \$7350) = \$742.00$
> State taxes saved equal:
> $.07 \times (\$8000 + \$2000 - \$7350) = \underline{\$185.50}$
> Total taxes saved equal: $\$927.50$

EXAMPLE 4-2: Now what if Jim and Sherry had substantial medical expenses such that their other deductions totaled $8500, which is greater than the standard deduction for both the federal and state governments. What is the approximate value of their first year home-ownership tax deductions?

ANSWER:

Federal taxes saved equal:

$.28 \times (\$8000 + \$2000) = \$2800$

State taxes saved equal:

$.07 \times (\$8000 + \$2000) = \underline{\$700}$

Total taxes saved equal: $\$3500$

Another tax benefit of homeownership occurs when the house is sold. Federal tax law allows the homeowner to escape income taxes on any profits of up to $250,000 for single taxpayers, and up to $500,000 for married taxpayers made from the sale of a house if the homeowner has used the house as a principal residence for at least two of the five years before the sale. Many states have similar laws. In the decisions examined in later topics, it will be assumed that homeowners escape taxes on profits made from the sale of their house.

Appreciation

Houses are durable goods which last a long time. As such, a house is an investment. The value of a house can rise, fall, or remain constant over time. If a house increases in value over time, it is said to appreciate. Appreciation is an investment return to the homeowner; that is, if appreciation occurs it is a benefit, or gain, to homeownership. Therefore, appreciation effectively reduces the cost of homeownership. Houses appreciated in value rapidly in the 1970s. During that period it was not uncommon for a house to appreciate by 12–15 percent annually. For many consumers this meant that it actually paid them to be homeowners.

For example, consider a house initially worth $50,000. Suppose it costs the owner $7000 annually in out-of-pocket costs to pay the mortgage, taxes, insurance, and operating and maintenance expenses. Also suppose the owner saves $1000 in taxes due to the homeownership tax deductions. If the house appreciates 15 percent during the year, this means a gain of $50,000 × .15, or $7500 to the owner. Since tax savings and appreciation effectively reduce the cost of home-ownership, the actual cost to the homeowner is $7000 – $1000 – $7500, or –$1500. That is, in this case it actually paid the consumer $1500 during the year to be a homeowner. Of course, the $7500 in appreciation would not be realized until the owner sold the house. (Investment analysts would call this a paper gain.) Alternatively, the owner could convert some of the appreciation to cash by taking out a loan based on realized appreciation—this is called a second mortgage or home equity loan and will be discussed later.

The Bottom Line

The tax deductions of homeowning reduce the dollar cost of owning. Appreciation in the house's value also reduces the cost of owing, but this benefit isn't realized until the house is sold or if the owner borrows against the house's equity.

4. How Good of an Investment Is a Home?

The previous section pointed out the importance of appreciation as a benefit to homeowning which reduces the cost, and increases the return, of owning a home. But how big has the appreciation in homes been? Have homes been an instant road to wealth?

In judging how good of an investment a home has been, it's important to be careful about what statistics are used. The news media frequently quotes statistics on home appreciation rates. Most of these quoted rates are misleading because they simply compare prices of houses that were sold this year to prices of houses sold last year. But if the houses sold this year are larger, or have more features, they should sell for more. What matters to the homeowner or homebuyer is how the *same* house has appreciated in value. The best statistic to use is the Housing Price Index (HPI) published by the Federal Housing Finance Agency. The HPI measures average price changes in repeat sales or refinancing on the *same* properties. The HPI serves as a timely, accurate measure of house price trends in the United States.

Figure 4-2 shows appreciation rates for homes, calculated from HPI, compared to rates of return for a broad stock portfolio (the S&P 500, including dividends) and 6 month Treasury securities for 1992–2012. Homes and Treasury securities have provided similar rates of return, but stocks have clearly been the superior investment.

Figure 4-3 shows how $100 invested in a home, a Treasury security, or the stock market would have grown over 1992–2012. Stocks (with dividends re-invested) win for

Figure 4-2. Home appreciation rate (based on Housing Price Index) vs. rates of return in stocks and short-terms Treasury securities.

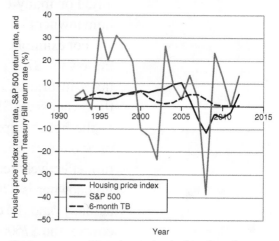

Data sources: Housing price index data from the Federal Housing Finance Agency. S&P 500 index data from Federal Reserve Bank of St. Louis. Six-month Treasury bill rate from the Federal Reserve System.

the entire period, followed by Treasury securities and homes. However, it should be noted that stock investment also had higher risk compared to Treasure security and housing.

A different way of looking at homes as investments is shown in Figure 4-4. In understanding Figure 4-4, first consider this proposition.

MEASURING HOUSE APPRECIATION RATES

C O N S U M E R   T O P I C

Newscasts frequently report something like the following: "The average price of a house sold this year is X percent greater than the average price of a house sold last year." Unknowing homeowners apply this information to their own house and expect that their house also increased X percent in value during the year.

But this isn't a correct assumption because comparing prices of houses sold this year to prices of houses sold last year is similar to comparing apples and oranges. There is no assurance that the houses sold this year were of the same size, had the same number of baths and bedrooms, and had the same amenities as the houses sold last year. In fact, it is likely that the average characteristics of houses sold this year are different than the average characteristics of houses sold last year. So, for example, if the houses sold this year are bigger and have more amenities, then that will account for part of their higher price.

The Federal Housing Finance Agency publishes the Housing Price Index (HPI) that measures average price changes in repeat sales or refinancing on the same properties. The National Realtors Association, on the other hand, publishes housing appreciation rate based on actual home sales. Fortunately, the appreciation rates have followed a similar pattern. Of the 21 years compared, the appreciation rate for homes with the same characteristics was lower in 11 years and higher in 10 years compared to the appreciation rate of homes actually sold.

So listen to and read news reports about house appreciation rates very carefully. The appreciation rate that the homeowner should be most interested in is the appreciation rate for houses with the same characteristics.

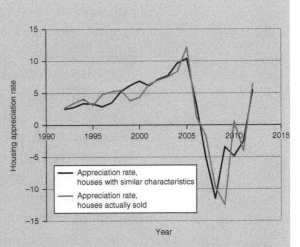

Data sources: Appreciation rates for houses with similar characteristics are based on housing price index data from the Federal Housing Finance Agency. Appreciation rate for houses actually sold from National Realtors Association.

Suppose you can borrow money at 5 percent interest. Also suppose you can deduct from your taxes all the interest paid on this loan, and let's say your tax bracket is 30 percent. Finally, suppose you can turn around and invest the borrowed funds and earn 9 percent interest. What is the effective cost of the 5 percent loan?

In order to answer this question, think first about the tax deduction. In the early years of the loan, when most of the loan payment is interest, the tax-deduction means the after-tax cost of borrowing is 5% − (.3 × 5%) = 3.5%. Next, you can invest this money and earn 9%, so your profit is 9% − 3.5% or 5.5%. So it actually pays to borrow after considering tax deductions and earnings by investing the borrowed funds. Stated another way, you can say the cost of borrowing in the example is −5.5%. This number is called the "real" after-tax cost of borrowing. The real after-tax cost of borrowing is negative when the value of tax deductions and investment returns exceed the cost of the loan; if they don't, real after-tax cost of borrowing is positive.

This way of looking at the cost of borrowing can be applied to

Figure 4-3. Value accumulations in homes, stocks and Treasury securities from 1992 to 2012.

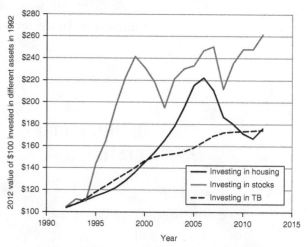

Data sources: Housing price index data from the Federal Housing Finance Agency. S&P 500 index data from Federal Reserve Bank of St. Louis. Six-month Treasury bill rate from the Federal Reserve System.

Figure 4-4. Real after-tax mortgage interest rates*.

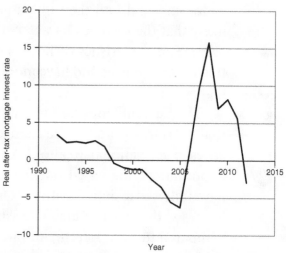

*Mortgage interest rates (1–30%)-house appreciation rate.

Data sources: Mortgage interest rate data from the Federal Reserve System. Housing price index data from the Federal Housing Finance Agency.

REAL AFTER-TAX MORTGAGE INTEREST RATE

homebuying. In this case the "real after tax mortgage interest rate" is calculated, which is the mortgage rate adjusted for tax deductions and further adjusted for the rate of house appreciation. Consider the rate of house appreciation to be the investment rate of return. Figure 4-4 shows the real after tax mortgage interest rate for 1992–2012. The real after-tax mortgage rate was very low in late 1990s and early to mid 2000s before the financial crisis of 2007 and the housing market downturn. This is one big reason why purchasing a home was so popular during that time.

The Bottom Line

Although not as good as the stock market in the 1990s, homes have provided steady investment returns.

5. Should You Own or Rent?

For many, owning a home is like apple pie and baseball—it's the American way of living. In fact, a greater percentage of Americans own homes than do citizens of any other country (including Japan). Some go so far as to think that a person is financially ignorant not to own a home. In the late 1970s—the "go-go" years of the homebuying market—this may have been true.

Today, homebuying requires a more thoughtful decision. After weighing the pluses and minuses of owning versus renting, many consumers find that renting is the financially smart option to take.

The decision to rent or to own shelter involves a consideration of many factors, with both owning and renting having certain advantages and disadvantages. Mobility is generally easier if you rent rather than own. It takes a considerable amount of time and expense when a homeowner desires to sell and move, whereas the consumer who rents can leave after the lease expires. On the other hand, owning gives you more control over the shelter than renting, which means the consumer who owns a house has greater ability to alter the structure to his/her preferences and tastes. With owning, the homeowner controls how much maintenance and upkeep are done to the dwelling, whereas in renting the landlord makes those decisions. The landlord's desires for maintenance and upkeep may not be the same as the tenant's desires. Additionally, the homeowner, as a property owner, possibly has more influence on public affairs in the community.

This section concentrates on evaluating the *financial* differences between renting and owning shelter. As you probably know, substantial *cost* differences are involved between renting and owning. Renting includes monthly payments to a landlord plus (usually) separate monthly payments for operating costs (utilities, etc.). As outlined

DETERMINANTS OF HOUSING APPRECIATION RATES

House values skyrocketed in the 1970s, slowed down in the 1980s and early1990s, but rose again in mid 1990s through mid 2000s until the financial crisis of 2007, when the housing market took a major downturn. Why do house values go up and down? This has been a question subjected to much research by economists interested in the housing markets. Before the financial crisis of 2007, three answers have resulted from this research: inflation, tax rates, and demographics.

In the 1970s inflation exploded: from 4 percent annually in the early 1970s to over 12 percent annually by the late 1970s. People who had invested in fixed rate investments, such as bonds or CDs, lost money; so they turned to "real asset" investments, such as gold, land, and houses, as havens for their money. Real asset investments are preferred during times of accelerating inflation because their value can automatically increase to keep pace with inflation. So the demand for houses as "inflation hedges" helped keep their value at pace with, and often exceeding, inflation.

In the 1970s federal income tax brackets were not indexed to inflation. This meant that as inflation pushed wages and salaries higher, taxpayers found themselves in high tax brackets. This meant that taxpayers paid a greater percentage of their income in federal taxes, even though the increase in wages and salaries only kept pace with the increase in prices. This was called "tax-flation," and it gave taxpayers an added incentive to invest in tax shelters. Since one of the easiest and well-known tax shelters was (and is) homeownership, "tax-flation" motivated investors to further increase the demand for homeownership, thereby adding to the appreciation rates achieved by homes.

The third factor explaining the superior investment performance in the 1970s was demographics. By the 1970s many of the "Baby-Boomers" had reached their 20s, thus causing an explosion in the number of first-time homebuyers. The increase in demand by first-time buyers caused an increase in demand for all houses as many owners traded up. The result, of course, was higher housing prices.

In the 1980s and 1990s these three factors, inflation, tax-flation, and demographics, reversed and meant a slowdown in housing appreciation rates. Largely due to policies followed by the Federal Reserve System, the annual inflation rate has been reduced to low single digits in the 1980s and 1990s. The attraction of homes as inflation hedges was therefore reduced.

"Tax-flation" in the federal tax code was eliminated in the 1980s. Federal tax brackets are now indexed to inflation, meaning that increases in a taxpayer's salary which is equal to the average inflation rate will not push the taxpayer into a higher tax bracket. Furthermore, federal tax brackets were dramatically lowered in the 1980s (the top federal tax rate was lowered from 70 percent to 33 percent). Both the indexing and lowering of federal tax brackets substantially reduced the benefit of homes as tax shelters.

C
O
N
S
U
M
E
R

T
O
P
I
C

Finally, a dramatic demographic change began in the 1980s. The "Baby Bust" of the late 1960s and 1970s began to show up as a *reduction* in the number of first time homebuyers in the late 1980s and 1990s. The housing market no longer had the fuel of growing numbers of first time buyers to propel it.

However, the housing boom from mid 1990s to mid 2000s has been attributed mainly to the unsustainable easing of mortgage lending standards during that time period. Such easing of lending standards led to a large amount of subprime mortgage lending (meaning making loans to people who may have difficulty maintaining the repayment schedule). Although such subprime lending led to initial high demand for housing that created the housing boom, the eventual rise of subprime mortgage delinquencies and foreclosures triggered a global financial crisis in 2007–2008 and a bust of the housing bubble.

Reference: N. Gregory Mankiw and David N, Weil. *The Baby Boom, the Baby Bust, and the Housing Market*. Working Paper No. 2794, National Bureau of Economic Research.

Luca Agnello & Ludger Schuknecht, 2011. *Booms and Busts in Housing Markets: Determinants and Implications*. Journal of Housing Economics, 20(3): 171–190.

John V. Duca, John Muellbauer, and Anthony Murphy, 2012. Shifting credit standards and the boom and bust in U.S. house prices. CEPR Discussion Paper No. DP8361. Available at http://demo2.sunnyvision.com/hkimr/uploads/seminars/3/sem_paper_0_441_oxdal-2012-june-8-us-house-prices-jd-jm-am.pdf

earlier, homeowning includes a large initial outlay for down-payment and closing expenses plus monthly payments for mortgage financing, taxes, insurance, and operating and maintenance costs. Also, as emphasized, homeownership enjoys substantial tax benefits which effectively reduce the cost of owning a house. Finally, the house can appreciate in value over time, which is a benefit to the owner.

The procedure for evaluating the *financial* differences between homeowning and renting boils down to this. Homebuyers should look at a house in two ways— as a place to live, but also as an investment. The investment part of the home is tied to the rate at which it appreciates in value after it is bought. The faster the home appreciates, the better it is as an investment.

The question then is this: Are you better-off (a) investing in a home, taking the tax benefits, and profiting from future appreciation, or (b) renting, probably spending less money, and being able to invest those saved funds elsewhere? Since future appreciation in the home's value is the major unknown, the real question is: At what average annual rate must a given home *appreciate* in value in order for homeownership to be preferred as an investment to renting and investing saved funds elsewhere?

The Procedure

The procedure for evaluating homeownership as an investment involves eight steps.[4] The goal of the procedure is to find the average annual rate of appreciation in the house such that at rates above this breakeven rate, home-ownership is preferred to renting, and at rates below this break-even rate, renting is preferred to homeownership.

Step 1:   Select a Holding Period for the Comparison

HOLDING PERIOD

First, select a period of time over which to compare homeowning to renting. At the beginning of this period we'll assume that you either purchase a home or sign a rental agreement, and at the end of the holding period you either sell the home or end the rental agreement. Let's call this holding period "n".

C O N S U M E R   T O P I C

THE TOWNHOUSE MARKET

All homes aren't created equal. Single family detached structures make up the largest part of the homeownership market. But in the last thirty years attached units, so-called townhouses, have also become an important part of the homeownership market.

Since single family detached structures and townhouses provide different characteristics, homebuyers don't consider them as perfect substitutes. Single family detached units provide more privacy than townhouses, whereas townhouses are usually cheaper per square foot of space. In general, a majority of homebuyers prefer single family, detached units to townhouses.

The demands for family detached units and townhouses respond differently to changes in mortgage interest rates. When mortgage interest rates fall, buying both single family units and townhouses becomes less expensive. But since the majority of buyers prefer detached units to townhouses, the demand for detached units increases much more than the demand for townhouses. In contrast, when mortgage interest rates rise, more buyers shift to townhouses due to their lower cost per square foot. Thus, townhouse demand can actually increase when interest rates rise.

---

[4] Waiden, Michael L. "A Simple Procedure for Evaluating Homeownership as an Investment". Journal of Consumer Affairs, Vol. 17, No. 2. © 1983. Reprinted by permission of the University of Wisconsin Press.

Step 2:   Calculate the Future Value of Net One-Time Costs of Homeownership

NET ONE-TIME
HOMEOWNERSHIP
COSTS

As described earlier, purchasing a home involves some substantial initial "one-time" costs, primarily in terms of the downpayment and closing costs. In comparison, the major initial one-time cost of renting is a modest security deposit. The net one-time costs of homeownership, which are calculated as the sum of the downpayment and closing costs minus the security deposit that would have been paid with renting, represent funds which you could have invested if renting had been chosen. Therefore, one opportunity cost of buying a home is the investment fund that could have been accumulated if the net one-time homeownership costs had been invested for the term of the holding period. Using an appropriate after-tax interest rate, this investment fund should be calculated to the end of the holding period using future value factors (FVF). Selected values of FVF are in Appendix Table A-1.

Step 3:   Calculate the Total Future Value of Monthly "Net Homeownership Investment Costs"

MONTHLY NET
HOMEOWNERSHIP
INVESTMENT COST

As a homeowner you must pay monthly homeownership costs equal to the sum of mortgage payments, property taxes, hazard insurance, and operating and maintenance expenses. These costs are reduced by any taxes which you save by being a homeowner. If you rent, you face monthly costs equal to the sum of rent plus any utility expenses paid separately from rent. Therefore, the monthly costs of homeowning exceed the monthly costs of renting by the amount: mortgage payment + property taxes + home hazard insurance costs + home operating and maintenance expenses − tax savings from homeownership − alternative rental costs. This amount is called the monthly "net homeownership investment cost." Again, these funds represent amounts which you could have invested if renting is chosen as the shelter option. Therefore, another opportunity cost of homeowning is the investment fund that could have been accumulated if the monthly net homeownership investment costs had been invested for the term of the holding period. Using an appropriate after-tax interest rate, this investment fund should also be calculated to the end of the holding period.

Step 4:   Calculate the Outstanding Loan Balance

The final outstanding loan balance represents funds which the homeowner owes to the lender. Any investment return from homeownership must be net of the final outstanding loan balance. Use either a financial calculator or Appendix Table A-7 for 30 year mortgages and Appendix Table A-8 for 15 year mortgages to calculate the loan balance at the end of the holding period.

Step 5: Sum the Results of Steps 2, 3, and 4

The sum of steps 2 and 3 represents that part of the house's value at the end of the holding period which is necessary to at least equal the investment accumulation that could be earned by renting and investing saved funds elsewhere. The result of step 4, of course, represents that part of the house's value at the end of the holding period which is necessary to cover the final outstanding loan balance, selling costs, and rental security deposit (if any). The sum of steps 2, 3 and 4 is termed the "minimum required future house value."

Step 6: Find the Breakeven Selling Price Taking into Consideration Realtor's Commission

The "minimum required future house value" requires one more adjustment before we can move to the next step. Typically consumers buy and sell houses through realtors. Realtors charge a commission to the seller when a house is sold. The commission often is 6% of the selling price but it can be lower in some cases. You need to add that commission to your "minimum required future house value" to come up with your "breakeven selling price." Assume the commission is 6%, the breakeven selling price is

$$Breakeven\ selling\ price = \frac{Minimum\ required\ future\ house\ value}{1-6\%}$$

Step 7: Find the Breakeven Annual Rate of Housing Value Appreciation

Let's call the breakeven annual rate of housing value appreciation associated with the breakeven selling price "A". "A" can be found by applying the following formula, where "n" is the holding period:

$$A = (\frac{minimum\ breakeven\ selling\ price}{initial\ house\ value})^{\frac{1}{n}} - 1$$

You can also find the value of "A" in the annual future value table (Appendix Table A-1) for the corresponding holding period "n".

Step 8: Compare the Calculated Breakeven Rate of Housing Value Appreciation to Forecasts of Housing Value Appreciation

As a final step you should gather forecasts of future housing value appreciation rates. These forecasts, to the extent possible, should be specific as to the house type and location being evaluated. From an investment perspective, if the forecasts indicate expected appreciation rates greater than the calculated breakeven rate, then homeownership is preferred to renting. If the forecasts indicate expected appreciation rates less than the calculated breakeven rate, then renting is preferred to homeownership. Figure 4-5 summarizes the procedure.

Figure 4-5. The own vs. rent comparison procedure.

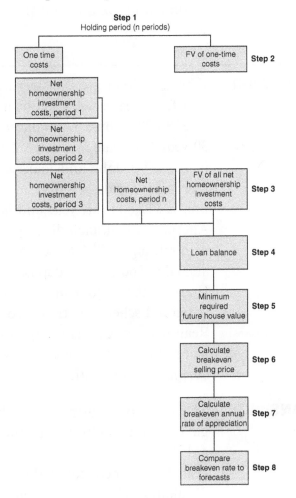

Two warnings should be sounded about the procedure. First, the procedure does not consider non-financial differences between home-ownership and renting. Abstracting from investment considerations, the accepted wisdom is that most consumers prefer homeownership to renting shelter. If the forecast of the annual rate of housing value appreciation is greater than the derived breakeven rate of appreciation, then non-financial aspects of homeownership need not be considered. If, however, the forecast of the annual rate of housing value apprecia-tion is less than the derived breakeven rate of appreciation, then you must subjectively decide if your preference for homeownership is worth the estimated foregone investment rate of return.

Second, the own-rent comparison may not be exact if the housing services supplied by owning and by renting are not approximately the same. For example, the alternative rental unit may be a much smaller dwelling unit than the house being considered for purchase. In this case, part of the annual net homeownership investment costs is due to the greater amount of housing services provided by the house. Therefore, for the procedure to be most effective, the house and rental unit should be similar in size and amenities.

EXAMPLE 4-3: John and Joan are considering buying a $350,000 house and living in it for three years. The down payment is 20% for a total of $70,000 so $280,000 would be financed at an 8% mortgage interest rate for a 30-year fixed rate mortgage. Other homeownership costs are as stated in Table 4-3. John and Joan's combined federal and state marginal tax rate is 35% and they have no other deductions. The standard deduction is $12,000 this year and is expected to increase by 5% each year. Alternative rent, including operating and maintenance costs associated with renting, is $1,800 per month in the first year and increases by 5% annually. The security deposit is $1,000 and is returned with no interest. However the forgone interest amount on the deposit is small enough in the grand scheme of things so it can be omitted from the calculation. Realtor commissions are 6% of the house's sales price. To reduce the number of calculations, do the own-rent analysis on an annual basis except for computations related to mortgage.

ANSWER: The value of housing tax deductions equals the homeowner's marginal tax rate multiplied by the housing tax deductions less the standard deduction ($12,000 in year 1, $12,600 in year 2, and $13,230 in year 3). Tax benefits in the first year are 35% x ($22,315 + $5,000-$12,000) = $5,360; tax benefits in the second year are 35% × ($22,121 + $5,000-$12,600) = $5,082; tax benefits in the third year are 35% x ($21,911+$5,000-$13,230) = $4,788.

The calculations of the procedure for evaluating owning vs. renting follow the steps outlined earlier.

Step 1: Select a Holding Period for the Comparison

The holding period is given as 3 years. That means n = 3.

Step 2: Calculate the Future Value of Net One-Time Costs of Homeownership

The net one-time costs of homeownership are $70,000 + $8,000 = $78,000. This amount represents money which John and Joan could invest if they rented. Using a 6% after-tax rate of return (i = 6%), the investment accumulation at the end of holding period is $78,000 × FVF(n=3, r=6%)=$78,000 × (1+6%)^3 = $78,000 × 1.191016 = $92,899.

A HOUSE OR A CHILD

C
O
N
S
U
M
E
R

T
O
P
I
C

Economics is called the "dismal science" in part because it forces us to consider trade-offs. Our limited resources mean we can't have everything we want, when we want it.

For many consumers, the shelter choice is not between a house and an apartment, but is between a house and a child. Children are expensive. Estimates indicate that a child costs a family $8,760 to $24,510 annually depending on the child's age and the family's income. This is money that could be used for a downpayment and for meeting the annual costs of owning a house.

The "trap" that many young families put themselves into is this. A couple marries and has a child immediately. The expenses of the child prevent them from accumulating enough savings to be able to buy and afford a house. Consequently, the couple must rent. The "trap" is deepened if the couple has additional children. Only when the couple's careers "take-off" are they financially able to afford both a house and children. However, this may only occur eight to twelve years after the couple married.

An alternative choice for young couples is to delay having children until a house has been bought and is affordable. The disadvantage of this option is that it may mean a required delay in the first child of five to eight years.

Neither option may be pleasant for young couples—have children now but rent versus buy a house now but delay having children. Couples will have to take into account their age, the circumstances in which they want to raise children (house or apartment), and the financial path of their careers. However, the one benefit of economics is that it exposes the choices and forces the decision-makers to consider them. It's better for couples to think about the choices and plan a decision rather than just letting things happen.

Reference: U.S. Department of Agriculture, *Expenditures on Children by Families, 2011* at website, *www.usda.gov.*

Step 3:   Calculate the Total Future Value of Periodic Net Homeownership Investment Costs

The net homeownership investment costs are calculated as item (9) in Table 4-3. To review, these costs represent money which John and Joan would have available to invest at the end of each year if renting. Assuming that money can be invested at an after-tax interest rate of 6%, at the end of the holding period, the investment accumulation of year 1 savings is $8,294 \times FVF(n = 2, r = 6\%) = \$8,294 \times (1+6\%)^2 = \$9,313$; the investment accumulation of year 2 savings is $\$7,992 \times FVF(n=1, r=6\%) = \$7,992 \times (1+6\%)^1 = \$8,472$; and investment accumulation of

Table 4-3. Evaluating homeownership as an investment: An example

One-time initial costs

Down payment	70,000
Closing costs	8,000
Total one-time costs	78,000

Periodical (annual) costs	Year 1	Year 2	Year 3
(1) Mortgage payment	24,654	24,654	24,654
(2) Loan balance	277,661	275,128	272,384
(3) Mortgage interest	22,315	22,121	21,911
(4) Property tax	5,000	5,000	5,000
(5) Homeowner insurance	600	600	600
(6) Operating and maintenance costs	5,000	5,500	6,050
(7) Tax benefits	5,360	5,082	4,788
(8) Alternative rent	21,600	22,680	23,814
Net homeownership periodical costs: (1)+(4)+(5)+(6)-(7)-(8)	8,294	7,992	7,702

Rent vs. own computation:

Step 1. Holding period	3
Step 2. Future value (FV) of net one-time costs of homeownership: $78,000 \times (1+6\%)^3$	92,899
Step 3. FV of net periodical costs: $8,294 \times (1+6\%)^2 + \$7,992 \times (1+6\%)^1 + \$7,702$	25,493
Step 4. Loan balance at the end of holding period	272,384
Step 5. Sum of results 2, 3, 4: $92,899+\$25,493+\$272,384$	390,777
Step 6. Breakeven selling price assuming 6% commission: $390,777/(1-6\%)$	415,720
Step 7. Breakeven annual rate of housing appreciation: $(\$415,720/\$350,000)^{(1/3)}-1$	5.90%

year 3 savings is simply $7,702 (no investment interest because that is at the end of the holding period). The total investment accumulation of all three years of net homeownership periodical costs is thus $9,313 + $8,472+$7,702 = $25,493.

Step 4:   Calculate the Outstanding Loan Balance

The outstanding loan balance at the end of the holding period is given in Table 4-3 as $272,384.

Step 5:   Sum the Results of Steps 2, 3, and 4.

Summing up the results of steps 2, 3, and 4 give us the minimum required future house value: $92,899+$25,493+$272,384=$390,777

Step 6:   Find the Breakeven selling price taking into consideration realtor's commission

Taking into consideration 6% realtor's commission, the minimum selling price needs to be $390,777/(1–6%)=$415,720

Step 7:   Find the Breakeven Annual Rate of Housing Value Appreciation

Using the formula given Step 7 above, the breakeven annual rate of appreciation needs to be ($415,720/$350,000)$^{(1/3)}$-1=5.90%

Step 8:   Compare the Breakeven Rate of Housing Value Appreciation to Forecasts of Housing Value Appreciation

If John and Joan find consensus forecasts of housing value appreciation rates above 5.90 percent annually, then homeownership is the preferred choice to renting. If the forecasts are below 5.90 percent, then John and Joan need to decide if any non-financial benefits of homeownership are worth the estimated foregone investment rate of return. For example, if houses are forecasted to appreciate 3 percent annually, then John and Joan would lose an annual investment return of approximately 2.90 percent by purchasing a home. In this case John and Joan must decide if any non-financial benefits of homeownership are worth giving up a 2.90 percent investment rate of return annually.

Some Answers

Every homebuyer's situation is different. The procedure for evaluating owning versus renting allows a homebuyer to "customize" the analysis to his situation.

Nevertheless, it is useful to have some answers for "typical," or "average," homebuying situations. Table 4-4 shows the minimum annual home appreciation rates required to make homeowning preferred to renting for six homebuying situations.

Two conclusions are obvious from the results. First, homebuying is more preferred to renting the higher the buyer's tax bracket. For example, for a $100,000 home purchased with a 9 percent mortgage and the owner staying 10 years, the house must appreciate annually at least

4.3 percent for owning to be better if the owner's tax bracket is 15 percent, but the appreciation rate can be as low as 3.6 percent if the owner is in the 33 percent tax bracket. Second, homebuying is more preferred to renting the longer the homeowner stays in the home. In fact, in some cases for 30 years of stay in the house, the home could actually depreciate in value and still be better than renting.

The Bottom Line

Owning is better than renting the higher your tax bracket and the longer you expect to stay in the house. If you expect to stay in the home less than 5 years, then homeowning should be evaluated very carefully.____

Table 4-4 Minimum annual rate of appreciation required for a home to make owning better than renting.

House purchase price: $200,000					
9% mortgage, 6% alternative investment rate			11% mortgage, 8% alternative investment rate		
#Yrs. Stay in House	Tax Bracket			Tax Bracket		
	15%	28%	33%	15%	28%	33%
2	8.7%	7.7%	7.3%	10.7%	9.3%	8.8%
5	5.1%	4.1%	3.7%	7.1%	5.8%	5.2%
10	3.9%	3.0%	2.7%	6.0%	4.8%	4.4%
20	2.4%	1.5%	1.1%	5.3%	4.1%	3.7%
30	–0.7%	–3.3%	–4.9%	4.7%	2.9%	2.1%

House purchase price: $100,000					
9% mortgage, 6% alternative investment rate			11% mortgage, 8% alternative investment rate		
#Yrs. Stay in House	Tax Bracket			Tax Bracket		
	15%	28%	33%	15%	28%	33%
2	9.2%	8.4%	8.2%	11.1%	10.1%	9.7%
5	5.6%	5.0%	4.7%	7.5%	6.6%	6.2%
10	4.3%	3.8%	3.6%	6.4%	5.6%	5.3%
20	2.7%	2.1%	1.8%	5.6%	4.6%	4.3%
30	0.0%	–2.4%	–4.0%	5.0%	3.5%	3.0%

		House purchase price: $70,000				
	9% mortgage, 6% alternative investment rate			11% mortgage, 8% alternative investment rate		
#Yrs. Stay in House	Tax Bracket			Tax Bracket		
	15%	28%	33%	15%	28%	33%
2	9.5%	9.0%	8.9%	11.4%	10.7%	10.4%
5	5.9%	5.6%	5.4%	7.9%	7.2%	7.0%
10	4.4%	4.1%	3.9%	6.6%	6.0%	5.8%
20	2.8%	2.3%	2.1%	5.7%	4.9%	4.6%
30	0.2%	−1.7%	−2.6%	5.1%	3.8%	3.3%

ASSUMPTIONS–FOR HOMEOWNING: Purchaser is married couple making 10% downpayment, closing costs equal to 4% of loan amount, fixed rate, 30-year mortgage, with 1 discount point, property tax equal to 1.2% of house value, annual home operating and maintenance costs equal to 3% of house value, hazard insurance of $3 per $1000; ASSUMPTIONS–FOR RENTING: Annual rent equals to 7.7% of initial house value, rental operating costs equal to 20% of rent. Operating and maintenance costs, hazard insurance, the standard deduction, and rent increase at an annual inflation rate of 4%.

6. Is There a Best Time to Buy a House?

Figure 4-6. Mortgage payment, constant-quality houses using fixed rate mortgage

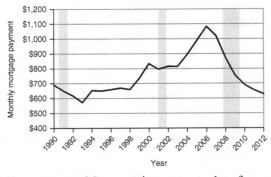

Year

Data sources: Mortgage interest rate data from the Federal Reserve System. Housing price index data from the Federal Housing Finance Agency. Mortgage payments computed assuming 20% down payment, average mortgage rate for 30-year conventional mortgage, and median housing price of $97,300 in 1990 (The Statistical Abstract of the United States) indexed by the Housing Price Index.

Realtors will say that the answer to the above question is "now." Realtors usually tell homebuyers that there is no advantage to waiting to buy a house—even if interest rates fall, the constant increase in prices of homes will swamp any savings in borrowing costs.

This isn't always true! If the prices of "constant-quality houses," that is, houses similar with respect to floor area, number of stories, number of bathrooms, lot size, presence or absence of air-conditioning, etc., are used to calculate the monthly mortgage payment on newly purchased houses, you can see that mortgage payments have generally risen from 1990 to 2006 before declines between 2006 and 2012. However, even during years of rise there were slowdowns or declines. Figure 4-6 shows that, holding quality equal, the monthly mortgage payment for an average house declined between 1990 and 1993, and then again between 2000 and 2001. This good news for consumers usually occurs at the end of, or immediately following, the economic bad news of a recession. In Figure 4-6 the shaded time periods indicate a national economic recession. At the end of such recession, or immediately following the recession, mortgage payments either stop rising or even decline. This is because a recession ultimately leads to lower interest rates and lower housing prices.

The Bottom Line

During periods of economic growth, buying a home now is better than buying a home later because mortgage payment are rising. But during economic recessions, it is better to wait to buy until after the recession because mortgage payments will fall. _____

C O N S U M E R   T O P I C

TRADING-UP

Trading-up refers to the selling of a home and the use of the equity and profit from that sale to purchase a larger home. Real estate agents often recommend trading-up as a strategy for improving a family's shelter at regular intervals and gaining wealth along the way.

For trading-up to work, however, homes must be appreciating at rates high enough to compensate for the realtor fees associated with sale of a house and the one-time costs associated with purchase of another house., The example below shows a situation where trading-up doesn't work and a situation where it does, The big difference in these two situations is the home's appreciation rate. At the higher appreciation rate trading-up works; at the lower appreciation rate, it doesn't,

	Trading-up doesn't work 8% appreciation	Trading-up works (15% appreciation)
Original price of 1st house	$200,000	$200,000
Sales price of 1st house	$216,000	$230,000
Appreciation gain	$16,000	$30,000
Equity gain from mortgage payments	$2,000	$2,000
TOTAL GROSS GAIN:	$18,000	$32,000
Realtor commission 6%	$12,960	$13,800
Closing costs on 2nd house	$8,000	$8,000
NET GAIN:	-$2,960	$10,200

Trading-up was popular, and profitable during housing boom years in the late 1970s, late 1990s and early 2000s when housing appreciation rates were high. With housing appreciation rates lower in the 1980s, early 1990s, and late 2000s homeowners must stay in their homes for longer time period before trading-up is profitable.

7. How Much of a Downpayment Should You Make?

For some homebuyers, especially first-time homebuyers, there's no decision to make about the down-payment. It usually takes all a first-time homebuyer's spare cash, plus maybe borrowing from relatives, to put together the minimum downpayment required to have the mortgage loan approved. If you're such a homebuyer you need read no further.

For homebuyers who can make more than the minimum downpayment, conflicting advice is often given about the suggested size of the downpayment. One side says to make a large downpayment in order to lower monthly mortgage payments and to increase ownership (equity) in the house. The other side says to make a smaller downpayment and take a larger loan in order to maximize the tax deductibility of mortgage interest costs and to use "other people's money" to purchase the house.

Neither side is necessarily correct. By now you should realize that there's an "opportunity cost" to making a larger downpayment. The opportunity cost is the interest which could have been earned if the homebuyer had invested the extra downpayment money. If a high enough interest rate can be earned by investing the extra downpayment money, then these investment returns will more than make up for the higher after-tax mortgage payments and reduced equity buildup in the house from a smaller downpayment. On the other hand, if only a low interest rate can be earned on the invested downpayment money, then the resulting investment returns will fall short of the extra after-tax mortgage payments and reduced equity.

An example is shown in Table 4-5. Ben borrows $100,000 at 10 percent interest, and Ben's tax bracket is 30 percent. Ben is trying to decide whether to make an extra $5,000 downpayment. When Ben can earn only a 7.25 percent interest rate on his investments, making the extra downpayment is financially wise. But when Ben can earn a 14.25 percent interest rate through investing, making the extra downpayment is not wise. In contrast, when the mortgage rate and investment rate are the same (10 percent), then using the $5,000 for an extra downpayment or investing the $5,000 is virtually a toss-up.

These results suggest a simple "rule of thumb"—use money for an extra downpayment if you can't invest that money at an interest rate higher than the mortgage interest rate. If you can invest the money in an investment paying an interest rate higher than the mortgage interest rate, then do so.

Unfortunately two other benefits of making a larger downpayment complicate this simple rule. First, since closing costs are a percentage of the loan amount, closing costs are lower for a higher downpayment. Second, private mortgage insurance costs are lower for higher downpayments. Private mortgage insurance is required on a conventional loan if the downpayment is 20 percent or less. Private mortgage insurance costs are higher for downpayments of 5 to 10 percent and lower for downpayments of 10 to 20 percent. The costs are added directly to the homebuyer's monthly mortgage payment.

The addition of these two other benefits of making a larger downpayment means that our simple rule of thumb must now be amended when considering downpayments of less than 20 percent. When the reduction of closing costs and private mortgage costs are included, the alternative investment interest rate must now be much higher than the mortgage interest rate for it to be wiser to invest money rather than add that money to the downpayment.

Table 4-6 shows the investment interest rates which must be exceeded for investing money to be better than adding that money to the downpayment for downpayment ratios of 20 percent or less. The very high interest rates for comparing 10 and 15 percent downpayments and for comparing 20 and 25 percent downpayments indicate that making an extra downpayment is most wise when doing so will put the homebuyer just over a 10 percent downpayment or just over a 20 percent downpayment. This is because at those two points the private mortgage insurance is reduced. Also, the necessary investment interest rates are lower, meaning that making the extra downpayment is less beneficial, the longer the homebuyer expects to stay in the house. This is because of the reduction in the private mortgage insurance rates for later years of the mortgage.

Table 4-5   Evaluation of making an extra downpayment.

Ben is examining the pros and cons of making an extra $5,000 downpayment on a $100,000 30-year mortgage charging 10% interest. Ben's tax bracket is 30%. Costs for the first 4 years are:

House purchase price: $100,000

	Year 1	Year 2	Year 3	Year 4	Loan Balance End of Yr. 4
Annual mtg. payment	$10,536	$10,536	$10,536	$10,536	
Tax savings	−2,992	−2,975	−2,956	−2,934	
After-tax payment	$ 7,544	$ 7,561	$ 7,580	$ 7,602	$97,402

House purchase price: $95,000

	Year 1	Year 2	Year 3	Year 4	Loan Balance End of Yr. 4
Annual mtg. payment	$10,009	$10,009	$10,009	$10,009	
Tax savings	−2,843	−2,826	−2,808	−2,788	
After-tax payment	$ 7,166	$ 7,183	$ 7,201	$ 7,221	$92,532
Savings if make extra	$ 7,544	$ 7,561	$ 7,580	$ 7,602	$97,402
downpayment	−7,166	−7,183	−7,201	−7,221	−92,532
	$ 378	$ 378	$ 379	$ 381	$ 4,870

If Ben can earn 7.25 percent on his investments, his after-tax investment rate is approximately 7.25% − (.3)(7.25%) = 5%. Using Appendix Table A-1, the future value of savings from making the larger downpayment is: $378(1.216) + $378(1.158) + $379(1.103) + $381(1.050) + $4,870 = $6,585.46. The future value of investing $5,000 for 4 yrs. at 5% is:$5,000(1.216) = $6,080.
Thus making the extra downpayment is financially better!

But, if Ben can earn 14.25 percent on his investments, his after-tax investment rate is approximately 14.25% − (.3)(14.25%) = 10%. Using Appendix Table A-1, the future value of savings from making the larger downpayment is:

$378(1.464) +$378(1.331) +$379(1.210) +$381(1.100) +$4,870 = $6,804.20.

The future value of investing $5,000 for 4 yrs. at 10% is: $5,000(1.464) =$7,320.
It's better to make a smaller downpayment and invest the $5,000.

But, if Ben can earn 10 percent on his investments, his after-tax investment rate is 10% − (.3) (10%) = 7%. Using Appendix Table A-1, the future value of savings from making the larger downpayment is:

$378(1.311) + $378(1.225) + $379(1.145) + $381(1.070) + $4,870 = $6,670.24.

The future value of investing $5,000 for 4 yrs. at 7% is:$5,000(1.311) = $6,555.
It's essentially a "wash" between using the $5,000 for an extra downpayment or investing the $5,000.

You might think that the advantage or disadvantage of making an extra downpayment depends on how fast the house appreciates in value. It doesn't. Regardless of the appreciation rate of the house, the difference in the homeowner's equity (house value minus outstanding loan balance) will remain the same for a given high downpayment and low downpayment.

Table 4-6 Minimum before-tax interest rate necessary to be earned on invested funds for lower downpayment to be better than higher downpayment

		5%	10%	15%	20%
Lower downpayment		5%	10%	15%	20%
Higher downpayment		10%	15%	20%	25%
9% mortgage					
Years of stay in house	2 years	12.5%	19.2%	12.5%	20.4%
	5	11.1	13.8	11.1	17.5
	10	10.4	12.4	10.4	16.5
	20	10.1	11.5	10.1	16.5
	30	10.1	11.4	10.1	16.5
11% mortgage					
Years of stay in house	2 years	15.3%	21.2%	15.3%	22.5%
	5	13.1	15.9	13.1	19.4
	10	12.4	14.5	12.4	18.6
	20	12.1	13.7	12.1	18.5
	30	12.1	13.7	12.1	18.5
13% mortgage					
Years of stay in house	2 years	17.3%	23.4%	17.3%	24.6%
	5	15.2	18.1	15.2	21.6
	10	14.5	16.7	14.5	20.8
	20	14.2	15.8	14.2	20.3
	30	14.2	15.8	14.2	20.3

Assumptions: 28% tax bracket, closing costs equal to 4% of loan amount, and the following private mortgage insurance schedule:

- for downpayments of 5% to 10%, 1% of loan amount plus $20 for first year and .25% of loan amount for each year thereafter;
- for downpayments of more than 10% to 20%, .5% of loan amount plus $20 for first year and .25% of loan amount for each year thereafter;
- for downpayments of over 20%, no private mortgage insurance.

The Bottom Line

Unless you're a very astute investor, making an extra downpayment is financially wise. However, don't rob the groceries, life insurance, or other necessities to do it!

C O N S U M E R   T O P I C

DO BROKERS EARN THEIR PAY?

Buyers use real estate brokers because they expect that brokers will find them a house that meets their needs and price range in a shorter time than buyers could by themselves. Sellers use brokers because they expect that brokers will be able to get a higher price for their house. Do we have evidence suggesting that brokers do perform these tasks?

One study by Donald Jud offers some interesting answers. Jud examined 529 house sales in North Carolina. Jud found that buyers using a broker did find a house in a shorter period of time. Buyers using a broker found a house in an average of 3.4 weeks, while buyers not using a broker took an average of 4 weeks to find a suitable house.

Do brokers earn their pay for sellers? Here Jud's findings are most interesting. Jud found that houses sold to buyers who used an agent to find the house did sell for more. However, Jud found no relationship between sales price and whether the house was *listed* by a broker or marketed by the owner.

Reference: G. Donald Jud. "Real Estate Brokers and the Market for Residential Housing." *American Real Estate and Urban Economics Association Journal,* Vol. 11, No. 1, Spring 1983, pp. 69–82.

8. Are Mortgages Rip-offs? The Meaning and Calculation of Mortgage Payments

Most homebuyers must deal with a mortgage. Few of us are fortunate enough to be able to come up with $100,000, $200,000, or $300,000 to buy a house outright. But consider this fact: If you take out a $200,000 mortgage at 8% interest rate for 30 years, you will repay $528,311 to the lender, not $200,000. That is, the $200,000 loan will be repaid, plus $328,311 in interest. That's right, the interest cost is more than the loan amount. Does this make the home mortgage a "rip-off?" Many say "yes," but the correct answer is "no."

First, look at the mortgage from the lender's perspective. If you borrow $200,000 today and repay the loan tomorrow, you owe the lender $200,000 plus some change in interest. The interest cost is low because you've used the lender's money for only a short period of time (one day). Even if you borrow the $200,000 for one year and then repay the loan, you will repay the lender $200,000 plus $16,000 in interest if the mortgage interest rate is 8 percent. Again, the interest cost is relatively small because you've used the lender's money for a short period of time (one year).

But most home mortgages are for 15 or 30 years. Although you don't use all of the lender's initial loan money for this entire length of time (with most mortgages, each mortgage payment includes some repayment of the loan—the principal payment), you are using some of the lender's money for the entire loan period. That's why the interest payment builds up to such a large amount— because you're borrowing the mortgage money for a long time. For example, if you borrowed $200,000 for 30 years and didn't repay any of the principal during the 30 year period, the simple interest costs would total $16,000 per year and $480,000 for the 30 years with an 8 percent loan. The fact that modern mortgages allow some payment of principal each month reduces the total interest charge to $328,311.

Another way to look at the mortgage is from the perspective of an investor. If you, as an investor, invested $200,000 in a security, like a Ginnie Mae security, that sent you a monthly check which included partial repayment of your money (principal) plus interest, then over 30 years you would receive a total of $528,311 in payments if the investment paid 8 percent interest. This is exactly how the lender looks at the investment of the home mortgage in the homebuyer.

Calculating Mortgage Payments

With the knowledge in hand that mortgages aren't rip-offs, yon can now move to a more technical discussion of how to calculate mortgage payments.

Consider a homebuyer taking out a $200,000 mortgage, paying 8 percent interest, and repaying the loan over 30 years. What should the homebuyer's mortgage payments be? The logical answer, keeping in mind the concepts of Chapter 1, is: *The mortgage payments should be such that the present value of the stream of mortgage payments, when discounted by the mortgage interest rate, equals the amount of the loan.* Given that mortgage payments are typically equal monthly payments, one can use the Present Value Factor Sum (PVFS) to convert all mortgage payments into present value. If we denote the loan amount as "L", the equal monthly mortgage payment as "M", the monthly interest rate as "rm", and the term of the mortgage (in months) as "n", then

$$L = M \times PVFS\,(r,n).$$

Typically the End-of-the-Month formula is used for mortgage payments computation. You can either use the Appendix Table A-6 to find out the PVFS for various combinations of interest rates and terms. Or, you can use the PVFS formula introduced earlier in this book:

$$PVFS(r,n) = \frac{1 - \frac{1}{(1+r)^n}}{r}$$

In the case of mortgage, because monthly compounding is used, we use monthly interest rate "rm" and number of months "n" in the PVFS computation. The monthly mortgage payments can be computed using:

$$M = \frac{L}{PVFS(rm,n)} = \frac{L}{1-\frac{\frac{1}{(1+rm)^n}}{rm}}$$

EXAMPLE 4-4: Bob wants to borrow $200,000 to purchase a house. The annual mortgage interest rate is 9 percent and the mortgage term is 30 years (360 months). What is the monthly mortgage payment?

Monthly interest rate rm = 9%/12 = 0.75% = 0.0075. n = 360 months. Monthly mortgage payment

$$M = \frac{L}{PVFS(rm,n)} = \frac{200,000}{1-\frac{\frac{1}{(1+0.0075)^{360}}}{0.0075}} = \frac{200,000}{124.2819} = \$1,609.25$$

You can also use Table A-6 to get the PVFS for 9% and 360 months. Because Table A-6 gives only three decimal points you get 124.282. Your monthly payment calculated using the table may be off by several cents due to rounding.

Calculating Principal and Interest Payments

Once the monthly mortgage payment is known, it is a straightforward procedure to divide each payment into principal and interest components. The interest payment equals the monthly interest rate multiplied by the outstanding loan balance. The principal payment equals the total mortgage payment minus the interest payment. The new outstanding loan balance equals the old outstanding loan balance minus the just made principal payment. The next period's division between principal and interest payments is then based on the new outstanding loan balance.

EXAMPLE 4-5: Calculate principal and interest payments for the first three months of the mortgage loan described in Example 4-4.

Original loan balance = $200,000
Monthly payment   = 1,609.25
Monthly interest rate = 9%/12=0.75%=0.0075

<u>Month 1:</u>
Interest payment   = Balance * Monthly interest rate = $200,000 × 0.0075 = $1,500
Principal payment   = Monthly mortgage payment – Interest payment = $1,609.25 – $1,500 = $109.25
New loan balance   = Original loan balance – Principal payment = $200,000 − $109.25 = $199,890.75

<u>Month 2:</u>

Interest payment = New loan balance * Monthly interest rate
= $199,890.75 × 0.0075 = $1,499.18

Principal payment = Monthly mortgage payment – Interest payment = $1,609.25–$1,499.18 = $110.06

New loan balance = End of month 1 balance – Principal payment
= $199,890.75 – $110.06 = $199,780.69

<u>Month 3:</u>

Interest payment = Month 2 loan balance * Monthly interest rate
= $199,780.69 × 0.0075=$1,498.36

Principal payment = Monthly mortgage payment – Interest payment = $1,609.25–$1,498.36 = $110.89

New loan balance = End of month 2 balance – Principal payment
= $199,780.69 - $110.89 = $199,669.90

Appendix Tables A-7 through A-12 gives loan balance factors for loans with terms of 30, 15, 5, 4, 3, and 2 years. The factor, when multiplied by the original loan amount, shows the remaining loan balance after a given number of years of payments have been made.

The Bottom Line

Mortgages are not "rip-offs." The reason the interest cost on mortgages is so high is because the homeowner takes a very long time to repay the mortgage. Mortgage payments can be calculated by using the rule that the present value sum of mortgage payments, when discounted by the mortgage interest rate, equals the mortgage loan.

9. How Much Home Can You Afford?

You can save time and trauma in shopping for a home if you know what you can afford. Old rules of thumb like, "You can afford a home 2½ times your income" are outdated in today's world of fluctuating interest rates.

How much home you can afford depends on the size of mortgage loan you acquire. Most mortgage lenders use a simple rule in evaluating whether to grant you a loan. The rule is that your monthly house payment, including the payment for the mortgage principal and interest, property taxes, and home hazard insurance, must be less than a certain percentage of your monthly gross income. Usually this percentage is around 28 percent, although it can be different at different lending institutions.

PITI
The monthly house payment for principal (P), interest (I), property taxes (T), and hazard insurance (I) is appropriately called the "PITI" payment.

EXAMPLE 4-6: The monthly principal and interest payment from the previous example is $1,609.25. Assume the monthly payments for property taxes and hazard insurance total is $300. If the prospective buyer earns $50,000 annually, and if the lender's cutoff percentage for PITI payments is 28 percent of gross income, will the buyer qualify for the loan? If not, what annual income is needed for the buyer to qualify

PITI= $1,609.25+$300 = 1,909.25
Monthly gross income = $50,000/12 = $4,166.67
PITI/monthly gross income = $1,909.25/$4,166.67 = 45.8%

The consumer would not qualify.

Income required to qualify:
        $1,909.25/28%=$6,818.75 monthly or $81,825 annually.

Some lenders use two ratios to qualify homebuyers for loans. The first is the PITI payment to income ratio. If the homebuyer passes this test, the second ratio will be the PITI payment plus other debt payments (car payments, furniture payments) as a percent of monthly gross income. This second ratio must usually be no more than 38 percent.

Some Answers

The above procedure can be used to derive "income multipliers" for home affordability. When the income multiplier is multiplied by the homebuyer's income, it shows the maximum house price which the homebuyer can afford for a given downpayment, interest rate, and PITI to income ratio.

Table 4-7 lists income multipliers for home affordability for various combinations of mortgage interest rates and downpayment percentages. The calculations assume a PITI to gross income ratio of 30 percent. Notice that the higher the downpayment percentage, the higher the income multiplier, but the higher the mortgage interest rate, the lower the income multiplier.

The Bottom Line

How much house you can afford depends on the mortgage interest rate, the size of the downpayment you make, and your income. Lenders use the ratio of the monthly PITI payment (principal, interest, taxes, and insurance) to your monthly gross income to decide if you can qualify for the loan.

Table 4-7 Income multipliers for home affordability.

Mortgage Interest Rate	----------Downpayment Percentages----------				
	5%	10%	15%	20%	25%
7%	2.55	2.64	2.73	2.83	2.95
8%	2.39	2.47	2.57	2.67	2.78
9%	2.16	2.33	2.42	2.52	2.62
10%	2.11	2.19	2.28	2.38	2.48
11%	1.99	2.07	2.16	2.25	2.35
12%	1.88	1.96	2.04	2.13	2.23
13%	1.78	1.86	1.94	2.02	2.12
14%	1.69	1.76	1.84	1.93	2.02

Assumes:
property taxes equal to 1.2% of the house price,
home hazard insurance equal to $3 per $1000 of home price,
30-year fixed mortgage rate,
and total monthly house payment to monthly gross income ratio of 30%.

HOW TO USE:
mortgage interest rate = 10%;
downpayment percentage = 5%;
homebuyer's gross income = $60,000;
maximum affordable house price = $60,000 × 2.11 = $126,600.

CONSUMER TOPIC

WHY ALL HOME IMPROVEMENTS DON'T PAY OFF

Once you buy a house, you can change the amount of housing you consume by making home improvements. However, home improvements should be considered very carefully. You may add a $10,000 family room to your home and expect the home's sales value to increase $10,000, but usually that's not the case. Studies show that rarely does a home improvement result in its full cost being added to the home's sale value. Most homeowners are lucky if they can recover 70 to 80 percent of a project's cost.

As a rule of thumb, the more consumers who would find a particular home improvement appealing, the greater will be the resale value percentage of that improvement. This means that more common home improvements will have more of their cost recovered than unusual home improvements. Common features like a fireplace, bath, and kitchen have a greater cost recovery than insulation, another room, or a swimming pool. Part of the reason for the low cost recovery of a pool might also be costs associated with maintaining the pool.

Owners must also be careful that the home improvement is consistent with the structural characteristics and decor of the house and with the house's price range. For example, if buyers wanting a swimming pool typically purchase homes in the $400,000 and over range, then adding a swimming pool to a $150,000 house would not be a good idea.

10. An Overview of Mortgages: What Are the Options?

Selecting a home mortgage is one of the most difficult and important personal finance decisions that a homebuyer will make. It's difficult because there are so many options today, and the options frequently seem like complex financial arrangements that only a financial wizard can understand. The selection is important because the mortgage is the biggest loan most consumers will take and the "correct" choice can save the borrower thousands of dollars.

Until the end of the 1970s homebuyers had no decision to make about the selection of a mortgage. This was because until that time there was only one type of mortgage—the fixed rate mortgage. All lenders offered the same garden variety of fixed rate, fixed payment mortgage.

What Changed?

In the late 1970s the dominance of the fixed rate mortgage began to crumble for two reasons. The unexpected rise in inflation rates in the late 1970s made lenders jittery about lending money at fixed interest

EARLY MORTGAGES: HOLDING ON TO A BALLOON

Mortgages have gone through a considerable transformation. In the 1920s the typical mortgage was a balloon, so-called because monthly payments included interest only and the original loan amount was due in one large final payment—the balloon. Mortgage terms were also much shorter, at most 20 years. In most cases, the homeowner would simply take out a new mortgage when the balloon came due. If the balloon couldn't be paid, the lender would take the home or farm.

The 1930s brought the demise of the balloon mortgage and the advent of the self amortizing (principal and interest payment) mortgage. The reason was that most lenders didn't want to take the risk of a balloon mortgage, with its large final payments, during the bad economic times of the 1930's Depression. The self-amortizing mortgage caught on in the Depression and has remained the mainstay of the mortgage market ever since. Balloon mortgages, however, can still be found and regained some popularity during late 1990s and early 2000s before the subprime mortgage crisis.

Early mortgages also differed in another important way from today's mortgages—they had higher downpayment requirements. Mortgages in the 1920s, for example, had downpayment requirements of 40 to 50 percent of the house value. Today, downpayments are frequently as low as 5 percent of the house value.

Reference: Randall J. Pozdena, *The Modern Economics of Housing,* Quorum Books, N.Y., 1988, pp. 127–128.

rates for long time periods. Lenders found that old 6, 7, and 8 percent mortgages which they were carrying were money losers with inflation rates in double-digits. Homebuyers also found problems with the fixed rate mortgage. As higher inflation rates pushed mortgage interest rates up, fewer homebuyers could qualify for mortgages. Many homebuyers became willing to accept a new type of mortgage which gave them a lower initial mortgage rate at the cost of potentially higher future rates.

For these reasons a number of alternative mortgage designs have been developed and offered since the late 1970s. Most of them have one thing in common—the homebuyer gets lower payments in the early years, but runs the risk of higher payments (including payments higher than with the fixed rate mortgage) in later years. The best example of this kind of mortgage is the adjustable rate mortgage (ARM). A major task of future topics of this chapter will be to design a framework for helping you decide which type of mortgage—fixed rate or adjustable rate—is better in which situation.

Other Options

Fixed rate mortgages and adjustable rate mortgages are the two major types of mortgage financing available today. But there are other options. These other options become particularly popular when all interest rates, including interest rates on fixed and adjustable rate mortgages, rise.

Two of these options are seller financing and shared equity financing. Seller financing is what the name implies—the seller acts as the bank and finances the purchase. The attractive feature of seller financing is that the seller can offer "below market" interest rates.

Shared equity financing involves a joint purchase by a homebuyer and an outside investor. The investor doesn't live in the house with the homebuyer, but the investor shares in the downpayment and mortgage payments. In return, the investor shares in the tax benefits and appreciation in the house.

This has been only an overview of home financing. Now on the some details and decision-making.

The Bottom Line

Selecting a mortgage today is complicated because there are so many options. A common option on many mortgages is to receive lower payments now in exchange for higher payments, or the risk of higher payments later.

11. What Are the Pluses and Minuses of a Fixed Rate Mortgage?

The fixed rate mortgage is easy to understand. The mortgage interest rate is fixed for the term of the mortgage, and this results in a fixed monthly payment for principal and interest. Fixed rate mortgage payments can change only if monthly payments for property taxes and hazard insurance change. Therefore, to a great extent, the homeowner with a fixed rate mortgage can perfectly predict future mortgage payments with not an ounce of uncertainty.

So are there any disadvantages to the fixed rate mortgage? Yes, there is possibly one, depending on your perspective. Recall from Chapter 1 our demonstration that, over time, a person's *nominal* income tends to rise. However, since the fixed rate mortgage payment doesn't change, this makes the burden, a "real" impact, of the fixed rate mortgage greatest in the early years of the mortgage and declining over time (see Figure 4-7). So the bad news is that the high "real" burden of the fixed rate mortgage in the early years of the term makes it more difficult for homebuyers to qualify, since they must qualify on the basis of the first year's comparison of payment to income. The good news is that if the homebuyer can qualify with a fixed rate mortgage, then the payment will become less burdensome as time goes on.

REAL BURDEN

Figure 4-7. The falling payment of the fixed rate mortgage.

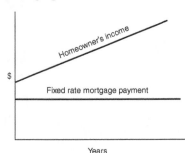

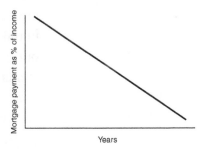

EXAMPLE 4-7:   Jack and Jill have bought a house using a fixed rate mortgage. Their fixed monthly house payment is $1,800, and their monthly income is $6,450. Show the burden of their house payment falls over three years if their income increases 5% annually.

$$\text{Payment burden, year 1: } \frac{\$1,800}{\$6,450} = 0.279 = 27.9\%$$

Income, year 2: $6,450*(1+5\%) = \$6,772.50$

$$\text{Payment burden, year 2: } \frac{\$1,800}{\$6,772.5} = 0.266 = 26.6\%$$

$$\text{Income, year 3: } \$6,772.5*(1+5\%) = \$7,111.13$$

$$\text{Payment burden, year 2: } \frac{\$1,800}{\$7,111.13} = 0.253 = 25.3\%$$

The Bottom Line

Fixed rate mortgages offer certainty—house payments only change if property tax or insurance payments change. But there are two costs to this certainty. Fixed rate mortgage payments start higher than payments for many alternative mortgages, so they are initially more expensive. Also, the burden of the fixed rate mortgage is highest in the early years and declines as the homeowner's income rises.

12. The Graduated Payment Mortgages: A Step-Ladder Mortgage

The graduated payment mortgage (GPM) was one of the earliest of the alternative mortgages. The idea of the GPM is to have mortgage payments rise over time, especially in the early years of the mortgage, to follow the expected rise in the homeowner's income. This eliminates the higher burden of the fixed rate mortgage in the early years of the mortgage's term. In practice, the initial payments of the GPM start out significantly lower than the payments on a comparable conventional mortgage. The GPM payments rise gradually each year, usually for 5-7 years, after which they are constant at a higher level than payments on a comparable conventional mortgage. In essence, the homebuyer trades-off lower payments in the early years of a GPM for higher payments in later years. The payment stream for a typical GPM is illustrated in Figure 4-8.

Figure 4-8. The graduated payment mortgage compared to the fixed rate mortgage.

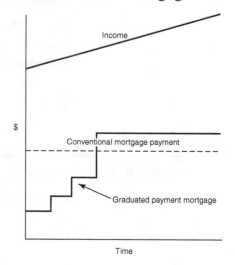

Is the GPM a "Rip-Off?"

Given a conventional mortgage and a GPM, having the same term and interest rate, the homeowner will pay more total dollars for the GPM. Hence some commentators claim that the GPM is a "rip-off." This is a false charge. You pay more in total dollars for GPM simply because dollars decline in value over time. Therefore, it takes more payment dollars in later years to compensate the lender for lower payments in the early years of the GPM when those dollars are worth more. The present value of the stream of graduated mortgage payments, when discounted by the mortgage interest rate, will still equal the amount of the loan.

GPM CALCULATIONS   To reinforce your understanding of the GPM, let's see how one might be constructed. Consider the previous example of a $50,000, 30-years mortgage loan at a 9 percent interest rate. The equal monthly payments were calculated to be $402.31. Now, if you want monthly payments to be $200 the first year, $250 the second year, $300 the third year, $350 the fourth year, and $400 the fifth year, what will be the equal monthly payments for the final 25 years? To find them, calculate the present value of the first five years of payments using a 9 percent discount rate, subtract this present value from the loan amount ($50,000), and then calculate the equal payments based on the remaining loan amount, a 9 percent discount rate, and a term of 25 years:

Present value of $200/month for
  first 12 months = $200 × present
  value sum for 9%, 1 yr. from
  Appendix Table A-6 = $200 × 11.435   = $2.287.00.

Present value of $250/month for second
  year (months 13-24). This requires some
  explanation. Appendix Table A-6 shows
  the present value sum for 9% and 1 year
  and for 9% and 2 years. The present
  value factor sum for months 13 to 24
  is thus the difference between these
  two. So $250 × (21.889 − 11.435)   = $2.613.50.

Present value of $300/month for third
  year (months 25−36) = $300 × (present
  value factor sum for 9%, 3 years −
  present value factor sum for 9%,
  2 years) = $300 × (31.447 − 21.889)   = $2.867.40.

Present value of $350/month for fourth
  year (months 37–48) = $350 × (present
  value factor sum for 9%, 4 years −
  present value factor sum for 9%,
  3 years) − $350 × (40.185 − 31.447)   = $3.058.30.

Present value of $400/month for fifth
  year (months 49–60) = $400 × (present
  value factor sum for 9%. 5 years −
  present value factor sum for 9%,
  4 years) − $400 × (48.173 − 40.185)   = $13195.20.

Total present value sum for years 1–5: $14,021.40

Remaining present value, end of year 5:
$50,000 – 14,021.40   = $35,978.60

The remaining present value loan, $35,978.60, will be repaid in equal monthly payments over years 6 through 30. To find these payments, $35,978.60 must be divided by the sum of monthly present value factors for 9 percent for years 6 through 30. This sum is found by subtracting the present value factor sum for 9 percent and 5 years in Appendix Table A-6 from the present value factor sum for 9 percent and 30 years: 124.282 – 48.173 = 76.109. The equal monthly payment for the last 25 years are thus:

$$\frac{\$35,978.60}{76.109} = \underline{\$472.72}$$

Possible Pitfalls in the GPM

INTEREST COSTS
NOT COVERED

It should be realized that the early GPM payments may not be large enough to cover interest costs. This is not a problem if the homeowner holds the mortgage long enough to make up this unpaid interest in later payments. It can present a problem if the homeowner sells the house in the early years of the GPM mortgage. In this case the interest not covered by payments is added to the loan amount. Furthermore, if the home doesn't appreciate rapidly the homeowner may find that the sales value of the house is not adequate to repay the loan balance.

EXAMPLE 4-8:   Assume you have the graduated payment mortgage just described above. How much would you owe to the lender if the house was sold at the end of the first year?

Original loan amount = $50,000, 9% interest rate.
First year's payments = $200/month.

Month 1

Interest owed = $50,000 × $\frac{.09}{12}$ = $375

Interest not paid = $375 – $200 = $175
New loan amount = $50,000 + $175 = $50,175

Month 2

Interest owed = $50,175 × $\frac{.09}{12}$ = $376

Interest not paid = $376 – $200 = $176
New loan amount = $50,175 + $176 = $50,351

Month 3

$$\text{Interest owed} = \$50{,}351 \times \frac{.09}{12} = \$378$$

Interest not paid = $378 – $200 = $178
New loan amount = $50,351 + $178 = $50,529

Month 4

$$\text{Interest owed} = \$50{,}529 \times \frac{.09}{12} = \$379$$

Interest not paid = $379 – $200 = $179
New loan amount = $50,529 + $179 = $50,708

Month 5

$$\text{Interest owed} = \$50{,}708 \times \frac{.09}{12} = \$380$$

Interest not paid = $380 – $200 = $180
New loan amount = $50,708 + $180 = $50,888

Month 6

$$\text{Interest owed} = \$50{,}888 \times \frac{.09}{12} = \$382$$

Interest not paid = $382 – $200 = $182
New loan amount = $50,888 + $182 = $51,070

Month 7

$$\text{Interest owed} = \$51{,}070 \times \frac{.09}{12} = \$383$$

Interest not paid = $383 – $200 = $183
New loan amount = $51,070 + $183 = $51,253

Month 8

$$\text{Interest owed} = \$51{,}253 \times \frac{.09}{12} = \$384$$

Interest not paid = $384 – $200 = $184
New loan amount = $51,253 + $184 = $51,437

Month 9

$$\text{Interest owed} = \$51{,}437 \times \frac{.09}{12} = \$386$$

Interest not paid = $386 – $200 = $186
New loan amount = $51,437 + $186 = $51,623

Month 10

$$\text{Interest owed} = \$51{,}623 \times \frac{.09}{12} = \$387$$

Interest not paid = $387 – $200 = $187
New loan amount = $51,623 + $187 = $51,810

<u>Month 11</u>

$$\text{Interest owed} = \$51,810 \times \frac{.09}{12} = \$389$$

Interest not paid = \$389 − \$200 = \$189
New loan amount = \$51,810 + \$189 = \$51,999

<u>Month 12</u>

$$\text{Interest owed} = \$51,999 \times \frac{.09}{12} = \$390$$

Interest not paid = \$390 − \$200 = \$190
New loan amount = \$51,999 + \$190 = \$52,189

So the loan balance at the end of the first year is \$52,189, \$2,189 more than the original loan amount. When the house is sold, \$52,189 is owed to the lender, not \$50,000.

Who Is the GPM for?

The GPM is best suited for the homebuyer who would have trouble making the payments of a conventional mortgage in the early years of homeownership, but who could more easily afford higher payments in later years. In other words, a GPM is designed for the homebuyer who wants to more closely match rising mortgage payments to rising income.

A young family buying a house for the first time will be most attracted to a GPM. In the early years the young family typically has major expenditures related to new children and appliances, auto, and furniture purchases. Making big mortgage payments may therefore be difficult. In later years, however, the major expenditures have tapered off and income earners in the family have received salary increases due to inflation. Such a family may be very willing to trade-off lower initial mortgage payments for higher later payments.

The Bottom Line

Take a Graduated Payment Mortgage (GPM) if you need lower mortgage payments in the early years of the mortgage and you can afford higher payments later. However, try to avoid selling the house too soon, because the loan amount will increase in the early years of the GPM. _____

13. The Adjustable Rate Mortgage: Roulette for the Homebuyer?

Adjustable rate mortgages, or ARMs, allow the mortgage interest rate to adjust. The mortgage rate can adjust up or down, depending on economic conditions, and this means the mortgage payment can also adjust up or down.

So why would you sacrifice the payment certainty of a fixed rate mortgage to take an ARM? The answer is that in the vast majority of cases, the initial ARM interest rate and payment are lower than for a fixed rate mortgage. This makes ARMs more affordable, at least in the beginning, and often easier to qualify for. However, many lenders now qualify ARM borrowers on the basis of the higher ARM interest rate which would prevail if the maximum first period adjustment occurred. This change has reduced some of the attractiveness of ARMs.

A Checklist of ARM Characteristics

Compared to the fixed rate mortgage, ARMs are complex contracts. Here are the most important characteristics of an ARM contract.

Index: The Index is a market interest rate which is not directly controlled by the lender and which the lender uses to adjust the ARM interest rate. The Index should be readily available in newspapers or government publications. We'll talk more about the Index later.

Spread: The Spread is the amount which, when added to the Index, produces the ARM interest rate. Common Spreads are 2-3/4 percent and 3 percent. The spread is sometimes called the "margin."

Frequency of Rate Change: This tells you how often the ARM mortgage rate can change. Some ARM rates change twice yearly, some change once per year; some change once every three years; and some change only once every five years. Research shows that ARMs which have rates that change more frequently will have *lower* initial interest rates.

Rate Caps: Rate Caps put limitations on the change in the ARM interest rate. Caps can be put on increases in the rate and decreases in the rate. Caps are generally put on periodic changes in the rate and lifetime (total) changes in the rate. For example, a Cap of "2/5" means that the maximum increase in the rate each time it changes is 2 percentage points, and the maximum increase in the rate over the lifetime of the ARM is 5 percentage points. Homebuyers obviously prefer ARMs which have lower Caps on increases in rates.

Frequency of Payment Change: This characteristic tells the homebuyer how often the ARM payment can change. Usually the frequency of payment change will be the same as the frequency of rate change, meaning the payment and rate change at the same time. However, ARMs in which the payment changes less frequently than the rate can result in negative amortization for the homebuyer (more on this below).

Payment Caps: Some ARMs put limits on how much payments can increase periodically and over the lifetime of the mortgage.

Storage of Rate Changes: Some ARMs allow for rate changes that weren't used (because they exceeded the cap) to be saved and potentially used later.

Lengthening of Term: Some ARMs allow the term of the mortgage to be lengthened in place of increasing the mortgage payment. However, this can generally only be done a few times.

"Teaser" Rate: A "teaser" rate is an initial ARM interest rate which is lower than that derived from adding the Index and Spread. Unless the Index rate falls significantly at the time of the first adjustment, an ARM with a teaser rate will usually mean an increase in the mortgage payment at the first adjustment.

In looking at the characteristics of ARMs, clearly the homebuyer would prefer some of the options over others. For example, homebuyers would prefer lower caps and lower teaser rates. However, options which homebuyers prefer and which are costly for the lender to provide will cost the homebuyer more. In ARMs, the cost of beneficial options usually occurs in the form of a higher initial interest rate, a larger spread between the index rate and interest rate, or greater discount points (prepaid interest; discussed later). A study by Michael Lea of actual ARM contracts generally found this to be true (see CONSUMER TOPIC).

THE IMPLICIT COST OF ARM CHARACTERISTICS

C O N S U M E R T O P I C

All ARMs are not alike. As explained in the text, ARMs have many characteristics. Some of these characteristics are beneficial to the homebuyer and some help the lender. Since there's no free lunch in economics, it makes sense that the homebuyer ultimately pays in some way for those beneficial ARM characteristics which are costly to the lender to provide.

A study by Michael Lea tried to put some numbers on the relationships between ARM characteristics and the cost of ARMs to the homebuyer. His findings are summarized in the table and they make a lot of sense.

ARMs in which the interest rate is fixed for a longer period of time are more risky for the lender because the lender must absorb any higher costs which occur for a longer period of time. Therefore, ARMs with longer adjustment periods tend to have higher initial rates.

ARMs with teaser rates are also more costly, in the long run, to the lender and, therefore, to the homebuyer, and the bigger the teaser rate discount, the bigger the ultimate cost. For example, the results can be interpreted as showing that an ARM with a 2 percentage point "teaser" discount will have an interest rate at the first adjustment period almost 1 percentage point higher than an ARM with no teaser. Also, teaser rates offered with longer ARMs are even more costly.

Lea found the impact of alternative ARM indexes not to be on the fully indexed initial interest rate, but to be on the "points" charged. Lenders prefer the Treasury rate index because it adjusts to their changing costs more rapidly. Indexes which don't adjust as rapidly, such as the cost-of-funds index and the Federal Home Loan Bank Board index, are less desirable to lenders. In compensation, the lender charges more "points" on ARMs with these indexes.

Surprisingly, Lea did not find any impact of "caps" on the cost of ARMs. One reason may be that his data did not identify if caps applied to limitations on interest rate *decreases* as well as increases. If caps apply to both interest rate increases and decreases, then a lender may believe that any additional costs due to having lower caps for rate upswings are counterbalanced by benefits from having limits on rate declines.

ARM CHARACTERISTIC	IMPACT ON FULLY-INDEXED INITIAL INTEREST RATE*
Rate adjusts every	**Percentage points relative to 1 yr. adjustment**
6 months	−0.73
2 years	+0.74
3 years	+0.28
5 years	+0.85
7 years	+0.47
Teaser rate discount of	Percentage points relative to no teaser rate discount
.25 to 1.00 percentage points	No change
1.00 to 2.00	+0.35
2.00 to 3.00	+0.97
Over 3.00	+2.49
Teaser rate discount is with	Percentage points relative to teaser rate discount with 1 yr. ARM
a 3 year ARM	+0.60
a 5 year ARM	+0.49
Type of Index	Impact on Points Charged
Cost of funds index	+0.38 higher points relative to Treasury rate index
Federal Home Loan Bank Board Index	+0.21 higher points relative to Treasury rate index

Reference: Michael J. Lea "An Empirical Analysis of the Value of ARM Features," *Housing Finance Review,* Vol. 4, No. 1, January 1985, pp. 467–481.

*The fully indexed initial rate is the rate found by adding the spread to the initial index value. The fully indexed initial rate is higher than the actual initial rate if the lender uses a teaser rate.

How ARMs Work

ARM payment calculations are made just like calculations for fixed rate mortgages. Given an initial interest rate, loan amount, and term, the ARM monthly payment is calculated as if the interest rate would never change over the life of the loan.

What happens at an adjustment period? First, the new interest rate is calculated. Then, the new interest rate is applied to the existing loan balance and to the *remaining* term to calculate the new payment.

EXAMPLE 4-9: Mary and Mike borrow $100,000 using a 3 year ARM with an initial interest rate of 8 percent and a term of 30 years. The monthly payments for principal and interest for the first three years are:

$$\frac{\$100,000}{136.283 \text{ (PVF sum, 8\%, 360 mos.)}} = \$733.77$$

After three years, assume the interest rate has risen to 10 percent. For the next three years, monthly payments are calculated using 10 percent and a term of 27years (324 months):

$$\frac{\$97,280}{111.845 \text{ (PVF sum, 10\%, 324 mos.)}} = \$870$$

Finally, at the end of 6 years the ARM rate falls to 7 percent. The remaining loan balance is $95,482. The new monthly payments are calculated using 7 percent and a term of 24 years (288 months):

$$\frac{\$95,482}{139.322 \text{ (PVF sum, 7\%, 288 mos.)}} = \$686$$

Knowing how to calculate ARM payments will allow you to double-check your lender when payment changes are made. The lender can make mistakes! To review, follow these steps in calculating an ARM payment:

1. Find the Index Value.
2. Add the spread to the Index value to obtain the new interest rate. Adjust the interest rate if it exceeds the caps.
3. Find the outstanding loan balance.
4. Calculate the new monthly payment by applying the new interest rate to the outstanding loan balance and the remaining term.

Beware of Negative Amortization

Most ARMs are structured to have both the interest rate and the monthly payment change at the same time. However, there are some ARMs which are structured to have the interest rate change more frequently than the payment. These ARMs should probably be avoided because they can result in something called *negative amortization.*

Negative amortization occurs when the mortgage rate rises but the mortgage payment remains the same. In this case the lender doesn't forget, or forgive, the extra interest costs which would be charged with the higher interest rate. Instead, the interest costs which aren't paid are added to the loan balance! Conversely, if the mortgage interest rate falls and the payment doesn't change, then principal payments out of each payment increase and the loan is repaid faster.

The Bottom Line

ARMs are complicated mortgages. Before you take an ARM, read the fine print of the contract and understand how the ARM stacks up on key characteristics. Avoid ARMs which allow for negative amortization. _____

14. Should You Take a Fixed or Adjustable Rate Mortgage?

Deciding whether to take a fixed or adjustable rate mortgage when buying a home is probably the most difficult decision a homebuyer must make. The difficulty arises because of the unpredictability of interest rates.

The advantage of ARMs is that their initial interest rate is usually 1 to 2 percentage points lower than the comparable fixed mortgage rate. Therefore, the homebuyer with an ARM begins in a better position, but faces the uncertainty of future changes in the interest rate and mortgage payment. How much of a disadvantage is this? Let's first consider some fundamentals:

MORTGAGE INTEREST RATE CYCLE

1. From 1972 to 2012, the average mortgage interest rate was 8.7%, and the standard deviation was 3.0%. The highest was 16.63% in 1981, while the lowest was 3.66% in 2012.
2. Mortgage interest rates move in cycles. From 1972 to 2012 there have been six cycles (See Figure 4-9). The average length of the cycle, from low point to low point in the mortgage interest rate, has been about 6 ½ years. The length of time of rate climbs was somewhat longer than the length of time of rate declines.
3. The peak of mortgage interest rates typically occurred at the end of an economic expansion and near the beginning of a recession. The lowest rates were typically found during the early part of an economic expansion.

If we assume this average cycle continues in the future (Figure 4-10), then some recommendations about the choice between fixed rate mortgages and ARMs can be made.

If mortgage rates are at point A, then a one-year ARM should be taken. Point A will usually occur in the middle of a recession. In this case, ARM mortgage rates will fall until point B. At point B, you should refinance to a fixed rate mortgage if you plan to remain in the home for a considerable length of time. Refinancing means you take out a new mortgage and pay off your old mortgage.

If mortgage rates are between point A and point B, then again a one-year ARM should be taken, and the mortgage should be refinanced at point B.

If mortgage rates are at point B, then you should take a fixed rate mortgage.

If mortgage rates are rising, that is, between point B and point C, then your decision is the most difficult. It can be approached in two ways. One

WORST CASE SCENARIO

way is to assume the "worst case scenario" happens if an ARM is taken. Assume the ARM increases the maximum it can each period, and then calculate how long it would take before the savings from earlier, lower ARM payments and faster principal pay-off, including their earnings if invested, are used up by later ARM payments higher than fixed rate mortgage payments. In other words, how long does it take before the present value of costs of the ARM exceeds the present value of costs of the fixed rate mortgage.

Another way to compare fixed rate mortgages and ARMs is to ask which is cheaper (in present value terms) if interest rates follow their average pattern. Fixed rate mortgages are more preferred when there is a low spread between the fixed rate and initial ARM rate, when the holding period is long, and when the adjustment period on the ARM is shorter.

Figure 4-9. 30-year fixed rate mortgage interest rate 1972–2012

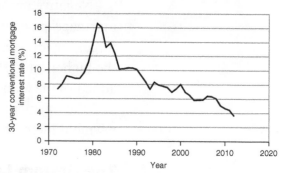

Data source: Mortgage interest rate data from the Federal Reserve System.

Figure 4-10. Average mortgage interest rate cycle.

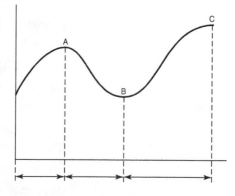

The Bottom Line _____

Take an ARM when mortgage rates are falling or if you plan to sell the house in a few years. Take a fixed rate if mortgage rates have "bottomed-out" or if you plan to stay in the house a long time. _____

15. Which ARM Index Is Best?

A major choice facing the homebuyer who takes an adjustable rate mortgage (ARM) is the selection of an ARM index. The index, when added to a spread of 2½ to 3 percentage points, determines the ARM interest rate at each adjustment anniversary. Thus, an important consideration for a homebuyer is how alternative indexes perform.

TREASURY INDEX

COST OF FUNDS
INDEX

There are two popular ARM indexes, the index based on U.S. Treasury securities adjusted to a constant maturity of one year, often abbreviated as CMT, and the index based on the median monthly cost of funds for Federal Savings and Loan Insurance Corporation (FSLIC) insured savings and loan associations, often abbviated as COFI.[5]

Figure 4-11 shows the performance of these two indices between 1982 and 2012. Although the trends in the two indices are very similar, there are some differences. First, the average rate is lower for the CMT than for the COFI. For the 1982–2012 period, the average CMT rate is 5.0% whereas the average COFI rate was 5.3%. Second, the difference between the highest rate and lowest rate is smaller for the COFI than for the CMT. For the 1982-2012 period, this difference is 10.8 percentage points for the COFI but 12.1 percentage points for the CMT. Third, when interest rates are rising, the COFI tends to rise less than the CMT. However, when interest rates are falling, the CMT tends to fall faster than the COFI. In other words, the CMT is more volatile than the COFI, but it also has a lower average rate compared to the COFI.

Figure 4-11. Performance of ARM indexes: constant maturity treasury index (CMT) and Cost of Funds Index (COFI)

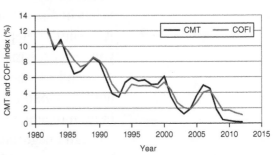

Data sources: CMT from the Federal Reserve System. COFI from the Federal Home Loan Bank of San Francisco.

_____

[5]The interest rate for U. S. Treasury securities adjusted to a constant maturity of one year should not be confused with the interest rate on one-year Treasury securities. They are different.

The ARM protects the lender against changes in inflation rates and interest rates and shifts much of this risk to the borrower. Since the COFI changes more slowly than the Treasury securities index, it provides less protection to the lender and more security to the borrower, especially when rates are rising. One study shows that because of this disadvantage to the lender, lenders may charge from .25 to .33 more points (1 point is 1% of the loan amount) to offer ARMs with the COFI (see Michael J. Lea, "An Empirical Analysis of the Value of ARM Features," *Housing Finance Review,* Vol. 4, No. 1, January 1985).

With this background, these lessons can be suggested for choosing an ARM index:

1. You can reduce fluctuations in the ARM index by choosing the COFI.
2. When interest rates are headed up, the COFI index is better because it will rise less than the CMT.
3. When interest rates are headed down, the CMT is better because it will fall faster and greater than the COFI.

The Bottom Line

If you'll keep the ARM for a long time, take an ARM with a COFI to reduce rate and payment fluctuations. If you'll keep the ARM for only a few years and interest rates are falling, take an ARM with a CMT. __

16. Should You Pay Points for a Lower Mortgage Rate?

When taking out a mortgage you'll run into something called "points." What in the world are "points," and are they good guys or bad guys! A "point" is 1 percent of the mortgage loan amount. For example, if you're borrowing $100,000, then one point is $1000.

Lenders charge points for two reasons. One reason is that points are used as a loan processing fee. Another reason is that points are charged in exchange for lowering the mortgage interest rate. Homebuyers usually can't negotiate on points charged as a loan processing fee (a typical fee is 1 point). However, homebuyers usually do have a choice in the number of points paid to lower the mortgage interest rate. Thus, the decision that you face is: Is it wise to pay more points to lower the mortgage interest rate?

By paying extra points, you benefit with lower mortgage payments but tax deductions will also be less. By not paying extra points, you face higher mortgage payments, but tax deductions are larger and you are free to invest the funds or use them to make a larger downpayment.

Federal income tax treatment of the payment of points depends on whether the mortgage is used to purchase a new home or to refinance an existing loan. If a new home is being purchased, points paid to reduce the mortgage interest rate can be deducted in their entirety in the year the house is purchased. In contrast, if the new mortgage is used to refinance an existing mortgage, then the deduction of points must be spread out over the life of the mortgage.

The key factor in this decision about points is how long you plan to stay in the house. The longer you stay, the more likely that the benefits of lower mortgage payments and faster equity build-up from paying extra points will outweigh the costs of the money for the points, the lower tax benefits, and the foregone investment interest earnings.

How would you calculate whether paying extra points is worthwhile? Once again, you'd pull out—that's right—our present value procedure. For a given holding period of the mortgage, calculate the present value sum of the after-tax mortgage payments and final loan balance if extra points aren't paid. Then compare this sum to the present value sum of the extra points payment plus the after-tax mortgage payments and final loan balance if the extra points are paid. Whichever present value sum is smaller is the better option.

These calculations are tedious and time-consuming. What's found is that the critical factor in determining which is better—paying extra points or not—is how long the homeowner will stay in the home. The longer you'll stay in the home and keep the mortgage, the more beneficial it is to pay the extra points in order to reduce payments. The reason is very intuitive: the longer you keep the mortgage, the greater will be the present value sum of savings on after-tax payments and equity build-up.

Table 4-8 shows the minimum number of months you must stay in the house for paying extra points to be worthwhile. Panels A and B show the results for a 30 and 15 year mortgage when a new purchase is involved, and panels C and D give the results when refinancing is involved. The required stay is shorter the fewer the number of points paid for a given interest rate reduction and the larger the reduction in the mortgage rate for a given points payment. The required stay is longer for refinancing since the tax deduction of points is not as generous in this case.

Is it better to spend money to pay points to reduce the interest rate or to increase the downpayment and decrease the loan? In the case of no refinancing, it is usually better to spend money to reduce the interest rate. For 30 year mortgages, as long as it takes fewer than 7 points to reduce the mortgage rate one percentage point, it's better to pay the points. For 15 year mortgages, as long as it takes fewer than 5 points to reduce the mortgage rate one percentage point, it's better to pay the points.

Table 4-8   Number of months mortgage must be held to make paying extra points financially beneficial, 28% tax bracket.

A. 30 Year Mortgage, New Home Purchase

Difference between interest rates is:	Number of extra points paid for lower mortgage interest rate				
	1	2	3	4	5
1 percentage point	13	26	40	55	72
2	7	13	19	26	33
3	5	9	13	17	22
4	4	7	10	13	16

B. 15 Year Mortgage, New Home Purchase

Difference between interest rates is:	Number of extra points paid for lower mortgage interest rate				
	1	2	3	4	5
1 percentage point	13	27	42	58	78
2	7	13	20	27	34
3	5	9	13	17	22
4	4	7	10	13	16

C. 30 Year Mortgage, Refinance

Difference between interest rates is:	Number of extra points paid for lower mortgage interest rate				
	1	2	3	4	5
1 percentage point	18	36	56	77	100
2	9	18	27	36	46
3	6	12	18	24	30
4	5	9	13	18	22

D. 15 Year Mortgage, Refinance

Difference between interest rates is:	Number of extra points paid for lower mortgage interest rate				
	1	2	3	4	5
1 percentage point	18	36	56	78	104
2	9	18	27	36	46
3	6	12	18	24	30
4	5	9	13	18	22

Assumes funds can be invested at an 8% before-tax rate.

However, even if you plan to stay in the house for a long time, you need to take into considertation the possibility of refinancing, especially no-cost refinancing if you have good credit. If you purchase a house when the mortgage interest rate is high, it is likley that the interest rate will go down at some point in the future so you can refinance. In that case, it may not be wise to pay points to buy down interest rate if you can refinance in the future to get an even lower interest rate.

The Bottom Line

The longer you plan to stay in the house, the more beneficial it is to pay "points" to get a lower mortgage interest rate. However, if you purchase a house when mortgage interest rate is very high, it might be wise to refinance to a lower rate in the near future instead of paying points to buy a lower rate.

17. Is a 15 Year Mortgage Better Than a 30 Year Mortgage?

Fifteen year mortgages have made a comeback in the American housing market. Homebuyers are attracted to the lower mortgage interest rates which the 15 year mortgage usually offers and to the faster loan pay-off and, consequently, smaller total interest expenses.

The 15 year mortgage will have higher monthly payments than the 30 year mortgage. Monthly mortgage payments are calculated just as with 30 year mortgages, except that the present value factor sum in Appendix Table A-6 is associated with 15 years (180 months) rather than 30 years. Table 4-9 shows differences between 30 year mortgage payments and 15 year mortgage payments.

If you can afford both the payments on a 15 year or 30 year mortgage, are you always better-off taking the 15 year mortgage? To answer this question, let's consider the advantages and disadvantages of the 15 year mortgage as compared to the 30 year mortgage.

There are two advantages to the 15 year mortgage. First, it results in faster repayment of the loan. Second, the mortgage interest rate is usually lower, generally ¼ to ½ percentage point lower. This means that if you stay in the house a long time (for example, 30 years), you can burn the mortgage after 15 years with the 15 year mortgage, whereas with the 30 year mortgage you'd have another 15 years of payments to make. However, even if you sold the house sooner than 15 years, your equity will be larger with the 15 year mortgage than the 30 year mortgage.

There are also two disadvantages to the 15 year mortgage. Since the loan is repaid faster, interest costs are lower and so too are interest tax

Table 4-9 15 year vs 30 year monthly mortgage payments.

$100,000 loan	15 year	30 year
3%	690.58	421.60
5%	790.79	536.82
7%	898.83	665.30
9%	1014.27	804.62
11%	1136.60	952.32
13%	1265.24	1106.20
$250,000 loan	15 year	30 year
3%	1726.45	1054.01
5%	1976.98	1342.05
7%	2247.07	1663.26
9%	2535.67	2011.56
11%	2841.49	2380.81
13%	3163.11	2765.50
$400,000 loan	15 year	30 year
3%	2762.33	1686.42
5%	3163.17	2147.29
7%	3595.31	2661.21
9%	4057.07	3218.49
11%	4546.39	3809.29
13%	5060.97	4424.80

deductions and the resulting income tax savings. The second disadvantage is an often overlooked one. Since 15 year mortgage payments are higher than 30 year payments, if the 30 year mortgage is taken there will be funds available which could be invested.

The question which is better, the 15 year or 30 year mortgage, really depends on the answer to this question: If the 30 year mortgage is taken, what investment interest rate would have to be earned by investing both the additional tax savings and the monthly payments savings, as compared to the 15 year mortgage, such that the additional 30 year mortgage payments could be made later and enough could be earned to equal the greater equity build-up with the 15 year mortgage?

These investment interest rates required to make the 30 year mortgage financially better than the 15 year mortgage are given in Table 4-10 for two 15 year, 30 year mortgage comparisons. In both comparisons the 15 year mortgage rate is 10 percent. As can be seen, in all situations the required investment rate is greater than the 15 year mortgage rate, and for short lengths of stay in the house, the required investment rate would have to be twice or three times greater than the 15 year mortgage rate.

There is a way to have most of the benefits of the 15 year mortgage without being committed to the higher payments. This is to take a 30 year mortgage but to make enough extra payments each month so as to repay the mortgage in 15 years. The advantage of this approach is that you aren't committed to the higher 15 year payments each month. If the budget won't allow the higher payment, you can pay the lower 30 year payment. The disadvantage of this approach is that you don't receive the slightly lower interest rate associated with the 15 year mortgage.

Table 4-10   Minimum interest rate required to be earned on invested funds for the 30 year mortgage to be preferred to the 15 year mortgage.

15 year mortgage rate = 10%	**30 year mortgage rate = 10¼%**		
	---------------TAX BRACKET-------------		
No. of years you stay in house	**15%**	**28%**	**33%**
2	20.4%	20.1%	20.0%
5	13.8%	14.2%	14.1%
10	11.9%	11.8%	11.8%
15	11.1%	11.1%	11.0%
30	10.7%	10.7%	10.7%
15 year mortgage rate = 10%	**30 year mortgage rate = 10½%**		
	--------------TAX BRACKET-------------		
No. of years you stay in house	**15%**	**28%**	**33%**
2	31.9%	31.4%	31.2%
5	18.0%	17.7%	17.7%
10	13.6%	13.6%	13.6%
15	12.2%	12.1%	12.1%
30	11.5%	11.4%	11.4%

EXAMPLE 4-10: Marilyn and Len have just taken an $200,000, 30 year mortgage with a 6% interest rate. What is their monthly principal and interest payments? How much extra would they have to pay each month to reduce the term to 15 years?

ANSWER: Monthly interest rate rm=6%/12=0.5%=0.005. n=360 months. Monthly mortgage payment

$$M = \frac{L}{PVFS(rm,n)} = \frac{200,000}{1 - \dfrac{1}{(1+0.005)^{360}}} = \frac{200,000}{166.7916} = \$1,199.10$$

You can also use Table A-6 to get the PVFS for 6% and 360 months.

If instead the mortgage term is 15 years with the same 6% rate, then n=180. Monthly mortgage payment

$$M = \frac{L}{PVFS(rm,n)} = \frac{200,000}{1 - \dfrac{1}{(1+0.005)^{180}}} = \frac{200,000}{118.5035} = \$1,687.71$$

The extra payment is: $1,687.71-$1,199.10=$488.61

The Bottom Line

Unless you are a very astute investor who can earn very high investment interest rates on your money, the 15 year mortgage is preferable to the 30 year mortgage. Furthermore, the advantage of the 15 year mortgage increases the shorter the length of time you stay in the house. But, of course, don't rob your grocery, insurance, or heating budget to make the higher 15 year mortgage payments!

18. Should You Prepay a Mortgage, or Pay-Down a Mortgage, or Make Extra Monthly Principal Payments?

Prepaying a mortgage means paying off the mortgage with one large payment. Paying-down a mortgage means making one large payment to reduce the mortgage loan balance, but not all the way to zero. Making extra monthly principal payments means writing an extra check each month to the mortgage company, in addition to your regular mortgage payment, which is directly applied to reducing the mortgage loan balance.

The benefit from prepaying, paying-down, or making extra monthly principal payments is that the mortgage will be paid-off faster, and consequently you will not make as many mortgage payments in the future. However, there are two disadvantages. First, by paying off the mortgage faster, you will reduce your total mortgage interest paid and, consequently, will reduce tax deductions and tax savings from having the mortgage. Second, the funds used to prepay, pay-down, or make extra principal payments could have been put to another use, such as investing, where interest income could have been earned.

So is it wise to prepay, pay-down, or make extra monthly principal payments? The answer is simple. If you can earn an interest rate on invested money which is *greater* than your mortgage interest rate, then it is *not* wise to prepay, pay-down, or make extra principal payments. In this case, it is better to invest the funds which would have been used to prepay, pay-down, or make extra monthly principal payments. These funds plus their after-tax interest earnings will be able to more than pay the extra mortgage payments incurred by not prepaying, paying-down, or making extra principal payments.

In contrast, if you cannot earn an investment interest rate which is higher than the mortgage interest rate, then you are better-off using spare funds to prepay, pay-down, or make extra monthly principal payments.

Another way of saying the same thing is to realize that every dollar of principal paid on the mortgage ahead of schedule saves you the mortgage interest cost each year. So, if you have a marginal dollar, a mortgage charging 10 percent, and an investment opportunity paying 7 percent (before taxes), it's better to take that dollar and pay down on the mortgage and save 10 percent annually than to invest that dollar and earn only 7 percent annually. But if 12 percent could be earned on the dollar, it's better to invest the dollar!

As an example, suppose Beth and Bob are considering paying off their mortgage loan balance of $10,775, on which they have one more year to pay. The mortgage rate is 11 percent and Beth and Bob are in the 33 percent tax bracket. If they can earn 12 percent on invested funds, Table 4-11 shows how Beth and Bob would be better off, by $41.60, by investing the $10,775 and using that investment fund to make the mortgage payments.

Most homeowners who have 10, 11, or 12 percent mortgages cannot invest funds safely and earn higher rates. Such homeowners are better-off prepaying, paying-down, or making extra monthly principal payments. However, homeowners who have 5, 6, or 7 percent fixed rate

Table 4-11 Paying-off a mortgage vs. investing.

Payment No.	After-tax payment[a]	Funds can be invested at a 12% before-tax annual rate (8% annual or .67% monthly, after-taxes)
		Investment fund balance
349	$919.73	$10775 × 1.0067 = $10847.19; $10847.19 – $919.73 = $9927.46
350	922.31	9927.46×1.0067 = 9993.98; 9993.98 – 922.31 = 9071.67
351	924.92	9071.67×1.0067 = 9132.45; 9132.45 – 924.92 = 8207.53
352	927.55	8207.53×1.0067= 8262.52; 8262.52– 927.55= 7334.97
353	930.20	7334.97×1.0067 = 7384.11 ; 7384.11 – 930.20 = 6453.91
354	932.88	6453.91×1 .0067 = 6497.15; 6497.15 – 932.88 = 5564.27
355	935.58	5564.27×1.0067 = 5601.55; 5601.55 – 935.58 = 4665.97
356	938.31	4665.97×1.0067= 4697.24; 4697.24– 938.31= 3758.93
357	941.06	3758.93×1.0067= 3784.11; 3784.11– 941.06= 2843.05
358	943.84	2843.05×1.0067 = 2862.10; 2862.10 – 943.84 = 1918.26
359	946.64	1918.26×1.0067= 1931.12; 1931.12– 946.64= 984.48
360	949.47	984.48×1.0067 = 991.07; 991.07 – 949.47 = 41.60

Assumptions: Original mortgage of 100,000, 11 percent mortgage rate, 30-year term, loan balance of $10,775 after 348 payments, payment due at the end of the month, homeowner's tax bracket is 33 percent.

[a]Mortgage payment after subtracting the tax savings due to mortgage interest deductions, assuming homeowner is in the 33 percent tax bracket.

mortgages are generally better off investing excess funds and keeping their mortgage.

The Bottom Line

Use spare funds to prepay or pay-down a mortgage, or to make extra principal payments, when those funds *can't* earn an interest rate higher than the mortgage interest rate.

19. Buydowns: Bargains or Gimmicks?

With a buydown, a builder pays a fee to a lending institution, such as a bank or savings and loan, and in exchange the lending institution offers a below-market interest rate to buyers of the builder's homes. Usually the buydown is for a limited amount of time, such as two or three years. After that time, the mortgage interest rate becomes the market rate prevailing at the time the mortgage was made. The buydown is therefore similar to the graduated payment mortgage.

3-2-1

2-1

Two buydowns are popular, the 3-2-1 and the 2-1. The 3-2-1 buydown means the first year's mortgage rate is 3 percentage points below market, the second year's rate is 2 percentage points below market, and the third year's rate is 1 percentage point below market; in the fourth and later years the rate is the market rate prevailing when the loan was made. In the 2-1 buydown, the first year's rate is 2 percentage points below market and the second year's rate is 1 percentage point below market.

In effect, the fee which the builder pays the lending institution is a prepayment of the interest which the lender would have received at the higher mortgage interest rate. Studies have shown that houses with buydowns have prices which are higher by the amount of the fee paid by the builder to get the buydown; that is, the builder adds the cost of the buydown to the price of the house. Houses with 3-2-1 buydowns will be 4½ to 5 percent higher in price, and houses with 2-1 buydowns will be 2 to 2½ percent higher in price.[6]

Does this mean that buydowns are worthless, that the benefit of a lower interest rate will be cancelled by a higher house price? No. First year mortgage payments (principal and interest) on 3-2-1 buydowns are 15 to 21 percent lower than payments on conventional mortgages, and on 2-1 buydowns first year payments are 10 to 14 percent lower. However, when the buydown ends and the mortgage rate reverts to the original market rate, the loan balance is higher and the buy-down payment is higher than the conventional mortgage payment.

Table 4-12 shows how a 3-2-1 buydown works compared to a conventional loan. Note how the 3-2-1 buydown payments gradually increase each year, and that both the loan balance at the end of three years and the final payments are higher for the 3-2-1 buydown compared to the conventional loan.

Is a buydown a good idea? Compared to an ARM, a buydown usually provides a bigger discount in the first year mortgage payment. This discount can increase if ARM rates rise rapidly after the first year, but more likely the discount decreases in future years as the buydown expires. Compared to a conventional fixed rate mortgage, the buydown reduces mortgage payments during the years of the buydown, but increases mortgage payments during years after the buydown expires.

---

[6] DeMagistris, Robin, "Impact of 'Buydowns' on Affordability and Home Prices" *Federal Reserve Bank of N. Y, Quarterly Review,* Summer 1982, pp. 41-45.

Table 4-12   Conventional loan compared to 3-2-1 buydown.

A. CONVENTIONAL LOAN, $100,000

Market Interest Rate	Monthly Payment	Loan Balance at End of Three Years
15%	$1264	$99,348
14%	1185	99,191
13%	1106	99,000
12%	1029	98,767
11%	952	98,487
10%	878	98,152

B. 3-2-1 BUYDOWN

Market Interest Rate	Initial Loan[a]	Monthly Payment			Loan Balance at End of 3 Years	Monthly Payment Yrs.4-30[b]
		Year 1	Year 2	Year 3		
15%	$104,800	$1078	$1158	$1239	$103,690	$1320
14%	104,800	998	1077	1156	103,391	1236
13%	104,800	920	997	1074	103,052	1151
12%	104,700	843	917	992	102,534	1067
11%	104,700	768	841	914	102,222	988
10%	104,600	696	766	835	101,425	906

[a]Assumes buydown loan is 4.8% higher for 15%, 14%, and 13% market interest rates, 4.7% higher for 12% and 11% market interest rates, and 4.6% higher for 10% market interest rate.
[b]Mortgage interest rate reverts to market interest rate.

The Bottom Line

Buydowns reduce mortgage payments during the years of the buydown (2 or 3 years) in exchange for higher payments when the buydown ends. However, the loan balance also falls more slowly with the buydown. Like the GPM, buydowns are best suited for homebuyers who need a big discount for one or two years in their mortgage payments, but who can afford higher payments after that. These are homebuyers who are at starting salary levels in their jobs, but who expect to receive significant salary increases in the future.

THE PRICE-LEVEL ADJUSTED MORTGAGE:
A MORTGAGE WHOSE TIME HASN'T COME

As already discussed, the real (inflation-adjusted) payments of the fixed rate mortgage fall over time. This makes the mortgage burden highest in the early years of the mortgage. The graduated payment mortgage, the adjustable rate mortgage with deep discounted teaser rates, and buydowns are ways of reducing the mortgage payment burden in the early years.

Yet the reductions in payments from these mortgages last only a few years, maybe five at most. There is a mortgage, called the price-level adjusted mortgage, or PLAM, which attempts to have the mortgage payment gradually increase over time with the homeowner's income. The PLAM works like this. The mortgage loan is made for a typical term, say 30 years, but at a "real" interest rate, such as *4 percent*. However, each year the mortgage balance is increased by the inflation rate and the mortgage payment is recalculated based on the remaining term.

For example, consider a $100,000 mortgage with a 30 year term. If the loan was made with a fixed rate 9 percent mortgage, monthly principal and interest payments would be $804.62. If the loan was made with a PLAM with a 4 percent interest rate and assuming a 5 percent annual inflation rate, then monthly payments would be as follows:

Monthly Principal and Interest Payments on PLAM: $100,000, 30 yr. loan, 4% interest rate, 5% annual inflation rate.

Year	PLAM Payment $	Year	PLAM Payment $
1	477.19	16	992,03
2	501.04	17	1,041.63
3	526.10	18	1,093.72
4	522.40	19	1,148.40
5	580.02	20	1,205.82
6	609.02	21	1,266.11
7	639.47	22	1,329.42
8	671.45	23	1,394.89
9	705.02	24	1,465.68
10	740.27	25	1,538.97
11	777.28	26	1,615.92
12	816.15	27	1,696.71

(*continued on next page*)

C O N S U M E R   T O P I C

(continued from previous page)

13	856.96	28	1,781.55
14	899.80	29	1,870.63
15	944.79	30	1,964.16

PLAM payments begin much lower than fixed rate payments. PLAM payments rise 5 percent annually in this example, matching the 5 percent inflation rate.

Two problems have hindered the introduction and use of PLAMs. First, negative amortization occurs with PLAMs in the early years of the mortgage term. Furthermore, the negative amortization lasts for a much longer time than with a graduated payment mortgage or a buydown. For example, in the PLAM loan considered here, negative amortization would occur until the 12th year. Therefore, PLAMs are unattractive to many homeowners who plan to move within 10 or 12 years.

The second disadvantage of PLAMs is that the total dollars repaid are much greater than the total dollars repaid on a fixed rate mortgage. In the example considered above, a total of $951,108 will be repaid on the PLAM compared to $289,663 repaid on the fixed rate mortgage. The reason this occurs, of course, in because dollars decline in value with time. To compensate for fewer, yet more valuable, dollars repaid in the early years of the PLAM, many cheaper dollars will have to be repaid later. In fact, the "real" dollars repaid on the PLAM and the fixed rate mortgage are the same. Nevertheless, most homebuyers look at nominal dollars and are "turned off" of the PLAM because of its large bill.

There is a cousin to the PLAM, called the GEM, which has received modest acceptance. GEM stands for growing equity mortgage. The initial payments on a GEM are also based on a very low interest rate, maybe 4 or 5 percent. Unlike the PLAM, there is a pre-established rate at which the payments increase each year. Payments are calculated based on a 30-year term, but GEMs are usually paid off in less than 20 years. GEMs, in essence, force the homeowner to make extra principal payments.

20. Should You Take a Biweekly Mortgage?

With a conventional mortgage, payments are made monthly, generally at the beginning of the month but with the payment designated for the previous month.

A different kind of mortgage, called the biweekly mortgage, requires two mortgage payments per month. Before throwing this book aside (who needs two mortgage payments per month!), realize that each biweekly mortgage payment is half the amount of the comparable monthly mortgage payment. Since there are 26 biweekly periods in a year, the homebuyer with a biweekly mortgage makes the equivalent of 13 monthly payments.

So why should a homebuyer consider making two smaller mortgage payments monthly rather than one payment? As Table 4-13 shows, the

Table 4-13 Terms of biweekly mortgages.

If mortgage interest rate is:	Biweekly mortgage will be full paid in
14%	17 years
12%	19 years
10%	21 years
8%	23 years
6%	24½ years

answer is that the biweekly mortgage reduces the term of the mortgage. The higher the mortgage interest rate, the greater the reduction in the term for the biweekly mortgage from the conventional monthly mortgage with a 30 year term.

So by paying absolutely no more money per month, and by paying the equivalent of one extra monthly payment per year, you can significantly reduce the term of your mortgage with the biweekly mortgage.

How can such an apparently minor change in the mortgage result in such a significant shortening of the mortgage's term? Paying one extra payment per year is definitely siginificant, but the effect of compound interest is also significant. The biweekly mortgage results in half of each monthly mortgage payment being made 2 weeks earlier than with the conventional monthly mortgage. This reduces the compound interest costs of the mortgage to the homebuyer and allows the mortgage to be paid off earlier.

There is one disadvantage to the homebuyer of the biweekly mortgage. The fact that half of each monthly payment is made two weeks earlier means that the homebuyer loses the chance to invest those funds for the two weeks (for example, in a short term money market fund). If you can earn an interest rate on investments higher than the mortgage interest rate, then the biweekly mortgage is not a good idea.

The Bottom Line

For all homebuyers except those who can earn very high interest rates on their invested funds, the biweekly mortgage is a good idea. The biweekly mortgage does require the discipline to send two mortgage checks per month to the lender rather than one.

21. Should You Share a Mortgage?

Upon first glance, you might say "yes, why not share a mortgage if this means sharing the mortgage payment with someone else." But why would anyone help someone else pay their mortgage payments!

Believe it or not, there are mortgage plans which have a second party help the homebuyer make the mortgage payments, and the second party doesn't live with the homebuyer. Two such mortgage plans are the *shared appreciation mortgage*, or SAM, and the *shared equity mortgage*, or SEM.

Shared Appreciation Mortgage

The Shared Appreciation Mortgage, or SAM, is a mortgage in which the lender gives the borrower a discount on the mortgage interest rate in return for ownership of a share of the house's value appreciation at a certain future date or when the house is sold. The lender is willing to do this if the lender thinks his/her share of the house's appreciation will at least make up for the foregone mortgage interest payments. That is, the lender expects the future value of the foregone mortgage interest payments, calculated as if invested at current market interest rates (for example, the current mortgage interest rate), to be less than the lender's appreciation share.

Evaluating the Shared Appreciation Mortgage

The key elements for the borrower to consider in the SAM contract are the lender's share percentage of appreciation and the corresponding discount in mortgage payments. The lender will calculate the share percentage and payment discount offered to the borrower based on his/her expectation of the house's appreciation. However, it is important for the borrower to apply his/her own *expectation* of the house's appreciation in order to evaluate the shared appreciation mortgage contract. For example, if the borrower thinks the house will appreciate faster than the lender's expectation, then the future value of the payment discounts will be *smaller* than the lender's appreciation share and, in the borrower's view, the payment discounts will be too *small*. In this case the borrower may well decide to reject the shared appreciation mortgage offer. Conversely, if the borrower believes the lender's appreciation rate estimation is too optimistic, then the future value of the payment discounts (assuming the borrower invests them at the initial mortgage interest rate or better) will more than make up for the lost appreciation and the shared appreciation mortgage will be a preferred contract. The following example illustrates these ideas.

EXAMPLE 4-12: Sally is contemplating purchasing an $85,000 house with a $5,000 downpayment and an $80,000 loan. A lender will finance the house with a shared appreciation mortgage at a 7 percent mortgage interest rate (fixed rate with payments calculated for 30 years) and a 40 percent share in the house's appreciation due no later than at the end of 10 years. The downpayment is included in calculating the house's appreciation and no improvements are assumed to be made to the house over the 10 years. Current mortgage interest rates are 10 percent. At what average annual rate is the lender implicitly assuming the house to appreciate? Should Sally take this shared appreciation mortgage?

ANSWER: $80,000 loan at 7 percent for 30 years.
PVFS (rm=7%/12, n=360) = 150.308

$$\text{Monthly payment} = \frac{\$80,000}{150.308} = \$532.24$$

If financed at 10 percent, payments would be:
PVFS (rm=10%/12, n=360) = 113.951

$$\text{Monthly payment} = \frac{\$80,000}{113.951} = \$702.06$$

So, in exchange for 40 percent of appreciation during the next ten years, Sally pays $532.24 monthly instead of $702.06, or $6,386.88 annually instead of $8,424.72. On an annual basis the lender foregoes $8,424.72 − $6,386.88 = $2,037.84. The lender could have invested this amount each year for ten years at 10 percent. This investment would have yielded a future value of $2,037.84 × (2.594 + 2.358 + 2.143 × 1.949 + 1.771 + 1.610 + 1.464 + 1.331 + 1.210 + 1.100) = $2,037.84 × 17.53 = $35,723.34. That is, the lender assumes that 40 percent of the house's value appreciation will at least equal $35,723.34. This means the lender assumes the house will appreciate by at least

$$\frac{\$35,723.34}{.40} = \$89,308.35 \text{ over ten years.}$$

Therefore, the lender assumes the total value of the house will be at least $85,000 + $89,308.35 = $174,308.35 at the end of ten years. The lender's assumed annual appreciation rate for the house is:

$$\left(\frac{\$174,308.35}{\$85,000} \right)^{\frac{1}{10}} - 1 = 0.0745 = 7.45\%$$

Therefore, if Sally thought the house would appreciate at less than 7.45% annually, the SAM would be preferable. If Sally thought the house would appreciate at more than 7.45% annually, then Sally would be better off not taking the SAM or negotiating for a larger payment discount from the lender.

Another way of looking at and evaluating the SAM is for the borrower to ask if the payment discounts can be invested to accumulate to the expected appreciation share owed to the lender at the specified future date. If so, then the SAM is a "good deal;" if not, then the SAM should not be taken or should be re-negotiated.

EXAMPLE 4-13: Take the $85,000 house considered in the previous example. Suppose at the end of ten years Sally expects the house to be worth $140,000. The lender offers Sally a shared appreciation mortgage which costs Sally $6,386.88 annually in mortgage payments rather than $8,424.72, a discount of $2,037.84 annually. In exchange, the SAM contract requires Sally to pay 40 percent of the house's appreciation at the end of ten years. Should Sally take the SAM contract if she can invest funds at an after tax interest rate of 6 percent and Sally's tax bracket is 28 percent?

ANSWER: If the house appreciates to a value of $140,000 at the end of ten years, that will be a total appreciation of $140,000 − $85,000 = $55,000. Sally will owe 40 percent of $55,000, or $22,000 to the lender in a lump sum at the end of ten years. Approximate after-tax payments with the SAM are 1 − .28, or .72 × $6,386.88, or $4,598.55, and .72 × $8,424.72 or $6,065.80, without the SAM. The SAM reduces after-tax payments by $1,467.25. The question is whether the annual after-tax mortgage payment discounts of $1,467.25 for ten years can be invested to accumulate at least $22,000. Investing $1,467.25 annually for each of ten years at 6 percent yields a final accumulation of:

$1,467.25 × (FVFS (r=6%, n=10)) = (1.080 + 1.166 + 1.260 + 1.360 + 1.469 + 1.587 + 1.714 + 1.851 + 1.999 + 2.159) = 15.645 = $22,955.

Since the expected investment accumulation of $22,955 is greater than the expected payment of $22,000, the SAM contract is a "good deal."

Possible Pitfalls in the Shared Appreciation Mortgage

The shared appreciation mortgage can lead to problems for borrowers. One obvious potential problem is that the borrower does not save enough funds to pay the lender's appreciation share. In this case the borrower may be forced to sell the house merely to pay the owed appreciation value. The homebuyer who is considering a SAM should check the contract for provisions for financing the lender's appreciation share if such funds are not available to the owner.

A second point to recognize is that most SAMs are short term; for example, a maximum of ten years. At the end of the SAM's term when the lender's appreciation share is due, the borrower must refinance the outstanding loan balance in order to remain in the house. Again, the SAM contract should be checked for any refinancing provisions.

Shared Equity Mortgage

The shared equity mortgage is a sister to the shared appreciation mortgage. The shared equity mortgage actually puts the homeowner somewhere between renting the house and fully owning the house. Under the shared equity mortgage there are two parties, the *owner-occupant* and the *owner-investor.* The two parties share in the downpayment, financing, taxes, and insurance costs of the house according to a specified percentage split. In addition, the owner-occupant typically pays all maintenance and operating costs and pays rent to the owner-investor for the privilege of living in the owner-investor's share of the house.

The shared equity mortgage contract specifies a term for the agreement between the owner-occupant and owner-investor. When the term is up, three options are generally available: (1) the contract can be renewed, (2) the house can be sold and the sales price distributed to the owner-occupant and owner-investor according to the percentage split, or (3) the owner-occupant can refinance his/her share of the mortgage and pay the owner-investor's share of the house's estimated current value in a lump sum.

OWNER-OCCUPANT
OWNER-INVESTOR

Restrictions Imposed by the Shared Equity Mortgage

The owner-occupant and owner-investor are joint owners of the house under the shared equity mortgage. Such joint ownership imposes important restrictions on both parties. The owner-occupant can make structural changes to the house only with the consent of the owner-investor. Similarly, if the owner-occupant wants to sell the house and move before the end of the agreement's term, the owner-investor's consent must be granted.

Evaluating the Shared Equity Mortgage

The shared equity mortgage allows a consumer to more easily afford homeownership because the sum of the owner-occupant's mortgage payment and rent to the owner-investor will be less than the owner-occupant's mortgage payment under a conventional mortgage. In exchange, of course, the owner-occupant shares ownership of the house with the owner-investor. Furthermore, if the owner-occupant wants to become sole owner of the house when the shared equity mortgage contract expires, the owner-occupant must "buy-out" the owner-investor's share of the house's value. Therefore, the same question and evaluation arises as with the shared appreciation mortgage: Can the owner-occupant invest the money that is saved in payments from the shared equity mortgage and accumulate a fund large enough to pay the owner-investor's expected share of the house's value at the end of the agreement? If the answer is yes, then the shared equity mortgage is advantageous; if the answer is no, then the homebuyer might be better off with another type of mortgage.

The Bottom Line

Shared appreciation and shared equity mortgages are ways of reducing homeownership costs that become popular when mortgage interest rates rise. But there's no free lunch. In exchange for lower mortgage payments, the homeowner must share the appreciation gained in the house's value.

22. What Is Seller Financing?

Seller financing is another alternative mortgage which becomes popular during inflationary times when conventional mortgage interest rates are nominally high. High nominal mortgage interest rates prevent many potential buyers from qualifying for conventional loans. Home sales decline, which hurts both sellers and potential buyers.

In a standard home purchase, the seller receives the proceeds of the sale, uses the proceeds to pay-off any outstanding mortgage loan the seller has, and keeps the remaining funds. The buyer finances the purchase with a mortgage from a bank or savings and loan association.

BELOW MARKET INTEREST RATE

In seller financing the seller merely acts as the lender to the buyer. The seller offers a loan to the buyer, usually a short term loan, at a below-market interest rate. Thus, instead of receiving in a lump sum the sales price of the house, the seller receives monthly payments from the buyer over a specified period of time. If the seller also has a mortgage, the seller must use part of the buyer's periodic payments to continue making his/her (the seller's) mortgage payments. Of course, the seller moves out of the house and the buyer moves in. At the end of the term of the seller-financed loan, the buyer owes the seller the outstanding loan balance of the seller-financed loan. In order to make this final payment the buyer usually must obtain conventional financing. Therefore, seller financing is usually viewed as a temporary arrangement designed to provide below-market financing until conventional financing can be acquired.

An Example of How Seller Financing Works

Paul wants to sell his house for a price of $330,000. Market mortgage interest rates are 15%, but at that price few buyers appear. After six months Paul advertises his house as offering seller financing at 12% with $30,000 down payment and a 10-year term with payments calculated as if the term is 30 years. Paul currently pays $1,800 monthly on a mortgage with $90,000 outstanding loan balance. In 10 years this mortgage will have $72,000 outstanding loan balance.

If Paul could have sold his house in the standard manner with the buyer obtaining market financing, Paul would have received $330,000 at the time of sale, used $90,000 to pay his outstanding mortgage loan balance, and pocketed the rest ($330,000-$90,000=$240,000). Instead, under seller financing, the buyer will pay Paul $3,085.84 monthly in principal and interest payments (based on a 12% interest rate and calculated for 30 years) for 10 years. Paul will use $1,800 to continue paying his mortgage and will pocket the rest ($3,085.84 -$1,800=$1,285.84). At the end of the 10 years the buyer will owe Paul the outstanding balance on the $300,000 loan, which will be $280,254. Paul can then use that amount to pay the $72,000 remaining on this loan and keep the remainder.

Alternatives to Seller Financing

There are a number of potential problems associated with seller financing. For example, there is no assurance that the buyer will be able to obtain conventional market financing when the seller-financed arrangement is terminated. This could put both buyer and seller in a difficult position. Also, seller financed arrangements frequently create legal problems, particularly regarding the *seller's* original mortgage. Often the holder of the *seller's* mortgage does not permit the seller financed arrangement. If, however, the seller nevertheless contracts a seller financed arrangement, but the arrangement is discovered by the seller's mortgage holder, the seller's original mortgage may be called. This simply means that the outstanding loan balance of the seller's original mortgage is due immediately. If the seller does not have the amount of the loan balance available, both the seller and the buyer could lose the house.

REDUCE THE HOUSE PRICE

One way to avoid these problems is for the seller to consider lowering the sales price of the house rather than offering seller financing. The price reduction merely has to be such that it, plus its interest earnings, would be enough to pay the difference in mortgage payments between the conventionally financed mortgage and the seller financed mortgage. The following example gives an illustration.

EXAMPLE 4-14: In the previous example a housing selling for $330,000, with a $30,000 down payment, could be financed conventionally with a 15% mortgage. Alternatively, Paul, the seller, offers seller financing at 12% for 10 years. If, instead of offering seller financing, Paul reduced the price of the house, what would be the necessary price reduction if the buyer's tax bracket is 28% and funds can be invested, after taxes, at 10%?

ANSWER: Annual payments on $300,000 loan at 15% =$45,520

Annual payments on $300,000 loan at 12% =$37,030
Approximate after-tax payments at 15% = $45,520*(1-28%)=$32,774
Approximate after-tax payments at 12% =$37,030*(1-28%)=$26,662
Difference in after-tax payments for each of the 10 years = $6,112

To find the necessary price reduction, find the present value (PV) which, if invested at 10%, will produce annual amounts of $6,112 for each of the 10 years in the future. Because this is an equal amount per year situation, one can apply present value factor sum (PFVS).

$6,112*PVFS(r=10%, n=10 years)=$6,112*9.5565= $58,410

Therefore, a reduction in price of $58,410 (to $330,000-$58,410=$271,590) would be equivalent to offering seller financing at 12% for 10 years if the average buyer is in the 28% tax bracket and can invest funds at an after tax rate of 10%.

The Bottom Line

Instead of engaging in seller financing, consider having the seller reduce the price of the house enough such that conventional financing can be used.

23. When Should You Refinance Your Mortgage?

Refinancing a mortgage means taking a new mortgage and paying off the existing mortgage. You would consider doing this if current mortgage rates are lower than the interest rate on your existing mortgage. By refinancing to a lower rate, you reduce your mortgage payment and build up home equity faster. In case of sale of the house, a higher profit would be earned.

If refinancing was costless, then every time mortgage rates fell lower than your mortgage rate, you refinance, assuming time cost is not an issue. Typically refinancing does have a cost – generally you must pay closing costs again, which may be as high as 4% of the loan. However, there is also no-cost refinancing, which has become more and more popular in recent years, especially if you have excellent credit. Of course, there is no free lunch, so no-cost refinancing typically has a higher interest rate than refinancing with cost. In the case of no-cost refinancing, the comparison is simple. If the no-cost refinancing has a lower interest rate than your current mortgage rate, then you should refinance. Here we focus on refinancing with a cost.

There are two situations in which refinancing with a cost can be considered. One situation is when you have an adjustable rate mortgage and think that interest rates have hit the low point of the interest rate cycle (see *Should You Take a Fixed Rate or Adjustable Rate Mortgage?*). In this case you refinance from an adjustable rate mortgage to a fixed rate mortgage. The new fixed rate mortgage may not be lower than the adjustable rate mortgage, but the expectation is that by refinancing, you will avoid future higher mortgage costs when the adjustable rate rises.

The second situation which lends itself to refinancing is when the current fixed rate mortgage is lower than your existing fixed rate mortgage. In this case the question is how much lower the new mortgage rate must be such that the benefits of refinancing overcome the closing costs, lost value of tax deductions, and lost interest earnings on the closing costs associated with refinancing. Table 4-14 gives some answers. The shorter the time you expect to stay in the house, the lower the new mortgage rate must be for refinancing to be financially wise.

The Bottom Line

Consider refinancing your home mortgage when mortgage rates have hit the bottom of a cycle.

Table 4-14   When mortgage refinancing is beneficial.*

Expected length of stay in house from time of refinancing.	For refinancing to be financially beneficial, new mortgage interest rate must be at least:
2 years	4 percentage points lower than existing rate
5 years	2 percentage points lower than existing rate
10 years	1 percentage point lower than existing rate
15 years	¾ percentage point lower than existing rate
25 years	¾ percentage point lower than existing rate

*Assumes closing costs equal to 4% of loan, 1% mortgage discount rate, 28% federal tax bracket, new mortgage term equal to remaining term of original mortgage, and an alternative before-tax investment rate of 8%.

24. Another Look—How Do the Various Mortgages Compare?

Table 4-15 gives a shorthand comparison of the alternative mortgages in the mortgage parade. There are no "good" or "bad" mortgages. Each mortgage can be matched to a certain type of homebuyer or to a certain type of economic situation.

If the homebuyer can afford them, the 15 year mortgage and the biweekly mortgage have large benefits with few drawbacks. The major drawback is the foregone interest earnings on the extra payments or on the payments made earlier than they would be. This drawback increases the higher the alternative investment interest rate which the homebuyer can earn.

25. What Can You Do to Sell Your House?

Most of this chapter has been concerned with buying and financing a home. But, if you buy a home, chances are that you'll also sell a home.

When the time comes for you to sell your home, what can you do to improve the chances? First, apply some common sense with needed cosmetic changes to your home. If the yard looks shabby and the flowers droopy, polish up your green thumb and make your landscaping look presentable. Apply a new coat of paint to the outside of the house if necessary. On the inside, keep the house picked-up, clean, and inviting. Remove stains on the carpet, fix windows or doors which don't work properly, and repaint walls which are faded or which are painted an "outlandish" color. Most of these cosmetic changes can be done by the homeowner with little expense. Remember that your home will frequently be competing with brand new, spic-and-span homes.

From an economic perspective, however, the pricing of a home for sale is critically important. As has been emphasized before, homes are collections of many characteristics, not only of the home but also of the surrounding neighborhood and community. The sale of a home is an all or nothing proposition. If the home is sold, the whole package of characteristics is bought; the characteristics cannot be sold individually. The longer a home is for sale, the more likely a buyer will be found who places a high value on the package of characteristics offered by the house, and the more likely the buyer will offer a high price for the house.

The downside to waiting for the "highest bidder" is that the seller bears an opportunity cost related to the delay in selling the house. For example, suppose Steve and Joanne could sell their home today for $100,000 or six months from now for $105,000. The advantage of waiting the six months is that an extra $5,000 is gained from the sale. The disadvantage of waiting is that Steve and Joanne give up the opportunity of having $100,000

Table 4-15   Another glance at alternative mortgages.

Mortgage Type	Major Features	Best Taken When
Fixed Rate Mortgage	Fixed interest rate. Fixed principal & interest payment. Payment burden declines over time.	Interest rates are at the bottom of their cycle. Homebuyer plans to stay in house a long time.
Graduated Payment Mortgage	Payment starts low then gradually rises for 3-5 yrs, then levels.	Homebuyer is young with low income but has good potential for increased future income.
Adjustable Rate Mortgage	Interest rate and payment can change. Caps on changes.	Interest rates are at the top of their cycle. Homebuyer plans to stay in house a short time.
15 Year Mortgage	Mortgage is repaid in 15 years. Interest rate can be fixed or variable.	Always, unless very high interest can be earned on invested money, or money used for extra payments would be taken from necessities.
Buydown	Interest rates start 3 or 2 percentage points below market, then rise to market rate and remain constant. House price will be higher than without buydown.	Homebuyer is young with low income, but has good potential for increased future income.
Biweekly Mortgage	Mortgage payment is made every two weeks. Each payment is one-half the regular monthly payment. Mortgage is repaid faster than with monthly payment scheme.	Always, unless budget won't permit or very high interest rates can be earned on invested money
Shared Appreciation Mortgage Shared Equity Mortgage	Mortgage payment is lower than with conventional financing. Lender or investor shares in home's appreciation. Appreciation payment is due in 5–10 years.	Homebuyer needs lower payments for 5–10 years.
Seller Financing	Seller offers below-market financing to buyer for specified time period. Seller must obtain conventional financing at end of time period.	Homebuyer can't afford conventional financing and seller won't reduce house price

WHY ARE REAL ESTATE BROKERAGE RATES ALL THE SAME?

With most products and services there are noticeable differences in price. But not so with real estate brokerage rates. Nine times out of ten, if you ask a real estate agent what her brokerage rate is, she'll say 6 percent. Why? Is there some sort of conspiracy among real estate agents?

The conspiracy argument is one view; but there's probably a more logical (and less diabolical) explanation. Information is a vital part of the real estate industry—information about what houses are for sale, their characteristics, and their price. This information changes daily. Real estate agents have found that it is cheapest to collectively gather this information and share it. In most markets this is done through the Multiple Listing Service (MLS), a central clearinghouse for real estate information in a local market.

For the MLS to work, it requires cooperation among real estate agents and firms. For example, if one agent lists a house but another agent sells it, then the agents share in the commission. But if agents charged different brokerage rates, then other agents would steer away from those houses with lower rates in order to concentrate on those with higher rates and commissions. This would result in a breakdown in cooperation and the demise of the MLS. So the desire for cooperation among brokers provides an incentive for a single "going rate" brokerage fee.

A related question is why most brokers charge a percentage rate rather than a flat fee. The answer here seems to relate to the difficulty sellers (homeowners) have in monitoring real estate agent's efforts. The seller typically has a difficult time judging how hard the agent is working to sell the house for the highest price in the shortest time. A percentage fee is a form of profit-sharing because the higher the price the agent gets for the house, the more will be the agent's commission. A percentage fee form of compensation should give the agent greater incentive to get a higher price for the house than a flat fee.

The Internet is changing the real estate market by making more information readily available to more people. It will be interesting to see if this changes how real estate agents are compensated.

Reference: John H. Crockett "Competition and Efficiency in Transacting: The Cash of Residential Real Estate Brokerage. *American Real Estate and Urban Economics Association journal,* Vol. 10, No. 2, Summer 1981, pp. 209–227.

to invest for six months, net their living costs, for that time. For example, if Steve and Joanne could rent for $400 per month, then six months rent is $2,400 and they would have $97,600 ($100,000 – $2,400) to invest for six months. If a 7 percent annual after tax interest rate could be earned, then the opportunity cost of waiting for six months is $3,416 ($97,600 × .07 × .5). So waiting six months to sell the house gains Steve and Joanne a net benefit of $1,584 ($5,000 – $3,416).

SELLING YOUR HOME: DO-IT-YOURSELF OR USE AN AGENT?

C O N S U M E R

T O P I C

When it is time to sell a home, many owners are tempted to go the "FSBO" route—that is, for-sale-by-owner. Many owners think, "why-not;" if the owner can sell the house, then the realtor commission is saved. This is no small matter, since realtor commissions are usually 6 percent of the sale price. Thus, if the owner goes the "FISBO" route, the saved commission can add to the seller's profit, can be used to reduce the selling price, or can be split between the two.

Before trying to sell a home via a FSBO, you should carefully consider one word: "information." Information is the currency of the real estate market. A home doesn't sell unless information about it is put in the hands of buyers. The seller must decide how to accomplish this. Certainly a sign in the yard and advertisements in the newspapers real estate section are necessary elements of a FSBO strategy.

Unfortunately, the FSBO seller begins at a distinct disadvantage. The major source of information in a local real estate market is the "Multiple Listings Service," or MLS. The MLS is a centralized listing of information about homes for sale in the local market. Local real estate firms cooperatively fund the MLS. When an agent is looking for a house for a buyer, the agent punches the buyer's desired house and neighborhood characteristics into the MLS computer and out pops a list of potential houses. Any agent can access a house listed for sale whether the house is listed by the agent's firm or some other firm. However, houses which listed as "FSBO" are not listed in the MLS. This disadvantage is probably why many FSBO sellers will turn to an agent to list the house after one or two unsuccessful months of trying.

Research by Kang and Gardner confirms that pricing of the house is related to the length of time for its sale.[7] Kang and Gardner found that the higher the initial asking price of a house compared to its ultimate sales price, the longer the time required for the house to sell. Furthermore, the researchers found this relationship to be most important for higher priced homes. This makes sense because there are relatively fewer buyers for homes in the upper price range.

Researchers Kang and Gardner made an interesting discovery regarding sellers who wait longer periods of time in hope of getting a higher price. The finding was that sellers who wait longer periods of time for a sale when mortgage interest rates are high may be able to get a higher price, but waiting when interest rates are low will not reap a higher price.

---

[7] Kang, Han Bin and Mona J. Gardner, "Selling Price, Listing Price, Housing Features, and Marketing Time in the Residential Real Estate Market" Paper presented at the 1988 American Real Estate and Urban Economics Association Meetings, New York, N. Y. 1988.

The Bottom Line

For a quick sale, make sure the home is competitively priced. Houses which are overpriced take longer to sell. Furthermore, keeping a house on the market for a longer period of time brings a higher price only when mortgage interest rates are high.

WORDS AND CONCEPTS YOU SHOULD KNOW

Housing prices and location
Location premium
Homeownership costs
Closing costs
Homeownership tax deductions
Appreciation
Real after-tax mortgage interest rate
Breakeven annual rate of appreciation
Mortgage payments and recessions
Private mortgage insurance
Calculation of mortgage payments
Purchasing power of mortgage payments
Calculation of principal and interest payments
PITI
Fixed rate mortgage
Real mortgage payment burden

Graduated payment mortgage
Adjustable rate mortgage
Interest rate spread
Rate caps
Teaser rate
Negative amortization
Mortgage interest rate cycles
Points
15 Year mortgage
Prepaying a mortgage
Buydowns
Biweekly mortgage
Shared appreciation mortgage
Shared equity mortgage
Seller-financing
Refinancing

SHELTER—A SUMMARY

1. Where to live:
   - living in the city is more costly, yet gives you accessibility to more services and employment.
   - living in the country is less costly, yet puts you far away from shops, hospitals, and entertainment.
   - there is no "free lunch" in choosing where to live—cities with more amenities have higher shelter prices and lower wages.

2. The price of homes and the rent of apartments are determined by structural characteristics and amenities (size, carpet, air conditioning, etc.) and by neighborhood characteristics and amenities and location.

3. Homeownership costs include up-front, or one-time costs (closing costs, points, downpayment, etc.) and periodic (monthly) costs, such as the mortgage payment, operating costs, and insurance.
   - Tax deductions and appreciation reduce the cost of homeownership.

4 In deciding whether to own or rent, calculate the "breakeven annual rate of appreciation" on the house. If the house appreciates more than this rate, then, from a financial point-of-view, owning is better than renting.
   - The longer you plan to stay in a house, the better the house is as a financial investment.
   - Mortgage payments for new homes typically fall following a national economic recession.

5. Putting extra money toward a downpayment is generally wise unless very high investment rates can be earned on that money.

6. Mortgages are not "rip-offs." The present value of the mortgage payments, when discounted by the mortgage interest rate, equals the amount of the mortgage loan.
   - Use this principle to calculate mortgage payments.
   - The monthly interest due on a mortgage loan equals the outstanding loan balance multiplied by the monthly mortgage interest rate.

7. The PITI payment is the monthly house payment for principal, interest, taxes, and insurance. Lenders look at the PITI payment as a percentage of your monthly gross income to decide

if you qualify for the mortgage loan. Generally lenders want the PITI to monthly gross income ratio to be less than 28%.

8. The fixed rate mortgage has the advantage of a fixed rate and fixed payment but the disadvantage of high "real burdens" in the early years.

9. The graduated payment mortgage (GPM) has payments which begin low in the early years and then gradually rise to a constant level after 5 or 7 years. More total dollars are paid, but the present value cost of the GPM is the same as a fixed rate mortgage with the same interest rate.
    • Watch out for negative amortization (payments don't cover interest costs) in the early years of the GPM.

10. The adjustable rate mortgage (ARM) is a complicated contract. At a minimum, check how any ARM contract stacks up on the index, spread, frequency of rate change, rate and payment caps, and the "teaser rate."
    • ARM payments are calculated in the same way as fixed rate payments, except that when the ARM rate and payment are changed the new loan is calculated based on the remaining term.
    • ARM contracts in which the rate changes more frequently than the payment can result in negative amortization.

11. ARMs are better mortgages when:
    • mortgage interest rates are high and headed down;
    • the buyer will stay in the house only a few years.

12. The Treasury security ARM index (CMT) changes rapidly and is best for the homebuyer when rates are falling. The cost-of-funds ARM index (COFI) changes slowly and is best for the homebuyer when rates are rising.

13. "Points" are money charged "up-front" when a mortgage is taken. One point is one percent of the loan amount. Paying more points gets the borrower a lower mortgage interest rate. The longer the borrower expects to keep the mortgage, the wiser it is to pay points.

14. Take a 15 year mortgage unless a high rate of return can be earned on the extra money paid each month for it. Also, use spare funds to pre-pay or pay-down a mortgage, or to make extra principal payments, when those funds *can't* earn an interest rate higher than the mortgage interest rate.

15. Buydowns are similar to GPMs. Mortgage payments are reduced for two or three years, then rise and remain constant for the remainder of the mortgage term. Buydowns are offered by builders.

16. With a bi-weekly mortgage, the homeowner makes a mortgage payment every two weeks, but each payment is half the regular monthly payment. The benefit of the bi-weekly mortgage is that the mortgage term is reduced to between 17 and 24 years from 30 years.

17. Shared appreciation mortgages (SAMs) and shared equity mortgages (SEMs) lower mortgage payments for the homeowner by having the bank or an investor share in the payments in exchange for a share of the house's future appreciation.

18. With seller financing, a seller of a home finances the sale at a below market interest rate for a limited period of time. After that time the buyer must obtain conventional financing. An alternative to seller financing is for the seller to lower the house price by an equivalent amount.

19. Refinancing your mortgage means paying off your existing mortgage and taking out a new mortgage, usually with a lower interest rate. The lower the new mortgage interest rate and the longer the new mortgage will be held, the more beneficial is refinancing.

20. In order to sell a house quickly, make sure it is competitively priced for its size, condition, and location.

DISCUSSION QUESTIONS

1. Consider two houses of the same size with the same features and amenities, one located in San Francisco and one located in rural South Dakota. Why is the San Francisco house much more expensive than the South Dakota house?

2. Why have researchers found that local public school quality affects local house prices? What does this imply for support of public schools?

3. Why would an *increase* in income tax rates actually *reduce* the after-tax cost of homeowning relative to renting?

4. If you're financially able to, should you always own a house rather than rent?

5. "Always buy now rather than later," state realtors. Is this good advice?

6. You borrow $100,000 with a mortgage but repay $300,000 over 30 years. Does this make the mortgage a "rip-off?"

7. Are there any disadvantages to the fixed rate mortgage?

8. How are the graduated payment mortgage and the buydown similar?

9. You're a homebuyer. How would you decide whether to take a fixed rate mortgage or adjustable rate mortgage?

10. What characteristics of an adjustable rate mortgage should you examine before taking an ARM?

11. What is negative amortization and how can it occur?

12. What are "points" and when is it in the homebuyer's interest to pay them?

13. Why do seller financing, shared appreciation mortgages, and shared equity mortgages always become popular when mortgage interest rates rise?

14. How can the homeowner use mortgage interest rate cycles to his or her advantage?

1. Calculate the monthly principal and interest payments for a $180,000 conventional mortgage loan at 11 percent for 30 years. Show that the present value of the stream of payments is equal to $180,000 (for this part use annual rather than monthly payments).

2. For the mortgage in Problem 1, approximately how much of the *monthly* mortgage payment goes for principal and for interest in month 1, in month 2, in month 3?

3. Assume the household seeking the mortgage in problem 1 earns a gross annual income of $75,000, Would the household qualify for the loan if the bank's limit for the PITI/monthly gross income is 27 percent and if monthly payments for hazard insurance and property taxes are $500?

4. Consider a married couple buying a $200,000 house using a $10,000 downpayment and financing the balance for 30 years at a conventional fixed rate of 10 percent. Initial closing costs are $2,500. Consider a holding period of 3 years. Property taxes are $200 monthly and hazard insurance is $30 monthly each year. Operating costs and maintenance are $200/month and increase 10 percent annually. Alternative rent including utilities and maintenance is $1,200/month and increases 7 percent annually. The couple's tax bracket is 33 percent with no other deductions. The standard deduction is $10,000 each year. Calculate the required annual rate of appreciation on the house assuming a 6 percent after-tax alternative investment rate of return.

5. A lender wants to structure a $240,000, 30 year loan with a 12 percent mortgage interest rate as a graduated payment mortgage. If the lender wants to offer monthly payments of $1,500 the first year, $1,800 the second year, and $2,100 the third year, what must the final equal monthly payments be?

6. You are ready to sign a contract to buy a house using an adjustable rate mortgage. The mortgage loan is for $100,000 for 30 years at an initial interest rate of 8 percent. The interest rate and payments are changed annually. The interest rate is tied to the Treasury security index, plus a spread of 3 percentage points. Assume the Treasury security index is 7 percent at the start of the next year. Show your interest payments, principal payments, and outstanding loan balance for the first 3 months of the mortgage in each year.

7. You want to buy a $250,000 house with $25,000 down and a $225,000 mortgage. A lender offers you a shared appreciation mortgage with the following agreement: an 11 percent mortgage interest rate (fixed rate with payments calculated for 30 years) in return for your giving 45 percent of the house's appreciation to the lender no later than at the end of 10 years. Current conventional mortgage interest rates are 16 percent. What average annual rate is the lender implicitly assuming the house to appreciate?

8. A couple comes to you (as an expert on consumer economics) for advice about the following proposition. The couple owes $8,000 on their home. Their bank wants them to pay off the mortgage, and offers them a $500 savings certificate if they do so. If the couple keeps the mortgage they will pay $3,000 in principal and interest payments for each of the next 3 years. Interest payments on the mortgage are not sufficient for the couple to itemize, hence, paying off the mortgage will not affect their taxes. Assume the couple can invest funds at an 11 percent after-tax rate of return regardless of whether they hold a mortgage or not. Should they prepay?

9. Describe how you would analyze the possibility of refinancing a 12 percent mortgage with a remaining balance of $60,000 and a remaining term of 20 years. Refinancing would cost you $2,000 in closing costs, but fixed rate mortgages are now 8 percent. Don't work the problem—simply set it up.

Buying Consumer Durables and Using Credit

Introduction

Consumer durables are products like cars, washing machines, television sets, and furniture—products which last a long time. The topics of buying consumer durables and using credit go hand in hand because credit is often used to purchase the durable product, or "good." (If you're using credit to buy non-durable goods, like food, then you're in trouble.)

Having plowed through the chapter on buying the biggest consumer durable of all—a house—this chapter should be a breeze. The ideas and concepts used in understanding consumer credit finance are exactly the same as those used in housing finance. The major difference is that mortgage loans are made for a much longer time period (15 or 30 years) than consumer credit loans, which are usually made for less than 5 years.

This chapter will arm you with the ideas and information necessary to evaluate consumer credit options. Personal loans, auto loans, credit cards, and home equity loans will all be studied. You'll discover what an APR is. You'll find out when it's better to take an auto dealer's low interest rate financing, and when it's better to by-pass that financing and take the price rebate. You'll see if rent to own contracts are simply disguised high interest rate contracts, or if they are the best option for some consumers.

This chapter will also show you how to calculate the total cost of a consumer durable good (it's more than the gas you put in your car or the water in your washing machine). In fact, one of the biggest costs, depreciation, is a cost which most consumers ignore. You'll learn that consumer durable goods, like refrigerators and TVs, earn "rates of return" for you just like a CD or bond does.

Perhaps most importantly, this chapter will show you the ways you can get into credit trouble and the ways you can get out of credit trouble. Consumer credit is a useful tool, but as many consumers have discovered, it can be overused.

1. Why Use Credit?

Why in the world would anyone use consumer credit if not forced to in order to survive? Isn't credit the automatic road to financial problems?

Consumer credit has gotten a bad reputation based on all the stories about families ruining their lives by living beyond their means on credit. Actually, if credit is properly used, it can serve a very valuable function.

Matching Consumption and Income

Consider the type of consumer credit discussed in the last chapter—the mortgage. If you didn't buy a home until you could pay for it with cash, then you and very few others would ever become homeowners. Use of a mortgage allows you to purchase a home and pay for the home while living in it. You're able to repay the mortgage loan with future earnings.

Borrowing and saving allow many of us to match our consumption needs with income across our life span. Figure 5-1 illustrates an economic theory called "life-cycle saving's hypothesis." The idea is that consumption needs typically rise somewhat over time, but income does not change at the same rate. Income is initially below consumption needs in the early years, but income rises above consumption needs in the middle years, before declining again after retirement. Without borrowing and saving, consumption needs exceed income in the early years and after retirement, but income exceeds consumption needs in the middle years. Borrowing allows the income stream to more closely match the desired consumption stream.

When you borrow, the lender is giving you a credit, or trust, against your future earnings. What do you get out of the deal? You get to use the credit to buy something now. You then pay for the product by repaying the credit while you're using the product. If you wait until you have saved enough money to pay cash for the product, then you avoid using credit, but you postpone use and enjoyment of the product. The returns or benefits that consumer durable goods give may be well worth the price of credit paid to buy the good now rather than later (Figure 5-2).

FUTURE EARNINGS

With this view of credit in hand, it makes sense that the major users of credit are young families. Young families are in precisely the early part of the life cycle illustrated in Figure 5-1. Consumption needs are high due to the need for buying furniture, appliances, cars, and products associated with raising young children. Income, however, is likely low because the income earner or earners are just beginning their careers. However, income potential may well be high. Table 5-1 shows that household debt payments as a percent of income declines with age of the household head.

Figure 5-1. Life-cycle saving's hypothesis: Matching consumption with income by borrowing and saving

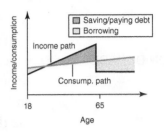

Figure 5-2. The function of credit.

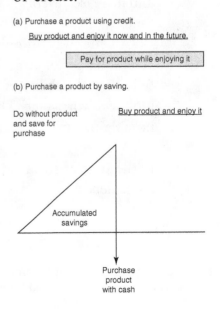

What Should Credit Be Used For?

DURABLE GOODS

Credit makes most sense when used to buy long lasting consumer goods, so-called durable goods. In this case you are paying for the product while using it. On a more practical level, if you can't continue making the credit payments, then the product can at least be sold and the proceeds used to repay some of the debt.

NON-DURABLE GOOD

Using credit makes less sense for purchase of a consumer good which is quickly used up, a so-called non-durable good. Here you continue paying for the non-durable good after you have finished using it and, of course, there's no chance of selling the good to help pay off the debt. Consumers who use credit to purchase food, to buy fuel, or to purchase non-durable clothing have a greater chance of developing credit problems.[1]

HAVE AMERICANS BEEN ON A CREDIT BINGE?

C O N S U M E R   T O P I C

Americans appear to have an appetite for credit. According to the Federal Reserve, consumer credit loans for everything except homes have risen from $352 billion in 1980 to $1.4 trillion in 2000, and to $2.8 trillion in 2012!

But, as you have already learned, looking at nominal dollars is misleading. Converting to 2012 dollars, the debt values in 1980 was $981 billion and in 2000 was $1.9 trillion. This is better, but it still shows a dramatic upward trend! However, these numbers do not show the whole picture because they do not account for the increased population size and increased average family income over time.

Household debt-service payments as a percentage of disposable income

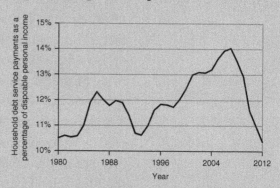

Data source: Federal Reserve System.

A better way of looking at the alleged "credit binge" of American consumers is to look at the ability of consumers to afford the debt. When this is done, the trends look less worrisome. The household debt-service payments as a percentage of disposable income have gone through ups and downs. However, between 1980 and 2012, the highest ratio was about 14% in 2007, the year when the financial crisis led to the start of so-called "great recession" in the United States. That sure was not a coincidence!

---

[1]Credit, especially credit cards, can be justifiably used to purchase non-durable goods if the credit is used as a convenience. Convenience credit is credit which is immediately repaid (or repaid within thirty days) and usually does not incur an interest charge.

Table 5.1. Median ratio of debt payments to family income, 2010

Age of head (years)	
Less than 35	16.4
35–44	20.9
45–54	19.2
55–64	17.6
65–74	17.0
75 or more	14.1

Data source: Federal Reserve System, Survey of Consumer Finances, 2010.

When to Use Credit Instead of Cash

For many consumers the question of whether to pay cash or use credit is easily answered. There's no cash available, so credit must be used if the product is to be purchased. In this case the cost of buying the product with credit is the interest rate charged, on the credit loan. We'll talk more about how to calculate the interest rate on credit loans later.

OPPORTUNITY COST OF CASH

If you could pay with cash, then the answer to whether using cash or credit is better is simple—use whichever is cheaper. You already know that the cost of using credit is the interest rate charged. But is there a cost to using cash? The cash is yours, so why should there be a cost? Of course there's a cost—*the opportunity cost* of what you could do with that cash.

SUBJECTIVE RATE OF RETURN

If you could invest that cash and earn, for example, a 7 percent after-tax rate of return, then the opportunity cost of using the cash to purchase the product is 7 percent. However, if the cash is your emergency savings which you will use to buy necessities (food, fuel, rent, or mortgage) in the case of a financial emergency, then your *subjective rate of return* from this cash may be much higher— maybe 15, 25, or 50 percent!

Table 5-2 illustrates a case where cash is cheaper than credit and a situation where credit is cheaper than cash. In Situation A the interest rate on the credit loan is 12 percent, and 9 percent (after-taxes) can be earned by investing cash. The calculations show that if the loan were taken and the cash invested, the cash and its investment earnings could not generate enough money to meet the credit payments. In Situation B, however, a 15 percent (after taxes) interest rate can be earned on the cash investment, so the cash can be invested to generate more than enough to meet the credit payments. So in this instance using credit is cheaper.

RULE

In general you will find that it is difficult to earn an after-tax rate of return on cash higher than the interest rate charged on consumer credit. So if you have the available cash, it's usually cheaper to pay with cash

Table 5-2 Using cash or using credit—which is cheaper?

Purchase Price of Product = $1,000

SITUATION A: Using cash is cheaper.

Month	Borrow $1,000 Loan = 12%, 12 mos. Payment	Invest $1,000 at 9% after-tax rate and use it to make credit payments (9% annual rate = 0.75% monthly rate)
1	$88.85	$1000 × 1.0075 = $1007.50, $1007.50 − $88.85 = $918.65
2	88.85	918.65 × 1.0075 = 925.54, 925.54 − 88.85 = 836.69
3	88.85	836.69 × 1.0075 = 842.97, 842.97 − 88.85 = 754.12
4	88.85	754.12 × 1.0075 = 759.78, 759.78 − 88.85 = 670.93
5	88.85	670.93 × 1.0075 = 675.96, 675.96 − 88.85 = 587.11
6	88.85	587.11 × 1.0075 = 591.51, 591.51 − 88.85 = 502.66
7	88.85	502.66 × 1.0075 = 506.43, 506.43 − 88.85 = 417.58
8	88.85	417.58 × 1.0075 = 420.71, 420.71 − 88.85 = 331.86
9	88.85	331.86 × 1.0075 = 334.35, 334.35 − 88.85 = 245.50
10	88.85	245.50 × 1.0075 = 247.34, 247.34 − 88.85 = 158.49
11	88.85	158.49 × 1.0075 = 159.68, 159.68 − 88.85 = 70.83
12	88.85	70.83 × 1.0075 = 71.36, 71.36 − 88.85 = −17.49

SITUATION B: Using credit is cheaper.

Month	Borrow $1,000 Loan = 12%, 12 mos. Payment	Invest $1,000 at 15% after-tax rate and use it to make credit payments (15% annual rate = 1.25% monthly rate)
1	88.85	$1000 × 1.0125 = $1012.50, $1012.50 − $88.85 = $923.65
2	88.85	923.65 × 1.0125 = 935.20, 935.20 − 88.85 = 846.35
3	88.85	846.35 × 1.0125 = 856.93, 856.93 − 88.85 = 768.08
4	88.85	768.08 × 1.0125 = 777.68, 777.68 − 88.85 = 688.83
5	88.85	688.83 × 1.0125 = 697.44, 697.44 − 88.85 = 608.59
6	88.85	608.59 × 1.0125 = 616.20, 616.20 − 88.85 = 527.35
7	88.85	527.35 × 1.0125 = 533.94, 533.94 − 88.85 = 445.09
8	88.85	445.09 × 1.0125 = 450.65, 450.65 − 88.85 = 361.80
9	88.85	361.80 × 1.0125 = 366.32, 366.32 − 88.85 = 277.47
10	88.85	277.47 × 1.0125 = 280.93, 280.93 − 88.85 = 192.09
11	88.85	192.09 × 1.0125 = 194.49, 194.49 − 88.85 = 105.64
12	88.85	105.64 × 1.0125 = 106.96, 106.96 − 88.85 = 18.11

than with credit. The only exception to this rule is if the cash is part of your emergency savings fund. Then the cash should be kept in the fund and credit used.

Using Credit to Beat Inflation

What if you face the following situation. You can buy a TV today using credit, or you can save enough in a year to pay cash. You can only earn 8 percent, after taxes, on your cash yet a personal loan will cost 10 percent, so using cash is cheaper, However, next year the price of the TV may be higher. So, is it better to wait until the TV can be bought with cash, or is it better to use credit now so the price of the TV can be locked in? The question you face is illustrated in Figure 5-3.

Using credit to purchase a product today and "lock in" the price is a clear advantage of credit purchases. For example, if the TV costs $1000 today and you finance it with a one-year personal loan charging 10 percent, then monthly payments will be $87.92. In comparison, if you wait a year and pay cash, yet you give up the opportunity of earning an 8 percent interest rate when you pay cash, then you are foregoing income of $91.34 a month for a year if the TV's price rises 5 percent to $1,050. If the TV's price rises 10 percent to $1,110, then using cash would mean an opportunity cost of $95.69 monthly.

Table 5-3 shows the relative benefits of buying now with credit, rather than waiting until next year to buy, for some typical financing alternatives. Negative entries in the table are the monthly savings in financing by buying today with credit. Positive entries in the table mean it's cheaper to wait until next year and buy with cash.

The table shows it is generally cheaper to buy today if the product is expected to increase in price next year, especially when the price increases are 5 percent or more. In contrast, if the product's price is expected to remain the same or fall next year, then it's cheaper to wait and pay with cash. Other conclusions resulting from Table 5-3 are:

- the smaller the difference between the credit interest rate and the opportunity cost rate of cash, the greater the advantage of buying today (compare entries for 12% credit rate and 7% opportunity cost rate to entries for 18% credit rate and 7% opportunity cost rate when next year's price is above $1000).

Figure 5-3. When to buy the TV.

Image (c) cobalt88, 2013. Used under license from Shutterstock, Inc.

♦ the higher the expected inflation rate for the product, the greater the advantage of buying today (compare entry for next year's price of $1,200 to entry for next year's price of $1,050 under any interest rate column).

Table 5-4 shows the average annual inflation rate for some typical consumer durable goods. Since computer prices have been falling, waiting

---

Table 5-3 Borrow today vs. pay cash next year. Difference between monthly payment if borrow today vs. monthly opportunity cost if pay cash tomorrow.

Today's price = $1.000.   12 month loan

(Positive numbers = cheaper to buy next year;
Negative numbers = cheaper to buy today.)

Credit interest rate today:		8%	10%	12%	18%
Opportunity cost rate of cash tomorrow:		5%	7%	7%	7%

Next Year's Price:	(Annual Inflation Rate)				
$ 900	–10%	$11.39	$10.04	$10.97	$13.80
950	–5%	7.19	5.72	6.65	9.48
1000	0%	2.99	1.39	2.32	5.15
1025	2.5%	0.89	–0.77	0.16	2.99
1050	5%	–1.21	–2.94	–2.01	0.83
1100	10%	–5.41	–7.26	–6.33	–3.40
1150	15%	–9.61	–11.59	–10.66	–7.83
1200	20%	–13.81	–15.92	14.99	–12.16

Table 5-4. Annual rates of inflation for typical consumer durable goods from 1983–2013.

Product	2013 January CPI	Annual inflation rate from 1983–2013
Household furnishing and operations	125.40	0.76%
Video and audio equipment	98.99	–0.03%
Personal computers	58.87	–1.75%
New vehicles	145.87	1.27%
Used cars and trucks	145.26	1.25%

Data source: U.S. Bureau of Labor Statistics, Consumer Price Index.

WHO'S IN DEBT?

As the accompanying table shows, almost 25 percent of all families have no consumer debt. Also, contrary to popular opinion, close to half of the poorest families (incomes in the lowest 20th percentile) have no consumer debt.

In fact, consumer debt is more prevalent the higher the family income, until the very highest family income range (top 20th percentile of income) is reached. Primary residence mortgage and installment loan debt especially follow this pattern.

The reverse pattern exists for age and debt. Here, families with heads aged 35 to 44 are the heaviest users of debt.

C O N S U M E R   T O P I C

Percentage of families holding debt by type of consumer debt, 2010

Family characteristic	Secured by residential property		Install-ment loans	Credit card balances	Lines of credit not secured by residential property	Other	Any debt
	Primary residence	Other					
All families	**47.0**	**5.3**	**46.3**	**39.4**	**2.1**	**6.4**	**74.9**
Percentile of income							
Less than 20	14.8	1.3	34.1	23.2	1.2	4.2	52.5
20–39.9	29.6	1.7	40.8	33.4	2.2	4.2	66.8
40–59.9	51.6	3.5	49.9	45.0	2.1	6.8	81.8
60–79.9	65.4	6.0	56.6	53.1	1.9	7.8	86.9
80–89.9	74.5	9.1	58.8	51.0	2.0	11.8	88.9
90–100	72.8	19.4	41.8	33.6	3.7	6.6	84.5
Age of head (years)							
Less than 35	34.0	2.9	61.9	38.7	1.8	5.5	77.8
Less than 35	34.0	2.9	61.9	38.7	1.8	5.5	77.8
35–44	57.6	5.1	60.0	45.7	2.2	8.6	86.0
45–54	60.4	7.6	49.8	46.2	2.7	9.7	84.1
55–64	53.6	7.6	40.7	41.3	3.0	6.7	77.7
65–74	40.5	5.0	30.3	31.9	1.2	2.3	65.2
75 or more	24.2	2.9	12.3	21.7	*	2.0	38.5

Data source: Federal Reserve System, Survey of Consumer Finances, 2010.

to buy a computer next year with cash is better. For the other products which have modest inflation rates of 1, 2, 3 percent, buying today on credit or tomorrow with cash is a toss-up unless today's financing would be done with a credit card (at 18 percent). Of course, if there's a spurt of inflation in the future, then this favors buying today with credit.

These conclusions, however, ignore one important point. By delaying purchase of a durable good for, say, a year, you give up the pleasure of having use of that good for the year. This cost must be weighed against any financial benefits of delaying the purchase.

In the next topic you'll learn how to calculate the monthly payments associated with a credit loan. Then you'll be able to easily calculate the benefits and costs of buying now or later for any situation.

The Bottom Line

Use credit to transfer future purchasing power to today. Use credit if the credit interest rate is lower than the opportunity cost rate on cash. Finally, use credit to buy goods now that are increasing rapidly in price. _____

2. How Do You Calculate the Cost of Credit?

The interest rate charged on consumer credit is the major determinant of consumer credit payments. The higher the interest rate, the higher will be payments, and the lower the interest rate the lower will be payments.

Interest rates charged on consumer credit loans are very variable. The interest rates charged on personal loans from banks and savings and loans vary between 8 and 14 percent. Credit card interest rates are between 15 and 22 percent, and interest rates from finance companies and other lenders may be even higher.

Consumer credit interest rates vary so much due to the variation in risk of the borrowing consumer. If the lender perceives that the borrower has a higher chance of not meeting the payments on the loan, then the interest rate charged will be higher.

Calculating Payments

PRESENT VALUE OF CREDIT PAYMENTS

How will a lender calculate the payments necessary to repay a consumer credit loan? You should by now anticipate the answer because, yes, discounting is involved again. The lender of a consumer credit loan will use the same logic as a banker making a mortgage loan. *The lender will want the present value of the future payments to equal the loan amount.*

So, if you have a loan amount and an interest rate, find the monthly payment by first summing the monthly present value factors associated with the interest rate and then dividing that sum into the loan amount. To save you time and aggravation, Appendix Table A-6 gives monthly present value factor sums for various interest-rate and loan term combinations.

EXAMPLE 5-1: Find the equal monthly payment for a $1000 loan charging an 18 percent annual interest rate and being repaid in 12 months. Payments are made at the end of each month.

ANSWER:

$$\text{Monthly payment} = \frac{Loan\,amount}{PVFS\left(rm,=\dfrac{18\%}{12},n=12\,months\right)}$$

$$= \frac{\$1,000}{10.9075} = \$91.68$$

You can either use the PVFS formula or Appendix Table A-6 to find the PVFS.

EXAMPLE 5-2: Find the equal monthly payment for a $1000 loan charging an 18 percent annual interest rate and being repaid in 24 months. Payments are made at the end of each month.

ANSWER:

$$\text{Monthly payment} = \frac{Loan\,amount}{PVFS\left(rm,=\dfrac{18\%}{12},n=24\,months\right)}$$

$$= \frac{\$1,000}{20.0304} = \$49.92$$

You can either use the PVFS formula or Appendix Table A-6 to find the PVFS.

This process can be used in reverse to find the interest rate charged on a consumer credit loan. If you know the original loan amount, the loan term, and the monthly payment, then calculate:

$$\frac{loan}{monthly\ payment}.$$

The result of this division is the present value factor sum (PVFS). Find this number in Appendix Table A-6 by reading across the row for the loan term until the number is found. Then read the corresponding interest rate.

EXAMPLE 5-3: A $2000 loan requires the repayment of $60.86 monthly for 48 months (each payment is at the end of the month). What is the associated annual interest rate?

$$\text{ANSWER} : \frac{\$2000}{\$60.86} = 32.86.$$

The interest rate in Appendix Table A-6 associated with a term of 48 months and a present value factor sum of 32.86 is 20 percent.

Don't be deceived by what is called "add-on" interest. In EXAMPLE 5-1, $91.68 is paid monthly for twelve months for a total repayment of $1100.16.

Total interest paid, or the "add on" interest, is thus $1,100.16–$1,000 = $100.16.

You might be tempted to say that the interest rate is equal to, or $\frac{\$100.16}{1,000}$,

or 10.02. This is incorrect since the actual interest rate is almost twice as large, at 18 percent.

ADD-ON INTEREST

The reason the "add-on" interest rate is incorrect is because it assumes the borrower has full use of the $1,000 for the entire loan term. This is wrong since each credit payment includes some repayment of principal (just as each mortgage payment does). This will be shown in the next section.

Calculating Payments for Principal and Interest

You already know how to do this. Interest and principal payments on consumer loans are calculated just as with a mortgage. That is:

interest payment = previous outstanding loan
balance × periodic interest rate,
principal payment = periodic payment – interest payment,
new outstanding loan balance = previous loan
balance – principal payment.

For example, consider a $10,000 loan to be repaid in 12 months with an interest rate of 12 percent. Table 5-5 shows the progression of principal and interest payments out of each payment and the change in the outstanding loan balance. Notice that the monthly interest rate is the annual rate of 12 percent divided by 12, or 1 percent.

Table 5-5 shows interest charged on a monthly basis—that is, the monthly interest rate is the annual rate divided by 12. However, lenders can use other techniques in allocating monthly payments to interest and principal. One technique calculates the monthly interest rate as ([yearly interest rate/365] × number of days in the month). This technique will produce results very similar to those shown in Table 5-5.

Table 5-5   Calculating the loan balance on a consumer credit loan.

$10,000 loan, 12% rate, term of 12 months, monthly payment = $888.49							
Month 1	Interest	=	$10,000.00	×	.01	=	$100.00
	Principal	=	$888.49	−	$100.00	=	$788.49
	Balance	=	$10,000.00	−	$788.49	=	$9,211.51
Month 2	Interest	=	$9,211.51	×	.01	=	$92.12
	Principal	=	$888.49	−	$92.12	=	$796.37
	Balance	=	$9,211.00	−	$796.37	=	$8,415,14
Months 3	Interest	=	$8,415.14	×	.01	=	$84.15
	Principal	=	$888.49	−	$84.15	=	$804.34
	Balance	=	$8,415.14	−	$804.34	=	$7,610.80
Month 4	Interest	=	$7,610.80	×	.01	=	$76.11
	Principal	=	$888.49	−	$76.11	=	$812.38
	Balance	=	$7,610.80	−	$812.38	=	$6,798.42
Month 5	Interest	=	$6,798.42	×	.01	=	$67.98
	Principal	=	$888.49	−	$67.98	=	$820.51
	Balance	=	$6,798.42	−	$820.51	=	$5,977.91
Month 6	Interest	=	$5,977.91	×	.01	=	$59.78
	Principal	=	$888.49	−	$59.78	=	$828.71
	Balance	=	$5,977.91	−	$828.71	=	$5,149.20
Month 7	Interest	=	$5,149.20	×	.01	=	$51.49
	Principal	=	$888.49	−	$51.49	=	$837.00
	Balance	=	$5,149.20	−	$837.00	=	$4,312.20
Month 8	Interest	=	$4,312.20	×	.01	=	$43.12
	Principal	=	$888.49	−	$43.12	=	$845.37
	Balance	=	$4,312.20	−	$845.37	=	$3,466.83
Month 9	Interest	=	$3,466.83	×	.01	=	$34.67
	Principal	=	$888.49	−	$34.67	=	$853.82
	Balance	=	$3,466.83	−	$853.82	=	$2,613.01
Month 10	Interest	=	$2,613.01	×	.01	=	$26.13
	Principal	=	$888.49	−	$26.13	=	$862.36
	Balance	=	$2,613.01	−	$862.36	=	$1,750.65

(continued on next page)

Table 5-5 Calculating the loan balance on a consumer credit loan (continued).

$10,000 loan, 12% rate, term of 12 months, monthly payment = $888.49

Month 11	Interest	=	$1,750.65	×	.01	=	$17.51
	Principal	=	$888.49	–	$17.51	=	$870.98
	Balance	=	$1,750.65	–	$870.98	=	$879.67
Month 12	Interest	=	$879.67	×	.01	=	$8.80
	Principal	=	$888.49	–	$8.80	=	$879.69
	Balance	=	$879.67	–	$879.69	=	$0.00

However, another technique calculates the monthly interest rate as ([yearly interest rate/360] × number of days in the month). Collins calls **365.25/360 METHOD** this the "365.25/360" method because on average it results in 5.25 additional days of interest charged per year.[2] This technique is very beneficial to the lender because it results in more interest and less principal being charged from each loan payment. Table 5-6 compares the allocations to principal and interest using the three techniques discussed. Obviously, the "365.25/360" method should be avoided, especially for long-term loans.

The Bottom Line

Consumer credit loan payments are calculated so that the present value sum of the payments equals the loan amount. Loans which use the "365.25/360" method of allocating interest and principal result in more of each payment for interest and less for principal. Avoid these kinds of loans.

3. What in the World Is the "Rule of 78"?

The "Rule of 78" (not to be confused with the "Rule of 72" in investing) is an alternative way of calculating the allocation of each credit payment to principal and interest. After reading this section, you'll probably say it's a bizarre way!

The "Rule of 78" is implemented by following these six steps:

Step 1: Add the digits for the number of months of payments. For example, for a 12-month payment term, add 1 + 2 + 3 + 4 +

---

[2] Robert A. Collins, "The Allocation of Monthly Payments to Principal and Interest: A Caveat for Consumers." *The Journal of Consumer Affairs,* Vol. 15, No. 2, Winter 1981, pp. 317–323.

Table 5-6 Alternative ways of calculating loan balances.

$1,000 loan, 12% annual rate, 12 months, payment = $88.81

	Monthly rate = .12/12 = .01	Monthly rate = $\frac{.12}{365}$ × days in mo.	Monthly rate = $\frac{.12}{360}$ × days in mo.
January	Int. = 1000 × .01 = $10.00	Int. = 1000 × $\frac{.12}{365}$ × 31 = $10.19	Int. = 1000 × $\frac{.12}{360}$ × 31 = $10 33
(month 1)	Prin. = 88.81 − 10.00 = 78.81	Prin. = 88.81 − 10.19 = 78.62	Prin. = 88.81 − 10.33 = 78.48
(31 days)	Bal. = 1000 − 78.81 = 921.19	Bal. = 1000 − 78.62 = 921.38	Bal. = 1000 − 78.48 = 921.52
February	Int. = 921.19 × .01 = $9.21	Int. = 921.38 × $\frac{.12}{365}$ × 29 = $8.78	Int. = 921.52 × $\frac{.12}{360}$ × 29 = $8.91
(month 2)	Prin. = 88.81 − 9.21 = 79.60	Prin. = 88.81 − 8.78 = 80.03	Prin. = 88.81 − 8.91 = 79.90
(29 days)	Bal. = 921.19 − 79.60 = 841.59	Bal. = 921.38 − 80.03 = 841.35	Bal. = 921.52 − 79.90 = 841.62
March	Int. = 841.59 × .01 = 8.42	Int. = 841.35 × $\frac{.12}{365}$ × 31 = $8.57	Int. = 841.62 × $\frac{.12}{360}$ × 31 = $8.70
(month 3)	Prin. = 88.81 − 8.42 = 80.39	Prin. = 88.81 − 8.57 = 80.24	Prin. = 88.81 − 8.70 = 80.11
(31 days)	Bal. = 841.59 − 80.39 = 761.20	Bal. = 841.35 − 80.24 = 761.11	Bal. = 841.62 − 80.11 = 761.51
April	Int. = 761.20 × .01 = $7.61	Int. = 761.11 × $\frac{.12}{365}$ × 30 = $7.51	Int. = 761.51 × $\frac{.12}{360}$ × 30 = $7.62
(month 4)	Prin. = 88.81 − 7.61 = 81.20	Prin. = 88.81 − 7.51 = 81.30	Prin. = 88.81 − 7.62 = 81.19
(30 days)	Bal. = 761.20 − 81.20 = 680.00	Bal. = 761.11 − 81.30 = 679.81	Bal. = 761.51 − 81.19 = 680.32

$5 + 6 + 7 + 8 + 9 + 10 + 11 + 12 = 78$. For a 24-month payment term, add $1 + 2 + 3 + 4 + 5 + 6 + 7 + 8 + 9 + 10 + 11 + 12 + 13 + 14 + 15 + 16 + 17 + 18 + 19 + 20 + 21 + 22 + 23 + 24 = 300$.

Step 2: Assign a number to each month of payment, but where the assigned number is the reverse of the month's order. For example, for a 12-month payment, the number assignments are:

Month 1 = 12	Month 7 = 6
Month 2 = 11	Month 8 = 5
Month 3 = 10	Month 9 = 4
Month 4 = 9	Month 10 = 3
Month 5 = 8	Month 11 = 2
Month 6 = 7	Month 12 = 1

Step 3: Calculate the total amount of interest paid on the loan, also called the finance charge. The total interest paid equals the total amount paid for the loan (number of payments × monthly payment) minus the original loan amount.

Step 4: To find the interest paid for a given month, first add the assigned number for that month to the assigned numbers for the earlier months. Divide this sum by the sum of all the numbers (or digits) (from STEP 1). Multiply this result by the finance charge to find the interest paid for the month.

Step 5: The principal paid for the month is the monthly payment minus the interest paid (calculated in STEP 4).

Step 6: The new outstanding loan balance is the previous outstanding loan balance minus the principal paid.

Table 5-7 shows how the Rule of 78 is applied to the $1,000, 12 percent, 12-month loan shown in Table 5-5. Table 5-8 compares the monthly loan balances using the Rule of 78 and using economic logic (as calculated in Table 5-5). Notice that the principal payments are always smaller and the interest payments and outstanding loan balances are always larger using the Rule of 78 than using economic logic to allocate principal and interest. This will always happen with the Rule of 78. If you want to pay off a loan early (called prepaying a loan) and the lender

Table 5-7   Calculating the outstanding loan balance by the Rule of 78.

\$10,000 loan, 12% rate, term of 12 months
Monthly payments = \$888.49
Total payment = \$10,661.88
Total interest charge = \$661.88
(1 + 2 + 3 + 4 + 5 + 6 + 7 + 8 + 9 + 10 + 11 + 12 = 78)

Month 1 $\dfrac{12}{78} \times 661.88 = 101.83 =$ total interest payment

$888.49 - 101.83 = 786.66 =$ total principal

$10,000 - 786.66 = \underline{9213.34 \text{ balance}}$

Month 2 $\dfrac{(12+11)}{78} \times 661.88 = 195.17 =$ total interest payment

$(888.49 \ 2) - 195.17 = 1,581.81 =$ total principal

$10,000 - 1,581 = \underline{8,418.19 \text{ balance}}$

Month 3 $\dfrac{(12+11+10)}{78} \times 661.88 = 280.03 =$ total interest payment

$(888.49 \ 3) - 280.03 = 2,385.44 =$ total principal

$10,000 - 2,385.44 = \underline{7,614.56 \text{ balance}}$

Month 4 $\dfrac{(12+11+10+9)}{78} \times 661.88 = 356.40 =$ total interest payment

$(888.49 \ 4) - 356.40 = 3,197.56 =$ total principal

$10,000 - 3,197.56 = \underline{6802.44 \text{ balance}}$

Month 5 $\dfrac{(12+11+10+9+8)}{78} \times 661.88 = 424.28 =$ total interest payment

$(888.49 \ 5) - 424.28 = 4,018.17 =$ total principal

$10,000 - 4,018.17 = \underline{5,981.83 \text{ balance}}$

Month 6 $\dfrac{(12+11+10+9+8+7)}{78} \times 661.88 = 483.68 =$ total interest payment

$(888.49 \ 6) - 483.68 = 4,847.26 =$ total principal

$10,000 - 4,847.26 = \underline{5,152.74 \text{ balance}}$

Month 7 $\dfrac{(12+11+10+9+8+7+6)}{78} \times 661.88 = 534.60 =$ total interest payment

$(888.49 \ 7) - 534.60 = 5,684.83 =$ total principal

$10,000 - 5,684.83 = \underline{4,315.17 \text{ balance}}$

Month 8 $\dfrac{(12+11+10+9+8+7+6+5)}{78} \times 661.88 = 577.02 =$ total interest payment

(continued on next page)

Table 5-7 Calculating the outstanding loan balance by the Rule of 78 (continued).

$10,000 loan, 12% rate, term of 12 months
Monthly payments = $888.49
Total payment = $10,661.88
Total interest charge = $661.88
(1 + 2 + 3 + 4 + 5 + 6 + 7 + 8 + 9 + 10 + 11 + 12 = 78)

$(888.49 \times 8) - 577.02 = 6,530.90 =$ total principal

$10,000 - 6,530.90 = \underline{3,469.10}$ balance

Month 9 $\dfrac{(12+11+10+9+8+7+6+5+4)}{78} \times 661.88 = 610.97 =$ total interest payment

$(888.49 \times 9) - 610.98 = 7,385.44 =$ total principal

$10,000 - 7,385.44 = \underline{2,614.56}$ balance

Month 10 $\dfrac{(12+11+10+9+8+7+6+5+4+3)}{78} \times 661.88 = 636.42 =$ total interest payment

$(888.49 \times 10) - 636.42 = 8,248.48 =$ total principal

$10,000 - 8,248.48 = \underline{1,751.52}$ balance

Month 11 $\dfrac{(12+11+10+9+8+7+6+5+4+3+2)}{78} \times 661.88 = 653.39 =$ total interest payment

$(888.49 \times 11) - 653.39 = 9,120.00 =$ total principal

$10,000 - 9,120.00 = \underline{880}$ balance

Month 12 $\dfrac{(12+11+10+9+8+7+6+5+4+3+2+1)}{78} \times 661.88 = 661.88 =$ total interest payment

$(888.49 \times 12) - 661.88 = 10,000 =$ total principal

$10,000 - 10,000 = \underline{0}$ balance

---

uses the Rule of 78, you'll find the lender will require a larger prepayment than if economic logic is used to calculate the outstanding loan balance. Bonker shows that the Rule of 78 becomes more unfavorable to the consumer the greater the term of the loan and the greater the interest rate.[3]

Why is the Rule of 78 used? Before the age of high speed computers and calculators, it was probably used as a shortcut to calculating the outstanding loan balance or, it may be used to discourage consumers from prepaying loans. Whatever the reason, the Rule of 78 is certainly biased in favor of the lender.

---

[3]Bonker, Dick. "The Rule of 78." *Journal of Finance,* Vol. 31, No. 3, June 1976, pp. 877–888.

Table 5-8   The Rule of 78 vs. Economic Logic.

Month	End-of-month outstanding loan balance Rule of 78	End-of-month outstanding loan balance Economic Logic	Difference
1	$9,213.34	$9,211.51	$1.83
2	8,418.19	8,415.14	3.04
3	7,614.56	7,610.80	3.76
4	6,802.44	6,798.42	4.02
5	5,981.83	5,977.91	3.92
6	5,152.74	5,149.20	3.54
7	4,315.17	4,312.20	2.97
8	3,469.10	3,466.8	2.27
9	2,614.56	2,613.01	1.55
10	1,751.52	1,750.65	0.87
11	880.00	879.67	0.33
12	0.00	0.00	0.00

The Bottom Line

Everything else equal, consumers should avoid loans which calculate the payment allocation to principal and interest using the Rule of 78. The Rule of 78 always results in a smaller payment allocation to principal and a larger outstanding loan balance. It results in a built-in prepayment penalty.

4. What Does the APR Mean?

APR is short for annual percentage rate. The Consumer Credit Protection Act of 1968 requires that lenders follow specified procedures in calculating the APR and presenting it to consumers. Fortunately these procedures use economic logic, so the APR is a useful characteristic for consumers to consider.

Definition of the Finance Charge

An important part of the definition of the APR is what is included as a cost of the loan. The Consumer Credit Protection Act gives a broad definition of the credit costs including "any charge payable directly or indirectly by the consumer." This includes interest payments but also these charges paid to the lender:

♦ any service or carrying charges,
♦ points, loan fees, and similar charges,
♦ appraisal, investigation, and credit report fees,
♦ premiums for life, health, or credit insurance if required by the lender.

Closing costs, application fees charged to all applicants of credit (whether credit is granted or not), charges for late payment or over-withdrawal of an account, and fees for title examination are not considered part of credit costs.

APR for Closed-End Credit Loans

APR AND UP-FRONT
COSTS

Specific calculation of the APR depends on whether the loan is closed-end credit or open-end credit. Closed-end credit is credit which must be repaid in a specific term, such as a mortgage loan, personal loan, or auto loan. The APR for closed-end credit loans is calculated in the way you have already learned. The APR is the interest rate which equates the present value of the credit costs to the loan amount. This means that loans with heavy up-front costs, such as points and loan fees, will have a higher APR, everything else equal.

Table 5-9 shows the calculation of APRs for two closed-end credit loans, one with up-front costs and one without up-front costs. For the loan with up-front costs, first subtract those costs from the loan amount. This is done because the up-front costs are paid now, so they shouldn't be discounted. Divide the result by the monthly payment. Find this number in Appendix Table A-6 corresponding to the number of monthly payments. For the loan without up-front costs, find the APR by dividing the loan amount by the monthly payment and then using Appendix Table A-6.

You will find the APR quoted for mortgage loans usually greater than the mortgage interest used to calculate the monthly principal and interest payments. Why? It's because the APR will include as credit costs the upfront costs of points, loan fees, and appraisal and credit report fees.

The APR can be calculated for any type of closed-end credit payment structure—for example, a loan with weekly payments, biweekly payments, or a loan with irregular or unequal payments. Appendix Table A-6 can't be used to calculate APRs for these loans; instead, more complex iterative methods or computer programs are used. Nevertheless, the same principle holds that the APR is the interest rate which equates the present value of the credit costs to the loan amount.

Table 5-9 Calculating the APR.

A.   *Loan with up-front costs:*

$3,000 loan, up-front costs of $500, monthly payments of $125 for 24 months:

$$\frac{\$3,000-\$500}{\$125}=\frac{\$2,500}{\$125}=20$$

In Appendix Table A-6, find the interest rate corresponding to an entry of 20 and a row value of 24 months.

Answer = 18 percent APR

B.   *Loan without up-front costs:*
$3,000 loan, no up-front costs, monthly payments of $140 for 24 months.

$$\frac{\$3,000}{\$140}=21.43$$

In Appendix Table A-6 find the interest rate corresponding to an entry of 21.43 and a row value of 24 months.

Answer = Between 11 and 11¼ percent APR.

APR for Open-End Credit Loans

Open-end credit loans are loans which do not have to be repaid in a specific term. Credit card loans and many other charge card loans are examples. Usually a minimum amount must be repaid each month, but generally some part of the loan can be carried over from month to month. Of course, interest is charged on each month's outstanding loan balance.

The APR on an open-end credit loan is calculated differently than the APR on a closed-end loan. For an open-end loan, the APR is calculated as the periodic rate multiplied by the number of payment periods in one year. If monthly payments are made, then the APR is the monthly interest rate multiplied by 12. For example, if the monthly rate is 1½ percent, then the APR is 1½ × 12 or 18 percent.

Technically, this calculation of the APR is in error. Remembering back to Chapter 1, if, for example, you have a monthly interest rate of 1 percent, then the annual interest rate is:

$$(1.01)^{12}-1=1.1268-1$$
$$=.1268$$
or 12.68 percent.

The APR calculation shows the annual interest rate to be .01 ×12, or 12 percent. The APR calculation is less than the actual annual interest rate. The error between the APR and the actual interest rate increases the higher the APR.

Why isn't the APR for open-end credit loans calculated in the correct way? That's a good question. The methods of calculating the APR were established by the 1968 Consumer Credit Protection Act. Clearly it would be in consumers' interests if the Act were amended to include the correct calculation of the open-end APR.

The Bottom Line

The APR (annual percentage rate) is a standardized measure of credit costs. In calculating the APR, periodic credit payments are included as well as up-front costs, such as points and fees. Loans with lower APRs are better for consumers. However, the APR calculation for open-end credit loans understates the true cost of credit.

5. What Are the Total Costs of a Consumer Durable Good?

Credit is used to buy consumer durable goods, like cars, washing machines, refrigerators, and furniture. Before you can analyze whether it is wise to use credit to buy a consumer durable good, you must understand the total costs of a consumer durable good.

Since the most expensive consumer durable good purchased by consumers is a car, a car will be used to illustrate most of the costs and concepts.

Rental Costs

RENTAL FEE

OPERATING COSTS

If a consumer durable good is rented, there are two costs that you face. One is the *rental fee* paid for using the product. For example, you might rent a car for $250 per month or a TV for $30 a month. The second cost is *operating costs* while using the product. Gasoline is the major operating expense for a car, and electricity is the major operating expense for a TV.

Ownership Costs

If a consumer durable good is owned, then just like with a house, total costs are more numerous and complicated than for renting. It is useful to separate durable good costs into two kinds, fixed costs and variable costs. Fixed costs are costs of owning the durable good which don't depend on how much the product is used. Variable costs are costs of owning the durable good which do vary by how much the product is used (see Table 5-10).

FIXED COSTS

Fixed Costs of owning a durable good include depreciation, finance costs, scheduled maintenance, insurance costs and other fees (where applicable), and foregone interest earnings.

DEPRECIATION

Depreciation means a decline in the market value, or worth, of the consumer durable good. Depreciation represents a "using up" of the durable good. When depreciation occurs, it means the owner of the durable good loses money because the good could now only be sold for less money. Depreciation is generally related to the age of the durable good. Also, more or less depreciation will occur each year depending on how much the good is used. However, for simplicity, assume that depreciation is directly related to the product's age, so it is a fixed cost. For autos, depreciation is the largest cost of ownership in the early years of the auto's life.

FINANCE COSTS

Finance costs are those expenditures made for the loan used to purchase the durable good, if such a loan was used. If no loan was taken to purchase the durable good, or if the loan has been completely repaid, then finance costs are zero.

SCHEDULED
MAINTENANCE
COSTS

Scheduled maintenance costs are those expenditures made to keep the durable good useful and in working order and which are made at certain intervals of time, unrelated to the use of the good. Oil changes, lubrication, and safety checks on cars are examples.

INSURANCE COSTS
AND FEES

Insurance costs and fees only occur for a few consumer durable goods, with autos being the best example. For autos, insurance coverage must be bought for potential personal and property damage (see Chapter 7). Also, various fees may be imposed by the state or locality, such as a titling fee (generally paid only once when the auto is purchased) and an annual license fee.

FOREGONE INTEREST
EARNINGS

Finally, an often overlooked cost of ownership of a consumer durable good is the *foregone interest earnings on net ownership*. This is an opportunity cost, just like the opportunity cost of a downpayment on a house. Net ownership of the consumer durable good is equal to

---

Table 5-10   Costs of owning durable goods.

Fixed costs:
   Depreciation
   Finance costs
   Scheduled maintenance
   Insurance costs and fees (where applicable)
   Foregone interest earnings

Variable costs:
   Fuel or power
   Unscheduled maintenance and repairs

the market value of the durable good minus any outstanding loan on the good. If you pay cash for the durable good, then you're giving up interest you could earn on that cash. The point is that by owning the durable good, you are passing up the opportunity of investing your net ownership value and earning interest. That is, you could sell the durable good, pay-off any outstanding loan value, invest any net value and earn interest. The foregone interest earnings is thus a cost of ownership of a durable good. Of course, if the net ownership value is zero, or even less than zero, then there are no foregone interest earnings.

Variable Costs

Variable costs of owning a consumer durable good include fuel or power costs and unscheduled maintenance and repair costs.

FUEL COSTS

Fuel and power costs are costs such as gasoline for an auto and electricity for a washing machine or air conditioner. Obviously these costs are greater the more the durable good is used.

UNSCHEDULED
MAINTENANCE
AND REPAIR COSTS

Unscheduled maintenance and repair costs are maintenance and repair costs which directly depend on the use of the durable good. For example, for an auto these costs include replacement of brake linings, shock absorbers, and fan belts and transmission repairs.

Total Costs of Owning an Auto

Table 5-11 shows an example of the total costs of the most expensive consumer durable good other than the home—the automobile. The example is for an intermediate size auto. It assumes a twelve year life for the auto and total mileage of 120,000. A four year, 7 percent auto financing loan is used. Notice the importance of the depreciation cost. Depreciation is the second most costly item, after finance costs, in the early years of auto ownership, and in the middle years of ownership depreciation is the most costly item. In the first year alone, 23 percent of the auto's value is lost in depreciation.

ACCELERATED
DEPRECIATION

Depreciation varies by type of vehicle. Table 5-12 shows depreciation rates for four vehicle types. All vehicle types display what is called "accelerated depreciation."

Accelerated depreciation simply means the depreciation rates are higher in the early years of vehicle ownership. In contrast, "straight line depreciation" means the depreciation rate is the same each year. The accelerated depreciation of vehicles is illustrated in Figure 5-4, which shows the remaining value of vehicles as a percent of the original value. Notice that the larger the vehicle, the more relative value is lost (depreciation) in the early years. This probably occurs because larger vehicles

Table 5-11 Total cost of owning an intermediate size auto (price = $20,000).

	Yr. 1	Yr. 2	Yr. 3	Yr. 4	Yr. 5	Yr. 6	Yr. 7	Yr. 8	Yr. 9	Yr. 10	Yr. 11	Yr. 12
FIXED COSTS												
Depreciation	$4621.67	$2715.00	$2350.00	$1853.33	$1745.00	$1695.00	$1348.33	$1085.00	$1005.00	$833.33	$833.33	$360.00
Finance costs[a]	5748.00	5748.00	5848.00	5748.00	—	—	—	—	—	—	—	—
(End of Year Loan Balance)	(15,510.60)	(10,696.80)	(5535.00)	–0–	—	—	—	—	—	—	—	—
Scheduled maintenance	97.96	161.78	164.60	161.78	97.96	345.51	97.96	161.78	164.60	214.75	35.48	35.48
Insurance	1354.71	1354.71	1354.71	1354.71	1354.71	801.35	801.35	801.35	801.35	801.35	801.35	801.35
Registration & license fees	812.28	29.25	29.25	29.25	29.25	29.25	29.25	29.25	29.25	29.25	29.25	29.25
Foregone int. earnings (7% × end of yr. value)[b]	–0–	137.66	334.48	592.20	470.05	351.40	257.02	181.07	110.72	52.38	25.20	—
VARIABLE COSTS												
(Miles driven)	(14,500)	(13,700)	(12,550)	(11,400)	(10,300)	(9700)	(9200)	(8700)	(8200)	(7800)	(7300)	(6700)
Fuel: gas[c]	906.25	856.25	784.38	712.50	643.75	606.25	575.00	543.75	512.50	487.50	456.25	418.75
Unscheduled maintenance incl. tires and oil	37.22	90.28	560.26	516.52	1425.48	1176.03	1719.44	844.02	457.73	125.20	112.93	105.34
TOTAL COSTS	13,578.09	11,092.93	11,325.68	10,968.29	5766.20	5004.79	4828.35	3646.22	3081.15	2543.76	1848.79	1750.17

[a] Annual payments for $20,000 loan financed at 7% for 4 years.

[b] ($20,000—Accumulated depreciation—end of year loan balance) × .07.

[c] Assumes 24 miles per gallon and $1.50/gallon gasoline.

Source: Federal Highway Administration, Cost of Owning and Operating Automobiles and Vans, 1984, updated to 1999 using price changes from the Consumer Price Index.

Table 5-12 Depreciation rates for vehicles.

Vehicle Size	Yr. 1	Yr. 2	Yr. 3	Yr. 4	Yr. 5	Yr. 6
Passenger van	.31	.14	.11	.07	.06	.05
Large auto	.25	.15	.13	.09	.08	.07
Intermediate auto	.23	.14	.12	.09	.09	.08
Compact auto	.18	.13	.12	.09	.08	.06
Subcompact auto	.13	.13	.12	.09	.09	.08
Vehicle Size	Yr. 7	Yr. 8	Yr. 9	Yr. 10	Yr. 11	Yr. 12
Passenger van	.05	.05	.05	.04	.04	.03
Large auto	.06	.06	.05	.03	.02	.01
Intermediate auto	.07	.05	.05	.04	.02	.02
Compact auto	.06	.06	.06	.06	.05	.05
Subcompact auto	.08	.08	.07	.06	.05	.02

Source: Federal Highway Administration.

are used, on average, by more people and are thus subject to more wear and tear.

Follow these steps in calculating your costs of owning a car:

1. *Depreciation:* Pick the rate corresponding to your vehicle type (Table 5-12) and multiply by the original price.
2. *Finance costs:* Insert your annual payments if financed.
3. *Scheduled Maintenance:* Maintenance costs are difficult to estimate. The 1999 estimated costs for an intermediate size auto are used in Table 5-13. Increase these costs by 20 percent for a large auto or van and decrease them by 20 percent for a compact or subcompact auto.

Figure 5-4. Remaining value of vehicles.

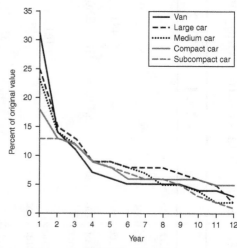

Source: Federal Highway Administration.

Table 5-13 Do it yourself—estimating your own total costs of auto ownership.

Price =

	Yr. 1	Yr. 2	Yr. 3	Yr. 4	Yr. 5	Yr. 6	Yr. 7	Yr. 8	Yr. 9	Yr. 10	Yr. 11	Yr. 12
FIXED COSTS												
(1) Depreciation (rate from Table 4-13 × price)	—	—	—	—	—	—	—	—	—	—	—	—
(2) Finance costs	—	—	—	—	—	—	—	—	—	—	—	—
(3) Scheduled maintenance	97.96	161.78	164.60	161.78	97.96	345.51	97.96	161.78	164.60	214.75	35.48	35.48
(4) Insurance	—	—	—	—	—	—	—	—	—	—	—	—
(5) Registration & license fees	—	—	—	—	—	—	—	—	—	—	—	—
(6) Foregone interest earnings	—	—	—	—	—	—	—	—	—	—	—	—
VARIABLE COSTS												
(7) Fuel (fuel factor × miles driven)	—	—	—	—	—	—	—	—	—	—	—	—
(8) Unscheduled maintenance (rate × miles driven [mi.])	.0026 × mi. =	.0066 × mi. =	.0446 × mi. =	.0453 × mi.=	.1384 × mi. =	.1212 × mi.=	.1869 × mi. =	.0970 × mi. =	.0558 × mi. =	.0161 × mi. =	.0155 × mi. =	.0157 × mi. =
TOTAL	—	—	—	—	—	—	—	—	—	—	—	—

4. *Insurance:* Insurance rates are sensitive to many factors—your age, type of auto, and driving record are among the more important. Write down estimates for your situation. After the auto is five years old, consider reducing the collision coverage (see Chapter 7).

5. *Registration and license fees:* These costs vary by state. Include state sales tax for purchase of the auto in the first year.

6. *Foregone interest earnings:* First, for each year calculate your equity in the auto. Your equity equals the original price of the car minus accumulated depreciation and minus any outstanding loan balance. Use Appendix Tables A7–A12 in calculating the outstanding loan balances.

7. *Fuel:* Fuel costs equal a fuel factor multiplied by your miles driven in a year. The fuel factor is based on the per-gallon price of gas and your average gas mileage. It is calculated as "price of fuel per gallon/average miles per gallon."

Total Costs of Other Consumer Durable Goods

The average annual total costs of other common consumer durable goods are shown in Table 5-14. The major cost components of these goods are depreciation, energy costs, maintenance and repair costs, and finance charges. For ease of comparison, financing of the full price of the product over the product's life is assumed. These ownership costs can be totaled and compared to the costs of renting a durable good to determine which option (own vs. rent) is least expensive (more on this later).

In recent years, consumers have paid increased attention to energy costs of consumer durable goods. In fact, average annual operating costs for major consumer appliances, such as refrigerators, are posted alongside the price. But there doesn't seem to be a free lunch here (again!). Comparison of price and energy usage for both air conditioners and washers shows that the more energy efficient appliances have a higher price (see CONSUMER TOPIC: *Will You Pay for Energy Efficiency?*).

Calculation of the "life cycle cost" of an appliance can help you decide which brand of a particular appliance is cheaper over its total life. The life cycle cost of an appliance is the purchase price plus the present value of the annual energy costs, that is

$$
\begin{aligned}
\text{Life cycle cost} = \text{Purchase price} + & (\text{Annual energy cost} \times \text{PVFS} \\
& (r = \text{real interest rate}, \\
& n = \text{life of the appliance}))
\end{aligned}
$$

Table 5-14   Total cost of selected consumer durable goods.

Product	Price	Average Life	Avg. Ann. Depreciation Cost[a]	Ann. Avg. Energy Cost[b]	Avg. Ann. Maintenance & Repair Cost	Annual Finance Charges (10%)[c]	Total Average Annual Costs
Refrigerator	$1,180	15 yrs.	$79	+ $130	+ $18	+ $152 =	$379
Washer	480	11 yrs.	44	+ 75	+ 7	+ 72 =	198
Dryer	440	12 yrs.	37	+ 55	+ 7	+ 63 =	162
Window air conditioner	346	12 yrs.	29	+ 50	+ 5	+ 50 =	134
Dishwasher	590	10 yrs.	59	+ 38	+ 9	+ 94 =	200
Range	704	14 yrs.	50	+ 20	+ 10	+ 94 =	174

[a]Assumes straight line depreciation, that is, annual depreciation cost = price/average life.
[b] Equals 1.5 percent of original product price.
[c]Annual payment for price financed at 10 percent interest rate and term equal to average life.

Source: Author's calculations using data from Consumers Union, Consumer Reports Buying Guide, 2000; *Dana Chase Publications, Inc., 1981, as reported in Pickett, Mary S., Mildred G. Arnold, and Linda E. Ketterer,* Household Equipment in Residential Design, *N.Y.: John Wiley, 1986.*

C O N S U M E R   T O P I C

WILL YOU PAY FOR ENERGY EFFICIENCY?

As you've learned many times by now, there is no free lunch in economics—or at least the free lunch is very rare. This means that services or benefits that consumers receive from products usually cost money.

Energy efficient appliances are a good example. There are two reasons to expect energy efficient appliances to be more expensive than other appliances. First, it's probably more expensive for a manufacturer to build an energy efficient appliance, since more insulation and better motors must be installed. Second, since consumers save money with energy efficient appliances, they're willing to pay a higher price.

To test this theory, data from *Consumer Reports* for side-by-side model refrigerators were examined. This appliance was chosen because the information from *Consumer Reports* included the purchase price and the estimated annual energy cost.

Analysis of the data showed that every $1 reduction in annual energy costs was associated with a $16 increase in the purchase price. So, at least for this appliance, consumers pay now to save money later—just what economic theory would predict!

Source of data: Consumer Reports, Buying Guide 2000.

Use of a real interest rate lets you avoid predicting inflation rates. The real interest rate used should be the difference between a safe investment rate and the inflation rate of energy prices. A typical rate is 3 percent. Use Appendix Table A-4 and sum the annual present value factors associated with the real interest rate and appliance life (in years).

For example, suppose you're comparing refrigerators. The purchase price of brand A is $1,000 with annual energy costs of $150. The purchase price of brand B is $800 with annual energy costs of $175. Both brands last 15 years, then their life cycle costs, using a 3 percent real interest rate, are:

$$\text{Life cycle cost, Brand A:}$$
$$\$1,000 + (\$150 \times \text{PVFS}(r = 3\%, n = 15))$$
$$= \$1,000 + (\$150 \times 11.936) = \$2,790.40$$

$$\text{Life cycle cost, Brand B:}$$
$$\$800 + (\$175 \times \text{PVFS}(r = 3\%, n = 15))$$
$$= \$800 + (\$175 \times 11.936) = \$2,888.80$$

The life cycle cost of Brand A refrigerator is almost $100 cheaper.

The Bottom Line

The total costs of renting a consumer durable good are the rental fee and operating expenses. The total costs of owning a consumer durable good are more complicated, and include depreciation and foregone interest earnings. For autos, depreciation is one of the largest costs of ownership.

6. What Are the Benefits of a Consumer Durable Good?

Consumer durable goods provide services for the owner. The refrigerator preserves fresh food, the washer cleans clothes, the TV entertains, and the auto moves you to and from work, shopping, and other destinations.

If you didn't have a consumer durable good, then you'll have to spend money in some other way in order to receive the services that the consumer durable good provides. This is very important, because these alternative expenditures are the best measure of the benefits from a consumer durable good. That is, *the annual benefit from a consumer durable good can be measured as what it would cost you to receive the same services (as you do from the consumer durable good) in the next best way*.

For example, if you don't own a washer and dryer, you'll clean your clothes at the local laundromat. Thus, the annual benefit from owning a washer and dryer can be measured as the annual cost of washing and drying your clothes at the local laundromat. Furthermore, these benefits are *tax-free!*

Calculation of Benefits

BENEFIT/COST RATIO   Table 5-15 shows the calculation of annual benefits and benefit/cost ratios for common consumer durable goods. The calculated benefits are only examples, and the benefits will vary from consumer to consumer. Costs are from Tables 5-11 and 5-14. So that you might calculate your own benefit/cost ratio for a consumer durable good, here's a brief summary of the factors that should be considered in the calculation.

Refrigerator: Benefits are calculated as the difference between the cost of eating meals out and the cost of eating meals at home, including time costs of preparation. The example shown is for one person. Benefits increase when more people use the refrigerator.

Washer/Dryer: Benefits are calculated as the cost of doing laundry at a laundromat, including the value of your time spent at the laundromat. Benefits increase the more loads of wash done per week.

Window air conditioner: These benefits are more subjective. One approach is to consider that a window air conditioner means you'll have a better night's sleep during the summer and you'll therefore be more productive at work. The value of the additional productivity is the benefit. Benefits increase the more hot nights per year.

Dishwasher: The major benefit from having a dishwasher is saved time. Therefore, benefits are greater the higher the value of time of the person who would do the dishwashing! If children do the dishes, then benefits will be much lower, and maybe zero!

Range: Benefits are the difference between buying hot food out and preparing hot food at home. Benefits are greater for larger families.

Auto: Benefits from owning an auto are what you would spend on public transportation or private taxi, plus the value of the travel time you save by having an auto. The more travelling you do, and especially the more travelling you do to destinations not served by public transportation, the greater the benefits. Also, the greater the value of your time, the greater the benefits.

Although the benefit/cost ratios in Table 5-15 are only examples, it is interesting to compare their relative sizes. Benefit/cost ratios for a refrigerator and dishwasher are the highest. It is therefore not surprising that almost every household now has a refrigerator and dishwasher.

Table 5-15 Benefits and benefit/cost ratios for common consumer consumer durable goods.

Durable Good	Total Average Annual Cost	Benefits = Annual Savings	$\dfrac{\text{Benefits}}{\text{Costs}}$
Refrigerator	$379	$20/day if eat out. $9/day if eat in. ___ Save$11/day or $4,015/yr.	$\dfrac{\$4,015}{\$379} = 10.59$
Washer	$198	Save 5 loads/wk. @ $2/load at laundromat, × 52 wks. = $520 Save 1 hr./wk @ $10/hr. × 52 wks. = $520	$\dfrac{\$1,040}{\$198} = 5.25$
Dryer	$162	Save 5 loads/wk. @ $1/load at laundromat, × 52 wks. = $260 Save 1 hr./wk @ $10/hr × 52 wks. = $520	$\dfrac{\$780}{\$162} = 4.81$
Window AC Unit	$134	Get good night's sleep; equal to 1 more hr. work per day; × $15 hr. × 5 days = $75/wk.; × 8 wks. = $600	$\dfrac{\$600}{\$134} = 4.48$
Dishwasher	$200	Save 3 hrs./wk. @ $10/hr. = $30/wk.; × 52 = $1,560 if adults; @ $0/hr. – $0, if children	$\dfrac{\$1,560}{\$200} = 7.80$ if adult $\dfrac{\$0}{\$200} = 0$ if children
Range	$174	Save $10/wk in buying hot food; × 52 = $520	$\dfrac{\$520}{\$174} = 2.99$
Auto	$6,286	Save 15 weekly round trips on public transportation @ $5/trip = $75/wk; × 52 = $3,900/yr. Save 6 hrs./wk. in time costs; × $10/hr. = $60/wk. × 52 = $3,120/yr. Save $600 in bus fare for one long trip annually	$\dfrac{\$7,620}{\$6,286} = 1.21$

The Bottom Line

Consumer durable goods provide benefits to the owner which can be measured by what it would cost to receive the same services (as from the durable good) in the next best way. The benefits from consumer durable goods generally increase the more members in a household and the greater the members' value of time.

7. When Should You Replace a Consumer Durable Good?

The simple answer to the question, "when should you replace a consumer durable good" is when it becomes more costly to keep and run it than to buy a new one. Actually, this simple answer is the right answer, but frequently consumers make mistakes in not correctly measuring costs of the existing and of the new durable good.

An example is probably the best way to illustrate the principles at work here. Suppose you've been driving your current car for six years. You've fully repaid the auto loan. What's the cost of driving the car for one more year? The total costs will equal depreciation, foregone interest earnings on the car's value, repair costs, and fuel costs. Since the car is six years old, depreciation and foregone interest earnings costs will be small. Repair costs and fuel costs will be the major expense items.

But what about the costs of a new car? Wait, you might say—surely the first year's cost of a new car is much greater than the repair costs and fuel costs of keeping the existing car, even if the new car is more fuel efficient. But this isn't a valid comparison, since the total cost of the new car will likely decline over time. Instead, the cost of keeping your existing car for another year should be compared to the average annual cost of a new car, where the annual cost is averaged over the same number of years as the age of your existing car (or the number of years you've had your existing car). Also, the average should be our old friend, "economic average"—the annuity value.

Thus, if the cost of keeping your existing car one more year is less than the annual average (annuity) cost of a

Figure 5-5. Costs of new vs. old car.

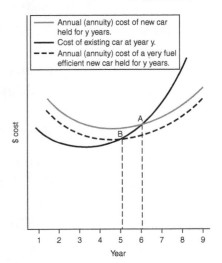

new car, then you should keep your old car at least one more year. But, when the cost of keeping your existing car one more year exceeds the annual average (annuity) cost of a new car, it's time to trash the old buggy and get a new one.

Figure 5-5 illustrates this principle. Beyond point A (year 6) it is more costly to keep your existing car than to buy a new one. Therefore, in this example, a new car should be bought at year 6. If the new car is very fuel efficient, this will have the effect of lowering new car costs and reducing the time at which a new car should be bought (to year 5 in Figure 5-5).

Complications

Data from the Federal Highway Administration show that the marginal yearly total cost of an existing car looks like that shown in Figure 5-6. Marginal costs rise until year 7, then fall until year 11, then rise again. This pattern occurs because major repairs made in years 7 and 8 "renew" the car and make repair and maintenance costs lower until years 11 and 12, when repair and maintenance costs begin to rise again.

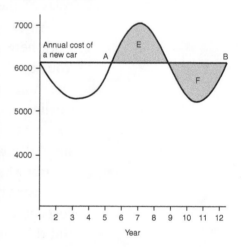

Figure 5-6. Actual costs of new vs. old

Figure 5-6 indicates there are two possible replacement points, A (year 6) or B (year 12). Whether A or B is chosen depends on how much repair and maintenance costs can be reduced in years 9 to 11. If these costs can be reduced such that the savings represented by area F are greater than the costs represented by area E, then replacement should be delayed to year 12. If not, then replacement should be done at year 6.

What about Comfort and Styling?

So far the decision about when to replace a car has been solely based on dollars and cents. But new cars often provide more comfort and styling than old ones. Should these qualities be ignored?

Comfort and styling should be considered, but their value is hard to quantify in money terms. The best approach is to estimate the extra cost of comfort and styling and then ask if these qualities are worth the cost.

The Bottom Line _____

Consumer durable goods should be replaced when the annual cost of keeping the durable good becomes more expensive than the annualized (annuity) cost of a new durable good, where the annual cost of the new durable good is averaged over the age of the existing durable good._____

Owners who heavily use their cars should probably replace them after six years. Owners who carefully maintain and use their cars can probably replace them much later—maybe only after 12 years.

8. Should You Rent or Buy a Consumer Durable: The Case of Cars[4]

Most consumer durable goods, including washers, refrigerators, TVs and cars, can be rented. However, there are two distinct consumer durable good rental markets, cars and everything else.

The principal behind judging whether renting or buying a consumer durable good is better is, again, very simple: do whichever is cheaper. Either compare the present value sums over the life of renting or buying to decide which is cheaper, or compare the annual average (annuity) values of each option.

The renting of consumer appliances, like refrigerators, washers, and dryers, and the renting of TVs, stereos, and other entertainment equipment is primarily handled by the "rent-to-own" business. This economic arrangement will be explored in the next topic. This topic focuses on comparing the renting or purchasing of cars.

Elements of Auto Leasing

We've already discussed extensively (meaning you were sick of it) the various costs of buying and owning an auto (see Table 5-11). In this section we'll discuss the costs of renting an auto before moving on to comparison of the own versus rent options.

ROLE OF DEPRECIATION

Auto renting is called auto leasing. The first thing you'll notice about auto leasing is that the monthly cost is usually much less than the monthly finance cost of buying the same auto. But there's a logical

---

[4]A reference for some of the information in this topic is the Federal Reserve System's "Keys to vehicle leasing" at http://www.federalreserve.gov/pubs/leasing/."

reason for this. When buying a car, your monthly finance payments are based on the full original market value of the car (less any downpayment). Taken together, all the finance payments will equal the original value of the car plus interest on the loan over the loan's term. With leasing, the dealer must also recover interest on the original value of the car (or whatever the dealer paid for it), since there's an opportunity cost to the dealer in having his/her money tied up in the car. But, in addition, the dealer only has to recover the amount by which the car *depreciates* over the term of the lease, rather than recover the entire value of the car. This is because the dealer gets the car back after the lease is up, and therefore has ownership to the remaining value of the car.

ROLE OF
DEPRECIATION

TYPES OF LEASES

There are a number of "bells and whistles" related to auto leasing. Some of the key ones follow:

Downpayment or Prepayment: Sometimes a leasee can obtain low monthly lease payments only by making a large downpayment and/or by prepaying the final few monthly payments. Obviously, any dollars paid up-front, rather than later, are more expensive.

Mileage: Some auto leases limit the mileage driven on the car. If mileage exceeds the limit, then a surcharge must be paid. The surcharge will be in cents per mile, with a typical range being six to 15 cents per mile.

Maintenance: You need to study the auto lease agreement very carefully to find out what maintenance and repair costs are covered by the dealer and what maintenance and repair costs must be paid by you. Typically the leasee must pay for oil changes, lube jobs, tune-ups, etc. But what about the replacement of a major part, such as shocks or tires? You might expect the dealer to pay for these, but make sure it's in writing.

Depreciation: Dealers set up leases and monthly lease rates based on some expected depreciation schedule. With a *closed-end lease* the dealer bears the risk that you will "use-up" the car more and depreciation will be greater than expected. With an *open-end lease* the leasee bears this risk, in that the lease must pay for an "extra depreciation" beyond that expected by the dealer. Payments will be somewhat higher for a closed-end lease than for an open-end lease. However, if you expect to "drive the daylights" out of the car and increase its depreciation beyond an average amount, the closed-end lease may be better.

Fuel and Insurance: You pay these.

Length of Lease: When you sign an auto lease, you agree to a certain lease period, or term. The lease payments are based on this lease term. If you end the lease before the end of the term, you might end up owing the dealer hundreds or thousands of dollars! Why? Part of the reason is depreciation. The lease payment is based, in part, on the average annual depreciation rate during the period the car is leased. As seen from Table 5-12, the longer a new car is leased, the lower the average annual depreciation rate will be. Hence, if a leasee "breaks the lease" and returns the car before the end of the lease term, the average annual depreciation rate will be higher than expected and monthly lease payments lower than necessary. The charges paid for this early termination of the lease will make up the difference.

Comparing Owning and Leasing

Determining which is cheaper, owning or leasing, is simple. Calculate the present value of the total costs of each option and select the option with the lowest present value cost.

Table 5-16 shows the present value calculations for owning and for two leasing options. The example is done on an annual basis to reduce the number of calculations, although to be very precise you'd want to do monthly calculations. The auto used is the $20,000 intermediate-sized auto shown in Table 5-11. It is assumed that maintenance, insurance, registration and license fees, and fuel are paid by the consumer under all options. This leaves depreciation, finance costs, and foregone interest earnings as the ownership costs to compare against leasing.

Note that ownership costs should be calculated and compared for the same length of time as the lease period. In the example in Table 5-16, this is four years. In this example, under the ownership option it is assumed that the car will be sold for its remaining value at the end of the comparison period (four years). Thus, the present value of the market value of the car at the end of the comparison period should be subtracted from ownership costs.

Lease 1 charges a straight $5,300 annually, and the cost of this lease is less than ownership costs by almost $4,000 ($17,952 compared to $23,883). Lease 2 also has a base leasee rate of $5,300 annually. However, to get this rate the leasee must pay an upfront fee of 20 percent of the car's value (.20 x $20,000 = $4,000) plus $2,650, which will be counted toward the final six months' payment. The present value cost of this lease is much more ($22,145.57).

The examples in Table 5-16 are only that—examples. They are not meant to imply that leasing is cheaper than owning. You should work the numbers for any ownership—lease comparison.

A Shortcut Way to Compare Owning vs. Leasing

The comparison of owning a car versus leasing a car can be simplified even more. First assume that maintenance, insurance, registration and license, and fuel costs are the same with both options. Now consider ownership costs versus the costs which the dealer must recover through the lease payments. Both the consumer buying a car and the dealer leasing the car face depreciation costs and foregone interest earnings costs.

Table 5-16 Comparing owning vs. leasing.

		Own	Lease 1	Lease 2
Year				
1	Depreciatjon	$4,621.67	$5,300	$4,000
	Finance costs	5,748.00		+ 5,300
	Foregone interest earnings	–0–		+ 2,650
		$ 10,369.67		
2	Depreciation	$ 2,715.00	$5,300	$5,300
	Finance costs	5,748.00		
	Foregone interest earnings	137.66		
		$ 8,600.66		
3	Depreciation	$ 2,350.00	$5,300	$5,300
	Finance costs	5,748.00		
	Foregone interest earnings	334.48		
		$ 8,432.48		
4	Depreciatjon	$ 1,853.33	$5,300	$2,650
	Finance costs	5,748.00		
	Foregone interest earnings	592.20		
		$ 8,193.53		

Value of car, end of year 4 = $8,460.00.

Present value of owning for 4 years and then selling (7% discount rate):

$$\$10,369.67 \times .9346 + \$8,600.66 \times .8734 + \$8,432.48 \times .8163 +$$
$$\$8,193.53 \times .7629 - \$8,460 \times .7629 = \$23,883.45$$

Present value of Lease 1 for 4 years:

$$\$5,300 \times .9346 + \$5,300 \times .8734 + \$5,300 \times .8163 +$$
$$\$5,300 \times .7629 = \$17,952.16$$

Present value of Lease 2 for 4 years:

$$(\$4,000 + \$5,300 + \$2,650) \times .9346 + \$5,300 \times .8734 +$$
$$\$5,300 \times .8163 + \$2,650 \times .7629 = \$22,145.57$$

The consumer buying a car faces finance costs based on the full value of the car, whereas the dealer faces an opportunity cost of this same amount but less the present value of the market value of the car at the end of the lease term. So this is the major way that ownership costs and lease payments differ—*lease payments do not have to cover the present value of the remaining market value of the car when the lease is up.*

Knowing this principle, you can easily calculate by how much the lease payment should understate the finance costs of buying when both the finance term and lease term are the same. First, find the value of the car at the end of the lease term. Use Table 5-12 or other sources for this. Second, convert this value to a present value using Appendix Table A-4. Third, convert this present value to a monthly annuity average using Appendix Table A-6. The monthly lease payment should be less than the finance payment by at least this amount.

EXAMPLE 5-4: Sam Spade is considering leasing a $25,000 new car for three years. How much lower, at a minimum, should monthly lease payments be compared to monthly finance payments? Use an 11 percent interest rate.

ANSWER: Using Table 5-13, the car should be worth [$25,000 − (.25 + .15 + .13) × $25,000] = $11,750 at the end of the third year. The present value of $11,750, using an 11 percent discount rate, is .731 x $11,750 = $8,589.25. The comparable monthly annuity amount, using an 11 percent interest rate and 36 months, is:

$$\frac{\$8,589.25}{30.545} = \$281.20.$$

Thus, for leasing to be preferable to buying, the monthly lease payment should be more than $281.20 lower than monthly finance payments.

Who Should Lease?

Even if leasing doesn't pay, financially, leasing may still be the best answer for some consumers. Leasing is particularly advantageous for consumers who want to drive new cars at regular intervals (e.g., every 2 or 3 years) but don't want the hassle of selling their old cars.

The Bottom Line

Calculate and compare the present values of the total costs of owning a car and the total costs of leasing a car to determine which is cheaper. Make sure you read the fine print of auto leases to find out all the charges and surcharges of leases.

9. Are Rent-to-Own Contracts Good Deals?

You've seen the advertisements many times—pay a low weekly or monthly amount and you can rent a new television, stereo, or washer. Furthermore, if you make all the payments for a certain number of weeks or months, all the rent payments will be applied to purchase of the product and, in fact, you'll own the product free and clear. These contracts are called rent-to-own (RTO) contracts, and to read the advertisements, they sound like the best thing since sliced bread.

However, many researchers have shown that if RTO payments are considered credit payments for purchase, then the implicit interest rate is very high. For example, Swagler estimated APRs as high as 200 percent for rent-to-own color televisions in Atlanta.[5]

CALCULATION OF APR How can these APRs on rent-to-own contracts be calculated? They are calculated in the same way as APRs on other credit loans. For example, if a color TV can be bought with cash for $600 or with 24 rent-to-own monthly payments of $43 then the approximate APR is found by:

$$\frac{\$600}{\$43} = 13.95.$$

The present value factor sum, 13.95, is found in Appendix Table A-6 corresponding to 24 months. The approximate APR is 58 percent.

However, there are two problems with using the rental payment as the finance payment. First, under rent-to-own contracts the dealer promises to maintain and repair the product while the rent-to-own payments are being made. Under a typical purchase agreement, the consumer assumes responsibility for maintenance and repair after an initial time period (e.g., after 30 days). Second, since the dealer doesn't know if the consumer will, in fact, make all payments and ultimately own the product, the dealer faces some cost for expected depreciation and the expected opportunity investment cost on the product. These costs are not faced by the dealer under a standard purchase agreement. Therefore, dealer maintenance and repair costs, expected depreciation, and expected opportunity investment costs must be subtracted from rent-to-own payments before a true APR is calculated. Doing this can lower the implicit APR. However, research by Walden indicates that even after these costs are subtracted, APRs on rent-to-own contracts are still very high.[6]

---

[5]Swagler, Roger M., "Rent-to-Own Programs: Is Consumer Protection Adequate?" *Proceedings of the 32nd Annual Conference of the American Council Consumer Interests,* April 9–12, 1986, pp. 267–271.

[6]Walden, Michael L. "The Economics of Rent-to-Own Contracts," *Journal of Consumer Affairs,* Winter 1990, 24(2), pp. 326–337.

WHY DO CONSUMERS USE RENT-TO-OWN CONTRACTS?

C O N S U M E R   T O P I C

Buying an appliance, TV, or piece of audio equipment with a rent-to-own contract is no bargain; in fact, it's very expensive. Implicit APRs on rent-to-own contracts can be 3 or 4 times as high as APRs on personal loans or even credit cards. Why, then, do some consumers continue to patronize rent-to-own dealers?

A study by Swagler and Wheeler provides some answers. Swagler and Wheeler questioned 61 individuals in the West Palm Beach, Florida area who had used rent-to-own contracts. On average, the individuals had low incomes ($13,000 annual income), less than high school educations, and had been denied credit (60 percent had previously been denied credit).

Swagler and Wheeler reported that two-thirds of the participants said that the ability to "get the product right away" was either their first or second reason for using RTO contracts, and almost one-half listed "no credit check" as their first or second reason.

These findings, together with the fact that 60 percent of the participants had been rejected for credit, indicate that higher risk borrowers are attracted to RTO contracts and dealers. However, the flip-side of this is that some of the higher implicit interest rates charged on RTO contracts is compensation to the dealer for the greater riskiness of the borrowers. Yet the importance of "getting the product right away" means that RTO participants have high personal rates of time preference and are therefore willing to pay the higher implicit APRs.

Source: Swagler, Roger M, and Paula Wheeler, "Rental-Purchase Agreements: A Preliminary Investigation of Consumer Attitudes and Behaviors. *The Journal of Consumer Affairs*, Vol. 23, No. 1, Sept. 1989, pp. 145–160.

WHO USES
RENT-TO-OWN
DEALS

Why, then, do consumers patronize rent-to-own dealers if the APRs are so high? There are at least three reasons. One is that consumers don't understand how to calculate the APR on rent-to-own contracts. A second reason is that consumers who use rent-to-own contracts do so because they can't obtain cheaper credit elsewhere and they put a high value on purchasing the product. Research by Swagler and Wheeler supports both these reasons (see CONSUMER TOPIC). Lastly, consumers who use rent-to-own contracts may do so because they're interested in only renting the product for a short period of time.

The Bottom Line

Rent-to-own contracts are very expensive ways of purchasing consumer durable goods. Only use rent-to-own contracts after you've exhausted all other credit sources, and then only if the benefits from the durable good exceed its cost.

**C
O
N
S
U
M
E
R

T
O
P
I
C**

PAYDAY LOANS

Payday loans are a relatively new way for consumers to obtain money, but often at a high cost. A payday loan is a loan based on your future paycheck. Say you are due to receive a paycheck of $1000 in two weeks. You borrow $100 today. You repay the $100, plus interest, when you receive your paycheck.

So what's the "rub" with paycheck loans? Like rent-to-own contracts, the "rub" can be in the interest rate on the loan. Some calculations show paycheck loans to have an APR as high as 780%.

So think twice about getting quick cash from your future paycheck. The cost may be astronomical!

Reference: Fox, Jean Ann, "Safe Harbor for Usury: Recent Developments in Payday Lending." *Advancing the Consumer Interest*, Winter 1999, Vol. 11, No. 2, pp. 7–12.

10. Where Can You Get Consumer Credit?

There are many kinds and sources of consumer credit. You can get credit from banks, savings and loans, credit unions, finance companies and pawn brokers to name a few. You can get credit requiring collateral (property pledged to the loan) or requiring no collateral. You can even get credit based on the equity in your house. Where should you start and where's the best deal?

RISK AND
INTEREST RATE

First, an obvious point should be made. Lenders will charge higher interest rates on loans which they perceive as carrying more risk. If Tenth National Bank thinks that Joe Sharkey, a gambler, is five times more likely *not* to repay a loan than Mary Tightwad, a conservative money handler with an impeccable record, then the interest rate charged to Joe Sharkey will be much higher than the interest rate charged to Mary Tightwad. Lenders use many characteristics for judging the credit worthiness of a borrower, including current income, current debt level, past credit repayment record, and job stability. We'll talk more about how lenders make decisions about lending money in *HOW TO GET CREDIT?*

Secured and Unsecured Loans

One way to reduce the interest rate on credit is to use *secured loans*. Secured loans are simply loans in which the borrower pledges some asset in the event of default (payments aren't made) on the loan. Often the asset is what the borrower is buying with the credit loan. For example, the new car is pledged as security on the auto loan. If the borrower does default on the loan, the lender can take possession of the asset to help pay-off the loan's outstanding balance.

In contrast, an unsecured loan is one in which there are no assets specifically pledged as collateral against the loan. Credit cards are the best example of an unsecured loan. If the borrower default on the loan, then the lender cannot seize any specific asset to help meet the loan balance. Instead, any fund or assets which the lender receives would only result from general bankruptcy proceedings against the borrower.

Obviously, since unsecured loans are more risky in the eyes of the lender than secured loans, the interest rate on unsecured loans will be higher. This is one reason why the interest rate on credit cards is so high.

Types of Lenders

In general, lenders target their loans toward specific risk categories of customers. This means the consumer credit market is stratified by average risk of loan and, consequently, by average interest rate charged. As Figure 5-7 shows, banks, savings and loan associations, and credit unions generally specialize in lower risk and, hence, lower interest rate loans. Next are sales finance companies, which are loan companies tied to specific sellers (e.g., retailers such as Sears and auto companies

Figure 5-7. Stratification of the consumer market.

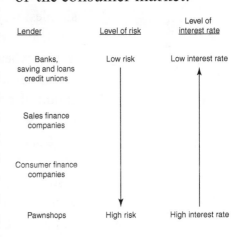

such as General Motors and Ford). These companies will accept loans slightly more risky than banks, S&Ls, and credit unions. Third are consumer finance companies, which target higher risk borrowers and loans. Finally, pawnshops will accept very high risk loans, but you'll also pay a very high interest rate—maybe as high as 30 or 35 percent. With a pawnshop you must physically turn over property used as collateral for the loan. The loan amount will be much less than the market value of the property. Generally the loan is for a short period, maybe no more than six months. If the loan isn't repaid, the pawnbroker keeps your property and sells it.[7]

STRATIFICATION
OF CREDIT MARKET

---

[7]There's actually another level to the consumer credit stratification, and this is "loan sharks." We'll define "loan sharks" as unconventional lenders who operate outside normal (and legal) channels. "Loan sharks" will make very high risk loans but, as a consequence, will charge very, very high interest rates (1000 percent or more). Furthermore, because of the high risk and large interest charge, strong-arm or violent tactics are sometimes used to enforce payment.

So what does the stratification of the consumer credit market mean to you as a borrower? Obviously, you want to pay as low an interest rate as possible on a loan. Therefore, you should begin searching for credit from banks, S&Ls, credit unions (if you're a member), and sales finance companies. If you can't qualify for a loan here, then gradually move up the risk/interest rate ladder. At the point where you qualify, you must then decide: (1) do you really want the loan—that is, does your personal rate of time preference exceed the interest rate charged? and (2) can you afford the loan payments without destroying your budget (see *How Much Is Too Much Credit?*).

Two Types of Loans

There are two fundamental types of consumer credit loans, closed-end credit loans and open-end credit loans.

CLOSED-END LOANS   *Closed-end credit loans* are loans which must be repaid over a certain period of time and according to a specific schedule. The loan's term and payment schedule can be structured in an infinite number of ways. The simplest way is a loan where one payment is made at the end of the loan term, and that payment includes both principal and interest. More common is where the loan is repaid in equal monthly payments of principal and interest. We've already discussed how the interest rate and the allocation of each payment to principal and interest are calculated in these loans (see Figure 5-5).

Open-end credit loans are loans which don't have a loan term (they're open-end) and consequently don't have a specific payment schedule. Instead, each credit statement will specify some minimum amount which must be paid for that month. The minimum amount is usually some percentage of the outstanding loan balance at that time. Credit cards are the best example of open-end credit loans.

The Bottom Line

Consumer credit is usually available if you're willing to pay the price. The consumer credit market is stratified by risk. Banks, S&Ls, and credit unions concentrate on lower risk loans and charge lower interest rates; consumer finance companies and pawnshops concentrate on higher risk loans and charge higher interest rates. Where you'll get a loan depends on the risk you present to the lender and how badly you want the loan.

11. What Kinds of Credit Cards Are Best?

There are three important factors to consider in analyzing the cost of a credit card: (1) the annual fee, (2) the periodic interest rate, and (3) calculation of the average daily balance. However, how important each

WHO USES CREDIT CARDS?

C
O
N
S
U
M
E
R

T
O
P
I
C

Consumer use of credit cards has gone through ups and downs over time. The Federal Reserve reports that in 1989, about 40% of families owed money on a credit card. By 1995, almost half (47%) of families had a balance on their credit card. The percentage remained around 45% until 2010, when it was back to about 40%. In 1989, the average debt owed on credit cards was about $1,800. However, in 2010, the average debt owed on a credit card increased to $7,100. Adjusting for inflation, it was an increase of 124%.

Middle income households have the highest percentage of credit card use while low income households have the lowest percentage of credit card use. In 2010, only 23.2% of households in the lowest 20th percentile carried a balance on their credit cards, while households in the 60th to 80th percentile had the highest credit card use percentage at 53.1%. Compared with other age groups, credit card use was the highest for those aged 45–54 at 46.2%, and the lowest for those 75 or older at 21.7%.

Source: Federal Reserve System, Survey of Consumer Finances, various years.

of these factors is to you depends on how you use the credit card. Therefore, which type of credit card, in terms of the combination of these factors, is best for you, also depends on how you use the card.

CREDIT CARD
CHARACTERISTICS

The *annual fee* is simply a flat fee paid each year for using the credit card. The fee does not vary by how much the card is used. In our economics lingo, the flat fee is a fixed cost.

The periodic interest rate is the *variable cost* of the credit card. The periodic interest rate used by a credit card is a monthly rate. The quoted annual rate (APR) is then the monthly rate multiplied by 12. To get the monthly finance charge, the monthly rate is multiplied by the average daily balance.

The *average daily balance* is a weighted average of loans during the billing cycle (usually a month). The average is calculated by multiplying each loan by the number of days the loan is held during the month. Payments are subtracted from loans on the day the payment occurs. The "weighted" loans are summed and then divided by days in the month to get the average daily balance. The calculations in Table 5-18 show how this is done.

GRACE PERIOD

Some credit cards will give you a *billing cycle (or month) grace period.* A billing cycle (month) grace period means that if you have paid *during this month* the *full balance* owed from the *previous month*, then no finance charge will be owed for purchases made with a credit card during the current month.

CONVENIENCE USER   Table 5-17 shows how the monthly finance charge is calculated under these different conditions. There is no grace period in cases A and B, and there is a grace period in cases C and D. Consumers who take advantage of grace periods and are always able to pay off their previous balance (Case D) incur no finance charge. They get a free ride on the credit card, except for the cost of the annual fee. They use credit cards as a convenience—preferring the convenience of writing one check at the end of the month rather than writing many checks during the month or carrying and paying with cash.

Obviously, then, someone who uses a credit card only as a convenience will prefer a card with a low fee, a high interest rate, and a grace period. The convenience user doesn't mind the higher interest rate because finance charges are never incurred.

In contrast, a consumer who always carries a loan balance and infrequently pays the previous month's balance in full will generally be better off with a card having a high annual fee and a low interest rate, although this trade-off will depend on the cardholder's average daily balance.

Table 5–17   Calculation of the monthly finance charge.

CASE A

No grace period; partial payment of previous balance.

Previous balance: $100   Monthly interest rate = 1.5%

June	June	June
1 –	11 –	21 –
2 –	12 –	22 –
3 –	13 –	23 –
4 – charged $50	14 –	24 –
5 –	15 –	25 –
6 –	16 – charged $170	26 –
7 –	17 –	27 –
8 –	18 –	28 – charged $20
9 – pmnt. of $40	19 –	29 –
10 –	20 –	30 –

Average daily balance:

4 days (June 1 – 3) of $100	= 4 × $100 =	$ 400
5 days (June 4 – 8) of 150 ($100 + $ 50)	= 5 × 150 =	750
7 days (June 9 – 15) of 110 (150 – 40)	= 7 × 110 =	770
12 days (June 16 – 27) of 280 (110 + 170)	= 12 × 280 =	3,360
3 days (June 28 – 30) of 300 (280 + 20)	= 3 × 300 =	900
		$6,180

$$\frac{\$6,180}{30 \text{ days}} = \$206 \text{ average daily balance for month}$$

Finance charge = $206 × .015 = $3.09

CASE B

No grace period; full payment of previous balance.

Previous balance: $100   Monthly interest rate = 1.5%

June	June	June
1 –	11 –	21 –
2 –	12 –	22 –
3 –	13 –	23 –
4 – charged $50	14 –	24 –
5 –	15 –	25 –
6 –	16 – charged $170	26 –
7 –	17 –	27 –
8 –	18 –	28 – charged $20
9 – pmnt. of $100	19 –	29 –
10 –	20 –	30 –

Average daily balance:

4 days (June 1 – 3) of $100	= 4 × $100 = $ 400	
5 days (June 4 – 8) of 150 ($100 + $ 50)	= 5 × 150 = 750	
7 days (June 9 – 15) of 50 (150 – 100)	= 7 × 50 = 350	
12 days (June 16 – 27) of 220 (50 + 170)	= 12 × 220 = 2,640	
3 days (June 28 – 30) of 240 (220 + 20)	= 3 × 240 = 720	
	$4,860	

$$\frac{\$4,860}{30 \text{ days}} = \$162 \text{ average daily balance for month}$$

Finance charge = $162 × .015 = $2.43

CASE C

Grace period; partial payment of previous balance.

Previous balance: $100   Monthly interest rate = 1.5%

June	June	June
1 –	11 –	21 –
2 –	12 –	22 –
3 –	13 –	23 –
4 – charged $50	14 –	24 –
5 –	15 –	25 –
6 –	16 – charged $170	26 –
7 –	17 –	27 –
8 –	18 –	28 – charged $20
9 – pmnt. of $40	19 –	29 –
10 –	20 –	30 –

Average daily balance calculations same as for Case A.

Finance charge = $206 × .015 = $3.09.

Continued

Table 5–17   Continued

CASE D

Grace period; full payment of previous balance.

Previous balance: $100

Monthly interest rate = 1.5%

June	June	June
1 –	11 –	21 –
2 –	12 –	22 –
3 –	13 –	23 –
4 – charged $50	14 –	24 –
5 –	15 –	25 –
6 –	16 – charged $170	26 –
7 –	17 –	27 –
8 –	18 –	28 – charged $20
9 – pmnt. of $100	19 –	29 –
10 –	20 –	30 –

Finance charge = $0 (since fully paid previous balance ($100) on June 9).

The total annual cost to the cardholder is: annual fee + (monthly interest rate × average daily balance × 12). The "frequent card user" will want to choose a card which minimizes this cost.

Table 5-18 shows the average daily balances above which the frequent card user is better off with a card having a *higher* annual fee and *lower* interest rate. For example, if the frequent user has a choice between a $30 fee and 16 percent card or a $50 fee and 14 percent card, the Table shows the user is better-off with the $50 fee and 16 percent card if her average daily balance is above $1,005.

Other Complications

Credit card companies may complicate your comparison process by competing on factors other than the annual fee, interest rate, and grace period. Some of these factors can be readily dismissed; others require more analysis.

A card company may offer to waive the annual fee—but only for a year. Likewise, a card company may offer cardholders the ability to earn "bonus dollars," which can be used to purchase catalog products. But the prices of the catalog products may be higher than the prices of similar products which can be bought elsewhere!

One offer that may be worth examining is the offer of a grace period in exchange for putting a certain amount of money in the issuing bank's CD. However, frequently this CD carries a below-market interest rate. Thus, you face a tradeoff—pay less interest on your credit card, but earn

Table 5-18   Which credit card is best for you?

If your average daily balance is *above* this amount, you're better off with the higher fee-lower interest rate credit card.

Higher Fee—Lower Interest Rate

Lower Fee, Higher Interest Rate	$15 16%	$15 14%	$15 12%	$30 16%	$30 14%	$30 12%	$50 16%	$50 14%	$50 12%
$ 0, 18%	$750	$375	$250	$1,500	$ 755	$ 500	$2,500	$1,255	$ 835
$15, 18%	0	0	0	750	375	250	1,750	880	585
$30, 18%	0	0	0	0	0	0	1,000	500	335
$ 0, 16%	X	$755	$380	X	$1,505	$ 755	X	$2,500	$1,255
$15, 16%	X	0	0	X	755	380	X	1,755	880
$30, 16%	X	0	0	X	0	0	X	1,005	505
$ 0, 14%	X	X	$750	X	X	$1,500	X	X	$2,500
$15, 14%	X	X	0	X	X	750	X	X	1,750
$30, 14%	X	X	X	X	X	0	X	X	1,000

X = comparison not valid

less interest on your CD money. To see if this is a good deal, compare the estimated savings on credit card interest to the lost CD interest earnings. If the interest saved is greater than the interest lost, then the CD-tied credit card is a good deal.

EXAMPLE 5-5:   You face two credit card options. Card A charges an 18 percent APR but has a grace period. However, to get this card you must deposit $1,000 in a CD paying only 3 percent interest. Card B charges 16 percent APR but has no grace period. Both cards have fees of $25. You can invest money in another CD paying 8 percent. Your average daily balance is $300. Is the CD-tied credit card a good deal?

If you always paid the balance within the grace period, then your annual credit card costs with Card A are simply the fee of $25. With Card B, your annual credit card costs are $25 + .16 ($300) = $73. Thus, the interest (and fee) saved with Card A is $48.

The cost of Card A is the foregone interest on the CD. Earning 8 percent, a $1,000 CD results in annual interest of $80. Earning 3 percent, a $1,000 CD pays $30, so the lost interest (before taxes) is $50. With a

WHY ARE CREDIT CARD RATES SO HIGH AND WHY DON'T THEY CHANGE?

C O N S U M E R

T O P I C

Two major consumer concerns about credit cards are: the rates are high, and the rates don't change much, even when other interest rates fall. These concerns have led many consumers to the conclusion that credit card companies must be conspiring to keep rates high.

But there are some alternative reasons explaining why credit card rates are high and relatively stable. The simple answer as to why credit card rates are higher than alternative consumer credit rates (e.g., bank personal loans, auto loans) is that credit card costs and risks are higher. Credit card loans require no collateral. When consumers take out a personal or auto loan they make one transaction. The average cardholder uses a credit card many times in a year, therefore making many transactions for the card issuer to handle and monitor. As a consequence, the cost to a bank handling a credit card is 10 to 12 times higher than the handling costs of a single personal loan or auto loan.

The existence of a grace period on most credit cards also increases their costs. About half of cardholders pay their balance within the grace period. Thus, these cardholders don't pay interest, and get free use of the credit card funds for the grace period (usually 30 days). It is estimated that credit card rates would fall from 18 percent to 15 percent if the grace period were eliminated.

Now what about the second complaint—that credit card rates don't change much, especially on the downside? The main reason for this stability is that the cost of money is a much less important component of the total cost of credit cards than for other loans. The cost of money accounts for 40 to 60 percent of credit card costs, compared to 80–90 percent for other types of loans. In contrast, operating costs account for a much larger share of credit card costs, 40 to 60 percent, compared to an average of only 15 percent for other loans. These differences mean that when other interest rates fall, meaning the cost of money falls, the fall in the cost of credit cards will be much smaller than the fall in the cost of other loans.

Public policies designed to help consumers may in fact hurt consumers with regard to credit card rates. Federal law requires that card issuers notify cardholders when credit card rates are increased. This, of course, is costly. Card issuers may not lower rates, when conditions allow them to, for fear that later they may have to raise rates and incur the notification costs.

Finally what about the theory that card issuers conspire to keep rates high? It's possible, but the evidence seems stacked against this explanation. For collusion to work, the number of colluders must be small. Yet there are thousands of banks issuing credit cards.

References: Becker, Michael, "Credit Card Caps Curtail Consumer Choices," Citizens for a Sound Economy; No. 14, July 15, 1987;

Sullivan, A., Charlene and Robert W. Johnson, "Responsiveness of Consumer Credit Rates to Changes in Short Term Interest Rates" *Monitor*, Credit Research Center, Purdue University, Vol. 9, No. 3, May–June 1983.

SHOULD CREDIT CARD RATES BE CONTROLLED?

C
O
N
S
U
M
E
R

T
O
P
I
C

Your immediate answer is probably yes, of course, credit card interest rates should be controlled so that they don't become excessively high. And you have plenty of company. Each year many bills are introduced in state legislatures and in the U.S. Congress to control credit card rates.

Legislators control credit card rate by passing usury ceilings. Usury ceilings are limits which credit card rates can't exceed.

If usury ceiling are set high enough, then they have little effect on credit card rates. But if usury ceilings are set low enough, then they may force credit card rates lower or prevent credit card rates from moving higher in the future. These are called *binding* usury ceilings.

What happens when usury ceilings become binding? You might be tempted to say—credit card rates are lower, consumers are better-off, and credit card companies just make lower profits. But if the credit card market is competitive (and evidence indicate it is), then credit card companies don't make excessive profits compared to the risk of their loans. Instead, if credit card companies are forced to lower rates, then they will attempt to reduce their high risk customers by imposing stricter standards on who can obtain cards. Typically these high risk customers are low income consumers, so the supply of credit to low income consumers is reduced. These consumers then turn to pawnshops and other high rate lenders for loans, or they must make larger downpayments in order to obtain lower interest rate loans from banks. In fact, research shows that, after taking account of the risk characteristics of customers, rate ceilings have no impact on the average interest rate charged.

References: Villegas, Daniel J. "An Analysis of the Impact of Interest Rate Ceilings," *Journal of Finance*, Vol. 37, No. 4, Sept. 1982, pp. 941–954.

Greer, Douglas F. "Rate Ceilings, Market Structure, and the Supply of Finance Company Personal Loans," *Journal of Finance*, Vol. 29, No. 5, December 1974, pp. 1363–1382.

Peterson, Richard L. "Effects of Creditor Remedies and Rate Restrictions," in The Federal Reserve Bank of Boston, *The Regulation of Financial Institutions*, MA, 1980, pp. 24–43.

28 percent tax bracket, this reduces to $36. So by taking Card A, you gain $48 at a cost of $36. Thus, Card A is a good deal. However, Card A becomes less beneficial the less advantage you take of die grace period.

The Bottom Line

Compare credit cards on the basis of annual fee, interest rate, and grace period. Convenience users are better off with low fee-high interest rate cards with grace periods. Frequent credit users, who can't take advantage of the grace period, are better off with high fee-low interest rate cards, although the advantage is dependent on the size of the frequent user's average daily balance. _____

CONSUMER TOPIC

DEBIT CARDS

Debit cards are different from credit cards. Debit cards allow a cardholder to pay for a product by transferring money directly from the cardholder's bank account to a merchant's account. Therefore, no loan is involved. Debit cards are simply an alternative to paying with cash or with a check.

Some years ago it was thought that debit cards would be the rave of the future. But this expectation hasn't been fulfilled. Several disadvantages of debit cards may be responsible. One disadvantage of debit cards is that users don't get the advantage of the 30 day grace period, or float, available with credit cards. Users of debit cards pay as soon as the product is purchased. Users of credit cards can get a 30-day free loan as long as balance is paid in full at the end of the month.

Record-keeping may also be more costly with a debit card than by paying with check. When a check is written, most people immediately record the amount and payee. You may be tempted to skip the recording of this information when paying with a debt card.

Also, a consumer who has second thoughts about a purchase can stop payment on a check or tell a credit card company to cancel a payment. This option is gone when using a debit card.

Debt cards also provide less consumer protection than credit cards. With credit cards, if your card is stolen, you are limited to $50 of liability for fraudulent use. However, if your debit card is stolen, you could lose as much as $500 if you do not tell the card issuer within two business days after learning of the card loss. If you do not report within 60 days then your risk is unlimited.

Reference: Finn, Edwin A., Jr. "Customers are Cool to Debit Cards Despite Growing Presence in Stores." *The Wall Street Journal*, August 20, 1985, p. 31.

---

12. How Can You Get Credit Out of Your Home, and Should You?

Home equity loans are another type of consumer credit loan. The collateral of a home equity loan is the equity (appraised value minus mortgage loan balance) the consumer has built-up in the house. Home equity loans have increased in popularity because of the greater ability to deduct interest charges on home equity loans for federal income tax purposes as compared to other kinds of consumer credit loans. Married couples can deduct interest payments on up to $100,000 of home equity loans, and single homeowners can deduct interest charges on up to $50,000 of home equity loans. Furthermore, there are no restrictions on the use of the home equity loan for its interest to qualify as deductible. The only other restriction is that total interest charges on the home only will be deductible on mortgage debt up to one million dollars (not a severe limitation for most homeowners). The total debt can be from one or two homes.

Second Mortgage

There are two major types of home equity loans. The traditional type has a fixed interest rate and a fixed term, thereby resulting in fixed payments. In addition, the homeowner receives the entire loan at once for use for the planned purpose. This type of home equity loan is called a *second mortgage*. The fixed interest rate on a second mortgage is higher than the fixed interest rate on new first (original) mortgages because the lender of the first mortgage has first claim on the house if the homeowner defaults. The term is usually between 10 and 15 years. The maximum amount which can be loaned by a second mortgage is some percentage (e.g., 75 percent) of the homeowner's house equity (difference between appraised value of house and outstanding loan balance on *first* mortgage).

Open-End Loan

A second type of home equity loan is really an open-end credit loan. Typically these loans are simply called home equity loans. The homeowner receives a line of credit through the home equity loan. Funds are borrowed when needed by the homeowner, sometimes by a method as easy as writing a check. The loan can be paid-off in a specified period of time or carried as long as the homeowner wants (but maybe with an outside time limit). A typical index is the "prime interest rate," so the home equity loan rate equals the prime rate plus a spread.[8] Some loans permit payments to be only of interest, meaning the entire principal payment will be due in a lump sum at some future date (termed a balloon payment).

Following is a checklist of considerations which the homeowner should heed before taking a home equity loan.

1. Are there minimum and maximum withdrawals from the loan?
2. If the loan has a variable interest rate,
   - what is the frequency of change?
   - what are the index and spread?

---

[8] The prime interest rate is the interest rate charged to the best (least risky) commercial customers.

- what are the caps?
- is the variable rate convertible to a fixed rate?

3. What are the closing costs?
4. Are there any "continuing costs," such as annual membership fees or a transaction fee, every time funds are borrowed?
5. Are there penalties for late payment or early prepayment?
6. Do payments include both interest and principal components, or only interest? If only interest, when does the balloon payment occur?

Which Is Best?

If you want to borrow money based on the equity in your home, which type of loan is best—the second mortgage or the open-end home equity loan? To answer this, consider the advantages and disadvantages of each type of loan.

If interest rates are at the bottom of the interest rate cycle when you are borrowing, the second mortgage is advantageous because a fixed interest rate can be locked in. In contrast, if interest rates are at a peak and are expected to fall, then an open-end home equity loan may be preferred in order to take advantage of a variable interest rate.

If you need the discipline of a fixed payment schedule, without the ability to borrow more and more money, then a second mortgage may be for you. A second mortgage forces the same kind of payment discipline as a first mortgage. In contrast, you can keep going back to the credit cookie jar with an open-end home equity loan as long as your loan limit isn't exceeded.

On the other hand, the flexibility of the open-end home equity loan can be advantageous for consumers who want to have a ready line of credit available for purchases which must be made quickly. Especially if such consumers borrow wisely, then the open-end home equity loan can be a real benefit.

The Bottom Line

A homeowner can borrow funds based on the equity in his/her home and all interest payments are tax deductible. Such home equity loans have become major alternative sources of credit. _____

13. How Can You Compare Consumer Credit Loans?

The annual percentage rate (APR) is the standardized way of comparing consumer credit loans. Loans with a higher APR are more expensive than lower APR loans. The calculation of the APR was discussed in an earlier chapter.

But all loan comparisons aren't so straight-forward. A good example is auto loans. Auto dealers will frequently make the following offer:

REBATE VS. LOW APR   buy this car using a dealer financed low APR loan, or receive a rebate on the price of the car and pay cash or obtain financing elsewhere. Dealer APRs can be as low as 0, 1, 2, 3, or 4 percent, and rebates can be as much as $1,000, $2,000, or $3,000. So the choice is between a larger loan financed with a lower APR, or a smaller loan financed with a higher APR. How can these alternatives be compared to determine which is the best deal?

If two loans are being compared with different APRs, but both loans have the same term and there are no tax deductions involved, then the loans can simply be compared by calculating and comparing the monthly payments.

EXAMPLE 5-6:   Which is cheaper, a $10,000 dealer loan with a 3 percent APR, or a bank loan at a 10 percent APR with a $1,000 rebate? Both loans are for 24 months.

ANSWER: For the first loan, the loan amount is $10,000 and the annual interest rate is 3%. The term of the loan is 24 months. This is a monthly compounding situation so the interest rate needs to be converted to monthly rate.

$$\text{Monthly payment for loan 1} = \frac{Loan\ amount}{PVFS\left(rm,=\dfrac{3\%}{12},n=24\ months\right)} = \frac{\$10,000}{223.2660} = \$429.81$$

You can either use the PVFS formula or Appendix Table A-6 to find the PVFS.

For the second loan, the loan amount is $9,000 since a $1,000 rebate is available. The annual interest rate is 10% with a 24-month term.

$$\text{Monthly payment for loan 2} = \frac{Loan\ amount}{PVFS\left(rm,=\dfrac{10\%}{12},n=24\ months\right)} = \frac{\$9,000}{21.6709} = \$415.30$$

Therefore, the bank loan is cheaper.

If the loans being compared have different terms, or if one loan involves tax advantages, then the loans must be compared by their present values. The next two examples illustrate this process.

EXAMPLE 5-7:   Which is cheaper, a $10,000 dealer loan with a 3 percent APR and a 12 month term, or a bank loan with a 10 percent APR, an 18 month term, and a $1,000 rebate? Use a discount rate of 8 percent.

ANSWER: For the first loan, the loan amount is $10,000 and annual interest rate is 3% with a 12-month term.

$$\text{Monthly payment for loan 1} = \frac{Loan\,amount}{PVFS\left(rm,= \frac{3\%}{12,}, n=12\,months\right)} = \frac{\$10,000}{11.8073} = \$846.94$$

For the second loan, the loan amount is $9,000 and annual interest rate is 10% with a 18-month term.

$$\text{Monthly payment for loan 2} = \frac{Loan\,amount}{PVFS\left(rm,= \frac{10\%}{12,}, n=18\,months\right)} = \frac{\$9,000}{16.6508} = \$540.51$$

In order to compare these two loans, we need to convert the monthly payments into present value using the same discount rate, which is 8% in this case.

Present value of loan 1 = Monthly payment of loan 1 * PVFS $\left(rm = \frac{8\%}{12}, n = 12\right) = \$846.94 \times 11.4958 = \$9,736.24$

Prevent value of loan 2 = Monthly payment of loan 1 * PVFS $\left(rm = \frac{8\%}{12}, n = 18\right) = \$540.51 \times 16.9089 = \$9,139.45$

The bank loan is cheaper.

EXAMPLE 5-8: Which is cheaper, a $10,000 dealer loan with a 1 percent APR, or a home equity loan with a 12 percent APR and a $1,000 rebate. The term of both loans is 12 months and the borrower's tax bracket is 28 percent. Use an 8 percent discount rate.

ANSWER: This is an interesting comparison because the interest payments on the home equity loan are tax-deductible.

For loan 1, the loan amount is $10,000, interest rate is 1%, and term is 12 months.

$$\text{Monthly payment for loan 1} = \frac{Loan\,amount}{PVFS\left(rm,= \frac{1\%}{12,}, n=12\,months\right)} = \frac{\$10,000}{11.9353} = \$837.85$$

For loan 2, the loan amount is $9,000, interest rate is 12%, and term is 12 months.

$$\text{Monthly payment for loan 2} = \frac{Loan\,amount}{PVFS\left(rm,= \frac{12\%}{12,}, n=12\,months\right)} = \frac{\$9,000}{11.2551} = \$799.64$$

From the comparison of monthly payments it is obvious that the home equity loan is cheaper, even without considering the interest tax deduction. To find the cost after considering tax deductions, first calculate the present value of the dealer loan:

Present value of loan 1 = Monthly payment of loan 1 * PVFS $(rm = \frac{8\%}{12}$, $n = 12) = \$837.85 \times 11.4958 = \$9,631.76$

Finding the present value cost of the home equity loan is more complicated, since the value of the tax deductions must first be subtracted as shown in the table below:

Month	Interest	Loan Balance	After-tax Payment	Present Value
1	$9000 ×.01 = $90	$9000 – (799.64 – 90) = $8290.36	799.64 – (.28 × 90) = 744.44	774.44 × .993 = 769.02
2	8290.36 ×.01 = 82.90	8290.36 – (799.64 – 82.90) = $7,573.62	799.64 – (.28 × 82.90) = 776.43	776.43 × .987 = 766.16
S	7573.62 ×.01 = 75.74	7573.62 – (799.64 – 75.74) = $6,849.72	799.64 – (.28 × 75.74) = 778.32	778.43 × .980 = 763.02
4	6849.72 ×.01 = 68.50	6849.72 – (799.64 – 68.50) = $6,118.52	799.64 – (.28 × 68.50) = 780.46	780.46 × .974 = 759.94
5	6118.58 ×.01 = 61.19	6118.58 – (799.64 – 61.19) = $5,380.13	799.64 – (.28 × 61.19) = 782.51	782.51 × .967 = 756.77
6	5380.13 ×.01 = 53.80	5380.13 – (799.64 – 53.80) = $4,634.29	799.64 – (.28 × 53.80) = 784.58	784.58 ×.961 = 753.75
7	4634.29 ×. 01 = 46.34	4634.29 – (799.64 – 46.34) = $3,880.99	799.64 – (.28 × 46.34) = 786.66	786.66 × .954 = 750.47
8	3880.99 ×.01 = 38.81	3880.99 – (799.64 – 38.81) = $3,120.16	799.64 – (.28 × 38.81) = 788.77	788.77 × .948 = 747.72
9	3120.16 ×.01 = 31.20	3120.16 – (799.64 – 31.20) = $2,241.72	799.64 – (.28 × 31.20) = 790.90	790.90 × .942 = 744.80
10	2351.72 ×.01 = 23.52	2351.72 – (799.64 – 23.52) = $1375.60	799.64 – (.28 × 23.52) = 793.05	793.05 × .935 = 741.86
11	1575.60 ×.01 = 15.76	1575.60 – (799.64 – 15.76) = $791.72	799.64 – (.28 × 15.76) = 795.23	795.23 × .929 = 739.06
12	791.72 ×.01 = 7.92	791.72 – (799.64 – 7.92) = 0	799.64 – (.28 × 7.92) = 797.42	797.42 × .923 = 736.31

PRESENT VALUE SUM = $9,028.88

The home equity loan is cheaper.

Some Conclusions on Car Loans

Can any conclusions be reached about loan alternatives, especially in auto financing? The car buyer faces three typical options: dealer financing (often at low APRs), a bank loan, and a home equity loan. If the dealer offers rebates, these can be used to reduce the loans for bank and home equity financing. Home equity financing offers the advantage of tax deductibility of interest costs, as noted above.

Table 5-19 compares dealer financing with low APRs to home equity loan financing that uses rebates and tax deductions. The present value methodology demonstrated above was used to arrive at the conclusions. As the table shows, it's usually better to take the rebate and finance with a home equity loan. Dealer loans do become more attractive the longer the loan term when the rebate is low.

Table 5-19   Comparing a low APR dealer loan to a home equity loan with a rebate.

Dealer loan vs. home equity loan with rebate, home equity loan = 10%

$10,000 auto, borrower's tax bracket is 28%, (DL = dealer loan cheaper; HE = home equity loan cheaper)[a]

Dealer Rebate/APR	Term of Loan (months)				
	12	**24**	**36**	**48**	**60**
$1000, 0%	HE	HE	DL	DL	DL
2%	HE	HE	HE	HE	DL
3%	HE	HE	HE	HE	HE
4%	HE	HE	HE	HE	HE
$2000, 0%	HE	HE	HE	HE	HE
2%	HE	HE	HE	HE	HE
3%	HE	HE	HE	HE	HE
4%	HE	HE	HE	HE	HE
$3000, 0%	HE	HE	HE	HE	HE
2%	HE	HE	HE	HE	HE
3%	HE	HE	HE	HE	HE
4%	HE	HE	HE	HE	HE

[a]Results hold for any alternative before-tax investment interest rate between 5 percent and 18 percent.

Dealer loan vs. home equity loan with rebate, home equity loan = 12%.

$10,000 auto, borrower's tax bracket is 28%, (DL = dealer loan cheaper; HE = home equity loan cheaper)[b]

Dealer	**Term of Loan (months)**				
Rebate/APR	12	24	36	48	60
$1000, 0%	HE	HE	DL	DL	DL
2%	HE	HE	HE	DL	DL
3%	HE	HE	HE	DL	DL
4%	HE	HE	HE	HE	DL
$2000, 0%	HE	HE	HE	HE	HE
2%	HE	HE	HE	HE	HE
3%	HE	HE	HE	HE	HE
4%	HE	HE	HE	HE	HE
$3000,0%	HE	HE	HE	HE	HE
2%	HE	HE	HE	HE	HE
3%	HE	HE	HE	HE	HE
4%	HE	HE	HE	HE	HE

[b]Results hold for any alternative before-tax investment interest rate between 5 percent and 18 percent.

Table 5-20 makes the same kind of comparison between dealer financing and bank financing. Of course, bank financing won't look as good because no tax deductions are available. Nevertheless, the same general conclusion holds: take the rebate and the bank loan except for long loan terms when the rebate is low.

Debt Consolidation Loan

A final kind of loan comparison involves debt consolidation loans. A debt consolidation loan is a loan which combines many smaller loans. Usually the company offering the consolidated loan advertises that their single loan will result in a lower monthly payment than the combined monthly payment of the several smaller loans. However, frequently this is only possible if the consolidated loan has a longer term than the several smaller loans. This means the consolidated loan may actually have a higher interest rate than the existing loans.

Table 5-20 Comparing a low APR dealer loan to a bank loan with a rebate.

Dealer loan vs. home equity loan with rebate, home equity loan = 10%

$10,000 auto, (DL = dealer loan cheaper; BL = bank loan cheaper)[a]

| Dealer Rebate/APR | Term of Loan (months) | | | | |
	12	24	36	48	60
$1000, 0%	BL	BL	DL	DL	DL
2%	BL	BL	DL	DL	DL
3%	BL	BL	BL	DL	DL
4%	BL	BL	BL	DL	DL
$2000, 0%	BL	BL	BL	BL	DL
2%	BL	BL	BL	BL	BL
3%	BL	BL	BL	BL	BL
4%	BL	BL	BL	BL	BL
$3000, 0%	BL	BL	BL	BL	BL
2%	BL	BL	BL	BL	BL
3%	BL	BL	BL	BL	BL
4%	BL	BL	BL	BL	BL

[a]Results hold for any alternative before-tax interest rate between 5 percent and 18 percent.

Dealer loan vs. home equity loan with rebate, home equity loan = 12%.

$10,000 auto, (DL = dealer loan cheaper; BL = bank loan cheaper)[b]

| Dealer Rebate/APR | Term of Loan (months) | | | | |
	12	24	SS	48	60
$1000,0%	BL	DL	DL	DL	DL
2%	BL	BL	DL	DL	DL
3%	BL	BL	DL	DL	DL
4%	BL	BL	DL	DL	DL
$2000,0%	BL	BL	BL	DL	DL
2%	BL	BL	BL	BL	BL
3%	BL	BL	BL	BL	BL

4%	BL	BL	BL	BL	BL
$3000,0%	BL	BL	BL	BL	BL
2%	BL	BL	BL	BL	BL
3%	BL	BL	BL	BL	BL
4%	BL	BL	BL	BL	BL

[b]Results hold for any alternative before-tax interest rate between 5 percent and 18 percent.

EXAMPLE 5-9:   Keith has three loans with the following characteristics:

> Loan 1, $131.87/mo., $1500 bal., 12 mos., 10% interest
> Loan 2, $198.20/mo., $3250 bal., 18 mos., 12% interest
> Loan 3, $ 99.81/mo., $1600 bal., 18 mos., 15% interest

Keith's total monthly payments are $429.88. EasyLoan Co. says it can consolidate Keith's loans into one monthly payment of $350. The term is 24 months. Is this a good deal?

ANSWER: The total loan being financed is $1500 + $3250 + $1600, or $6350. With a monthly payment of $350, the present value factor sum is $\dfrac{\$6350}{\$350}$, or 18.143. Looking in Appendix Table A-6, a present value factor sum of 18.143 and a term of 24 months is associated with an annual interest rate of almost 28.5 percent. The consolidated loan is not a cheaper alternative.

The Bottom Line

Compare loans by their present value amounts. With regard to auto loans, in most cases it's better to take the dealer's rebate and use bank or home equity loan financing.

14. How Can You Get Credit?

In the U.S., there are credit bureaus that collect financial information from various sources and provide consumer credit information on individual consumer's borrowing and bill-paying habits for a variety of uses. Often a consumer's credit risk is summarized into a "credit score," which is a numerical expression based on a statistical analysis of a person's credit habits. Lenders, such as banks and credit card companies, use credit scores to evaluate the potential risk posed by lending money to consumers. Your credit score can not only determine if you qualify for a loan, but also how high your interest rate is if you do qualify.

The best-known and most widely used credit score model in the U.S. is called the FICO score. The score is sold by the FICO company. Although the exact formulas for calculating credit scores are kept as a trade secret, FICO has disclosed several factors that can affect your

CREDIT SCORES

credit score, including payment history, credit utilization, length of credit history, types of credit used, and recent searches for credit. As you would expect, a credit history of late payments on bills will lower your FICO score. If your ratio of current revolving debt such as credit card balances to the total available revolving credit limit is too high, your FICO score will be lower. Consumers can improve their credit scores by paying off debts and lowering the credit utilization ratio. In addition, as your credit history gets longer, your FICO score will improve if the history is a good one. Consumers can also benefit by having a history of managing different types of credit. Finally, hard credit inquiries, which

C O N S U M E R

T O P I C

CREDIT DISCRIMINATION AND WOMEN

Several states have passed laws prohibiting lenders from discriminating in the granting of loans on the basis of sex. The intent of the law is to remove sex of the applicant as a consideration in the granting of a loan. Instead, the framers of the law want the economic characteristics of female applicants to be used as the basis of loan grants in the same way as they are for men.

Such laws can be passed, but do they work? This question was the object of a study by Cathleen Zick of the University of Utah. In 1973 California became one of the first states to pass a sex anti-discrimination law in the area of consumer credit. Zick used data for a sample of female loan applicants, some of whom applied for credit before the enactment of the law, and some of whom applied after the law was put in force. If the law had its intended effect, then Zick expected to find that lenders put more weight on the economic characteristics of women in the granting of credit for those applicants after the law's enactment than for those applicants before the law.

This is, in fact, exactly what Zick found. Economic characteristics such as work experience, credit history, and length of residence, had much more influence on the credit decision for applicants after the law was in force than for those before the law. Lenders apparently changed their decision rules in the direction intended by the law.

Reference: Zick, Cathleen D. "Equal Credit Opportunity Legislation and Indicators of Credit Worthiness: An Economic Study of Women Applicants for Credit in California." The Journal of Consumer Affairs, Vol. 17, No, 2, Winter 1985, pp. 370–387.

can occur when consumers apply for a credit card or loan, can hurt scores, especially if it is done frequently.

Each consumer actually has three credit scores because there are three national credit bureaus: Equifax, Experian, and TransUnion. Each bureau has its own database so the FICO scores computed using their databases can be slightly different. The Fair Credit Reporting Act requires each of the three credit bureaus to provide you with a free copy of your credit report, at your request, once every 12 months. It is important for you to obtain a free report to make sure your credit information is accurate. You can visit www.annualcreditreport.com or call 1-877-322-8228 to order your free report.

Other than credit scores, the better you look financially to the lender in terms of your income and assets compared to your debts, the more likely you will get a loan.

The Bottom Line

You can increase your chances of getting credit by reducing your existing debt, increasing your credit score, and increasing your income. Consider getting a job for a non-working spouse before you seek credit.

15. How Much Credit Is Too Much Credit?

Use the 20 *percent warning signal* to tell if you're overextended on consumer credit. That is, if your consumer credit payments (not including the mortgage payment) exceed 20 percent of your after-tax income, then you're probably headed (or you're already there) for credit problems.

20 PERCENT RULE

Where does this 20 percent warning signal come from—is it pulled out of the air? The 20 percent is based on the fact that for the average household, spending on necessities (food, clothing, shelter, auto, fuel, medical care) and other common purchases take up 80 percent of the household's after-tax income. This leaves 20 percent for savings, consumer credit payments, and other expenses. For the average household spending more than 20 percent on consumer credit payments, these payments cannot be sustained and will eventually lead to skipped payments and credit problems.

Of course, all consumers are not average. Some consumers may be especially frugal in expenditures on necessities and therefore be able to carry debt payments more than 20 percent of after-tax income. On the other hand, other consumers may spend a higher share of after-tax income on necessities and therefore aren't able easily to carry a 20 percent consumer debt load.

The Bottom Line

For the average consumer, consumer debt payments equal to 20 percent of after-tax income are the maximum that can safely be carried. The greater the consumer debt payment share is above 20 percent, the greater the debt problem that the consumer may face._____

16. How Can You Get Out of Credit Problems?

Before talking about how you can get out of credit problems, let's first briefly talk about how you can get into credit problems.

SOURCES OF CREDIT PROBLEMS

There are two ways of getting into credit problems. The first way is that your income remains the same but your debt rises; that is, you overextend yourself with consumer credit. This shouldn't happen as a result of consumer loans for which you must apply. For these loans the lender will examine your debt load and not extend you the loan if, by doing so, your credit will be overextended. Instead, this cause of credit problems is more likely to happen from overuse of credit cards, for which you don't undergo a credit examination.

The second way of getting into credit problems is that your debt remains the same but your income drops unexpectedly. Typical reasons for a drop in income include unemployment or reduction in work time and divorce.

There are no magic, painless ways of escaping from credit problems. Any program for reducing or eliminating credit problems involves three steps:

1. Don't take on more debt,
2. Reduce other expenditures so as to free-up resources to pay off, or reduce, existing debt,
3. Begin a regular monthly program of paying off the existing debt.

In other words, this is a belt-tightening program. Don't be led to believe there is any other way out of debt.

CALCULATING A PAYMENT SCHEDULE

Present Value Factor Sum (PVFS) can be helpful in calculating a payment plan necessary to retire consumer debt. Again, you can either use the PVFS formula given in Chapter 1 or use Appendix Table A-6 to find PVFS for given annual interest rate and term. The loan amount divided by the PVFS equals the equal monthly payment for a given number of months.

$$\frac{\text{Loan amount}}{\text{PVFS}} = \text{monthly payment for N months}$$

Now, if you have a loan amount and you know how much you can pay per month, Appendix Table A-6 can be used in reverse to find how long it will take to retire the debt. That is,

**C
O
N
S
U
M
E
R

T
O
P
I
C**

WHO HAS DEBT PROBLEMS?

Two statistics indicating debt problems are regularly published by the Federal Reserve System using data from the Survey of Consumer Finances. One is debt-to-income ratio greater than 40%, and the other is any debt payment past due 60 days or more. In 2010, 13.8% families had a debt-to-income ratio greater than 40%, while 10.8% families had debt payments past due 60 days or more.

The profile of families that have consumer debt problems is not surprising. The lower the family income, the higher the percentage of families in debt trouble. In 2010, 26.1% families in the lowest 20th percentile of the income distribution had debt-to-income ratio above 40%, while only 2.9% families in the top 20th percentile of the income distribution had the same debt problem. Those in the middle ages (35–54) were more likely to have debt problems, compared to either younger or older families. While the percentage of homeowners with high debt-to-income ratio was much higher than renters (17.1% vs. 5.0%, respectively), the percentage of debtors with any payment past due 60 days or more was much higher among renters than homeowners (16.6% vs. 8.7%, respectively).

Source: Federal Reserve System, Survey of Consumer Finances, 2010.

$$\frac{\text{Loan amount}}{\text{Monthly payment for N months}} = \text{PVFS associated with interest rate and term of N months.}$$

Find the calculated PVFS under the given interest rate and read off the associated term. The term is how long it will take you to retire the debt by making these monthly payments.

EXAMPLE 5-10: Jack and Jill are in credit trouble. They have accumulated a credit card debt of $3,000. If they pay $100 a month to the credit card company, how long will it take to pay off the debt if the credit card APR is 18 percent?

ANSWER:

$$\frac{\$3,000}{100} = 30.$$

Look for 30 in Appendix Table A-6, under 18 percent, and then read off the value of "N" (number of months). The PVFS of 30 falls almost halfway between 27.66 (36 months) and 34.04 (48 months), so it would take Jack and Jill approximately 42 months (halfway between 36 and 48) to retire the debt of $3,000.

The Bottom Line

Tighten the household financial belt to get out of credit problems. Don't take on more credit, reduce other household spending, and begin a regular monthly program of paying off loans in order to get out of credit problems.

WORDS AND CONCEPTS YOU SHOULD KNOW

Life-cycle saving's hypothesis
Consumer durable goods
Consumer non-durable goods
Opportunity cost of cash
Present value of credit payments
Add-on interest
Interest payment
Principal payment
Outstanding loan balance
Periodic interest rate
365.25/360 method of principal and interest allocation
The rule of 78
APR
Up-front costs
APR and closed-end credit loans
APR and open-end credit loans
Rental costs of a consumer durable good
Ownership costs of a consumer durable good
Fixed costs
Depreciation
Foregone interest earnings
Variable costs
Accelerated depreciation
Straight line depreciation
Life cycle cost

Benefit-cost ratio
Rule for replacing consumer durable goods
Cost of leasing
Closed-end lease
Open-end lease
Role of depreciation in lease costs
Rent-to-own contracts
Relationship between risk of borrower and interest rate charged
Secured loans
Unsecured loans
Stratification of the credit market
Closed-end loans
Open-end loans
Annual credit card fee
Monthly finance charge
Average daily balance
Debt consolidation loan
Grace period
Convenience user of credit cards
Second mortgage
Home equity loan
Rebate on auto purchase
20 percent rule
Credit scores
Credit bureaus

CREDIT—A SUMMARY

1. Credit allows the borrower to match consumption needs and income. Credit transfers future purchasing power to the present.

2. Credit makes most sense when used to buy long-lasting consumer goods (consumer durable goods). Credit makes less sense when used to buy goods that are used up quickly (consumer non-durable goods), unless credit is simply used as a convenience.

3. Using cash to buy a product is not free. The cash has an opportunity cost because it could have been invested and earned interest. Charge yourself the after-tax rate of return as the cost of using cash.

4. Using credit to buy today is wise if the product being purchased has a high inflation rate and if the difference between the credit interest rate and the opportunity cost of cash is small.

5. Credit payments are calculated in the same way as mortgage payments. The present value of credit payments, using the credit interest rate as the discount rate, equals the loan amount. Find the monthly credit payment by dividing the loan amount by the monthly present value factor sum (PVFS) associated with the credit interest rate and term.

6. Calculate the interest payment out of a credit payment by multiplying the periodic interest rate by the outstanding loan balance. The principal payment then equals the credit payment minus the interest payment. The new outstanding loan balance is the old balance minus the principal payment.

7. The "365.25/360" method of principal and interest allocation results in 5.25 additional days of interest charged per year.

8. The Rule of 78 is an alternative method of allocating principal and interest payments out of a credit payment. It results in more of each credit payment going to interest and less to principal as compared to allocation using economic logic (see 6 above).

9. The APR of a loan is the annual percentage rate. The APR is based on charges for borrowing money plus other fees (e.g., points) required by the lender.

    A. The APR for closed-end loans is calculated using economic logic. Any up-front fees, such as points, are first deducted from the loan amount before calculating the APR.

    B. The APR for open-end loans is simply the periodic rate multiplied by the number of periods in a year. This understates the true cost of borrowing.

10. Ownership costs of a consumer durable good include fixed costs and variable costs. Fixed costs include depreciation, finance costs, scheduled maintenance, insurance costs and fees, and foregone interest earnings. Fixed costs are paid regardless of how much the good is used. Variable costs include fuel and unscheduled maintenance. Variable costs increase with use of the good.

    A. Depreciation is a "using up" of the durable good. Depreciation is a major cost of autos.

    B. Foregone interest earnings is an opportunity cost related to net ownership (market value minus outstanding loan balance) of the durable good. The owner could sell the durable good, invest the net ownership cost, and earn interest.

11. Life cycle cost of an appliance takes into account both purchase price and operating costs. The life cycle cost equals the purchase price plus the present value of the annual energy costs over the life of the appliance.

12. The annual benefit from a consumer durable good can be measured as what it would cost to receive the same services as received from the consumer durable good in the next best way. Calculation of benefit-cost ratios for common consumer durable goods shows that most return benefits are greater than their costs.

13. A consumer durable good should be replaced when the cost of keeping the good for one more year is greater than the annual average (annuity) cost of a new durable good, where the average of the new good is calculated over the number of years equal to the age of the existing durable good. For cars, replace them an average of every six years if they are heavily used or every 12 years if they are carefully maintained and used.

14. Compare the present value cost of owning to the present value cost of leasing to evaluate which is cheaper. Annual lease payments should always be less than annual ownership payments, since leasees don't use the full value of the durable good.

15. Rent-to-own (RTO) contracts are common for consumer durable goods other than autos. RTO contracts allow the consumer to apply the rental payments to purchase of the consumer durable good as long as all payments are made. However, if RTO contracts are considered purchase agreements, then the APR is very high. Research shows that users of RTO contracts are high-risk consumers who have been denied credit elsewhere.

16. The consumer credit market is stratified by risk level. More risky borrowers pay higher interest rates. Secured loans, which have some asset pledged as collateral for the loan, charge lower interest rates than unsecured loans. Closed-end loans must be repaid in a specific term, whereas open-end loans don't have a specific payment schedule.

17. There are two costs of using a credit card: the annual fee and the monthly finance charge. Many credit cards have a grace period, meaning that if the amount owed from the previous month (previous balance) has been paid this month, then no finance charge is due on amounts charged this month.

   A. A convenience user is a consumer who always pays the previous balance each month and thus never pays a finance charge.

   B. Convenience users are better off with credit cards charging a low fee and a high interest rate.

   C. Credit card users who carry a high balance owed and never use the grace period are better off with high fee and low interest rate credit cards.

18. Second mortgages and home equity loans are two ways of borrowing against the equity in a consumer's home. The second mortgage is usually a fixed rate, fixed term loan. The home equity loan is an open-end credit loan that often has an adjustable interest rate.

19. Auto purchasers frequently face two financing options: use the dealer's low APR loan or finance elsewhere but get a rebate on the price. Such options can be compared by their monthly payments or after-tax present value costs. In the majority of cases, it's better to take the dealer's rebate and finance elsewhere.

20. Debt consolidation loans combine a number of smaller debt payments into one payment. The one large payment is usually less than the sum of the smaller payments. However, the interest rate on the consolidated loan can be higher if the term of the loan is longer than the terms on the smaller loans.

21. Consumer credit problems arise when a consumer's income drops unexpectedly or when borrowing increases substantially. The average consumer shouldn't spend more than 20 percent of after-tax income on credit payments.

22. There are three steps to getting out of credit trouble:

   a. don't take on more debt,

   b. reduce other expenditures to free-up money to pay down on the debt, and

   c. begin a regular monthly program of paying off the debt.

PROBLEMS

1. You can purchase a $900 refrigerator today using a 12 percent loan (24-month term) or you can pay cash in a year. Which is better if the after-tax opportunity cost of your cash is 6 percent and the refrigerator is expected to cost 14 percent more next year?

2. What is the equal monthly payment for a $10,000 loan charging a 16 percent annual interest rate and being repaid in 36 months?

3. A $5,000 loan requires the repayment of $101.38 monthly for five years. What is the associated annual interest rate?

4. Take a $5,000 loan charging an 18 percent annual interest rate and with a term of 24 months. First, calculate the monthly payment. Then calculate the monthly payment to principal and to interest and calculate the outstanding loan balance for the first three months using both economic logic and using the Rule of 78.

5. Calculate the APR for:
   a)   a $6000 loan with monthly payments of $200 for 36 months.
   b)   a $6000 loan with up-front fees of $500 and monthly payments of $200 for 36 months.

6. Use Table 4-14 to calculate the annual total costs of owning a new intermediate-sized auto for the first five years. Use the following information in the calculation:
   a)   the car's price is $20,000,
   b)   the car's purchase is financed with a $2,000 downpayment and the remainder borrowed at 8 percent for a term of five years,
   c)   insurance costs are $1,000 annually,
   d)   registration and fees are $300 the first year and $30 annually thereafter,
   e)   you can earn 6 percent, after taxes, on invested money,
   f)   the car averages 35 miles per gallon and gas costs $1,45 per gallon, and
   g)   you expect to drive 15,000 miles each year.

7. Which is cheaper over its expected life, a washer costing $500 and having an annual energy cost of $100 or a washer costing $750 and having an animal energy cost of $65? Assume both washers have a life of ten pars. Use a 3 percent real interest rate.

8. Estimate the annual benefits to you of owning a washer and dryer.

9. Peter can rent a $600 TV from a rent-to-own dealer for $64 a month. If Peter makes 36 monthly payments he can own the TV. If all the payments are considered as purchase payments, and if Peter makes all 36 payments, what is the approximate APR?

10. You're considering leasing a $17,000 compact car for two years. How much lower, at a minimum, should monthly lease payments be compared to monthly finance payments? Use an 8 percent interest rate.

11. Credit card A has a $50 annual fee and a 14 percent interest rate. Credit card B has a $15 fee and an 18 percent interest rate. If your average credit card debt is $1,000, and if you don't take advantage of the grace period, which card is cheaper for you?

12. Which is cheaper, a $12,000 car dealer loan with a 4 percent APR and a 24-month term or a bank loan with a 10 percent APR, a 24-month term, and a $1,500 rebate?

13. Which is cheaper, a $12,000 car dealer loan with a 4 percent APR and a 24-month term or a bank loan with a 10 percent APR, a 36-month term, and a $1,500 rebate? Use a discount rate of 7 percent.

14. Laura and Hen have accumulated $8,000 in credit card debt. If they can discipline themselves not to take on any more debt, and if they can make monthly payments of $200, how long will it take them to pay off the debt if the credit card interest rate is 18 percent?

CHAPTER 6

Life Insurance

Introduction

Many people think life insurance is a complicated topic. Life insurance agents often don't help simplify life insurance decision-making. Agents overwhelm the consumer with numbers, dollars, and sometimes false comparisons.

In this chapter you'll learn how to uncomplicate life insurance. You'll learn that not everyone needs life insurance. You'll learn how to calculate life insurance needs (it's present value time again!) and you'll learn the proper way to compare life insurance policies. Most importantly, after digesting this chapter you will be armed to do battle with life insurance agents, never again afraid to ask the right questions and to evaluate the answers.

1. Why Insurance?

Insurance is protection against risk. We face many risks in our lives—the risk of a car accident, the risk of slipping on ice and breaking an arm, the risk of dying from a heart attack. Consumers buy insurance to pay the costs associated with the risks if they do occur. For example, if you have an auto accident, auto insurance will pay to repair your car; if you have an extended illness or injury, medical insurance will pay the hospital and doctor bills; and if you die, life insurance (as we shall see) is designed to help meet the expenses of your financial dependents. If insurance is purchased and none of these evils occur, is the cost of

RISK

insurance wasted? Absolutely not—the insurance has still served to protect—to provide peace of mind—since you had no way of accurately predicting if the risk would occur (more on this later).

But who needs insurance and insurance companies! Why doesn't the smart person save a little each month, put the money aside in a savings account, and use money to pay for repairs if a car accident happens, or to pay the hospital and doctor bill if an illness occurs? This is called

SELF INSURANCE

self insurance. The reason most consumers don't self insure is that it's *cheaper* to purchase market insurance. It would be impossible for a person to save enough money to replace his future income if he were to die, yet spending $200 to $2000 a year for life insurance will do exactly this.

The Bottom Line _____

Buy insurance to protect against those risks which are unavoidable or which are expensive to avoid. _____

2. How Does Life Insurance Work?

Life insurance (and, in fact, any insurance) operates on a "pooling" principle. Out of a given population of consumers, some will die during the year. However, which particular consumers will die is unknown to

WHY WE DIE

The accompanying table shows the causes of death in the United States in 2010. Heart disease and cancer each accounted for a little less than a quarter of all deaths. Combined they were responsible for almost half of all deaths in 2010.

The death rate fell significantly from 9.6 per 1000 population in 1950 to 8.5 per 1000 population to 8.0 per 1000 population in 2010. The life expectancy in 2010 was 78.7 years, with male life expectancy at 76.2 and female life expectancy at 81.1. States in the southeast region generally have higher death rates than those in other regions of the country.

Causes of Death in 2010

Cause	Number	% of total
Diseases of heart	597,689	24.2
Malignant neoplasms (cancer)	574,743	23.3
Chronic lower respiratory diseases	138,080	5.6
Cerebrovascular diseases	129,476	5.2
Accidents (unintentional injuries)	120,859	4.9
Alzheimer's disease	83,494	3.4
Diabetes mellitus	69,071	2.8
Nephritis, nephrotic syndrome and nephrosis	50,476	2
Influenza and pneumonia	50,097	2
Intentional self-harm (suicide)	38,364	1.6
Septicemia	34,812	1.4
Chronic liver disease and cirrhosis	31,903	1.3
Essential hypertension and hypertensive renal disease	26,634	1.1
Parkinson's disease	22,032	0.9
Pneumonitis due to solids and liquids	17,011	0.7
All other causes (Residual)	483,694	19.6
Sum	2,468,435	100

Data source: National Vital Statistics System, Centers for Disease Control and Prevention.

RISK POOLING

both consumers and to life insurance firms.[1] Based on past experience of similar populations, each consumer only knows that he or she faces some probability of dying during the year. Therefore, each consumer is motivated to pool his/her probability of dying with other consumers. Each consumer contributes a relatively small amount of money to

[1]If life insurance companies know which consumers will die, those consumers would not be offered life insurance, or would only be offered insurance at a very high price.

a common fund or pool. The fund is then used to pay the insurance benefits to those consumers who die. It should be stressed that the reason consumers are willing to engage in this "pooling" of resources for insurance, is that none of them knows exactly if he or she will die. If a consumer did know, steps could be taken to avoid the risk, and insurance firms would be reluctant to sell policies to the consumer.

For example, suppose ten consumers each want $1000 of life insurance. Suppose each consumer faces a 10 percent chance of dying during the year. Each consumer would then pay $100 (10 percent of $1000) to the life insurance fund, and the fund would accumulate $1000 (10 consumers × $100 per consumer). One consumer would die during the year (10 percent of 10), and that consumer's family would collect the $1000.

In reality of course, the insurance company would have costs (administrative costs, marketing costs, advertising costs) and would have to make a profit, so the cost to the consumer in our example would be more than $100.

The Bottom Line

Life insurance works on the principle of pooling of risk. Consumers are motivated to buy life insurance because no one knows who will die or when.

3. What Questions Should You Ask About Life Insurance?

Life insurance is probably one of the most mysterious and misunderstood of consumer products. Part of the reason is that, like home mortgages, life insurance involves costs and benefits paid and received over time; hence, life insurance involves comparing dollars at different points in time over a long time period. Another problem with life insurance is that the cost of a policy is not always obvious. The money paid for some policies may buy only protection, while the money paid for other policies may buy a combination of protection and savings. How is the consumer to compare such policies? Life insurance policies aren't bought frequently, so some consumers may not want to invest the time learning about alternative policies. Lastly, inflation adds complexity to life insurance planning. Inflation has prompted many consumers to reexamine old policies and to consider cancelling those policies and purchasing alternative protection. Inflation has also encouraged product innovation by the industry in the form of different types of policies, specifically the so-called "universal" life insurance policies.

There are three life insurance questions which the consumer must answer: (1) who needs life insurance; (2) how much life insurance is needed; and (3) what kind of life insurance is needed. The consumer who has answered these questions will have successfully navigated through the life insurance channel.

INSURED   OWNER

Before addressing the life insurance questions, we must establish some terminology. The *insured* is the person who is covered by the life insurance. The *owner* of the life insurance policy pays the premiums. Usually the owner is the same as the insured, and this will be assumed in future discussions unless otherwise stated. *Beneficiaries* are the people who will receive the proceeds of the life insurance policy if the insured were to die. The policy face value is the amount of life insurance purchased, which is the money received by the beneficiaries if the insured dies.

BENEFICIARIES
FACE VALUE

PREMIUM

Finally, the *premium* is the price paid by the consumer for the life insurance policy. Premiums can generally be paid monthly, quarterly, or twice-yearly.

The Bottom Line

The consumer should answer three questions about life insurance: (1) Is it needed? (2) How much is needed? (3) What kind should be purchased?

4. Who Needs Life Insurance?

FINANCIAL
DEPENDENTS

Life insurance serves a simple purpose: to provide income to the *financial dependents* of an income producer, in the event that the *income producer* dies. For example, consider the traditional family in which the husband works and the wife maintains the household and cares for the children. In this case, the income producer is the husband and the financial dependents are the wife and children. Life insurance is bought on the husband in order to provide income to the wife and children if the husband dies.

"NON-TRADITIONAL"
FAMILIES

But, of course, the "traditional" family is long gone in America. Over half of wives now work. Should life insurance be considered on working wives? Yes, if the working wife has financial dependents, such as children. What if both husband and wife work? Then, if there are children or other financial dependents, life insurance should be considered for both husband and wife.

TRADITIONAL
FAMILIES

Life insurance agents today are pushing families to also consider life insurance on wives, or house-husbands, who work in the home rather than the market-place. This is a sound idea. Although housewives and house-husbands don't earn explicit salaries, they certainly perform valuable services which would cost money for the family to replace. Therefore, it is reasonable to consider life insurance on housewives and house-husbands based on the value of the services (child care, cleaning, cooking, etc.) they perform.

C O N S U M E R   T O P I C

SUBSTITUING EDUCATION FOR LIFE INSURANCE

There are substitutes for life insurance. One of the best substitutes is a better-educated spouse. Instead of spending money on life insurance, the same money could be spent by the spouse in acquiring more education and skills. If the insured were to die, the spouse could then use the education and skills to acquire a better job and earn more money. Hence, less life insurance would be needed.

Is there evidence that families do, in fact, substitute education for life insurance? Based on research by Goldsmith, the answer is yes. Using an analysis of over 4000 households, Goldsmith found that households with more educated wives, everything else equal (including income), were likely to have less life insurance. A better educated spouse, who therefore could replace more of the insured's income upon his death, can be a substitute for life insurance.

Reference: Goldsmith, Art. "Household Life Cycle Protection: Human Capital versus life Insurance." *Journal of Risk and Insurance,* Vol 50, No, 3 Sept, 1983, pp.473–486.

Who shouldn't have life insurance? Many families buy life insurance on their children (the children are the insured), but, other than an amount for burial expenses, life insurance on children is silly. Children aren't major income earners and they don't have financial dependents. Money spent on life insurance premiums for children is better invested in an educational savings fund.

SINGLES, CHILDLESS COUPLES

Singles and childless couples also have very little need for life insurance. If a couple plans to have children in the future, it's best to wait until that time to purchase life insurance. The only reason for an individual with no financial dependents to purchase life insurance would be in the following special situation. The individual expects to have financial dependents in the future. Furthermore, the individual is in good health now but expects to be in poorer health in the future when he applies for life insurance. Buying life insurance now, before the individual needs it but while he/she is in good health, can "lock" the individual into lower life insurance premiums.

Families shouldn't expect to make money from life insurance. Life insurance's main purpose is to provide protection. If the insured doesn't die and the beneficiaries don't collect, the premiums paid for the life insurance policy *haven't* been wasted. The premiums have paid for protecting against the possibility of death of the insured.

The Bottom Line

The highest priority for life insurance should be for an income earner with financial dependents.

5. How Much Life Insurance? The Income Approach

Most people use the "sound rule" to select an amount of life insurance—they pick the amount of life insurance that "sounds right." This rule obviously won't do; it will result in the family buying too much or too little life insurance.

There are two "correct" approaches to calculating the required life insurance face value amount: the *income approach* and the *expense approach*. This section discusses the income approach; the next section tackles the expense approach.

General Principle

The income approach calculates the life insurance face value amount as the investment fund necessary to replace the insured's future income (if the insured were to die today) that is not replaced by Social Security survivor's benefits or other family savings.

Let's ignore Social Security survivor's benefits and other family savings for a moment and focus only on replacing the insured's income. How would we do this—would we simply add up the insured's future income? No. This will give us more than necessary, because the smart consumer (or his insurance company) will invest that part of the insurance fund which is not needed each year in the event that the insured does die.

DISCOUNTING   What we should do is to discount the insured's future income in order to find the life insurance face value amount. For example, if we want to find the face value amount necessary to replace $20,000 for each of five years, and we begin discounting in year 2 using a 3 percent discount rate, then the required face value amount is:

$20,000 × 1.000 (no discounting since this is needed immediately if the insured dies now) = $20,000

$20,000 × 0.971 (PV factor for 1 yr., 3%) = 19,420

$20,000 × 0.943 (PV factor for 2 yrs.,3%) = 18,860

$20,000 × 0.915 (PV factor for 3 yrs.,3%) = 18,300

$20,000 × 0.888 (PV factor for 4 yrs.,3%) = 17,760

Sum = Face Value Amount = $94,340

To prove to yourself that $94,540 would produce $20,000 each year for five years if the insured were to die today, work through the following calculations:

	Beginning Amount		Amount Used		Remainder to Invest		F.V. Factor for 1 yr, 3%		Amount Available for Year
Year 1	$94,340.00	−	$20,000	=	$74,340.00	×	1.03	=	$76,570.20
Year 2	76,570.20	−	20,000	=	56,570.20	×	1.03	=	58,267.31
Year 3	58,267.31	−	20,000	=	38,267.31	×	1.03	=	39,415.33
Year 4	39,415.33	−	20,000	=	19,415.44	×	1.03	=	20,000.00
Year 5	20,000.00	−	20,000	=	0		—		—

What about Inflation?

In the income approach calculations, inflation can be handled in one of two ways. One alternative is to directly incorporate it. This would mean inflating the future income values to their expected actual (nominal) amount. It would also mean adding an inflation component to the real discount rate and using the resulting nominal interest rate for discounting.

The major problem with this way of handling inflation is in predicting inflation, A look at Figure 2-2 shows the variability in inflation.

Fortunately there is another way of handling inflation and that is to ignore it! In technical terms, this means to deal in "real numbers"—real income and real interest rates. If, for example, we assume that any salary increases received by the insured will simply keep up with inflation (meaning real income is constant), then we can use the insured's current income for all future income earning years. This also means that a real interest rate is used as the discount rate; 3 percent would be a typical rate.

Furthermore, both ways of handling inflation will give the same answer. Table 6-1 shows three "income approach" calculations. Calculation A is the "real" approach which does not inflate income and which discounts using a real interest rate. Calculation B assumes an inflation rate of 5 percent, and Calculation C assumes an inflation rate of 10 percent. All three calculations give the same answer, subject to some rounding error. Note in Calculations B and C that it is important to use the correct discount rate [(1 + real rate) × (1 + inflation rate)]. If the short-cut rate [1 + real rate + inflation rate] is used, the results will be slightly different. Also, the value factors are not from Appendix Table A-4, but are calculated to four places to give more precision to the results. For example, in calculation B, 0.8550 is 1/(1.0815).

The Importance of Social Security Survivor's Benefits

Social Security survivor's benefits are substantial. The surviving family of most workers covered by Social Security qualify for the survivor's benefits. Benefits are paid to the surviving spouse and children until the last child is age 18. Benefits vary by the income of the insured worker

Table 6-1   The income approach, with and without inflation.

A. Inflation rate of 0%, discount rate of 1.03.

$20,000 × 1.0000 = $20,000

20,000 × 0.9709 = 19,418

20,000 × 0.9426 = 18,852

20,000 × 0.9151 = 18,302

20,000 × 0.8885 = 17,770

$94,342

B. Inflation rate of 5%, discount rate of 1.0815 (1.03 × 1.05).

$20,000 × 1.0000 = $20,000	$20,000 × 1.0000 = $20,000
20,000 × 1.0500 = 21,000	21,000 × 0.9246 = 19,427
20,000 × 1.1025 = 22,050	22,050 × 0.8550 = 18,852
20,000 × 1.1576 = 23,152	23,152 × 0.7905 = 18,302
20,000 × 1.2155 = 24,310	24,310 × 0.7310 = 17,770
	$94,341

C Inflation rate of 10%, discount rate of 1.1330 (1.03 × 1.10).

$20,000 × 1.0000 = $20,000	$20,000 × 1.0000 = $20,000
20,000 × 1.1000 = 22,000	22,000 × 0.8826 = 19,417
20,000 × 1.2100 = 24,200	24,200 × 0.7790 = 18,852
20,000 × 1.3310 = 26,620	26,620 × 0.6876 = 18,303
20,000 × 1.4641 = 29,282	29,282 × 0.6068 = 17,770
	$94,342

---

and by how long the insured worker was employed. Social Security survivor's benefits are also indexed for inflation, meaning they rise each year by the inflation rate.

Some Answers: Putting the Income Approach to Work

The income approach is put to work in Table 6-2 by assuming a 35 year old insured wants his/her income replaced until the children are age 18 and assuming a real discount rate of 3 percent. The calculations assume only Social Security survivorship benefits; no pension or other savings are assumed to replace some of the insured's income.

All life insurance policy amounts are shown as multiples of annual income. So, for example, a family with an annual income of $30,000 needs $195,000 ($30,000 × 6.5) of life insurance coverage. The calculations assume children are very young. The multiples would be lower if children were older because there would be less years to cover until they are 18.

Table 6-2 Life insurance policy amount, as a multiple of annual income, necessary to replace income of a 35 year old, not replaced by Social Security survivor's benefits, until children are age 18.

Annual Income	Multiple of Annual Income
$ 10,000	3.0
15,000	4.0
20,000	5.0
25,000	6.0
30,000	6.5
35,000	7.5
40,000	8,0
45,000	8.5
50,000	9.0
60,000	10.0
70,000	10.5
100,000	11.5

Source: Author's calculations.

Rather than insuring 100 percent replacement of the insured's income, families may want to insure only 70 or 75 percent of the insured's future income. In this case, use 70 or 75 percent of the insured's income as the income number in Table 6-2 and find the corresponding multiple for the life insurance face value amount.[2] If both spouses work, then a life insurance face value amount should be found from Table 6-3 for each spouse's income. Social Security survivor's benefits are the same for both male and female workers.

Do It Yourself

A six step procedure can be used to calculate an individual's life insurance face value amount using the income approach.

Step 1: Decide on the number of years of the insured's work career to be insured. A common possibility is to insure until the youngest child is out of school, either at age 18 or age 22. Call this number of years the *life insurance term*.

LIFE INSURANCE
TERM

---

[2]Actually this will over-estimate somewhat the life insurance amount because the actual Social Security survivor's benefit will be based on the insured's total income.

THE AVERAGE SIZE OF LIFE INSURANCE POLICIES

C O N S U M E R   T O P I C

The average face value amount of life insurance policies purchased by consumers has generally increased over time, from $36,339 in 1985 to $98,130 in 2010. So are consumers increasing their amount of protection? No necessarily! What really counts is the amount of real (inflation adjusted) protection. Has the increase in the size of polices kept up with increases in prices of goods and services?

The graph shows the average face value of new life insurance policies over time, both in nominal values and in inflation-adjusted 2010 dollars. While there were ups and downs in the average face value amount, the general trend between 1985 and 2010 is an increasing one even after adjusting for inflation. This makes sense because household income has increased in real value during that period. As a result, consumers need higher overage amounts to replace their higher income and higher expenditures over time.

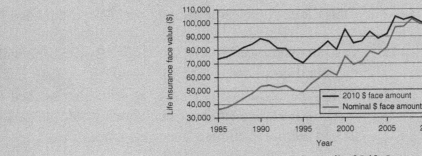

Data source: American Council of Life Insurance.

Step 2:
REAL INCOME
For each year of the life insurance term, write down the insured's real income. If the insured expects pay raises which will only equal inflation, then each year's *real* income equals the insured's current income. If the insured expects pay raises which will exceed inflation, then the rate by which the pay raise is expected to exceed the inflation rate should be used to increase the salary each year. Multiply the real income by a percentage (e.g., 70 or 75 percent) if only a percentage of real income is to be replaced by life insurance.

Step 3:
For each year of the life insurance term but only until the youngest child is 18, write down the Social Security survivorship benefit received from the Social Security office.

Step 4:
NET REAL INCOME
Subtract the Social Security survivorship benefit from the insured's real income for each year. Also subtract any other annual income (such as pension income) which would be received by the beneficiaries due to death of the insured. Call the remaining real income the "net real income."

Step 5: Use a real discount rate, such as 3 percent, to calculate the present value of the "net real income" over the life insurance term.

Step 6: Subtract from the present value amount calculated in STEP 5 any current family savings which will be used to replace the insured's income. The resulting number is the life insurance face value amount.

EXAMPLE 6-1: Joe Gregory, age 35, earns $30,000 annually and expects to receive pay raises only equal to the inflation rate. Joe has three financial dependents: his wife Jean, a 13 year old child, and a 10 year old child. Joe finds Social Security will pay an annual survivorship benefit to his wife and children of $19,155 when both children are under age 18, $16,411 when one child is under age 18, and $0 when both children are age 18. The Gregory family has $5,000 in savings which will be applied to replace some of Joe's future income. Joe wants a life insurance face value amount which will replace 70 percent of his future real income until the youngest child is age 22.

Step 1: The life insurance term is 22 − 10 = 12 years. Joe will have two children under age 18 for years 1 to 5, then one child under age 18 for years 6 to 8. If Jean also worked in the marketplace, then similar calculations would be performed to find her life insurance face value amount.

Yr.		STEP 2	STEP 3	STEP 4	STEP 5
1	$30,000 × .7 =	$21,000 −	$19,155 =	$ 1,845 × 1.000 =	$ 1,845.00
2	30,000 × .7 =	21,000 −	19,155 =	1,845 × 0.971 =	1,791.50
3	30,000 × .7 =	21,000 −	19,155 =	1,845 × 0.943 =	1,739.84
4	30,000 × .7 =	21,000 −	19,155 =	1,845 × 0.915 =	1,688.18
5	30,000 × .7 =	21,000 −	19,155 =	1,845 × 0.888 =	1,638.36
6	30,000 × .7 =	21,000 −	16,411 =	4,589 × 0.863 =	3,960.31
7	30,000 × .7 =	21,000 −	16,411 =	4,589 × 0.837 =	3,840.99
8	30,000 × .7 =	21,000 −	16,411 =	4,589 × 0.813 =	3,730.86
9	30,000 × .7 =	21,000 −	−0− =	21,000 × 0.789 =	16,569.00
10	30,000 × .7 =	21,000 −	−0− =	21,000 × 0.766 =	16,086.00
11	30,000 × .7 =	21,000 −	−0− =	21,000 × 0.744 =	15,624.00
12	30,000 × .7 =	21,000 −	−0− =	21,000 × 0.722 =	15,162.00

$83,676.04

Minus savings −5,000.00

LIFE INSURANCE FACE VALUE AMOUNT $78,676.04

EXAMPLE 6-2: Suppose now that Joe Gregory assumes his salary will increase 2 percentage points above inflation annually. How will this affect the required life insurance face value amount?

The $30,000 salary should now be increased by 2 percent each year after year 1. This is done by multiplying $30,000 by the future value factor associated with 2 percent and the corresponding number of years. The rest of the calculations are then the same.

Step 1: The life insurance term is 22 − 10 = 12 years.

Yr.		STEP 2	STEP 3	STEP 4	STEP 5	
1	$30,000 × 1.00	× .7 = $21,000 −	$19,155 =	$1 845 × 1.000 = $		1845.00
2	30,000 × 1.020 (FV factor, 2%, 1 yr)	× .7 = 21,420 −	19,155 =	2265 × 0.971 =		2199.32
3	30,000 × 1.040 (FV factor, 2%, 2 yrs)	× .7 = 21,848 −	19,155 =	2693 × 0.943 =		2539.50
4	30,000 × 1.061 (FV factor, 2%, 3 yrs)	× .7 = 22,285 −	1.9,155 =	3130 × 0.915 =		2863.95
5	30,000 × 1.082 (FV factor, 2%, 4 yrs)	× .7 = 22,731 −	19,155 =	3576 × 0.888 =		3175.49
6	30,000 × 1.104 (FV factor, 2%, 5 yrs)	× .7 = 23,186 −	16,411 =	6775 × 0.863 =		5846.83
7	30,000 × 1.126 (FV factor, 2%, 6 yrs)	× .7 = 23,649 −	16,411 =	7328 × 0.837 =		6058.21
8	30,000 × 1.149 (FV factor, 2%, 7 yrs)	× .7 = 24,122 −	16,411 =	7711 × 0.813 =		6269.04
9	30,000 × 1.172 (FV factor, 2%, 8 yrs)	× .7 = 24,605 −	−0− =	24605 × 0.789 =		19413.35
10	30,000 × 1.195 (FV factor, 2%, 9 yrs)	× .7 = 25,097 −	−0− =	25097 × 0.766 =		19224.30
11	30,000 × 1.219 (FV factor, 2%,10 yrs)	× .7 = 25,599 −	−0− =	25599 × 0.744 =		19045.66
12	30,000 × 1.243 (FV factor, 2%,11 yrs)	× .7 = 26,111 −	−0− =	26111 × 0.722 =		18852.14

	$107,332.79
Minus savings:	5,000.00
LIFE INSURANCE FACE VALUE AMOUNT:	$102,332.79

The Bottom Line

Use the income approach to calculate life insurance needs based on the future income of the insured.

6. How Much Life Insurance? The Expense Approach

The expense approach is a more complete method of calculating the necessary life insurance face value amount but it is more tedious than the income approach and more calculations are required. The idea of the expense approach is simple. A life insurance face value amount is calculated which will provide enough funds to pay the expected expenses of the beneficiaries which won't be covered by Social Security or other income. If the insured dies, the life insurance face value amount is invested and used as the expenses occur. It's important that the expenses which are budgeted will not provide a *higher* standard of living than the insured could provide if he/she lived. This would make the family better off, at least financially without the insured. Families shouldn't want this, and it also makes life insurance companies nervous.

Discounting and Inflation

As with the income approach, the simplest way to handle inflation is to ignore it. Simply write down expenses in current dollars and then discount using a real discount rate, such as 3 percent This method assumes that expenses will increase at the average inflation rate. If some expenses are expected to rise faster than average inflation, then they can be increased each year by their "real" inflation rate. This principle will be demonstrated later with examples.

Family Expenses—Where to Find the Numbers

In implementing the expense approach, it is best if a family uses its own particular expenses. This will give a "customized," or "personalized" life insurance face value amount.

But many families don't have a good idea about their expenses. This section will provide some average family expenses calculated by government researchers and statisticians.

The most important expense which life insurance should cover is child expenses. Table 6-3 shows annual costs of raising a child from birth to age 18 for four regions of the country, as estimated by the U.S. Department of Agriculture. The annual costs include amounts for house operating and maintenance costs but exclude amounts for mortgage costs or rent. Mortgage costs and rent are handled separately.

If a family has one child, the costs should be taken directly from Table 6-3. However, studies show that the costs of raising children dis-

ECONOMIES
TO SCALE

play, what economists call, *economies to scale.* This means that the second child doesn't cost quite as much as the first child, and the third child costs even less. This happens because some child-rearing products can be shared or re-used. Also, savings can be achieved by purchasing some products in bulk or economy size when the family is larger. Studies by the U.S. Bureau of Labor Statistics and the U.S. Dept. of Agriculture show that the following percentages should be applied to the costs in Table 6-3 for multiple children:

> for second child: 91% of costs
> for third child: 85% of costs
> for fourth child: 79% of costs
> for fifth child: 76% of costs.[3]

---

[3]Sources: U. S. Bureau of Labor Statistics, *Consumer Expenditure Survey;* U. S. Dept. of Agriculture, "USDA Estimates of the Cost of Raising a Child: A Guide to Their Use and Interpretation," Miscellaneous Publication No. 1411.

Table 6-3.   Estimated annual costs of raising a child in an
urban area, 2011

Age of Child	Total Expenditure
Lower income (before tax income < $59,410)	
0–2	$ 9,050
3–5	$ 9,100
6–8	$ 8,760
9–11	$ 9,520
12–14	$ 9,960
15–17	$ 9,970
Total	$169,080
Medium income (before tax income between $59.410 and $102,870)	
0–2	$ 12,370
3–5	$ 12,390
6–8	$ 12,290
9–11	$ 13,110
12–14	$ 13,820
15–17	$ 14,320
Total	$234,900
Higher income (before tax income over $102,870)	
0–2	$ 20,460
3–5	$ 20,480
6–8	$ 20,420
9–11	$ 21,320
12–14	$ 22,700
15–17	$ 24,510
Total	$389,670

*Source: US Department of Agriculture, Expenditure on children by families,
2011. http://www.cnpp.usda.gov/Publications/CRC/crc2011.pdf*

College Expenses

Average annual public college costs for tuition, room, board, books and
transportation in 2011–2012 was $17,136 for four-year in-state colleges
and $29,703 for four-year out-of-state colleges. For private four-year
schools, the average cost was $37,971.[4]

---

[4]The College Board, www.collegeboard, com. The expenses are for the 2011–2012
academic year.

Education costs are one of the expenses which have been increasing faster than the average rate of inflation in recent years. For example, from 2002 to 2012 annual public college tuition and fees increased 3.8% point faster than the average inflation rate. College costs are therefore a prime example where it may be wise to assume that future costs increase faster than the average rate of inflation.

Spousal Expenses

The surviving spouse must eat and also be clothed. The annual estimated expenditures for a single person in 2011, excluding rent or mortgage expenses, but including utilities and fuel, is $27,837 (Table 6-4).

Housing Expenses

If the family owns a home, housing expenses should be listed in two parts. First, the outstanding mortgage balance should be listed as an expense which will be paid in full if the insured were to die.[5] Second, property taxes should be listed as an annual expense. Property taxes average 1.7 percent of the house's value.

If the family rents, then housing expenses should be listed as the annual rent, excluding fuel and utilities. Average annual rent in 2011 is $7,872 (Table 6-4). Fuel and utility expenses are included in the expenses for the children and the spouse.

Homemaker Expenses

The expenses for child rearing discussed earlier do not include expenses for child care, or more generally, homemaker services. Homemaker services include meal preparation, cleaning, laundry, and child supervision. It is important to consider these expenses when life insurance is being examined for a spouse who works only in the home (a homemaker). In the event of death of this spouse, homemaker services would have to be purchased. If the homemaker services are "picked up" by the surviving spouse, that spouse still faces an opportunity cost which can be approximated by the purchase of the homemaker services.

Using results from research the value of annual home-maker services for a 30 hour workweek is $20,204 in 2011 (Table 6-4).

---

[5]Why not simply budget annual mortgage payment expenses? There are two reasons why this approach isn't used. First, if the mortgage payments are fixed, then they won't increase with the rate of inflation and won't fit into our discounting procedure. If the mortgage is variable, then changes in mortgage rates would have to be predicted in order to project mortgage payments. Including the mortgage balance in the life insurance face value amount is the simplest and most direct approach.

Table 6-4. College, spousal, housing, and homemaker service expenses, 2011

Average annual public college in-state costs	$17,136[a]
Average annual public college out-of-state costs	$29,703[a]
Average annual private college costs	$37,971[a]
Annual living costs of a single person	$27,837[b]
Average annual rent	$ 7,872[b]
Average homemaker service	$20,204[c]

[a]The College Board, www.collegeboard.com

[b]Average annual expenses of a single person, excluding shelter. Bureau of Labor Statistics, 2011 Consumer Expenditure Survey

[c]Cathleen D. Zick and W. Keith Bryant. "Alternative strategies for pricing home work time," Home Economics Research Journal 1986. Estimates updated to 2011 using CPI.

Other Expenses

This list of family expenses is not necessarily comprehensive. A family may want to budget funds for other expenses—for example, savings for an emergency fund or burial expenses of the insured. Amounts may also be specified for expenses made to ease the family's trauma upon death of the insured. Other debts besides mortgage debt may also be included. Income earned by the surviving spouse, and Social Security survivorship benefits, should be included as "offsets" to the expenses.

Do It Yourself

Armed with this information about family expenses, you can now calculate the life insurance face value amount by the expense approach. The expense approach is implemented in six steps.

Step 1: Decide on the number of years for which family expenses will be covered by life insurance. This is the life insurance term. It is useful to divide the life insurance term into three parts: the child rearing years, the post-children—pre-retirement years, and the retirement years.

Step 2: For each year of the life insurance term, list the annual expenses for child rearing, college, spousal costs, housing (property taxes), and other costs which the family wants covered by life insurance. Use the family's own estimated expenses or use the averages from Tables 6-3 and 6-4. Use current dollar values for each of the years unless an expense is expected to rise faster or slower than the average rate of inflation. If an expense is expected to rise faster than the average rate of inflation, then increase the expense each year by its "real" inflation rate. If an expense is expected to rise slower than the average rate of inflation, then decrease the expense each year by its "real" deflation rate.[6]

Step 3: If the insured is a homemaker, then add an annual amount to pay for replacement of homemaker services.

Step 4: For each year of the life insurance term, subtract the Social Security survivorship benefit and subtract the income of the surviving spouse (if the spouse will work upon death of the insured) from the total annual expenses. Call the result the family's annual net expenses.

NET EXPENSES

Step 5: Use a real discount rate, such as 3 percent, to calculate the present value of the "net expenses" over the life insurance term.

Step 6: If the family owns a home with a mortgage, add the mortgage balance to the present value calculated in STEP 5. Also add the balance of any other debts and other immediate expenses which the family wants life insurance to cover. The result is the life insurance face value amount.

EXAMPLE 6-3: John and Mary's Family.

John and Mary are both age 35. John works in the marketplace and Mary works at home as a "homemaker." John earns $100,000 annually. John and Mary have two children, Tommy, age 5, and Jenny, age 7. John and Mary own a home with a $240,000 mortgage balance, pay $4,248 annually in property taxes, and have $12,000 in other debts. Find the life insurance face value amount for John and for Mary if expenses are to be covered until the children are aged 22, after completion of public college. Assume college expenses will rise 2 percentage points faster than inflation.

Table 6-5 shows the life insurance calculation for John. Expenses are budgeted for Jenny and Tommy's child rearing, assuming a moderate standard of living, and for college expenses. When Jenny and Tommy are both living at home, Tommy's expenses are reduced (multiplied by .91)

---

[6]For example, if utility expenses are expected to rise 2 percentage points faster than the average inflation rate, and if today's utility expenses are $1,000, then next year's expenses are $1,000 × 1.02, or $1,020, the third year's expenses are $1,000 × 1.02 × 1.02, or $1,040.40, etc. If food costs are expected to rise 2 percentage points slower than the average inflation rate, and if today's food costs are $1,000, then next year's food expenses are $1,000 × 0.98, or $980, the third year's expenses are $1,000 × 0.98 × 0.98, or $960.40, etc.

Table 6-5. The traditional family – life insurance on John for the child rearing years

	Step 1			Step 2				Step 4		Step 5	
Year	Mary's Age	Jenny's Age	Tommy's Age	Mary's Expenses	Jenny's Expenses	Tommy's Expenses	Property Taxes	SS Survivor-ship	Net Expenses	PVF(3%)	PV
1	35	7	5	$27,837	$12,290	$12,390x0.91	$4,248	$40,344	$15,306	1.0000	$15,306
2	36	8	6	$27,837	$12,290	$12,290x0.91	$4,248	$40,344	$15,215	0.9709	$14,772
3	37	9	7	$27,837	$13,110	$12,290x0.91	$4,248	$40,344	$16,035	0.9426	$15,114
4	38	10	8	$27,837	$13,110	$12,290x0.91	$4,248	$40,344	$16,035	0.9151	$14,674
5	39	11	9	$27,837	$13,110	$13,110x0.91	$4,248	$40,344	$16,781	0.8885	$14,910
6	40	12	10	$27,837	$13,820	$13,110x0.91	$4,248	$40,344	$17,491	0.8626	$15,088
7	41	13	11	$27,837	$13,820	$13,110x0.91	$4,248	$40,344	$17,491	0.8375	$14,649
8	42	14	12	$27,837	$13,820	$13,820x0.91	$4,248	$40,344	$18,137	0.8131	$14,747
9	43	15	13	$27,837	$14,320	$13,820x0.91	$4,248	$40,344	$18,637	0.7894	$14,712
10	44	16	14	$27,837	$14,320	$13,820x0.91	$4,248	$40,344	$18,637	0.7664	$14,284
11	45	17	15	$27,837	$14,320	$14,320x0.91	$4,248	$40,344	$19,092	0.7441	$14,206
12	46	18	16	$27,837	$17,136 \times 1.03^{11}$	$14,320	$4,248	$37,224	$32,901	0.7224	$23,769
13	47	19	17	$27,837	$17,136 \times 1.03^{12}$	$14,320	$4,248	$37,224	$33,613	0.7014	$23,575
14	48	20	18	$27,837	$17,136 \times 1.03^{13}$	$17,136 \times 1.03^{13}$	$4,248		$82,415	0.6810	$56,120
15	49	21	19	$27,837	$17,136 \times 1.03^{14}$	$17,136 \times 1.03^{14}$	$4,248		$83,924	0.6611	$55,484
16	50		20	$27,837	$17,136 \times 1.03^{15}$	$17,136 \times 1.03^{15}$	$4,248		$58,782	0.6419	$37,730
17	51		21	$27,837	$17,136 \times 1.03^{16}$	$17,136 \times 1.03^{16}$	$4,248		$59,583	0.6232	$37,130
									PV Sum		$396,271

Step 6   Mortgage balance   **$240,000**

Other debts   **$12,000**

Life insurance face value amount   **$648,271**

to account for economies of scale in child rearing. Expenses are budgeted for Mary's living expenses, but homemaker services are not budgeted since Mary will continue performing these services if John dies. All expenses are budgeted in current dollars except college expenses. College expenses are assumed to rise 3 percentage points faster than the average inflation rate each year. For example, if current college expenses (year 1) are $17,136 annually, then college expenses in year 12 (11 years in the future) will be $17,136 \times 1.03^{11}$.

Mary, Jenny, and Tommy will receive Social Security survivorship benefits until Tommy is age 18. The amount is reduced in year 12 when Jenny reaches age 18. These benefits are deducted from the total expenses to equal net expenses. The present value of the net expenses is calculated, and to this is added the mortgage and other debt to equal John's life insurance face value amount ($648,271).

A life insurance policy could also be bought with John as the beneficiary in the event Mary dies. The calculations would be similar to those in Table 6-5 except that the Social Security survivorship benefits would be replaced by John's income.

Alternatively, the life insurance face value amount for Mary could be calculated as simply the present value of homemaker expenses, since these are the services which would have to be replaced if Mary died.

What if both Mary and John work in the marketplace? Then, separate life insurance policies face value amounts can be calculated for both. The key difference will be in Step 4. If both parents work, then each will generate Social Security survivor's benefits in the case of death. Therefore, in calculating a life insurance face value amount in the event of John's death, Step 4 includes Social Security survivor's benefits from John and Mary's income. And, in calculating a life insurance face value amount in the event of Mary's death, Step 4 includes Social Security survivor's benefits from Mary and John's income.

The Bottom Line

Use the expense approach to calculate life insurance needs based on the future net expenses of the beneficiaries. _____

7. Inflation Again! Life Insurance Requirements as the Insured Lives!

We've already talked about inflation's impact on life insurance requirements and how to handle it. We showed how the actual future rate of inflation could be ignored by discounting future incomes and expenses by a real interest rate.

But there's another problem created by inflation which occurs if the insured continues to live. As the insured lives an additional year, inflation has occurred during that year. This increases all future projected expenses. The face value amount would have kept up with the year's inflation if it had been invested, but it wasn't since the insured lived. The face value amount is now inadequate to cover the higher future expenses. Call this the "inflation effect."

INFLATION EFFECT

Counterbalancing the inflation effect, however, is the fact that as the insured lives a year longer, there is one less year of insurance coverage needed. This reduces the needed life insurance face value amount. Call this the "term effect."

TERM EFFECT

How the combined inflation effect and term effect influence the life insurance face value amount as the insured ages depends critically on the size of the past inflation rate, term effect, and the original number of years of insurance coverage. The higher the past inflation rate, the more likely that the inflation effect dominates the term effect, especially in the early years of the life insurance term. As the life insurance term nears its end, the term effect will become more dominant. Likewise, the greater the original number of years of insurance coverage, the more likely that the inflation effect dominates the term effect for a longer period of the life insurance term.

Figure 6-1 shows how the inflation effect and term effect combine assuming life insurance is to provide $1000 of real protection each year for an initial coverage term of 22 years. The initial policy is for $16,415 of protection.

Figure 6-1. Life insurance requirements, initial $1000 annual need, 3% discount rate, 22-year term (I = inflation rate).

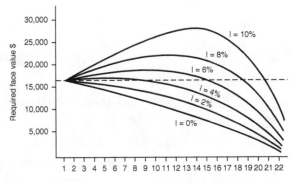

If the annual inflation rate is 4 percent or less then there's no problem— the term effect dominates and the required face value amount declines each year. Problems do arise for inflation rates higher than 4 percent. In order to maintain the amount of "real protection," additional life insurance will need to be purchased.

Figure 6-2 shows how the inflation effect and term effect combine for $1,000 of real protection and assuming an initial coverage term of 50 years. Now the required face value amount increases for all inflation rates except zero. Again, the rates of increase in the face value amount are greater the greater the inflation rate, and the peak in the required face value amount occurs later the higher the inflation rate.

How can more life insurance be purchased? One way is simply to buy more coverage, but this requires another medical exam and proof of insurability. Other ways include:

Buying universal life insurance—one form of universal life insurance allows the protection amount to increase each year (see *Who Should Buy Universal Life Insurance?* later in this chapter).

Figure 6-2. Life insurance requirements, initial $1000 annual need, 3% discount rate, 50-year term (I = inflation rate).

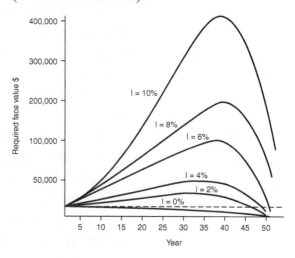

Purchase a policy with a guaranteed insurability option—this option allows more protection to be purchased without evidence of insurability.

Purchase a policy with a cost-of-living rider—this rider will increase the protection amount each year by the change in the Consumer Price Index.

Purchase a policy which pays dividends and use the dividends to buy paid-up amounts of life insurance.

The annual inflation rate from 1980 to 2012 averaged 3.2 percent. If this average inflation rate is expected to continue in the future, then the face value amount can continually decline if the original coverage term is 22 years (Figure 6-1). However, if the original coverage term is 50 years (Figure 6-2), then the face value amount must increase modestly until year 30 before declining! Therefore, it's important for the insured to use one of the techniques listed above to change coverage as needed.

The Bottom Line

If you have a need for life insurance for more than 22 years, or if the annual inflation rate is more than 4 percent, then your life insurance needs will increase for at least some years.

8. How Often Should You Re-evaluate Your Life Insurance?

You shouldn't purchase life insurance and then forget it! If you have a new child, then certainly your required face value amount will increase (by the expense approach) and more life insurance will be needed. On the other hand, if a child graduates from college and becomes financially independent, then your face value amount will decrease. However, as the previous section showed, even if your financial dependents don't change, your face value requirements can change due to inflation or a reduced life insurance term.

The point is that you should reevaluate your life insurance requirements periodically. Certainly if a financial dependent is added or subtracted, then your life insurance needs should be re-evaluated immediately. In other cases every *five* years is probably a good rule of thumb.

FIVE YEAR
EVALUATION

When your life insurance requirements are re-evaluated, use the same procedures as outlined before. The major change is to use current incomes and expenses, *at the time of the new evaluation.* For example, let's say you're re-evaluating your life insurance in 2018. The child expenses in Table 6-3 are for 2011. To use Table 6-3, simply increase the child expenses by the total inflation rate between 2011 to 2018. For example, if prices had increased 25 percent between 2011 to 2018, then increase all child expenses in Table 6-3 by 25 percent before using them.

It's relatively easy to buy more life insurance—at the very least, you buy another policy. But what about reducing life insurance coverage? With most policies, as we'll see, that's impossible to do; you can't simply chop off $10,000 of protection from your $100,000 policy. But with one type of policy, called universal life, this flexibility is possible (see *Who Should Buy Universal Life Insurance?*).

The Bottom Line

Reevaluate life insurance needs when family members change, or every five years.

9. How Are Life Insurance Premiums Calculated?

Consumers are price-takers, meaning that no individual consumer can influence the average price of any product. Consumers observe and compare prices and make their decisions on purchases.

Nevertheless, it's important for consumers to understand how some prices are arrived at by producers, and life insurance is one of those situations.

Benefits Equal Costs

The guiding principle behind life insurance policy pricing is simple. Premiums will be charged to the consumer such that the present value of revenues received from the consumer equals the expected present value of benefits paid to the consumer. Benefits include payments to beneficiaries of the policy if the insured dies plus services provided by the insurance company.

Expected benefits received by the consumer of life insurance depend on the likelihood of the insured dying during the insurance coverage period. The likelihood or probability of dying is determined from past observations on death rates at various ages. These death MORTALITY TABLE rates by age are grouped together in a mortality table. You can find a mortality table (or an actuarial life table) on Social Security Administration's website.

The Cost of Annual Life Insurance

Let's take the simplest case first. Let's see how the premium for annual life insurance (called annual term insurance) would be calculated.

Suppose a male aged 39 wants to buy $100,000 of life insurance for a year and the chance that he will die in the year is 0.00214, or 0.214 percent. So, the life insurance company would expect to pay to the average 39 year old male:

$$0.00214 \times \$100,000 = \$214$$

Thus, $214 in premiums would have to be received from the man.

However, if premiums are paid at the beginning of the year, but claims are paid at the end of the year, the $214 could be *discounted* for

UNISEX LIFE INSURANCE RATES

**C
O
N
S
U
M
E
R

T
O
P
I
C**

Life insurance campanies have an incentive to charge different premiums to different individuals if those individuals have significant differences in their probabilities of dying. Traditionally, different rates have been charged based on two characteristics: the sex of the individual and whether the individual smokes. Smokers have been found to have noticeably higher chances of dying in any given year, and women have a significantly longer life span than men.

Modern society has removed many of the barriers and differences between men and women. In this environment, different life insurance rates for men and women have been questioned.

Insurance firms, like most of us, use the best information available after considering the cost of acquiring information. It may be that difference in life spans between men and women are not due to genetic differences between the sexes, but are due to environmental factors based on traditional lifestyle differences between males and females. For example, the average male may experience more stress than the average female, and this may contribute to life-span differences. While these environmental factors are difficult and expensive to measure, the sex of the insured is easy to observe.

As medical researchers discover more about the environmental and lifestyle factors affecting death rates and life span, we may see insurers using more of these findings and relying less on the simple, yet easily observable, sex of the insured. However, the current reliance on sex of the insured benefits females since their longer life span results in lower life insurance premiums.

one year. If a 3 percent discount rate is used, the required premium payment is: $214 \times PVF$ (r = 3%, n = 1) = $214 \times 0.9709 = \$207.77$.

Finally, if servicing costs are $20, then $20 will be added for a final premium of $227.77.

Notice that since the chance of dying increases with age, the premiums for annual life insurance will also increase with age.

Calculating Level Life Insurance Premiums

There is a type of life insurance policy where premiums are constant each year, even though the probability of dying increases with age. Premiums for this kind of policy, called whole life insurance, are calculated in a way similar to the calculation of fixed rate mortgage payments.

First, calculate the single premium which, if paid today, would equal the expected benefits of the policy to the consumer. For example, take our 39 year old male. He wants to buy a $100,000 policy over five years.

Death rates are taken from a mortality table. The single premium to pay for this policy is:

Age	Insurance		Death Rate		PVF (3%)		Cost
39	100000	×	0.00214	×	0.9709	=	$207.77
40	100000	×	0.00232	×	0.9426	=	$218.68
41	100000	×	0.00253	×	0.9151	=	$231.53
42	100000	×	0.00275	×	0.8548	=	$235.07
43	100000	×	0.00299	×	0.8626	=	$257.92
							$1,150.97

To repay a current mortgage loan amount in equal annual payments, we divided the loan by the sum of the present value factors associated with the mortgage interest rate. The same principle is used to convert the single insurance premium to equal annual payments, but with one change. Since the insured may die before the end of the policy term and hence may not make all payments, each present value factor after the first (since the insured is alive today and will make the first payment) must be multiplied by the associated probability of the insured *being alive* during that year. These probabilities are taken from a mortality table. The resulting "probability-scaled" present value factors are then added and divided into the policy's single premium to find the equal annual premium payment:

Age	Probability of Being Alive at the Beginning of the Year		PVF (3%)		Probability-scaled PV Factor
39	1.00000	×	1.0000	=	1.0000
40	0.99786	×	0.9709	=	0.9688
41	0.99768	×	0.9426	=	0.9404
42	0.99747	×	0.9151	=	0.9128
43	0.99725	×	0.8548	=	0.8525
			Sum	=	4.6745

$$\text{Equal annual payment} = \frac{\$1150.97}{4.6745} = \$246.22$$

Calculation of Cash Values

Before leaving the topic of premiums and their calculation, the origin and meaning of "cash value" should be discussed. Cash values result solely from the method of calculation of premiums on a life insurance

RESERVES

policy. When premiums are calculated to be equal over the term of the policy, policyholders will pay more to the company than what is needed to cover claims in the early years of the policy and less than what is needed to cover claims in the later years of the policy. The insurance company covers future claims not paid for by premiums by investing and accumulating the "excess" payments in the early years. The built-up excess is called the *reserve*. Note that the reserve is not an overpayment charged by the company, but is due only to the method of equal premium payments throughout the policy's term.

CASH VALUE

When an individual cancels a policy that has equal annual premiums there will remain reserves that haven't been used. Some of these reserves are returned to the individual in the form of a cash value. Individuals are usually allowed to receive the cash value as cash or the equivalent in paid-up insurance. The individual won't receive all of his reserve due to a number of factors, such as:

1. the company is staffed and equipped for a given number of policyholders; reducing the number of policyholders means some excess staff and excess costs,
2. the company may have to cancel some of its investments and possibly take losses when a policy is cancelled, and
3. the bulk of service expenses occurs when the policy is written; part of the reserve may be needed to fully recover these expenses when the policy is cancelled.

Policies which are priced on a "pay as you go" basis (e.g., most term policies) do not accumulate cash values.

The Bottom Line

Life insurance policies are priced such that the cost to the average policyholder equals the benefits received by the average policyholder. Policies with level premiums may generate cash values, which the policyholder receives if the policy is cancelled.

10. Who Should Buy Term Insurance?

Term insurance is plain life insurance with no frills. Term insurance has no side investment fund which accumulates as the years pass. Term insurance works very simply. If the insured dies, the beneficiaries collect the face value amount of the term insurance. If the insured doesn't die, the beneficiaries (and the insured) collect nothing.

If the insured doesn't die while the term insurance is in force, is the term insurance wasteful? Of course not. If the insured continues to live, the term insurance has still done the job of providing protection.

Typical Policies

Table 6-6 shows two typical term insurance policies. The policies are for $100,000 of face value for a non-smoker. Premiums are higher for a smoker.

NON-PARTICIPATING
POLICY

Look first at the policy on the left, the non-participating policy. Non-participating means the policy pays no dividends back to the insured. Notice how the premiums rise each year. This directly reflects the increasing chance that, the insured will die as the insured ages. This is called the mortality cost. Mortality costs increase with the age of the insured for all life insurance policies, but as we will see, some policies handle rising mortality costs differently.

PARTICIPATING POLICY
DIVIDENDS

The term policy on the right of Table 6-6 is a participating term policy. This means that the life insurance company will pay back to the insured each year an amount of money called *dividends*. Dividends are derived from the investment which the life insurance company makes. In order to receive dividends, the insured must pay slightly higher

Table 6-6. Sample term insurance policies.
Face value = $100,000

| | Policy 1 | | Policy 2 | | Net Premium |
Age	Premiums	Age	Premiums	Dividends	(Premiums-Dividends)
35	$163	35	$130	$ 20	$110
36	166	36	160	31	129
37	169	37	212	72	140
38	176	38	275	123	152
39	185	39	289	129	160
40	196	40	320	135	185
41	214	41	341	141	200
42	231	42	362	147	215
43	249	43	383	153	230
44	265	44	410	160	250
45	288	45	463	188	275
46	310	46	536	216	320
47	336	47	604	244	360
48	369	48	692	272	420
49	406	49	754	299	455
50	432	50	792	312	480
51	461	51	825	325	500
52	494	52	888	338	550
53	535	53	951	351	600
54	574	54	1015	365	650

premiums. Notice in Table 6-6 that the premiums for the participating policy are higher than for the non-participating policy except in the first year.

NET PREMIUMS

Dividends can be thought of as a partial return of premiums. "Net premiums," or premiums minus dividends, are what the insured pays "on net" to the insurance company for a participating policy. Net premiums are the true annual cost of the participating policy. In the case of a non-participating policy, net premiums are the same as premiums.

In this example, the premiums of the non-participating policy are generally lower than the net premiums of the participating policy, meaning the non-participating policy is cheaper. This is not always the case. Whether a participating or non-participating policy is a better buy will be discussed in a later topic.

Is Term Insurance Not Permanent?

It is sometimes stated that term insurance is "not permanent." This is misleading. Generally, as long as the policyholder pays premiums on time, the policy is automatically renewed each year without additional medical exams. This automatic renewal sometimes ends at age 65 or 70, at which time the insured would have to undergo a medical exam to provide "evidence of insurability." There are term policies, however, which are renewable to age 100.

Calculating the Cost of Term Policies

Look back at the sample term policies in Table 6-6. How would you calculate the total cost of the two policies? Before you've read this book (and maybe some of you even now), you would probably say to simply sum the premiums for the non-participating policy and sum the premiums for the participating policy. In fact, there's a name for this, and it's called the "traditional cost method."

TRADITIONAL COST METHOD

What's wrong with the traditional cost method? The answer has been given a number of times by now (and by now you're probably tired of hearing it), but again the answer is that simply summing the premiums or net premiums ignores the time value of money. The financial fact of life is that paying $1 today is more expensive than paying $1 later. Why? Because if you had $1 today, you could invest it in something safe (U.S. savings bond, CD), accumulate more than $1, and be able to pay the $1 later and have money left over. This means that two life insurance policies which charge the same total amount of premiums may not have the same "true" cost. The policy which charged higher premiums in the early years and lower premiums later would be more expensive than the policy which charged lower premiums in the early years and higher premiums later.

In calculating the true cost of a term policy, either of two methods could be used: the present value of premiums, or net premiums, can be figured, or the future value of premiums, or net premiums, can be calculated. Because the life insurance industry uses the future value approach, we will use it here.

INTEREST-ADJUSTED NET COST

The industry name for the true cost of a term policy is the *interest-adjusted net cost*. Follow these 4 steps to calculate the interest-adjusted net cost:

Step 1: Select the number of years that the policy will be kept. Call this the *policy term.*

Step 2: Select an interest rate which corresponds to the nominal after-tax rate expected to be earned on investments. (A nominal interest is used because the life insurance premiums are nominal payments.)

Step 3: For each year of the policy term, multiply the policy premium, or net premium, by the *future value factor* (Appendix Table A-1) associated with the selected interest rate and the years remaining to the end of the policy term. Call the result the *interest adjusted net premium.*

Step 4: Sum the interest adjusted net premiums. The result is the interest adjusted net cost.

INTEREST ADJUSTED NET COST INDEX

A *fifth step* can be added which converts the interest adjusted net cost to the *interest-adjusted net cost* index. The interest adjusted net cost index is calculated by simply dividing the interest adjusted net cost by the future value factor sum associated with the selected annual interest rate and the policy term. Often this index is expressed as the cost per $1000 of policy face value.[7]

Table 6-7 shows the calculation of the interest adjusted net cost and interest adjusted net cost index for two term policies. Policy 2 is the cheaper policy. However, if the premiums had simply been added, then policy 1 would have been indicated as the cheaper policy (policy 1's sum of premiums equals $6219, compared to $6381 for policy 2).

---

[7]The interest adjusted net cost index is best used for comparing different policies at the same point in time, for example comparing policy A and policy B in 2013. The interest adjusted net cost index is *not* appropriate for comparing the costs of policies in different years; for example, comparing policy A issued in 2010 to policy B issued in 2013. The reason is that the index is expressed as a cost per $1000. For policies in the same year, $1000 of face value provides comparable protection. But for policies issued in different years, $1000 of face value for the policy issued in the later year provides less "real" protection due to inflation— the higher cost of goods and services, (See David F. Babbel, "Measuring Inflation Impact on Life Insurance Costs." *Journal of Risk and Insurance*, Vol 46, No. 3, Sept .1979, pp. 425–440).

Table 6-7   Interest adjusted net cost calculations for term policies ($100,0000 face value, using 5% interest rate).

POLICY 1	POLICY 2
35 $163 × 2.653 (FVF, 5%, 20 yrs) = $ 432.44	35 $110 × 2.653 (FVF, 5%, 20 yrs) = $ 291.83
36 166 × 2.527 (FVF, 5%, 19 yrs) = 419.48	36 129 × 2.527 (FVF, 5%, 19 yrs) = 325.98
37 169 × 2.407 (FVF, 5%, 18 yrs) = 406.78	37 140 × 2.407 (FVF, 5%, 18 yrs) = 336.98
38 176 × 2.292 (FVF, 5%, 17 yrs) = 403.39	38 152 × 2.292 (FVF, 5%, 17 yrs) = 348.38
39 185 × 2.183 (FVF, 5%, 16 yrs) = 403.86	39 160 × 2.183 (FVF, 5%, 16 yrs) = 349.28
40 196 × 2.079 (FVF, 5%, 15 yrs) = 407.48	40 185 × 2.079 (FVF, 5%, 15 yrs) = 384.62
41 214 × 1.980 (FVF 5%, 14 yrs) = 423.72	41 200 × 1.980 (FVF, 5%, 14 yrs) = 396.00
42 231 × 1.886 (FVF, 5%, 13 yrs) = 435.67	42 215 × 1.886 (FVF, 5%, 13 yrs) = 405.49
43 249 × 1.796 (FVF, 5%, 12 yrs) = 447.20	43 230 × 1.796 (FVF, 5%, 12 yrs) = 413.08
44 265 × 1.710 (FVF, 5%, 11 yrs) = 453.15	44 250 × 1.710 (FVF, 5%, 11 yrs) = 427.50
45 288 × 1.629 (FVF, 5%, 10 yrs) = 469.15	45 275 × 1.629 (FVF, 5%, 10 yrs) = 447.98
46 310 × 1.551 (FVF, 5%, 9 yrs) = 480.81	46 320 × 1.551 (FVF, 5%, 9 yrs) = 496.32
47 336 × 1.477 (FVF, 5%, 8yrs) = 496.27	47 360 × 1.477 (FVF, 5%, 8 yrs) = 531.72
48 369 × 1.407 (FVF, 5%, 7yrs) = 519.18	48 420 × 1.407 (FVF, 5%, 7 yrs) = 590.94
49 406 × 1.340 (FVF, 5%, 6yrs) = 544.04	49 455 × 1.340 (FVF, 5%, 6 yrs) = 609.70
50 432 × 1.276 (FVF, 5%, 5 yrs) = 551.23	50 480 × 1.276 (FVF, 5%, 5 yrs) = 612.48
51 461 × 1.216 (FVF, 5%, 4yrs) = 560.58	51 500 × 1.216 (FVF, 5%, 4 yrs) = 608.00
52 494 × 1.158 (FVF, 5%, 3yrs) = 572.05	52 550 × 1.158 (FVF, 5%, 3 yrs) = 636.90
53 535 × 1.103 (FVF, 5%, 2yrs) = 619.53	53 600 × 1.103 (FVF, 5%, 2 yrs) = 661.80
54 574 × 1.050 (FVF, 5%, 1 yrs) = 602.70	54 650 × 1.050 (FVF, 5%, 1 yrs) = 682.50
Interest adjusted net cost: $9,648.71	Interest adjusted net cost: $9,557.48
FV factor sum, 5%, 20 yrs: 34.715	FV factor sum, 5%, 20 yrs 34.715
(Sum of all FVFs used in above calculations.)	

$$\text{Interest adjusted net cost index} = \frac{9,648.71}{34.715} = 277.94$$

or

$2.78 per $1000 of face value.

$$\text{Interest adjusted net cost index} = \frac{9,557.48}{34.715} = 275.31$$

or

$2.75 per $1000 of face value.

The interest adjusted net cost index is generally calculated by life insurance companies and shown to consumers as part of the policy presentation. However, several words of caution should be followed. First, in using the interest adjusted net cost index to compare term policies, make sure you're comparing apples and apples, and not apples and oranges. That is, make sure the policies have the same face value amount and the same characteristics (more on characteristics of life insurance policies later).

Second, most companies calculate the interest adjusted net cost index using a 5 percent interest rate. This is probably a conservative rate. Results can vary if different interest rates are used.

Last, the interest adjusted net cost index for the same policy can change depending on the policy term used. For example, if a policy term of 10 years is used, then the interest adjusted net cost index is $3.21 per $1000 for policy 1 and $2.79 per $1000 for policy 2.

Variations on the Term Theme

ANNUAL RENEWABLE TERM

The type of term life insurance policy just described is called *annual renewable term*. Premiums increase each year, and the policy is automatically renewable to a maximum age as long as premiums are paid on time.

N-YEAR LEVEL TERM

There are term policies which have constant premiums for a certain number of years. These are called *N-year level term* policies, where N is the number of years during which the premiums are constant. Five-year level term and ten-year level term are the most popular of this variety. To determine if an N-year level term policy is better than an annual renewable term policy, compare the interest adjusted net costs of the policies.

CONVERTIBLE TERM

A *convertible term* insurance policy is one where the insured can exchange the term policy for another policy, usually a whole life policy, during a specified period of time and without evidence of insurability. Consumers who really want whole life insurance, but can't afford it (premiums for whole life policies are initially higher than term insurance premiums) like this type of term policy.

Term Policies are Best Suited for • • •

Term policies are best suited for the person who (1) wants lower life insurance premiums in the early years of the policy so that more money can be spent on other things or on investing, and (2) will not need life insurance in the later years of life (past 65) when term insurance becomes very expensive.

Persons who want very long life insurance coverage or who want to use life insurance as a form of (forced) savings will find other policies more attractive.

The Bottom Line

Term life insurance is plain insurance with no investment frills. The interest-adjusted net cost shows the true cost of a term policy. Buy term insurance for the cheapest coverage, except during retirement.

C O N S U M E R   T O P I C

FLIGHT INSURANCE

Are you often tempted to buy flight life insurance? Think of it—for only a few dollars you can buy life insurance in the six figures that will be paid to your loved ones in the event of your death on the flight. What a great deal!

Let's examine the "deal" a little more closely. Flight insurance is nothing more than term insurance—where the term is 3 or 4 hours (the time of the air flight). It is "cheap" for two reasons. First, the short term, and second, the fact that the death rate on airline flights is very low, in fact lower than travel by car. So what looks like a cheap product—a "good deal"—is really not a free lunch when the costs to the life insurance company of flight insurance are considered.

But there's a more fundamental reason why a flyer might want to pass up flight insurance. Consumers should plan their life insurance requirements not on the basis of specific events—like flying or having an accident—but on the general chance of dying. If the consumer has used the economic logic described in this chapter to develop a sensible life insurance plan, then flight insurance should be bypassed on the way to the destination.

11. Who Should Buy Whole Life insurance?

Whole life insurance provides permanent protection for the "whole life" of the insured, which is generally through the age of 100. As long as premiums are paid on time, the insured is guaranteed protection until age 100. The face value of the policy is paid to the beneficiaries if the insured dies anytime during his "whole life."

CONSTANT PREMIUM   An important element of the standard whole life policy is its *constant premium,* even as the policyholder ages. That is, the same premium is paid each year for the whole life policy.

But since the chance of dying for a given person increases as the person ages, how can whole life policies be kept constant each year? This was discussed earlier (see *How Are Life Insurance Premiums Calculated?*) and will only be summarized here. The premium is set at a level which is higher than expected mortality costs in the early years of the policy, but is set at a level which is lower than expected mortality costs in the later years of the policy. The policyholder is overpaying in the early years of the whole life policy in order to prevent premiums from rising in the later years of the policy.

The "excess payments" made by the policyholder of a whole life policy are accumulated by the life insurance company as a *cash value.* If the policyholder cancels the whole life policy, the cash value will not be needed by the company and will be returned to the policyholder. Also, while the policy is in force, the policyholder can borrow against the cash value.

A Typical Whole Life Policy

A typical whole life policy is shown in Table 6-8. Only the first 20 years of the policy are shown. Notice the constant premiums over the policy term. Most whole life policies are participating, so anticipated dividends are shown in the second column. Net premiums (premiums minus dividends), which are the effective annual cost of the policy, are shown in the third column. The cash value in each year is shown in the last column. The accumulation of interest on the cash value is not taxed unless the policy is cancelled, and usually not even then.

Calculating the Cost of Whole Life Policies

The total cost of a whole life policy is calculated by the interest-adjusted net cost, just as with a term policy, but with one major difference. After the sum of the interest adjusted net premiums are found, the cash value at the end of the policy term is subtracted. Why? The reason is that if the insured holds the whole life policy to the end of the policy term and

Table 6-8 A whole life policy ($100,000 face value).

Age	Premiums	Dividends	Net Premiums	Cash Value
35	$1,316	$ 0	$1,316	$ 0
36	1,316	151	1,165	0
37	1,316	189	1,127	500
38	1,316	231	1,085	1,500
39	1,316	273	1,043	2,600
40	1,316	322	994	3,740
41	1,316	371	945	4,880
42	1,316	420	896	6,020
43	1,316	469	847	7,160
44	1,316	518	798	8,300
45	1,316	581	735	9,500
46	1,316	644	672	10,700
47	1,316	707	609	11,900
48	1,316	770	546	13,100
49	1,316	834	482	14,300
50	1,316	909	407	15,480
51	1,316	984	332	16,660
52	1,316	1,059	257	17,840
53	1,316	1,134	182	19,020
54	1,316	1,213	103	20,200

Cash value at age 65: 25,500

then cancels the policy, the insured will receive the cash value. The cash value is a benefit to the insured, so it should be subtracted from the cost of the policy represented by the sum of the interest adjusted net premiums. Sometimes the interest adjusted net cost is called the *surrender cost* when applied to whole life policies.

SURRENDER COST

Therefore, there are 5 steps to the calculation of the interest adjusted net cost for whole life policies (STEPS 1–4 are the same as for the term policy):

Step 1: Select the number of years that the policy will be kept (the *polity term*).

Step 2: Select an interest rate which corresponds to the nominal after-tax rate expected to be earned on investments.

Step 3: For each year of the policy term, multiply the policy net premium by the *future value factor* (Appendix Table A-1) associated with the selected interest rate and the years remaining to the end of the policy term. These are the interest adjusted net premiums.

Step 4: Sum the interest adjusted net premiums.

Step 5: Subtract the cash value for the final year of the policy term from the sum of the interest adjusted net premiums. The result is the interest adjusted net cost.

Again, a **sixth step** can be added by dividing the interest adjusted net cost by the future value factor sum (derived from Appendix Table A-1) associated with the selected interest rate and the policy term. This is the interest adjusted net cost index, or surrender cost index.

What about taxes on the cash value if the whole life policy is cancelled? Federal income taxes are only paid on that part of the cash value which exceeds the sum of the *net premiums*. Call this excess of cash value over net premiums the net cash value. The tax can then be calculated by multiplying the net cash value by the insured's marginal tax rate. If the interest adjusted net cost is used to only compare one whole life policy to another, then taxes on the cash value do not need to be considered.

Table 6-9 shows the interest adjusted net cost and interest adjusted net cost index calculations for the whole life policy presented in Table 6-8. The calculations are made both with and without taxes considered on the cash value (a 28 percent marginal tax rate is assumed). For whole life policies, the interest adjusted net cost index will usually decline the longer the policy term.

Table 6-9 Interest adjusted net cost calculation for a whole life policy ($100,000 face value and 5% interest rate).

Age	Net Premiums				
35	$ 1316	×	2.653 (FVF, 5%, 20 yrs.)	=	$ 3,491.35
36	1165	×	2.527 (FVF, 5%, 19 yrs.)	=	2,943.96
37	1127	×	2.407 (FVF, 5%, 18 yrs.)	=	2,712.69
38	1085	×	2.292 (FVF, 5%, 17 yrs.)	=	2,486.82
39	1043	×	2.183 (FVF, 5%, 16 yrs.)	=	2,276.87
40	994	×	2.079 (FVF, 5%, 15 yrs.)	=	2,066.53
41	945	×	1.980 (FVF, 5%, 14 yrs.)	=	1,871.10
42	896	×	1.886 (FVF, 5%, 13 yrs.)	=	1,689.86
43	847	×	1.796 (FVF, 5%, 12 yrs.)	=	1,521.21
44	798	×	1.710 (FVF, 5%, 11 yrs.)	=	1,364.58
45	735	×	1.629 (FVF, 5%, 10 yrs.)	=	1,197.32
46	672	×	1.551 (FVF, 5%, 9 yrs.)	=	1,042.27
47	609	×	1.477 (FVF, 5%, 8 yrs.)	=	899.49
48	546	×	1.407 (FVF, 5%, 7 yrs.)	=	768.22
49	482	×	1.340 (FVF, 5%, 6 yrs.)	=	645.88
50	407	×	1.276 (FVF, 5%, 5 yrs.)	=	519.33
51	332	×	1.216 (FVF, 5%, 4 yrs.)	=	403.71
52	257	×	1.158 (FVF, 5%, 3 yrs.)	=	297.61
53	182	×	1.103 (FVF, 5%, 2 yrs.)	=	200.75
54	103	×	1.050 (FVF, 5%, 1 yrs.)	=	108.15
	$13,778				$28,507.70

$$\text{Minus cash value} \quad -20,200.00$$

Interest adjusted net cost: $ 8,307.70

FV factor sum, 5%, 20 yrs: 34.715

Interest adjusted net cost index: $\dfrac{\$8,370.70}{34.715} = \$ 239.31$ or

$ 239 per $1000

Tax on cash value ($20,200 − $13,778) × .28 = $ 1,798.16

After-tax cash value = $18,401.84

Interest adjusted net cost: $28,507,70

$$-18,401.84$$

$$\$10,105.86$$

$$\$10,105.86$$

Interest adjusted net cost index: $\dfrac{\$10,105.86}{34.715} = \$ 291.11$ or

$ 2.91 per $1000

Policy Loans

Most whole life insurance policies allow the policyholder to borrow against the cash value of the policy. Interest is charged on the loan, and under current tax law the interest is not deductible.

Years ago the interest charged on whole life policy loans was very low. This made it very advantageous for policyholders to borrow on the cash value and invest the borrowings when interest rates to investors rose to lofty levels.

Life insurance companies learned from this experience and new whole life policies either charge higher interest rates on cash value borrowings, or charge variable interest rates.

It is sometimes said that life insurance policy loans are more expensive than taking the same money from a savings account because interest is paid on the policy loan but no interest is paid on a withdrawal from a savings account. This is incorrect because it ignores the concept of opportunity cost. When you take money from your savings account, you are "giving up" the interest which could have been earned on that money. You are, in effect, borrowing from yourself, so you should count as a cost the interest you could have earned. As the example in Table 6-10 shows, withdrawing from a savings account can be just as costly as borrowing from the cash value of a life insurance policy.

Some participating whole life policies reduce the dividend payments when the policyholder takes out a policy loan. The "lost" dividends should certainly be counted as another cost of the loan (treat them like interest).

CONSUMER TOPIC

CHEAP POLICES?

What could be better? Buying life insurance through the mail, with guaranteed acceptance and no medical exam, and with low dollars per month cost! Furthermore, coverage won't be cancelled if the insured's health fails.

There are plenty of disadvantages to these policies! First, they're usually only sold in small face value amounts, may be $5,000, $15,000, or $25,000. Premium costs can work out to be only dollars per month, but when calculated as dollars per $1000 coverage, the policies aren't cheap.

What about the offer that coverage is guaranteed? If you're a smoking, obese, unhealthy person, then this is an advantage. But for a healthy average person, it's a bad deal. The fact that all consumers of the same age pay the same rate means that healthy consumers subsidize unhealthy ones. The promise that coverage won't be cancelled in the event of poor health is worthless. All life insurance policies maintain coverage as long as premiums are paid.

The recommendation: Compare the cost of "cheap" mail order policies, either using the cost per $1000 of coverage or using the interest adjusted net cost, to the cost of agent marketed or group policies.

Table 6-10 Borrowing from a whole life policy vs. taking from savings.

Cash value Loan Rate = 8%		Savings Account, 8% annual interest	
Year 1: CV=	$14,300	Year 1:	10,000
Year 2: CV =	15,480	Year 2: ($10,000 × 1.08)	10,800
Borrow	$ 1,000	Withdrawal	−$ 1,000
		Amount, end year 2	$ 9,800
Year 3: Return ($1000 + 8% int.)	$ 1,080	Year 3: ($9,800 × 1.08)	$10,584
CV =	$16,660	Deposit	$ 1,000
		Amount, end year 3	$11,584
If hadn't taken loan:		If hadn't made withdrawal:	
Year 1: CV =	$14,300	Year 1:	$10,000
Year 2: CV =	$15,480	Year 2: ($10,000 × 1.08)	10,800
Year 3: CV=	$16,660	Year 3: ($10,800 × 1.08)	11,664
Cost to you of borrowing the $1,000 for a year = $80 interest.		Cost to you of taking the $1,000 out for 1 year = $11,664 − $11,584 = $80	

Variations on the Whole Life Theme

There are several variations to the standard whole life policy (also some-times called ordinary life). These variations are depicted in Figure 6-3. The variations generally make some minor adjustment to the standard whole life policy, but advertising "hype" is sometimes used to make consumers think the variations are something unique and better. However, the whole life variations should still be judged by the same criterion as whole life policies (e.g., interest adjusted net cost).

Figure 6-3. Variations on the whole life theme.

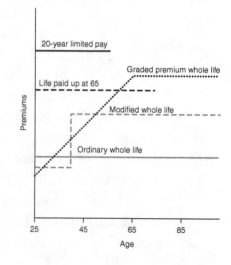

LIMITED PAY
20-YEAR PAY

A *limited pay whole life policy* is a whole life policy in which the term of the payment is less than the term of the coverage. For example, a *20 year limited pay* whole life policy means the policy premiums are completely paid in 20 years, yet the coverage continues for the insured's "whole life" (until age 100). *A life paid-up at 65* policy means premiums are only paid until age 65 but coverage lasts until age 100.

PAID UP AT 65

Agents sometimes push limited pay whole life policies by saying that it's better to pay premiums for only 20 years, or until age 65, than to pay premiums to age 100. Agents may even show consumers that the sum of premiums paid with a whole life policy are less than the sum of premiums paid for an ordinary whole life policy if the insured lived to age 80 or 85. This may be so, but it's meaningless. As you now know, the correct way to compare the total cost of a whole life policy is by the interest adjusted net cost or cost index. To decide if a limited pay whole life policy is better than an ordinary whole life policy, compare the interest adjusted net cost indexes for the desired policy term.

Limited pay whole life premiums will always be higher than ordinary whole life premiums. A limited whole life policy should only be considered if the consumer wants life insurance coverage for a period longer than the pay period of the limited pay policy. If not, then an ordinary whole life policy will be better.

MODIFIED WHOLE LIFE

GRADED PREMIUM WHOLE LIFE

The *modified whole life policy* and the *graded premium whole life policy* are to life insurance what the graduated payment mortgage is to housing finance. With both policies, premium payments are made initially lower than they would be under an equal annual premium method and then rise to a higher level (higher than under the equal annual premium method) later. With the modified whole life policy, there are only two levels of premium payments, a low initial level and a high later level. With the graded premium policy, the premium payments rise in many steps before leveling off. These policies may be favored by consumers who want a whole life policy, can't afford the premiums in their younger years, but could afford higher premiums later. Again, however, use the interest adjusted net cost to compare the total costs of modified whole life and graded premium whole life policies.

INDEXED WHOLE LIFE

An *indexed whole life insurance policy* is one in which the face value amount increases with the inflation rate, generally measured by the Consumer Price Index. The cost of the increasing face value amount can be handled in two ways. Under one method, the extra cost of the added face value amount is added to the policyholder's premium as the additions occur. This results in rising premiums for the indexed whole life policy. Under the other method, the company estimates the future increases in the face value which will occur and spreads these costs equally over all premiums. This preserves the constant premium of the whole life policy. Indexed whole life insurance policies are one way of addressing the problem created by inflation on the required face value amount (see *Inflation Again! Life Insurance Requirements as the Insured Lives*).

C
O
N
S
U
M
E
R

T
O
P
I
C

LIFE INSURANCE AGENT COMMISSIONS

Life insurance agents are paid by commissions which are a percent of premiums paid by the consumer. Commissions are typically front-loaded, meaning that they are higher when the policy is first sold than in later years. This obviously gives agents an incentive to sell new policies.

Commissions vary by the type of policy. Commissions are typically higher for cash value policies than for term policies. For example, an agent might earn 55 percent of premiums in the first year of a whole life policy but only 35 percent of first year term premiums.* Since premiums are much higher for whole life policies, this means many more dollars in commissions for the agent selling whole life policies.

It makes sense that commissions are higher for cash value insurance than for term insurance. The life insurance company receives money which it can invest when cash value insurance is bought, but no investment money is received when term insurance is bought. Although the accumulated cash value can be returned to the consumer, the life insurance company, like any other investment company, keeps a "cut" of the investment returns.

The buyer of life insurance should keep these agent incentives in mind when shopping for life insurance. Agents will try to push cash value insurance over term insurance.

*Mark S. Dorfman and Saul W. Adelman. *Life Insurance,* Dow-Jones Irwin, Homewood, Illinois, 1988.

ECONOMATIC WHOLE LIFE POLICIES

Economatic whole life policies are participating policies which don't return dividends to the policyholder. Instead, dividends are kept by the company and used to buy additional paid-up whole life insurance. At the same time, the company offers lower premiums and a lower face value amount. However, the company expects that the sum of the face value and the whole life additions will make the total face value amount the same as for a competitive policy with higher premiums.

The economatic strategy is dependent on the investment fortunes of the company and the resulting dividends. If dividends are lower than the company forecasted, then the economatic strategy won't work and the face value will be less than advertised.

Beware of Advertising Gimmicks

The whole life insurance buyer will usually be overwhelmed with mountains of numbers and comparisons presented by the life insurance agent. Some of these numbers and comparisons will be meaningless and inaccurate. The smart life insurance buyer will know what questions to ask, what information to seek, and what information to ignore.

If the policy is participating, sometimes the agent will say, "Look, the policy pays for itself by year X," if, at year X, dividends are greater than premiums. That's nice, but so what! This could be done by making the premiums very high, so that in the early years the company has a large investment fund to generate the big dividends.

Sometimes the agent may state, "This policy costs you nothing," by showing you that the sum of dividends and the cash value at a future date exceed the sum of premiums. This is a meaningless comparison because it ignores the time value of money.

The smart consumer will use the interest adjusted net cost and cost index as a way of judging the total cost of a whole life policy.

Whole Life Policies Are Best Suited for • • •

Whole life policies should be considered by the person who (1) wants guaranteed life insurance coverage well into retirement years, or for considerably longer than age 65 or 70, and (2) doesn't have the discipline to save and wants to use life insurance as a form of forced savings.

Persons who only need life insurance protection for a short period of time, ending at or before retirement, and who have the discipline to save and invest competitively should not consider whole life insurance.

The Bottom Line

Whole life insurance provides protection at a constant cost each year. An investment fund is received if the policy is cancelled. Initial costs are much higher than for term protection.

12. How to Compare a Term and a Whole Life Policy

Term and whole life insurance policies can be compared in two ways: by the interest adjusted net cost or cost index, which we've already discussed, or by the side-by-side comparison, which we'll discuss in this topic.

Interest Adjusted Net Cost

The interest adjusted net cost can be used to compare term and whole life policies as long as (1) the same interest rate is used in the calculations for both policies; and (2) taxes are taken out of the cash value for the whole life policy. For example, look back to Tables 6-7 and 6-8. In Table 6-7, the two term policies were calculated to have interest adjusted net cost indexes of $2.78 and $2.75 per $1000. In Table 6-8 the whole life policy was calculated to have an interest adjusted net cost index of $2.91 per $1000 after considering taxes on the cash value. Thus, the total costs of the term policies are less than the total cost of the whole life policy.

C O N S U M E R

T O P I C

THE A. L. WILLIAMS STORY

In the late 1970s interest rates rose to unprecedented levels in the U.S. This had a profound effect on the life insurance industry. Whole life policies which had been issued when interest rates were lower had fixed cash value accumulations based on those lower rates. Many consumers found that they were better off cancelling their whole life policies, buying term insurance, and investing the difference at high interest rates.

An entrepreneur who took advantage of this situation was A. L. Williams. Mr. Williams built a life insurance empire based on convincing consumers to cancel their whole life policies, buy term, and invest the difference. Mr. Williams' agents also offered the investment funds for the "invest the difference" part of the process.

Needless to say, the A. L. Williams organization created a stir in the industry because many life insurance companies lost business to A. L. Williams. A. L. Williams was accused of "churning," meaning that agents made money in commissions when old policies were cancelled and new ones purchased. Of course commissions were earned, but probably in most cases the life insurance consumer benefitted also.

The A. L. Williams organization didn't do anything unique; they simply did it on a large scale and with much publicity. The term policies offered by A. L. Williams should be evaluated by the interest adjusted net cost, just as other term policies are evaluated. In fact, a 1986 evaluation by Consumers Union showed A. L. Williams policies to be among the highest cost policies.

Side by Side Comparison

A second, and perhaps more revealing, way to compare term and whole life policies is by the *side-by-side comparison*. This is also called the "buy term and invest the difference" comparison. The approach is simple. Begin with a whole life and term policy which are similar in all respects, including their face value amount. For each year of the policy term, subtract the net term premium from the net whole life premium. Assume this difference is invested at same after-tax interest rate, and develop an investment fund with these investments. Accumulate the investment fund over the investment term. Compare the final after-tax investment fund with the after-tax cash value of the whole life policy at the end of the policy term. If the after-tax cash value is larger, then the whole life policy is better. If the after-tax investment fund accumulated with the term policy is larger, then the term policy is better.

Table 6-11 illustrates the side-by-side comparison for the non-participating term policy from Table 6-6 and the whole life policy from Table 6-8. Since the investment fund is larger with the term

Table 6-11   Side-by-side comparison for a term and whole life policy.

Age	Whole life Policy Net Premiums	Term Policy Net Premiums	Side Investment Fund with Term Policy After-Tax Return of 5%		
35	$1,316	$163	$1316−163 = $1153,	$1,153	× 1.05 = $ 1,210.65
36	1,165	166	1165−166 =	999, (1999 + 1210.65) × 1.05 =	2,320.13
37	1,127	169	1127 −169 =	958, (958 + 2320.13) × 1.05 =	3,442.04
38	1,085	176	1085 −176 =	909, (909 + 3442.04) × 1.05 =	4,568.59
39	1,043	185	1043 −185 =	858, (858 + 4568.59) × 1.05 =	5,097.92
40	994	196	994 −196 =	798, (798 + 5697.92) × 1.05 =	6,820.71
41	945	214	945 − 214 =	731, (731 + 6820.71) × 1.05 =	7,929.30
42	896	231	896 − 231 =	665, (665 + 7929.30) × 1.05 =	9,024.01
43	847	249	847 − 249 =	598, (598 + 9024.01) × 1.05 =	10,103.12
44	798	265	798 − 265 =	533, (533 + 10103.12) × 1.05 =	11,167.92
45	735	288	735 − 288 =	447, (447 + 11167.92) × 1.05 =	12,195.67
46	672	310	672 − 310 =	362, (362 + 12195.67) × 1.05 =	13,185.55
47	609	336	609 − 336 =	273, (273 + 13185.55) × 1.05 =	14,131.48
48	546	369	546−369 =	177, (177 + 14131.48) × 1.05 =	15,023.90
49	482	406	482−406 =	76, (76 + 15023.90) × 1.05 =	15,854.90
50	407	432	407 − 432 =	−25, (−25 + 15854.90) × 1.05 =	16,621.40
51	332	461	332 − 461 =	−129, (−129 + 16621.40) × 1.05 =	17,317.02
52	257	494	257 − 494 =	−237, (−237 + 17317.02) × 1.05 =	17,934.02
53	182	535	182−535 =	−353, (−353+17934.02) × 1.05 =	18,460.07
54	103	574	103−574 =	−471, (−471 + 18460.07) × 1.05 =	18,888.52

<table>
<tr><td>After-tax cash value with
whole life policy, at age 54: $18,401.84.</td><td>After-tax side investment fund
with term policy, at age 54: $18,888.52.</td></tr>
</table>

policy the term policy is preferred. This is the same answer found by comparing the interest adjusted net cost indexes of the policies.[8] Note that in the later years of the policy comparison the term premiums are higher so they reduce the accumulated investment fund.

---

[8]The two approaches will give the same answer because they really are the same method. The difference is in how the whole life cash value is handled. With the interest adjusted net cost method, the cash value is subtracted from the accumulated interest adjusted whole life net premiums before comparing the result to the accumulated interest adjusted term net. premiums. With the side-by-side comparison, the investment fund accumulated with the term policy is like the term policy's "cash value," and this fund is compared to the final whole life cash value.

**C
O
N
S
U
M
E
R

T
O
P
I
C**

THE LINTON YIELD

Another way of comparing term policies and cash-value policies is with the Linton Yield. To calculate the Linton Yield, set up the following comparison. First, match a whole life policy and a term policy that both provide the same amount of protection. (Both policies should have similar provisions too.) Second, subtract the net premiums of the term policy from the net premiums of the cash value policy. These are monies that could be invested if the term policy were bought. Third, find the interest rate which, when applied to the monies available for investing with the term policy, would accumulate to the same amount as the cash value with the cash value policy at a given year. This interest rate is the Linton Yield. It represents the implicit interest rate earned in the cash value policy. A cash value policy with a higher Linton Yield is considered better.

Linton Yields typically vary over the policy term of a cash value policy. In the early years of the policy Linton Yields are very low, and maybe negative! Linton Yields then rise as the cash value is held longer.

Words of Caution

When comparing a term and whole life policy, make sure the policies are comparable with respect to face value amount and policy characteristics, such as riders, settlement options, etc. (see *Is the Fine Print of Life Insurance Policies Important?* later in this chapter). Participating policies and non-participating policies can be compared as long as the dividends on participating policies are subtracted from premiums to form net premiums.

The selection of the after-tax interest rate used to calculate the interest adjusted net cost or to do the side-by-side comparison is very important. The higher the interest rate selected, the more favorable the term policy will be. In the interest adjusted net cost approach, a higher interest rate means a higher time value of money, which means a greater "penalty" for the higher whole life premiums, compared to term premiums, in the early years of the policy. In the side-by-side approach, a higher interest rate means more interest is accumulated in the term policy's side investment fund.

The Bottom Line

Compare term and whole life policies by the interest adjusted net cost method or side-by-side method. However, make sure the policies being compared have the same face value amount and similar policy characteristics.

13. Who Should Buy an Endowment Policy?

Endowment insurance is often advertised as life insurance which allows you to "have your cake and eat it too." Like other life insurance policies, endowment insurance will pay the face value amount to the beneficiaries if the insured dies while the insurance is in force. However, unlike other policies, endowment insurance will also pay the face value amount to the insured if the insured lives to a certain age. If the face value is received in this way it is called an endowment. If the endowment policy is cancelled before the end of the policy term, a cash value is paid to the insured.

For the right to this double-barrelled benefit, endowment life insurance premiums are much higher than whole life insurance premiums for the same face value amount. This is because endowment life insurance must insure not only against the probability of the insured dying, but also against the probability of the insured living to a certain age! Endowment life insurance is generally only offered for policy terms of 20 or 30 years.

Endowment life insurance takes the idea of forced savings a step beyond that provided by whole life insurance. So is this a good deal? As we have seen time and time before, it depends critically on what else you could do with your money. Table 6-12 shows a side-by-side comparison of an endowment policy and a whole life policy. Both are for $100,000 of coverage. The endowment policy ends at age 65, at which time the insured collects $100,000 (before taxes) if he is living. The endowment is taxed to the extent that it exceeds the sum of net premiums paid.

This particular example shows that if the insured bought the whole life policy and invested the difference in net premiums in an investment earning 5 percent (after-taxes), then the sum of this investment fund and the after-tax cash value received from the whole life policy at age 65 would far exceed the after-tax endowment. The same kind of side-by-side comparison can be done between an endowment policy and a term policy.

Endowment Policies Are Best Suited for • • •

Endowment life insurance policies provide an extra element of forced savings as compared to whole life policies, but at the cost of higher premiums. Also, endowment policies only provide protection for a limited time period, not for your "whole life."

Endowment policies should be considered by a person who (1) needs life insurance protection for a limited time period, and not past age 65, (2) wants a high level of forced savings, and (3) can afford high premiums.

Table 6-12 Side-by-side comparison of endowment and whole life policies.

Age	Endowment at 65 $100,000 Premiums	Endowment Dividends	Net Premiums	Whole Life Policy $100,000 Premiums	Dividends	Net Premiums	Side Investment Fund with Whole life Policy, After-tax Return of 5%
35	$3280	0	$3280	$1316	0	$1316	$3280 – $1316 = $1964, (1964) × 1.05 = $ 2062.20
36	3280	160	3120	1316	151	1165	3120 – 1165 = 1955, (1955 + 2062.20) × 1.05 = 4218.06
37	3280	205	3075	1316	189	1127	3075 – 1127 = 1948, (1948 + 4218.06) × 1.05 = 6474.36
38	3280	250	3030	1316	231	1085	3030 – 1085 = 1945, (1945 + 6474.36) × 1.05 = 8840.33
39	3280	295	2985	1316	273	1043	2985 – 1043 = 1942, (1942 + 8840.33) × 1.05 = 1132.45
40	3280	340	2940	1316	322	994	2940 – 994 = 1946, (1946 + 11326.45) × 1.05 = 13930.82
41	3280	387	2893	1316	371	945	2893 – 945 = 1948, (1948 + 13930.82) × 1.05 = 16672.76
42	3280	434	2846	1316	420	896	2846 – 896 = 1950, (1950 + 16672.76) × 1.05 = 19553.90
43	3280	481	2799	1316	469	847	2799 – 847 = 1952, (1952 + 19553.90) × 1.05 = 22581.20
44	3280	530	2750	1316	518	798	2750 – 798 = 1952, (1952 + 22581.20) × 1.05 = 25759.87
45	3280	595	2685	1316	581	735	2685 – 735 = 1950, (1950 + 25759.87) × 1.05 = 29095.36
46	3280	660	2620	1316	644	672	2620 – 672 = 1948, (1948 + 29095.36) × 1.05 = 32595.53
47	3280	725	2555	1316	707	609	2555 – 609 = 1946, (1946 + 32595.53) × 1.05 = 36268.61
48	3280	790	2490	1316	770	546	2490 – 546 = 1944, (1944 + 36268.61) × 1.05 = 40123.24
49	3280	856	2424	1316	834	482	2424 – 482 = 1942, (1942 + 40123.24) × 1.05 = 44168.50
50	3280	939	2341	1316	909	407	2341 – 407 = 1934, (1934 + 44168.50) × 1.05 = 48407.63
51	3280	1022	2258	1316	984	332	2258 – 332 = 1926, (1926 + 48407.63) × 1.05 = 52850.31
52	3280	1105	2175	1316	1059	257	2175 – 257 = 1918, (1918 + 52850.31) × 1.05 = 57506.73
53	3280	1188	2092	1316	1134	182	2092 – 182 = 1910, (1910 + 57506.73) × 1.05 = 62387.57
54	3280	1275	2005	1316	1213	103	2005 – 103 = 1902, (1902 + 62387.57) × 1.05 = 67504.05
55	3280	1346	1934	1316	1281	35	1934 – 35 = 1899, (1899 + 67504.05) × 1.05 = 72873.20
56	3280	1417	1863	1316	1349	-33	1863 – (–33) = 1896, (1896 + 72873.20) × 1.05 = 78507.66
57	3280	1488	1792	1316	1417	-101	1792 – (–101) = 1893, (1893 + 78507.66) × 1.05 = 84420.69
58	3280	1559	1721	1316	1485	-169	1721 – (–169) = 1890, (1890 + 84420.69) × 1.05 = 90626.23
59	3280	1630	1650	1316	1553	-237	1650 – (–237) = 1887, (1887 + 90626.23) × 1.05 = 97138.89
60	3280	1693	1587	1316	1621	-305	1587 – (–305) = 1892, (1892 + 97138.89) × 1.05 = 103982.43
61	3280	1756	1524	1316	1689	-373	1524 – (–373) = 1897, (1897 + 103982.43) × 1.05 = 111173.40
62	3280	1819	1461	1316	1757	-441	1461 – (–441) = 1902, (1902 + 111173.40) × 1.05 = 118729.17
63	3280	1882	1398	1316	1825	-509	1398 – (–509) = 1907, (1907 + 118729.17) × 1.05 = 126667.98
64	3280	1945	1335	1316	1893	-557	1335 – (–557) = 1892, (1892 + 126667.98) × 1.05 = 134987.98
65	3280	2011	1269	1316	1969	-653	1269 – (–653) = 1922, (1922 + 134987.98) × 1.05 = 143755.48

Endowment at age 65: $100,000

Sum of net premiums: $ 70,987

Tax on endowment at 28%: (100,000 – 70,987) × .28 = $8,147.84

After-tax endowment = $91,851.16

Cash value at age 65 = $25,500

Sum of net premiums = $11,198

Cumulative after-tax side investment fund = $143,755.48

After-tax cash value = $25.500 – ($25,500 – $11,198) × .28 = $21,496

Total after tax investment fund and cash value = $165,251.48

The Bottom Line _____

Buy an endowment life insurance policy if you want a short-term policy with a big dose of forced savings._____

14. Who Should Buy Universal Life Insurance?

Origin

In the late 1970s interest rates earned on investments rose to double-digits. Many consumers who had bought whole life policies found those policies were not competitive because the cash value was growing at a much lower interest rate. Many consumers cancelled their whole life policies, bought term policies, and invested the difference at high interest rates.

In response, the life insurance industry developed a new policy, called "universal life" (UL), so called because the industry advertised it as being able to meet any life insurance need. Consumers immediately took to universal life, but tax law changes eventually took away some of UL's luster. Nevertheless, it remains a valuable option for life insurance consumers.

What Is Universal Life?

Universal life is a combination of term insurance plus a side investment fund. Unlike whole life insurance, UL's side investment fund earns a current competitive interest rate. Like whole life policies, the side investment fund is sheltered from taxes until withdrawals are made or until the UL policy is canceled.

FLEXIBILITY

One of the big benefits of a UL policy is its *flexibility.* After some required minimum payments are initially made, the policyholder has some degree of control over premium payments. The policyholder can make whatever premium payment desired—make lower premium payments or even skip premium payments—as long as there is enough money in the side investment fund to pay annual mortality costs. The IRS does put limits on the maximum UL premium payments.

The amount of life insurance coverage can be decreased or increased with a UL policy. In the case of an increase, however, the policyholder will have to show evidence of insurability.

The interest rate paid on the side investment fund is determined by the life insurance company and is changed periodically. Two interest rates will be presented to the consumer, a minimum guaranteed rate (usually 4 or 4½ percent) and a current rate. Policy projections with both interest rates should be examined.

Another benefit of UL policies is the breakdown of where each premium payment goes, which will be provided by the company. A periodic report will show how much of each premium goes to pay the mortality cost, administrative cost, other costs, and how much goes to the side investment fund.

Two Types of UL Policies

OPTION A
OPTION B

There are two types of UL policies, so-called Option A and Option B. They differ by the calculation of the death benefit. In Option A the death benefit is constant over most of the life of the contract, then rises only when the investment fund exceeds the original death benefit. In Option B the death benefit is the sum of an original fixed benefit plus the investment fund. Thus, in Option B the death benefit rises over time as the investment fund increases. Premiums will be higher in Option B for the same amount of initial coverage, or, if premiums are the same in the two options, the investment fund will be smaller in Option B. Figure 6-4 shows how Options A and B differ. Option B is best if the insured expects to require more life insurance coverage as he ages [see *Inflation Again! Life Insurance Requirements as the Insured Ages*].

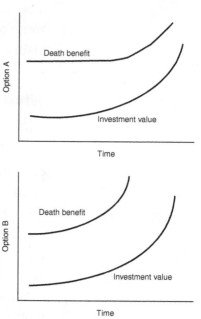

Figure 6-4. Universal life insurance policy options.

Examples of these two universal life policy options are shown in Tables 6-13 and 6-14. Two investment funds are shown, a guaranteed rate of 4 percent and a current rate of 10½ percent. The fourth column of both figures shows the surrender charge which must be paid to the life insurance company if the policy is cancelled. The fifth column shows the investment fund which the policyholder would receive, before-taxes, if the policy is cancelled. The last column shows the death benefit. In Table 6-13 the death benefit is a constant $100,000 (Option A); in Table 6-14 the death benefit is the sum of $100,000 and the surrender investment value.

Notice that since both policies have premiums of $2000 annually, Option B has lower investment values.

Surrender Charges and Loads

Most UL policies have surrender charges and loads. Surrender charges occur if the policyholder cancels the policy or withdraws some of the

Table 6-13   A universal life policy. Option A.

Male age 45, non-smoker, $100,000 benefit.

End of Year	Premium	Investment Value, 4%	Surrender Charge	Surrender Investment Value, 4%	Death Benefit
1	$2,000	$ 1,437	$1,135	$ 302	$100,000
2	2,000	2,901	1,135	1,766	100,000
3	2,000	4,392	1,135	3,257	100,000
4	2,000	5,911	1,135	4,776	100,000
5	2,000	7,456	1,135	6,321	100,000
10	2,000	15,462	0	15,462	100,000
15	2,000	23,596	0	23,596	100,000
20	2,000	31,362	0	31,362	100,000

End of Year	Premium	Investment Value, 10½%	Surrender Charge	Surrender Investment Value, 10½%	Death Benefit
1	$2,000	$ 1,629	$1,135	$ 494	$100,000
2	2,000	3,406	1,135	2,271	100,000
3	2,000	5,345	1,135	4,209	100,000
4	2,000	7,463	1,135	6,328	100,000
5	2,000	9,778	1,135	8,643	100,000
10	2,000	25,083	0	25,083	100,000
15	2,000	49,627	0	49,627	100,000
20	2,000	90,926	0	90,926	100,000

investment fund. Surrender charges are typically higher in the early years of the policy and may be zero in later years. The UL policies in Tables 6-13 and 6-14 display this pattern of surrender charges.

LOADS "Loads" are fees taken "off the top" of each premium payment. Typically they are a flat dollar amount or a percentage of the premium payment. Usually there is a higher "initial load" for the first year and a lower "renewal load" for the subsequent years. Make sure in UL policy presentations that load charges are identified and not included in the investment fund accumulation.

Surrenders and Loans

PARTIAL SURRENDER Some of the investment fund in UL policies can be directly withdrawn by the policyholder. This is called a *partial surrender.*

Table 6-14 A universal life policy, Option B.

Male, age 45, non-smoker, $ increasing benefit, initial 100,000.

End of Year	Premium	Investment Value, 4%	Surrender Charge	Surrender Investment Value, 4%	Death Benefit
1	$2,000	$ 1,430	$1,135	$ 295	$101,430
2	2,000	2,879	1,135	1,744	102,879
3	2,000	4,345	1,135	3,210	104,345
4	2,000	5,828	1,135	4,693	105,828
5	2,000	7,322	1,135	6,187	107,322
10	2,000	14,756	0	14,756	114,756
15	2,000	21,330	0	21,330	121,330
20	2,000	25,581	0	25,581	125,581

End of Year	Premium	Investment Value, 10½%	Surrender Charge	Surrender Investment Value, 10½%	Death Benefit
1	$2,000	$ 1,623	$1,135	$ 488	$101,623
2	2,000	3,386	1,135	2,250	103,386
3	2,000	5,299	1,135	4,163	105,299
4	2,000	7,377	1,135	6,242	107,377
5	2,000	9,634	1,135	8,499	109,634
10	2,000	24,120	0	24,120	124,120
15	2,000	45,653	0	45,653	145,653
20	2,000	77,600	0	77,600	177,600

As with whole life policies, loans can be taken against the investment fund in the UL policy. The money in the investment fund is not reduced; in fact this money continues to earn interest. The money in the investment fund does serve as collateral for the loan.

NET COST OF BORROWING

UL policies will often quote a "net cost of borrowing" for such loans. The net cost of borrowing is the difference between the interest rate charged on the loan and the interest rate earned on money in the investment fund. For example, if 10 percent interest is charged on the UL policy loan and 9 percent is earned on the UL policy investment fund, the UL policy (or agent) may say that the net cost of borrowing is "only" 10 percent minus 9 percent, or 1 percent.

The idea of a "net cost of borrowing" is deceptive and incorrect. The opportunity cost of the UL policy loan is still the interest rate charged.

THE RISE AND FALL OF UNIVERSAL LIFE

The life insurance industry rolled merrily on until the late 1970s. Whole life, endowment, and a little term insurance were the mainstays of the industry just as the fixed rate mortgage was in the real estate industry.

The high inflation rate and interest rates of the late 1970s and early 1980s unraveled this peaceful world. Consumers became disenchanted with the low interest rates earned by whole life policies and many cancelled their policies and bought term and invested the difference (see "The A. L. Williams Story").

The life insurance industry counterattacked with a new policy called universal life, which promised to pay competitive market interest rates on the investment accumulation. Universal life grew from 2 percent of all new premium dollars in 1981 to 38 percent in 1985.

But since 1985, universal life has slipped. Two reasons account for the fall of universal life. First, the fall in interest rates, beginning in 1982, reduced the attractiveness of universal life and raised the status of the old standby whole life. Second, the competitive tactics of same companies and agents came back to haunt them. Some companies promised very high interest rates on universal life policies, and calculated the required premium payments assuming these rates would continue. When interest rates fell, holders of these universal life policies either had to pay more premiums or accept less protection. Such situations put a blemish on universal life.

Source: *Financial Planning*, January 1989, pp. 52–55.

Furthermore, some UL policies reduce the interest earned on that part of the investment fund covering the policy loan when such a loan is received. If this happens, it's another cost of the loan.

For example, suppose a policyholder borrows $1000 from his UL policy and is charged 10 percent interest, However, because of the loan, $1000 in the UL investment fund which was earning 9 percent interest now earns only 5 percent interest, a loss of 4 percent. The total interest rate cost of the loan is 10 percent plus 4 percent, or 14 percent.

Tax Implications

The above discussion of surrenders and loans in UL policies is somewhat academic due to changes in federal tax law. Prior to 1988, money could be withdrawn from a UL policy, either through partial withdrawals or loans, with no tax consequences. This was a big selling point for UL policies.

This benefit of UL policies was closed in 1988. Now, in many cases all of partial surrenders and loans from UL policies are taxed.[9] To find the withdrawals which are taxed, first calculate:

$$\text{Max} = \begin{array}{c} \text{Investment value of} \\ \text{UL policy before} \\ \text{withdrawal is made} \end{array} - \begin{array}{c} \text{Sum of net} \\ \text{premiums paid.} \end{array}$$

All of the UL withdrawals less than "Max" are subject to taxation.

For example, suppose $5000 is withdrawn from a UL policy. If $10,000 in net premiums had been paid, and if the investment value is $19,000, then:

$$\text{Max} = \$19,000 - \$10,000 = \$9,000.$$

Since $3000 is less than $9000, then the entire $3000 is taxed.

It gets worse! If the policyholder is younger than 59½ years old, then that part of the UL withdrawal which is taxable ($3000 in the above example) is also subject to a 10 percent penalty. The only exceptions are if the policyholder is disabled, or if the withdrawal is made in equal payments over the life expectancy of the policyholder.

Needless to say, these two tax laws have reduced the partial surrenders and loans from UL policies.

Evaluating UL Policies

Interest-adjusted net cost indexes can be calculated for UL policies using the same formula as for whole life policies. However, be sure to take account of surrender charges and the taxes on UL's investment accumulation.

UL policies can also be evaluated using a standard side-by-side comparison. The UL policy is compared to alternative life insurance policies which provide the same level of protection.

Table 6-15 shows the after tax investment fund received by the policyholder if the UL policy shown in Table 6-13 was cancelled after 10 years and after 20 years. After 10 years the policyholder would take home, after taxes, $23,151.46, and after 20 years the take-home value is $76,666.72.

By comparison, Table 6-16 shows what could be accumulated in a side investment fund if a term policy is bought instead of the UL policy. A 7 percent after-tax interest rate is assumed since the UL policy uses

[9]Withdrawals from UL policies are potentially subject to taxation when the UL policy fails the 7-pay test. The 7-pay test is failed if the sum of the UL policy premiums, at any time during the first 7 years of the policy, exceeds the sum of the whole life premiums which would have been paid to provide the same face value coverage. UL policies with Option A (constant death benefit) are more likely to fail the 7-pay test than UL policies with Option B (increasing death benefit.).

Table 6-15   Surrender of a UL policy.

(UL policy, $100,000 constant death benefit—Option A—male, age 45, non-smoker)

End of Year	Surrender Premium	Investment Value 10½%
1	$2,000	$ 494
2	2,000	2,271
3	2,000	4,209
4	2,000	6,328
5	2,000	8,643
10	2,000	25,083
15	2,000	49,627
20	2,000	90,926

Total surrender at end of year 10:
 (policyholder is age 55)

Surrender investment value	= $	25,083
Sum of premiums paid	= $	20,000
Max = $25,083 − $20,000	= $	5,083
Part of surrender value taxed	= $	5,083
Tax at 28% = .28 × $5,083	= $	1,423.24
10% penalty = .10 × $5,083	= $	508.30
After-tax surrender value	=	
$25,083 − $1,423.24 − $508.30	=	$23,151.46

Total surrender at end of year 20:
 (policyholder is age 65)

Surrender investment value	= $	90,926
Sum of premiums paid	= $	40,000
Max = $90,926 − $40,000	= $	50,926
Part of surrender value taxed	= $	50,926
Tax at 28% = .28 × $50,926	=	$14,259.28
No 10% penalty.	=	
After-tax surrender value	=	
$90,926-$14,259.28	=	$76,666.72

Table 6-16 Comparing a universal life and term policy.

Age	UL Premium		Term Premium		Buy Term and Invest the Difference (7% after-tax rate)
45	$2000	–	$288	=	$1712, $1712 $\times 1.07 = $ $ 1831.84
46	2000	–	310	=	1690,(1690 + 1831.84) $\times 1.07 = $ 3768.37
47	2000	–	336	=	1664, (1664 + 3768.37) $\times 1.07 = $ 5812.63
48	2000	–	369	=	1631, (1631 + 5812.63) $\times 1.07 = $ 7964.69
49	2000	–	406	=	1594, (1594 + 7964.69) $\times 1.07 = $ 10227.80
50	2000	–	432	=	1568,(1568 + 10227.80) $\times 1.07 = $ 12621.50
51	2000	–	461	=	1539, (1539 + 12621.50) $\times 1.07 = $ 15151.74
52	2000	–	494	=	1506, (1506 + 15151.74) $\times 1.07 = $ 17823.78
53	2000	–	535	=	1465, (1465 + 17823.78) $\times 1.07 = $ 20638.99
54	2000	–	574	=	1426, (1426 + 20638.99) $\times 1.07 = $ 23609.54
55	2000	–	627	=	1373, (1373 + 23609.54) $\times 1.07 = $ 26731.32
56	2000	–	680	=	1320, (1320 + 26731.32) $\times 1.07 = $ 30014.92
57	2000	–	740	=	1260, (1260 + 30014,92) $\times 1.07 = $ 33464.16
58	2000	–	809	=	1191,(1191 + 33464.16) $\times 1.07 = $ 3708.1.02
59	2000	–	897	=	1103, (1103 + 37081.02) $\times 1.07 = $ 40856.90
60	2000	–	971	=	1029, (1029 + 40856.90) $\times 1.07 = $ 44817.92
61	2000	–	1060	=	940, (940 + 44817.92) $\times 1.07 = $ 48960.97
62	2000	–	1162	=	838, (838 + 48960.97) $\times 1.07 = $ 53284.90
63	2000	–	1304	=	696, (696 + 53284.90) $\times 1.07 = $ 57759.56
64	2000	–	1431	=	569, (569 + 57759.56) $\times 1.07 = $ 62411.56

If purchase no life insurance and invest $2000 annually and earn 7% after tax, value at end of:

   10 years: $2,000 $\times$ 14.784 (Sum of FVFs from Appendix Table A-1) = $29,568;

   20 years: $2,000 $\times$ 43.867 (Sum of FVFs from Appendix Table A-1) = $87,734.

a 10½ percent before-tax rate. After 10 years the "term and invest the difference" strategy is slightly better ($23,609.54 investment fund with term compared to $23,151.46 after-tax surrender value for the UL), but after 20 years the UL policy clearly is better ($76,666.72 UL after-tax surrender value compared to $62,411.56 investment fund with terms).

The UL policy evaluated in Table 6-15 is the Option A kind. If it were the Option B type, then the term policy premiums in Table 6-16 would have to be changed to purchase the same amounts of increasing coverage as provided by the UL policy.

Although this comparison is only an example, studies of many UL policies have reached the same conclusion: a "buy-term and invest the difference" strategy is better if the UL policy is only kept for 7 to 8 years; after this the UL policy is better.[10] Of couree, UL policies can also be compared to whole life policies using a side-by-side comparison.

As already noted, the UL policy does have a substantial tax advantage—interest earnings on the investment fund are accumulated tax-free. Does this make the UL policy a better investment vehicle, even if life insurance is not needed? To decide this, calculate the after-tax investment accumulation if all UL premiums are invested, and compare the result to the after-tax surrender value of the UL policy. The bottom of Table 6-16 shows the comparison. In our example, the UL policy does not beat a pure investment.[11]

Beware of Advertising Gimmicks

Universal life policies are a welcome addition to life insurance policy options. However, probably more advertising gimmickry has been used with UL policies than with any other kind of life insurance policy. The buyer of life insurance must be cautious to see through this gimmickry.

One technique which has been used to sell UL policies is to show policy projections which use very high interest rates on the investment fund. This allows the company to either show very high investment fund accumulations or to show low-premiums.

As learned in Chapter 2, you now know that high interest rates don't last. In fact, in the middle 1980s when interest rates were falling, many policyholders who bought UL policies with high projected interest rates had a rude awakening: either the death benefit of the policy would have to be reduced, or more premiums would have to be paid.

The moral of the story for the consumer is this. Beware of UL policies which project high interest rates forever. Use UL policy projections that assume a conservative interest rate earned on the investment fund.

---

[10]See Stephen P. D'Arcy and Keun Chang Lee, "Universal/Variable Life Insurance Versus Similar Unbundled Invest Strategies," *The Journal of Risk and insurance,* Vol. 54, No. 3, Sept 1987, pp. 452–477.

[11]The investor interested in tax-deferment of interest earnings can buy tax-deferred annuities (see the chapter on Retirement Planning).

UL Policies Are Best Suited for

Universal life insurance policies are best suited for consumers who (1) can afford premiums higher than with term or whole life policies, (2) want to use life insurance to develop a large side investment fund which earns current interest rates tax free, and (3) want flexibility in their premium payments and face value amount. The benefits from UL policies increase the longer the policy is held. Under UL option B, it is possible to transfer the face value amount and investment fund totally tax-free to beneficiaries upon death of the insured.

The Bottom Line

Universal life policies provide the greatest flexibility in face value amount and premiums. However, premiums are much higher than for term or whole life policies. Look at interest rate and investment projections with a skeptical eye. _____

15. Who Should Buy Single Premium Life Insurance?

Single premium life insurance (SPL) can be thought of as an "extreme" version of universal life insurance. The "extreme" part is that only one large premium is paid with SPL. This large single premium is paid at the beginning of the policy and is usually several thousand dollars.

A typical SPL policy is shown in Table 6-17. A single premium of $15,000 is paid in year 1, and this buys $100,000 of guaranteed protection. Most SPL policies are the "Option B" kind, where the death benefit equals the guaranteed death benefit plus the investment value. Two series of investment values and death benefits are shown in Table 6-17, one using the guaranteed investment rate (4%) and the other using the current investment rate (9%).

After the 1986 Tax Reform Act SPL became very popular as a tax shelter. Since very little of the single premium paid in the first year is needed to cover the cost of protection, the vast majority of that premium goes into the investment fund (notice the current investment value of $14,445 in year 1 of Table 6-17, based on a single premium payment of $15,000). Like all cash value life insurance products, this investment fund accumulates interest tax-free. Furthermore, until 1988, withdrawals could be made from the investment value of SPL policies with no tax consequences.

Since 1988, SPL policy withdrawals have been subject to the same tax rules as UL policies. Most withdrawals from SPL policies are now taxed and are subject to a 10 percent penalty if the policyholder is under

Table 6-17   A single premium life insurance policy.

Male, age 45, non-smoker.

End of Year	Premium	Guaranteed Investment Value	Guaranteed Death Benefit	Current Investment Value	Current Death Benefit
1	$15,000	$ 0	$100,000	$14,445	$1,14,445
2	0	0	100,000	14,109	114,109
3	0	610	100,610	14,424	114,424
4	0	1,724	101,724	15,301	115,301
5	0	2,878	102,878	16,292	116,292
10	0	9,531	109,531	24,370	124,370
15	0	17,366	117,366	38,120	138,120
20	0	26,288	126,288	57,261	157,261

Surrender charges: year 1, 8% of investment value
year 2, 7% of investment value
year 3, 6% of investment value
year 4, 4% of investment value
year 5, 2% of investment value
year 6+, 0% of investment value

Guaranteed interest rate earned on investment value: 4%

Current interest rate earned on investment value: 9%

If surrender at end of year 20, after-tax current surrender value (28% tax bracket):

$$\$57,261 - .28(57,261 - 15,000) = \$57,261 - \$11,833.08 = \underline{\$45,427.92}$$

age 59½. Needless to say, these new rules have considerably reduced the luster of SPL policies.

SPL policies are probably not a good idea for most life insurance consumers. The large up-front payment puts SPL policies out of range of most buyers. Also, if the policyholder dies prematurely, then many more dollars will have been invested in the SPL policy than in other types of policies. If the consumer is looking for the tax-free build-up of investment value that SPL offers, then *single premium tax-deferred annuities* can fill this need [see chapter on Retirement Planning].

Table 6-18 shows a side-by-side comparison of an SPL policy and a term policy. In this case the SPL policy is better for the 20-year comparison.

The Bottom Line _____

Only wealthy individuals can afford to make the one large payment required for a single premium life insurance policy. _____

Table 6-18 Side-by-side comparison of SPL policy and a term policy.

Age	SPL Premium		Term Premium		After-tax Investment Fund if Buy Term (6%)
45	$15,000	–	$ 288	=	$14712, $14712 × 1.06 = $ 1831.84
46	0	–	310	=	−310, (− 310 + 15594.72) × 1.06 = 16201.80
47	0	–	336	=	−336, (− 336 + 16201.80) × 1.06 = 16817.75
48	0	–	369	=	−369, (− 369 + 16817.75) × 1.06 = 17435.68
49	0	–	406	=	−406, (− 406 + 17435.68) × 1.06 = 18051.46
50	0	–	432	=	−432, (− 432 + 18051.46) × 1.06 = 18676.62
51	0	–	461	=	−461, (− 461 + 18676.62) × 1.06 = 19308.56
52	0	–	494	=	−494, (− 494 + 19308.56) × 1.06 = 19943.44
53	0	–	535	=	−535, (− 535 + 19943.44) × 1.06 = 20572.94
54	0	–	574	=	−574, (− 574 + 20572.94) × 1.06 = 21198.88
55	0	–	627	=	−627, (− 627 + 21198.88) × 1.06 = 21806.19
56	0	–	680	=	−680, (− 680 + 21806.19) × 1.06 = 22393.76
57	0	–	740	=	−740, (− 740 + 22393.76) × 1.06 = 22952.99
58	0	–	809	=	−809, (− 809 + 22952.99) × 1.06 = 23472.63
59	0	–	897	=	−897, (− 897 + 23472.63) × 1.06 = 23930.17
60	0	–	971	=	−971, (− 971 + 23930.17) × 1.06 = 24336.72
61	0	–	1060	=	−1060, (−1060 + 24336.72) × 1.06 = 24673.32
62	0	–	1162	=	−1162, (−1162 + 24673.32) × 1.06 = 24922.00
63	0	–	1304	=	−1304, (−1304 + 24922.00) × 1.06 = 25035.08
64	0	–	1431	=	−1431, (−1431 + 25035.08) × 1.06 = 25020.32

SPL after-tax current surrender value at end of year 20: $45,427.92 (Table 6-17).

16. What is Decreasing Term Life insurance?

Earlier we discussed term insurance as a type of life insurance in which premiums increase each year in line with increasing mortality costs. There is a type of term insurance in which premiums remain constant. It's called *decreasing* term insurance because, in order to keep the premiums constant, the face value amount must decline each year (see Figure 6-5).

Decreasing term insurance is usually used to provide protection for the insured's home mortgage balance. The policy is structured in such a way that the declining coverage matches the declining mortgage balance over time. This means that the cost of the decreasing term insurance will depend on the mortgage term and the mortgage interest rate. For adjustable rate mortgages the insured must select an average interest rate that is expected to prevail over the mortgage term.

Figure 6-5. Term vs. decreasing term life insurance.

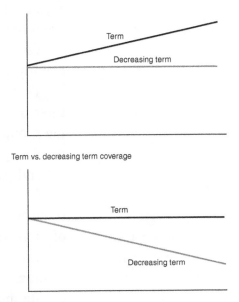

Term vs. decreasing term coverage

Decreasing term insurance should primarily be purchased for mortgage protection, rather than for general protection for child rearing and spousal expenses. Even if the protection needs of the insured are expected to decline each year, inflation will counteract some of this decline (see *Inflation Again! Life Insurance Requirements as the Insured Lives*), and it would be rare if the insured's general life insurance needs followed the pattern of a decreasing term policy.

The Bottom Line

Buy decreasing term life insurance for your home mortgage balance.

17. Are Group Life Insurance Policies Better?

Frequently, consumers can purchase life insurance policies through their place of work or maybe through a club or organization to which they belong, like an auto club, a church, or a labor union. These life insurance policies are called group policies. Evidence that the consumer is a member of the group is generally sufficient to guarantee eligibility for a group policy.

With a group policy you still receive individual coverage. You are eligible for coverage, and can purchase the group policy, as long as you remain a member of the group. Once you leave the group, however, the group coverage is generally ended. Group policies are usually either term policies or whole life policies.

The big advantage of group policies is that they can be cheaper than other individual policies for three reasons. First, since the policies are marketed through the group, administrative and servicing costs are lower. Rather than an agent directly visiting you, group policies are marketed as part of an employer's fringe benefit package or through the mail. Second, if the mortality costs of the group are lower than for society at large, these lower costs will be passed on in the form of lower premiums. Last, some group life insurance may be paid by the employer. However, the cost of coverage above $50,000 must be reported by the employee as income for income tax purposes.

These potential advantages of group life insurance are countered by three disadvantages. First, as mentioned earlier, if you leave the group, the group policy is usually ended. This could force a situation where a middle aged consumer in poor health must enter the life insurance market and pay high premium rates for a new policy.

FACE VALUE
AMOUNT

A second disadvantage of group policies is that coverage is based on some group-related characteristic such as your salary, position, or years of membership in the group. But, as seen earlier in this chapter, there's no simple and automatic relationship between life insurance needs and income, for example. In most cases group policies will provide an inadequate amount of protection. This means you will probably have to supplement the group policy with other individual coverage.

Finally, often group life insurance is offered to all members of the group at the same price per $1000 of coverage regardless of the person's age. This obviously means that older members get a bargain at the expense of younger members. For younger members this may make the group life insurance more expensive than alternative individual coverage. Comparisons of the cost of group insurance versus individual policies should be made by the consumer.

The Bottom Line

Consider group coverage if offered by your employer or group. However, individual policy coverage may still be needed as a supplement. _____

18. Should You Switch Life Insurance Policies?

Imagine the following situation. You have owned a whole life policy for ten years. You have just read a magazine article showing how life insurance premiums can be reduced by buying term insurance rather than whole life. You're tempted to cancel your whole life policy and buy a term policy, but you're not sure. How would you decide what to do?

SIDE-BY-SIDE
COMPARISON

The answer is easy. You would do a standard "side-by-side" comparison, but with two changes. First, you start the comparison at your current age. Second, in calculating the potential side investment fund developed with the term policy, you include the cash value received when the whole life policy is cancelled.

Table 6-19 gives an example of this comparison. The policyholder bought the whole life policy at age 35. The policyholder is now age 45 and wants to compare the policies through age 54. The standard side-by-side comparison is done from age 45 to age 54. Note that when the whole life policy is cancelled at age 45, a cash value of $10,160 is received (no taxes are paid on the cash value because it is less than the sum of premiums paid to that point). The $10,160 cash value is immediately added to the side investment fund and accumulated through age 54. This example shows that switching from the whole life policy to the term policy would be wise because the potential after-tax investment accumulation with the term policy ($30,184.36) exceeds the after-tax cash value with the whole life policy ($24,200).

Table 6-19   Switching from a whole life policy to a term policy.

| | $100,000 Whole Life Policy non-participating | | $100,000 Term Policy | |
| | | | | Side Investment Fund (assume 6% after-tax rate of return) |
Age	Net Premiums	Cash Value	Net Premiums	
35	$1263	0		
36	1263	0		
37	1263	200		
38	1263	1300		
39	1263	2400	Ignore—"sunk costs"	
40	1263	3660		
41	1263	4920		
42	1263	6180		
43	1263	7440		
44	1263	8700		
45	1263	10160	$289	[10160 + (1263 − 289)] × 1.06 = 11802.04
46	1263	11620	309	[11802.04 + (1263 − 309)] × 1.06 = 13521.40
47	1263	13080	335	[13521.40 + (1263 − 335)] × 1.06 = 15316.36
48	1263	14540	368	[15316.36 + (1263 − 368)] × 1.06 = 17184.04
49	1263	16000	405	[17184.04 + (1263 − 405)] × 1.06 = 19124.56
50	1263	17640	431	[19124.56 + (1263 − 431)] × 1.06 = 21153.95
51	1263	19280	460	[21153.95 + (1263 − 460)] × 1.06 = 23274.37
52	1263	20920	494	[23274.37 + (1263 − 494)] × 1.06 = 25485.97
53	1263	22560	535	[25485.97 + (1263 − 535)] × 1.06 = 27786.81
54	1263	24200	574	[27786.81 + (1263 − 574)] × 1.06 = 30184.36
	Sum of premiums = 1263 × 20 = $25,260		After-tax cash value = $24,200	After-tax investment accumulation = $30,184.36

Another Example

Your life insurance agent calls you and says "Janice, 1 have a great deal for you. You have an old whole life policy for $54,000 of coverage which has a cash value of $11,000. If you cancel this policy, take the $11,000 and buy this other policy, I can make you two guarantees. First, I can *guarantee* you that you'll never pay another penny in life insurance premiums, and you'll still have $54,000 in coverage. Second, I can guarantee you that at age 65 you'll have $40,000 in an investment fund which will be available to you. You can't miss!"

Should Janice take the "deal" or pass it up? To answer, Janice will have to do some number crunching. Two options can be examined. Option one is to take the agent's deal, which is really buying a single premium policy. If Janice does this she'll have $54,000 of protection unti age 65, at which time she can surrender the policy and receive $40,000. Taxes will be paid on the difference between the $40,000 and what Janice paid, $11,000. Assuming a 28 percent tax bracket, the after tax surrender value would be:

$$\$40,000 - (\$40,000 - \$11,000) \times .28 = \underline{\$31,880}.$$

Option two is to invest the $11,000, but to use this investment fund to pay premiums each year for a term policy for $54,000 of coverage. Table 6-20 shows how this option would work out. At the end of the period, Janice would have *$22,815.45* (after taxes) in the investment fund. Based on these numbers, Janice should take the agent's deal.

There are many possible combinations of comparing the switching of life insurance policies. Just remember to compare apples and apples. Make sure the policies being compared provide the same coverage.

HELP IN BUYING LIFE INSURANCE

Several services offer cost comparisons between life insurance policies. A web search on "life insurance quotes" reveals several sites that provide premium quotes.

These services are quick, easy ways for consumers to obtain information about life insurance companies, but they should be used cautiously. Little information is given by the services on policy provisions. Side-by- side comparisons are not always offered.

Help of a different sort is available from the National Insurance Consumer Organization (N.I.C.O.). NICO will do a side- by-side comparison of a cash value policy to a term policy using the "Linton Yield" method (see "Another Way of Analyzing Policies—the Linton Yield). The consumer must provide the appropriate policy information to NICO.

Table 6-20   Analyzing Janice's options.

Age	Annual Cost of $54,000 of Term Protection		After-tax Side Investment Fund if Buy Term
45	$156	$11,000.00 − $156 = $10,844.00	$10,844.00 × 1.06 = $11,495.00
46	167	11,495.00 − 167 = 11,328.00	11,328.00 × 1.06 = 12,007.68
47	181	12,007.68 − 181 = 11,828.68	11,828.68 × 1.06 = 12,536.28
48	199	12,536.28 − 199 = 12,337.28	12337.28 × 1.06 = 13,077.52
49	219	13,077.52 − 219 = 12,858.52	12,858.52 × 1.06 = 13,630.03
50	233	13,630.03 − 233 = 13,397.03	13,397.03 × 1.06 = 14,200.85
51	249	14,200.85 − 249 = 13,951.85	13,951.85 × 1.06 = 14,788.96
52	267	14,788.96 − 267 = 14,521.96	14,521.96 × 1.06 = 15,393.28
53	289	15,393.28 − 289 = 15,104.28	15,104.28 × 1.06 = 16,010.53
54	310	16,010.53 − 310 = 15,700.53	15,700.53 × 1.06 = 16,642.57
55	339	16,642.57 − 339 = 16,303.57	16,303.57 × 1.06 = 17,281.78
56	367	17,281.78 − 367 = 16,914.78	16,914.78 × 1.06 = 17,929.67
57	400	17,929.67 − 400 = 17,529.67	17,529.67 × 1.06 = 18,581.45
58	437	18,581.45 − 437 = 18,144.45	18,144.45 × 1.06 = 19,233.11
59	484	19,233 11 − 484 = 18,749 11	18 749 11 × 1 06 = 19 874 06
60	524	19,874.06 − 524 = 19,350.06	19,350.06 × 1.06 = 20,511.06
61	572	20,511.06 − 572 = 19,939.06	19,939.06 × 1.06 = 21,135.41
62	627	21,135.41 − 627 = 20,508.41	20,508.41 × 1.06 = 21,738.91
63	704	21,738.91 − 704 = 21,034.91	21,034.91 × 1.06 = 22,297.01
64	773	22,297.01 − 773 = 21,524.01	21,524.01 × 1.06 = 22,815.45

Investment fund accumulation of $22,815.45 beginning at age 65.

Then analyze the potential investment funds which could be developed with each.

The Bottom Line

Do a side-by-side comparison to evaluate switching life insurance policies.

19. Are Participating Policies Better Than Non-Participating Policies?

As already discussed, one way that life insurance policies differ is whether they are participating or non-participating policies. Owners of participating policies participate in, or share in, the investment fortunes of the life insurance company. The participation comes in the form of dividends which are credited to the policyholder. Dividends can be directly returned to the policyholder, can be kept by the company to earn interest, or can be used to purchase paid-up insurance.

For the privilege to participate in the investment fortunes of the life insurance company premiums for participating policies will be higher than premiums for non-participating policies. This raises the obvious question: Is it better for the life insurance consumer to pay higher premiums and participate in the dividend earnings of the life insurance company or is it better for the life insurance consumer to buy a non-participating policy, pay lower premiums and invest, the saved money elsewhere?

The only way this question can be answered is to compare the track records of both options. To date, the evidence seems to be on the side of participating policies. A study by Myers and Pritchett compared paying higher participating policy premiums and earning dividends versus paying lower non-participating policy premiums and investing elsewhere.[12] They found that, on average, buying participating policies was the wiser choice over the study period (1959–1979) as long as the participating policy was not surrendered before 10 years. The dividend returns earned by participating policies exceeded any investment returns which could have been earned by investing the difference between the participating policy premiums and the non-participating policy premiums. One reason may be the large investment portfolios of life insurance companies which allow for a diversity of investments which can't be matched by the individual.

Another advantage of participating policies is that they provide a form of inflation protection. The schedule of premiums and cash values on non-participating policies is fixed. If future inflation rates are higher than expected by the life insurance company, then the cash values won't be worth as much in terms of real purchasing power. However, with participating policies, higher than expected inflation rates will result in higher than expected dividends, thereby reducing the net premiums of the participating policy. Although cash values won't increase, policyholders will receive greater cash values per dollar of net premiums.

The Bottom Line

Current evidence indicates that participating policies are "better buys" than non-participating policies.

---

[12]Phyllis S. Myers and S. Travis Pritchett, "Rate of Return on Differential Premiums for Selected Participating Life Insurance Contracts," *Journal of Risk and Insurance,* Vol. 50, No. 4, December 1983, pp. 569–586.

20. One More Time—Which Policy Is Best for You?

All the discussion about life insurance policies boils down to one simple distinction. There are really only two kinds of life insurance policies, pure protection policies, and policies which provide protection and an investment fund. Term policies are the only kind of pure protection policies, whereas whole life, endowment, universal life, and single premium life are all examples of protection and investment policies.

For the person who wants to spend as little as possible on life insurance, especially during the child rearing years, and who wants to manage his own investment outside of a life insurance company, then term insurance is the best choice. Decreasing term provides a decreasing amount of protection over time.

For the person who wants to use life insurance for protection and as a means of forced savings, then whole life, endowment, universal life, and single premium life should be considered. In order of the degree of forced savings, whole life provides the least, followed by universal life, endowment, and single premium life. One disadvantage, however, of these forced savings plans is that the funds may not be as easily accessible as funds in other investments. For example, many investments provide easy access via checks (e.g., money market funds at brokerage houses, checking accounts), yet the investment funds in life insurance policies don't have this option. Also, a 10 percent penalty is imposed on withdrawals from universal life and single premium life policies if the insured is under age 59½.

Table 6-21 summarizes the major features of alternative life insurance policies.

C O N S U M E R   T O P I C

CONSUMERS UNION'S POLICY RATINGS

Most consumers don't have the time to collect price information on more than a handful of life insurance companies. Fortunately, a consumer research organization, called Consumers Union, periodically collects information on a large number of life insurance policies, including term, whole life, and universal life policies, and calculates the policies' interest adjusted net costs. The results are published in Consumer Unions' monthly magazine, *Consumer Reports*.

Table 6-21   Life insurance policies—a wrap-up.

Type	Premiums	Protection	Investment Fund	Investment Risk	Best for:
Term	Low first, gradually rise over time	Constant protection	None	—	Young consumers who do own investing.
Decreasing term	Low and constant	Decreasing protection	None	—	Mortgage protection.
Whole life	Moderate size and constant	Constant protection	Yes, but access only if cancel.	Guaranteed investment fund. Non-par policies subject to erosion by high inflation.	Long term protection with small forced savings.
Endowment	High and constant	Constent protection	Yes, can receive if live to certain age.	Guaranteed investment fund. Non-par policies subject to erosion by high inflation.	Protection until retirement with high forced savings.
Universal life	Variable depending on amount to investment fund	Can be constant protection or variable protection	Yes, can access if cancel policy or can add to death benefit.	Low guaranteed fund, but variable current investment fund.	Consumers wanting flexibility in protection and payments, and wanting variable investment fund.
Single premium life	One very large premium.	Can be constant protection or variable protection	Yes, can access if cancel policy or can add to death benefit.	Low guaranteed fund, but variable current investment fund.	Very few consumers.

The Bottom Line

Compare life insurance policies on the basis of their protection and investment characteristics.

21 Do You Need Life Insurance After the Kids Are Gone?

Earlier in this chapter we argued that the main purpose of life insurance is to insure that income will be provided to financial dependents of the insured in the event that the insured dies. The greatest need for life insurance occurs during the child rearing years.

Yet the basic principle of life insurance need can be applied anytime during the individual's life. For example, suppose John is unmarried, has no children, yet has an elderly mother who lives with him and is financially dependent on John. John may want to purchase life insurance to insure that, in the event of his death, his mother could continue living the standard of living that John has provided her.

Life Insurance After the Kids Leave but Before Retirement

Life insurance requirements after the children become financially independent usually decline substantially. The question to be addressed is: If the insured dies, will the spouse have enough income to maintain the desired standard of living? More life insurance will be needed if the spouse doesn't work; less or maybe no life insurance will be needed if the spouse works.

Table 6-22 shows an example of a life insurance calculation for a couple aged 50 after children have become financially independent. The

Table 6-22 Life insurance requirements after kids, but before retirement (expense approach)

Year	Mary's age	Mary's expenses	Property taxes	SS Survivor-ship	Net expenses	PVF (3%)	PV
1	50	$27,837	$4,248	$ 0	$32,085	1.0000	$ 32,085
2	51	$27,837	$4,248	$ 0	$32,085	0.9709	$ 31,150
3	52	$27,837	$4,248	$ 0	$32,085	0.9426	$ 30,243
4	53	$27,837	$4,248	$ 0	$32,085	0.9151	$ 29,362
5	54	$27,837	$4,248	$ 0	$32,085	0.8885	$ 28,507
6	55	$27,837	$4,248	$ 0	$32,085	0.8626	$ 27,677
7	56	$27,837	$4,248	$ 0	$32,085	0.8375	$ 26,871
8	57	$27,837	$4,248	$ 0	$32,085	0.8131	$ 26,088
9	58	$27,837	$4,248	$18,612	$13,473	0.7894	$ 10,636
10	59	$27,837	$4,248	$18,612	$13,473	0.7664	$ 10,326
11	60	$27,837	$4,248	$18,612	$13,473	0.7441	$ 10,025
12	61	$27,837	$4,248	$18,612	$13,473	0.7224	$ 9,733
13	62	$27,837	$4,248	$18,612	$13,473	0.7014	$ 9,450
14	63	$27,837	$4,248	$18,612	$13,473	0.6810	$ 9,174
15	64	$27,837	$4,248	$18,612	$13,473	0.6611	$ 8,907
						Sum	$300,235
					Step 6. Mortgage balance at 52		$ 80,000
						Total	**$380,235**

example assumes one spouse works and earns $100,000 and the other spouse doesn't work. Since the children are gone, homemaker expenses are ignored. Social Security survivor benefits for a spouse with no children under age 18 don't begin until the spouse is 60. In this example, if the spouse worked and earned at least $32,085 annually, then the life insurance requirement would only equal the mortgage balance.

Life Insurance During Retirement

Income needs of individuals during retirement are best handled by financial retirement planning (see the chapter on Retirement Planning). Nevertheless, in the case of a husband and wife, for example, we can ask our standard life insurance question: if one spouse were to die, would the financial position of the other spouse be affected adversely? If a financial gap is left by the death of a spouse, then life insurance can fill the gap.

To determine if a gap is left, estimate the expenses of the surviving spouse and subtract estimates of the surviving spouse's income. The surviving spouse's income would include income from the deceased spouse's pension, the surviving spouse's pension, Social Security, and any labor income or annual investment earnings. Do this calculation for both the husband and the wife.

LIFE INSURANCE AND ESTATES

Does life insurance play a role in settling the estate of a deceased person? Life insurance can play two roles. First, it can be used as a source of liquid (cash) funds for payment of estate taxes. Estate taxes are taxes which must be paid when an individual dies and the individual's estate (wealth) is passed to inheritors. However, for most families estate taxes will be small, or zero, because an entire estate can be passed tax-free to a spouse. Also, in 2013, estates under $5.25 million in value escape all estate taxes.

A second role that life insurance can play in estate planning is in the following situation. Suppose Sarah and George Rogers' main estate is a large illiquid asset such as a farm, and the farm is difficult to subdivide. The Rogers have several children. They want to pass the farm to one child, but provide comparable amounts of cash to the other children. Enough life insurance would be bought to provide those amounts of cash.

The Bottom Line

After the children leave home and become financially independent, life insurance needs are reduced. Estimate remaining life insurance needs by examining the income of the spouse if the insured were to die.

22. Is the Fine Print of Life Insurance Policies Important?

The major elements of life insurance policies which we've already discussed are face value amount, premium, cash value (or investment fund), dividends, and death benefit. You should be thoroughly familiar with these names and their meanings by now.

But when you examine a life insurance policy you'll be hit with more terminology in the contract's *policy provisions*—the so-called "fine print." The policy provisions spell out the details of the life insurance policy. The purpose of this section is to define the meaning of these provisions and to tell you which ones are worth having (and paying for!).

Waiver of Premium

This is an important policy provision. It means that premiums don't have to be paid (yet the policy remains in force) if the insured becomes totally disabled before a specified age (e.g., 65) and remains disabled for at least six months. Having the waiver of premium provision will mean modestly higher premiums, but it's worth it.

DISABILITY

Pay close attention to the policy's definition of *disability*. Generally the definition will be liberal in the first few years of the policy, meaning that the inability to perform your current job is enough to be classified as "totally disabled." Thereafter, the definition may switch to a more restrictive one, where total disability means the inability to do any job for which you are reasonably trained, or maybe simply any job.

Convertibility

The convertibility option allows the buyer of a term policy to later convert it to a whole life policy. Generally this option must be exercised within a limited number of years.

The convertibility option is wise for an insurance buyer who really wants whole life insurance, can only afford term insurance now, but who will be able to afford whole life premiums later. However, for a consumer who has evaluated term and whole life and who favors term, there is no need to pay for the convertibility option.

Accidental Death Benefit

If this provision is present in the policy, it means that the face value amount paid to beneficiaries will be double or triple the stated amount if the insured dies from an accident (e.g., auto accident) than if the insured dies in some other way (e.g., an illness). An explicit extra premium will be charged for this provision.

Adding an accidental death benefit is not recommended. Why should the income requirements of the beneficiaries be higher if the insured died accidentally than if the insured died in some other way! If anything, the income needs would be higher in the case of death by a lingering illness where medical costs would be higher.

Guaranteed Insurability

This provision allows the policyholder to buy additional life insurance at certain specified future dates without evidence of insurability, that is, without undergoing new medical exams. The maximum amount which can be purchased each time is called the *option amount*. An explicit additional premium will be charged for this provision.

OPTION AMOUNT

Guaranteed insurability is a good idea for young consumers who (1) may want to add coverage due to inflation (see *Inflation Again! Life Insurance Requirements as the Insured Lives*) or due to added beneficiaries, and (2) who think their health will deteriorate to below the average with age. For consumers who don't anticipate needing more protection, or who believe their health status will be maintained or will improve, the guaranteed insurability provision is not necessary.

Reinstatement Time Limit

This provision states the maximum length of time (in years) before which a lapsed policy can be reinstated without evidence of insurability. A lapsed policy is one where the consumer has stopped making premium payments and protection has stopped. Longer reinstatement time limits are obviously more favorable to consumers.

Incontestability Time Limit

This is the length of time after which the life insurance company cannot challenge information (about age or health status, for example) which the insured provided. After this time period, the company cannot challenge, and possibly cancel, the policy if it is found that the insured provided inaccurate information. Shorter incontestability time limits benefit consumers.

Suicide Time Limit

The suicide time limit is the number of years before which the policy won't pay because of suicide by the insured. Again, shorter suicide time limits are more favorable to consumers.

Premiums Can Be Reduced

Some policies include a provision stating that premiums can be reduced in the future if mortality costs fall.

Smoker/Non-Smoker Status

Most policies today reduce premiums if the insured is certified as being a non-smoker.

Minimum Dividend Interest Rate

If the policy is participating, a minimum, interest rate will be guaranteed to be paid on dividends if dividends are left to be invested by the company.

Loan Provisions

If the policy has a loan option, these provisions will state the conditions under which loans can be made, the interest rate charged and, for UL and SPL policies, the implications of the loan for the interest rate paid on the investment fund.

Guaranteed and Current Investment Interest Rate

For UL and SPL policies, a minimum guaranteed interest rate will be stated for the investment fund as well as a variable current rate.

Settlement Options

These provisions refer to the features and options available to the beneficiaries for receiving the death benefit in the event of death of the insured. Two common options are to receive the death benefit in a lump sum and to receive the death benefit in monthly checks, with the balance invested by the life insurance company. In the case of the latter option, an important feature is the minimum interest rate the company guarantees to pay on the remaining balance.

The Bottom Line

The "fine print" of life insurance policies describes provisions which can affect the cost, face value amount, loans, and settlement options of the policy.

23. Why Do Prices of Life Insurance Policies Differ?

Let's say you look in the yellow pages and dial the offices of ten different insurance agents. If you ask each agent for the premium cost of their best term policy, you'll likely get ten different answers. The same is true if you ask for their best whole life policy; or their best universal life policy. In other words, the prices of the same kind of life insurance policy vary from company to company. Why?

One reason may be that costs of companies vary, and that high cost companies pass along their higher costs to consumers. This might make sense for a short time, but it wouldn't make for a logical explanation over a longer time period. Why would consumers continue to buy from a high cost company if they could get the same policy from another company at a lower cost?

The answer to this puzzle seems to be in the words "same policy." As the previous section showed, life insurance policies are complex contracts which contain many provisions. Some of the provisions, like waiver of premium, the accidental death benefit, and guaranteed insurability, carry explicit additional charges which the consumer can see. But other provisions, like the type and number of settlement options, the loan provisions, and a provision for possibly reducing premiums, are not separately priced by life insurance companies. So, just like houses which have better characteristics are expected to cost more, life insurance policies which have better provisions are expected to cost more.

There's another reason why life insurance policies vary in cost. It seems logical that consumers of life insurance policies will be concerned about the risk involved with the life insurance company—risk in terms of the company not being able to pay claims. Therefore, consumers may be willing to pay more for a policy from a company which they consider "less risky." Risk may be measured by a number of factors, such as company size (larger companies are less risky) and the "Best" rating for the company (see *Rating Life Insurance Companies*).

C O N S U M E R   T O P I C

RATING LIFE INSURANCE COMPANIES

The A. M Best Company is a publisher of financial and policy information about life insurance companies. Best uses this information to publish annual ratings of the financial quality of life insurance companies. There arc six levels to the rating system:

A+ — Superior
A — Excellent
B+ — Very Good
B — Good
C+ — Fairly Good
C — Good

Consumers can use this rating system to judge the financial quality of a company and the risk that a claim won't be paid. Most companies are rated A or A+. Ask your insurance agent to provide the Best's rating for the life insurance companies you are considering.

A study by Walden seems to support the theories about why life insurance policy costs vary.[13] The study analyzed 59 whole life policies issued in 1982. The study found that policy characteristics and risk characteristics of the company could largely explain differences in policy costs, and company expenses were *not* related to policy *costs*. For example, policies which guarantee a high minimum interest rate on the settlement options and policies which state that premiums can be reduced were more expensive. Also, policies issued by companies with more assets and with a Best rating of A+ were more expensive.

The Bottom Line

Life insurance policies with characteristics more favorable to the policyholder will be more expensive. Also, life insurance policies issued by companies with a better financial rating will be more expensive. _____

24. Credit Life Insurance: Rip-Off or Convenience?

Credit life insurance is life insurance purchased in connection with purchase of a consumer durable good (e.g., appliance, furniture) using debt. Credit life is usually structured as decreasing term insurance where the face value amount declines over time to match the declining debt balance. If the insured dies, the face value of the credit life policy is used to pay the remaining debt owed on the loan.

Credit life insurance is usually much more expensive than other life insurance. Some estimates indicate that it is at least twice as expensive (Rubin[14]). One reason is that often a medical exam is not required to obtain credit life insurance. Credit life insurance is usually available to anyone between 18 and 65. Thus, credit life insurance would be expected to be more costly due to its generous insurability provisions. Another reason for credit life insurance's higher premiums is that it is convenient—it is available at the time the consumer durable good is purchased and in the precise amount necessary to cover the loan.

You should consider conventional life insurance coverage as an alternative to credit life insurance. Your existing life insurance may already be adequate to cover the credit payments associated with the durable good loan. If not, a decreasing term insurance rider can often

---

[13]Walden, Michael L., "The Whole Life insurance Policy as an Options Package: An Empirical Investigation." *Journal of Risk and Insurance,* Vol. 52, 1, March 1985, pp. 44–58.

[14]Harvey W. Rubin, "Credit Life Insurance and Its Alternatives," *The Journal of Consumer Affairs,* Vol, 12, No. 1, Summer 1978, pp. 145–153.

be added to existing life insurance coverage to cover the durable good debt payments.

The Bottom One

Credit life insurance is easy and convenient to purchase, but is much more costly than other kinds of life insurance. You'll save money by using standard kinds of life insurance to insure consumer credit debt payments.

25. Do Life Insurance Policies Save You Taxes?

This is a summary section, because the tax implications of life insurance policies have been discussed in many of the previous sections.

Table 6-23 summarizes the tax implications of life insurance policies. There are currently two major tax advantages of life insurance policies. First, no income tax is paid on the death benefit, although in some cases an estate tax is paid. The easiest way to avoid the estate tax is to name your spouse as the beneficiary.

The second big tax advantage is that the investment fund in cash value policies (whole life, endowment, universal life, single premium life) is not taxed while left untapped. That is, the investment fund can earn interest tax-free. This is similar to one aspect of Individual Retirement Accounts (IRAs) and is a big plus for life insurance policies. Tax is ultimately paid if the policy is surrendered, but in the meantime, money which would have been paid in taxes is left to earn interest and accumulate. It's always better to pay taxes later rather than sooner. Furthermore, the investment fund will never be taxed if it is included as part of the death benefit when the insured dies. This option is available with universal life and single premium life policies.

The Bottom Line

The two major tax advantages to life insurance policies are (1) no taxes are paid on death benefits, and (2) interest earned on policies with investment funds is not taxed while left untouched.

WORDS AND CONCEPTS YOU SHOULD KNOW

Risk
Self-insurance
Risk-pooling
The insured
Beneficiaries
Face value
Financial dependents
Income Approach
Expense Approach
Social Security survivors benefits
Homemaker expenses
Inflation effect
Term effect
Mortality table
Reserves
Cash value
Term insurance
Non-participating policy
Participating policy
Dividends
Net premiums
Traditional cost method
Interest adjusted net cost
Interest adjusted net cost index
Annual, renewable term
N-level term
Convertible term
Whole life insurance
Surrender cost

Policy loan
Limited pay whole life
Life paid up at 65
Modified whole life
Graded premium whole life
Indexed whole life
Economatic whole life
Side-by-side comparison
Buy term and invest the difference
Endowment life insurance
Universal life insurance
"Option A"
"Option B"
Loads
Single premium life insurance
Decreasing term life insurance
Group policies
Policy provisions
Waiver of premium
Convertibility
Accidentel death benefit
Guaranteed insurability
Reinstatement time limit
Incontestability time limit
Suicide time limit
Settlement options
Best rating
Credit life insurance

LIFE INSURANCE—A SUMMARY

1. Life insurance
   - is protection against risk of death,
   - works by a pooling of risk.
   - Three questions should be addressed:
     (a) who needs it,
     (b) how much is needed, and
     (c) what kind of policy is needed?

2. Who needs life insurance?
   - Top priority to income earners who have financial dependents.
   - House-husbands and housewives also.
   - Not children.

3. Calculating the amount of life insurance:
   - income approach: face value amount is present value of insured's future income not replaced by Social Security or other family savings;
   - expense approach: face value amount is present value of beneficiary's future expenses not replaced by Social Security or other family savings or income;
   - use real dollars and a real discount rate;
   - recalculate at least every five years to account for family changes and inflation.

4. Life insurance premiums are calculated so that the average policyholder costs equal the average policyholder benefits. Policies with level premiums accumulate reserves in the early years which are used to pay greater costs in the later years.

5. Term insurance is pure insurance protections. Premiums rise with the insured's age to reflect the increasing probability of death. Use the interest-adjusted net cost to compare term policies. Term is generally the cheapest protection except during retirement.

6. Whole life insurance provides protection with annual premiums which are the same each year. A reserve, or cash value, is developed, and the policyholder receives the cash value if the policy is cancelled.

7. Use the interest-adjusted net cost or the "side-by-side comparison" to compare term and whole life policies.

8. Endowment policies pay the face value amount if the insured dies or if the insured lives to a certain age (e.g., 65). Endowment policy premiums are very high.

9. Universal life insurance is a combination of protection and an investment fund. The face value amount, premiums, and investment fund are all flexible. The death benefit can include or exclude the investment fund. Use a side-by-side comparison to evaluate universal life policies.

10. Buyers of single premium life insurance pay one large premium for the policy at the beginning of the coverage term. Single premium life insurance policies also accumulate an investment fund.

11. Decreasing term policies have constant premiums but declining face value with time. Decreasing term policies are bought for mortgage protection.

12. Group life insurance policies are often cheaper but may not provide adequate protection.

13. Do a side-by-side comparison to evaluate switching life insurance policies.

14. Participating policies have higher premiums but pay dividends to the policyholder. Evidence shows that participating policies are better than buying non-participating policies and "investing the difference."

15. Life insurance is most needed during the child rearing years. Use the "expense approach" to decide how much life insurance is needed after the children are financially independent.

16. The fine print of policies describes important provisions, such as the conditions under which premiums arc waived, convertibility, guaranteed insurability, loan provisions, and settlement options.

17. Policies which contain more provisions favorable to the consumer, and policies issued by more financially secure companies have higher costs.

18. Credit life insurance insures that consumer debt payments will be made if the insured dies. Credit life insurance is convenient and easily available, but also very expensive.

19. Life insurance has two major tax benefits:
   • death benefits are not taxed, and
   • interest is accumulated tax-free in cash-value policies.

DISCUSSION QUESTIONS

1. Why does anyone need life insurance? Why can't a family simply save money to cover the risk of an income earner dying?

2. Should an unmarried college student with no financial dependents buy life insurance?

3. Skeptical Sam says, "The chances of me dying this year are so small. Why should I buy life insurance?" What reply would you give to Sam?

4. In calculating the amount of life insurance needed by the expense approach, why not simply sum the future net expenses of the family?

5. What problems does inflation cause for life insurance calculations, and how are those problems handled?

6. How often should a family's life insurance face value amount be re-calculated, and why?

7. If the insured doesn't die during the life insurance term, therefore meaning that the beneficiaries collect nothing, is life insurance a wasteful expenditure?

8. Are term policies, which don't have an investment fund built-in, not as good as cash-value or investment fund policies?

9. In calculating the cost of a life insurance policy, what's wrong with simply adding the premiums and subtracting the dividend sum and the cash value?

10. Describe how the interest-adjusted net cost and interest-adjusted net cost index are calculated.

11. How can whole life policies charge a constant premium each year when mortality costs rise with age?

12. Is a whole life policy which is fully paid-up in twenty years "cheaper" than a whole life policy which the insured must pay for every year?

13. Name some advantages and some "cautions" of universal life policies.

14. Is life insurance needed after the children are financially independent?

15. Is life insurance a tax shelter?

16. What are the advantages and disadvantages of credit life insurance?

17. Why do life insurance policy prices vary?

PROBLEMS

1. The Everett family is composed of Ed, the father, age 35, Beth, the mother, age 30, and two children, Tiffany, age 8, and Ronnie, age 5. Both Beth and Ed work in the marketplace and each earns $60,000 annually. Tiffany and Ronnie plan to attend public college. The Everett's have a $140,000 mortgage balance and pay $2,400 yearly in property taxes.

   The Everetts want to consider life insurance for the child-rearing years (until Ronnie is out of college).

   (a) Find the life insurance face value amount for Ed and for Beth by the income approach. Use a 3 percent discount rate and assume 100 percent replacement.

   (b) Find the life insurance face value amount for Ed by the expense approach. Use a 3 percent discount rate. Assume college expenses rise 2 percent annually in real terms.

2. It is now five years later. The Everetts now owe $120,000 on their home mortgage. Find the life insurance face value amount for Beth by the income approach assuming the inflation rate has been 5 percent a year.

3. Three life insurance policies follow, a term policy, a whole life policy, and universal life policy. Each is for $100,000 in face value.

   Do side-by-side comparisons to determine which policy is best assuming you can earn a 5 percent after-tax interest rate on invested funds and your tax bracket is 28 percent.

Age	Term --- Term	Premiums	Whole Life --- Dividends	Cash Value	Premiums	Universal life --- Surrender-Investment Value	Death Benefit
35	$165	$1,250	$ 0	$ 0	$2,100	$ 300	$100,000
36	170	1,250	160	0	2,100	300	100,000
37	175	1,250	200	500	2,100	2,500	100,000
38	177	1,250	240	1,500	2,100	4,000	100,000
39	180	1,250	280	2,500	2,100	6,000	100,000
40	183	1,250	320	3,500	2,100	8,000	100,000
41	190	1,250	380	4,500	2,100	10,000	100,000
42	195	1,250	420	6,000	2,100	13,000	100,000
43	200	1,250	470	8,000	2,100	17,000	100,000
44	230	1,250	500	10,000	2,100	20,000	100,000
45	260	1,250	570	11,000	2,100	22,000	100,000
46	300	1,250	620	12,000	2,100	26,000	100,000
47	340	1,250	700	12,750	2,100	28,000	100,000
48	370	1,250	770	13,500	2,100	31,000	100,000
49	420	1,250	900	14,250	2,100	33,000	100,000
50	440	1,250	1,000	15,000	2,100	35,000	100,000

4. Calculate the interest-adjusted net cost and the interest-adjusted net cost index for the term policy in problem 3.

5. Calculate the interest-adjusted net cost and the interest-adjusted net cost index for the whole life policy in problem 3.

6. You can buy $ 100,000 in coverage at age 35 with a single premium life policy for $18,000. Is this a better buy than the term policy in problem 3?

7. You bought the whole life policy in problem 3 at age 35. You are now age 40. Should you cancel the whole life policy and buy the term policy?

CHAPTER 7

Health, Property, and Auto Insurance

Introduction

Insurance is now not new to you. You've already plowed your way (hopefully successfully) through life insurance. You'll now apply many of the same principles you learned with life insurance to the new topic of health, property, and auto insurance.

But there are some major differences between this chapter and life insurance. Perhaps the biggest difference is one of emphasis. In life insurance we spent much time deciding how to calculate how much life insurance is needed. We designed two fairly precise approaches to this calculation.

Unfortunately, we can't always be as precise in this chapter, particularly with respect to health insurance. How on earth can we estimate what our future health expenses will be, especially with medical technology changing so rapidly? An operation that can't be performed today may be feasible in the future, but at what cost? Instead of making elaborate calculations for expected health expenses, the principle we'll employ is to insure for large and catastrophic expenses but self-insure for small expenses.

Another way that this chapter will differ from life insurance is in the attention to policy provisions and characteristics. Policy provisions and characteristics are much more important for health, property, and auto insurance than for life insurance, particularly in regard to when the policy will pay. With life insurance, the determination of whether the policy will pay is very simple—the policy pays if the insured dies. With health, property, and auto insurance, there are many more "gray" areas. For example, will your health insurance policy pay for all nursing home care or only for nursing home care which follows a hospital stay? Why might your health insurance policy pay for a broken leg you suffered in a fall down the stairs but not for a broken leg you suffered while skydiving? The provisions and characteristics of health, property, and auto insurance policies will define when the policy will pay, so we will pay much more attention to them here than we did in the life insurance topic.

In this chapter you'll learn about the advantages of deductibles and co-insurance, about the very important definitions of "accident" and "disability," and about what government health insurance plans (Medicaid and Medicare) will and will not pay. After studying this chapter, you'll be ready to make intelligent decisions about health, property, and auto insurance.

1. What Should You Insure?

PURE RISK

Risks can be categorized into two types, pure risks and speculative risks. Pure risks are risks in which only a loss can result if the risk occurs. Being injured in an auto accident is an example of a pure risk. Nothing good can happen from an auto accident. At best your car will be repaired to its state before the accident and any physical injuries to you will be treated and you will be rehabilitated. People try to avoid auto accidents because they are pure risks— because only losses can result.

SPECULATIVE RISK

In comparison, if you face a speculative risk, the result can be either a loss or a gain. The best example of a speculative risk is gambling. Say you buy $5 of lottery tickets. One outcome is that none of your tickets wins and you lose $5. The other outcome is that one or more of your tickets win and you win a prize much greater than $5.

Another example of a speculative risk is in investing. Say you buy a share of stock for $20. You face speculative risk because there's some chance that the stock's price will rise (and you will gain) and there's some chance that the stock's price will fall (and you will lose).

In this chapter we'll only be concerned about insurance for pure risks. Later in the chapter on investing you'll learn some techniques for "insuring" against speculative risks in investments. As far as gambling is concerned, you're on your own for finding ways to improve your odds and cut your losses in the lottery.

Classification of Pure Risks

Each of us faces a multitude of pure risks in our everyday living. The risks range from the minor and trivial, such as the risk of stubbing a toe or losing a pencil, to the serious and severe, such as the risk of injury from an auto accident or the risk of death. Pure risks therefore differ by the size of their potential loss.

SEVERITY OF LOSS

FREQUENCY

Pure risks also differ by their frequency. For some risks there is only a very small chance that they will occur. Being struck by lightning, suffering losses from an earthquake (except in California) and misplacing and losing your shoes are examples. For other risks there is a much greater chance that they will happen. Being involved in an auto accident and losing an umbrella are examples of more frequent risks.

We can therefore consider pure risks on the basis of two dimensions, severity of loss and frequency of occurrence. Figure 7-1 illustrates these dimensions and gives examples of risks classified by severity and frequency. Losing a pencil is a frequent occurrence but it is a small loss. In contrast, if you tried to jump the Grand Canyon on a motorcycle, death is highly likely and the severity is obviously great.

Figure 7-1. Classification of pure risks.

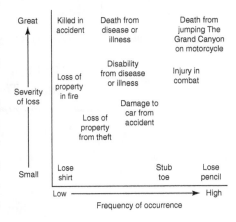

What to Do about Pure Risks

AVOID RISK

There are four options the consumer can follow in addressing pure risks. One option is to *avoid the risk*. For some risks this is a reasonable option, for other risks it's not. For example, it's reasonable for most consumers to avoid death from an attempt to jump the Grand Canyon on a motorcycle by simply not attempting this feat. Also, a person can avoid the risk of death in combat by not joining the military. But in our modern society, it's not reasonable for most of us to avoid driving a car or to avoid owning private property.

A second option is to try to reduce the risk. For example, drive defensively to reduce the chance of an auto accident, install a home security system to reduce the chance of theft, and eat healthy foods and get regular exercise to reduce the chance of death from disease or illness.

SELF-INSURE

The problem with this option is that even with these efforts, the risks cannot be reduced to zero. Careful drivers still have accidents, homes with security systems are still burglarized, and healthy people still get diseases and illnesses. A third option for addressing pure risks is self-insurance. Set aside small amounts of money each month into a separate savings account, and then dip into this savings to replace losses when they occur. This option is fine (and, in fact, is recommended as you will see) for small potential losses. But it's impossible for most consumers to build up enough savings to replace their house if it burned down or to pay the medical bills in the case of a serious and prolonged illness. So self insurance won't work for catastrophic losses.

BUY INSURANCE

The fourth option for addressing pure risks is to *buy insurance*. With insurance, the consumer pays a relatively small periodic amount, and in exchange, the insurance pays for the loss if a loss occurs.

Insurance on What?

We can use a simple rule to decide where to best spend our insurance dollars. *The rule is to buy insurance on those pure risks that have the highest expected loss.* The expected loss of a pure risk is simply the risk's frequency of occurrence multiplied by the risk's severity of loss:

$$\text{Expected loss} = \text{Frequency of occurrence} \times \text{Severity of Loss}$$

How do we measure frequency of occurrence and severity of loss? Frequency of occurrence can simply be measured as the chance, or probability, that the loss will occur. You may be tempted to measure severity of loss by the dollar amount of loss. But what is really meant by severity of loss is the value, or utility, to you of the loss. How this differs from the dollar amount of the loss is best explained with an example.

Say your car is worth $5,000 so the maximum property loss you would suffer if your car was "totaled" in an accident is $5,000. Let's also assume your annual income is $50,000, so that if personal injury to you from a car accident meant you were disabled and couldn't work for a year, your lost income is $50,000 (medical bills from the accident are ignored here). Is the severity of loss from the one year disability ten times ($50,000/$5,000 = 10) as great as the severity of loss from totaling your car?

The severity of loss from the one year disability is probably *greater* than ten times the severity of loss from totaling your car. Why? It's greater if consumers put more value, or utility, on the early dollars they earn than on the later dollars they earn. Early dollars are more valuable to consumers because those dollars are used to purchase necessities like food, clothing, and housing. This idea is in line with the notion that an additional dollar to a poor consumer is worth more than an additional dollar to a rich consumer. It's also in line with the concept of diminishing marginal utility (see *Why Is Your 10th Hot Dog Not as Good as Your First Hot Dog?*).

EARLY DOLLARS, LATE DOLLARS UTILS

Figure 7-2 illustrates a relationship between income and utility of income where "early" dollars are worth more than "later" dollars. Call the units for utility of income *"utils"* Notice that the reduction of income from $50,000 to $45,000 reduces the utility of income by one-half util. The reduction of income from $50,000 to $0 reduces utility by 13 utils, 26 times as much! This is because the loss of $50,000 dips into more of those early "higher-valued" dollars than does the loss of $5,000.

Figure 7-2. Total utility and income.

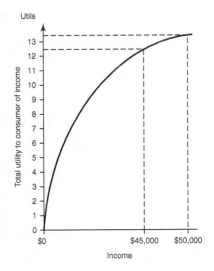

What does this all mean for calculation of severity of loss and expected loss? Look at Table 7-1. Suppose the probability of having your auto "totaled" is 10 percent and the auto's value is $5,000, and the probability of a year-long disability is ½ percent with a resulting loss of salary of $50,000. If the severity of loss is taken as the simple dollar value of loss, then panel A in Table 7-1 shows that the expected loss from the auto damage is greater than the expected loss from the year-long disability.

Table 7-1 Alternative calculations of expected loss.

A. For severity of loss, use simple dollar value of loss.

	Frequency of Occurrence	Severity of Loss	Expected Loss
Auto damage (totaled)	.10	$ 5,000	$500
Year-long disability	.005	$50,000	$250

B. For severity of loss, use consumer value of loss.

	Frequency of Occurrence	Severity of Loss	Expected Loss
Auto damage (totaled)	.10	$ 5,000	$500
Year-long disability	.005	$130,000	$650

However, if the consumer values the severity of loss of the yearlong disability at more than ten times the severity of loss from the auto damage, then panel B shows how the expected loss calculations are altered. In panel B, the consumer values the severity of loss from the year-long disability at twenty-six times the severity of loss from the auto damage. This is enough to make the expected loss from the year-long disability now greater than the expected loss from the auto damage. So, in this example, the consumer would want to buy disability insurance before buying auto damage (collision) insurance.

Some Practical Answers

Now you know, conceptually, how to calculate expected loss, and you know that you want to consider buying insurance on those pure risks having the highest expected loss.

Unfortunately, however, there's no easily available source for numbers on probability of occurrence for various risks and, even worse, there's no easy way to convert dollar value of loss to consumer utility of loss. Should we, therefore, throw out the concept of expected loss?

No, we still want to keep expected loss as a guide to selecting those risks to insure. The principle of expected loss, taken together with the knowledge that consumers value "early" dollars more than "later" dollars, suggests that you should first insure unavoidable risks with high severity of loss and high frequency of occurrence, next insure all other unavoidable risks with high severity of loss and, lastly, insure those unavoidable risks with moderate severity of loss and high frequency of occurrence. Following this suggestion, Table 7-2 lists pure risks in order of their priority for insurance.

RISK-BENEFIT ANALYSIS

**C
O
N
S
U
M
E
R**

**T
O
P
I
C**

The use of many products entails risk-taking. When you drive a car you run the risk of having an accident. When you ride a bike you run the risk of taking a fall. When you push a power lawn mower you run the risk of slipping and cutting a hand or foot.

Why then do we use products if, by doing so, we run the risk of an injury? The answer is simple—because we reap benefits from using the products. Think how much your mobility would be restricted if you didn't use a car for travel. Think how long it would take to mow a lawn without a power lawn mower. So we accept risks of harm and injury from using products because the products yield us benefits. Presumably we only use products where our value of the benefits exceed the expected losses from the risks.

What are the benefit-risk comparisons for some common consumer products and activities? Rachel Dardis, Gail Davenport, Janet Kurin, and Janet Marr attempted to answer this question for cars, ranges, cycling, skiing and clothing. The risk in clothing is the possibility of injury from burns if the garment catches fire.

For each product or activity the economists calculated a risk-benefit ratio. The risk-benefit ratio is the expected loss from using the product or performing the activity divided by the expected benefit. The expected loss equals the probability of a loss occurring multiplied by the severity of the loss. Losses include property damage, medical costs and income lost due to injuries. Where the loss included loss of life, the average present value of future earnings was used as the economic cost of loss of life. Potential losses from clothing (daywear, nightwear) are due to flammability.

The researchers calculated the risk-benefit ratios for ranges, clothing, skiing, and standard and intermediate sized autos to be very low—under .08, or 8 percent. This means that expected losses from these products and activities are all less than 8 percent of expected benefits. Therefore, it's logical for consumers to worry very little about risk from these products and activities. On the other hand, bicycles, compact autos when seat belts aren't used, and subcompact autos when seat belts aren't used have the highest risk-benefit ratios at between .12 and .20, or 12 to 20 percent. This means that for every $1 of benefits, consumers suffer an average of 12¢ to 20¢ in losses when using these products. Therefore, it makes sense for consumers to use seat belts when using subcompact and compact cars and to exercise caution in using bicycles.

Reference: Dardis, Rachel, Gail Davenport, Janet Kurin, and Janet Marr. "Risk-Benefit Analysis and the Determination of Acceptable Risk." *Journal of Consumer Affairs*, Vol. 17, No. 1, Summer 1983, pp. 38–56.

The Bottom Line

Reduce your exposure to risk by taking actions to reduce risk and by avoiding (as much as possible) activities with high expected losses. Buy insurance first on unavoidable pure risks that could result in large losses.

Table 7-2 Suggested priority for insuring pure risks.

Death (if have dependents)

Disability

Medical costs

Liability (e.g., you are sued for injury to someone else)

Property damage to home (if homeowner)

Property damage to possessions

Property damage to car

---

2. What Determines Insurance Prices?

PV OF PREMIUMS AND BENEFITS

The principle behind the pricing of health, property and auto insurance is exactly the same as the principle behind the pricing of life insurance. Premiums are charged to the insured such that the present value of those premiums equal the present value of the expected benefits received by the insured. Benefits include expected payments received by the insured plus services provided by the company. Expected payments received by the insured are based on the probabilities of various injuries, illnesses, and accidents occurring to the insured and the expected payments associated with each injury, illness, or accident. Services include commissions for agents, taxes, administrative expenses, profit, and margins to allow for unexpected claims.

An Example

Table 7-3 gives a simple example of how premiums for a health insurance policy would be calculated. The policy will pay a maximum of $100,000 annually for the insured who is a male aged 40. For simplicity, premiums are based on the likelihood of paying three levels of claims, 100 percent, 50 percent, and 10 percent. Column 3 shows the probability of paying each level of claim in each year. An insurance company would derive these probabilities using personal characteristics of the insured (such as age, sex, and health status) and experience of the company.

The calculation of equal annual premiums is done in the same way as for premiums of whole life policies (see *How Life Insurance Premiums Are Calculated*). Column 4 shows the calculation of expected claim costs each year, and the present value of these costs is calculated in column 5 using a three percent discount rate. Service costs are given in column 7. Service costs are typically highest in the first year when the policy is written. Column 8 is the present value of service costs. Column 9 is the sum of the present value of expected claims and service costs for each year.

Table 7-3 Calculation of Five Year Health Insurance Premiums, $100,000 maximum annual medical expense, male age 40.

(1) Year	(2) Claim Type	(3) Probability of Claim Occurring	(4) Expected Cost of Claim	(5) PV of Expected Claim Cost (3%)	(6) Survival Rate	(7) Service Costs	(8) PV of Service Costs	(9) PV of Expected Claims & Service Costs
1	100% Claim	.001	$100,000 × .001 = $100	$100 × .971 = $ 97.10	.999	$15	$15 × .971 = $14.57	$223.33 + $14.57 = $ 237.90
	50% Claim	.002	50,000 × .002 = 100	100 × .971 = 97.10				
	10% Claim	.003	10,000 × .003 = 30	30 × .971 = 29.13				
				$223.33				
2	100% Claim	.001	100,000 × .001 = 100	100 × .943 = 94.30	.999	5	5 × .943 = 4.72	216.89 + 4.72 = 221.61
	50% Claim	.002	50,000 × .002 = 100	100 × .943 = 94.30				
	10% Claim	.003	10,000 × .003 = 30	30 × .943 = 28.29				
				$216.89				
3	100% Claim	.001	100,000 × .001 = 100	100 × .915 = 91.50	.998	5	5 × .915 = 4.58	210.45 + 4.58 = 215.03
	50% Claim	.002	50,000 × .002 = 100	100 × .915 = 91.50				
	10% Claim	.003	10,000 × .003 = 30	30 × .915 = 27.45				
				$210.45				
4	100% Claim	.001	100,000 × .001 = 100	100 × .888 = 88.80	.998	5	5 × .888 = 4.44	257.52 + 4.44 = 162.96
	50% Claim	.003	50,000 × .003 = 150	150 × .888 = 133.20				
	10% Claim	.004	10,000 × .004 = 40	40 × .888 = 35.52				
				$257.52				
5	100% Claim	.001	100,000 × .001 = 100	100 × .863 = 86.30	.998	$5	5 × .863 = 4.32	250.27 + 4.32 = 254.59
	50% Claim	.003	50,000 × .003 = 150	150 × .863 = 129.45				
	10% Claim	.004	10,000 × .004 = 40	40 × .863 = 34.52				
				$250.27				

Single premium if paid at beginning of year 1: $ 1,191.09

"Probability scaled" sum of present value factors: $(.971 \times .999) + (.943 \times .999) + (.915 \times .998) + (.888 \times .998) + (.863 \times .998) = 4.572$

Equal Annual Premium $= \dfrac{\$1,191.09}{4.572} = \$260.52$

If the insured were to pay a single premium at the beginning of year 1 for the five years of coverage, the premium would simply be the sum of the five annual costs calculated in column 9. This single premium is $1,191.09. However, if the insured wants to pay an equal annual premium each year, then $1,191.09 is divided by the "probability-scaled" sum of present value factors, where the probability-scales are the probability of the insured surviving each year. These probabilities are given in column 6. The equal annual premium is $260.52.

Lessons Learned

You will never do a premium calculation like that in Table 7-3. Insurance companies make these kinds of calculations and present consumers with the premium they must pay to purchase the coverage.

However, consumers can learn much about insurance pricing, such as why insurance prices might go up or might go down, by studying the ingredients of Table 7-3. Here are some lessons:

CHANCE OF CLAIMS RISE

A. Premiums rise if probabilities of claims rise: You've already learned the principle that insurance is based not on knowing who will file claims (i.e., who will have an injury, illness, or accident), but on the principle of knowing the probability that a claim will be filed from anyone in a group. Insurance companies rely heavily on knowing these probabilities in order to set premiums. Anything that increases the probabilities that claims will be filed will increase premiums.

This is one reason why insurance companies can often appear "stingy" or "picky" in agreeing to pay claims. Kidney transplants are a good example. Recent advances in medical technology have made kidney transplants much more feasible. However, if a company wrote a policy before kidney transplants were common, such that the company did not work transplants into their probabilities, then they will be very reluctant to set the precedent for paying for the transplants.

UNCERTAINTY

B. Uncertainties about future claims increase probabilities and premiums: If the insurance company has much uncertainty about what probabilities of future claims will be, then the company will err on the high side and increase both probabilities and premiums. Any new disease or illness (such as AIDS) which increases the uncertainty of future claims will increase premiums.

SIZE OF CLAIMS

C. Increases in the size of claims lead to increases in premiums: As the average size of claims increases, expected claim costs increase. These higher claim costs will ultimately have to be recovered through higher premiums.

REAL INTEREST RATES

D. Increases in real interest rates decrease premiums by increasing the investment returns earned by premium revenue.

The ups and downs in liability insurance rates in the 1980s (see CONSUMER TOPIC) provide a good example of these factors at work.

THE INSURANCE LIABILITY CRISIS OF 1985–86

C
O
N
S
U
M
E
R

T
O
P
I
C

Liability insurance protects you against claims for property damage or personal injury to others. In the mid-1980s a crisis developed in liability insurance. Insurers began suffering losses in liability claims greater than their income. For example, in 1984 commercial auto liability insurers paid $1.31 in costs for every $1.00 in income, and medical malpractice insurers paid $1.45 in costs for every $1.00 in income. As a result, liability insurers dramatically raised rates (rates increased as much as 300 to 1200 percent) and made liability insurance unaffordable to many consumers and firms. The high cost of liability insurance had widespread implications. For example, many doctors stopped delivering babies because they couldn't afford to carry adequate medical liability insurance.

What caused the liability insurance crisis? There are two reasons. The first reason has to do with the roller coaster of interest rates to the 1980s. Recall from Chapter 2 that real interest rates (interest rates after subtracting the inflation rate) rose to very high levels in the early 1980s. This meant that investors received a very good return on their money invested in such things as bonds, CDs and money-market funds. Insurance companies earned such a great return on their investments that they could afford to cut premiums to order to take on more business. So liability insurance rates actually fell in the early 1980s.

When real interest rates dropped like a rock in the mid-1980s, liability insurers also fell into trouble. The lower investment returns insurers were now receiving combined with income from premiums were no longer adequate to meet claim costs. Premiums had to be increased.

The second reason for the liability crisis in the mid-1980s was the increase in the frequency and size of liability claims. For example, more medical malpractice liability suits were filed between 1980 and 1987 than in the entire previous U.S. history. Also, many states and judges began applying the concept of "strict liability" to liability suits. Previously, if a consumer was injured by a product because he improperly used it, the manufacturer was not held at fault. For example, if a consumer put his hand under a running lawn mower, the lawn mower manufacturer wouldn't be liable for injury to the consumer's hand. Under strict liability, however, a manufacturer can be held at fault if it can be shown that the product was improperly designed or manufactured, or if the manufacturer had provided inadequate warnings. So, for example, if the consumer who had stuck his hand under a running lawn mower could show that the manufacturer hadn't adequately warned him not to do this, then the manufacturer could be held at fault for the injury.

The increase in the frequency and size of liability claims is reflected in increased costs to insurance companies. In 1960 legal defense work for commercial liability

(*continued on next page*)

**C
O
N
S
U
M
E
R

T
O
P
I
C**

(*continued from previous page*)

cases took 5 percent of premium income, but in 1982 legal defense work took 25 percent of premium income.

The liability insurance crisis of the mid-1980s has retreated. In the second half of the 1980s and in the 1990s interest rates were much more stable. Also, since 1986 several states have passed laws limiting the size of liability awards and making it more difficult to file claims.

Reference: Meier, Kenneth J. *The Political Economy of Regulation: The Case of Insurance.* Albany, NY: State University of New York Press, 1988, pp. 88–108.
Huber, Peter W. *Liability: The Legal Revolution and Its Consequences.* New York: Basic Books, 1988, p. 9, pp. 30–40.
Miller, Roger LeRoy, Daniel Benjamin, and Douglass North. *The Economics of Public Issues*, NY: Harper & Row, 1990, pp. 75–83.

The Bottom Line

Insurers set insurance premiums so that expected claim costs and operating costs equal revenues from premiums. Anything that increases the probability of claims, the uncertainty of future claims, or the size of claims will lead to higher premiums to consumers.

3. How Much of a Deductible Should You Take?

Choosing the right sized deductible is one of the most important insurance decisions you will make. A deductible is the dollars you pay out of your pocket on a claim before the insurance company pays anything. For example, suppose you have a claim for $1000 of damage suffered on your car in an accident, and suppose you have a $500 deductible. The $500 deductible means you pay the first $500 on the damages and the insurance company pays the rest. In this case, the rest is $500.

Before we talk about why buying an insurance policy with a deductible might be good, let's first talk about why insurance companies might like you to buy policies with deductibles. One obvious reason might be that companies won't pay as much on claims if a policy has a deductible, because the consumer shares in paying the damages. But a more INCENTIVES important reason has to do with incentives. If the consumer must share in paying the damages, then it might be reasonable to think that the consumer will try harder to avoid accidents and injuries. So insurance companies like policies with deductibles because they think that consumers with such policies will try harder to avoid losses.

Benefits of Deductibles

If insurance companies like policies with deductibles, do they give consumers something in exchange for buying policies with large deductibles? The answer is yes. The benefit of policies with large deductibles is that they lower the cost of insurance and make it easier for you to afford larger coverage. A doubling of the deductible can easily cut the premium cost by 50 percent or more on a standard individual health insurance policy.

Why is there such a dramatic drop in the cost of insurance when the deductible rises? There are two reasons. One we already talked about—that with higher deductibles insurance companies believe that consumers will be more careful to avoid losses because more of their money is at stake. In economics this is to reduce or avoid the so-called "moral hazard." A moral hazard is a situation where a party will have a tendency to take risks because the costs that could occur will not be felt by the party taking the risk. The second reason is administrative costs. With low deductible policies, the insurance company must pay-off on more small claims. Administrative costs (the paperwork) per claim tend to be the same regardless of the size of the claim. This means administrative costs are higher for small claims than for large claims. Of course, administrative costs are passed on to consumers in premiums. So another reason that low deductible policies are more costly per dollar of coverage is that administrative costs are higher.

ADMINISTRATIVE COSTS

High Deductible Policies Make Economic Sense

High deductible policies make economic sense. Why? Remember the last topic where we discussed what you should insure. The conclusion was that your insurance dollar is best spent insuring against large losses rather than small losses. Your insurance dollar should first be spent insuring against losses that would be catastrophic to you and your family's financial well-being.

INSURE CATASTROPHIC LOSSES

Buying a policy with a large deductible allows you to do just this. By buying a policy with a large deductible, you reduce the premium cost per dollar of insurance, thereby allowing you to afford more total coverage. For example, suppose you can afford to spend $1000 annually on health insurance. If you take a $250 deductible the $1000 will only buy you $50,000 of coverage. But if you take a $750 deductible, the $1000 will buy you $150,000 of coverage. Economic logic says to take the $750 deductible policy because it will provide more coverage against catastrophic losses.

Is there any way for you to calculate precisely the size of the deductible that is best for you? Unfortunately, the answer is no. It's impossible to know what your optimal insurance deductible is unless the precise shape of your income-utility function (the relationship between income and your utility from income—see Figure 7-2) is known. Hanna made some reasonable assumptions about the income-utility function (in essence, Hanna assumed the income-utility function looked like the curve in Figure 7-2) and derived that consumers should choose a deductible equal to 3 percent of their net worth.[1] So, for example, if your net worth is $30,000, then Hanna's results suggest that insurance deductibles of $900 should be sought.

Co-Insurance

A policy characteristic similar to the deductible is the co-insurance rate. The co-insurance rate is the percentage of the loss, after the deductible, which the insured must pay. For example, suppose your policy has a $500 deductible and a 10 percent co-insurance rate. If you suffer a loss of $10,000, then you will first pay a deductible of $500. Of the remaining loss of $9,500, you will further pay 10 percent of this amount, or $950. The remaining loss of $8,550 ($10,000 – $500 – $950) will be paid by the insurance company.

Most co-insurance rates have a cap, meaning that the insured will only pay up to a certain amount. For example, the policy might say that the co-insurance rate is 10 percent with a cap of $1,000. This means that, after subtracting the deductible, the insured is responsible for paying 10 percent of the loss, but if the 10 percent is greater than $1,000, then no more than a $1,000 co-insurance amount will be paid. Figure 7-3 gives an example of how a co-insurance cap would work.

Should you buy a policy with a co-insurance rate? The disadvantage of such policies is that you will pay more out of your pocket for any losses than you would pay with a policy with no co-insurance rate. The advantage of policies with coinsurance rates is that they're cheaper, both because consumers share in the losses and because insurance companies expect consumers with co-insurance rates to be more careful and to act to reduce total claims.

You should consider insurance policies with co-insurance clauses for the same reasons that you consider policies with deductibles. Policies with co-insurance clauses are cheaper, and the money you

Figure 7-3. How a co-insurance cap works.

Policy has a $500 deductible and a 10% co-insurance rate with a $1,000 cap.

Insured suffers a loss of $50,000.

Insured pays $500 deductible.	10% of $49,500 equals $4,950. But cap of $1,000.	Insurance company pays balance of $50,000–500– –$1,000 = $48,500.

---

[1] Hanna, Sherman. "Risk Aversion and Optimal Insurance Deductibles." *Proceedings of the 35th Annual Conference of the American Council on Consumer Interests,* March 29-April 1, 1989, Baltimore, Maryland, pp. 141–147.

DO CONSUMERS RESPOND TO RELATIVE PRICES?

C O N S U M E R   T O P I C

As you learned in Chapter 1, economists believe that consumers buy less of a product when the product's (real) price rises. This is because, with the product's price higher, consumers are motivated to purchase substitutes for the product.

But does this theory work for medical care? If there are few substitutes for medical care, consumers may find it difficult to substitute other products for medical care when medical care prices rise. Also, with private insurance and government picking up most of the direct cost of medical care, consumers feel a very small direct impact of increases in medical care prices.

The table summarizes a wealth of research which has been conducted on how consumers respond to changes in medical care prices. The term "price elasticity" simply means the percentage change in consumer use of the product or service divided by the percentage change in the product or service's price. If consumers reduce use of a product or service when its price rises, then the price elasticity is negative. Also, the more that consumers reduce use of a product or service when its price rises, the more negative will be the price elasticity. For example, a price elasticity of −1.00 means that in response to a 10 percent increase in price, consumers reduce use of the product or service by 10 percent. But a price elasticity of −.10 means that in response to a 10 percent increase in price, consumers reduce use of the product or service by only 1 percent.

The estimates of the demand for health care are consistently found to be price inelastic. In a literature review conducted by Ringle et al (2005), the price elasticity of health care was reported to center around -0.17, meaning that a 1% increase in the price of health care will lead to only a 0.17% reduction in demand for health care expenditures. Studies have also consistently found lower levels of demand elasticity at lower levels of cost-sharing.

Reference: Ringel, Jeanne S., Susan D. Hosek, Ben A. Vollaard, & Sergey Mahnovski, "The Elasticity of Demand for Health Care – A Review of the Literature and Its Application to the Military Health System." Rand report prepared for the Office of the Secretary of Defense. 2005. Available at http://www.rand.org/content/dam/rand/pubs/monograph_reports/2005/MR1355.pdf.

save can he used to buy more coverage. This is consistent with the general recommendation of buying insurance for large potential losses and self-insuring for small losses. However, make sure that the co-insurance clause has a dollar cap.

The Bottom Line

Consider buying insurance policies with a large deductible and with a coinsurance rate. This will lower your costs of buying more coverage and allow you to increase your coverage to include potential catastrophic losses. You're better off self-insuring for potential small losses. _____

4. How Much Disability Insurance Do You Need?

Disability insurance is similar to life insurance in that it is meant to replace income of the insured. It is different in that it replaces income of the insured when the insured is disabled rather than dead. Also, as we discussed, life insurance is only needed if the insured has dependents. However, all income earners should consider buying disability insurance because if the insured becomes disabled, he will still need income.

Becoming disabled is a relatively small risk. For example, the odds of a professional person becoming disabled for more than 60 days during her career is only four percent. Yet, if it occurs, disability can be a catastrophic loss. If you can't work and earn income, how will you live? In the "old days," disabled persons would live with their relatives or become beggars. These are still options today, but there's also the option of disability insurance.

What Is Disability?

In evaluating disability insurance policies, one of your main concerns should be the policy's definition of disability. All policies do not define disability in the same way. The policy's definition of disability will determine whether or not you receive money from the insurance company when an injury or accident prevents you from working.

There are three major ways that disability can be defined:

1. Inability to do your current job.
2. Inability to do any job for which you're reasonably trained.
3. Inability to do any job.

Obviously the first definition is the most favorable for the consumer, the third definition is the most favorable for the company, and the second definition is in-between. Most consumers will want to buy a disability insurance policy that uses the first or second definition. A policy using the third definition will pay income to a consumer after a disability much less frequently than a policy using the first or second definitions. Of course, policies using the first two definitions will cost more than policies using the last definition.

Some disability policies may use a combination of the definitions. A common kind of policy uses the first definition for the first couple years of coverage and then switches to the second definition.

Table 7-4 Alternative definitions of disability.

Best	Can't do current job.
	Can't do any job for which you're trained.
Worst	Can't do any job

Types of Disability Insurance

There are three major kinds of disability insurance policies. Two of the policies are publicly supported programs—Workmen's Compensation and Social Security disability insurance—and the third are private policies.

WORKMEN'S COMPENSATION

Workmen's Compensation is a state operated program which pays benefits to workers if they are injured and disabled on the job. The money paid to disabled workers comes from contributions from employers. Employers agree to fund Workmen's Compensation in exchange for employees who are injured on the job giving up the right to sue the employer for negligence.

Workmen's Compensation replaces some percentage of the income lost due to the injury. The replacement rate is usually no higher than 67 percent. Also, frequently there are dollar caps on what can be replaced. The cap is not automatically indexed to inflation.

There can also be limits on the number of weeks of payment of Workmen's Compensation benefits (e.g., maximum of 400 or 500 weeks). If the worker can return to work but must take a lower paying job, Workmen's Compensation will make a lump sum payment to the worker. There may be a waiting period before benefits begin. Benefits from Workmen's Compensation aren't taxed.

There are two reasons why you shouldn't rely on Workmen's Compensation as your only disability insurance policy. First, Workmen's Compensation won't cover disability from injury or illness sustained off the job. Second, there is no assurance that Workmen's Compensation will provide you with an adequate income during your disability.

SOCIAL SECURITY DISABILITY

The *Social Security* disability insurance program is a federal program which is funded by the Social Security payroll tax. Social Security uses the most restrictive definition of disability. Social Security will only pay if you are disabled to the extent that you can't do any job.

If you qualify for Social Security disability benefits, the amount you get is based on your lifetime average earnings. According to Social

Security Administration, the average disability monthly payment in February 2013 was $978.52. Generally the amount of working income replaced declines as income rises. Benefits are, however, indexed to inflation. Benefits are not taxed and don't begin until the sixth month of disability.

It should be very obvious that you shouldn't rely only on Social Security for disability income benefits. Social Security will only pay if you can't do any job. So, for example, if a surgeon is disabled such that she can no longer operate but she can sell hamburgers at McDonald's, Social Security will not pay. Also, the income replacement rates for Social Security may not be adequate to maintain your standard of living.

Private disability insurance policies are the third type of policy. Private policies can be sold directly to individuals or can be provided as part of fringe benefits by an employer. Before buying a private disability insurance policy, it's important to check and fully understand the policy's provisions. These provisions are highlighted in the next section.

Provisions of Disability Policies

1. *Definition of Disability:* The first characteristic of a disability insurance policy that you should check is the policy's definition of disability. You should favor a policy that defines disability as the inability to do your current job, followed by policies that only pay if you can't also do a comparable job for which you were trained.
2. *How Much Coverage:* An obviously important characteristic of a disability insurance policy is how much income it will provide you if you are disabled. Most policies will not sell coverage for 100 percent replacement of income because they don't want people to have an incentive to "manufacture" or "fake" injuries or illnesses.

Most people won't need 100 percent replacement of income anyway. If you're disabled and can't work, you won't have work related expenses. Also, if the disability benefits are from a private policy for which you paid the premiums, these benefits won't be taxed so you won't have income taxes. If work expenses and income taxes account for approximately 35 percent of income, then a disability insurance policy replacing 65 percent of income would be adequate. (Medical expenses related to the disability will be covered by medical insurance—discussed in the next topic.)

If the disability insurance policy is provided by your employer and the employer paid for it, then benefits you receive will be taxed. In this case you'd probably want to replace 80 percent of income.

Although you will calculate the coverage you want as a percentage of your income, the large majority of policies will convert this percentage

Table 7-5 A checklist of disability insurance policy provisions and recommendations.

Disability definition—take coverage for inability to do current job.

Coverage amount—65–80% of income.

Inflation protection—take "future increase option" and "cost of living rider."

Waiting period—take longer periods and self-insure for short disability periods.

Time limit on payments—take longer.

Social Security rider—take.

Residual rider—valuable for self-employed and business people whose business can suffer even after the disability period.

Cancellation provisions—want a policy that can't be cancelled as long as premiums are paid.

to a dollar amount. This means that coverage will be specified as a certain dollar amount. However, this can present a problem as the insured's future income rises, but the dollar amount of disability insurance protection remains constant.

3. *Inflation Protection:* To address this problem—that coverage is stated in dollar amounts which won't change as inflation occurs—companies offer provisions which provide inflation protection. These provisions are optional, meaning that it's up to the consumer to ask that they be included in the policy. Of course, since the provisions provide a benefit to the consumer, they will add to the cost of the policy.

FUTURE INCREASE OPTION

The first provision is the "future increase option," which allows the insured to add to the dollars of benefits provided by the policy without undergoing a new exam. This provision may add as much as 10 percent to the policy's premium.

COST OF LIVING RIDER

The second provision is called a "cost of living rider." This provision will increase benefits by the rate of inflation (CPI) but only *after* you start receiving benefits. The provision provides no protection against the inflation which occurs between the time you bought the policy and the time you become disabled and start receiving benefits.

Obviously, both provisions are needed to provide full inflation protection. With the "future increase option" you can add to coverage as your income and expenses rise.

With the "cost of living rider" you can be assured that benefits will increase, once you start receiving them, with the rate of inflation.

4. *Waiting Period:* This provision is similar to a deductible. The waiting period is the period of time after a disability occurs and before payments begin. The disadvantage to a longer waiting period is

ADVANTAGE OF
WAITING PERIOD

that you'll have to fend for yourself during the waiting period. The advantage of a longer waiting period is that longer waiting periods reduce your premium costs. Premium costs are reduced for two reasons. First, as with deductibles, companies think that consumers will be more careful if they must pay for the first few months of disability. Second, administrative costs per claim for policies with longer waiting periods will be lower because the company will not have many claims for short time periods, where administrative costs per claim are higher.

So you can reduce your premium costs per dollar of coverage and therefore be able to afford more coverage by buying a disability insurance policy with a longer waiting period. Of course, this means you must self-insure for short periods of disability. But this fits in with the recommendation of self-insuring for small losses and buying insurance for catastrophic losses.

Before you decide about the waiting period provision, check your company's sick leave policy. If your company provides, say, 15 days of paid sick leave each year, then there's no need to begin disability benefits until after the sick leave is exhausted.

One final word about waiting periods. After the waiting period is over it usually takes another 30 days before the first benefits check arrives. So a waiting period of 30 days is effectively a waiting period of 60 days, and a waiting period of 60 days is effectively a waiting period of 90 days.

5. *Time Limit on Payments:* Check the policy to see if it will only pay benefits for a certain time period. You'd like a policy with a longer time limit in the event that your disability is very serious and long. Consider increasing the waiting period in order to buy a longer time period on payments.

6. *Social Security rider:* This provision means that if the insured qualifies for Social Security disability benefits, the company will reduce the benefits paid in its policy by the amount of the Social Security benefits.

This is a worthwhile provision to have. This rider will not reduce the total coverage you receive, it just changes the source of the coverage. As long as you have adequate coverage on your private policy, there's no reason to receive more total benefits just because you qualify for Social Security disability benefits. Take this rider and reduce your premium costs.

7. *Residual rider:* This is a relatively new provision designed for self-employed people and business persons. Say you're a doctor and you've been disabled for a year. You return to work and you find your business has suffered as former patients have found new doctors. In other words, since many of your patients have left, you suffer a loss in income.

A disability policy with a residual rider will replace some percentage of the loss or the entire loss up to a certain dollar limit for a certain length of time or until the insured is age 65. This provision is valuable for self-employed or business people whose business could shrink during the disability period and remain smaller even after the insured returns to work.

8. *Cancellation provisions:* This provision states the conditions under which the policy can be cancelled. You prefer a policy that can't be cancelled as long as you pay premiums. You don't want a policy that could be cancelled after you file a claim.

The Bottom Line

Buy disability insurance to replace your income in the event that you're sick or injured and can't work. Policies which pay benefits if you can't do your current job are the best (and most expensive). Consider buying a policy with a longer waiting period in order to free-up money to buy more coverage. Also consider policies with inflation protection both before and after benefits begin. _____

5. What are the typical health insurance provisions you need to know?

Everyone faces uncertain risks of illness or injury which can result in large medical bills. So the smart consumer pays a relatively small amount of money each year for health insurance in exchange for health insurance paying the medical bills if an injury or illness occurs.

As with any kind of insurance, you don't buy health insurance to make money. If you buy health insurance and stay healthy and injury-free, you haven't wasted money. You've bought protection. You don't want to have a big injury or illness just to collect more from your insurance company than you've paid in.

How Much Health Insurance?

We know it's beginning to sound repetitious, but you want to buy health insurance to guard against big medical expenses that could destroy your savings and net worth. It's better to spend a dollar insuring against major medical expenses and hospital stays than against minor expenses such as office visits and cough syrup. With medical technology changing rapidly and medical expenses increasing so much (see CONSUMER TOPIC: *What's Driving Up Medical Care Costs?*), medical insurance coverage really can't be too high. Coverage in the multiple six figure range (between $100,000 and $1,000,000) is very reasonable.

The way to afford such high coverage is to purchase policies with large deductibles and with co-insurance clauses.

WHAT'S DRIVING UP MEDICAL CARE COSTS?

According to the Centers for Medicare and Medicaid Services, in 2011, the United States spent over $2.7 trillion or $8,680 per person on health care, representing roughly 18% of GDP, much higher than other developed nations such as the UK (9.6%), Germany (11.6%), or Japan (9.5%). The rapid growth in health care spending creates an unsustainable burden on America's economy, with far-reaching consequences.

CONSUMER TOPIC

Many factors contribute to these increases. A 2012 report by the Bipartisan Policy Center (BPC) described a range of complex "drivers" that are responsible for our high levels of health spending today. A PBS news report summarized the following seven main drivers from the BPC report:

U.S. National Health Care Expenditure as Share of GDP: 1960–2011

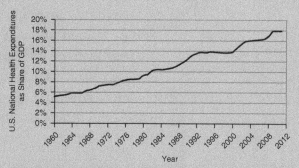

Data source: National health care expenditures data from the Center for Medicare and Medicaid Services. GDP data from U.S. Department of Commerce, Bureau of Economic Analysis

1. We pay our doctors, hospitals and other medical providers in ways that reward doing more, rather than being efficient. This encourages overtreatment, including repetitive tests.

2. We are growing older, sicker, and fatter. As we get older, we tend to need more medical care. Additionally, nearly half of the U.S. population has one or more chronic conditions, which drive up costs. And two-thirds of adults are either overweight or obese, which can also lead to chronic illness and additional medial spending.

3. We want new drugs, technologies, services and procedures. While medical advances help us get well and delay death, they also drive up spending.

4. We get tax breaks on buying health insurance—and the out-of-pocket cost to patients of seeking care is often low. This encourages more expensive plans with richer benefits. Low deductibles and/or small co-payments can encourage overuse of care. Increasingly, however, employers are moving towards high-deductible plans as a way to slow premium growth.

5. We don't have enough information to make decisions on which medical care is best for us. There is no broad standard for evaluating individual treatments so it is difficult for doctors and patients to make optimal decisions. Also, Americans vary widely in how they view end-of-life issues, with some desiring every possible medical intervention to stave off death in every situation, no matter how small the possibility of success.

6. Our hospitals and other providers are increasingly gaining market share and are better able to demand higher prices.

7. We have supply and demand problems, and legal issues that complicate efforts to slow spending. While malpractice premiums and jury awards are part of what drives spending, "defensive medicine" –when doctors prescribe unnecessary tests or treatments out of fear of facing a lawsuit is a larger problem. The U.S. faces a shortage of primary care doctors. However, state laws sometimes limit nurse practitioners or other medical professionals, who are paid less than doctors, to fully perform work for which they are trained.

Reference: Bipartisan Policy Center (BPC). "What is Driving U.S. Health Care Spending?" September 2012. Available at http://bipartisanpolicy.org/sites/default/files/BPC%20 Health%20Care%20Cost%20Drivers%20Brief%20Sept%202012.pdf
Public Broadcasting Services (PBS). "Seven Factors Driving Up Your Health Insurance Costs." October 24, 2012. Available at http://www.pbs.org/newshour/rundown/2012/10/seven-factors-driving-your-health-care-costs.html.

Provisions of Health Insurance Policies

This is the most important section of this topic. Health insurance policies are very complex. The policy provisions will tell you what illnesses and injuries are covered, what services are covered, and what the coverage and limits of coverage are. In 2010, the Patient Protection and Affordable Care Act, commonly called ObamaCare, was signed into law by President Barack Obama. It represents one of the most significant expansion and regulatory overhaul of the U.S. healthcare system since the passage of Medicare and Medicaid in 1965, and has important implications for consumer decision-making.

Table 7-6 lists twenty-three of the most important questions to ask about a health insurance policy. Many of the questions are self-explanatory but here's a rundown on those that need more explanation.

A. *What is the elimination period?*

This is an initial period of time after an injury or illness when benefits are paid by the insurance policy. Companies utilize this period to investigate the nature of the injury or illness to determine if benefits should be paid. The elimination period is like a deductible. Companies like elimination periods because they discourage consumers from filing claims for short time periods. You can reduce your premiums for health insurance by buying a policy with a longer elimination period.

B. *Is policy renewed with payment of premium?*

If the policy is automatically renewed when premiums are paid, then the policy can't be cancelled if you file a large claim.

C. *How is "accident" defined?*

What do you mean, how is "accident" defined? Doesn't an accident occur when an injury occurs as a result of an unfortunate event? Not necessarily. Companies have very specific definitions of "accident," and coverage won't be provided unless the injury meets the company's definition of accident.

Table 7-6 Twenty-three questions to ask about a health insurance policy.

What is the elimination period?

What are the deductible and co-insurance rate?

Is the deductible per injury or illness per year?

Is the premium waived if you become disabled?

Can benefits change if you switch to a more hazardous job?

Is policy automatically renewed with payment of premium?

How does the policy define accident?

How many days of hospitalization are covered?

How soon are you covered for pre-existing conditions?

Are doctor's visits covered?

What hospital expenses are covered?

What surgical expenses are covered?

Are ambulance costs covered?

Are X-rays and lab tests covered?

Is anesthesia covered?

Are prescription drugs covered?

Are some injuries or illnesses excluded from coverage?

Is there a dollar limit or a percentage of cost limit on expenditure items?

Are there limits per injury or illness?

Are there annual limits?

Are there lifetime limits?

Is nursing home care included?

Is home care included?

CAUSE AND RESULT   There are two major alternative definitions of accident. One definition defines an injury as an accident only if both *cause and result were unintended and unexpected.* The second definition of accident only requires that the *result be unintended and unexpected.*

RESULT   These two definitions can have very dramatically different results. Say you are skydiving and you break your leg in landing. Under the "cause and result" definition of the accident, your injury wouldn't be covered under a health policy because the skydiving was intended. That is, the cause of the injury—the skydiving—was *intended.* Under the "result" definition of the accident, you would be covered by a health policy because the result—the leg injury—was unintended.

On the other hand, if you're hit by someone else's car and injured, and the other person was at fault, you would be covered under both definitions.

Obviously you're better off with a policy which defines accident under the "result" definition. Fortunately, most major policies have begun to exclusively use the "result" definition.

C O N S U M E R   T O P I C

WHO PAYS THE MEDICAL BILL?

There are three parties that pay medical bills: consumer out-of-pocket payment, private insurance, and government. The share paid by each of these parties has changed over the years (see graph). The share paid directly by consumers has fallen dramatically from 48% in 1960 to 11% in 2011. The shares paid by private insurance and government increased substantially during that period of time. Of course, consumers indirectly pay the bills of both insurance companies and the government through premiums and taxes.

Does it matter who initially pays the bill? Yes, it does. Economists believe that the falling share directly paid by consumers had reduced their concern about monitoring the kind and cost of care they receive. After all, if the government or insurance companies will pick up the tab, why worry about the cost? This kind of "moral hazard" is one reason why insurance programs need to have deductibles and co-payments.

Percentage of health care expenditures paid by source

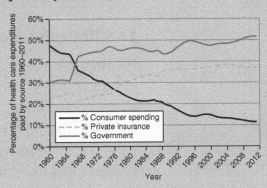

Data source: National health care expenditures data from the Center for Medicare and Medicaid Services.

D. *Pre-existing conditions:*
    Most policies have restrictions on paying benefits for an illness or injury which existed before the policy was issued. Policies may restrict payment of benefits on these conditions for as long as two years. You can't get around this provision by not mentioning the condition on the application for the policy.

E. *Limits:*
    Policies can put numerous kinds of limits on benefits. Limits can be put on each injury or illness (called "episode" limits), on total benefits each year, and on total benefits over the lifetime of the policy. For example, a policy may have a limit of $10,000 for heart surgery, $250,000 on all claims per year, and $1,000,000 on all claims over the lifetime of the policy. Alternatively, a policy may promise to pay a certain percentage of medical expenses. The Obamacare bill prohibits lifetime limits on coverage starting from 2010, and will prohibit health plans from imposing annual limits on the amount of coverage an individual may receive starting from 2014.

F. *Nursing home or home care:* With more people living longer and unable to care for themselves, professional care in nursing homes maybe required or a professional nurse may be required to care for the person in his home. Some general health insurance policies may include coverage for these services. Increasingly however, these services are sold separately under long-term care policies (see next topic).

PROVISIONS
AND PREMIUMS
A major reason why prices of health insurance policies vary is because policy provisions vary. Policies with provisions more favorable to the consumer will cost more, and policies with provisions less favorable to the consumer will cost less.

The moral of the story is that you get what you pay for. Health insurance policies with lower deductibles, lower coinsurance rates, and more coverage and benefits will cost more.

The Bottom Line

Health insurance policies are complex. It is important to educate yourself about the various definitions and provisions used in health insurance policies so you can evaluate the costs and benefits of different policies. Typically you can reduce your health insurance costs by buying policies with larger deductibles and bigger coinsurance rates if you are generally in good health.

6. What Kinds of Health Insurance Are Out There?

Health insurance plans are available to consumers either through private insurance such as employer-sponsored group insurance, social insurance such as Medicare, or social welfare programs such as Medicaid and Children's Health Insurance Program (CHIP). Depending on your age, employment status, income, and net worth, you may have access to some or all of these options. Your first task is to figure out what you qualify for. Then, within what you qualify for, you can evaluate different provisions and costs associated with these provisions.

Medicare

Medicare is a national social insurance program, administered by the U.S. federal government since 1965, that guarantees access to health insurance for Americans ages 65 and older and younger people with disabilities as well as people with end stage renal disease and persons with Lou Gehrig's Disease. Medicare has four parts, commonly referred to as Medicare Part A, B, C, and D. The Medicare program is frequently changed by the Congress. The following description is based on the Medicare program as it stood in 2013.

CONSUMER TOPIC

Health Care and Health Care Reform in the United States

Health care in the United States is provided by many distinct organizations. Health care facilities are largely owned and operated by private sector businesses. Health insurance helps pay for medical expenses, whether through private insurance such as employer-sponsored group insurance, social insurance such as Medicare, or social welfare programs such as Medicaid and Children's Health Insurance Program (CHIP).

According to the Census Bureau, in 2011, roughly 55.1% of Americans obtain insurance through an employer, 9.8% purchase private health insurance directly, and 32.2% were enrolled in a public health insurance program. The remaining 15.7% were uninsured.

Percentage of Population Covered by Type of Health Insurance: 2010 and 2011

Coverage type	2010	2011
Any private plan	64.0	63.9
Any private plan alone	52.5	52.0
Employment-based	55.3	55.1
Employment-based alone	45.7	45.1
Direct-purchase	9.9	9.8
Direct-purchase alone	3.7	3.6
Any government plan	31.2	32.2
Any government plan alone	19.7	20.4
Medicare	14.6	15.2
Medicare alone	4.7	4.9
Medicaid	15.8	16.5
Medicaid alone	11.1	11.5
Military health care	4.2	4.4
Military health care alone	1.3	1.3
Uninsured	16.3	15.7

**Data source: U.S. Census Bureau, Current Population Survey 2011 and 2012.*

**The estimates by type of coverage are not mutually exclusive; people can be covered by more than one type of health insurance during the year.*

(continued on next page)

(continued from previous page)

International comparisons of health care have found that the U.S. spends more per capita than other similarly-developed nations but falls below similar countries in various health outcomes, suggesting inefficiencies and waste. Further, the U.S. has significant underinsurance and significant impending unfunded liabilities from its aging demographics and its social insurance (Medicare) and social welfare programs (Medicaid). The fiscal and human impact of these issues have motivated a long history of health care reform proposals, many of them failed efforts.

Since World Word II, there are four major reform achievements at the national level. In 1965 President Lyndon Johnson enacted legislation that introduced Medicare and Medicaid. Medicare is a national social insurance program that covers Americans ages 65 and older, people with disabilities as well as people with certain specific diseases. Medicaid is a mean-tested social welfare program for certain people and families with low income and resources. It is jointly funded by the state and federal governments, and is managed by the states. The most significant legislative change to Medicare was the Medicare Modernization Act, signed into law by President George W. Bush in 2003.

The Consolidated Omnibus Budget Reconciliation Act of 1985 (COBRA) amended the Employee Retirement Income Security Act of 1974 (ERISA) to give some employees the ability to continue group health insurance coverage after leaving employment.

In 1997 the State Children's Health Insurance Program (SCHIP) was established to provide health insurance to children in families at or below 200% of the federal poverty level but do not qualify for Medicaid.

In 2010 the Patient Protection and Affordable Care Act, often referred to as the "ObamaCare", was enacted, providing for the introduction over ten years of a comprehensive system of mandated health insurance through mandates, subsidies, and tax credits to employers and individuals in order to increase health insurance coverage rates, including a controversial individual mandate to purchase health insurance coverage or otherwise pay a financial penalty starting from 2014. ObamaCare also requires insurance companies to eliminate pre-condition screening and premium loadings, policy rescinds on technicalities when illness seems imminent, and annual and lifetime caps.

Part A is Hospital Insurance that covers inpatient hospital stays, including semiprivate room, food, and tests. Skilled nursing facility and hospice benefits are provided if certain criteria are met. You usually do not pay a monthly premium for Part A if you or your spouse paid Medicare taxes while working.

Part B is Medical Insurance that helps pay for costs generally associated with out-patient services, including physician and nursing services, x-rays, laboratory and diagnostic tests, and other outpatient medical treatments administered in a doctor's office. Medication administration is covered under Part B if it is administered by the physician during an office visit. Part B also helps with durable medical equipment, including canes, walkers, wheelchairs, and mobility scooters for those with mobility impairments. Complex rules are used to manage the benefit, with coverage information available on the website of the Centers for Medicare and Medicaid Services. Most people pay the Part B premium of $104.90 each month in 2013.

Medicare Part C refers to Medicare Advantage plans. With the passage of the Balanced Budget Act of 1997, Medicare beneficiaries were given the option to receive their Medicare benefits through private health insurance plans, instead of through the original Medicare plan (Parts A and B). These programs were known as "Medicare+Choice" or "Part C" plans. Pursuant to the Medicare Modernization Act of 2003, "Medicare+Choice" plans were made more attractive to Medicare beneficiaries by the addition of prescription drug coverage and became known as "Medicare Advantage" (MA) plans. Medicare Advantage plans are offered through private companies known as Medicare Advantage Organizations (MAO). Medicare Advantage plans are required to offer coverage that meets or exceeds the standards set by the original Medicare program, but they do not have to cover every benefit in the same way. If a plan chooses to pay less than Medicare for some benefits, like skilled nursing facility care, the savings may be passed along to consumers by offering lower co-payments for doctor visits. Medicare Advantage plans use a portion of the payments they receive from the government for each enrollee to offer supplemental benefits. All plans limit their members' annual out-of-pocket spending on medical care. Some plans offer dental coverage, vision coverage and other services not covered by Medicare Parts A or B, which makes them a good value for the health care dollar, if you want to use the provider included in the plan's network. The Part C monthly premium varies by plan.

Medicare Part D covers outpatient prescription drugs exclusively through private plans or through Medicare Advantage plans that offer prescription drugs. It went into effect on January 1, 2006. Anyone with Part A or B is eligible for Part D. It was made possible by the passage of the Medicare Modernization Act. In order to receive this benefit, a person with Medicare must enroll in a stand-alone Prescription Drug Plan (PDP) or Medicare Advantage plan with prescription drug coverage (MA-PD). These plans are approved and regulated by the Medicare program, but are actually designed and administered by private health insurance companies. Unlike Original Medicare (Part A and B), Part D coverage is not standardized. Plans choose which drugs (or even classes of drugs) they wish to cover, at what level (or tier) they wish to cover, and are free to choose not to cover some drugs at all. Plans that cover excluded drugs are not allowed to pass those costs on to Medicare, and plans are required to repay CMS if they are found to have billed Medicare in these cases. The Part D monthly premium varies by plan.

If you choose Original Medicare, you also need to decide if you need Medigap insurance. Medigap insurance (also called "Medicare Supplement Insurance") is private insurance designed to pay medical expenses not met by the original Medicare, such as deductibles and co-insurance payments not paid by Medicare, hospital charges on hospital visits beyond day 150, and doctor expenses higher than those approved by Medicare. Note that Medicare does not pay any of the costs for you to get a Medigap policy.

Each Medigap policy must follow Federal and state laws designed to protect consumers, and the policy must be clearly identified as "Medicare Supplement Insurance." Medigap insurance companies in most states can only sell you a "standardized" Medigap policy identified by letters A through N. Each standardized policy must offer the same basic benefits. Cost is usually the only difference between Medigap policies with the same letter sold by different insurance companies.

If you are eligible for Medicare, you can use these steps outlined by the CMS to make a decision about what type of plan to get.

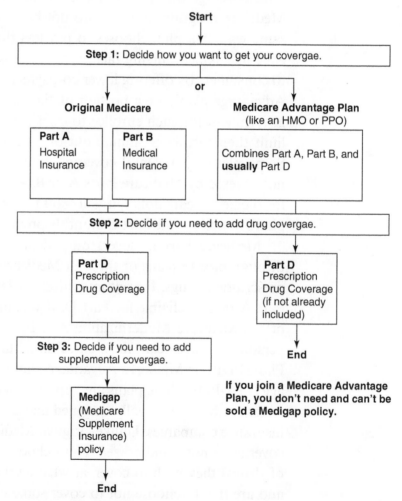

Source: Centers for Medicare and Medicaid Services, 2012. Choosing a Medigap Policy: A Guide to Health Insurance for People with Medicare. Available at http://www.medicare.gov/pubs/pdf/02110.pdf.

Medicaid and the Children's Health Insurance Program (CHIP)

Medicaid is a health care program for certain people and families with low incomes and resources. It is a means-tested program that is jointly funded by the state and federal governments, and is managed by the states. The Children's Health Insurance Program (CHIP) provides health coverage to children in families with incomes too high to qualify for Medicaid, but cannot afford private coverage. Like Medicaid, CHIP is administered by states, but is jointly funded by the federal government and states.

Medicaid was created by the Social Security Amendments of 1965 as an entitlement program to help states provide medical coverage to low-income families. The Patient Protection and Affordable Care Act of 2010 (ObamaCare) expanded Medicaid eligibility starting in 2014. Each state establishes their own eligibility standards, determines the scope and types of services they will cover, and sets the rate of payment. Historically and by statue, the standard delivery system for Medicaid is fee for service where health care providers are paid for each service. However states are increasingly moving to the use of managed care and other integrated care models. You should visit your state's Medicaid website to find out state-specific information.

Types of Health Insurance and Health Care Delivery Methods

Many of the common health insurance plans today offer several choices for coverage, based on factors including cost, flexibility and how much of a role you want to play in managing and paying for your own health care. These include:

Indemnity (fee-for-service) plans

With an indemnity or fee-for-service plan, you can go to the doctor of your choice, and you, your doctor or your hospital submits a claim to your insurance company for reimbursement. Just note that you will only be reimbursed for "covered" medical expenses, a list of which can be found in your benefits summary. The good news is that the vast majority of procedures will be covered under an indemnity plan.

Indemnity plans pay a sizable percentage of what they consider the "usual and customary" charge for covered services in your area. The insurer generally pays 80 percent of the usual and customary costs and you pay the other 20 percent coinsurance. If the provider charges more than the usual and customary rates, you will have to pay both the coinsurance and the excess charges.

For example, if your insurer determines that the usual and customary fee for "X medical service" is $100, the insurer will pay $80 and you will be required to pay the remaining $20. However, if your doctor charges more than the usual and customary fee, $105 for example, you would be required to pay the additional $5, making your total expense $25. Many indemnity plans reimburse at the 80/20 level, but some reimburse at other levels, such as 70/30.

In addition to the coinsurance, most indemnity plans have deductibles. These might range from $100 to $300 per year per individual, or $500, $1,000 or more per family.

Indemnity policies typically have an out-of-pocket maximum. This means that once your covered expenses reach a certain amount in a given calendar year, the insurer will pay the usual and customary fee in full. However, if your doctor charges you more than the usual and customary fee, you still may have to pay a portion of the bill.

Health maintenance organizations (HMOs)

Many of these plans focus on preventing diseases and staying healthy. If you join an HMO, you typically must receive all your care from network providers, except in medical emergencies. One common model of HMOs is that they deliver care directly to patients. Patients may go to an HMO's medical facility to see the nurses and doctors. Another common model is a network of individual practitioners. In these individual practice associations (IPAs), you will get your care in the office of a physician who may accept patients from different health plans.

With an HMO, you choose a primary care physician affiliated with your plan, usually a general practitioner, to coordinate your care. Generally, you must receive a referral from your primary care physician before visiting a specialist in your provider network. With rare exceptions, your HMO will require that you seek care within its network of providers—doctors, hospitals, and labs—with whom your HMO has negotiated a fee schedule. Negotiating discounts from providers is one of the main ways HMOs keep healthcare costs in check. HMOs are generally the most affordable type of health insurance plan.

In addition to your premiums, most HMOs require a copayment for certain services, for example, $10 or $20 for an office visit. Some, but not all, HMOs will apply copayments to hospitalizations as well.

Preferred provider organizations (PPOs)

A preferred provider organization (PPO) is the form of managed care closest to an indemnity plan, which typically allows you to see any doctor, any time. A PPO negotiates discounts with doctors, hospitals and other providers, who then become part of the PPO network.

When you see a physician in the network, you typically make a copayment, such as $25. When you see a physician out of the network, you'll still receive coverage, but your insurance will cover only a portion of the bill, usually 70, 80 or 90 percent. The remaining amount is your responsibility. For example, the insurer may reimburse you for 80 percent of the cost of the doctor's visit if you go to a provider outside the network. So after an office visit, you'll owe 20 percent of the total bill, plus your copayment.

In addition to the coinsurance, PPOs may also have deductibles. These are amounts of covered expenses you must pay before the insurer will start reimbursing you for your medical bills. These might range from $100 to $300 per year per individual, or $500 or more per family.

One of the things people like about PPOs is the ability to make self-referrals. That means you can see any doctor you want, including specialists inside and outside the PPO network, without a referral. Also, premiums are usually lower than indemnity plans because of the negotiated provider discounts.

Point-of-service organizations (POS)

A point-of-service plan (POS) combines elements of both a health maintenance organization (HMO) and a preferred provider organization (PPO). The plan allows you to use a primary care physician to coordinate your care, or you can self-direct your care at the "point of service."

When medical care is needed, you generally have two or three options, depending on the particular health plan. You can go through a primary care physician, in which case the services will be covered under HMO-like guidelines (i.e., usually just a copayment will be required). You can access care through a PPO provider and the services will be covered under in-network PPO guidelines (i.e., a copayment is required, and you may have to pay coinsurance as well). You can obtain services from a provider outside of the HMO and PPO networks. These services will be reimbursed according to out-of-network rules (i.e., usually a copayment and higher coinsurance charge will be required). In addition to the coinsurance, POS plans may have deductibles.

Consumer-directed health plans

These newer health plans give you more control over your own health care, both in choosing the care you receive and paying for it. They often require you to pay a substantial deductible (often $2,000 or more) before coverage starts, and are combined with a Health Savings Account (HAS) that allows you to save money to pay for current and future medical expenses on a tax-free basis. In order to be eligible for a HSA, you must be covered by a high-deductible plan and not have any other health insurance. HSAs are a good option for individuals who want to protect themselves from catastrophic healthcare costs, but don't anticipate many day-to-day medical costs. They also can serve as a lower-cost alternative to more traditional health plans for small businesses.

Here's how the program works. You can sign up for an HSA if your employer offers such a plan (individuals can buy these plans as well, though not in every state). An HSA must be paired with a health insurance plan that requires an annual deductible of at least $1,250 for individuals or $2,500 for families in 2013. Total out-of-pocket costs for these plans, including deductibles and copayments, can't exceed $6,250 for an individual or $12,500 for a family in 2013, though these amounts change from year to year. Despite the high deductibles, some plans still offer full coverage or require only a small copayment for preventative care, such as an annual physical or a well-child checkup.

High-deductible health plans typically have lower premiums than HMOs, PPOs or POS plans, but they come with the potential for higher out-of-pocket costs. To offset that risk, you (or your employer) can contribute up to $3,250 annually (individual) or $6,450 (family) to a tax-advantaged HSA account in 2013. Again, these figures change from year to year. These contributions reduce your taxable income (or they are tax-free if made by your employer), and money in your HSA can be used to pay any qualified medical expense now or in the future. An attractive feature of HSAs is that they can pay for expenses that your regular health plan ordinarily doesn't cover, such as eyeglasses and hearing aids. In addition, while the money is in the account, it can be invested, and the investment gains are tax-free as long as they are used for qualified medical expenses.

The Bottom Line

Health insurance in the U.S. is quite complicated, including private insurance such as employee group insurance, social insurance such as Medicare, and social welfare programs such as Medicaid and CHIP. You must understand the overall picture in order to know what programs you are eligible for. Once you know what you are eligible for, you need to read and understand policies' provisions – the fine prints - in order to know what benefits you will get under various policies and the costs associated with them. In general, you pay more for better coverage and more flexibility.

ARE NON-PROFIT HOSPITALS BETTER AND LESS EXPENSIVE?

C O N S U M E R   T O P I C

In the "old days," most hospitals were run by the government or by non-profit organizations such as schools and churches. This has changed. Many hospitals are now run by for-profit corporations.

With corporate hospitals interested in making a profit for their shareholders, we might suspect such hospitals to be more costly and not as good.

To address this issue in a careful way, a study tracked the experience of 2600 patients admitted to 1378 different hospitals throughout the United States. Perhaps surprisingly, the researchers found very little difference in cost and quality of care between for-profit and nonprofit hospitals.

Reference: Sloan, Frank, Gabriel Picone, Donald Taylor, Jr. and Shin-Yi Chou, "Hospital Ownership and Cost and Quality of Care: Is There a Dime's Worth of Difference?, Working Paper 6706, National Bureau of Economic Research, August, 1998.

7. How Can Yon Pay for Long-Term Health Care?

As medical technology and other factors keep people alive longer, there's an increasing chance that people will need some type of long-term care. Long-term care is medical or personal care received by a person at home or in a care facility on a continuing basis. For example, the probability that a person will need nursing home care tends to increase dramatically after age 65.

MEDICAID

As you learned in the last topic, Medicare does not pay for long-term care. Medicaid, the federal health insurance program for the poor, does pay for long-term care, but you must be "asset-poor" to qualify. You must deplete your assets first in paying for long-term care before you are eligible for Medicaid. Only a home, a car, a limited amount of household possessions, and a limited amount of cash can be protected and do not have to be "used up" before eligibility for Medicaid is approved.

Payment Options

Long term care in a nursing care facility is expensive. Annual costs can easily range between $30,000 and $60,000. The big question is, how to pay for these costs?

LIVE WITH CHILDREN

One option is for the elderly individual to live with his or her children rather than live in a nursing care facility. This, of course, was the traditional form of long-term care. But this option may not be possible for two reasons. First, the type of long-term medical care required may make it necessary to be in a nursing care facility. Second, your children may not have the space or time to provide you with long-term care.

USE MONEY-FROM HOME SALE

A second option is to sell your home (assuming you own a home) and other physical assets (like cars and boats) and use the cash to fund long-term care. The problem with this approach, of course, is that it may not be sufficient to fund long-term care for the necessary number of years. For example, suppose your asset sale nets you $125,000. Using an annual nursing facility cost of $22,000 and a real interest rate of 3 percent, the $125,000 and its interest earnings would last a little longer than six years ($125,000/$22,000 = 5.68 where 5.68 is the sum of annual FV factors for 3 percent for between six and seven years, Appendix Table A-4).

SAVE WHILE WORKING

A third option is to budget for nursing care facility costs in your retirement planning. Essentially this means saving enough while you're working to be able to find nursing facility care if you need it (see Chapter 10, Retirement Planning, for the methodology). However, this is an expensive option and many consumers simply wouldn't be able to save the necessary amounts.

LIVING BENEFIT POLICY

A fourth option is called a "living benefit policy." A living benefit policy is a life insurance policy which allows the policyholder to withdraw some part of the policy under certain health conditions. There are two versions of this policy. Under one version, the policy pays a specified lump sum amount when the policyholder contracts a specified illness. For example, the policyholder may be allowed to withdraw 25 percent of the policy's face value. Under the second version, the policy pays a certain percent of the face value (e.g., 2 percent) each month after a specified illness hits.

There are two problems with living benefit policies. First, life insurance is not bought to be used by the policyholder (the insured), but by

Table 7-7 Options for funding long-term care.

Live with children.
Sell home and other assets.
Save while working.
Living benefit policy.
Long-term care policy.

the insured's financial dependents in the event of the insured's death. If the face value money is used by the insured for long term care, then it won't be available for the financial dependents. Second, there is no assurance that the life insurance face value that can be withdrawn will be adequate to pay for the needed long term care.

LONG-TERM CARE POLICY

The fifth option is a long-term health care policy. A long-term health care policy is an insurance policy specifically designed to pay long-term care expenses. The cost of the policy increases dramatically with age due to the increasing chance of needing care as the insured ages. For example, at age 55 a long-term care policy might cost $500 annually. This increases to $1,000 annually if the policy is bought at age 65, and $4,000 annually if the policy is bought at age 70.

Long Term Care Policy Provisions

As with general health insurance policies, it's very important to consider the provisions of long-term care policies to know what you're buying. Here's a rundown of the more important provisions and how they vary.

A. *Daily expense coverage:* Some policies set a dollar limit on daily expenses and some pay a percentage of all expenses.

B. *Inflation protection:* You should look for a policy that provides some inflation protection as costs of nursing facility care increase. Policies that pay a percentage of expenses will pay more as expenses increase. Policies that pay a dollar limit should definitely have that dollar limit increased with the inflation rate.

C. *Hospitalization first?:* Many policies require that the insured be hospitalized first before entering a long-term care facility. Obviously this limits the policy's coverage. A policy that doesn't first require hospitalization will cost more.

D. *Can premiums increase?:* Some companies are allowed to increase premiums for a group of policyholders.

E. *Time limit on payments:* Some policies limit the number of years of payments. Policies with longer limits, or no limits, will obviously cost more.

F. *Waiting period:* Most policies won't pay benefits until after a waiting period. Companies use this time to investigate claims. Waiting periods can be as short as 20 days or as long as a year. Waiting periods are like a deductible. You can reduce the costs of a long-term policy by taking a longer waiting period.

G. *Home care also?:* Some policies only pay for care in a nursing care facility and others pay for care in both a nursing facility and at home.

The Bottom Line

With the chance of being confined to a nursing care facility increasing, insurance against long-term care costs becomes more important. One option is to use up your assets and then go on Medicaid. If you don't like this, buy long-term care insurance. Of course, note the policy's provisions, in particular, the dollar or percentage limits and inflation protection. You can reduce the costs of long-term care policies by taking a longer waiting period.

8. How Much Property Insurance Do You Need?

Property insurance insures your physical property against damage or destruction. Insurance on your home (if you're a homeowner), clothing, furniture, audio-visual equipment, and appliances are included under property insurance. Auto insurance is a separate category of property insurance and will be discussed in the next topic. Also, don't confuse property insurance with warranties. Property insurance covers physical damage and destruction. Warranties insure against malfunctions in the operation of the product not caused by physical damage. Warranties are addressed in a later chapter.

What's Covered in Homeowners Insurance

The biggest kind of property insurance is homeowners insurance. Homeowners insurance covers damage to your home and its contents and covers personal damages (liability) to anyone injured at your home.

There are a number of questions you should ask about the provisions of any homeowners insurance policy. Foremost are the types of risk covered. Table 7-8 lists the typical risks covered by a homeowner's insurance policy. Obviously the more risks covered by the policy the more expensive the policy. In addition to the risks listed in Table 7-8, you might also want coverage for buildings other than the main house on your property (e.g., detached garage, storage building), for debris removal and landscaping, and for a living allowance while you live elsewhere during the home's repair.

What dollar amount of coverage should you buy on a homeowner's policy? First recognize that most homeowners don't need to insure their land and the home's foundation. In most cases the land and foundation can't be destroyed by typical disasters. Instead, you want to insure for the *replacement value* of your home's *structure*. The replacement value is what it would cost to replace the home's structure everything except

REPLACEMENT
VALUE

Table 7-8   Typical risks covered by a homeowner's insurance policy.

Fire, lightning	Theft
Windstorm, hail	Glass breakage
Explosion	Falling Objects
Riots	Weight of ice, snow, sleet
Damage by aircraft	Collapse of building
Damage by others' vehicles	Water damage
Smoke damage	Freeze damage
Vandalism	Electrical damage

the land and foundation) if the home were totally destroyed. You can determine the replacement value by paying for an appraisal of the home or by estimating it from a knowledge of land prices.

For example, suppose you purchase a house on a ½ acre of land for $150,000. If land in the neighborhood costs $50,000 an acre, then your ½ acre of land is worth $15,000. Also, suppose the house's foundation cost $3,000 to construct. The replacement value of the house's structure is therefore $132,000 ($150,000 −$15,000 −$3,000).

Some insurance companies use as a rule of thumb to set the amount of home insurance equal to the mortgage amount held by the homeowner. This protects the mortgage company's interest, but it may not be enough to fully replace the structure for the homeowner.

80% RULE   Most insurance companies also use the "80 percent rule." This rule says that 80 percent of the home's replacement value (not including the value of the lot) at any time must be insured for full replacement of losses to be made. If less than 80 percent of the home's replacement value is insured, then the insurance company will only pay a fraction of losses equal to the actual amount of coverage divided by 80 percent of the home's replacement value. The following examples will illustrate this principle at work.

EXAMPLE 7-1:   Martha and George own a home whose replacement value is $100,000. They have insurance coverage equal to $60,000. They suffer a fire loss equal to $20,000. How much of the $20,000 will the insurance company pay?

ANSWER:

$$\$20,000 \times \frac{\$60,000}{\$100,000 \times .80} = \$15,000$$

EXAMPLE 7-2: Roselyn and jimmy bought a house three years ago that, at that time, had a replacement value of $100,000. They bought insurance then with coverage of $90,000. Today their home has a replacement value of $150,000. They suffer wind damage equal to $5,000. How much of this $5,000 will the insurance company pay?

ANSWER: Eighty percent of the current replacement value is $120,000 ($150,000 × .8). Roselyn and Jimmy's coverage is now less than this at $90,000. The company will therefore pay:

$$\$5,000 \times \frac{\$90,000}{\$120,000} = \$3,750.$$

When analyzing a homeowner's insurance policy, make sure you understand the company's definition of "replacement cost." Does it refer only to the structure's value without the foundation, or does it include the structure and foundation?

Inflation Protection

EXAMPLE 7-2 demonstrates that inflation and the increasing dollar value of homes is an important consideration in homeowner's insurance. The point is simply that replacement costs of homes will rise over time with inflation. If your homeowner's insurance policy doesn't take this into account, then the "real" value of your coverage will decline over time.

Most insurance companies offer a provision in their homeowner's policies which provides inflation protection. The provision automatically increases the coverage amount each year in line with some national inflation index (like the CPI). To pay for this additional coverage, premiums also rise.

Is such an inflation provision adequate to keep your coverage up with the rising replacement costs of your home? The answer depends on how fast your home's replacement costs are rising compared to the national inflation rate. If your home's replacement costs are rising no faster than the national inflation rate, then the provision is adequate. But if you live in an area of the country where housing costs are rising faster than the national rate of inflation, then the provision would not be adequate. You would need to purchase additional coverage in excess of that provided by the inflation provision.

Coverage of Contents

Homeowners insurance also covers damage or destruction to the contents of your home, items like furniture, appliances, clothing, and audio-visual equipment. There are two ways—an easy way and a hard way—to estimate the coverage amount required for these contents. The easy way is to estimate the value of the contents as some percent (say 15–20 percent) of the value of the structure. The hard way is to itemize all the contents and attach a value to each.

There are also two ways that an insurance company can reimburse you for a loss. One way is to reimburse you for the actual (depreciated) value of the damaged or destroyed item, not the replacement value. The depreciated value will be less than the replacement value. For example, suppose you bought a TV for $500 four years ago. If the average TV has a useful life of eight years, then the current depreciated value may be only $250 because half of the TV has been "used up." A policy reimbursing only depreciated value would give you only $250 for the TV if it were destroyed. The best you could do would be to purchase a used four-year old TV to replace the destroyed TV.

DEPRECIATED VALUE OF CONTENTS

REPLACEMENT VALUE OF CONTENTS

The second method of reimbursement for contents is to reimburse replacement cost. In the TV example, this would mean a reimbursement payment sufficient for to buy a new TV comparable in style, size, and performance to the destroyed TV. Most consumers would probably prefer this form of reimbursement. To get it, however, policy premiums will be 10 to 15 percent higher.

Deductibles

Deductibles are available for homeowner's insurance, and as with other kinds of insurance, taking a larger deductible can save you money on premiums. For example, increasing the deductible from $100 to $250 can reduce premiums by as much as 25 percent, and increasing the deductible from $250 to $500 can slash another 10 percent from premiums. Again, it makes economic sense to take a larger deductible, self-insure for small losses, and use the savings to buy greater coverage.

Renter's Insurance

If you're not a homeowner, do you still need property insurance? The answer is a definite yes! If you rent an apartment and the apartment building burns, the landlord loses the apartment building but you lose your possessions in the apartment. The landlord is under no obligation to reimburse you for loss of your possessions. So you need property insurance on your possessions and contents in the apartment. You might also want this policy to include living expenses if you must temporarily move out of the apartment while repairs are being made.

Another reason to purchase renter's insurance is for liability protection. If someone injures himself inside your apartment and has substantial damages and medical expenses, the liability part of a renter's policy will protect you and pay any claims you are found responsible for.

The Bottom Line

Buy homeowner's insurance to protect your home and its contents against damage or destruction and to protect yourself (and your net worth) against injury claims filed by those injured on your property. Add an inflation provision to the policy to make sure coverage keeps up with replacement costs. Contents can be insured for their depreciated value or their replacement value. If you're a renter, buy renter's insurance to protect your possessions and to protect against injury claims.

9. What Kind of Auto Insurance Should You Buy?

Why buy auto insurance, you might say. You're a careful driver and have never had an accident. Wouldn't buying auto insurance be just a waste of money?

One reason you buy auto insurance is because it's required in most states. But, also, buying auto insurance makes good economic sense. No driver can perfectly predict if and when an accident will occur and how extensive it will be. Potential damages from an accident include not only damage to the auto, but also personal physical injury. Personal physical injury to others caused by you and your auto is the largest potential claim on you and your wealth.

Premiums

Insurance companies use characteristics such as age, occupation, sex, driving record, and miles driven to predict the probability of an accident and the expected pay-out. Also, if a driver has one accident, the probability of having another accident increases, so premiums rise.

Among the characteristics cited above as influencing auto premiums, age is first and foremost. For example, a study in Wyoming showed that drivers aged 15–24 were 24 percent of the population but were involved in 52 percent of the accidents with an arrest and 40 percent of the accidents without an arrest.[2]

---

[2]Spahr, Ronald W. and Edmond L. Escolas, "1979 Automobile Accident Reports: Do Driver Characteristics Support Rate Discrimination?" *Journal of Risk and Insurance*, Vol. 49, No. 1, March 1982, pp. 91–103.

Types of Auto Insurance Coverage

Auto insurance covers a number of risks. Not only must you worry about injury and damage to you and your car, but you must also worry about injury and damage to other people and their cars in the event that you are at fault in the accident.

Let's first consider the coverage you need for injury and damage to others in the event that you were the cause of the accident. There are two components to this coverage, bodily injury coverage and property damage coverage.

BODILY INJURY
COVERAGE

Bodily injury coverage pays for injury or death to other people resulting from the accident which you caused. Suppose, for example, you run a red light and plow into the side of Fred's car. Fred has extensive injuries and is in the hospital for months. If it's determined that you were the cause of the accident, then your bodily injury coverage will pay Fred's medical bills and related expenses.

PROPERTY DAMAGE
COVERAGE

Property damage coverage pays for damage your auto causes to someone else's property, again in the event that you were the cause of the accident. If, when you ran the red light and hit Fred's car, you did $4,000 of damage to Fred's car, property damage coverage would pay the bill.

The limits which your insurance company will pay on bodily injury and property damage are usually expressed in a shortcut form by "XXX/YYY/ZZZ." "XXX" is the maximum payment in thousands of dollars per accident for bodily injury to any one person, "YYY" is the maximum payment in thousands of dollars per accident for bodily injury to all persons, and "ZZZ" is the maximum payment in thousands of dollars per accident for all property damage. For example, if your limits are "100/300/500," then a maximum of $100,000 will be paid for bodily injury to any single person, a maximum of $300,000 will be paid for bodily injury to all persons, and a maximum of $500,000 will be paid for all property damage, including damage to others' autos.

Collision, comprehensive, medical, and uninsured motorist are all coverages that pay money to you in the event of an accident or other damage to your car.

COLLISION

Collision pays for damage to your car resulting from an accident in which you were the cause (if the other driver was at fault, then her insurance pays for damages to your car). The cost of collision protection increases with the value of your car. That is, collision protection for a $30,000 Mercedes will cost more than protection for a $7,000 Yugo.

Since cars depreciate in value over time, you should periodically reduce your collision coverage to keep it in line with the car's current value. Collision will pay no more than the current depreciated value of your car. Suppose, for example, you have a ten year old car worth $500, the car is damaged in an accident, and it would cost $2,000 to repair the car. The most the insurance company will pay you is $500. The philosophy of the insurance company is that you can buy a used car of the same condition for $500 and you'll be no worse off. There is no provision in auto insurance, as there is in home insurance, where you can be reimbursed enough to buy a new car.

COMPREHENSIVE   *Comprehensive* coverage pays for damage to your car resulting from non-accidents, such as fire, windstorms, vandalism, and theft. Again, keep your comprehensive coverage in line with your car's current value.

MEDICAL INSURANCE   *Medical insurance* pays for medical and hospital costs for you and your passengers as a result of an accident and in the event that you are at fault in the accident.

Finally, what if you're in an accident the other driver is at fault, but the other driver doesn't have enough insurance? What happens then; are you up a creek without a paddle? This situation is what the final type of coverage, called uninsured motorists insurance, is for. *Uninsured motorists insurance* pays for injuries to you and your passengers should injury be caused by a motorist whose insurance is inadequate. Usually only bodily damage is covered. Damage to your car is not generally covered by uninsured motorists insurance.

UNINSURED
MOTORISTS
INSURANCE

C O N S U M E R   **T O P I C**

AWARDS FOR LOSS OF ENJOYMENT OF LIFE

Juries in accident trials have typically awarded plaintiffs money to pay for damages to their property (e.g., car) and money for medical expenses or lost income. Recently juries have begun awarding a new type of damage called "compensation for loss of enjoyment of life." For example, suppose Sally loses an arm in an accident. Not only is Sally compensated for medical expenses and lost income, but she's also compensated for loss of enjoyment of life due to having only one arm. The loss of enjoyment of life is due to the fact that, with one arm, Sally can't enjoy many activities like golf, baseball, basketball, and can't perform many tasks around the house.

Economists working for lawyers have begun estimating the "loss of enjoyment of life" due to various injuries and illnesses. Often these estimates are in the millions of dollars. This has greatly inflated jury awards and brought calls for guidelines to control awards for "loss of enjoyment of life." Currently there are no restrictions on the amount that can be awarded for this kind of loss. One suggestion is not to prohibit the awards, but to legislate allowable ranges for them.

Reference: "Computing Damages for Personal Injury." *The Urban Institute,* Policy and Research Report, Vol. 19, No. 3, Fall 1989, pp. 14–16.

Table 7-9 Components of an auto insurance policy.

For injury and damage to others:

1. Bodily injury coverage—pays for injury or death to other people resulting from an accident caused by you.

2. Property damage coverage—pays for damage your auto causes to other's property.

For injury and damage to you and your car:

1. Collision—pays for damage to your car if you caused the accident.

2. Comprehensive—pays for damage to your car resulting from non-accidents.

3. Medical insurance—pays for medical costs for you and your passengers if you caused the accident.

4. Uninsured motorists insurance—pays for injuries to you and your passengers if other driver is at fault and his insurance isn't adequate.

Deductibles and Amount of Coverage

Deductibles are available with the collision and comprehensive components of auto insurance. As with other types of insurance, taking a larger deductible will save you money on premiums. For example, increasing the deductible from $100 to $250 can reduce premiums by 23 percent, increasing the deductible to $500 can save another 22 percent and increasing the deductible to $1,000 can save another 15 percent on premiums.

If you follow the recommendation of insuring against big losses and self-insuring for small loss, then you should take big deductibles and use the savings to buy more coverage. In particular, you should buy large coverage ($300,000–$500,000) for bodily injury, uninsured motorists insurance, and medical coverage. Coverage for collision and comprehensive should be kept close to the depreciated value of your car.

Fault and Auto Insurance Costs

As you have learned from the above discussion, the assignment of fault in an auto accident determines who pays the damages and injuries in the accident. If you're at fault, then your insurance company pays, but if the other driver is at fault, then that driver's company pays.

But how is fault assigned? What happens if one driver bears most of the fault, but the other driver is also a little bit at fault? There are two alternative legal approaches to these questions. The legal concept of

CONSUMER TOPIC

VARIATION IN AUTO INSURANCE RATES

Substantial variation in auto insurance rates can be seen by examining average rates by state. In 2008, average annual spending per vehicle for auto insurance ranged from a low of $503 in North Dakota to a high of $1126 in D.C.

Although many factors affect the level of auto insurance rates, the influence of living patterns can be easily seen by identifying the highest and lowest cost states. Five states and D.C. had average costs above $1,000: Delaware, D.C., Florida, Louisiana, New Jersey, and New York. Also, seven states had average costs below $600: Idaho, Iowa, Kansas, Nebraska, North Carolina, North Dakota, and South Dakota.

Clearly, the degree of population density in the state affects auto insurance rates. Notice that most states with high costs are urban, high-density states, whereas most states with low costs are much more rural. It makes sense that auto insurance rates are higher in states with high density. The chances of having an auto accident increase as more people and cars are packed into a given land area.

Data Source: US, Bureau of the Census, Statistical Abstract of the U.S., 2012.

CONTRIBUTORY NEGLIGENCE

COMPARATIVE NEGLIGENCE

contributory negligence says that in order for you to be awarded damages from the other driver, you must be free of all fault, however slight, in causing the accident. Alternatively, the legal concept of *comparative negligence* says that you can still recover damages from the other driver even if you are slightly at fault. The damages you recover will be in proportion to the fault of the other driver. For example, if it is found that the other driver was 80 percent responsible for the accident, then 80 percent of your damages would be paid by the other driver's insurance company.

From the consumer's perspective, comparative negligence is better because the driver can collect even if he is partially at risk. Most states have comparative negligence (only Alabama, D.C., Maryland, North Carolina, South Carolina, and Virginia have contributory negligence). However, research shows that comparative negligence costs the consumer more in auto insurance premiums because companies face larger expected pay-outs with comparative negligence compared to contributory negligence. Flanigan, Johnson, Winkler, and Ferguson found auto insurance premiums 12 percent higher in comparative negligence states, even after accounting for other factors affecting auto insurance premiums.[3]

---

[3] Flanigan, George B., Joseph E. Johnson, Daniel T. Winkler, and William Ferguson. "Evidence from Early Tort Reforms: Comparative Negligence Since 1974," *Journal of Risk and Insurance*, Sept, 1989, Vol. 56, No. 3, pp. 525–531.

IS STATE REGULATION OF AUTO INSURANCE BENEFICIAL?

A special law passed by Congress in 1945 allows states to regulate the auto insurance industry. The rationale for such regulation is that it protects the financial solvency of the auto insurance industry and prevents "excessive" competition. Regulation is also supposed to keep auto insurance premiums at affordable levels for consumers.

But in a market with many competitors, what are the effects of regulating prices? Suppose State A says that insurers can't charge auto premiums higher than $500 per year. What will auto insurers do? They will insure all drivers whose risk characteristics and driving record indicate a premium of no more than $500 annually, and they won't insure more risky drivers.

But if State A requires that all drivers have auto insurance (as most states do), then there's the dilemma of what to do with the drivers that companies don't want to insure at the regulated premiums. Most states have solved this problem by setting up an involuntary auto insurance market (also called a reinsurance market). Drivers who can't get insurance on their own are put in this market. All insurance companies share in the risk of insuring these drivers. If the involuntary market results in losses to the insurers (because they can't charge rates high enough to pay for losses), then the companies will have to charge higher rates to all other drivers, or insurers will have to make up the difference by reducing their levels of service, promotion, and advertising.

What, then, does state regulation of the auto insurance industry, and particularly of auto insurance premiums, accomplish? First, it probably results in more drivers being put into the "involuntary" market. Second, it probably results in "safe" drivers paying more to subsidize "unsafe" drivers in the involuntary market. So safe drivers pay higher premiums and unsafe drivers pay lower premiums. It's unclear, however, whether average premiums are lower or unaffected under regulation.

Many studies have attempted to estimate the effects of state regulation of the auto insurance market. There is strong evidence from these studies that the percentage of drivers in the involuntary market is higher in those states with stricter regulations. For example, Grabowski, Viscusi, and Evans found that those states with the strictest regulation of the auto insurance industry had at least 25 percent of their drivers in the involuntary market, whereas other states had ten percent or less. Annual subsidies per driver in the involuntary market are as high as $300 in those states with the tightest regulations.

The studies show no consistent impact of regulation on average auto insurance premiums. For example, Pauly et al., and Harrington found that regulation lowered premiums, Joskow and D'Arcy found that regulation raised premiums, and

(continued on next page)

C
O
N
S
U
M
E
R

T
O
P
I
C

(continued from previous page)

Ippolito found that regulation had no impact on auto premiums. These mixed results shouldn't be surprising if regulation's main impact is not to reduce total cost but simply to change who pays those costs.

References: D'Arcy, S. "An Economic Theory of Insurance Regulation," Ph.D. dissertation, University of Illinois, 1982

Grabowski, Henry, W. Kip Viscusi, and William N. Evans. "Price and Availability Tradeoffs of Automobile Insurance Regulation," *Journal of Insurance Regulation*, Vol. 56, No. 2, June 1989, pp. 275–299.

Harrington, S. E, "A Random Coefficient Model of Interstate Differences in the Impact of Rate Regulation on Auto Insurance Prices." Working Paper, Wharton School, University of Pennsylvania, 1984.

Ippolito, R. "The Effects of Price Regulation in the Automobile insurance Industry," *Journal of Law and Economics,* Vol. 22, April 1979, pp. 55–89.

Joskow, P. "Cartels, Competition and Regulation in the Property-Liability Insurance Industry," Bell Journal of Economics and Management Science, Vol. 4, 1973, pp. 375–427.

Pauly, M., H. Kunreuther, and P. Kleindorfer. "Regulation and Quality Competition in the U.S. Insurance Industry," in J. Finsinger and M. Pauly, eds., The Economics of Insurance Regulation, London: Macmillan, 1986, pp. 65–107.

No-Fault Auto Insurance

No-fault auto insurance was once thought to be a way to reduce auto insurance costs. No-fault insurance is auto insurance in which fault does not have to be established before insurance payment is made. Instead, if Joe Jaguar had an auto accident, Joe Jaguar's insurance company would pay for damages to Joe's car and injuries to Joe, whether the accident was Joe's fault or not (under the "fault" system, the insurance company of the driver who was proven to have caused the accident pays for the bulk of the damages). The idea was that if fault did not have to be proven in accidents, then legal fees could be saved and auto insurance premiums lowered.

However, some economic studies have found just the opposite; that is, no-fault auto insurance is associated with higher, not lower, auto insurance premiums (see CONSUMER TOPIC). This result shouldn't, perhaps, be surprising. Since no-fault weakens the link between individual responsibility and payment, no-fault auto insurance gives drivers, in general, less incentive to be cautious of their actions and gives insurance companies less incentive to penalize drivers who have frequent accidents. Therefore, the institution of no-fault auto insurance may in fact, have the effect of promoting more accident-causing behavior.

WHAT'S WRONG WITH NO-FAULT?

C O N S U M E R

T O P I C

No-fault auto insurance was heralded as a way to reduce auto insurance costs by cutting out the middleman—the lawyer. But two studies have found this not to be the case. A study by Elizabeth Landes found that states with no-fault did not have fewer accidents. Landes' results took account of differences in population densities (which likely influence accident rates) and differences in definitions of no-fault.

A study by Johnson, Flanagan, and Weeks (JFW) directly examined the impact of no-fault insurance on auto insurance premiums between states. The study recognized that many factors other than the type of fault system influence differences in average driver premiums between states. The factors that JFW "controlled for" included population density, the average hourly manufacturing wage, and motor vehicle fatalities per registered driver JFW found all three factors were positively related to auto insurance premiums.

Even after controlling for these three factors, JFW still found that states with no-fault systems had higher insurance premiums than states without no-fault. JFW found that states with true no-fault system had average premiums $12 to $13 higher.

So, based on the evidence of these two studies, no-fault auto insurance has not saved money for drivers.

References: Landes, Elizabeth M. "Insurance, Liability, and Accidents." *Journal of Law and Economics*, Vol. 25, No. 1, April 1982, pp. 49–65.

Johnson, Joseph F., George B. Flanigan, and James K. Weeks, "An Empirical Investigation of the Costs of Adopting No Fault Insurance Systems, 1971–80. *Journal of Insurance Regulation*, Vol. 2, No, 2, December 1983, pp. 168–175.

The Bottom Line

Auto insurance is a must, but be careful not to over-insure on some components and under-insure on others. Don't over-insure on collision and comprehensive coverage. Reduce this coverage as the value of your car depreciates. Don't under-insure on bodily insurance and medical insurance. Take large deductibles on collision and comprehensive to reduce premiums.

WORDS AND CONCEPTS YOU SHOULD KNOW

Pure risks
Speculative risks
Frequency of loss occurring
Severity of loss
Self insurance
Expected loss
Utils
Deductible
Co-insurance
Disability insurance
Definition of disability
Workmen's Compensation
Social Security disability insurance
Future increase option
Cost-of-living rider
Waiting period
Social Security rider
Residual rider
Elimination period
Definition of accident
Group health insurance
Medicare
Medigap

Medicaid
CHIP
Indemnity (fee-for-service) plans
Health maintenance organizations (HMOs)
Preferred provider organizations (PPOs)
Point-of-service organizations (POS)
Consumer-directed health plans
Health Savings Account (HSA)
Long-term care
Living benefit life insurance policy
Property insurance
80 percent rule
Replacement value
Depreciated value
Renter's insurance
Bodily injury coverage
Property damage coverage
Collision coverage
Comprehensive coverage
Uninsured motorists insurance
Contributory negligence
Comparative negligence
No-fault auto insurance

HEALTH, PROPERTY AND AUTO INSURANCE—A SUMMARY

1. Many products and activities involve risk. You can do four things about risk. You can avoid the risk, reduce the risk, self-insure (accept the risk), or buy insurance.

    A. Insurance should be bought on those products or activities that have the highest expected loss. Expected loss equals the frequency of a risk occurring multiplied by the severity of loss.

    B. "Big losses" are proportionally more severe to consumers than "small losses" (for example, a $50,000 expected loss is more than ten times as severe as a $5,000 expected loss). This means that more importance should be given to insuring large, catastrophic losses. A suggested priority for insurance coverage is:
       - death (if have dependents)
       - liability
       - medical costs
       - liability
       - property damage to home
       - property damage to possessions
       - property damage to car.

2. Insurers set insurance premiums so that the present value of premiums collected over time equal the present value of expected benefits paid by the insured plus the present value of service costs. Insurance premiums rise if:
   - the probabilities of claims rise,
   - uncertainties of future claims rise,
   - the average size of claims rise.

3. A deductible is the dollars you pay out of your pocket on an insurance claim before the insurance company pays anything. The advantage of taking a larger deductible is that it lowers the cost per dollar of insurance coverage. Costs are lower with a higher deductible because administrative costs per claim are lower for large claims and because consumers will be more careful to avoid losses when there is a deductible.

Buying an insurance policy with a larger deductible makes economic sense. With a large-deductible policy, you self-insure for small losses. However, the lower cost per dollar of insurance allows you to afford greater coverage and insure against catastrophic losses. Some economists recommend choosing deductibles equal to 3 percent of the consumers's net worth.

4. A co-insurance rate is the percentage of a loss, after subtracting the deductible, which the insured must pay. For example, with a policy with a $500 deductible, a 10 percent co-insurance rate and a $10,000 loss, you pay the $500 deductible and 10 percent of the remaining loss (10 percent of $9,500). Usually there's a cap on the co-insurance amount.

The advantage of taking a policy with a co-insurance rate is that such policies are cheaper, thereby allowing you to afford more coverage.

5. Disability insurance pays benefits if you are sick or injured for an extended time period and can't work.
   A. There are two public disability insurance programs. Workmen's Compensation and Social Security. Workmen's Compensation only pays if you're injured or become ill on the job. Benefits are usually low. Social Security disability insurance only pays if you are totally disabled and can't do any kind of work. Benefits depend on your income and work history.
   B. Carefully study the provisions of private disability policies.
      a. Definition of disability:
         Inability to do current job (least restrictive),
         Inability to do any job for which you're trained,
         Inability to do any job (most restrictive).
      b. Amount of coverage:
         Replace 65–80 percent of income.
      c. Future increase option—allows you to buy more coverage as your income rises.
      d. Cost of living rider—means that once benefits begin, they are periodically increased with the cost of living.
      e. Waiting period—is the period of time after a disability occurs and before payments begin. It is similar to a deductible because premiums are lower for policies with longer waiting periods.
      f. Time limit on payments—states how long benefits are paid.
      g. Social Security rider—if the insured qualifies for Social Security disability benefits, it reduces your benefits by the amount of the Social Security benefits.
      h. Residual rider—makes up some of the income lost by self-employed and business persons who have been disabled and return to work to find their business has shrunk.

6. Buy health insurance to guard against big medical expenses that could destroy your savings and net worth. Buy policies with larger deductibles in order to afford greater coverage.

   A health insurance policy's provisions will determine its cost. Carefully study a policy to see what treatments and care it will cover and how much it will pay. Other important provisions are:
   A. Elimination period—time period after an injury or illness when no benefits are paid. It is like a deductible because policy costs are lower for policies with longer elimination periods.
   B. How is "accident" defined?—One definition says an injury is an accident only if the cause and result were unintended and unexpected. The second definition is less restrictive, specifying an injury as an accident if the result was unintended and unexpected.
   C. Pre-existing condition—specifies the time period during which the policy won't pay benefits for an illness or injury which existed before the policy was issued.
   D. Limits—specifies limits on dollars paid for treatments and services.

7. Health insurance is the U.S. is provided through three mechanisms: private insurance (employment-based or individual plans), social insurance (Medicare), and social welfare programs (Medicaid and CHIP).

8. Medicare is federally funded health insurance for consumers over age 65. Medicare has four parts. Part A is hospital insurance. Part B is if for physician services. The original Part A and Part B are fee-for-service plans that may need to be supplemented by a private Medigap plan. Part C is Medicare Advantage plans that combine Part A, Part B, and usually Part D benefits into a HMO or PPO type of arrangement. Part D is prescription drug coverage.

9. Medicaid is the joint federal and state program that pays medical expenses for the poor. CHIP is the joint federal and state program that provides health insurance for children in lower-income families that do not qualify for Medicaid. Eligibility varies by state, but usually consumers must have income below or near poverty level and have very few assets to qualify to Medicaid.

10. Health insurance and care delivery method can be roughly classified into five types. The traditional indemnity plan, also called fee-for-service plans, pays physicians and hospitals on a per-service basis. Health maintenance organizations (HMOs) cover care rendered by

those doctors and professionals who have agreed by contract to treat patients in accordance with the HMO's guidelines and restrictions in exchange for a steady stream of customers. In turn HMOs are able to lower costs. Preferred provider organizations (PPOs) negotiate discounts with doctors, hospitals and other providers, who then become part of the PPO network. When you see a physician in the network, you typically make a copayment. When you see a physician out of the network, you'll still receive coverage, but your insurance will only cover a portion of the bill. Point-of-service organizations (POS) combine elements of both a health maintenance organization (HMO) and a preferred provider organization (PPO). The plan allows you to use a primary care physician to coordinate your care, or you can self-direct your care at the "point of service." Consumer-directed health plans give you more control over your own health care, both in choosing the care you receive and paying for it. They often require you to pay a substantial deductible before coverage starts, and are combined with a Health Savings Account (HSA) that allows you to save money to pay for current and future medical expenses on a tax-free basis.

11. Long-term health care is medical or personal care received by a person at home or in a care facility on a continuing basis. Medicare pays for only a very limited amount of long term care.

   Living benefit policies are life insurance policies which allow some of their face value amount to be accessed for long term care for the insured.

   Long-term health care policies are insurance policies specifically designed to pay for long term care. Important provisions of long term care policies include:
   A. Inflation protection will increase benefits along with inflation,
   B. A provision requiring hospitalization first will limit use of the policy,
   C. Time limit on payments specifies how long benefits can be paid,
   D. The waiting period specifies how long the consumer must wait before benefits begin. Policies with longer waiting periods cost less.
   E. Are benefits also paid for home care?

12. Property insurance protects your physical property, such as your home, clothing, furniture, audio-visual equipment, and appliances, against destruction or damage.

    A. For your home, insure for replacement costs. Land costs and the house's foundation are not included in replacement costs. Add an inflation rider to the policy to keep coverage in line with rising replacement costs.

    B. Most insurance companies require that 80 percent of a home's replacement value at any time be insured for full replacement of losses.

    C. Contents can be insured in two ways: as some percent of the value of the structure, or based on their itemized value. Also, contents can be insured for their actual, depreciated value or their replacement value. The replacement value method is more expensive.

    D. Take large deductibles to reduce the cost of homeowner's insurance.

    E. If you rent, you still need insurance on contents and against claims made by those injured in your apartment.

13. There are six components of an auto insurance policy:

    A. Bodily injury coverage—pays for injury or death to other people resulting from accident you caused.

    B. Property damage coverage—pays for damage your auto causes to other's property,

    C. Collision—pays for damage to your car if you caused the accident.

    D. Comprehensive—pays for damage to your car resulting from non-accidents.

    E. Medical insurance—pays for medical costs for you and your passengers if you caused the accident.

    F. Uninsured motorists insurance—pays for injuries to you and your passengers if other driver is at fault and his insurance isn't adequate.

       States with contributory negligence laws say that you must be free of all fault in an accident in order to collect from someone else.

       States with comparative negligence laws say you can recover damages from someone else even if you are partially at fault. You recover damages in proportion to the fault of the other driver.

       No-fault auto insurance is a system where everyone's insurance company pays for their insured's damage. Fault does not have to be established. Research shows that no-fault has not lowered insurance costs.

DISCUSSION QUESTIONS

1. Define the difference between a pure risk and a speculative risk.

2. If you pay thousands of dollars for auto insurance over the years and never have an accident, has the expenditure been wasted? Why, or why not?

3. How do pure risks differ? What can be done about pure risks?

4. If you had only enough money to buy medical insurance or to buy collision insurance for your car, which should you buy and why?

5. If many Congressmen and legislators begin talking about passing laws to make it easier for consumers to sue and collect damages from producers, why might product liability insurance premiums rise even before the new legislation is passed?

6. Why do insurance policies with high deductibles make economic sense?

7. What are the three ways that a disability can be defined?

8. Why is a waiting period provision in a disability insurance policy like a deductible? Why is an elimination period in a health insurance policy like a deductible?

9. What is the major reason why the prices of health insurance policies differ?

10. What are the different types of health insurance plans?

11. Name several options for addressing long-term health care.

12. What is the difference between insuring depreciated value and insuring replacement value on personal possessions?

13. What is no-fault auto insurance?

14. What are some advantages and disadvantages of national health insurance?

PROBLEMS

1. If the chance that you'll fall off your bicycle is 20 percent, and the severity of loss of the fall is $250, what is the expected loss from riding your bicycle?

2. If the probability of you dying in the next year is 1 percent, and the severity of loss from your death to your dependents is $1,000,000, what is the expected loss from you dying in the next year?

3. You have an insurance policy with a $250 deductible and a 15 percent co-insurance rate with a $500 maximum. You suffer a $20,000 loss. How much do you pay and how much does the insurance company pay?

4. Gail and Fred own a home whose replacement value is $150,000. They have insurance coverage for only $80,000. They suffer a fire loss equal to $30,000. How much of the loss will the insurance company pay?

Fundamentals of Investing

Introduction

When people think of personal finance, they immediately think of investing. You now know that investing is only a part of personal finance and consumer economics, yet it is a very important part. Most of us have some kind of investments at any point in time. We use investing for many different reasons—we invest for our children's education, for a house downpayment, for a Hawaiian vacation, and for our retirement, to name a few examples.

It's important to realize that investing doesn't mean just putting money in the bank or stock market. You and your family are also important assets, and investing in yourself and your family, via formal education, on-the-job training, and even child-rearing are issues also considered in this chapter.

To the uninformed, investing can appear very bewildering. The menu of potential investments, even for the small saver, has exploded in recent years, as have the number of "financial advisers" pushing those investments. Furthermore, the national economy, over which we have no control, can affect our investments, and this introduces another degree of uncertainty. For example, a particular investment that performs well when inflation is low may be a disaster when inflation is high. The economic roller coaster which you learned about in Chapter 2 can pull particular investments up and down as it goes through its twists and turns and peaks and valleys.

This is the first of two chapters about investing. This chapter discusses the fundamentals of investing, that is, that basic knowledge that you need to know before you invest your money or time. In this chapter you'll learn why investment goals should be modest, you'll learn about the multiple kinds of risk and the relationship between risk and return, and you'll work your way through the maze of calculating investment returns (it's really not that bad). You'll also learn about investing in yourself and in your family. After conquering these fundamentals, you'll be ready to forge ahead into the next chapter, Types of Investments.

1. Why Should You Invest?

Investing is the opposite of borrowing. As explained in Chapter 5, with borrowing you are transferring resources (money) you will have in the future to the present for current use. With investing, you are transferring resources (money) you have now to the future for use then.

In fact, at the aggregate level, borrowing and investing are interrelated. Those people who invest are providing the funds to those people who borrow. Also, those people who borrow pay an interest rate for their loans, and the interest paid by borrowers provides the rate of return earned by investors (see Figure 8-1). Of course, the rate of return earned by investors is frequently lower than the interest rate paid by borrowers. This is because brokers (banks, savings and loans, stockbrokers), whose job is to match investors to borrowers, earn a "cut" of the interest rate paid by borrowers.

Figure 8-1. The investing/borrowing cycle.

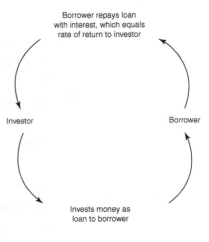

Borrower repays loan with interest, which equals rate of return to investor

Investor

Borrower

Invests money as loan to borrower

Saving Is Not Investing

INVESTING

Saving is not investing. Savings means taking money and putting it in a mattress, home safe, or safe deposit box. Investing means taking the money you have saved and "putting it to work" to earn a rate of return. The disadvantage of investing is that you usually take some risk of losing your money when investing (more about risk later). So, why take the chance and invest?

INFLATION AGAIN

The answer is simple (you've probably guessed it already). If you put your money in a mattress or safe deposit box, you really lose money over time. Why? Because of our old bug-a-boo, inflation. As time marches on, inflation rolls on, and every dose of inflation reduces the purchasing power of dollars you have in your mattress or safe deposit box. For example, if you put $1000 in your safe deposit box today and inflation averages 5 percent a year, then in 10 years your $1000 will only be worth $614 in purchasing power. Your goal of transferring purchasing power has gone haywire. The reason you take a chance and invest is so the purchasing power of your saved dollars will at least keep pace with inflation, and maybe exceed inflation. Therefore, when, at some future date, you're ready to use the money you've saved, its purchasing power will at least be the same as, and hopefully higher than, when you initially invested it.

This viewpoint of investing is much different from the viewpoint of those who think that investing means trying to "get rich quick." Of course, if you can "get rich quick" by investing, so much the better, but it usually means taking a lot of risk in your investment plans. Here, we want to stress a much more modest goal of investing. You invest in order to transfer purchasing power to the future. In investing, your goal is to earn a rate of return that at least compensates for the erosion caused by inflation.[1] This is illustrated in Figure 8-2. As you'll see, sometimes even this goal is hard to achieve.

---

[1]Taxes also erode purchasing power, so the investment rate of return really should compensate for the erosion caused by inflation and taxes.

Rate of Time Preference Again

Figure 8-2. Invest to counteract inflation.

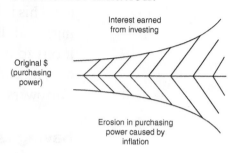

You've already learned about your personal rate of time preference in Chapter 1, but let's review it again because it's a very important determinant in how much you invest.

Your personal rate of time preference indicates the trading you're willing to do between present consumption and future consumption. The personal rate of time preference is expressed as a percent, such as 5 percent, 10 percent, or 20 percent. Your personal rate of time preference tells how many extra dollars of consumption you'll need next year in order to give up one dollar of consumption this year. So, if, for example, your personal rate of time preference is 10 percent, this means you need $1.10 of consumption next year in order to be willing to give up $1.00 this year. The higher your personal rate of time preference, the more you like consumption today as compared to consumption in the future.

The implication of your personal rate of time preference for investing should be obvious. The higher your personal rate of time preference, the less willing you are to transfer current purchasing power to the future, so the less willing you are to invest and the more willing you are to borrow. In contrast, the lower your personal rate of time preference, the more willing you are to transfer current purchasing power to the future, and so the more willing you are to invest. In short, consumers with a high personal rate of time preference will invest a smaller percentage of their income than people with a low personal rate of time preference.

BORROWING VS. INVESTING

AGE

What determines your personal rate of time preference? Two important factors are age and economic circumstances. In general, your rate of time preference falls as you age and so your willingness to invest should rise with age. This is related to the maturing process; as you age you're able to look farther ahead and consider consumption over a longer time period. When you reach senior citizen status, however, your rate of time preference may rise since your time horizon is now shorter. However, counteracting this impact may be the desire to pass wealth on to your descendants and to their future consumption.

ECONOMIC SITUATION

Economic circumstances also influence a consumer's personal rate of time preference. Consumers whose economic circumstances are poor and whose economic outlook is no better have little motivation to postpone consumption for tomorrow. Such consumers will have a high rate of time preference and will generally save very little. In contrast, consumers whose economic circumstances are good and whose economic outlook is bright will have a low rate of time preference. Such consumers have a strong motivation to "live for tomorrow" and will be much more willing to delay consumption.

The Life Cycle of Investing

Consistent with the Life Cycle Saving's Hypothesis discussed in Chapter 5, the investing behavior of most consumers follows a typical pattern with age. Consumers in their 20s and 30s have a high rate of time preference due to demands for current consumption from establishing a household and raising children. Savings and investing during this time is low. When they reach their 40s and 50s, consumers' rate of time preference falls as children have left the nest and are on their own, and large household purchases (house, autos, appliances) have been made. Saving and investing during this time is high. Then, in the retirement period (60s and above), consumers' personal rate of time preference rises again and investing falls. In fact, during this time consumers dissave (draw down on investment funds) to convert accumulated funds to income.

Borrow and Invest?

FINANCIAL
EMERGENCIES

Most consumers are both borrowers and investors. That is, most consumers have both loans on which they pay interest and investment on which they earn interest. Does this make sense?

For many consumers, especially young consumers, the answer is yes. For young consumers, investments are used mostly as an emergency source of funds in the event that a big purchase is needed or an unexpected expense is incurred.

But for middle aged consumers who have loans but who also have large investments, the question of whether borrowing and investing at the same time is wise should be examined. Remember that paying down on the balance of a loan is like earning the interest rate charged for that loan. For example, a dollar spent to reduce the balance of an 18 percent loan is like earning 18 percent interest on an investment. So, if you have $2000 which you could invest at 10 percent, or which you could use to pay down on your 18 percent credit card balance, reducing the credit card balance is the wise move.

The Bottom Line

The purpose of investing is to transfer purchasing power to the future. Your modest investment objective should be to earn enough to counteract the erosive power of future inflation. Consumers with lower personal rates of time preference save and invest more (as a percent of

C O N S U M E R

T O P I C

ARE AMERICANS NOT SAVING?

A recent complaint about Americans is that they don't save. Statistics published in the Statistical Abstract of the United States show that the "personal savings rate" steadily fell starting from the mid-1980s until the mid-2000s, as illustrated in the graph. In 2004 this measure showed Americans only saving 1.4% of their after-tax income.

The "personal savings rate" receives much attention in the media. This is unfortunate because it's really a bad measure of the actual saving done by Americans. Simply put, the "personal savings rate" excludes a lot of real saving. For example, the personal savings rate calculation doesn't include all the savings which Americans and their employers put into pensions. A pension account certainly is saving. The personal savings rate also doesn't include the savings built up in home equity by Americans. Some economists argue that Social Security contributions are really savings, albeit, forced savings, and so these monies should be added to what Americans are setting aside for the future.

Personal Savings Rate in the U.S.1929–2010

Data Source: Statistical Abstract of the United States 2012.

But perhaps the biggest recent influence on American savings has been the stock market. The reported savings rate doesn't include the savings earned in the stock market. For example, if you have $1000 in the stock market at the beginning of the year; and your stock portfolio increases 30%, then $300 has been added to your savings without you adding a dime. So, when stock market gains are high, there's less motivation to save because the stock market is generating the savings for you.

So there's more than meets the eye to the savings rate and savings behavior.

---

income) than consumers with higher personal rates of time preference. In general, a consumer's personal rate of time preference declines with age and with improved economic status. _____

2. How Does the Economy Influence Investments?

Remember the economic roller coaster from Chapter 2? The economic roller coaster simply means that the economy goes through a predictable cycle of ups and downs, although the timing of the cycle is almost never the same. A major part of the economic cycle is the fluctuation in interest rates.

It should make sense to you that particular investments fare differently during different parts of the economic roller coaster. In fact, there is a fairly predictable pattern to the fortunes of investments in the economic roller coaster, or business cycle.

What's Hot, What's Not, and When

Figure 8-3 shows a typical business cycle. For purposes of investment recommendations it's useful to divide the economic cycle into four parts, A, B, C, and D. Part A is the *Expansion* phase of the cycle. Economic growth is strong and growing, interest rates are low, and the inflation rate is low. In other words, economic optimism is high. This is an ideal time to buy and hold stocks. Growth in the economy will increase the value of stocks.

EXPANSION

PEAK

Part B is the *Peak* phase of the business cycle. The economy peaks during this phase, then begins to slow down and recede. The economy reaches capacity in terms of output and employment, so prices begin to be bid up faster and faster. An accelerating inflation rate is the major feature of this phase. Higher and higher inflation results in higher and higher interest rates. Real estate, gold, other precious metals, and even collectibles are the best investments to hold during this phase as investors look for investments which are

Figure 8-3. The investing/borrowing cycle.

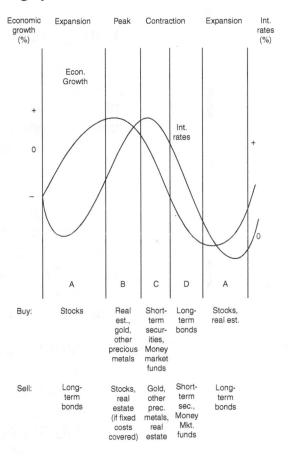

considered inflation hedges. The stock market peaks during this phase, so stocks should be sold.

CONTRACTION

Parts C and D compose the *Contraction* phase of the economy. During the beginning of the economic contraction (Part C), interest rates continue rising, then peak, then begin to decline. Short-term financial investments, like Treasury bills, short-term certificates of deposit, and money market mutual funds, will pay the highest interest rates. The inflation rate will begin to fall at the end of Part C, so real estate, gold, and other precious metals should be sold then.

Part D is the major part of the economic contraction. During Part D a recession occurs. The inflation rate and interest rates fall during Part D. Long-term bonds should be bought at the beginning of Part D for two reasons. First, interest rates paid on long term bonds are at their height (and are higher than interest rates paid on short-term financial securities at the beginning of Part D). Second, as interest rates in the economy fall during Part D, the value of long-term bonds bought at the beginning of Part D rises because their interest rate is so attractive (more on this later). So long-term bonds should be bought in Part D and short-term financial securities should be sold.

Following Part D, the cycle begins again, so stocks should be purchased in the new Part A.

Hitting the Turning Points

It's all well and good to look at a picture like Figure 8-3 and, with *hindsight,* observe how different investments perform better in different phases of the business cycle. A picture like Figures 8-3 is no big surprise to investment professionals. If an investment professional knows where in the business cycle the economy is, the professional can recommend the appropriate investment. The problem with using the investment roller coaster as a guide to investment strategy is knowing when the turning points occur, that is, knowing when the economy moves from one phase to the next phase. At any point in time there is usually disagreement about the "best investments" precisely because investment advisers disagree about the turning points.

Although not foolproof, here is some help on detecting when the turning points occur in the investment roller coaster:[2]

> MOVE FROM PART D TO PART A: The so-called *coincident* economic indicators, including employment, industrial production, manufacturing and trade sales, and personal income stop decreasing and begin to increase. At this point you should buy stocks.
>
> MOVE FROM PART A TO PART B: The *leading economic indicators* decline and the spread between long-term interest rates and short-term interest rates is very positive. At this point, buy gold and real estate.
>
> MOVE FROM PART B TO PART C: The coincident economic indicators begin to fall. Move your investment funds to short term financial securities.

INDICATORS

[2] Much of this discussion is taken from David L. Smith, "As the World Turns," *Financial Planning,* November 1988.

MOVE FROM PART C TO PART D: The so-called *lagging economic indicators,* including the prime rate, the average duration of unemployment, commercial and industrial loans outstanding, labor costs per unit of output, and the ratio of consumer installment credit to personal income, begin to decline, and the interest rate spread between long- and short-term rates is very negative. Here, shift into long-term bonds,

Because the detection of investment turning points is not an exact science, many investment advisers don't recommend an all-or-nothing approach, where, for example, if you think the economy is in Part A, you put all your investments in stocks, or, if you think the economy is in Part B, you put all your investments in gold and real estate. An alternative approach is to always have some of your money in each of the major investments (stocks, gold and real estate, short-term financial securities, long-term financial securities), but to alter the shares in each investment as it becomes evident where the economy is in the business cycle. We'll add more to this discussion later.

The Bottom Line

As the economy moves through the business cycle, different investments perform well at each phase of the cycle. If an investor can predict turning points in the phases of the business cycle, then an optimal investment strategy can be designed. The challenge to investors is to use information about the economy to accurately predict when the turning points occur.

3. What Does Investment Risk Mean?

Unfortunately, there's more to investment risk than you probably think. Most people think of risk in investing as meaning the chance that invested money will be lost. This, however, is only one type of risk. Broadly speaking, risk is uncertainty and there can be numerous uncertainties in investing.

Types of Risk

There are at least five major kinds of investment risks. Here's a summary of them:

DEFAULT RISK

Default risk is the risk of losing all, or a major part, of your original investment. Default risk is present for bonds, stocks, gold, and real estate.

LIQUIDITY RISK

Liquidity risk is the risk of not being able to "cash-in" your investment for all of your money. Liquidity risk is high for investments in rapidly changing markets (changing both up and down) and in markets in which it may take a long time to sell the investment (like real estate).

RATE RISK

Rate risk is the risk of not earning the rate of return you expect on an investment. For example, you may buy a stock or a real estate property expecting it to earn a 10 percent annual rate of return. However, there is no guarantee it will earn that rate of return, so there's a risk of not getting the rate of return you expect.

INFLATION RISK

Inflation risk is the risk that the investment returns won't keep up with inflation. You now know that the major reason for investing is to transfer purchasing power to the future, and to do this the investment returns must keep up with inflation. All investments can't guarantee that their returns will keep up with inflation. For example, short-term financial investments like one or three month CDs or money market funds have little inflation risk because their interest rates will change fast enough to keep up with changing inflation rates. But long-term financial investments, like long-term bonds that pay a fixed interest rate, have substantial inflation risk. When the long-term bond is issued, the interest rate will incorporate the *expected* future inflation rate. But if the actual inflation rate is higher than the expected inflation rate, then the long-term bond will lose money (more on this later).

REINVESTMENT RISK

Reinvestment risk is the risk associated with needing to reinvest investment returns and not knowing at what rate those returns can be reinvested. For example, let's say you have a bond paying 10 percent interest, so each year you get a check for 10 percent of your original investment. You cannot necessarily reinvest that money and earn 10 percent because new bonds may be paying less than 10 percent. So bonds carry reinvestment risk. On the other hand, if you have a share of stock that pays dividends, you can reinvest those dividends in the same stock, and those dividend dollars will earn the same rate of return as the other dollars invested in the stock.

As we consider different investments in the next topic, we will evaluate how the investments stack up on each of the risk categories.

Measuring Risk

VARIABILITY OF RETURN

In a nutshell, risk is uncertainty about the rate of return you will earn from an investment. Therefore, the best way to measure risk is to use the *variability* in an investment's rate of return. Investments with more variability in their rate of return are riskier. Stocks, especially small company stocks, tend to have a much greater variability in their rate of return than bonds. Investments from the government, such as Treasury securities, have the lowest variability in their rate of return.

What do you notice about the relationship between average return and risk, as measured by the standard deviation? There is a positive relationship between the two—that is, the higher the average return, the higher the risk. We'll talk more about this later.

BETA

There are two other more specific measures of risk, one pertaining to stocks and one pertaining to bonds. Beta is a measure of risk for individual stocks. A beta equal to 1 is representative of the general risk of the entire stock market. Betas of individual stocks are then compared to 1 to gauge the relative riskiness of the stock. For example, if stock A has a beta of .5, this means its risk (variability of its rate of return) is only half that of the entire stock market. On the other hand, if stock B has a beta of 2, this means its risk (variability of rate of return) is twice that of the entire stock market. Betas for individual stocks are available from most stockbrokers and from the investment service called Value Line.

BOND RATINGS

Two investment services, Standard and Poor's and Moody's, have designed rating systems for bonds (see Table 8-1). The ratings only

Table 8-1   Bond rating systems.

Standard and Poor's Rating System

AAA	capacity to repay is very strong.
AA	capacity to repay is very strong; only slightly less than AAA.
A	capacity to repay is strong.
BBB	capacity to repay is adequate.
	Bonds rated below **BBB** are regarded as predominately speculative with respect to capacity to repay.
BB	small near-term vulnerability but faces major on-going uncertainties.
B	has adequate capacity to repay now, but greater vulnerability to default.
CCC, CC, C	is currently vulnerable to default
CI	reserved for income bonds on which no interest is being paid.
D	bond is in default

Moody's Ratings

Aaa	best quality.
Aa	high quality.
A	good quality, but elements may be present that suggest possible future problems.
Baa	adequate quality, but; lack outstanding protective elements and may contain some speculative elements.
Ba	have some speculative elements.
B	lack characteristics of the desirable investment; assurance of repayment over long time is small.
Caa	poor standing.
Ca	high degree of speculation.
C	poor prospect.

measure default risk. The ratings are based on current information, but any bond's rating is subject to change as new information becomes available.

Dancing Partners: Risk and Return

It should not be surprising that risk and rate of return go hand in hand. Why would you put your money in a small, risky company just starting a business instead of in a sure thing (like a bank certificate of deposit) unless you were promised a higher return from the small company. Of course, you only get the higher return if the small company is successful—that's the risk.

If you can find an investment that has the same amount of risk as another investment but pays a higher rate of return, then this invest-
"GOOD BUYS" ment is a "good buy."

Likewise, investments which pay a lower rate of return for the same amount of risk are "bad buys."

Look at Figure 8-4. Here, hypothetical investments are plotted according to risk and rate of return. Risk could be measured by the investment's standard deviation, or by beta if the investment is a stock, or by Standard and Poor's or Moody's rating if the investment is a bond. Investment B is better than investment D because B pays the same rate of return as D but has lower risk. However, investment C is superior to both investments B and D. C pays a higher return and has lower risk than D. Also, C has the

Figure 8-4. Comparing the risk and return of investments.

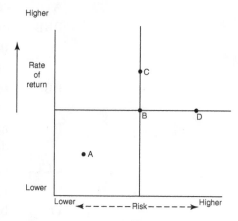

same risk as B but pays a higher return. We can't say whether C is better than A or A is better than C, since C pays a higher return than A but has more risk. Whether the investor is better off with investment A, investment C, or a combination of A and C is a complicated question. We'll only begin to answer the question in the next section.

How Much Risk Should You Take?

RISK-AVERSE Economists believe that most consumers are *risk-averse*. Consumers who are risk averse turn down opportunities to participate in bets with equal chances of winning $X or losing $X. That is, a risk averse

TRADEOFFS BETWEEN INVESTMENT CHARACTERISTICS

**C
O
N
S
U
M
E
R**

**T
O
P
I
C**

As you've learned, there are a number of characteristics to any individual investment. One way that investments differ is by how they stack up with respect to these characteristics. An interesting question is whether an investment's characteristics affect its rate of return.

In some very interesting research, Anthony Schiano addressed this question. Schiano considered the impact of four investment characteristics—liquidity, divisibility, predictability, and reversibility—on the investment's rate of return. Schiano measured liquidity as the minimum amount of time that the investment must be held or the minimum trading time required to realize the full current value of the investment. Longer holding or trading times mean less liquidity, and investors dislike less liquidity and prefer more liquidity. Divisibility was measured by the smallest dollar amount in which the investment could be held, and investors prefer greater divisibility, meaning lower minimum dollar amounts. Predictability was measured as the variability in the investment's rate of return, so predictability is a measure of risk, and investors prefer less risk. Lastly, reversibility measured the loss in the investment from tax and trading costs. Consumers prefer lower losses, so consumers prefer less reversibility.

Schiano used data from over 2500 investors in 1983 to estimate the relationship between investment characteristics and rate of return. His results were what we might expect. Investors were willing to give up some rate of return in order to have greater divisibility (lower minimum investments), greater liquidity, greater predictability, and lower reversibility. Or, thought of in the opposite way, in order to entice investors to take investments with lower divisibility, lower liquidity, lower predictability, and greater reversibility, higher rates of return must be paid.

Source: Schiano, Anthony G. *A Lancasterian Approach to Examining the Composition of Household Asset Portfolios.* Unpublished Ph.D. dissertation, Cornell University, 1987.

consumer would not participate in a bet which had 50 percent odds of winning $1000 and 50 percent odds of losing $1000. For a risk averse consumer to participate in a bet, either the odds of winning must be considerably sweetened, or the winning prize must be considerably increased. For example, a risk averse consumer might participate in a bet with a 20 percent chance of losing $1000 but an 80 percent chance of winning $1000. Or, a risk averse person might participate in a bet with a 90 percent chance of losing $100 but a 10 percent chance of winning $1000.

However, studies show that consumers' aversion to risk declines as consumer wealth increases. Studies show that either the dollar amount of money put in risky investments increases with consumer wealth or the proportion of total money invested which is in risky investments increases with consumer wealth. This means that as your income or wealth increases, you should take a closer look at more risky investments.

CONSUMER TOPIC

Measuring Risk Tolerance

Risk tolerance is a measurement of an individual's willingness to accept risk, making it a valuable tool for investors and financial planners. There are several different methods of measuring risk tolerance. One commonly used method is the risk question in the Federal Research Board's Survey of Consumer Finances (SCF). The question reads: "Which of the following statements comes closest to the amount of financial risk that you are willing to take when you save or make investments? (1) Take substantial financial risk expecting to earn substantial returns; (2) Take above average financial risk expecting to earn above average returns; (3) Take average financial risk expecting to earn average returns, and (4) Not willing to take any financial risk". Sung and Hanna found that only a minority of respondents are willing to take above average risks to make an above average return on investments. Risk tolerance increases with education and income. Female-headed households have lower risk tolerance than otherwise similar married couple and male-headed households. Whites are more risk tolerant than other races and ethnicities.

Barskey and colleagues proposed a measure based on presenting a set of hypothetical questions. Their measure links the theoretical concept of relative risk aversion with the survey questions. The initial question looks like this: "Suppose that you are the only income earner in the family, and you have a good job guaranteed to give you your current (family) income for life. You are given the opportunity to take a new and equally good job, with a 50–50 chance it will double your after-tax income and a 50–50 chance that will cut your income by X% (for example, a third). Would you take the new job"? One can start from a 50% cut and go down to 30%, 20%, 10%, etc. By asking what percentage cut the respondent is willing to take, one can figure out the risk tolerance level of the respondent. In Barskey and colleagues' study of older adults, the majority were found to have very low risk tolerance.

References   Barsky, R.B., Juster, F.T., Kimball, M.S. & Shapiro, M.D. (1997). Preference parameter s and behavioral heterogeneity: An experimental approach in the Health and Retirement Study. Quarterly Journal of Economics, 112(2), 537–579.

Sung, J. & Hanna, S. (1996). Factors related to risk tolerance, Financial Counseling and Planning, 7, 11–20.

The Bottom Line

Risk is uncertainty, and there are many uncertainties in investing: uncertainty about default, about what rate of return will be earned, about cashing-in your investment, about inflation, and about reinvesting. You should only take on more risk in your investments if you are promised a higher average rate of return. Studies show that most of us don't like risk, but that as our income and wealth increase, we will put more money in riskier investments.

4. How Do You Calculate the Return on Your Investments?

You might ask, "What's there to talk about here—just look at the interest rate paid by the investment." Unfortunately, it's not that simple. First, not all investments earn a return in the same way. Second, interest rates are not always calculated in the same, economically logical way.

Types of Investment Returns

There are three basic ways that an investment can earn a return for an investor: an income return, a capital gain return, and an income plus capital gain return.

INCOME RETURN

An *income return* is the type of return you're most used to seeing. The amount invested, the principal, doesn't change in nominal amount, but income is paid periodically to the investor. The income paid is the income return. Interest paid on a CD, money market fund, or bond, dividends paid by a stock, and rent collected from an apartment are examples of income returns.

CAPITAL GAIN

A *capital gain* is returned by an investment when you can sell it, or "cash-it-in" for a price higher than what you paid for it. In this case the original amount invested, the principal, does change in value, and the change in value is the capital gain. For example, if you buy a stock for $50/share and sell it for $90/share, then you've made a capital gain of $40/share. Stocks, real estate, precious metals, bonds and collectibles (baseball cards, antiques) are examples of investments that can earn capital gains. Unfortunately, they can also earn capital losses, meaning you sell the investment for less than you bought it.

Finally, there are some investments that can pay both income returns and capital gain returns. Stocks which pay dividends, rental apartments and houses, and bonds are examples of investments which can pay this double-barreled return.

Is one type of investment return necessarily better than another kind? The answer to this question depends on your investment goal.

**C
O
N
S
U
M
E
R**

**T
O
P
I
C**

ARE CONSUMERS CONSISTENT IN THEIR ATTITUDE ABOUT RISK?

As stated in the text, consumers who don't play "fair games," that is, consumers who don't play games which give an equal chance of winning $X or losing $X, are said to be risk-averse. Consumers who will play "fair" games or who will play "unfair" games (games which have a higher chance of losing $X than of winning $X) are said to be risk-seeking.

Can the same consumer be both risk-averse in some cases and risk-seeking in other cases? For example, the fact that most of us buy auto and health insurance means that we're risk-averse. But most of us will also engage in small, unfair gambles, where the chance of losing, say, $10, is much greater than the chance of winning $10. Are such consumers inconsistent in their attitude toward risk?

You'll probably say no—that there's nothing inconsistent with protecting yourself against a big loss by buying auto and health insurance, but being willing to gamble and lose small amounts of money. You're right, but it actually took economists a long time to come to this same conclusion! What's happening is that consumers are risk-averse with respect to large losses in income. Most consumers won't gamble with substantial portions of their current income and, in fact, they will pay to buy insurance to protect that level of income. At the same time, consumers are willing to bet and almost certainly lose a relatively small amount of money in order to have a minuscule chance of winning a large pot of money (as in a lottery). Even insurance agents buy lottery tickets!

WHICH IS BETTER?

Investments which only pay capital gain returns don't pay off until they are sold. Obviously, this is a disadvantage to investors who want periodic income from their investments for use to meet living expenses. Younger investors, who are investing primarily for the long run and not for immediate income returns, are more likely to favor capital gain investments than income investments.

The returns from capital gain and income investments also perform differently over the investment cycle (see Figure 8-3). Capital gain investments (stocks, gold, real estate) tend to do better when the economy is expanding, whereas investments paying income returns do better when the economy has peaked and is beginning to contract. An exception is long-term bonds. The capital gain return of long-term bonds does best when the economy is contracting.

RETURNS AND
TAXATION

Finally, there are different tax implications of capital gain and income investments. In general, investment returns are taxed in the year they are received by the investor. In the case of income returns, this is usually every year, as the income from the investment occurs and is paid to the investor every year. Capital gain investments can earn a return every year, but that gain is not taxed until the investor has cashed-in the investment. This is beneficial because the present value of taxes paid later is always less than the present value of the same taxes paid earlier. Table 8-2 demonstrates this with an example. Notice that the investor reaps more after-tax gain from the investment with taxation of the total gain when the investment is sold (part B) than when the annual gain is taxed each year (part A). The comparison assumes a 28% marginal tax rate. Capital gains tax rate varies over time. In 2013, capital gains tax rate can be 0%, 15%, or 20%, depending on income level. Most middle-class consumers are likely in the 15% capital gains tax bracket.

Table 8-2   The benefits of delayed taxing of capital gains.

Purchase stock, value	= $3,000	⎤ capital gain = $1,000
Value, end of 1 year	= $4,000	⎦
Value, end of 2 years	= $5,500	capital gain = $1,500
Value, end of 3 years	= $7,200	capital gain = $1,700

Sell stock at end of 3 years.

A. Present value of total after-tax gain, if tax each year (28% tax rate, 9% discount rate).

First year gain	= $1,000
Tax = .28 × $1,000	= $ 280
PV of tax = $280 × .917	= $ 256.76
Second year gain	= $1,500
Tax = .28 × $1,500	= $ 420
PV of tax = $420 × .842	= $ 353.64
Third year gain	= $1,700
Tax = .28 × $1,700	= $ 476
PV of tax = $476 × .772	= $ 367.47

Total gain over 3 years = $7,200 – $3,000	= $ 4,200
PV of total gain = $4,200 × .772	= $3,242.40
PV of total after-tax gain = $3,242.40 – $256.76 – $353.64 – $367.47	= $2,264.53

B. Present value of total after-tax gain if only tax when sell (28% tax rate, 9% discount rate).

Total gain over 3 years = $7,200 – $3,000	= $4,200
Tax = .28 × $4,200	= $1,176
After-tax gain = $4,200 – $1,176	= $3,024
PV of total after-tax gain = .772 × $3,024	= $2,334.53

Return Calculation

YIELD

How the return, or *yield* (return and yield are used interchangeably), on an investment is calculated depends on the type of investment. As you'll see, yield calculation can actually be easier for capital gain investments than for income investments.

1. *Yield Calculation on Capital Gain Investment.*

Calculating the yield on a capital gain investment for one year is very simple. Just calculate the gain (hopefully) as a percent of the price at the beginning of the year. So if a stock increases from $100/share to $110/share, the yield is $10/$100 or 10 percent.

What about calculating the yield over a number of years? There are two ways to do this, a simple but not quite correct way, and a more difficult but more correct way!

SIMPLE WAY

The simple way is to first calculate the yield in proportional form by dividing the total gain over the number of years by the original price. This is the total proportional gain. Then, to express the yield as an annual percent, divide the total proportional gain by the number of years the investment was held and multiply by 100. So, for example, if your stock rises from $50/share to $80/share in three years, the gain is $\frac{\$30}{\$50}$, the total proportional gain is $30 or .60, and the annual percentage yield is .60/3 years, or .20 or 20 percent.

However, this annual yield overstates the true yield because some of the gain occurred from the increases in the stock's price being automatically reinvested in the stock. To account for this, first remember the formula for the future value of $1: future value = $1 × (1 + r)^n$ where r is the annual yield or rate of return. The factor $(1 + r)^n$ is the future value factor associated with r and the number of years, n. The value (1 + total proportional gain) is a future value factor. So the annual yield can be calculated using this formula:

CORRECT WAY

$$\text{Annual yield} = [1 + \text{total proportional gain}]^{\frac{1}{n}} - 1.$$

EXAMPLE 8-1: You buy a stock for $80 and sell it after five years for $115. What is the annual percentage yield?

ANSWER: *Simple Way:* Total Gain = $115 − $80 = $35

$$\text{Total Proportional Gain} = \frac{\$35}{\$80} = .438$$

$$\textit{Annual percentage yield} = \frac{0.438}{5} = 0.088 = 8.8\%$$

More correct way:

$$1 + \textit{total proportional gain} = 1 + 0.438 = 1.438$$

$$\textit{Annual percentage yield} = 1.438^{\frac{1}{5}} - 1 = 0.075 = 7.5\%$$

You can also use Appendix Table A-1 to find the annual interest rate, or yield that corresponds to 1.438 for five years.

CALCULATIONS WITH A LOSS   What if the stock, or capital gain investment, falls in price? Obviously this results in a negative annual yield. EXAMPLE 8-2 shows how to do the calculations in this case.

EXAMPLE 8-2:   The stock which you bought for $80 five years ago now sells for $60. What is the annual percentage yield?

ANSWERS: *Simple Way:* Total Gain = $60 – $80 = –$20

$$\text{Total Proportional Gain} = \frac{-\$20}{\$80} = -.25$$

$$\text{Annual Percentage Yield} = \frac{-.25}{5} = -0.05 = -5\%.$$

More correct way:

$$1 + \textit{total proportional gain} = 1 - 0.25 = 0.75$$

$$\textit{Annual percentage yield} = 0.75^{\frac{1}{5}} - 1 = 0.944 - 1 = -0.056 = -5.6\%$$

You cannot use Appendix Table A-1 because the table does not have negative interest rates.

---

2. *Yield Calculation on Capital Gain and Income Investment*

The yield on an investment paying both a capital gain and an income return is the simple combination of the two returns.

EXAMPLE 8-3:   CANCO stock has an annual capital gain yield of 8.3 percent and pays 6 percent annual dividends. What is the total annual yield?

ANSWER: Total annual yield = 8.3% + 6.0% = 14.3%.

---

3. *Yield Calculation on Income Investment.*

Now the fun begins. Most consumers have money in income-producing investments like CDs, bonds, or money market accounts. Extreme care must be taken in comparing interest rates quoted on these investments because all interest rates, or yields, are not calculated in the same way. In fact, there are over 100 different ways of calculating yields on income earning investments.

One way that interest rate calculations differ is by the compounding period. There is no compounding (also called simple interest), annual compounding (one compounding period per year), quarterly compounding (four compounding periods per year), monthly compounding (12 compounding periods per year), daily compounding (360 or 365 compounding periods per year depending on the definition of a year), and continuous compounding. Everything else equal, the more frequent the compounding period per year, the higher the effective interest rate.

EFFECTIVE YIELD   The effective yield takes into account the compounding period of an investment. By convention, effective yields are quoted on an annual basis, even though the investment may not be for a year. This allows direct comparison of investments which are held for different time periods. However, this can be tricky and confusing. *For investments of less than a year, you should compound out to a year. For investments of more than a year, also compound for a year. This will allow direct comparison of the investment yields.*

The general formula to use for finding the effective yield, which is the return using compounding, for all but continuous compounding, is:

$$Annual\ Effect\ Yield\ (AEY) = (1+\frac{R}{n})^n - 1$$

In this formula, R is the quoted or stated interest rate before compounding. The number of compounding period per year is denoted as n (2 or semiannual, 4 for quarterly, 12 for monthly, and either 360 or 365 for daily).

EXAMPLE 8-4: The quoted (uncompounded) interest rate on a one-year CD is 9 percent. Find the annual effective yield using no compounding, semi-annual compounding, quarterly compounding, monthly compounding, and daily (365 days in a year) compounding.

ANSWERS: No compounding: AEY=quoted rate=9%

Semi-annual compounding: R = 0.09, n = 2:

$$AEY = (1+\frac{0.09}{2})^2 - 1 = 0.092 = 9.20\%$$

Quarterly compounding: R = 0.09, n = 4:

$$AEY = (1+\frac{0.09}{4})^4 - 1 = 0.0931 = 9.31\%$$

Monthly compounding: R = 0.09, n = 12:

$$AEY = (1+\frac{0.09}{12})^{12} - 1 = 0.0938 = 9.38\%$$

Daily compounding: R = 0.09, n = 365:

$$AEY = (1+\frac{0.09}{365})^{365} - 1 = 0.0942 = 9.42\%$$

EXAMPLE 8-5:   The quoted (uncompounded) interest rate on a six-month CD is 9 percent. Find the annual effective yield using no compounding, semi-annual compounding, quarterly compounding, monthly compounding, and daily (365 days in a year) compounding.

ANSWERS: The calculations are the same as for EXAMPLE 8-4. The CD is compounded as if it is held for a year.

EXAMPLE 8-6:   The quoted (uncompounded) interest rate on a 3-year CD is 9 percent. Find the annual effective yield using no compounding, semiannual compounding, quarterly compounding, and daily (365 days in a year) compounding.

ANSWERS: Again, the calculations are the same as for EXAMPLE 8-4. For comparability, the CD is compounded as if it is held for a year.

For continuous compounding, the procedure for finding the annual effective yield is slightly different. The following formula, which we won't derive, is used:

Effective Yield for Continuous Compounding $= 2.71828^R - 1,$

where R is the quoted or stated interest rate in decimal form. (Readers with a math background will recognize 2.71828 as "e".) In most cases, continuous compounding will give an effective yield only slightly larger than for daily compounding.

EXAMPLE 8-7:

CONTINUOUS
COMPOUNDING

Compare the annual effective yield for a 9.5% quoted interest rate which is compounded daily (365 days) versus one that is compounded continuously:

Daily compounding: AEY $= [(1+0.095/365)]^{365} - 1 = 0.0996 = 9.96\%$
Continuous Compounding: AEY $= [2.71828]^{0.095} - 1 = 0.0997 = 9.97$

BOND EQUIVALENT
BASIS

CD BASIS

Stock brokers and bank, savings and loan, and credit union executives often quote effective yields on a "bond equivalent basis" or a "CD basis." An effective yield calculated on a bond equivalent basis is compounded daily first by dividing the quoted interest rate by 365 and then compounding over 365 days. An effective yield calculated on a CD equivalent basis is compounded daily by first dividing the quoted interest rate by 360 and then compounding over 365 days. This will result in a higher effective yield than the yield calculated from a bond-equivalent basis, as EXAMPLE 8-8 shows.

EXAMPLE 8-8: Calculate the effective yield from a 10 percent quoted interest rate CD using a bond equivalent basis and a CD equivalent basis.

ANSWERS: BOND EQUIVALENT BASIS:

$$(1+\frac{.10}{365})^{365}-1=10.52\%$$

CD EQUIVALENT BASIS:

$$(1+\frac{.10}{360})^{365}-1=10.67\%$$

DISCOUNT INVESTMENTS

However, beware! Just because an investment's yield is *advertised* on a bond equivalent basis or a CD equivalent basis doesn't necessarily mean your interest is calculated that way. It's up to you to find out what compounding method is used to produce interest on your account and to double-check the stockbroker's or bank's figures. There are some income-producing investments—mainly Treasury bills, which you buy for less than face value, then later when the investment is cashed in you receive back the face value. This is called "buying at discount." The difference between the face value and the price you paid is your interest income. R is then calculated as

$$\frac{\text{Face Value Price} - \text{Price}}{\text{Price}}$$

If the investment is for a year, then R is the effective yield. More commonly, such investments are for 3 months or 6 months. In these situations, R should be compounded to a year to equal an annual effective yield.

EXAMPLE 8-9: You buy a Treasury bill for $9,400 and six months later you cash it in for $10,000. What is the annual effective yield?

$$R = \frac{10,000 - 9,400}{9.400} = .0638$$

Since the Treasury bill is for six months, compound it for two periods to produce the annual effective yield:

$$[(1+.0638)^2 - 1] = 13.17\%$$

4. *Deposits and Withdrawals.*

There's one more issue to cover, and this particularly pertains to savings accounts at banks, thrifts, and credit unions. It's the method of calculating the interest earnings on a savings account when a number

DAY-OF-DEPOSIT TO DAY-OF-WITHDRAWAL

of deposits or withdrawals are made in the month. You probably think that a savings institution would determine the interest you earn on a savings account each day on the amount of money you have on deposit that day. This method is called the day-of-deposit to day-of-withdrawal and means deposits begin earning interest on the day of deposit and continue to earn interest until the day of withdrawal.

LOW BALANCE METHOD

FIFO

But surprise—all institutions don't use this logical method. One other method, the "low balance method," pays interest for the month on only the lowest balance you have in the account for the month. The "first-in, first-out" (FIFO) method subtracts a withdrawal not from the balance existing on the day of withdrawal, but from the earliest balance or deposit of the month. This means the earliest balances, which have the most days to earn interest, will be smaller. The "last-in, first-out"

LIFO

(LIFO) method subtracts a withdrawal not from the balance existing on the day of withdrawal, but from the most recent deposit or balance.

Table 8-3 shows the interest earnings calculations for these four methods—day-of-deposit to day-of-withdrawal, low balance method, first-in/first-out, and last-in/first-out. The day-of-deposit to day-of-withdrawal method produces the greatest amount of interest for the investor. Note that in the low balance method interest is only paid on the lowest balance during the month, $2,000. In the first-in/first-out method, the November 30 withdrawal of $1,000 is not deducted from the balance on November 30, but is deducted from the $2,000 balance on November 1. Therefore, the investor starts with only $1,000 on November 1 rather than $2,000. In the last-in/first-out method, the November 30 withdrawal of $1,000 is deducted from the November 17 deposit of $3,000.

DAILY INTEREST

There are other "tricks" which savings institutions can use to pay less interest on deposits. *Daily interest* (not to be confused with daily compounding) means daily earnings are not added to the principal (and therefore are not compounded) until a time specified in the savings contract, which is usually at the end of the month or quarter. *"Dead days"*

DEAD DAYS

are days at the end of a month or quarter during which the institution computes interest earnings. However, the institution doesn't calculate and add interest for these days! Institutions which "round-down"

ROUNDING

will count only dollar deposits and interest earnings and ignore cents, and some may only count $5 shares (for example, $9.99 would only be counted as $5).

Fixed vs. Floating Interest Rates

An important characteristic of the rate of return of an investment is whether the rate is *fixed* over the term of the investment or whether the rate can *float* with market interest rates over the term of the investment. Each option presents potential opportunities and costs to the investor.

Table 8-3 Alternative ways of calculating savings account interest earnings.

An Example:

5% annual interest rate;

$$\text{daily interest rate} = \frac{.05}{365} = 0.000137.$$

November 1	Deposit	$2,000
November 3	Deposit	800
November 17	Deposit	3,000
November 30	Withdraw	1,000

A. Interest earned on day-of-deposit to day-of-withdrawal.

11/ 1 to 11/ 2 (2 days), $2 \times \$2,000 \times 0.000137$ = $ 0.548
11/ 3 to 11/16 (14 days), $14 \times (\$2,000 + \$800) \times 0.000137$ = $ 5.370
11/17 to 11/30 (14 days), $14 \times (\$2,800 + \$3000) \times 0.000137$ = $11.124
11/30 (1 day), $1 \times (\$5,800 - \$1,000) \times 0.000137$ = $ 0.658
                                 TOTAL = $17.700

B. Low balance method.

Lowest balance is $2,000 on November 1–2.
Interest earned for month based on $2,000 balance:

$$30 \times \$2,000 \times 0.000137 = \underline{\$8.22}$$

C. First-in/First-out method.

November 30 withdrawal of $1,000 is deducted from November 1 deposit of $2,000.
Start November 1 with only $1,000.

11/ 1 to 11/2 (2 days), $2 \times \$1000 \times 0.000137$ = $0.274
11/ 3 to 11/16 (14 days), $14 \times (\$1,000 + \$800) \times 0.000137$ = 3.452
11/17 to 11/30 (14 days), $14 \times (\$1,800 + \$3,000) \times 0.000137$ = 9.206
11/30 (1 day), $1 \times (\$4,800) \times 0.000137$ = 0.658
                                 TOTAL = $13.59

D. Last-in/Last-out method.

November 30 withdrawal of $1,000 is deducted from November 17 deposit of $3,000.
Start November 17 with deposit of only $2,000.

11/ 1 to 11/ 2 (days), $2 \times \$2,000 \times 0.000137$ = $ 0.548
11/ 3 to 11/16 (14 days), $14 \times (\$2,000 + \$ 800) \times 0.000137$ = 5.370
11/17 to 11/30 (14 days), $14 \times (\$2,800 + \$2,000) \times 0.000137$ = 9.206
11/30 (1 day), $1 \times (\$4,800) \times 0.000137$ = 0.658
                                 TOTAL = $15.782

For example, a fixed rate carries the opportunity that it may turn out to be a high rate over the term of the investment.

This would happen if market interest rates fell over the investment term (Figure 8-5). Conversely, investing in a fixed interest rate carries

RICHARD MORSE AND THE CRUSADE FOR CONSISTENT INTEREST ACCOUNTING

Richard Morse, former Professor of Family Economics at Kansas State University, was long a crusader for consistent reporting of interest earnings. Through his publication "Check Your Interest," he informed thousands of consumers about the variety of ways in which interest can be calculated on savings accounts.

Morse's efforts paid off. In 1993, the Truth in Savings Act took effect. The Act requires financial institutions to quote interest rates as an "annual percentage yield," or APY. The APY enables direct comparison of interest rates with different compounding periods.

the possible cost that the rate can turn out to be a low rate over the investment term if market interest rates rise (Figure 8-5). A floating rate has the opportunity of out-performing a fixed rate if market interest rates rise in the future (Figure 8-5); conversely, a floating interest rate will cost an investor if market interest rates fall over the term of the investment (Figure 8-5).

As we've already discussed, there's no foolproof method for predicting the future direction of interest rates. Interest rates tend to rise during the expansion phase of the business cycle and when there's a large positive spread between long and short term rates. Thus, when these conditions are present, investments with floating interest rates are preferred. On the other hand, interest rates tend to fall during the contraction phase of the business cycle and when there's a large negative spread between long and short term rates. When these conditions appear, fixed rate investments are the way to go.

Figure 8-5. Fixed and floating rates of returns.

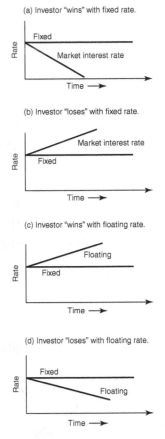

(a) Investor "wins" with fixed rate.

(b) Investor "loses" with fixed rate.

(c) Investor "wins" with floating rate.

(d) Investor "loses" with floating rate.

Impact of Taxes

You already know how to take taxes into account in your investment returns. If the investment return is fully taxed, multiply the return or yield by your tax bracket, then subtract this result from the yield to get the after-tax yield:

After-tax yield = Yield – (tax bracket * yield).

EXAMPLE 8-10: A three year CD has an annual yield of 8.7 percent. Joe's marginal tax rate is 28 percent. What is the after-tax annual yield?

$$\text{After-tax yield} = 8.7\% - .28 \times 8.7\%$$
$$= 6.3\%$$

Currently capital gains are frequently taxed at lower rates by the federal government than are other earnings. However, this hasn't always been the case. The capital gains tax has a history of being adjusted by Congress (see Consumer Topic: The Fall and Rise and Fall of the Capital Gains Tax).

TAX-FREE INTEREST   Some investment returns escape taxation altogether. Interest earned on municipal bonds is not taxed by the federal government and frequently is not taxed by state governments. The capital gain from sale of your home is not taxed if you buy a home of comparable or greater expense within two years.

A Final Word of Caution

A final word of caution should be sounded about calculating total returns when the annual yield varies each year. This is particularly important with stock yields or other investments where returns are reinvested and compounded.

Consider the following simple example. Suppose you invest $1,000 in Stock XYZ. In the first year the stock's yield is 100 percent but in the second year its yield is -50 percent. You might be tempted to say that the average annual yield is the simple average of 100 percent and –50 percent, which is 25 percent, so that you would have more than $1,000 at the end of two years. Actually, you'll have exactly $1,000 at the end of two years, just what you started with. What happened?

To understand what happened, let's work through the numbers. Starting with $1,000, the first year's yield is 100 percent. This means that at the end of one year you have $1,000 × (1 + 100%) or $2,000. In the second year the rate of return is –50 percent. This means that at the end

THE FALL AND RISE AND FALL OF THE CAPITAL GAINS TAX

**C
O
N
S
U
M
E
R**

**T
O
P
I
C**

Historically, U.S. capital gains tax rate has been subject to many policy changes. The highest marginal tax rate on capital gains has been either the same or lower than the highest marginal tax rate on earned income. Proponents of a lower capital gains tax rate argue that the lower tax motivates investment in the stock market, which in turn provides funds for fueling American business that translates into job growth. Opponents of a lower capital gains tax argue that the benefits of the lower tax would go primarily to higher income stock holders and real estate developers and thus lead to higher income inequality.

From 1913 to 1921, capital gains were taxed at the ordinary rates. The Revenue Act of 1921 allowed a maximum capital gains tax rate of 12.5%, which was substantially lower than the highest marginal tax rate on ordinary income. Although the rate changed often after that, prior to 1987, capital gains were always taxed at a much lower tax rate than ordinary income returns. Also, for quite a few years before 1987, only 40 to 50 percent of capital gains were taxed by the federal government. The highest tax bracket in 1986 was 50 percent with only 40% gains taxed. This meant that in 1987, the maximum capital gains tax was 20 percent (40% × 50%).

This benefit to capital gains investments disappeared with the 1986 Tax Reform Act. From 1987 to 1990, capital gains income was taxed at the same rates as other investment income. For taxpayers in the 28 and 33 percent tax brackets, this meant an increase in the tax on capital gains. The commercial real estate industry especially felt the effects of this increase in capital gains tax. Beginning in 1991, the maximum capital gains tax was capped at 28% but the effective rate was a bit higher due to interactions with other tax provisions. Lower rates for long-term investments (held longer than 18 months) were introduced in 1997. The Economic Growth and Tax Relief Reconciliation Act of 2001 during the Bush years cut the top rate for capital gains to about 15%. In 2013 Obama brings the top rate on capital gains back to 25%.

of the second year you have $2,000 × (1 + (−50%)) or $1,000. The reason you are back to where you started is because the second year's yield of −50 percent is applied to your balance at the end of the first year, $2,000, and not to your original balance of $1,000.

In general, to find the total yield from an investment over n number of years, when the annual yield varies, use this formula:

(1 + year 1's yield) × (1 + year 2's yield) × (1 + year 3's yield) × . . .
(1 + year n's yield) −1 = total yield.

EXAMPLE 8-11: The annual yields for stock XYZ over five years were:

$$Year\ 1 = 20\%$$
$$Year\ 2 = -5\%$$
$$Year\ 3 = 15\%$$
$$Year\ 4 = 7\%$$
$$Year\ 5 = -10\%$$

What's the total yield over the five years? If you started with a $1,000 investment in stock XYZ, how much would you have at the end of the five years?

ANSWER: Total yield $= (1+.20) \times (1-.05) \times (1+.15) \times (1+.07) \times (1-.10) -1$
$= 1.20 \times .95 \times 1.15 \times 1.07 \times .90 -1$
$= 1.262 -1$
$= 0.262 = 26.2\%$

Amount at the end of 5 years $= \$1,000 \times (1 + 1.262) = \$1,262$

ARITHMETIC AVERAGE

How would we calculate an average annual yield for the yields in EXAMPLE 8-11? One way is to take the simple arithmetic average, that is, sum the annual yields and divide by five. This method gives (20% + –5% + 15% + 7% + –10%)/5, or 5.4 percent.

However, if annual earnings in the investment are reinvested, the arithmetic average is incorrect. In this case we again use our formula

$$[(1 + year\ 1's\ yield) \times (1 + year\ 2's\ yield) \times$$
$$(1 + year\ 3's\ yield) \times \ldots (1 + year\ n's\ yield)]^{\frac{1}{n}} - 1$$

GEOMETRIC AVERAGE

to find the annual yield. Or, calculate (1 + total yield) and find it and the associated interest rate in Appendix Table A-1. This average is called the geometric average.

EXAMPLE 8-12: Find the geometric average yield for the annual yields posted by stock XYZ in EXAMPLE 8-11.

ANSWER: $[(1.20) \times (.95) \times (1.15) \times (1.07) \times (.90)]^{.20} - 1 = 1.262.20 - 1$
$= 0.0476$ or 4.76%.

Or, find 1.262 in Appendix Table A-1 in the year 5 row. It falls halfway between 4.50 percent and 5.00 percent. What this means is that receiving annual yields of 20 percent, –5 percent, 15 percent, 7 percent, and –10 percent for five years is the same as receiving a compound annual yield of 4.76 percent.

The Bottom Line _____

Calculating the return on an investment can be a complicated process. When comparing yields of alternative investments, make sure they're calculated in comparable ways. As a last resort, simply ask the investment advisor or salesperson, "How much money will I have in this account at the end of a year?" _____

5. How Many Baskets Should Hold Your Investment Eggs?

The ideal investment strategy is to know what's "hot" at any point in time and to have all of your money invested in it. This is the "have all your eggs in one basket, but keep switching baskets strategy." This strategy would follow a process like that depicted in Figure 8-3.

The problem with this "ideal" investment strategy is that it requires the investor to correctly predict the turning points in the economy and to rapidly move money from one investment to another as these turning points dictate. If the turning points and moves are missed, then the ideal investment strategy breaks down.

An alternative to the ideal strategy of all your eggs in one basket is the strategy of having your eggs spread around into many investment baskets. This is the strategy of *diversification.*

IDEAL STRATEGY

DIVERSIFICATION

How Diversification Works

Suppose there are two alternative investments, Investment A and Investment B. Half of the years Investment A gives an annual yield of 20 percent, and half of the years it gives an annual yield of –5 percent. Investment B has the same pattern; half of the years it gives an annual yield of 20 percent and half of the years it gives an annual yield of –5 percent. If you invest all your money in Investment A, your (geometric) average yield is 6.8 percent $[((1.20 \times .95)^{1/2} – 1) = 6.8\%]$. If you invest all your money in Investment B your geometric average yield is also 6.8 percent.

Now suppose that when Investment A's yield is 20 percent, Investment B's yield is –5 percent, and when Investment A's yield is –5 percent, Investment B's yield is 20 percent. This means that Investment A and Investment B are *perfectly negatively correlated;* in other words, when Investment A is up, Investment B is down, and when Investment A is down, Investment B is up.

Look at Figure 8-6. Let's assume (and there's no reason that this is the case) that the positive and negative returns of both Investment A and Investment B alternate with a one-year cycle.[3]

If you had the ability to perfectly predict the future, meaning you could predict the years when Investment A yielded 20 percent and when Investment B yielded 20 percent, what would be your investment strategy? You would invest in Investment A in year 1, then move all your money to Investment B in year 2, then back to Investment A in year 3, then back to Investment B in year 4, etc.[4] This is the *ideal strategy* and is shown in Panel (c).

But if you don't have perfect foresight, meaning you don't know exactly when

[3]The fact that Investment A and Investment B have a 20 percent yield half the time doesn't necessarily mean that the yields occur in alternate years. For example, over a 10 year span it could be that Investment A has a 20 percent yield for years 1 to 4, then a –5 percent yield for years 5 and 6, then a 20 percent yield for year 7, and then a –5 percent yield for years 8–10. Over the 10 year period, this still works out to be 20 percent yields half the time and –5 percent yields half the time.

[4]You might say, "Won't commissions on all this buying and selling eat up the investment yields?" Not necessarily. There are ways of reducing commissions, such as through discount brokers and no-load mutual funds. This is discussed later.

Figure 8-6. Diversifying with Investment A and Investment B.

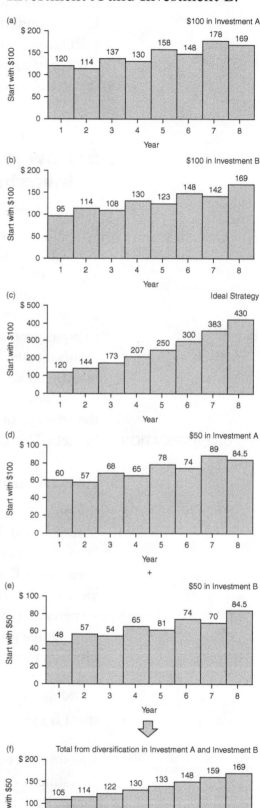

Investment A or Investment B will have a –5 percent yield, then there's a big risk to having all your money in either Investment A or Investment B at any point in time. The big risk is that you might have to "cash in" the investment during a year or during a string of years when the investment's annual yield is –5 percent. For Investment A this would be years 2, 4, 6, 8, and for Investment B, this would be years 1, 3, 5, and 7.

The alternative is diversification. Diversification means that you spread your money around into a number of investments. But they can't be just any investments. For diversification to work, they must be investments whose yields are not perfectly positively correlated, meaning that they don't always move in the same direction (both up and down). In fact, diversification works best when the yields of the investments are perfectly negatively correlated.

Our example with Investment A and Investment B gives a perfect example of how diversification works. In Figure 8-6, Panel (d) shows how half the funds would grow with Investment A, Panel (e) shows how half the funds would grow with Investment B, and Panel (f) shows how your total would grow. Notice that you end up at the same place, $169, as with Investment A or B, but you never have a "down" year. Your money increases at a steady rate.

Diversification is the safe, or risk-averse, approach to investing. You diversify to avoid having your money tied-up in an investment which, unexpectedly, does very poorly. You diversify when you can't perfectly predict the future, meaning you can't perfectly predict what investment is "hot" each year. The benefit of diversifying is that you avoid years with big losses and you don't lose much, if any, on your average annual yield over a long time period. The cost of diversifying is that you give up the opportunity of really "hitting it big" in any given year or over a number of years. You give up a chance at the "ideal strategy."

Diversification in Stocks

The idea of diversification has been most widely applied to stocks. In order to diversify in the stock market, two questions must be addressed: (1) how many stocks should be bought, and (2) how should those stocks be selected?

In order to answer the first question we must think about what we're trying to accomplish by diversifying within the stock market. The risk associated with investing in any particular stock will be composed of two parts: the risk associated with the whole stock market (i.e., the individual stock moves up when the whole stock market moves up and the individual stock moves down when the whole stock market moves down), and the risk associated with particular characteristics of the individual stock's company. By diversifying we try to get rid of the second risk. Diversification within the stock market will not eliminate the risks associated with ups and downs in the whole stock market.

HOW MANY STOCKS
TO DIVERSIFY

Studies have shown that by buying as few as fifteen different stocks, most of the second kind of risk—that associated with individual companies—can be eliminated.[5]

Now to the second question. How should the diversified set of fifteen stocks be picked? The answer might surprise you. The best way to insure that the stocks' individual company risks are unrelated is to *randomly* select the stocks. If you think this is too easy, you may want to first divide stocks into business groups (for example, energy and transportation, technology, consumer non-durables, financial, manufacturing, and utilities), and then randomly select two or three stocks within each group. However, one study showed that the benefits from doing this are not very big.[6]

Another way of diversifying in the stock market is to invest in all the stocks on the stock market; that is, to invest in the entire stock market. You might think that this would require a fortune to do. Fortunately, it doesn't. There are stock mutual funds which effectively invest in the entire market, or at least invest in a broad part of the market, such as the Standard and Poor's 500 stocks. These are called "index funds" as they usually follow particular market indexes. Buying into these mutual funds means that you get rid of all risk associated with individual companies, and your risk will be composed of entirely that risk associated with the stock market as a whole.

Diversification Between Types of Investments: Asset Allocation

ASSET ALLOCATION

Diversification between different types of investments is called *asset allocation*. The idea here is simple. If you aren't able to perfectly predict where the economy is going and what investment type will do best at any point in time, a reasonable approach may be to cover all the bases—to have some of your money invested in each major investment type at all times. That is, always have some of your money invested in stocks, gold (or precious metals) and real estate, short-term financial investments, and long-term bonds at all times.

Two major questions to address for asset allocation are: (1) What should be the initial allocation among investments? and (2) Should the allocation be periodically rebalanced? The answer to the first question

---

[5]One of the most famous studies on this topic is by John L. Evans and Stephen N. Archer, "Diversification and the Reduction of Dispersion: An Empirical Analysis," *Journal of Finance,* Vol. 23, December 1968, pp. 761–767.

[6]See L. Fisher and J. H. Lorie, "Some Studies of Variability of Returns on Investments in Common Stocks," *Journal of Business,* April 1970, pp. 99–134.

Table 8-4 Asset allocation over the life cycle.

	Early Career	**Mid-Career**	**Late Career**	**Retirement**
Stocks	20%	55%	40%	10%
Bonds	20%	10%	25%	25%
Gold/real estate	10%	25%	15%	5%
Cash	50%	10%	20%	60%

Early Career:	Career uncertainties and family demands suggest taking low risk.
Mid Career:	Earnings are at highest level and family demands are reduced—maximum risk can be taken.
Late Career:	As move toward retirement, take moderate risk.
Retirement:	Move to safety.

is that, assets should be invested in such a way that the rate of return is maximized for a given level of risk.[7] In general, the greater the risk that the investor is willing to take and the greater the time horizon for the investments, the greater the percentage of funds allocated to stocks. In contrast, the safer the investor wants to be and the shorter the time horizon, the greater the percentage of funds allocated to cash and bonds. A typical asset allocation pattern is shown in Table 8-4. In this case, the investor increases acceptable risk between early career and mid-career, and then reduces acceptable risk in late career and retirement.

Regarding the second question about periodically rebalancing the asset allocated portfolio, you probably should monitor and rebalance the portfolio from time to time, but not for the *wrong* reasons. The wrong reason to rebalance would be because you suddenly thought you knew which investment type is to become "hot." This defeats the whole idea of diversification. You're diversifying your investments with an asset-allocated portfolio in the first place because you don't know what investment type will become hot and for how long.

There are two "right" reasons for rebalancing an asset-allocated portfolio. One reason is because you've moved into a different stage of the life cycle and you want to change the mix of the assets (see Table 8-4). Another reason is because one or two of the investment types have grown so much that you desired percentage mix of investment types is not met.

---

[7]Computer programs exist which will compute these allocations. To run them, the programs require information on the average returns of the investment types, their standard deviations, the relationships (correlations) between the investment types, and the investor's acceptable level of risk.

The Bottom Line

Diversification means spreading investment funds into different investments whose returns are at least partially unrelated. The goal of diversification is to reduce risk without sacrificing average return. Diversification in the stock market can be achieved by randomly buying as few as 15 stocks. Diversification among different investment types is called asset allocation.

6. Should You Invest in Yourself?

Investing doesn't just mean putting money in the stock market or buying bonds. You can also invest in yourself by obtaining additional education in school, getting more training on-the-job, or improving your health. These kinds of investments are called *human capital investments* by economists, as contrasted with financial investments (stocks, bonds, mutual funds) or physical investments like houses, cars, and appliances. However, investments in yourself—in your human capital—can be just as important or maybe more important than financial or physical investments.

HUMAN CAPITAL INVESTMENTS

Before getting into the details, here's the "big picture" of what will be discussed in this section. Attaining more education or training or achieving better health are investments because they involve a classic tradeoff: you sacrifice time and/or money now in order to get a bigger paycheck and more happiness in the future.

For example, suppose Eddie has finished high school. He has two options— he can work full-time and earn more money than he's ever had before, or he can go to college. By going to college, Eddie will not only sacrifice the income from the full-time job, but he will also have to pay tuition, fees, books, and school supplies. He certainly won't live as well in college as he would with the income from a full-time job.

But there's a payoff for Eddie from going to college. Although he will live like a pauper while in college, his income will likely be much higher in the job he can land with a college education than with only a high school diploma. So Eddie's decision is this: Does he sacrifice some income and spend some money for the next four years in order to earn significantly more income over the following 30 to 40 years? As you will see, your old friend "present value analysis" will be indispensable in studying this question.

A Framework for Decision-Making

Eddie's decision and similar ones in human capital investing lend themselves to some number-crunching. The formula for making the calculations is to compare the costs of the investment to the benefits. Specifically, the question is:

Is the PRESENT VALUE OF COSTS > the PRESENT VALUE OF BENEFITS, or

Is the PRESENT VALUE OF COSTS < the PRESENT VALUE OF BENEFITS, or

Is the PRESENT VALUE OF COSTS = the PRESENT VALUE OF BENEFITS?

If the PRESENT VALUE OF COSTS of the investment is greater than the PRESENT VALUE OF BENEFITS, then the investment (i.e., going to college) shouldn't be made. Conversely, if the PRESENT VALUE OF COSTS is *less* than the PRESENT VALUE OF BENEFITS, then the investment should be made. If the costs and benefits are exactly equal, which is rare, then the investment is a toss-up.

RATE OF TIME PREFERENCE AGAIN   Before getting to an example, we need to refresh your memory about an important element of the present value framework—the discount rate. Recall from Chapter 1 that the discount rate should include a measure of your *rate of time preference,* or how you trade-off present dollars (and the purchases they provide) for future dollars (and the purchases they provide). Since almost everyone prefers dollars and goodies now to dollars and goodies later, the rate of time preference will be some positive number, like 5%, 10%, or 20%. To get the discount rate, the expected annual rate of inflation is added to the rate of time preference. Thus, for example, an annual inflation rate of 3% and a rate of time preference of 10% implies a discount rate of 13%. This means a person must get back $1.13 one year from now in order to be willing to give up $1.00 today, (You learned all this when we discussed present value and discounting. We are sure it's coming back to you!)

Anyway, the reason the rate of time preference is important here is that someone with a higher rate of time preference—someone who must get back much more in the future to give up resources today—will be less likely to make investments in human capital than someone with a lower rate of time preference. In other words, someone who is very "now oriented" will be less likely to make human capital investments in education than someone who is less "now oriented". Hopefully, this will become clearer, if it already isn't crystal clear, in the following example.

EXAMPLE 8-13:   Susan and Josie have both graduated from high school and are considering going to college for four years. If they were not to go to college and to take a fulltime job now, the job would pay $40,000 per year (real income). Going to college is expected to require the following costs for each of four years (again, real income)

ANSWER: Tuition and fees: $30,000
Books and supplies: $5,000
Total : $35,000

However, if both Susan and Josie graduated from college, the jobs they could obtain are expected to pay $60,000 each year (real income). If Susan's rate of time preference is 3% and Josie's is 15%, and both expect to work 26 years after college, who will go to college?

Since everything is stated in real incomes and real dollars, inflation can be ignored (remember, we did this with life insurance). Hence, in this example, the discount rate for each person equals her rate of time preference.

For Susan, the PRESENT VALUE OF COSTS equals the present value of costs of four years of college plus the present value of foregone income from working full-time:

$$(\$35,000 + \$40,000) \times \text{PVFS } (n = 4 \text{ years, } r = 3\%)$$
$$= \$75,000 \times 3.717$$
$$= \$278,782$$

Susan's PRESENT VALUE OF BENEFITS equals to the present value of the additional income she would earn over 26 years by going to college:

$$(\$60,000 - \$40,000) \times \text{PVFS (year 5 to 30, } r = 3\%)$$
$$= \$20,000 \times [\text{PVFS}(n = 30, r = 3\%) - \text{PVFS } (n = 4, r = 3\%]$$
$$= \$20,000 * (19.600 - 3.717)$$
$$= \$20,000 * 15.883$$
$$= \$317,667$$

Since the PRESENT VALUE OF BENEFITS exceeds the PRESENT VALUE OF COSTS, Susan will go to college. For Josie, the PRESENT VALUE OF COSTS is similarly calculated, but this time using a discount rate of 15%:

$$(\$35,000 + \$40,000) \times \text{PVFS } (n = 4 \text{ years, } r = 15\%)$$
$$= \$75,000 \times 2.855$$
$$= \$214,123$$

Josie's PRESENT VALUE OF BENEFITS also equals the present value of the additional income she would earn over 26 years after going to college, but again using a 15% discount rate:

$$(\$60,000 - \$40,000) \times \text{PVFS (year 5 to 30, } r = 15\%)$$
$$= \$20,000 \times [\text{PVFS } (n = 30, r = 15\%) - \text{PVFS } (n = 4, r = 15\%]$$
$$= \$20,000 * (6.596 - 2.855)$$
$$= \$20,000 * 3.711$$
$$= \$74,220$$

Josie won't go to college because, due to her higher discount rate, the PRESENT VALUE OF COSTS is greater than the PRESENT VALUE OF BENEFITS.

ROOM AND BOARD
COSTS

Notice in this example that room and board costs were not included as college costs. Why? Easy, because whether you go to college or not, you will still live somewhere and eat. So you have room and board expenses if you're in college or if you're working full-time.

Some Answers for Education

In Chapter 1 you learned about the substantial increase in annual income earned by the average college graduate compared to the average high school graduate. Why, then, doesn't everyone go to college?

One reason is that not everyone can be successful in college. Some individuals who attend college may flunk-out or do so poorly that their degree is relatively worthless. Their payoff to college is very low, and the present value of costs of attending college exceed the present value of benefits.

Other people who could potentially do well in college don't attend because they simply don't like going to classes, studying, and taking tests. In short, they don't like school. For these people, there's a huge distaste, or dissatisfaction, associated with attending school that overwhelms any net payoff from a college degree.

AGE AND EDUCATION

A third reason some individuals may not go to college is simply because they're too old. No, I don't mean their age means they couldn't do well in school. But, notice that the present value of benefits from a college education depends, in part, on how many years the person has remaining to work. The more years left to work, the greater the present value of benefits, and the fewer the remaining years to work, the smaller the present value of benefits. So, everything else equal, older people will be less motivated on economic grounds to attend college.

RISK AND PAYOFF

Individuals who perceive there is a great deal of risk associated with the payoff to going to college may decide the effort is not worth the cost. For example, suppose you're interested in one of the humanities fields. You may run the numbers and find that, assuming you are able to get a job with your humanities degree, going to college would be beneficial. But what if a significant number of graduates with humanities degrees can't find jobs in their field? If they end up working in retail sales, for example, then the time and money used to obtain the humanities degree may not have been worthwhile.

There are two ways to handle this possibility in our formula and calculations. One way is to use our friend "expected value" in forming the college degree salary. If half of humanities graduates obtain humanities jobs paying $50,000, but the other half work in retail sales paying $30,000, then the *expected value* of a humanities degree salary is $50,000 \times 0.5 + $30,000 \times 0.5$, or $40,000. The other way is to add a "risk premium" to the discount rate, where the "risk premium" is higher the greater the chances of not finding a job in the college degree field.

DISCRIMINATION AND PAYOFF

Last, if certain groups of individuals perceive they won't realize the same payoffs from going to college as the average person, then such groups will be discouraged from attending college. For instance, in the past, women and some ethnic and racial groups have alleged that discrimination has kept them from earning what the average college graduate has earned. If the discrimination was *thought* to have occurred, whether it did or not, then it could have kept some talented individuals from attending college. Hopefully, any such discrimination has been much reduced today.

On-Job-Training

You can also increase your skills, and potentially your future income, through on-job-training. However, unlike formal schooling at a college, university, or trade school, you don't *directly* pay for on-job-training in the sense that you write a check for tuition and fees. However, you may *indirectly* pay for on-job-training. Let's see how, and also see how this affects your willingness to go through on-job-training.

GENERAL ON-JOB TRAINING

There are two types of on-job-training. "General on-job-training" provides skills the employee can use not only at the specific job he has now, but also the learned skills can be used at similar jobs in the same industry. For example, if you take a job as a carpenter with Jones Brothers Carpenters and learn carpentry skills of measuring, cutting, and nailing while on-the-job, then these are general skills you can use if you leave Jones Brothers and work for Smith Brothers Carpenters.

SPECIFIC ON-JOB TRAINING

In contrast, "specific on-job-training" includes skills the worker uses that are specific to this job and can't be used at other jobs. Let's say Joe is a word processor who works at Skyland University. While there, he is taught, to use some software that only Skyland University uses. Learning this software is specific on-job-training because it's a skill that Joe can only use at Skyland U.

The distinction between general and specific on-job-training is important because it affects a worker's salary. In general, you have learned in this text and elsewhere that a worker's pay tends to rise the more useful skills she learns. But this is not always the case for skills learned that are "general on job-training". At the job where the worker learns general on-job-training, the company *won't* be willing to immediately pay more for these skills because the company knows the worker can take those skills and move to another job. The company looks at the general skills it teaches workers as a cost, and the company is compensated for these costs by not paying a salary commensurate with those skills at least for a while.

From the worker's standpoint, the learning of general skills in on-job-training can be viewed as a human capital investment. The worker accepts the lower salary from the company providing the general on-job-training in exchange for a higher salary later, either at the same company or another company. So, once again, the worker must decide if this tradeoff is worthwhile, as illustrated by the following example.

EXAMPLE 8-14: Jeff can take a job with Jones Brothers Carpentry as a laborer paying $35,000/year. However, the company promises to teach him carpentry skills which will eventually allow him to earn $45,000/year. Alternatively, Jeff can work at the local building supply store for $38,000/year. If the initial $35,000/year salary at Jones Brothers Company would last for three years, should Jeff take the job at Jones Brothers if his rate of time preference is 10% and he expects to work for 30 years? All incomes are real incomes, so inflation can be ignored.

The same framework is used here as was used in EXAPLE 8-13 when the decision was whether to go to college.

First, calculate the **PRESENT VALUE OF COSTS** for Jeff of working at Jones Brothers as the present value of the lower salary there for three years:

($38,000 − $35,000) × PVFS (n = 3 years, r = 10%)

= $3,000 × 2.487

= $7,461

Jeff's **PRESENT VALUE OF BENEFITS** equals the present value of the difference between $45,000 and $38,000 for the 27 years of working starting at year 4 and going until year 30:

($45,000 − $38,000) × PVFS (year 4 to 30, r = 10%)

= $7,000 × [PVFS (n = 30, r = 10%) − PVFS (n = 3, r = 10%)]

= $7,000 *(9.427 − 2.487)

= $7,000 * 6.940

= $48.580

Since the **PRESENT VALUE OF BENEFITS** is greater than the **PRESENT VALUE OF COSTS**, Jeff should take the job with Jones Brothers Carpentry.

The situation is entirely different with specific on-job-training. Since specific on-job-training skills are not useful anywhere except at the specific job where they're learned, the worker learning those skills can't benefit by moving to another job and earning a higher salary. Thus, the employer providing the specific on-job-training can't get away with paying a lower salary while the specific on-job-training skills are learned. Employers couldn't get workers to accept the lower salary because workers know the specific on-job-training skills aren't marketable anywhere else. There is no effect of specific on-job-training on the worker's salary.

Good Health as an Investment

If you think about it, practicing healthy living habits can often cost resources—either in money or time. Buying leaner cuts of meat costs more than buying fatty meats. A gym or health club membership obviously costs money. And, don't forget the time it takes to exercise, learn about nutrition, and cut fresh fruits and vegetables for a salad.

So there is an investment now in terms of money and time in order to be healthy. And what are the payoffs? One payoff is looking and feeling better. Also, there's a probable monetary payoff. The healthier one is, the fewer days that will be missed from work and the longer a person's work career. Thus, healthier people will likely have greater lifetime incomes than less healthy people.

WHY ISN'T EVERYONE HEALTHY

Then why doesn't everyone follow a healthy lifestyle and only eat good-for-you foods and exercise regularly? There are three possible reasons. First, living a healthy lifestyle involves the classic economic tradeoff found with all human capital investments—costs are paid now in order to reap benefits later. People with a lower rate of time preference will be more willing to pay the costs now for good health later, but those with a higher rate of time preference will be less likely to do so. The latter group—the "live for now group"—would rather use the extra money and time needed for the gym and better food in ways that give immediate satisfaction.

A second reason is based on our old friend "opportunity cost", but with a twist. The opportunity cost of "eating right and exercising" is "eating bad and being lazy", and "eating bad and being lazy" can be fun and pleasurable. If the benefits from this pleasure are valued to be large enough, they can overwhelm the perceived present value of benefits of good health later.

Third, although, there is a perceived link between healthy eating and exercise habits today and good health later, the link isn't solid. Everyone has heard stories of people who eat well and exercise daily dying young. Conversely, there are equally as many stories of people living a very long life who ate horribly and never did a strenuous thing in their life! The problem is that many other factors, such as genetics, climate, and stress, besides food and exercise, determine general health and wellbeing. The uncertainty of what exactly determines a long and healthy life make the calculations between investments in a healthy lifestyle and future payoffs in income and enjoyment very problematic.

CAN SMOKING PAY-OFF?

C O N S U M E R   T O P I C

For decades it's been widely thought that smoking can have negative consequences for personal health. Although the rate of smoking in the country has declined, millions of people still smoke, and people take up the smoking habit everyday. Why? Why would anyone begin or continue a habit that may hurt them in the long-run?

As explained in the text, one answer is that smokers calculate the benefits from smoking to exceed their costs. To put some specifics on this generality, economists Rachel Dardis and Thomas Keane estimated the benefits and costs of smoking for male smokers.

The major personal cost of smoking is the reduction in the smoker's life span. Dardis and Keane found that male smokers lose between five and six years in their life span. However, these lost years occur at the end of the smoker's life. Just like a future dollar is worth much less than a dollar today, living five less years fifty years from now is worth much less than living five less years in the near future. In fact, Dardis and Keane calculated that a male smoker translates losing five to six years at the end of their file to losing between one month to seven months of life when they begin smoking.

Dardis and Keane calculated the benefits of smoking as the willingness of smokers to pay for cigarettes, a common economic technique. Then, after putting a monetary value on the present value reduction in life span due to smoking, the researchers were able to compare the benefits from smoking to their costs.

Their results are instructive. When a discount rate of 10% is used, Dardis and Keane found that over 90 percent of their comparisons resulted in smoking benefits exceeding smoking costs. If a 5% discount rate is assumed, the findings are reversed—in most of the cases, costs outweigh benefits.

These findings are just what we would expect from economic theory. Smokers are likely very "now oriented", meaning they put a great deal of weight on the current pleasure from smoking, and they heavily discount the future costs.

Reference: Dardis, Rachel and Thomas Keane, "Risk-Benefit Analysis of Cigarette Smoking: Public Policy Implications," *The Journal of Consumer Affairs*, Winter 1995, Vol 29, No. 2. pp. 351–367.

UNHEALTHY HABITS   Now let's take the opposite perspective. Why would someone indulge in a habit, and, indeed, spend money on that habit, if they knew the habit was very unhealthy? Based on our framework of analyzing human capital investments, this would appear to be irrational because money is being spent today in order to reduce, not increase, future income.

You probably already know the answer because we've touched on it. If the bad habit returns enough pleasure today, if the person has a high enough rate of time preference (meaning they are very much a "live for now" person), and if the negative consequences of the habit would occur far enough in the future such that their present value is very low, then such behavior will be rational. For people practicing these habits, the pleasures today of the unhealthy behavior are high enough to outweigh the future negative effects on their health. The CONSUMER TOPIC on cigarettes and smoking gives an excellent example of the rationality of unhealthy actions.

The Bottom Line

When you invest in yourself, through formal education, on-job-training, and even a healthy lifestyle, you are investing in your *human capital*. Human capital investments cost money and time, but the payoff is usually a higher future income. There are some expenditures today that cause a probable decline in future income. Rational people engage in these habits if the current pleasure and enjoyment from the habits are greater than the present value of expected future costs. _____

7. Should You Invest in Your Family?

In addition to investing in yourself, you can also invest in a family. There are four familial types of investments we will study in this section: marriage, divorce, having children, and working in the marketplace versus working in household tasks.

We understand that you are probably extremely skeptical about the relevance of economics to these subjects, except perhaps the last one. After all, aren't marriage and having children the result of love and divorce is the end product of falling out of love? What possible insights could economics give us about the affairs of the heart?

While many disciplines and fields—psychology, sociology, family counseling, religion—can give very important insights into marriage, divorce, and children, so too can economics for one significant reason. Marriage, divorce, and children all involve the use of resources (time and money). Since economics is the discipline devoted to putting our resources to their best use, marriage, divorce, and children are "fair game" for economics.

The Benefits and Costs of Marriage

Simply put, people marry if they think their total enjoyment in life will be greater compared to being single. That is, if the total amount of benefits net of costs for a married couple is greater than the sum of benefits net of costs for the two individuals if single, then the two people will marry rather than remaining single. If you will indulge some mathematics, two people will marry if:

$$B_m - C_m > (B_{1s} - C_{1s}) + (B_{2s} - C_{2s}).$$

In this equation:

B_m = total benefits to person 1 and person 2 combined when married,

C_m = total costs to person 1 and person 2 combined when married,

B_{1s} = total benefits to person 1 when single,

C_{1s} = total costs to person 1 when single,

B_{2s} = total benefits to person 2 when single,

C_{2s} = total costs to person 2 when single.

To get some more insights into the economics of marriage, let's see how marriage could increase the total benefits from life to two people and reduce the total costs.

MARRIAGE BENEFITS On the benefit side, marriage is a way of recognizing and institutionalizing the love two people have for each other. Certainly two people can love each other outside of marriage, but marriage is a way of legally proclaiming that love to the world and legally binding two people together. Some people may recognize the love to be stronger and more serious if it is sanctioned through marriage. So, with respect to our current institutions and social perceptions, marriage confers some special benefits on love that non-marriage can't.

Marriage also assists in having and raising children. Why you might say—certainly there are many examples of children being born and raised outside of marriage. This is true, but again, like love, the raising of children within a marriage often implies a greater resource commitment from the parents to the children. Although not always true (in economics, we talk about tendencies and likelihoods, not absolutes), marriage means a greater chance that both parents will be present to raise the children. If unmarried, there is a greater chance one parent will not be present or will be committed to other endeavors or people. In short, marriage helps provide a firm foundation for the raising of children.

MARRIAGE REDUCES TRANSACTION COSTS Now let's look on the cost side. How might marriage reduce the total costs of living of two people? There are two ways. First, marriage can reduce the "transactions costs" of activities requiring partners. Think about dating, like going out to dinner or taking in a movie or concert. Single people must take the time to find a partner for such activities. And even if a person has a favorite boyfriend or girlfriend, that boyfriend or girlfriend may be busy or have other activities planned when called for a date. It may take several calls and much time to complete the "transaction" of setting up the date.

MARRIAGE ALLOWS SPECIALIZATION For married couples, there are no transaction costs of establishing dates, or at least the transaction costs are much lower. A married person has a built-in date with his/her partner. Presumably, the dates are willingly and easily established because the married partners have many similar likes and pursuits.

To understand the second way that marriage can reduce the costs of two people living, it helps to think of a household as a business. There are two major activities of the household—earning money, which we'll call *market work,* and accomplishing all the tasks of keeping a household running, such as shopping, cleaning, preparing meals, and, if children are present, child care and rearing. We'll call all these household tasks, *household work.* Marriage may allow two people to specialize in the activities of running a household and thus be able to maintain a household at lower total costs than the combined cost of running two households if each person were single.

This specialization and cost reduction can take many forms. One way is by taking advantage of the old adage that "two can live cheaper than one." When two single persons' households are combined, they can specialize with some of their household furnishings and appliances and sell or discard unneeded pieces. Economies of scale (remember this term from Chapter 6) can make the total costs of running a two-person household less than the combined cost of two one-person households.

ECONOMIES OF SCALE

Perhaps more important, a married couple may reduce total household costs by having one partner specialize in some household activities while the other handles the remaining activities. Furthermore, this specialization would be based on the best skills of each partner. Through this specialization, the total household tasks and activities can be completed more cheaply and efficiently than the same tasks and activities would be done in two single-person households.

"TRADITIONAL MARRIAGES"

In marriages of previous eras, so-called "traditional marriages," the specialization generally took the form of the male being totally engaged in market work—i.e., working at a market job for pay—while the female specialized in household work. This specialization was entirely logical at the time because males were taught marketable skills and trades while females were only taught household tasks. Marriage was highly desirable in those eras. Although a single male could work and earn money, it was very difficult and costly for him to maintain a household. In fact, most single males would either continue living with parents or reside in a boarding house where meals and other household tasks were provided for a fee.

The situation was even more daunting for single females. Since good-paying market work opportunities were scarce, single females often lived with the families of male relatives in exchange for performance of household tasks.

Traditional households are now a minority, and also the marriage rate has dropped. Part of the reason for both is the increased market work opportunities for females. Clearly, as females have more

Table 8-5   Trends in Birth Rates, Marriage Rates, Divorce Rates, Female Labor Force Participation Rates, and Real Female Earnings, 1970–2010

	1970	1980	1990	2000	2010
Birth rate	18.4	15.9	16.7	14.4	13.0
Marriage rate	10.6	10.6	9.8	8.3	7.1
Divorce rate	3.5	5.2	4.7	4.1	3.5
Female labor force participation rate	43.3	51.5	57.5	59.4	59.5
Female real median weekly earnings, 2010 $ (Current $)	$601(107)	$564 (213)	$616 (369)	$654 (516)	$704

Birth, marriage, and divorce rates are per 1000 population. Female labor force participation rate is percent of the female civilian noninstitutional population 16 and over.

Data source: Statistical Abstract of the United States, multiple years.

opportunities to earn significant salaries, the need to be married "just to survive" is reduced. Notice in Table 8-5 that the marriage rate has fallen as the real earnings of females have risen.

"MODERN MARRIAGES"   So, you're probably asking, what is the reason for two people, each wish the ability to earn income in market work, to be married? The answer is that there can still be benefits from specialization among household tasks in today's modern marriage. For example, in the case of one of the authors, Dr. Walden: He is a better breakfast cook and landscaper than his spouse, while she is better at preparing dinners and decorating. Thus, Dr. Walden and his wife reap the benefits of their respective specializations in household tasks by being married compared to being single. Dr. Walden eats better dinners and enjoys a better decorated home while his wife enjoys better breakfasts and receives pleasure from a better landscaped yard compared to being single.

In today's society with many employment opportunities for women, why hasn't marriage just been replaced by "living together"? Well, "living together" is certainly more prevalent today than in past years. However, marriage still has benefits over "living together". Marriage is a contract for the specialization of tasks among the partners. It is an implicit contract for the agreed upon division of labor, and it makes it more likely the partners will invest in their specialized skills. In summary, marriage motivates the partners to stay together and reap the benefits of their specialization.

ERRORS IN CALCULATING MARRIAGE BENEFITS

The Economics of Divorce

Divorce can occur if a marriage fails. Marriage fails if the total net benefits of being married fall short of the combined net benefits of the two people becoming single again.

Before marriage, the prospective partners must estimate the net benefits from being married. One reason marriages fail and end in divorce is that the partners simply overestimated the net gains from marriage. This can particularly occur if an individual has not searched very long for a partner. In this case, little information will have been gathered about potential partners, thereby making it more difficult to estimate the net benefits from marriage. Individuals who marry at a very young age will have had less time to collect information about potential mates. Thus, it makes sense that we observe higher divorce rates for individuals who have married at a very young age.

"FREE-LOADING" PARTNERS

Marriages can fail not only if the total net benefits are less than the combined net benefits when the partners are single, but failure can also occur if the total net benefits are weighted too much in favor of one partner. For example, if the partners initially agreed upon a division of the household tasks, but one partner didn't complete the assigned tasks, then the other partner could decide the net benefits to him/her from the marriage are much less than originally thought. Unless changes are made, the "put-upon" partner would be motivated to consider divorce from the "freeloading" partner.

Last, significant changes in the market work opportunities of the partners can alter the net benefits from marriage. This can come from two sources. If the partner specializing in market work suffers a significant decline in income, then the gains from marriage for the partner specializing in household work will diminish. In common terms, the partner specializing in household work will consider the income-earning partner to no longer be a "good provider."

INCOME CHANGES

Conversely, if the partner specializing in household work experiences a big increase in his/her market work opportunities, then the net gains from marriage will also be reduced. This partner will have less need for the other partner as a source of income.

It's little wonder, then, that many divorces result from income changes, both up and down, of the partners in the marriage.

Having Children

Ask any parent and they will agree there are certainly benefits, but also costs, to having children. Hence, the decision to have children again sets up the typical economic comparison of benefits and costs.

CHILDREN'S LOVE

There are three benefits to having children, but the relative importance of each has changed over time. First and foremost, children provide the benefit of love to parents. The love comes from watching the children grow and develop, and also from knowing children will carry on the parents' genes and traits. In essence, children are a biological extension of the parents, and one benefit of having children is that parents can effectively perpetuate themselves through time.

CHILD WORK

A second benefit of children is that they can contribute to market work and household work. Although the market work aspect of children has diminished for most households, in some enterprises, such as farming and other small, family-owned businesses, children's work is still very important. Here, children can provide a reliable labor supply.

PARENTAL OLD-AGE SECURITY

A third benefit of children is the security and care they can provide to parents in the parents' old age. In traditional societies, this was a very important consideration. For example, Dr. Walden can remember his grandparents in the 1950's living with their children's families. However, the development of company pensions and Social Security has considerably lessened this role of children. Nonetheless, even if parents can be assured of greater financial security in their old age, children can still play a key role in assisting parents make financial, living, and medical decisions.

The financial cost of children can be substantial, as was discussed in Chapter 6. But children also create non-financial costs. Parents often experience the mental stress of coping with the typical growing pains of children. Some would say this stress has increased in recent years as communication technologies (television, the internet) have made it more difficult for parents to control what is exposed to their children.

TIME COSTS OF CHILDREN

Also, don't forget the time costs associated with raising children. Rearing children takes time. This time either comes directly from the parents or can be hired through the use of child care and nannies. However, there is considerable debate among child psychologists and educators about the degree to which the time of hired child caregivers is a good substitute for parental time.[8]

So partners will evaluate the benefits and costs of children in determining whether to have children. A long-standing interesting question in this regard is whether the desired number of children in a household increases or decreases as the hourly earnings of the parents increase.

To answer this question, let's look at how the benefits and costs of children might change as parents' hourly earnings rise. One benefit that may be affected is the benefit of children to care for parents in old age. The greater the parents' hourly earnings, the less need parents may perceive for children to care for them in old age. Thus, on the basis of this benefit, we might expect parents with higher hourly earnings to desire fewer children.

---

[8]Some of the references include: Clarke-Stewart, K. Alison, "A Home is Not a School: The Effects of Child Care on Children's Development" *Journal of Social Issues,* 47, No.2, 1991, pp 105–123; Belsky, Jay, "The 'Effects' of Infant Day Care Revisited" *Early Childhood Research Quarterly* 3, 1988, pp. 235–272; and Blau, Francine and Adam Grossberg, "Maternal Labor Supply and Children's Cognitive Development," *Review of Economics and Statistics,* 74, No.3, August 1992, pp. 474–481.

PARENTS' HOURLY
EARNINGS AND
CHILDREN

On the cost side, the impact of parents' higher hourly earnings on their number of children can have conflicting impacts. If children are "normal goods," then an increase in parents' hourly earnings can increase the desired number of children. You may recall (hopefully) from Chapter 1 that a "normal good" is simply a good that consumers want more of when their income rises. So, just like consumers' desires to purchase more shirts or food when income rises, so too will they probably want to have more children when their income rises in response to an increase in hourly earnings.

But remember, one cost of having children is the time commitment from parents. As parents are paid more per hour, their time used in rearing children becomes more expensive (remember opportunity cost). A fundamental concept in economics is that less of a product is purchased and used as that product becomes more expensive. So we can say that children and child rearing become more expensive as parents' hourly earnings rise. This effect suggests that parents earning higher hourly pay will have fewer children. This is an application of the "substitution effect" you also learned in Chapter 1.

So the impact of an increase in parents' hourly earnings on the desired number of children is a combination of these opposing "income" and "substitution" effects. Research suggests that the substitution effect dominates, especially for the female's hourly earnings since females are still the major caregivers of children. Notice in Table 8-5 that birth rates have fallen as the female labor force participation rate and female earnings have increased.

Work versus Home

One of the biggest decisions for today's parents is whether to work for pay in the marketplace or devote time to household tasks, including caring for children. Wives, in particular, face this decision because they still perform most of the household tasks. But, as market work opportunities and real wage rates have increased for women, many have become increasingly torn between staying at home versus working for pay. Indeed, the percentage of married women working in the marketplace increased from 32% in 1960 to 62% in 2009, and, even more dramatically, the percentage of married women with children working in the market place jumped from 28% in 1960 to 70% in 2009.[9]

It's often claimed that in today's economy, wives must work in order to maintain the family's standard of living. The assumption is that it takes incomes from two parents working today to equal the income of one working parent decades ago. For most households, this isn't true!

---

[9]U.S. Bureau of the Census, *Statistical Abstract of the U.S.,* multiple years.

For example, research by Walden shows that only households headed by a single-earner without a college degree experienced declines in real income between 1960 and 1996.[10]

As with any of our economic decisions, the decision about how much to work in the marketplace versus in household tasks depends on an evaluation of benefits and costs. To explore these in further detail, let's look at this decision from the perspective of a married woman with young children.

HOUSEHOLD INCOME BENEFITS CHILDREN

The major benefit of the mother working is that more income will be available to the household for purchase of market produced goods and services, including those used for children. That is, the household can use some of the mother's income to buy clothes and computers and establish a college saving fund for the children. These purchases certainly contribute to the well-being of children.

A major cost of the mother working is that she will have less time available for household tasks, including time in child rearing. For some of these household tasks, there are good substitutes in the form of market purchased alternatives, such as cleaning services, dry-cleaners, and prepared meals (although the household will want to carefully calculate if there are monies remaining from the mother's salary after paying

SUBSTITUTES FOR PARENTAL TIME

for these services and additional taxes—see the CONSUMER TOPIC in Chapter 3). But a big question some would say THE question—is whether there are good substitutes for a mother's time in child rearing. That is, how will a child's development be affected by time spent in child care, with nannies or babysitters, or simply alone as compared to time with the child's mother? This is a very controversial subject for which there is currently no settled answer.

The main point is that child rearing involves the use of both purchased goods and services and parental time. Increased market work by the mother increases the ability to purchase goods and services for the child but decreases the amount of time spent with the child. Parents must choose the combination of purchased goods and services and parental time which, in the parents' evaluation, produces the best outcomes for children. This best combination will differ across households and will depend, in part, on the hourly earnings of the parents (especially the mother), the skills of the parents in child rearing versus the skills of child care and similar providers, and the preferences of the parents for spending time with their children. Clearly, one size, or better—one combination, does not fit all households here.

---

[10]Walden, Michael L. "Absolute and Relative Income and Consumption Trends of Married U.S. Households in 1960 and 1996, or The Cleavers and Kramdens Meet the Taylors and Conners", paper presented at the Annual Conference of the American Council on Consumer Interests, March, 2000, San Antonio, Texas.

The Bottom Line

Economics can provide some useful insights into decisions about marriage, divorce, having children, and working for pay or in household tasks. Each of these decisions involves resource use and benefits and costs. Individuals will evaluate these decisions, in part, on a comparison of their benefits and costs. However, as with many decisions, a prospective calculation of the benefits and costs won't always match reality.

WORDS AND CONCEPTS YOU SHOULD KNOW

Saving
Investing
Personal rate of time preference
The life cycle of investing
The economic roller coaster, or business cycle
Coincident economic indicators
Leading economic indicators
Lagging economic indicators
Default risk
Liquidity risk
Rate risk
Inflation risk
Reinvestment risk
Variability in rate of return
Standard deviation
Relationship between risk and return
Beta
Standard and Poor's bond rating system
Moody's bond rating system

Risk-averse
Income return
Capital gain return
Yield
Compounding period
Bond equivalent basis
CD equivalent basis
Effective yield
Effective yield on a Treasury bill
Day-of-deposit to day-of-withdrawal
Low balance method
First-in, first-out
Last-in, first-out
Daily interest
Dead days
Fixed interest rate
Floating interest rate
After-tax yield
Arithmetic average yield
Geometric average yield
Ideal investment strategy
Diversification
Asset allocation

FUNDAMENTALS OF INVESTING—
A SUMMARY

1. Investing and borrowing are part of a cycle. Those people who save and invest are providing the funds that are used by borrowers.

2. Saving is not investing. Saving means not to spend money on consumption products. Investing only occurs when saved funds are "put to work" to earn a rate of return.

3. Your goal from investing should not be to "get rich quick." Investing is done to transfer purchasing power to the future. Your goal in investing should be to earn enough to keep ahead of inflation.

4. A consumer's personal rate of time preference shows how many extra dollars of consumption are needed next year to compensate for giving up one dollar of consumption this year. The higher a consumer's personal rate of time preference, the less willing the consumer is to save and invest.

5. There is a general life cycle pattern to investing. Saving and investing is low when consumers are in their 20s and 30s. Saving and investing peaks when consumers reach their 40s and 50s. During retirement, consumers draw down on their accumulated investments.

6. The economic roller coaster, or business cycle, has a profound impact on the performance of alternative investments. During the expansion phase of the cycle, stocks perform best. Gold and real estate perform best at the peak of the business cycle. At the beginning of the contraction phase short term financial investments, like money market funds, do best. Finally during the main part of the contraction phase, long term bonds outperform other investments. The problem with using the business cycle to direct investments is knowing where in the cycle the economy is.

7. There are many types of risks involved with investing.
   DEFAULT RISK is the risk of losing a major part of your original investment.
   LIQUIDITY RISK is the risk of not being able to "cash-in" the investment for all your money.
   RATE RISK is the risk of not earning the rate of return you expect.

INFIATION RISK is the risk that your investment returns don't keep pace with inflation. REINVESTMENT RISK is the risk associated with reinvesting investment returns.

8. Risk is measured by the variability in an investment's rate of return. Typically this variability is measured by the investment's standard deviation of the rate of return.

   BETA is a measure of risk for stocks. Stocks with betas greater than 1 are more risky. BOND RISK is measured by rating systems developed by Standard and Poor's or Moody's.

9. Risk and rate of return move together. Superior investments are any investments which pay a higher rate of return for the same level of risk. Inferior investments are investments which pay a lower rate of return for the same level of risk.

10. Most consumers are risk-averse, meaning that consumers turn down opportunities to participate in bets with equal chances of winning $X or losing $X. However, studies show that consumers' aversion to risk declines as consumer wealth increases. This means that higher income or higher wealth consumers will have a greater proportion of their investments in more risky investments.

11. There are three ways that an investment can earn a return: income, capital gain, and income plus capital gain. An income return is a periodic cash payment. A capital gain occurs when an investment sells for a higher price than its purchase value. Capital gains are not taxed until the investment is sold and the gain received.

12. Calculate the average annual yield from a capital gain using the formula:

$$[1 + \text{total proportional gain}]^{\frac{1}{n}} - 1,$$

where n is the number of years over which the capital gain occurred. Alternatively, find [1 + total proportional gain] in Appendix Table A-1 for the number of years and read off the associated interest rate.

13. Calculate the average annual yield from a capital gain plus income investment as the combination of the two yields.

14. Calculate the annual effective yield (AEY) from an income investment using the formula

$$Annual\ Effect\ Yield\ (AEY) = (1 + \tfrac{R}{n})^n - 1$$

where R is the quoted or stated interest rate before compounding and n is the number of compounding period per year.

15. An effective yield calculated on a bond equivalent basis is compounded daily using a 365 day year. An effective yield calculated on a CD basis is compounded daily using 360 to form the daily interest rate but 365 for the number of compounding periods per year.

16. The effective income earned on investments which sell at discount is the difference between the face value and the price.

17. Day-of-deposit to day-of-withdrawal, the low balance, first-in/first-out, and last-in/first-out are alternative ways of calculating interest on a savings account.

    DAY-OF-DEPOSIT TO DAY-OF-WITHDRAWAL pays interest on each dollar from when it's deposited to when it's withdrawn.

    LOW BALANCE pays interest for the month only on the lowest balance during the month.

    FIRST-IN/FIRST-OUT withdrawals are subtracted not from the balance on the day of withdrawal but from the earliest deposit.

    LAST-IN/FIRST-OUT withdrawals are subtracted not from the balance on the day of withdrawal but from the most recent deposit.

18. Floating interest rates on investments are best when interest rates in the economy are headed up. Fixed interest rates on investments are best when interest rates in the economy are headed down.

19. Use this formula to calculate the after-tax yield:

    $$\text{Yield} - (\text{tax bracket} \times \text{yield}).$$

20. The average annual yield is calculated as the simple average of a number of individual yields. The geometric annual yield takes into account compounding and is calculated as

    $$[(1 + \text{year 1's yield}) \times (1 + \text{year 2's yield}) \times (1 + \text{year 3's yield}) \times \ldots$$

    $$(1 + \text{year n's yield})]^{\frac{1}{n}} - 1$$

21. Diversification means spreading investment funds into different investments whose rates of return are at least partially unrelated. The goal of diversification is to reduce the variability in rate of return without reducing the average rate of return.

    Complete diversification in the stock market can be achieved by randomly selecting as few as 15 stocks.

    Diversification among different investment types is called asset allocation. The best asset allocation varies by the consumer's age and income.

22. Investments in yourself and your family, such as going to college, marrying, and having children, involve, in part, an evaluation and comparison of economic benefits and costs.

DISCUSSION QUESTIONS

1. Borrowers want low interest rates and investors want high interest rates. Can both exist at once? Why or why not?

2. Uncle Joe, who doesn't trust anyone, growls, "I'll keep my savings in a mattress where I know it's safe rather than give it to some stranger who might lose it." What other kind of losses will Uncle Joe face with his "mattress saving"?

3. Besides having few dollars to save and invest, what other reason might explain why low income households save very little?

4. If everyone knows how the economy influences investments, why is there so much differing advice about what the "best" investments are?

5. When someone says they want to take little risk in their investments, why do you now have trouble knowing what they mean?

6. When considering risk (variability of rate of return) and rate of return, what would be a "bad" investment, and what would be a "good" investment?

7. Are you a risk-averse person?

8. Jeff and Joanne are 35, and Joanne's parents are 60. What are the pro's and con's of income investments and capital gains investments for Jeff and Joanne and for Joanne's parents?

9. If short term interest rates are currently higher than long term interest rates, would that motivate you to put your money in a floating interest rate investment or fixed interest rate investment?

10. Bob wants to "get rich quick" by investing in the stock market. Sam wants to take a more conservative approach to the stock market. Who will choose to diversify and why? After ten years, who do you think will come out ahead?

PROBLEMS

1. You bought WALDENCO stock four years ago for $25/share and today it sells for $45/share. What is the average annual yield?

2. WALDENOO stock has also paid dividends of 3 percent annually. What is WALDENCO's total average annual yield (dividends plus capital gains)?

3. The quoted interest rate on a 3-month CD is 7 percent. Find the annual effective yield using no compounding, semi-annual compounding, quarterly compounding, monthly compounding, and daily compounding.

4. The quoted interest rate on a 4 year CD is 7 percent. Find the annual effective yield using no compounding, semi-annual compounding, quarterly compounding, monthly compounding, and daily compounding.

5. Calculate the effective yield from a 12 percent quoted CD using a bond equivalent basis and a CD equivalent basis.

6. You buy a Treasury bill for $9,800 and three months later you cash it in for $10,000. What is the annual effective yield?

7. Here's the schedule of Sally's savings account deposits and withdrawals for March. Calculate the interest Sally would earn with (1) the-day-of-deposit to day-of-withdrawal method, (2) the low balance method, (3) the first-in/first-out method, and (4) the last-in/first-out method. March has 31 days. The annual interest rate is 7 percent.

> March 1 Balance of $3,000
> March 5 Withdraw $500
> March 10 Deposit $750
> March 20 Withdraw $250

8. Joe's tax bracket is 30 percent. Calculate Joe's after-tax annual yield from an investment paying an annual yield of 10 percent.

9. WALDENCO stock's annual yield for the last seven years were:

> Year 1   4%
> Year 2   10%
> Year 3   3%
> Year 4   −5%
> Year 5   6%
> Year 6   7%
> Year 7   −2%

Calculate the arithmetic average annual yield and the geometric average annual yield for WALDENCO stock.

CHAPTER 9

Types of Investments

Introduction

In this chapter you will apply the investment fundamentals you have learned to evaluate specific kinds of investments. Unfortunately, there's no perfect investment for all times. All investments have advantages and disadvantages and, as you've already learned, alternative investments perform differently in different stages of the economic roller coaster.

Two factors that influence your choice of investments are your economic circumstances (specifically your income and wealth) and your age, or stage in the life cycle as economists like to call it. In this topic you'll explore the kinds of investments which are best suited for different wealth and life cycle stages.

You've already learned that there are many kinds of risk, so that, technically speaking, there's no such thing as a risk-free investment. Nevertheless, the major kind of risk that worries most consumers is default risk (the risk of losing all, or a major part, of your original investment). In this chapter we'll look at the alternative investments in order of default risk, starting with those having the lowest default risk.

And now, armed with your knowledge of investment fundamentals, let's plunge ahead into the jungle of investments.

1. Why Should You Consider Investments from the Federal Government?

Investments from the federal government—you've got to be kidding! With the way the federal government runs its financial affairs, why would anyone in their right mind invest with the federal government?

The truth of the matter is that investments with the federal government—that is, those issued and backed by the U.S. government—are considered to have virtually no default risk. This is because the federal government can do something that no private corporation or bank can do. It can tax money away from consumers, or it can simply create money (remember that the Federal Reserve controls the money supply). This means the federal government can always get money to pay its debts. The fact that the federal government has never once missed an interest payment on its debt is the reason that federal government investments are assigned the lowest default risk.

WHY SAFE?

Why does the federal government sell investments? Simple. It does so to raise money—that is, to make up the difference between federal spending and federal tax revenues. You know what this gap between federal spending and federal tax revenues is, it's the budget deficit. So when the federal government runs a budget deficit, it funds the deficit by borrowing money from you and me.[1] No one holds a gun to our head and says we must loan money to the federal government. Many consumers willingly invest with the federal government because they consider federal government investments to be good, safe investments, which indeed they are.

Types of Federal Government Investments

The two major types of federal government investments are Treasury securities and U.S. savings bonds.

Treasury Securities

TREASURY BILLS

Treasury securities come in three varieties: bills, notes, and bonds. *Treasury bills* are issued in denominations of $10,000 to $1 million and for terms of 13, 26, or 52 weeks. Treasury bills don't pay an interest rate. Instead, Treasury bills are bought at a "discount" from their face value. This just means you don't pay the full face value for the Treasury bill—instead, you pay something less than full lace value—but when the bill matures you do receive back the bill's full face value.

EXAMPLE 9-1: Jack buys a $10,000 Treasury bill for $9,600. The bill matures in 26 weeks. What's the effective annual yield?

ANSWER: Jack has effectively earned interest of $400 ($10,000 − $9,600) up-front on an investment of $9,600. Compounding for two periods produces the effective annual yield of:

$$(1+\frac{\$400}{\$9,600})^2 - 1 = 8.5\%$$

TREASURY NOTES AND BONDS

Treasury notes and bonds are more standard investments in that interest is paid periodically after their purchase. Treasury notes and bonds differ only in their term: notes are for terms of 2 to 10 years, and bonds are for terms of 10 to 30 years. The minimum denomination on both notes and bonds is $1,000.

In "normal" times, the interest rate paid on Treasury bonds is highest, followed by the rate on bills. However, when interest rates in the economy are expected to fall, the differences can be very small, or, in fact, the rate on bills can be the highest.

---

[1]The federal government can also borrow money from foreigners by selling U.S. government investments to foreigners. The share of foreigner held debt has been increasing over time, from about 22% in 1999 to about 47% in 2013.

All Treasury securities (bills, notes, bonds) have one tax benefit, which is that their interest earnings are not taxed by state and local governments. Treasury securities can be bought and sold through a broker, who will charge a fee, or can be purchased directly from a Federal Reserve bank. Since Treasury securities have virtually no default risk, the interest rate paid on Treasury securities is generally lower than the rate on CDs or corporate bonds.

How do Treasury securities stack-up on the various kinds of risk? As already mentioned, they have the lowest default risk, since the federal government has a perfect record of paying its debts. Treasury securities are liquid, meaning they can be sold before maturity. However, for the long term Treasury securities, called Treasury bonds, there's a risk that the owner may not be able to sell the bond for its full face value. This would happen if higher inflation rates pushed interest rates up since the bond was issued. (We'll talk more about this in the topic on bonds). This means Treasury notes and bonds have inflation risk, because there's no assurance that the fixed interest rate paid on them will keep up with inflation rates.

RISK OF TREASURY SECURITIES

There's no rate risk for Treasury securities because the interest rate is fixed and you'll know exactly how much interest the securities will pay.

U.S. Savings Bonds

U.S. SAVINGS BONDS As of 2013, there are two types of U.S. Savings bonds offered, Series EE bonds and Series I bonds. In addition, there is a Series HH bonds that were discounted in August 2004. However, because HH bonds earn interest for up to 20 years, some investors may still have HH bonds that earn interest. The interest earned on U.S. saving bonds is subject to federal income tax, but not state or local income tax.

Series EE bond is a security that earns the same rate of interest (a fixed rate) for up to 30 years. Interest accrues monthly and is paid when the holder cashes the bond. When you buy the bond, you know what rate of interest it will earn. Treasury announces a fixed rate each May 1 and November 1 for new EE bonds. For example, if you want to buy an EE bond between November 1, 2012 and April 30, 2013, the annual interest rate is 0.20%. However, EE bonds bought from May 1997 through April 2005 earn a variable interest rate that changes every six months. EE bonds bought before May 1997 earn interest at different rates depending on when they were bought. The minimum purchase amount for EE bonds is $25, and the maximum is $10,000 each calendar year for each Social Security number. EE bonds can only be bought electronically; paper EE bonds are no longer available.

Series I savings bond is a security that earns interest based on combining a fixed rate and an inflation rate that usually changes every six months. The interest accrues for up to 30 years. The fixed rate is given at the time of purchase, and does not change during the life of the bond. The inflation rate, on the other hand, is set every six months in May and November, based on changes in the nonseasonally adjusted Consumer Price Index for all Urban Consumers (CPI-U) for all items. For example, if you want to buy an I-bond between November 1, 2012 and April 30, 2013, the fixed rate is 0.00%. The inflation component is 0.88%, reflecting the CPI-U from March to September 2012, for an effective annual inflation rate of 1.76%. Thus the composite rate for I-bonds purchased between November 2012 and April 30, 2013 is 1.76% (0.00%+1.76%). Like EE bonds, the minimum purchase for I bonds is $25, and the maximum purchase is $10,000 each calendar year for each Social Security number. However, tax payers may purchase an additional $5,000 paper I-bonds using their tax refunds.

RISK OF SAVINGS BONDS

How do U.S. Savings Bonds measure up on risk characteristics? Like Treasury securities, there is no default risk. You can cash EE bonds and I-bonds after 1 year of purchase. However if you cash them before 5 years you lose the last 3-months' interest. EE bonds and I-bonds can be redeemed online at TreasuryDirect and the cash amount can be credited to the investor's checking or savings account within one business day of the redemption date so liquidity risk is low but not zero. EE bonds pay a fixed interest rate so there is some inflation risk whereas I-bonds takes inflation into consideration so there is no inflation rate. However, as a tradeoff of this inflation risk protection, the fixed interest rate portion of I-bonds is typically lower than the interest rate for EE bonds.

When Should You Buy Treasury Securities and Savings Bonds

In order to answer a question like this for any investment, you must decide what kind of investment strategy you want to follow. As discussed in Chapter 8, there are two alternative strategies, the "ideal" strategy which moves your money around according to the phases of the economy, and the realistic, or diversified strategy.

WHAT INVESTMENT STRATEGY

If you follow the ideal strategy, then you should buy and hold Treasury bills and U.S. savings bonds in Phase C at the early period of a recession. Here, short term interest rates are rising to their highest level. However, remember that U.S. savings bonds must be held at least five years to receive the full amount of interest. Treasury notes and Treasury bonds would best be held in Phase D of the economy.

If you follow the realistic strategy and always hold a diversified set of investments, then Treasury notes and Treasury bonds would fit into the "long-term bond" category, whereas Treasury bills and U.S. savings bonds would fit into the cash category.

How U.S. Government Investments Stack Up: A Summary

Table 9-1 summarizes the investment characteristics of Treasury securities and U.S. savings bonds. All the investments have no default risk, which is the hallmark of U.S. government securities. All of them also enjoy a tax break from state and local governments and, in addition, EE bonds enjoy the advantage of delayed taxation on interest. There is also no reinvestment risk for EE bonds because interest is not paid periodically but is automatically reinvested at the EE bond's interest rate.

The Bottom Line

If you want investments with absolutely no default risk, then Treasury securities and U.S. savings bonds are for you. However, you'll pay for safety by sacrificing some percentage points on the rate of return.

If you had perfect knowledge about the economy, then you'd want to hold Treasury bills and EE bonds during Phase C (early recession) of the economic roller coaster and Treasury notes and bonds during Phase D (recession) of the economic cycle. If you follow the strategy of diversifying your investments, then you want to hold Treasury bills and HH and EE bonds as cash investments and Treasury notes and bonds as bond investments.

2. Are CDs the Lazy Person's Investment?

Let's quickly answer the question heading this chapter with a definite "no." Certificates of Deposit, or CDs, are a very popular investment because they're easy to understand and there's little that can go wrong with them. But just because they're not "flashy" or risky doesn't mean they're not a good investment. CDs should be an important part of most investor's portfolios.

Characteristics

A CD works very simply. You give money to a bank, S&L, credit union, or maybe a stockbroker for a certain period of time. Periodically, within that time period, you'll earn interest. At the end of the time period you get your original investment back, plus the earned interest.

Most CDs are insured by an agency of the federal government: the FDIC. This insurance says that if the issuer of the CD goes "belly-up,"

FEDERAL INSURANCE you won't lose the money in your CD. Currently the federal insurance covers up to $100,000 in an individual's accounts at a single institution. The $100,000 limit includes the original money you invested (the principal) plus interest earnings. Any amount over $100,000 is not insured.

Table 9-1 A summary of federal government investment characteristics

	T-bills	T-notes	T-bonds	EE bonds	I-bonds
Minimum denomination	$100	$100	$100	$25	$25
Term	4–52 weeks	2–10 years	30 years	Up to 30 years	Up to 30 years
Purchasing price and interest rate	Determined at auction. Typically issued at a discount from face value. Redeemed at face value.	Determined at auction. Can be greater than, less than, or equal to face value. Redeemed at face value.	Determined at auction. Can be greater than, less than, or equal to face value. Redeemed at face value.	Fixed rate announced by Treasury each May 1 and November 1 for new bonds. Purchased at face value.	Combined rate of a fixed rate known at the time of purchase, and an inflation rate calculated twice a year based on CPI-U. Purchased at face value.
Interest accrue method	Pay no interest before maturity. The interest is equal to the face value minus the purchase price.	Pay interest every six months until maturity	Pay interest every six months until maturity	Interest earned monthly and compounded semiannually but not distributed. Principal and interest paid at time of redemption.	Interest earned monthly and compounded semiannually but not distributed. Principal and interest paid at time of redemption.
Default risk	None	None	None	None	None
Rate risk	None	Moderate	High	None	None
Inflation risk	Low	Moderate	High	High	None
Reinvestment risk	None	Moderate	Moderate	None	None
Tax advantages	Exempt from state and local taxes	Exempt from state and local taxes	Exempt from state and local taxes	Exempt from state and local taxes. Deferred until redemption.	Exempt from state and local taxes. Deferred until redemption.

This federal deposit insurance is considered very good. It's not quite as good as the backing provided by the federal government to Treasury securities, because if the federal insurance agency runs short of funds (see CONSUMER TOPIC), it must ask Congress for help—Congress doesn't automatically provide the help. Nevertheless, the default risk of federally insured CDs is generally considered only a cut below the safety of Treasury securities.

CDs come in denominations as low as $1 and in terms of one week to five years. As with most investments, in normal times the interest rate earned on a CD increases with its term.

A disadvantage of CDs, as compared to Treasury securities, is that frequently you can't cash them in before their maturity without paying a penalty. Say you have a three year CD and you decide you need the money after two years. For many CDs, you could only cash them in if you paid a penalty, such as the equivalent of six months interest. There are CDs that charge no penalty for early withdrawal, but usually you pay for this benefit with a lower interest rate.

EARLY EXIT PENALTY

Not all CDs are insured. CDs with denominations of more than $100,000— so-called "jumbo" CDs—are not insured. However, as a result of this greater risk, they pay higher interest rates.

Where to Get CDs

Most investors buy CDs from banks, S&Ls, or credit unions. Because of their non-profit tax status, credit unions can sometimes pay higher interest rates.

CDs are also sold by stockbrokers. Why would you want to consider buying a CD from a stockbroker? There can be several advantages to buying from a broker. One is the interest rate earned. CDs bought from brokers often pay a higher interest rate than CDs bought at banks. There are two reasons for this. First, brokers can offer a wider choice of CDs than a local bank, and second, brokers can be more efficient than banks in selling CDs. Another advantage of broker CDs is convenience—they can be bought and sold over the phone. Last, CDs from brokers can be more "liquid," meaning that if you want to sell the CD before maturity, the broker can often find another buyer, and no "early withdrawal" penalty will be paid.

STOCKBROKER CDs

These advantages to broker-bought CDs must be countered by a couple of disadvantages. First, brokers will often charge a commission or fee for their services. Compare the fee to the extra interest earned and make sure you're still ahead. Second, and more importantly, make sure the broker-bought CD is insured. This can be tricky to determine and may require asking some tough questions. For example, if the broker had bought the CD on the "secondary market," simply meaning that it's a CD which has already been owned, and the broker paid a premium (a price above face value) for the CD because it paid a very high interest rate, then the premium part of the price will not be insured.

Insurance Again

As mentioned earlier, federal insurance covers up to $100,000 for individual accounts at a single institution. This means that to be totally insured, the sum of your individual CD accounts at a single institution must sum to less than $100,000. Obviously, if you have more than $100,000 to invest in CDs, one thing to do is to open accounts at many institutions.

INSURANCE AND JOINT ACCOUNTS

What about joint accounts at the same institution. The same rule applies. An individual is covered for up to $100,000 in joint accounts at a single institution. Unless otherwise stated, the rules assume equal ownership in the accounts. This means that an individual's shares in joint accounts will be calculated and then summed to determine if they are fully insured. The following examples will illustrate this rule.

EXAMPLE 9-2:   Jennifer has a CD in her own name for $40,000, a joint CD with her husband for $60,000, and a joint CD with her daughter for $50,000, all at the same bank. Are Jennifer's accounts fully covered by federal insurance?

ANSWER: Jennifer's own CD is covered up to $100,000. Since Jennifer's own CD is $40,000, this CD is fully covered. The coverage of Jennifer's joint accounts is:

$$\text{Joint CD with husband} = \tfrac{1}{2} \times \$60,000 = \$30,000$$

$$\text{Joint CD with daughter} = \tfrac{1}{2} \times \$50,000 = \underline{\$25,000}$$

$$\text{TOTAL JOINT ACCOUNT} \qquad = \$55,000$$

Since $55,000 is less than $100,000, Jennifer's investments in the joint accounts are totally insured.

EXAMPLE 9-3:   Larry has a CD in his name for $60,000, a joint CD with his wife for $150,000, and a joint CD with his son for $80,000, all at the same S&L. Are Larry's accounts fully covered by federal insurance?

ANSWER: Larry's own CD ($60,000) is fully covered. The coverage of Larry's joint accounts is:

Joint CD with wife = $\frac{1}{2}$ × $150,000 = $ 75,000

Joint CD with son = $\frac{1}{2}$ × $ 80,000 = $ 40,000

TOTAL JOINT ACCOUNT   = $115,000

$15,000 of Larry's joint account is not insured.

Variable Rates and Other "Bells and Whistles"

Most CDs carry fixed interest rates, but you may come across variable rate CDs. Typically, such variable rate CDs are tied to some external index, like the prime rate, the stock market, or the price of gold. Variable rate CDs tied to the stock market would obviously do well during Phase A of the economic cycle, whereas variable rate CDs tied to the prime rate or gold would do well during Phase B.

C O N S U M E R T O P I C

IS DEPOSIT INSURANCE CAUSING MORE HARM THAN GOOD?

A strong argument can be made that the "savings and loan crisis," which cost taxpayers over hundreds of billions of dollars in the 1980s and 1990s, is at least in part a result of the very system designed to protect the S&Ls—the system of federal deposit insurance.

As discussed in the text, federal deposit insurance insures the first $100,000 in an account at a bank or S&L which is part of the federal insurance program. Deposit insurance (at much lower amounts) started in the Depression years of the 1930s as a way of restoring public confidence in the banking system. Relatively stable interest rates and strict government regulation and supervision of the investments of S&Ls combined to make deposit insurance run smoothly until the late 1970s.

The system began to fall apart in the late 1970s. First, skyrocketing inflation pushed interest rates to double digit levels in the late 1970s. This hurt S&Ls because restrictions on their investments prevented them from paying the high, competitive rates. Congress and federal regulators responded by deregulating the S&Ls—allowing them to pay competitive interest rates but also allowing them to invest in a wider range of investments, including more risky investments.

Just as this deregulation was occurring the second economic tidal wave hit S&Ls—the economic roller coaster of the 1980s. Many of the newly deregulated S&Ls, who had previously been sheltered by federal restrictions, simply weren't ready to cope with the topsy-turvy 80s. The 1980s began with a severe recession, which bankrupted many of the S&L's new "riskier" investments. The mid-80s was a period of strong economic growth, and this encouraged a big wave of new investments from S&Ls. However, the economy again slowed in the late 80s, and many investments, particularly in real estate, went sour. By the end of the 1980s, scores of

References: Kane, Edward J. *The S&L Insurance Mess: How Did It Happen ?* Washington, D.C.: The Urban Institute Press, 1989.

Tobin, James. "Deposit Insurance Must Go." *The Wall St. Journal,* Nov, 22, 1989.

S&Ls had to throw in the towel, and the federal insurance system, and ultimately the taxpayers, were left holding the bag.

But how was the federal deposit insurance system to blame for this? The federal deposit insurance system was to blame in one big way—the system charged all S&Ls the same fee for the federal insurance, regardless of the risk taken by the S&L in its investments. This violates a cardinal law of insurance, that insurance rates should be adjusted in line with the risk of the activity being insured. Riskier activities should be charged higher insurance rates. The same fee for all principle worked well as long as S&Ls were limited in their investments. But after deregulation, the same fee was charged to the conservative S&L as to the S&L that was "playing poker" with depositor's money.

There are a number of ways to solve this problem. Certainly the insurance fee can be graded to the risk of the S&L's investments. Alternatively, federal deposit insurance can be limited to accounts which the S&L invests only in safe securities, such as Treasury securities and other federally guaranteed obligations. Finally, the insurance amount ($100,000) may be too high. If the point of the federal insurance is to insure depositors of moderate means, maybe the insurance amount should be halved, or maybe a cap should be put on the total coverage per family. The point of these reforms is to return market discipline to the S&L industry. If an S&L wants to take more risk in its investments, that's fine, but the federal government shouldn't insure that risk.

BUMP-UP CD

STEP-UP CD

There's also something called a "bump-up CD" and a "step-up CD." A "bump-up" CD is a CD in which you get one chance to have your rate "bumped-up" if future interest rates do in fact rise. A "bump-up" CD would be best during Phase C of the economic cycle where you're trying to hit the peak in interest rates. A "step-up" CD is a CD that has an interest rate which regularly rises over the term of the CD. However, you pay for this rise by having the rate start very low.

Short Term or Long Term

A big question for many CD investors is whether to buy a long term CD or a short term CD. Obviously, if you had perfect foresight about the economy and future interest rates, the answer would be easy. You'd buy long-term CDs when interest rates had peaked and are heading down. In this case you'd be able to "lock-in" a higher than average rate for the future. In terms of the economic roller coaster, you'd buy a long term CD at the beginning of Phase D.

In contrast, you'd buy short term CDs when interest rates were rising. In this situation you would be constantly "turning over" your money into higher yielding CDs. You'd want to buy short term CDs in Phases A, B, and C of the economic cycle.

DIVERSIFIED CDs

But if you don't know where interest rates are headed, what do you do, guess? No, you diversify. You buy a mixture of short term CDs and long term CDs. For example, you might put half your money into 3 month CDs and half into 3 year CDs. On average, this strategy will maintain the average interest rate earned, but will reduce the risk of earning a very low return.

Cashing in Old CDs for New Ones

What if you face this situation: Last year you bought a five year CD paying 8 percent. This year new five year CDs are paying $8\frac{1}{2}$ percent. Does it pay to cash-in your existing CD, perhaps pay a penalty, and then invest in the new higher-yielding CD? How would you figure this out?

Follow this three step procedure to determine if cashing-in an old CD for a new one pays.

1. Calculate the future value of your existing CD, including interest, to the end of the CDs term. Call this future value A.
2. Calculate the net value you would receive if you cashed in your existing CD. This net value equals the current value of your existing CD, with interest, minus any after-tax interest penalty. The interest penalty is tax-deductible, so the after-tax penalty equals (1 – tax bracket) multiplied by the penalty. Call this net value B.
3. Calculate the value $\frac{A}{B}$. $\frac{A}{B}$ is the future value factor that will increase today's net value B to the final value $\frac{A}{B}$. Then find A in the future value table, Appendix Table A-1, corresponding to the number of years left on your existing CD. The interest rate associated with this future value factor is the interest rate you'd have to receive on the new CD for cashing-in to be beneficial.

Let's illustrate this procedure with an example.

EXAMPLE 9-4: Doris has an 8 percent CD with a three-year remaining term. Doris originally invested $2000 in the CD. The value of the CD today, with its accumulated interest, is $2,332. If Doris cashes in the CD today she must pay a penalty equal to six months interest. Doris' tax bracket is

28 percent. What must the annual interest rate be on a new three-year CD for cashing-in to be financially smart?

ANSWER: (1) Future value of $2,332 at 8% for three years:

$$\$2,332 \times 1.260 \text{ (future value factor)} = \$2,938.32$$

(8%, 3 years)

$$A = \$2,938.32$$

(2) If Doris started with $2,000, then six months simple interest is: $\$2,000 \times .08 \times \frac{1}{2} = \$80$. However, Doris can use the $80 as a tax deduction. If Doris' tax bracket is 28 percent, then the after-tax penalty is $(1 - .28) \times \$80 = \$57.60$.

Therefore, Doris would receive $2,332 – $57.60, or $2,274.40, if she cashed-in the CD.

$$B = \$2,274.40$$

(3) $\dfrac{A}{B} = \dfrac{\$2,938.32}{\$2,274.40} = 1.292$

For a term of three years, 1.292 is very close to 9 percent in Appendix Table A-1. Therefore, Doris would need to find a three year CD paying more than 9 percent for cashing-in her existing CD to be worthwhile.

Table 9-3 gives some answers to the question of cashing-in an existing CD for a new higher-paying CD. The table shows the minimum interest rate needed on a new CD for cashing-in to be profitable. The calculations use a six month interest penalty and 28 percent tax bracket. Notice that the required interest rate rises the shorter the period of time left on the existing CD.

How Do CDs Measure Up?

Table 9-3 summarizes how CDs stack up with respect to risk and return characteristics. The very low default risk is, of course, a major feature of CDs. Liquidity risk is present for CDs with early withdrawal penalties. There is no rate risk since you know the interest rate paid on the CD. If inflation rates rise in the future, the interest rate paid on long term CDs will look progressively worse and worse. Interest is paid on interest for most CDs so there's no reinvestment risk.

CDs are very similar to Treasury securities, but the fact that they're not quite as safe means they usually pay a higher interest rate. To compare their return to Treasury securities, subtract state and local taxes paid on CD interest. In most cases, CDs will still pay more after taxes.

Table 9-2 Breakeven rate for cancelling your existing CD and buying a new CD.*

	Breakeven rate if have held your 3-yr. CD	
Your CD Rate	**1 Year**	**2 Year**
5%	6.0%	6.8%
6	7.0	8.0
7	8.2	9.5
8	9.5	10.8
9	10.6	12.0
10	11.9	13.5
11	13.0	14.7
12	14.0	16.0

	Breakeven rate if have held your 5-yr. CD			
Your CD Rate	**1 Year**	**2 Year**	**3 Year**	**4 Year**
5%	5.5%	5.6%	5.8%	6.5%
6	6.5	6.6	7.0	7.8
7	7.8	7.8	8.3	9.0
8	8.7	9.0	9.8	10.5
9	9.8	10.0	10.4	11.6
10	10.9	11.1	11.5	12.8
11	12.1	12.2	12.8	14.0
12	13.1	13.3	13.8	15.0

*Assumes a tax deductible early withdrawal penalty of six months interest, annual compounding, and tax bracket of 28 percent.

EXAMPLE 9-5: A 3-year CD pays 8 percent interest, and a 3-year Treasury note pays 7 percent interest. If the investor's state income tax bracket is 10 percent, which has the highest after-tax (after state tax) rate?

ANSWER: CD after state tax rate = 8% − .1 × 8% = 7.2%. Treasury note after state tax rate = 7%. The CD rate is higher.

Treasury securities are more liquid because they can always be sold, whereas many CDs can only be cashed in if a penalty is paid.

In terms of implementing the ideal strategy, short term CDs would be bought and held during Phase C, whereas long term CDs would be

Table 9-3 The risk and return of CDs: A summary.

	Summary
Minimum denomination	$1
Term	One week to 5 years.
Interest rate	Usually fixed, ½% to 1% higher than Treasury securities.
Default risk	very low.
Liquidity risk	Yes, if early withdrawal penalty.
Rate risk	None.
Inflation risk	Yes for long-term CDs unless a variable rate is paid.
Reinvestment risk	None—interest is compounded.
Tax advantages	None.

bought and held during Phase D. In the realistic investment strategy, short term CDs are part of "cash" investments, and long term CDs are part of "bond" investments.

The Bottom Line

CDs are insured, safe (in terms of default risk) investments which pay slightly higher interest rates than Treasury securities. CDs should be part of the "cash" and "bond" components of a diversified portfolio.

When buying CDs from brokers, be very careful to make sure that the entire cost is insured. Likewise, make sure your total CD account at a bank, S&L, or credit union is insured.

Finally, remember that all bank investments are *not* insured CDs. Banks do sell uninsured, and thus more risky, investments.

3. How Can Bonds Earn More Than Stocks or Gold?

You've already learned about one type of bond, Treasury bonds. Bonds are simply a way for governments and corporations to raise money and use it for a long period of time. Typically the term of a bond is 30 years.

A bond works like this. You buy a $1,000 bond from ABC Corporation, and the bond has a term of 30 years. This means you give ABC Corporation $1,000 today and they return the $1,000 to you at the end of 30 years. The $1,000 is called the "face value." In addition, each year ABC

FACE VALUE

Corporation pays you interest on the $1,000. If, say, the interest rate is 10 percent, this means you get a check from ABC Corporation each year for $100. If you keep the bond for its full term, this means you receive 30 checks of $100 each for the 30 years. Notice that this is *simple interest.* Bonds *do not* keep your interest and pay interest on interest. So one thing
REINVESTMENT RISK you should remember is that there is *reinvestment risk* with bonds, meaning that you have to find someplace else to invest the interest earnings.

USED BONDS Once you buy a bond, you don't have to keep it for its full term. There is an active market for "used bonds," which means you can buy and sell bonds which have been previously owned. This means there are existing bonds for sale with all kinds of remaining years. In fact, as you will see, more money can be made (and lost) by selling bonds before the end of their term than can be made from the bond's interest earnings. In short, bonds can earn substantial *capital gains.*

Bond Characteristics

You can buy safe bonds, you can buy pretty-safe bonds, and you can buy risky bonds. In other words, the default risk of bonds varies across the board. Bonds issued by the federal government (Treasury bonds) and bonds issued by "blue-chip" (large and established corporations)
DEFAULT RISK OF will have very low default risk. At the other end of the spectrum, bonds
BONDS issued by unknown corporations or corporations in bad financial shape will have much higher default risk. These bonds, obviously, will have to pay higher interest rates.

The default risk of a bond can be judged by noting the bond's rating. Bond ratings were discussed in Chapter 8. The advantages and disadvantages of high risk-high interest rate bonds, so-called junk bonds, will be discussed later in this topic.

Bonds pay a fixed interest rate. Obviously, investors like bonds with high interest rates, and companies and governments issuing the bonds
CALL PROVISION like lower interest rates. Most corporate bonds contain "call provisions." When a bond is "called" it means the issuer cashes in the bond for you—that is, pays you the face value of the bond—plus some extra. So why isn't this good for the investor? Because governments and corporations will only call bonds when current interest rates have fallen below the interest rate paid by the bond.

For example, your $1,000 bond from ABC Corporation is paying 10 percent interest. Suppose interest rates have fallen to 8 percent. ABC Corporation calls your 10 percent bond by paying you $1,000 plus maybe a premium of $50. ABC Corporation does this in order to retire the 10 percent bond and refinance their debt with new 8 percent bonds. So having a bond called is a disadvantage to the investor. Furthermore, the premium paid above the face value ($50 in our example) does not usually make up for the future higher lost interest earnings (e.g., the

$50 paid now would be less than the present value of losing $20/year in interest for the remaining life of the bond).

The call provisions of a bond tell the investor the conditions under which the bond can be called and the premium which must be paid when the bond is called. Most corporate bonds cannot be called until after 5 to 10 years. A big advantage of Treasury bonds is that they are generally not callable until the last 2–5 years of their term. This advantage is another reason why Treasury bonds pay lower interest rates than corporate bonds.

How Can You Make "Big Money" or Lose "Big Money" on Bonds

At first glance, you might think that bonds are just like CDs, except that their term is much longer (30 years). You give $1,000 to ABC Corporation, and ABC Corporation agrees to pay you $100 per year (10 percent interest) for each of 30 years, then gives back your $1,000 at the end of the 30 years.

BONDS MARKET VALUE CAN CHANGE However, there's a very important way in which bonds differ from CDs. *The market value of a bond (what you can sell the bond for) can fluctuate, whereas the value of the CD never changes.* This means, for example, that if you buy a $1,000 bond from ABC Corporation and then decide to sell it after two years, you may be able to sell it for more than $1,000 or less than $1,000; that is, you may be able to sell it for more or less than its face value. In contrast, say you buy a 5 year, $1,000 CD from XYZ Bank and there's no early withdrawal penalty. If you cash-in the CD at the end of two years you'll receive $1,000 plus any accumulated interest. But the underlying value of the $1,000 will never change.

CURRENT INTEREST RATES AND BOND VALUE What causes the market value of bonds to fluctuate? The answer is simple: interest rates. The simple rule is that if current interest rates paid on new bonds are *higher* than the interest rate paid on your existing bond, then you'll only be able to sell your existing bond for *less* than its face value. Conversely, if current interest rates paid on new bonds are *lower* than the interest rate paid on your existing bond, then you'll be able to sell your existing bond for *more*.

How much will the market value, or price, of an existing bond change in response to changes in current interest rates? The rule is this. *The market value of a bond will equal the present value of its future interest payments and the present value of its face value when the bond matures.* For a bond which pays an interest rate lower than the current market rate, the market value will be lower than the current face value.

Table 9-4 shows three examples of the calculation of bond prices. Each example uses an existing bond with a face value of $1,000, paying annual interest of $100 (for a 10% yield) and maturing in ten years. In panel (a), assume market interest rates have risen to 15 percent. If the bond was sold today, it would not sell for $1,000, but would sell for

HAVING YOUR CASH AND "CONVERTING" IT TOO: CONVERTIBLE BONDS

**C
O
N
S
U
M
E
R**

**T
O
P
I
C**

Convertible bonds look like bonds but can talk like stocks. Specifically, a convertible bond is a bond which can be converted to a specific number of stock shares by the investor. The number of stock shares received when the bond is converted is called the *conversion ratio.* Usually the conversion can take place anytime during the life of the bond.

When analyzing convertible bonds, there are three values to consider. The bond's *conversion value* is the conversion ratio multiplied by the stock's share price. The conversion value rises as the stock's share price rises. The bond's *investment value* is the value of the convertible bond if it were a regular bond and not convertible. The convertible bond's investment value is equal to the market value of a regular bond issued at the same time and with the same risk rating as the convertible bond. As with regular bonds, the investment value falls as market interest rates rise, and rises as market interest rates fall. Finally, the *market value* of a convertible bond is what the bond would sell for, unconverted, on the open market. The market value will equal the higher of the conversion value and investment value, plus a slight premium to account for the value of the convertibility option. The premium is lower the closer the bond is to maturity. The graph shows the relationship between these three values of a convertible bond.

There are two questions to address about convertible bonds. First, why do companies issue them? Second, are they good investments?

Companies issue convertible bonds in the hope that they can raise more money than they could by issuing regular bonds or straight stock. If investors believe the company's stock price will rise in the future, then investors will pay more than the investment value of the convertible bond when it's issued (e.g., investors will pay more than $1000 for a convertible bond with a face value of $1000). The company will also raise more money issuing convertible bonds than they could by issuing the stock, since the stock's price today is lower than it is expected to be in the future. In essence, the company can sell convertible bonds today based on future stock prices (which is an advantage as long as future stock prices are expected to be higher).

Should you consider buying convertible bonds? Compared to stocks, convertible bonds have the advantage of never falling below their investment value. So, compared to stocks, convertible bonds have the advantage of having a floor to their value.

Clearly, however, if you're buying a bond to hold until maturity, you should always buy a regular bond and never buy a convertible bond. Convertible bonds will always sell for more than a regular bond as long as investors think the stock's price will rise. Only buy a convertible bond if (1) you plan to convert it to stocks, or you plan to sell it before maturity, and (2) you expect the stock's share price to rise.

Reference: Stigum, Marcia and Frank J. Fabozzi, *The Dow Jones-Irwin Guide to Bond and Money Market Investments*, Homewood, Illinois, Dow Jones-Irwin, 1987, pp. 225–240.

less than $1,000. The present value calculations show the bond is worth only $748.90 today. Panel (b) shows that if current interest rates remain at 10 percent, then the bond would sell for $1,000. In contrast, panel (c) shows that if current interest rates had fallen to 5 percent, then the 10 percent bond would sell for a premium at $1,386.30. Notice that the final interest payment and face value are discounted by the same factor because they occur at the same time.

Changes in current interest rates will have a greater impact on bonds with a longer term than with bonds having a shorter term. This is because the shorter the term, the more impact a capital gain or capital loss realized when the bond matures will have on the current price. Table 9-6 illustrates how the price of the five year bond is influenced less by the increase in interest rates than is the ten year bond. The five year bond

sells at a discount of $\left(\dfrac{\$1,000 - \$832.30}{\$1,000}\right) = 16.8$ percent, whereas the

ten year bond sell at a discount of $\left(\dfrac{\$1,000 - \$748.90}{\$1,000}\right) = 25.1$ percent.

This means long term bonds are more subject to inflation risk.

Table 9-4   Determination of bond prices.

Existing bond face value = $1,000, paying $100 annually, and maturing in 10 years.

(a) $748.90 = 15% discount rate	(b) $1000.00 = 10% discount rate	(c) $1386.30 5% discount rate
100 × .870 = 87.00	100 × .909 = 90.90	100 × .952 = 95.20
100 × .756 = 75.60	100 × .826 = 82.60	100 × .907 = 90.70
100 × .658 = 65.80	100 × .751 = 75.10	100 × .864 = 86.40
100 × .572 = 57.20	100 × .683 = 68.30	100 × .823 = 82.30
100 × .497 = 49.70	100 × .621 = 62.10	100 × .784 = 78.40
100 × .432 = 43.20	100 × .564 = 56.40	100 × .746 = 74.60
100 × .376 = 37.60	100 × .513 = 51.30	100 × .711 = 71.10
100 × .327 = 32.70	100 × .467 = 46.70	100 × .677 = 67.70
100 × .284 = 28.40	100 × .424 = 42.40	100 × .645 = 64.50
100 × .247 = 24.70	100 × .386 = 38.60	100 × .614 = 61.40
1000 × .247 = 247.00	1000 × .386 = 386.00	1000 × .614 = 614.00
748.90	1000.40*	1386.30

*not exactly $1000 due to rounding error

Table 9-5 Long term bonds are influenced more by interest rate changes.

Existing bond face value = $1,000, paying $100 annually (10% interest) Assume current interest rates are now 15%.	
5 Yr. Remaining Term	**10 Yr. Remaining Term**
$ 100 × .870 = 87.00	$ 100 × .870 = 87.00
100 × .756 = 75.60	100 × .756 = 75.60
100 × .658 = 65.80	100 × .658 = 65.80
100 × .572 = 57.20	100 × .572 = 57.20
100 × .497 = 49.70	100 × .497 = 49.70
	100 × .432 = 43.20
1000 × .497 = 497.00	100 × .376 = 37.60
$832.30	100 × .327 = 32.70
	100 × .284 = 28.40
	100 × .247 = 24.70
	1000 × .247 = 247.00
	$748.90

To reinforce your knowledge of bond prices, here's another example of their calculation.

EXAMPLE 9-5: Pete owns a bond with a face value of $10,000 and which pays an annual interest of 7 percent (meaning payments of $700 annually). If the bond has six years remaining before it matures, what could Pete sell the bond for today if comparable new bonds are paying an interest rate of 9 percent?

ANSWER: Use discount rate of 9 percent.

$$
\begin{aligned}
\text{Price} = \$ \quad & 700 \times .917 = \$ \quad 641.90 \\
& 700 \times .842 = \quad 589.40 \\
& 700 \times .772 = \quad 540.40 \\
& 700 \times .708 = \quad 495.60 \\
& 700 \times .650 = \quad 455.00 \\
& 700 \times .596 = \quad 417.20 \\
& 10,000 \times .596 = \quad 5,960.00 \\
& \overline{\qquad \$9,099.50}
\end{aligned}
$$

PREMIUM BOND, DISCOUNT BOND

Pete could sell the bond for $9,099.50. Bonds which sell at a price greater than their face value are called *premium bonds.* Bonds which sell at a price less than their face value are called *discount bonds.*

Investors who try to implement the "ideal strategy" try to buy bonds when long term interest rates have peaked, and then sell them when interest rates have bottomed out. In terms of the business cycle, this means buying bonds at the beginning of Phase D and selling them at the end of Phase D. If this is done successfully, the investor will be able to sell the bond for much more than was paid for it. This is how "big money" can be made in bonds. Obviously, if the reverse is done—buying bonds when interest rates are low and selling when rates are high—then "big money" will be lost.

Calculating the Return from a Bond

There are two ways to calculate the return, or yield, from a bond. The first way is called the current yield. The current yield equals the annual interest payment divided by the price you paid for the bond:

CURRENT YIELD

$$Current\,Yield = \frac{Annual\,Interest\,Payment}{Price\,Paid\,for\,Bond}$$

If you bought the bond when it was issued, then the price paid should include any premium or discount paid.

EXAMPLE 9-6:   Calculate the current yield for a bond for which you paid $1300 and which pays $100 annually.

ANSWER: Current Yield $= \dfrac{\$100}{\$1300} = .077$ or 7.7%.

If the interest payment is taxed, then an after-tax current yield can be calculated by simply reducing the current yield by the product of the investor's tax bracket and the current yield.

EXAMPLE 9-7:   Calculate the after-tax current yield for the bond in EXAMPLE 8-6 if the investor's tax bracket is 30 percent.

ANSWER: After-tax current yield $= 7.7\% - .3 \times 7.7\%$
$$= 5.4\%$$

The current yield is a fine measure of the return from a bond for bonds which are bought at face value and are held to maturity. But for bonds which are bought at discount or at premium, or for bonds which are sold at discount or at premium, then the current yield is insufficient. In this case, a measure of yield for a bond is needed which takes into account both the annual interest payment and the capital gain or capital loss when the bond is sold or cashed-in. This measure is called the *holding period yield.*

$$Holding\ Period\ Yield = \frac{Annual\ Interest + AD}{\dfrac{Bond\ Purchase\ Price + Bond\ Sell\ Price - AD}{2}}$$

$$Where\ AD = \frac{Bond\ Selling\ Price - Bond\ Purchase\ Price}{Years\ Bond\ Held}$$

You can think of the holding period yield as the current yield with the gain or loss received when the bond is sold averaged into the calculation. If the bond is held to maturity, then the "Bond Selling Price" equals the "Bond Face Value," and the holding period yield is called "Yield to Maturity" (YTM).

Technically, the YTM should be the discount rate which will make the present value of the stream of interest payments and the present value of the final sales price of the bond at maturity (face value). The holding period yield formula given above serves as a close approximation. Conceptually, yield to maturity (YTM) can be found by solving the following equation:

YIELD TO MATURITY

Denote *PVFS (YTM, n)* as the Present Value Factor Sum with YTM as the annual interest rate and n as the number of years till maturity. *Bond Face Value* is the same as *Bond Selling Price* at maturity. You can use a spreadsheet or a financial calculator to figure out the exact YTM. Alternatively you can use the holding period yield formula given above to get a close approximation.

EXAMPLE 9-8: Calculate the holding period yield for a bond purchased for $833.33, which will pay $1000 when its term ends in five years, and which pays $100 interest each year.

ANSWER: Annual interest payment = $100

$$AD = \frac{\$1000 - \$833.33}{5} = \$33.33$$

Price of bond when bought = $833.33
Price of bond when sold = $1000

$$Holding\ period\ yield = \frac{\$100 + \$33.33}{(\$833.33 + \$1000 - 33.33)/2}$$

$$= .148\ or\ 14.8\%.$$

EXAMPLE 9-9:   Calculate the holding period yield for a bond purchased for $1300, which pays $100 interest each year, and which will pay $1000 when its term ends in eight years.

ANSWER: Annual interest payment = $100

$$Ad = \frac{\$1000\text{-}\$1300}{8} = -\$37.50$$

Price of bond when bought = $1300
Price of bond when sold = $1000

$$\text{Holding period yield} = \frac{\$100 + (-\$37.50)}{(\$1300 + \$1000 - (-\$37.50))/2}$$

$$= .053 \text{ or } 5.3\%.$$

After-tax holding period yields can be calculated in the same way as for other after-tax yields—just reduce the yield by the product of the investor's tax bracket and the yield.

EXAMPLE 9-10:   Calculate the after-tax holding period yields for the yields calculated in EXAMPLES 9-8 and 9-9 if the investor's tax bracket is 33 percent.

ANSWER: $14.8\% - (.33 \times 14.8\%) = 9.9\%$
$5.3\% - (.33 \times 5.3\%) = 3.6\%$[2]

Reinvestment Risk

A feature of bonds already mentioned is that interest is paid annually to the bondholder and not reinvested in the bond. This means the bondholder must find someplace else to invest the interest. Since the interest

---

[2] Alternatively, you could recalculate the holding period yields using after-tax interest and after-tax average annual gains or losses. The same answer will be found. In the case of a bond sold at a loss (as in EXAMPLE 9-9), the annual loss is a tax deduction. The calculations for the after-tax holding period yield for EXAMPLE 9-9 are:

$$\frac{\$100 - (.33 \times \$100) + [-\$37.50 + (.33 \times \$37.50)]}{(\$1300 + \$1000 - (-\$37.50))/2} = \frac{\$67 + [-37.50 + \$12.38)]}{\$1168.75}$$

$$= \frac{\$41.88}{\$1168.75} = 0.36 \text{ or } 3.6\%$$

The value of $(.33 \times \$37.50)$ is added to the numerator because it represents the value, in saved taxes, of the deduction of the loss of $37.50.

rate earned on future interest earnings can't be perfectly predicted, bonds have "reinvestment risk." Reinvestment risk simply means there is a risk related to not knowing the interest rate which will be earned on future interest earnings.

The reinvestment risk of bonds explains why investors are sometimes interested in buying premium bonds or discount bonds rather than new bonds bought at face value.[3] The rule investors use is this. If future interest rates are expected to be *higher* than current bond interest rates, then buying a *premium* bond is better so that more future interest will be earned to invest at the higher rate. On the other hand, if future interest rates are expected to be *lower* than current bond interest rates, then buying a *discount* bond is better so that not as much future interest will be earned to invest at the lower rate.

ZERO-COUPON BOND   An extreme form of the discount bond is the *zero-coupon bond*. A zero-coupon bond is simply a bond which pays no interest year to year. Instead, the interest is automatically reinvested at the bond's stated interest rate and accumulated until the bond matures. Therefore, zero-coupon bonds have no reinvestment risk because you know exactly what interest rate will be earned on the interest earnings. Zero coupon bonds are bought at a very low price compared to their redemption value. For example, a $2000 zero-coupon bond paying 9 percent interest would be redeemed in 30 years for $26,535. (How do we know this? Just multiply $2000 by the future value factor associated with 9 percent and 30 years, 13.268.)

PLUSES AND MINUSES   Zero coupon bonds should obviously be bought when interest rates
OF "ZEROS"   are at their peak. "Zero's" have the advantage of no reinvestment risk and of producing a specified amount of money at a specified future date. But zeros do have some disadvantages. First, the market price of zeros is very sensitive to interest rates. This means that if you need to sell a zero before it matures and interest rates are then higher than when you bought the zero, you may have to sell at a substantial loss. *To find out how much an existing zero-coupon bond is worth, simply divide its final value by the future value factor associated with the bond's remaining term and the current market interest rate.*

EXAMPLE 9-11: Joan bought a $2000, 30-year, 9% zero-coupon bond two years ago. At the end of 30 years Joan will cash-in the bond for $26,536. Joan wants to sell the bond today. Interest rates on comparable zero-coupon bonds are now 12%. How much would Joan get for her zero?

---

[3] Another reason for buying used discount or premium bonds is to match the remaining term to the investor's preference.

ANSWER:
$$\text{Current value} = \frac{26,536}{\text{FVF} (r = 12\%. \ n = 28)}$$
$$= \frac{26,536}{23,884}$$
$$= \$1,111.04$$

A second disadvantage of zero-coupon bonds is tax treatment. Although the zero-coupon bond owner doesn't receive annual interest payments, the IRS will calculate what these payments would be, and tax the investor each year. A way to avoid this problem is to buy tax-free, or municipal, zero-coupon bonds.

Municipal Bonds

Municipal bonds refer to any bonds issued by state and local governments or state and local public authorities (e.g., water districts, school districts). The bonds have all the characteristics of corporate or federal bonds except one—interest earnings are not taxed by the federal government. However, any capital gains earned by selling a municipal bond at a price higher than the purchase price are taxed. Also, municipal bond interest may be subject to state and local income taxes.

Of course, to compare yields for comparable corporate and municipal bonds, calculate the after-tax yield for each.

EXAMPLE 9-12: A municipal bond pays 8 percent interest and a corporate bond pays 9.5 percent interest. Which is better if the investor's federal tax bracket is 28 percent?

ANSWER: Municipal bond after-tax yield = 8%
Corporate bond after-tax yield = 9.5% − (.28 × 9.5%)
= 6.84%
In this case, take the municipal bond!

Junk Bonds

HIGH RISK BONDS

Junk bonds are simply high-risk, high-yield bonds. Although there is no precise definition of junk bonds, a rule of thumb is that a bond is considered "high" risk if its rating is *below* BBB by Moody's system.

How risky are junk bonds? A study spanning the years 1970–1984 showed the average default rate on junk bonds to be 2.24 percent

Table 9-6 How bonds measure up.

	Taxable Bonds	Municipal Bonds	Zero Coupon Bonds	"Junk" Bonds
Minimum denomination	$1000	$1000	$1000	$1000
Term	30 yrs., but can buy and sell existing bonds	30 yrs., but can buy and sell existing bonds	30 yrs., but can buy and sell existing bonds	30 yrs., but can buy and sell existing bonds
Interest rate	Fixed, and 1 to 2 percentage points higher than Treasury bonds	Fixed, and lower than rate for Treasury bonds	Fixed, and 1 to 2 percentage points higher than Treasury bonds	Fixed, and 3 to 4 percentage points higher than for taxable bonds
Default risk	Varies with rating	Varies with rating	Varies with rating	Very high
Liquidity risk	None	None	None	None
Rate risk	Low	Low	Low	Low
Inflation risk	High	High	High	High
Reinvestment risk	High	High	None	High
Tax advantages	None	Interest earnings not taxable	None, unless buy municipal zero-coupon bonds	None

compared to 0.15 percent for all bonds.[4] For this additional risk, the yield to maturity of junk bonds has averaged about $3\frac{1}{2}$ percentage points higher than the yield to maturity on government bonds.[5]

Should junk bonds be part of your portfolio? Clearly, the risk-averse investor would include them only as part of a diversified portfolio. However, Altman has concluded that the higher returns from junk bonds more than compensates for the additional risk (see reference in footnote 5).

How Bonds Measure Up

Table 9-6 summarizes how bonds measure up on risk and return characteristics. The major "problem" with bonds is their high inflation risk. The interest rate on bonds is fixed. If interest rates rise after a bond is bought, then the investor loses, especially if he cashes in the bond before it matures.

---

[4]Altmans, Edward and Scott Naumacher. "The Default Rate Experience on High-Yield Corporate Debt." *Financial Analysts Journal,* July/August 1985, pp. 25–41.
[5]Altman, Edward. "Analyzing Risks and Returns in the High-Yield Bond Market." *AAII Journal,* February 1988, pp. 7–11.

The Bottom Line

"Big" money can be made on bonds by buying them when interest rates are high and selling when interest rates are low. This strategy would best be implemented during a recession. So, "ideally," bonds should be bought at the beginning of a recession and sold at the end of a recession. However, if you forecast incorrectly and buy bonds when rates are low and sell when rates are high, then "big" money will be lost. Bonds can also be part of a "realistic" investment strategy. Here the idea is to buy and hold bonds until they mature, and not to try to sell to make large capital gains.

4. How Can You Invest in Mortgages?

You spent a lot of time and effort in Chapter 4 learning how to get a mortgage and how to evaluate alternative mortgages. Now, rather than being a borrower, how would you like to be on the other end, as a lender of mortgage money?

No, we are not suggesting that you set up your own bank and lend your money to homebuyers. Instead, what we'll discuss in this topic is investing in existing mortgages. You pay money to buy parts of existing mortgages, and in return you receive the mortgage payments from the homeowners.

Types of Mortgage Investments

MORTGAGE-BACKED SECURITIES   The generic name for mortgage investment is "mortgage-backed securities." Mortgage-backed securities are debt obligations that represent claims to the cash flows from pool of mortgage loans. This simply means that mortgage loans are purchased from banks and mortgage companies and then assembled into pools by a governmental, quasi-governmental, or private entity. The entity then issues securities that represent claims on the principal and interest payments made by homeowners paying these mortgages, a process known as securitization.

MORTGAGE PASS-THROUGH'S   Mortgage-backed securities exhibit a variety of structures. The most basic types are mortgage pass-through's, which means that mortgage payments made by the homeowners are "passed-through" the bank or brokerage firm to the investor. More complicated mortgage-backed securities, known as collateralized mortgage obligations (CMOs), may be designed to protect investors from or expose investors to various types of risk.

GINNIE MAE
FANNIE MAE
FREDDIE MAC   Most mortgage pass-through's are issued by the Government National Mortgage Association (Ginnie Mae), a U.S. government agency, or the Federal National Mortgage Association (Fannie Mae) and the Federal Home Loan Mortgage Corporation (Freddie Mac),

both of which are U.S. government-sponsored enterprises. Ginnie Mae's are backed by the full faith and credit of the U.S. government, which guarantees that investors receive timely payments. As such Ginnie Mae's default risk is the same as for Treasury securities. However, the interest rate earned on Ginnie Mae's are not fixed and is not guaranteed. Interest earned from Ginnie Mae's is not exempt from any taxes. Fannie Mae and Freddie Mac also provide certain guarantees and, while not backed by the full faith and credit of the U.S. government, have special authority to borrow from the U.S. Treasury. Some private institutions, such as brokerage firms, banks, and homebuilders, also securitize mortgages, known as "private-label" mortgage securities.

An important risk with regard to residential mortgages involves prepayments, typically because homeowners refinance when interest rates fall. Because of this the monthly payment an investor can receive from a simple mortgage pass-through such as a Ginnie Mae is unknown.

COLLATERALIZED MORTGAGE OBLICATIONS (CMOs)

A collateralized mortgage obligation (CMO) is a type of mortgage-backed security that is supposed to reduce this type of uncertainty. CMOs are backed by a trust that holds Ginnie Mae and other federal government-supported mortgages. When a CMO is created, it is subdivided into classes called "tranches." The principal repayments received by the CMO are initially paid to the first tranche until it has been entirely retired. Once the first tranche is retired payments are directed to the second tranche, then third tranche, so on and so forth until all the tranches have been repaid. Each tranche may have different principal balances, coupon rates, risks, and maturity dates. CMOs are highly sensitive to changes in interest rates.

What Can Go Wrong

There are several disadvantages to investing in mortgages. First, the minimum investment for Ginnie-Mae's, $25,000, is very high. However, this can be overcome by investing in mutual funds (discussed later).

Since the monthly check the investor receives includes both a principal and interest payment, mortgage pass-through's such as Ginnie-Mae's have reinvestment risk because the investor must find someplace else to invest this money.

INTEREST RATE NOT GUARANTEED

But the big potential problem with mortgage pass-through's is their interest rate. The interest rates on mortgage pass-through's are not fixed. The reason for this is because homeowners can refinance their mortgages. Say you buy a Ginnie Mae that initially pays 12 percent interest. After a couple of years the interest rate on new mortgages falls to

10 percent. Some homeowners with 12 percent mortgages will refinance to 10 percent mortgages. Some of the mortgages backing your Ginnie Mae will therefore be replaced with 10 percent mortgages. Your interest rate may not fall to 10 percent, but it will certainly fall to less than 12 percent, so the interest rate earned on mortgage pass-through's tends to fall when interest rates in the economy fall.

OK, you might say, the investor can lose on a mortgage pass-through if interest rates fall, so does the investor win if interest rates rise? No, because in this case the mortgage pass-through acts very much like a bond (and you know that owners of bonds lose when interest rates rise). If, for example, you own a 12 percent Ginnie Mae, and new Ginnie Mae's are paying 14 percent, then you'd lose money if you tried to sell your 12 percent Ginnie Mae. Of course, you could avoid losing money by not selling your Ginnie Mae, but you'd still be earning a below-market rate of return.

To make matters worse, owners of existing pass-through's don't get as much of a capital gain when market interest rates drop due to the likelihood that homeowners will refinance their higher rate mortgages to lower rate mortgages. So mortgage pass-through's are like bonds which can be called.

UNCERTAIN TERM   Another disadvantage of mortgage pass-through's is their uncertain term. Lenders and investors have no control over how long a homeowner will keep a mortgage. By convention, mortgage pass-through's are assumed to have a term of 12 years, but the actual term can be considerably less if homeowners move more frequently and prepay their mortgages.

Mortgage pass-through's based on adjustable rate mortgages have also been developed. In this case, the interest rate paid on an existing mortgage pass-through's would eventually rise if market rates rose.

CMOs reallocate risks among the different classes. As a result some classes receive less risks of a particular type while other classes more risk of that type. How much the risk is reduced or increased for each class depends on how the classes are structured.

When Should You Invest in Mortgages

If you're trying to implement the "idealistic strategy," then mortgage-backed securities are best bought at the beginning of Phase D (recession), when long-term interest rates are at their peak, and sold at the end of Phase D. However, if this strategy is followed, it is probably best to buy Ginnie Mae pass-through's, which have virtually no default risk, since mortgage defaults will increase during recessions.

Table 9-7 A summary of mortgage pass-through characteristics.

Maximum denomination—$25,000

Term—Unpredictable, but average of 12 years.

Interest rate—Varies as interest rates of the underlying mortgages change.

Default risk—Zero for Ginnie Mae's, higher for Freddie Mac's and Fannie Mae's.

Rate risk—Moderate.

Liquidity risk—None

Inflation risk—Moderate.

Reinvestment risk—High.

Tax advantages—None.

GINNIE-MAE AS
A RETIREMENT
INVESTMENT

If mortgage-backed securities are bought as part of the "realistic strategy," then they would compose part of the "bond" category. Their advantage over Treasury bonds is their higher average interest rate.

Finally, mortgage-backed securities can be a special kind of investment for retired consumers. Suppose, for example, that Joe and Betty Anson, aged 70, have $50,000 available to invest. They would like to use the $50,000 to partially live on over the next ten years. If the $50,000 is invested in a ten year Treasury note paying 10 percent, then Joe and Betty would receive $5000 each year for ten years and then $50,000 at the end of the ten years. If the $50,000 was invested in a mortgage-backed security with a term of 10 years and also paying 10 percent, then Joe and Betty would receive $7,932 each year, and no principal would be left at the end of the term. The mortgage-backed security would provide Joe and Betty with a larger annual income.

A Summary of Characteristics

Table 9-7 summarizes the risk and return characteristics for mortgage pass-through's. Rate risk exists because the interest rate and term are unpredictable. Inflation risk exists because the interest rate earned will not immediately increase if inflation rises. The risks of CMOs vary depending on how the CMO is structured.

The Bottom Line

Mortgage-back securities allow you to invest in mortgages and receive monthly payments which are part principal and part interest. Mortgage pass-throughs are fairly safe but pay higher interest rates than Treasury securities and some corporate bonds.

The disadvantage of mortgage pass-throughs is in the unpredictability of their interest rate. In some ways it's a "heads you lose, tails I win" situation with the interest rate on mortgage pass-through's. If market interest rates rise, then like bonds, the value of an existing mortgage pass-through falls. But if market interest rates fall, homeowners refinance their mortgage and the interest rate on the mortgage pass-through falls.

Compared to mortgage pass-through's, CMOs are more complicated and have various amounts of risk exposure depending on the particular CMO structure. —————

5. Should You Plunge into the Stock Market?

Stocks are perhaps the premier kind of investment. When an individual thinks of investments, she usually thinks of stocks and the stock market.

WHAT IS A STOCK   Technically, ownership of a stock represents ownership of a *claim* on the net earnings of a company after the claims of creditors are satisfied. In other words, if the company whose stock you own goes bankrupt, you'll only be paid from whatever's left after all creditors are paid.

Kinds of Returns

DIVIDENDS   There are two kinds of returns you can get from stocks. One is dividends. Dividends are periodic payments to the stockholder much like interest payments on a bond or CD. However, unlike bond or CD interest payments, dividend payments are generally not pre-determined but are established periodically, such as each quarter or each year after the company's financial position is reviewed. In bad years dividends will often not be paid; in good years dividends are usually high.

APPRECIATION   The second kind of return to a stock is appreciation in value between the purchase price of the stock and the sales price. In fact, some stocks never pay dividends, but instead reinvest dividends back into the company in order to (hopefully) increase appreciation. Such stocks are

GROWTH STOCKS   called *growth stocks.*

Where to Get Stocks

STOCK EXCHANGES   Stocks are bought and sold in financial markets, or exchanges. The major exchanges are the New York Stock Exchange, the American Stock Exchange, six regional exchanges, and the "Over-the-Counter" Exchange. The last market is unique in that it is not a physical market (it is not located in one physical place), but instead is simply a market between brokers. There are also a number of foreign stock exchanges.

BROKERS   In order to buy or sell stocks, you'll usually need the assistance of a *broker.* There are two kinds of brokers, full-service brokers and discount brokers. Full-service brokers will execute your buy and sell orders, but will also give you advice about what to buy and what to sell. For the buying and selling and the advice you'll pay a commission. The commission includes a flat fee and a percentage of the value of the purchase or sale. The percentage typically declines the greater the value of the transaction. For example, a full-service broker might charge a flat fee of $25 plus 2.8 percent of transactions under $1000, 1.8 percent of transactions between $1000 and $2500, and 1.5 percent on transactions over $2500.

DISCOUNT BROKERS   A discount broker will only execute your buy and sell orders; no advice is given. However, the benefit is that commissions are much lower than for full-service brokers. Commission for discount brokers can be 75 percent lower than for full-service brokers. Obviously, if you know what you want to buy and sell, you're better-off going through a discount broker.

Stocks can also be bought and sold through *mutual funds.* We'll talk about this later in the topic on mutual funds.

Measuring the Market

Following the progress of an individual stock is easy. You simply watch what the price per share is doing and also pay attention to the dividends.

But how do you keep track of what the entire stock market is doing? **STOCK MARKET** To do this you need to watch some stock market average, or index. Any **INDEX** stock market index is simply an average of a number of stocks in the stock market.

The key word in the last sentence is "number." How many stocks are used to construct the index, and how representative are they of the entire market? This is what distinguishes the various measures of the stock market.

DOW JONES   The most widely quoted market average is the *Dow Jones Industrial* **INDUSTRIAL AVERAGE** *Average* (DJIA). Originally the DJIA represented the average share price of the stocks in the average, but due to stock splits and dividend payments over the years, this is no longer true. There are two problems with the DJIA. First, it is calculated using only 30 leading stocks (there are thousands of stocks from all industries), and second, the more expensive stocks have a greater influence on the average.

S&P 500   Probably the second most popular market measure is the *Standard and Poor's 500 Stock Composite Index* (S&P 500). The S&P is an index much like the Consumer Price Index. The index value itself is meaningless; its only use is in comparison to previous index values. The base period for the index is 1941–43, where the index value was 10. So, for example, if the current index value is 1000, this means that the average price of the 500 stocks in the S&P 500 has increased 100 times since 1941–43.

INTERNATIONAL INVESTING

C O N S U M E R   T O P I C

U.S. investors are not limited to investing in American stocks. There are many foreign companies that issues stocks. The London and Japanese stock markets are the largest foreign stock markets. Keep in mind that even if you only invest in stocks of U.S. companies you already may have some international exposure in your investment portfolio. Many of the factors that affect foreign companies also affect the foreign business operations of U.S. companies. The fear that economic problems around the globe will hurt the operations of U.S. companies can cause dramatic changes in U.S. stock prices.

There are different ways you can invest internationally: through mutual funds, exchange-traded funds, American Depositary Receipts, U.S.-traded foreign stocks, or direct investments in foreign markets.

There are different kinds of mutual funds that invest in foreign stocks, including global funds, international funds, regional or country funds, and international index funds. International mutual funds provide more diversification than most investors could achieve on their own. Like other international investments, mutual funds that invest internationally probably will have higher costs than funds that invest only in U.S. stocks.

An exchange-traded fund is a type of investment company whose investment objective is to achieve the same return as a particular market index. ETFs are listed on stock exchanges and, like stocks (and in contrast to mutual funds), trade throughout the trading day. A share in an ETF that tracks an international index gives an exposure to the performance of the underlying stock or bond portfolio along with the ability to trade that share like any other security.

The stocks of most foreign companies that trade in the U.S. markets are traded as American Depositary Receipts (ADRs) issued by U.S. depositary banks. Each ADR represents one or more shares of a foreign stock or a fraction of a share. Although most foreign stocks trade in the U.S. markets as ADRs, some foreign stocks trade here in the same form as in their local market. For example, Canadian stocks trade in the same form in the United States as they do in the Canadian markets, rather than as ADRs. You can purchase ADRs and other foreign stocks that trade in the United States through your broker.

Finally, if you want to buy or sell stocks in a company that only trades on a foreign stock market, your broker may be able to process your order for you. These foreign companies do not file reports with the SEC, however, so you will need to do additional research to get the information you need to make an investment decision.

(*continued on next page*)

**C
O
N
S
U
M
E
R

T
O
P
I
C**

(continued from previous page)

Investors are attracted to foreign stocks for two chief reasons: diversification and growth. With international investing, you can spread your investment risk among foreign companies and markets that are different than the U.S. economy. In addition, you can take advantage of the potential for growth in some foreign economies, particularly in emerging markets.

There is one factor that U.S. investors in foreign stocks must worry about that investors in U.S. stocks don't. This additional worry is the foreign exchange rate. U.S. investors in foreign stocks will want the U.S. dollar to fall against foreign currencies, because this will mean more U.S. dollars received when each share of foreign stock is cashed in. Strengthening of the U.S. dollar against foreign currencies hurts investors in foreign stocks, because fewer dollars will be received when the foreign stocks are cashed in.

The S&P 500 is obviously a much broader index than the DJIA. High-priced stocks aren't given more importance because the index is constructed using weights based on the stock's total market value. However, the S&P 500 is still dominated by stocks from the largest corporations.

The two major stock exchanges, the New York Stock Exchange and the American Stock Exchange, each have their own market indices based on the stocks traded on their exchanges. These indices are constructed in a way similar to the construction of the S&P 500, but they include a broader range of stocks.

The National Association of Security Dealers produces a Composite Index which is based on over 2300 companies. It is constructed in a similar fashion as the S&P 500.

WILSHIRE 5000

The broadest stock market index is the Wilshire 5000, which is based on over 5000 stocks. The Wilshire 5000 is the total price of all stocks which are quoted on a daily basis.

Despite the wide variety of stock market indices, the nice thing for the investor is that all the indices tend to move together. Although the DJIA is the most widely quoted average in the media, the S&P 500 is the index used most frequently in economic studies.

Historical Performance of Stocks

There is one simple reason why all investors should consider stocks as part of their portfolio. Over long periods of time, stocks have consistently paid returns much higher than inflation. Studies show that the stock market pays an annual average return of approximately 7–9 percentage points higher than the inflation rate.[6]

A very important feature of stocks is that the longer the holding period, the less fluctuation in the rate of return. Although average returns are very similar regardless of the holding period, the spread between the highest and lowest returns dramatically shrinks with longer holding periods. What this means is that ups and downs in the stock market are smoothed out over long periods.

RECESSIONS AND THE STOCK MARKET

There are two economic conditions which the stock market doesn't like, recession and rising inflation. Recession, as you've learned, means bad economic times, and these bad times affect businesses as well as consumers. Recessions reduce consumer sales and reduce business profits. This, in turn, depresses stocks.

INFLATION AND THE STOCK MARKET

The relationship between the stock market and inflation is a little more tricky. As long as the inflation rate is steady and predictable (at whatever level), the stock market will keep ahead of inflation and act as an inflation hedge. However, the stock market will usually fall when the inflation rate rises. Why? Because a rising inflation rate creates unpredictability for business. Where will the rising inflation rate stop? What will the rising inflation rate do to wages and other costs that business must pay? Will the rising inflation rate cause the Federal Reserve to take corrective action which will lead to a recession? All of these questions make business planning difficult and uncertain, which in turn clouds the business outlook and depresses stock prices.

In terms of implementing the ideal strategy, this obviously means that the investor would try to buy stocks at the end of Phase D and sell them at the end of Phase A, thereby avoiding the phases of rising inflation and recession.

Stock Market Risks and Taxes

Everything said so far has been rather positive about the stock market. But there are a number of risks involved with stock market investing and these should be recognized before you "plunge in."

DEFAULT RISK

Default risk—the risk of losing all, or a substantial part, of your initial investment—is very high with stock market investing. A stock's price can fall and there's no limit to how far it can fall. As discussed earlier, "beta" is a measure of a stock's price volatility (a beta greater than 1 is more risky; a beta less than 1 is less risky). One way to reduce default risk is to diversify. We've already talked about the benefits of diversification. Diversification means spreading your stock market money in

---

[6]Davis, J., Aliaga-Diaz, R, and Thomas, C.J. "Forecasting Stock Returns: What Signals Matter, and What Do They Say Now?" Vanguard publication. Retrieved online 4/17/2013 at https://personal.vanguard.com/pdf/s338.pdf.

CAN YOU INSURE YOUR STOCK RETURNS?

As you've already learned, investing in the stock market is risky. When you put money in the stock market, you don't know for certain what rate of return you'll earn. Is there any way to get around this problem? Is there any way to guarantee, or insure, the rate of return you'll get from the stock market?

One approach combines a stock portfolio with a safe, liquid investment like a money market fund. The investor begins with a specified percentage split between the stock portfolio and money market fund (say 90% in stocks and 10% in the money market fund). The greater the decline in stocks, the more money that is transferred out of stocks and into the fund. In contrast, the greater the rise in stock prices, the more money that is transferred from the money market fund into stocks. The investor must decide on the percentage change in stock prices which will trigger a shift of money between stocks and the money market fund and the amount of money to be shifted each time.

There are disadvantages to this technique. The strategy results in stocks being sold when prices are low and bought when prices are high. Also, potential losses from the stock market aren't totally eliminated; instead, they are simply reduced.

An alternative form of stock market "insurance" does limit the losses you could suffer in stocks. This technique makes use of something called the "options" market and works like this. You buy a "put" in the options market for each stock you own. A "put" guarantees that you can sell a stock in the future at a specified price. In effect, a "put" locks in a price you can get for a stock in the future. You buy a "put" which will guarantee you can sell your stock for its current price. If the price of your stock increases in the future, then you sell your stock for that price and you ignore the "put." On the other hand, if the price of your stock falls in the future, you can use your "put" and get back the original price of the stock.

For example, Gary has 100 shares of WALDENCO worth today at $100/share. Gary buys 100 "puts" at $5/share which guarantees he can sell WALDENCO in six months at $100/share. Gary's total cost of the "puts" is $500. Say in six months WALDENCO has dropped to $70/share. Without the "puts" Gary would have lost $3,000 ($30 × 100); but he can exercise his "puts" and still sell WALDENCO for $100/share. If, however, WALDENCO rises to $130/share, Gary obviously will sell for $130/share and ignore the "puts." "Puts" provide a floor for losses.

The price paid for the "put insurance" depends importantly on the stock price guaranteed and past volatility in the stock price. The price paid for the "put" will be higher the higher the stock price guaranteed and the greater the past volatility in the stock's price.

many different, unrelated stocks. Again, the full benefits of diversification can be achieved with about 15 different stocks.

LIQUIDITY RISK   *Liquidity risk* is also present for stocks. Stocks can be readily converted to cash by selling them, but there's no guarantee that a "good" price would be received if the owner was forced to sell. Therefore, stocks should be viewed as relatively illiquid assets.

Stocks also have *rate risk,* meaning that the rate of return actually earned on a stock may be very different than what the buyer expected. Rate risk can also be reduced by diversification.

INFLATION RISK   Stocks have a moderate amount of inflation risk. As long as the inflation rate is consistent and steady from year to year, stock values will keep up with inflation and act as inflation hedges. But when the inflation rate is rising and is unpredictable, stock prices don't keep up with inflation and tend to fall in real (inflation-adjusted) terms. So stocks have inflation risk when inflation rates are rapidly rising.

Stocks don't have reinvestment risk because their returns, including dividends, can be reinvested in the stock.

TAX TREATMENT OF STOCK LOSSES   There is a federal tax advantage to owning stocks, but only if you sell for a loss. If you sell some stock for a loss, first you can use those losses as a deduction against any gains you've made by selling other stocks or other property. After doing this, if you have some losses left over, you can use $3000 of the losses as a deduction against your wages and salaries or other income. Finally, if after doing this you still have some losses left over, those losses can be "saved" and used as deductions in future years.

EXAMPLE 9-13: Frank sells ABC stock and makes a profit of $5000, but Frank takes a "bath" when he sells XYZ stock for a loss of $12,000. How can Frank use the $12,000 in losses?

ANSWER: Frank can use $5000 of the XYZ stock losses to offset the $5000 ABC gain. So Frank won't have to pay federal taxes on the ABC gain. Frank can use $3000 of the $12,000 XYZ loss to reduce his taxable salary. So Frank won't have to pay federal taxes on $3000 of his salary.s Frank can save the remaining $4000 in losses for use as deductions in future years.

Table 9-8 summarizes the risk, return, and tax characteristics of stocks.

Table 9-8   A composite look at stocks.

Minimum denomination	1¢
Term	Any
Rate of return earned	Varies
Default risk	Varies from high to low
Rate risk	High
Liquidity risk	High
Inflation risk	High when inflation rate is rising
Reinvestment risk	None
Tax advantages	Losses can be used to offset other gains, plus $3000 of losses can be used to offset wages and salaries.

IS THERE A POLITICAL STOCK MARKET CYCLE?

**C
O
N
S
U
M
E
R

T
O
P
I
C**

You've already learned how the state of the economy can affect the stock market. Since presidents can affect the economy through their power over national economic policy, it might make sense to think that presidents can have an impact on the stock market.

One theory claims that there is a four year cycle to the stock market. The theory goes like this. Presidents are elected for terms of four years. Presidents want to be re-elected, or if they can't run for re-election, they want their party to win the election. Presidents know that sometimes they have to enact policies that will cause temporary pain (e.g., possibly a recession) so that the economy will be better in the long run. If such "painful" policies must be enacted, it's better to do it in the first two years of the president's term so that the pain will be gone by the time the president runs for re-election. In contrast, in the second two years of a president's term, the president will enact policies that will "pump up" the economy so that everything is rosy for election time. Therefore, this theory predicts that the stock market should do much better in the second two years of a president's term than in the first two years.

How well has reality supported this theory? From 1960 to 2000 there were ten presidential terms. In seven of those terms, the stock market rose more in the second two years of the term than in the first two years. The exceptions were President Reagan's second term, President Bush's term, and President Clinton's second term. However, in President Bush's term the stock market performance was very dose between the first two years (26%) and second two years (24%).

So perhaps the exception to the rule is when a president is in his second term. Since a president is limited to two terms, without the incentive of future victory or defeat, the political cycle may weaken.

Approaches

ACCEPT MARKET
AVERAGE

There are two alternative approaches to the stock market. One approach says that the best way to invest in the stock market is to buy a representative, diversified set of stocks and be content to earn the *average* rate of return of the stock market. If you're following the ideal strategy, then you'd want to buy and sell this diversified stock portfolio according to the phases of the business cycle. If you're a realistic investor, then you buy the diversified portfolio and hold it. But, in either case, you don't try to "beat" the stock market.

BEAT THE MARKET

The second approach is the exact opposite; you do try to "beat the market" by selecting stocks that will outperform the market. Again, you could do this as part of the "ideal" strategy where you also buy and sell according to the business cycle, or as part of the realistic strategy in which you buy and hold for a long period. The next topic will examine alternative approaches to stock selection in order to "beat the market."

Figure 9-1.   Approaches to stock market investing.

APPROACH TO STOCK MARKET

	Accept average market	Try to "Beat the Market"
Ideal strategy– "Beat the Business Cycle	(B) Moderate risk. Buying and selling of entire portfolio according to business cycle.	(A) Most risky. Very frequent buying and selling of individual stocks and of entire portfolio.
Realistic strategy	(D) Least risky. Very little buying and selling. Hold stock portfolio through entire business cycle.	(C) Moderate risk. Hold a stock portfolio through entire business cycle but buy and sell individual stocks.

APPROACH TO BUSINESS CYCLE

C O N S U M E R   T O P I C

HOW GOOD ARE FINANCIAL NEWSLETTERS?

If you are an investor with a moderate or large investment portfolio, you've probably received offers to subscribe to an investment newsletter. For a price ranging from $100 to $500 annually, you can receive a weekly or monthly newsletter which tells you how to invest to receive the highest rate of return.

Are investment newsletters worth the price? Can investment newsletters show you how to "beat the market."

If the latter part of the 1980s are a representative time period, then the answer has to be "no." The Hulbert Financial Digest, which tracks newsletter performance, calculated the five year rate of return between September 30, 1984 and September 30, 1989 from the recommendations of 97 newsletters (the returns are not adjusted for risk). Out of the 97 newsletters, only one (Zweig Forecast) beat the Dow Jones Industrial Average, and only three beat the S&P 500 Index. Furthermore, there's little correlation in the rankings from year to year. The leading newsletter one year is usually not the leading newsletter, or even one of the leading newsletters, the next year.

These results are consistent with the idea that the stock market is "efficient," and that efforts to "beat the market" are largely fruitless.

Reference: Herman, Tom. "Scoop on Newsletters May Be Bad News," *The Wall Street Journal*, November 13, 1989.

The combination of either trying to beat the market or accepting the market average paired with the idealistic strategy versus the realistic strategy results in four approaches to stock market investing (Figure 9-1). Approach A (Try to Beat the Market and Beat the Business Cycle) is the most risky and results in the most trading of stocks. Investors using Approach A will buy and sell their entire stock portfolio to try to beat the business cycle, and they will buy and sell individual stocks to try to beat the market. The exact opposite strategy is followed by investors using Approach D. The investor using Approach D believes that the best that can be achieved is to earn the average return produced by the stock market over the entire business cycle. The Approach D investor owns stocks as part of a diversified portfolio (e.g., along with cash, bonds, gold, and real estate) and does very little buying and selling.

Approaches B and C are middle approaches but are very different. The investor following Approach B believes that individual stocks can't be found which beat the market, so this investor buys a diversified set of stocks designed to give the market average. However, the Approach B investor does try to beat the business cycle by buying and selling the entire stock portfolio according to phases of the cycle. In contrast, the Approach C investor doesn't try to time the business cycle but does try to buy and sell individual stocks in order to beat the market average.

The Bottom Line

Over the long run the returns from investing in the stock market have far exceeded inflation. However, over short periods of time stock market investing can be very risky. The stock market nose-dives during recessions and also performs poorly when the inflation rate is rising. Stock market investors can try to both "beat the market" and "beat the business cycle." This is a very risky approach which requires frequent trading. At the opposite extreme is the approach which accepts the market average rate of return and which holds stocks over the entire business cycle. Little buying and selling is done with this approach. _____

6. How Can You Pick Stocks?

There are three major approaches to picking stocks: the fundamental analysis approach, the technical analysis approach, and the efficient markets approach. Stock brokers and others who think the market can be beaten rely on either fundamental analysis or technical analysis. Economists are the big fans of the efficient markets approach, which says that stocks can't be consistently picked which beat the market! Obviously, the efficient markets approach takes all the fun out of picking stocks. You'll have to decide which approach or combination of approaches makes the most sense.

Fundamental Analysis

STOCK'S INTRINSIC
VALUE

Followers of fundamental analysis believe that each stock has an intrinsic, or basic, value. The task of fundamental analysis is to find the stock's intrinsic value and compare it to the stock's current price. If the stock's intrinsic value is greater than the stock's current price, then the stock should be bought. In this case the investor expects the stock's current price to rise to eventually equal the intrinsic value. In contrast, if the stock's intrinsic value is less than the stock's current price, then the stock shouldn't be bought or, if the investor already owns the stock, it should be sold. In this case the investor expects the stock's current price to fall to eventually equal the intrinsic value.

Sounds easy, right? Unfortunately, it's not as easy as it sounds. The big question with fundamental analysis is how to calculate a stock's intrinsic value? Conceptually, there's no problem in answering this question. People own stock in companies because companies (hopefully) make profits. Profits generate earnings (net income after expenses and taxes) for each share of stock. Earnings are paid out to stockholders in the form of dividends. The intrinsic value of a share of stock equals the present value of the expected future earnings, or dividends, paid to that stock. If earnings or dividends are expected to grow at some constant rate in the future, then this concept of intrinsic value can be simplified to this equation:

$$Intrinsic\ Value\ = \frac{D}{k-g}$$

where D = the stock's expected dividends per share one year from now, k = discount rate, and g = growth rate of dividends.

EXAMPLE 9-14: Suppose WALDENCO stock is expected to pay a dividend next year of $5/share. If WALDENCO dividends are expected to increase 4 percent annually, then calculate the intrinsic value of WALDENCO stock using a discount rate of 8 percent. If WALDENCO is selling at $100/share, should you buy it?

ANSWER: Intrinsic value $= \dfrac{\$5}{8\% - 4\%} = \dfrac{\$5}{.08-.04} = \$125/\text{share}.$

WALDENCO should be bought.

Although this appears simple enough, there are many questions associated with the equation for intrinsic value. Information on dividends is easy to find, but what about g, the dividend growth rate? The past dividend growth rate can be used, but there's no assurance that the future dividend growth rate will equal the past rate. Also, what discount rate should be used? Clearly, the more risk associated with the projection of future earnings and dividends, the higher the discount rate that should be used. But how high is high? Again, this is a matter of judgement.

PROBLEMS WITH FUNDAMENTAL ANALYSIS

In short, fundamental analysis requires peering into the future in order to calculate current value for a stock. Obviously, unpredictable events can occur in the future which will affect a stock's value (in our equation, these unpredictable events will affect k). For example, how many people successfully predicted the oil crises of the 1970s, which

CAN YOU MAKE MONEY IN THE STOCK MARKET BEING "CONTRARY"?

C O N S U M E R   T O P I C

Some investors and investment advisors like to call themselves "contrarians." A contrarian investor follows a simple rule: Do the opposite of what the crowd is doing. A contrarian investor buys stocks that have been losers and sells stocks that have been winners.

This strategy is based on the assumption that stock market investors overreact to both good news and bad news. This means stocks of companies experiencing good news will be pushed above their "true value" as everyone gets on the bandwagon for buying the stock. The contrarian, therefore, sells this stock at the height of its popularity because he knows it's overvalued and its price will fall. Just the same, stocks of companies experiencing bad news will be pulled below their "true value" as everyone dumps the stock. In this case, the contrarian buys the stock at its bleakest point because he knows the stock is undervalued and will rebound. So at the heart of the contrarian strategy is investor psychology, not economic fundamentals.

Does the contrarian strategy work? A study by Chan says no. Chan used stocks in the New York Stock Exchange over the period 1932–1983. He divided the study period into segments of 3 year periods and used the stocks' performance in the three year periods to separate winners and losers. The performance of the winners and losers were then examined in the next three year period. New winners and losers were then identified and the process was continued.

Chan found that when the stocks' risk, as measured by their betas, is taken into account, buying losers and selling winners does not give above-average returns. If contrarians make more money, it is only because they are taking more risk.

Reference: Chan, K. C. "On the Contrarian Investment Strategy," *Journal of Business*, Vol. 61, No. 2, 1988, pp. 147–163.

hurt the big, gas-guzzling U.S. car companies and helped the small, fuel-efficient Japanese car companies? Fundamental analysis relies on accurate predictions, but such predictions are hard to come by.

Technical Analysis

In many ways technical analysis is the opposite of fundamental analysis. Technical analysts don't try to compute the intrinsic value of a stock, nor do they look at general trends in the economy. Instead, technical analysts try to detect patterns in the movements of individual stock prices or in the movements of the general stock market. Technical analysts don't really care what causes the patterns; the movements may be caused by economic fundamentals, by investor psychology, or by some natural phenomenon like sunspots! The job of the technical analyst is to identify the pattern and then make decisions about buying and selling stocks based on the pattern. One of the disadvantages of technical analysis is that a change in the direction of a stock's price usually can't be identified until after the change has occurred. So the technical analyst will usually miss the absolute peaks and absolute bottoms in a stock's price.

As you might expect, technical analysts make frequent use of graphs of stock prices in order to identify patterns and trends. Two common patterns are shown in Figure 9-2. In the "head and shoulders" pattern, the stock price peaks at the head. The "head" is flanked by two lower peaks called "shoulders." A "neckline" is formed by connecting the two valleys between the left shoulder and the head and the right shoulder and the head. When the stock's price falls below the neckline, it should continue to fall and so the stock should be sold. If the stock's price doesn't fall below the neckline, then it should continue to trend upward.

HEAD AND SHOULDERS

"NECKLINE"

Figure 9-2. Two common patterns of stock prices.

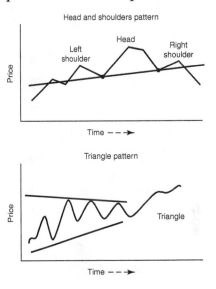

In the "triangle" pattern, the fluctuations in the stock's price gradually narrow to form a triangle.

TRIANGLE PATTERN
MOVING AVERAGE

When the stock's price "breaks-out" of the triangle, then the price will move in the direction of the breakout. In Figure 9-2 the stock's price moves abruptly higher, so the stock should be bought.

Technical analysts also use indicators to determine trends both for individual stocks and for the entire stock market. A moving average of a stock's price is an average which is re-calculated each day. However, on each recalculation the new day's price is added to the average and the first day's price is dropped. A "sell" signal is given when the current price of the stock falls below the moving average on a day in which there was active trading of the stock. A "buy" signal is given when the current price of the stock rises above the moving average on an active trading day. Figure 9-3 shows the calculation of moving averages for ABC Stock and XYZ Stock. The moving average indicator gives a "sell" signal for ABC stock since the most recent prices on both May 13 and 14 are less than the moving average. In contrast, a "buy" signal is given for XYZ stock since the most recent prices on May 13 and 14 are above the moving average.

Figure 9-3.   Calculation of 12-day moving averages.

	Price of ABC Stock		Price of XYZ Stock	
May 2	**$100**	—	**$80**	—
3	100	$100	82	$82
4	95	95	81	81
5	98	98	84	84
6	105	105	86	86
7	106	106	82	82
8	107	107	90	90
9	103	103	89	89
10	102	102	86	86
11	100	100	88	88
12	99	99	88	88
13	97	97	90	90
14	—	99	—	92
	12 day moving average for	12 day moving average for	12 day moving average for	12 day moving average for
	May 13 = $101.83	May 14 = $100.92	May 13 = $85.50	May 14 = $86.50

Other technical indicators are used not for evaluating individual stocks, but for judging where the general stock market is going. If the number of stock price advances compared to the number of stock price declines is increasing, then the stock market (in general) should move upward. Likewise, if the number of new stock price highs is greater than the number of new stock price lows, then the market is also expected to improve.

The Efficient Markets Approach

The efficient markets approach is very different from both fundamental analysis and technical analysis. Fundamental analysis and technical analysis both assume that stocks can be found which will outperform other stocks; they just differ on how those superior stocks can be found.

The efficient markets approach says that no stock bargains can he found. The efficient markets approach says that the stock market is efficient. This means that current stock prices always reflect all information, both current and future, about that stock's company the industry, and the general economy. If something happens which benefits or hurts a stock, this information will be rapidly incorporated into the stock's

NO STOCK

WHAT IS "PROGRAM TRADING"?

Program trading is a type of stock market trading which involves three elements: (1) a computer model which tells the investor when to trade, (2) trades between stocks held today and "futures" contracts for purchase or sale of stocks in the future, and (3) direct access to the stock market exchanges without going through brokers. Program trading is done by managers of large investment portfolios and usually not by individual investors. The direct access to the stock exchanges by program traders significantly reduces the costs of trading and therefore encourages more trading.

As mentioned, program trading involves use of *futures contracts.* A futures contract is simply a contract which locks in the investor to a price for buying or selling a stock in the future.* An investor who purchases a futures contract to sell locks in a price for selling a stock at a specified dale in the future. An investor who purchases a futures contract to buy locks in a price for buying a stock at a specified date in the future. Futures contracts are bought for a fraction (10 to 25 percent) of their face value. Futures contracts are different than options (see *Can You Insure Your Stock Returns?*) in that the futures contract must be acted upon. With an option, the investor can act on the option or can let it expire with no action.

Most program trading involves stock indexes rather than individual stocks. Stock indexes are simply collections of stocks designed to reflect the entire stock market. The most widely used index is the S&P 500 Index.

There are two types of portfolio trading, *risk reduction* and *arbitrage.* Risk reduction is illustrated in Figure 1. As an example, let's say the computer model projects that stocks will decline in the future. The investor owns a stock index fund today but doesn't want to sell it. To reduce the risk that the stock market will decline, the investor purchases a futures contract to sell that permits the investor to sell a stock index at some specified future date at the current price. If the stock market does in fact decline, the investor will lose money on the stock index he owns today. But he will be able to buy the same stock index at the lower price and resell it at the contracted higher price, thereby exactly offsetting his losses.

For example, in Figure 1 the stock index today is at 100. The investor purchases a futures contract to sell that locks in the value of 100 for sale of the index in nine months. In nine months the index value falls to 50. The investor loses 50 on the stock index he owned at the beginning of the period, but he can now buy another index at 50 and sell it at the locked-in value of 100, thus exactly offsetting his losses.

This procedure can backfire. If stocks actually rise in the future (say from 100 to 200), the investor will have to buy the stock index in the future at 200 and sell it at 100. This will result in a loss which will exactly offset the gain earned on the stock index owned at the beginning of the period.

*There are futures contracts for many other investments, including bonds, Ginnie Mae's, agricultural products, and metals.

(*continued on next page*)

**C
O
N
S
U
M
E
R**

**T
O
P
I
C**

(*continued from previous page*)

The second type of program trading is *arbitrage*. Here the investor compares the value of the stock index today to the value of that same stock index on a futures contract. If, for example, today's value is 100 and the value on a futures contract to sell is 110, then the investor will purchase the futures contract to sell and earn a guaranteed return of 10 percent (see Figure 2). In contrast, if today's value is 100 and the futures value is 90, the investor will sell the stock index today at 100 and purchase a futures contract to buy the same index at 90, again guaranteeing a return of 10 percent. Computer programs keep track of today's value, and futures values and tell the program trader what to do.

Program trading has been criticized for increasing the volatility of the stock market. How can this happen? Let's say the stock market is declining. To reduce risk, program traders purchase futures contracts to sell at a locked in price. However, the increased popularity of the futures contracts to sell eventually reduces the locked-in price that new contracts will guarantee. This creates a discrepancy between the value of stock indexes today and their value on futures contract—in this case, the futures value is lower. This, in turn, motivates arbitragers to enter and purchase futures contracts to buy and to sell stock indexes today (Panel (b) of Figure 2). This action depresses today's stock prices and makes for a greater downward trend.

Figure 1. Reducing risk.

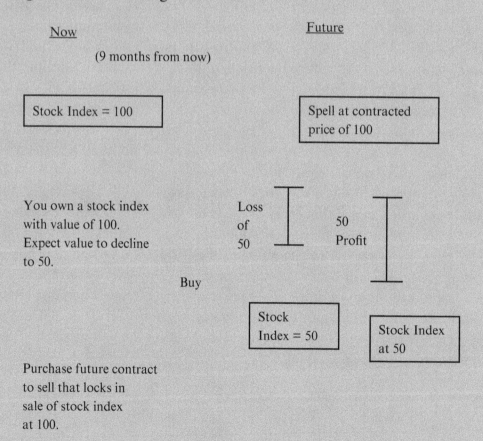

Figure 2.   Reducing risk.

(A)   Today's value   Futures' value

100   110

Result: Investor purchases stock Index today at 100 and purchases future contract to sell same stock index at 110 in future. This guarantees a profit of 10%.

(B)   Today's value   Futures' value

100   90

Result: Investor sells stock Index today at 100 and purchases futures contract to buy same stock index at 90 in future. This guarantees a profit of 10%.

Because of the impact of program trading on stock market volatility, some people want to ban or restrict program trading. However, supporters of program trading argue it keeps the stock market efficient.

Reference: Luft, Carl F. and Frederic B. Shipley III, "Program Trading and Individual Investors," *American Association of Individual Investors Journal*, January 1988, pp. 13–15.

BARGAINS

price. Only an investor possessing "inside information" (information that only a few people know) can expect to find stock bargains. But especially for the small investor, there are no bargains to be found. Only by buying a risky stock can the small investor earn an above-average return.

What is the investor to do if he follows the efficient market approach? The efficient market investor should concentrate on three things: (1) buying a diversified set of stocks in order to reduce risk, (2) reducing taxes on investment earnings, and (3) reducing the costs of buying and selling stocks.

Which Approach Is Best?

There have been many studies comparing the three different approaches to picking stocks. The results of these studies come closest to supporting the efficient markets approach, but not entirely. The following techniques have been found to select stocks which give above average returns, even after adjusting for risk. The techniques are all derived from the fundamental analysis approach.

1. *Buy stocks with low P/E ratios.* The P/E ratio is the stock's current price per share divided by the stock's current earnings per share. If

the current earnings per share is representative of future earnings, then stocks with low P/E ratios are undervalued because their price should rise in the future to reflect the stock's earnings. Studies have shown that buying stocks with low P/E ratios will earn the investor above average rates of return, even after adjusting for risk.[7] How low is a low P/E ratio? To determine this, Coulson[8] recommends randomly selecting 50 stocks and then picking the ten stocks among this group having the lowest P/E ratios. Out of this group of ten, use the *highest* P/E ratio as the ratio which should not be exceeded when stocks are selected.

Stock market guru Peter Lynch has modified the low P/E ratio method in the following way.[9] He calculates the number $\frac{P/E}{(g+d)}$, where g is the stock's annual average growth rate in earnings (in percentage terms) and d is the stock's dividend payments as a percentage of its price. If P/E/(g + d) is .5 or less, Lynch recommends buying the stock.

Why does the low P/E ratio method work? Actually, economists don't have a good answer for this. The best explanation seems to be that many investors may avoid low P/E stocks because they think such stocks are riskier, or have poor prospects, precisely because their price is low compared to their earnings.

2. *Buy neglected stocks.* According to Coulson, only 2000 of 9000 stocks are actively followed and analyzed by the research departments of Wall Street brokerage houses. This leaves 7000 "neglected" stocks. A study by Arbel and Strebel showed that investors can earn an above-average return, even after adjusting for risk, by investing in these "neglected" stocks.[10] Why?

Because investors perceive that the neglected stocks are riskier since they aren't followed by the brokerage houses. Investors think the stocks followed by the brokerage houses are safer and better, so investors are willing to accept a lower rate of return from them.

3. *Mergers.* Research has shown that superior returns can be earned by buying stocks of firms which are merged with other firms.[11]

[7]Goodman, David A. and John W. Peavy III, "The Interaction of Firm Size and Price-Earning Ratio on Portfolio Performance," *Financial Analysts Journal,* Jan.-Feb., 1986, pp. 9–12.

[8]Coulson, D. Robert. *The Intelligent Investor's Guide to Profiling from Stock Market Inefficiencies,* Probus Publishing, Chicago, 1987.

[9]Markese, John, "A Thumbnail Sketch: What is Growth Worth?" *AAIA Journal,* August 1989.

[10]Arbel, Avner and Paul Strebel, "Pay Attention to Neglected Firms," *Journal of Portfolio Management,* Winter 1983, pp. 37–42.

[11]Asquith, Paul, "Merger Bids, Uncertainty and Stockholder Returns." *Journal of Financial Economics,* 1988, Vol. 11, pp. 51–83.

HOW GOOD ARE STOCK BROKERS?

C
O
N
S
U
M
E
R

T
O
P
I
C

Anyone who can convince a brokerage firm to put them through a four month training course and can then pass a six-hour exam can become a stockbroker (or more precisely, a securities broker). Contrary to what you might think, brokers do not have to have a college degree in economics, business, or accounting!

With this in mind, there are several characteristics you should look for in a broker and several features or tactics you should avoid. First, at the initial meeting with you, the good broker will do a lot of listening and little talking. The good broker will want to find out from you your investment goals (why you are investing), how much you can invest, and most importantly, what level of risk you're willing to take. The good broker will explain to you the tradeoff between risk and return and the various ways in which risk can be handled (e.g., diversification). Given this information, the good broker will map out an investment plan which will meet your goals within your acceptable level of risk.

Brokers rely either on their own analysis or the analysis of the research departments of their brokerage company for making recommendations about specific investments. For stocks, the analysis is typically a combination of fundamental and technical analyses. When a broker recommends a particular stock, bond, or other investment, ask the broker what methods were used to derive the recommendation. Also, always check the risk of the recommendation. Of course, if you believe the stock market is "efficient," then you may put little faith in the recommendations of brokers.

Brokers are paid from commissions derived from buying and selling of securities, and this creates several potential conflicts with the client's interest. One potential conflict is that the broker may recommend more trading than is in the client's interest in order to generate more trades and more commissions. Frequent trading, designed to buy low and sell high, usually doesn't consistently work, so brokers who recommend frequent trading probably should be avoided. The commission basis of a broker's compensation also means the broker has an incentive to devote more time to large accounts than to small accounts.

Evaluate a broker's track record over at least five years and compare the rate of return earned from the broker's recommendations to the rate of return earned by the Dow-Jones average or the S&P 500 Average. If the broker's recommendations are not beating these broad market indices, then you're better off investing in a mutual fund which matches one of these indices and saving the brokerage commissions.

Reference: Rolo, Charles J. *Gaining on the Maket,* Boston: Little, Brown and Company, 1982, pp. 58–62.

However, the superior returns are only earned for the period between the announcement of the merger bid and the actual merger. Furthermore, the superior returns are only earned for firms which are successfully merged (below average returns are actually earned if the merger is unsuccessful), and the superior returns are only earned for the firm being taken over (the target firm) and not for the purchasing firm.

The Bottom Line

Research to date indicates that there are few "bargains" in the stock market. The realistic investor doesn't expect to consistently "beat the market." Instead, the realistic investor holds a diversified set of stocks and is satisfied to earn the average return of the stock market.

However, three techniques have been shown to select stocks which earn above average (risk-adjusted) rates of return: buying stocks with low P/E (price/earnings) ratios, buying stocks not followed by the large stock brokerage houses, and buying stocks of firms targeted for a takeover. In the last case, however, the above average returns are only earned for a short period of time.

7. When Does Gold Glitter?

Gold is the premiere inflation hedge. When the inflation rate is rising, investors flee bonds and the stock market for gold and real estate (real estete is discussed in the next topic). Figure 3 shows that gold prices skyrocketed precisely during those years when the inflation rate rose substantially. But in those years when inflation rates fell, gold prices plunged.

Why is gold such an inflation hedge? As with any product, the price of gold is determined by supply and demand. However, there are some unique features to the

Figure 3. Percentage changes in gold prices and inflation rate: 1970-2012

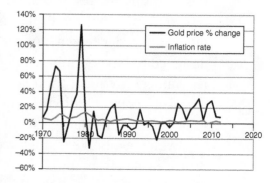

GOLD AND INFLATION

supply and demand of gold. The production of gold is relatively small and constant (South Africa and Russia are the largest producers). This means the supply of gold responds very slowly to changes in price. With respect to demand, gold has very few "productive" uses; its major use is as a speculative investment. Owning gold is viewed as a major alternative to holding currencies (paper money). Therefore, when the inflation rate is rising, meaning paper money is depreciating more rapidly, the demand for gold increases and the price skyrockets. Conversely, when the inflation rate cools, the demand for gold falls and so does its price.

**C
O
N
S
U
M
E
R**

**T
O
P
I
C**

MAKING MONEY FROM BASEBALL CARDS

Baseball cards that kids bought for pennies in the 1950s and 60s and then discarded have become hot investment properties. The investment returns of baseball cards of Hall-of-Fame players, as well as many of today's favorite players, have often out-paced other investment returns. Of course, not all baseball cards have increased in value at the same rate. Factors influencing a card's rate of return include the popu-larity of the player portrayed on the card, the year of issue, the physical condition of the card, whether the card contains an error, and whether the card is a rookie card.

Baseball cards are part of a general category of investments called collectibles. Collectibles include items like stamps, coins, art work, ceramics, rugs, and antique furniture. If a particular collectible becomes highly sought, its price can appreciate rapidly because supplies are very limited (Van Gogh isn't painting anymore!). In this way collectibles are like gold. Yet collectibles are subject to the whims of consumers. In part, baseball cards are popular today because of the 50s and 60s nostalgic craze of the "yuppies." This popularity could pass just as rapidly as it appeared.

There are other disadvantages of collectibles. Collectibles can deteriorate or be destroyed. Special efforts must be taken to care for and preserve them, and these efforts cost money. Insurance should be purchased for valuable collectibles.

The main mover of gold prices is therefore the inflation rate: when the inflation rate rises, gold prices rise, and when the inflation rate falls, gold prices fall. Gold prices are also partially influenced by interna-tional events. Any international incident which causes investors world-wide to doubt the stability of the major world currencies (particularly the dollar) will motivate investors to "flee to gold," and consequently gold prices will increase.

PURCHASING GOLD

Gold can be purchased in a number of ways: gold coins, gold certifi-cates, gold mutual funds, bullion accounts, and stock shares of mining companies. The last way is considered to be the most risky.

OTHER PRECIOUS METALS

Other precious metals, particularly silver and platinum, also serve as inflation hedges. Silver and platinum prices also rise and fall with the inflation rate.

The moral of the story is this. Investing in gold protects you against unexpected increases in the inflation rate and, to a certain extent, pro-tects you against the adverse economic effects of international crises. But the cost of this protection is high. Nothing is guaranteed with gold. You don't know what rate of return you'll earn and, furthermore, you could lose some or all of your original investment. So both rate risk and default risk are high. There is a tax advantage in that any losses you suffer from investing in gold can be used to offset capital gains from other investments, plus up to $3,000 of losses can be used to offset wages and salaries. The risks and rewards of gold are summarized in Table 9–9.

Table 9-9 Risk and rewards of gold.

Minimum denomination	$50
Term	Any
Rate of return earned	Varies
Default risk	High
Rate risk	High
Liquidity risk	High
Inflation risk	Low
Reinvestment risk	None
Tax Advantages	Losses can be used to offset other gains, plus $3,000 of losses can be used to offset wages and salaries.

The Bottom Line

Gold is the premier inflation hedge. When the inflation rate rises, gold prices rise, and when the inflation rate falls, gold prices fall. However, nothing is guaranteed with gold—neither your original investment nor the rate of return earned.

The investor following the idealistic strategy will try to buy gold just as inflation is heating up and then sell when the inflation rate has peaked and the Fed is embarked on an anti-inflation campaign. The realistic investor will always hold some gold as an investment, but never more than 15 percent of the total portfolio.

8. What Are the Returns from Real Estate?

Besides gold, the other important inflation hedge is real estate. Real estate means investments in houses (other than the one you live in), apartments, commercial buildings, and land. In most years the total return from investing in real estate exceeds the inflation rate. Real estate returns rise when the inflation rate is rising, and real estate returns fall in the years immediately following a recession.

What Do You Get from Real Estate?

There are two ways an investor can benefit from real estate. First, the investor can earn income from the property, and second, the value of the property can increase, so that when the property is sold a profit is made.

RETURN

For example, say you buy a rental house for $300,000. During the year you collect $12,000 in rent. At the end of the year you sell the rental house for $330,000. During the year you have earned a return of $12,000 in rental income and $30,000 in appreciation for a total return of $42,000.

TAX BENEFITS

There are also major tax benefits to owning real estate. The following rental expenses can be used as tax deductions. (Remember, a tax deduction doesn't reduce your taxes by the amount of the deduction, but taxes are reduced by the amount of the deduction multiplied by your tax bracket.)

1. Mortgage interest—If you have borrowed money to purchase the rental property, you can deduct the interest paid on the mortgage loan.
2. Real estate taxes—Any real estate taxes you pay on the rental property can be used as a deduction.
3. Operating expenses—Money you pay to manage or maintain the rental property can be used as a deduction. Operating expenses include things like heating and cooling costs (if paid by the owner and not the tenant), security costs, and costs of finding and screening tenants.
4. Repairs—You can deduct expenses made to repair the property and keep it in its current condition. For example, when the furnace dies or when the roof needs replacing, expenses for a new furnace and roof can be used as a deduction.
   Expenses paid to improve the property are not considered repairs and cannot be fully deducted in the year they're paid. For example, a room added to the rental property is an improvement and not a repair. Only part of the expenses for the room can be deducted each year according to depreciation rules (see below).
5. Insurance—Money spent for insurance on the property can be deducted each year.
6. Depreciation—The ability to deduct depreciation costs is a major advantage of owning rental property. Depreciation works like this. Say you buy a rental house for $100,000. The IRS says the house will wear out—that is, depreciate—over a certain length of time. The IRS therefore allows the owner of the rental property to deduct an amount each year equal to the amount by which the property depreciates that year. The IRS currently allows residential property

DEPRECIATION

to be depreciated over $27\frac{1}{2}$ years and non-residential property to be depreciated over $31\frac{1}{2}$ years. This means 3.64 percent (100/27.5) of the price you paid for a residential property can be taken as a depreciation deduction each year, and 3.17 percent (100/31.5) of the price you paid for a non-residential property can be taken as a depreciation deduction. (These percentages are subject to change by Congress.) However, only the value of the residential or nonresidential *building* can be depreciated. Land cannot be depreciated.

EXAMPLE 9-15: Susan and Sam buy a rental house for $115,000. The building is valued at $90,000 and the land at $25,000. How much can Susan and Sam deduct for depreciation each year?

ANSWER: $95,000 × .0364 = $3,458.

In some respects, depreciation is a fictitious concept. There is no reason to think that a rental unit will totally fall apart after 27 ½ years, especially if timely repairs are made. So depreciation is a big benefit (gift!) for rental property owners.

Table 9-10 shows how these deductions influence the after-tax return earned on rental property. Taxes are only paid on the difference between rental income and the sum of mortgage interest, real estate taxes, operating expenses, repairs, insurance, and depreciation. The after-tax return is rental income plus appreciation minus cash expenses (mortgage, real estate taxes, operating expenses, repairs, and insurance) and taxes. The rate of return is the after-tax return as a percentage of the investor's equity in the property.

Case A shows the rate of return calculation when the investor has little of his own money in the property, but consequently has high mortgage expenses. This is called being highly leveraged. If things go right (rental income is adequate and the property appreciates) this situation can result in a very high rate of return. But if things go bad, the leveraged investor can be left holding a large bag of debt. Case B is the opposite situation; the investor totally owns the property. Case C is a highly leveraged situation where the property has fallen in price during the year, thereby substantially lowering the investor's rate of return. Case D is discussed below.

How "Losses" Can Become Gains

Rental real estate can generate "paper losses" for the investor. This happens when, economically, the property makes money, but for tax purposes the property loses money.

Table 9-10   Alternative "Bottom Lines" for real estate.

	Case A	Case B	Case C	Case D
Beginning of year value	$100,000	$100,000	$100,000	$100,000
Investor's equity	20,000	100,000	20,000	20,000
(1) Rental income	15,000	15,000	15,000	15,000
(2) Appreciation	5,000	5,000	−1,000	5,000
(3) Mortgage interest	6,000	0	6,000	7,000
(4) Real estate taxes	3,000	3,000	3,000	3,000
(5) Operating expenses	1,000	1,000	1,000	2,000
(6) Repairs	500	500	500	1,500
(7) Insurance	500	500	500	500
(8) Depreciation (80,000 × .0364)	2,912	2,912	2,912	2,912
(9) Taxes* [.28 × (1) − (3) (4) − (5) − (6) − (7) − (8)]	304.64	1,984.64	1,90464	−535.36
(10) After-tax return [(1) + (2) − (3) − (4) − (5) − (6) − (7) − (9)]	8,695.36	13,015.36	1,015.36	6,535.36
(11) After-tax rate of return $\dfrac{(10)}{\text{Investor's Equity}}$	43.5%	13.0%	5.1%	32.7%

*Assumes a 28% tax bracket.

PAPER LOSSES

Look at Case D in Table 9-10. Economically, the property makes money because rental income and appreciation total $20,000 and cash expenses total only $14,000. But for tax purposes the investor reports only the rental income of $15,000 and reports cash expenses of $14,000 and depreciation of $2,912, for total expenses of $16,912. This means a loss for tax purposes (a "paper" loss) of $1,912. If this loss can be deducted, it will save the owner $535.36 in taxes.

Once upon a time such "paper" losses from real estate could be totally deducted. Thus, even though economically, the owner made money on the rental property, paper losses would be shown for tax purposes, and these losses could be used to actually reduce the owner's taxes. So instead of paying income taxes on the economic gains from the rental property, taxes could be reduced by owning real estate. What an investment!

LIMITATIONS ON
LOSSES

The 1986 Tax Reform Act put an end to the party, almost. Owners can deduct up to $25,000 in losses if they actively manage the rental property and their adjusted gross income is less than $100,000.[12] In order to "actively" manage the property, the owner must participate in selecting tenants, approving rental agreements, and deciding on repairs and other expenses. If the owner's adjusted gross income is between $100,000 and $150,000, the owner can also deduct losses, but the $25,000 limit is reduced by 50 percent of the amount by which adjusted gross income exceeds $100,000. No rental property losses can be deducted if the owner's adjusted gross income is greater than $150,000. These limits are up to date as of 2013.

However, all is not lost if you can't deduct all your paper rental property losses in the year they occur. When you sell the property, any losses which you haven't been able to deduct can be deducted at that time from the profits made on the sale.

Valuing Real Estate

PRESENT VALUE
AGAIN

Valuing real estate is similar to valuing stocks using the fundamental approach. The price an investor is willing to pay for a parcel of real estate equals the present value of the annual net incomes (income received minus cash expenses) plus the present value of the expected sales price when the parcel is sold. In calculating the annual net incomes, mortgage expenses are not deducted since this is only a consequence of the financing chosen for the property

This present value approach can be used in two ways. One way is to put all dollar amounts in nominal terms, and then discount using a nominal interest rate. The other way is to put all dollar amounts in real terms, and then discount using a real interest rate. This is the same choice we had with life insurance. Since predicting inflation rates are difficult, it's usually easier to use real dollars and real interest rates.

Table 9-11 gives an example of valuing a rental house. All dollar amounts are real dollars, and a real interest rate of 5 percent is used for discounting. In this example, Ben would be willing to pay $46,146 for the property.

Notice in Table 9-11 that the net incomes, in real dollars, are all the same ($2,000). In this case, the property's value can be determined in a very simple way with the following formula:

$$\text{Value} = \frac{\text{Annual Net Income}}{\text{Discount Rate}}$$

---

[12] Adjusted grass income is your total income minus certain adjustments, such as IRA deductions and alimony paid.

Table 9-11 Valuing a rental house.

Ben plans to buy a rental house, rent it, and sell it after 10 years. What will Ben offer for the house?

Year	Rental Income	Operating Expenses	Repairs	Insurance	Property Taxes	Net Income	Present Value (5% real discount rate)
1	$12,000	$5,000	$1,000	$1,000	$3,000	$2,000	$2,000 × .952 = $ 1,904
2	$12,000	$5,000	$1,000	$1,000	$3,000	$2,000	$2,000 × .907 = $ 1,814
3	$12,000	$5,000	$1,000	$1,000	$3,000	$2,000	$2,000 × .864 = $ 1,728
4	$12,000	$5,000	$1,000	$1,000	$3,000	$2,000	$2,000 × .823 = $ 1,646
5	$12,000	$5,000	$1,000	$1,000	$3,000	$2,000	$2,000 × .784 = $ 1,568
6	$12,000	$5,000	$1,000	$1,000	$3,000	$2,000	$2,000 × .746 = $ 1,492
7	$12,000	$5,000	$1,000	$1,000	$3,000	$2,000	$2,000 ×. 711 = $ 1,442
8	$12,000	$5,000	$1,000	$1,000	$3,000	$2,000	$2,000 × .677 = $ 1,354
9	$12,000	$5,000	$1,000	$1,000	$3,000	$2,000	$2,000 × .645 = $ 1,290
10	$12,000	$5,000	$1,000	$1,000	$3,000	$2,000	$2,000 × .614 = $ 1,228
							$15,446

Sales price at end of year 10: $50,000 $50,000 × .614 = $30,700

$46,146

CAPITALIZATION APPROACH

This is called the "capitalization" approach.[13] For example, using the data from Table 9-11, the property's value is:

$$\frac{\$2,000}{.05} = \$40,000.$$

The capitalization approach assumes the property will be held forever and that investors are only interested in the property for its rental income. Thus the capitalization approach doesn't allow for the investor to benefit from any property appreciation which is greater than inflation. Therefore, the present value approach is a more realistic approach, but it has the disadvantage that the investor must estimate the future sales price of the property. If this is difficult to do, then the capitalization approach can be used to give a "baseline" value for the property.

---

[13] The capitalization approach is merely a shortcut for taking the present value of a constant net incoine over an infinite number of years! When a constant value C is to be discounted and summed over an infinite number of years, the discounted present value sum turns out to simply be $\dfrac{C}{discount\,rate}$.

Not all investors will value a specific piece of real estate in the same way. Why? There are two major reasons. First, alternative investors may use the property in different ways, which in turn will produce different net incomes. For example, developer A may look at a rental building and see luxury apartments, whereas developer B may look at the same building and see student housing. Obviously, these alternative uses will produce different net incomes and different evaluations by the developers. Second, there's also a question about what discount rate to use. The greater the risk perceived for the property, the greater the discount rate used and the lower the evaluation. Again, different investors may use different discount rates, which in turn will result in different estimated values.

Risks with Real Estate

Although the returns from investing in real estate can be high, there are a number of risks associated with real estate investing.

ILLIQUIDITY

Real estate is a very illiquid asset. It may take substantial time and resources to convert a parcel of real estate to cash. Furthermore it's usually difficult to convert part of a property to cash (you can't sell off a room)—it's usually an all or nothing proposition.

Real estate investing is subject to default risk and rate risk. You can lose some or all of your investment and there's no guarantee as to the rate of return you'll earn. A major problem with real estate investing is that the investor-owner doesn't control his own destiny. What happens to surrounding properties and the surrounding neighborhood can profoundly affect your property. For example, construction of a noisy highway or factory in the immediate neighborhood of your property will likely reduce the property's value, whereas the development of new-

ZONING

parks and open spaces will increase the property's value. "Zoning" laws are used by local governments to try to control these neighborhood effects on properties. Investors in real estate should learn about the local zoning laws which relate to their property. Table 9-12 identifies important neighborhood factors which influence real estate.

How to Invest in Real Estate

The most direct way of investing in real estate is to purchase it yourself. Many people invest in real estate by owning one or two rental houses or by owning small parcels of land.

TIME COST OF
DIRECT REAL ESTATE
INVESTING

The disadvantage of this way of investing in real estate is the *time cost.* Not only must the direct real estate investor find and screen properties to purchase, but time must be devoted to managing the properties. Tenants must be found and supervised, contractors must be located to make repairs, and sometimes tedious accounting must be maintained.

Table 9-12 Neighborhood factors influencing real estate values.

Local property values are enhanced by:

• a growing local economy

• an adequale supply of fuel and water

• good municipal services

• a low crime rate

• good local schools

• compatible surrounding land uses

• accessibility to jobs, shopping, and recreation

• proximity to highways, but major highways with their noise and pollution shouldn't be too close.

Calls may be received in the middle of the night about broken plumbing or a malfunctioning furnace.

REAL ESTATE MANAGERS

One way to reduce this time cost is to hire people to manage your real estate properties. This, of course, costs money; typically real estate management firms charge a fee equal to 3 to 5 percent of rental income. Hiring a real estate management firm doesn't reduce your time costs to zero. You still must watch the management firm to make sure they're acting in your best interest.

REIT MLP

There are several indirect ways of investing in real estate. Real estate investment trusts (REITs) and master limited partnerships (MLPs) are two ways to invest in real estate without taking the time to find and manage the properties. REITs and MLPs are like stocks in that you buy shares of an investment group that is investing in real estate. The investment group makes all the selection and management decisions about the real estate. Your receive dividends based on income and capital gains generated from the real estate. The shares of REITs and MLPs can be traded on stock exchanges, so liquidity is not a problem as it is with direct real estate investing.

The major problem with REITs and MLPs is exactly their advantage—yon don't control the real estate decisions. You're entrusting your real estate investments to the decisions of others. This means that REITs and MLPs should be chosen carefully. Make sure the REIT and MLP you choose is well diversified (properties are selected from a number of cities and regions) and that the REIT and MLP management is well aware of the fundamentals influencing real estate returns (see Table 9-12).

Real Estates A Wrap-Up

Table 9-13 summarizes the risks and rewards of real estate investing. Inflation risk is very low for real estate, but other risks are high.

The Bottom Line

Real estate, like gold, is an inflation hedge. Real estate outperforms other investments when inflation is on the upswing. Real estate investing also still enjoys substantial tax advantages.

An investor who wants to "cover all the investment bases" should have some funds in real estate. Direct investment in real estate (i.e., owning a rental house) gives the most control to the owner but is also most costly in time. Indirect investing in real estate (REITs, MLPs) reduce the investor's time cost but also reduce the investor's control. _____

Table 9-13   A summary on real estate.

Minimum denomination	$1,000's
Term	Any
Rate of return earned	Varies; includes annual income and depreciation.
Liquidity risk	High for direct investment; low for investment in REITs and MLPs.
Default risk	High
Rate risk	High
Inflation risk	Low
Reinvestment risk	Low (income returns must be reinvested).
Tax Advantages	Mortgage interest and other expenses are deductible; depreciation expenses are deductible; "paper losses" can offset other income for "low" income (adjusted gross income under $100,000) investors.

9. Are the Benefits of Mutual Funds Worth Their Cost?

Mutual funds are not a type of investment. Yes, you read the sentence correctly, we said mutual funds are *not* a type of investment. Instead, mutual funds are a *way* of investing. Mutual funds can only make money for you because the managers of the fund invest in something else, such as stocks, bonds, gold, real estate, etc.

HOW MUTUAL FUNDS
WORK

Mutual funds work like this. You and other investors pool your money together. The pool is called a fund. The fund hires a professional manager who makes all the specific investment decisions—what to buy, how much to buy, and when to sell. The fund makes money from its investments. The money made by the fund is passed back to investors based on their contribution to the fund. Investors don't directly own the investments bought by the mutual fund. Instead, investors own shares in the mutual fund. But, of course, how well the mutual fund does is based on how well the fund's investments perform.

TYPES OF MUTUAL
FUNDS

There are many kinds of mutual funds. Mutual funds are distinguished by what they invest in. There are mutual funds which invest in stocks, bonds, Treasury securities, Ginnie-Mae's, gold, and real estate, to name a few. Within stocks, there are mutual funds which specialize in conservative stocks and funds which specialize in risky stocks. There are mutual funds which invest in certain sectors of the economy, which invest in certain regions of the country, and which invest in certain countries or regions of the world. There are mutual funds which invest in combinations of investments (so-called "asset-allocation" funds), and there are mutual funds which invest in a representative sample of all stocks (so-called "index" funds). In short, there is probably a mutual fund for just about every investment objective and every type of investment. The "prospectus" (pamphlet describing the fund's operations) of a mutual fund will tell you the kinds of investments the fund will buy. Legally, the fund can only do what is stated in its prospectus.

Why Invest Through a Mutual Fund?

At this point you may be confused. Why invest through a mutual fund and add a middleman (the fund manager) who must be paid? Isn't it always wise to cut out the middleman? Why not just directly invest in stocks, bonds, T-bills, gold, real estate, etc. rather than investing through a mutual fund? There are three potential benefits to mutual fund investing: less time involvement, professional management, and diversification.

1. *Less Time Involvement.* One advantage of mutual funds is that they reduce the amount of time the investor must devote to investing. The investor doesn't have to pore over volumes of information about specific stocks, bonds, or other specific kinds of investments. The managers of the fund do this. Investors don't have to struggle through information influencing when to buy and sell; again, the fund managers do this.

    However, time costs aren't reduced to zero. Investors still must decide what mutual fund shares to purchase and when to buy and when to sell,

2. *Professional Management.* With a mutual fund you buy professional management. The fund managers make all the day-to-day decisions about buying and selling. If you think professional managers can make better investment decisions than you can, then this is an advantage. If you don't think professional managers can make any better decisions (e.g., you think the stock market is "efficiently" priced), then this isn't an advantage.

Of course, if you bypass a mutual fund and directly buy investments you can still use professional management by having a stockbroker handle your investments.

3. *Broader Diversification.* You can achieve more diversification per dollar invested in a mutual fund than you can be investing that dollar directly. This happens because your dollars are combined with other investors' dollars in the mutual fund. The mutual fund has more dollars with which to purchase a wider range of investments than you could using just your own money.

But mutual funds can over-diversify. Recall from our discussion of diversification in Chapter 8 that the full benefit of diversification for stocks can be achieved with as few as 15 different stocks! The diversification benefits from mutual funds may therefore be overblown.

Why Not Invest in a Mutual Fund

All is not rosy with mutual funds. There are two big disadvantages to investing through mutual funds. Both disadvantages stem from the fact that the investor doesn't have direct control over the investments in the mutual fund.

DISTRIBUTION OF CAPITAL GAINS

1. *Taxes:* One disadvantage has to do with taxes and is most important for mutual funds investing in stocks. Recall that one advantage of investing in stocks is that, taxation of the appreciation in the stock's value—that is, taxation of the capital gain—is delayed until the stock is sold. You may initially think that the same advantage transfers to mutual funds. You may think that you won't be taxed on any appreciation in your mutual fund shares until you sell them. If you think this, then, unfortunately, you're wrong!

Each year managers of stock mutual funds usually do some selling of stocks in the fund's portfolio. When such sales are made, capital gains usually result. By law the mutual fund must distribute 90 percent of these capital gains back to the mutual fund shareholders in order to avoid having the fund taxed on the gains. The fund can "distribute" the capital gains to shareholders in three ways. One way is in cash. If this occurs, the shareholders receive the cash and taxes must be paid on the cash (makes sense, right?). A second way is that the fund keeps the cash but uses the cash to buy more shares for the shareholders. This seems OK too, except that the IRS will still make you pay taxes on the cash, even though you didn't receive it! The third way will seem the most bizarre to you. The fund can keep the capital gains cash, not buy more shares for you, but you still must pay taxes on the capital gains even though you didn't get anything!! This is called an *undistributed capital gain.* Later, however, you will get a "refund" of sorts in that when you actually sell some mutual fund shares and report a gain, you'll only pay taxes on that part of the gain which exceeds the undistributed capital gains you've already been taxed on.

UNDISTRIBUTED CAPITAL GAIN

It gets worse. If a fund distributes capital gains as cash to shareholders, it can wait until February 1 of the next year to do so. However, you still must pay taxes on this cash (which you haven't yet received) this year. Also, you will be allocated a full share of the capital gains distributions, and taxed accordingly, regardless of when you buy the mutual fund shares during the year.

Last, recall that when selling stocks directly, if you sell at a loss you can use those losses to offset other capital gains and sometimes to offset some of your wage and salary income. There's no such deal

CONSUMER TOPIC

INVESTMENT CLUBS

There's an alternative to investing on your own or investing with the advice of a broker or newsletter. The alternative is an investment club. An investment club is simply a group of "average" investors who make decisions together about buying and selling investments. Members of the investment club investigate individual investments and then make recommendations about buying or selling. Recommendations are voted on by the club members. Most investment clubs deal only with stocks.

An advantage of investment clubs is time. Each club member studies a limited number of stocks and shares the information with other club members. Club members therefore spend much less time on investment decisions than if they invested on their own. Another advantage of investment clubs is that they're not subject to the potential pressure from brokers to rapidly turn over their portfolio and run up large commissions. Studies show that investment clubs hold their stocks twice as long as individual investors.

One possible disadvantage of investment clubs is that they may encourage a "beat the market" attitude. Before joining an investment club, evaluate its average returns compared to the risks taken over a long period of time.

Reference: "Secrets of Successful Investment Clubs," *Changing Times*, February 1990, pp. 83–87.

with mutual funds. Any capital losses suffered by the mutual fund managers are not passed on to shareholders. You can only deduct capital losses if they occur when you sell some mutual fund shares (e.g., you sell a share for less than what you bought it at).

2. *Selling Mutual Fund Shares.* Another disadvantage of mutual funds arises when you want to sell some shares. To illustrate the problem, we must contrast to the situation where you directly own the investment.

Say you own 100 shares of WALDENCO stock which you bought in 2009 at $50 a share and another 100 shares which you bought in 2012 at $75 a share. Today WALDENCO sells at $100 a share and you want to sell 100 shares. Which 100 shares should you sell? For tax purposes, you want to sell the 2012 shares because then you'll only have to report a gain of $25 a share.

Generally, you don't have this flexibility in selling mutual fund shares. You either must assume that the shares sold are the first shares you bought (the first-in, first-out method), or you use the average purchase price of all shares owned. In the previous example, if WALDENCO were a mutual fund, the first-in, first-out method would mean that the first shares sold would be the 2009 shares ($50 a share). Alternatively, the first shares sold could be assumed to have a price of $62.50 (($50 + $75)/2).

FIRST-IN, FIRST-OUT METHOD

3. *Marking-to-Market:* This is a disadvantage for mutual funds which buy bonds, Treasury securities (notes and bonds) and Ginnie Mae's. In describing this problem we'll use the example of a bond mutual fund.

You already know the relationship between the price of a bond and market interest rates. When market interest rates rise, existing bonds become less valuable and their prices fall. In contrast, when market interest rates fell, the prices of existing bonds increase.

This fluctuation in the price of an existing bond matters most if you sell a bond before it matures. However, if you keep a bond until it matures you receive the face value for the bond. So if you buy a bond directly, you always know that you'll receive back the bond's face value if you hold it until maturity.

Again, not so with a bond fund. The managers of a bond mutual fund are required to each day price the fund *as if* all of the fund's bonds were sold that day. This is called "marking to market." This means changes in market interest rates will always have an impact on the value of shares in a bond mutual fund. So there's no such thing as holding a bond mutual fund until it matures. Owners of bond mutual funds must always worry about the potential for rising interest rates to reduce the value of their investment. The longer the average term of the bonds in the mutual fund's portfolio, the greater is this potential risk. To reduce this risk, buy bond and related funds with short maturities.

So mutual funds have some advantages, but they also have some big disadvantages (Table 9-14 summarizes these pluses and minuses). For the investor who wants to control his own destiny, the minuses probably outweigh the pluses.

Table 9-14   Pluses and minuses of mutual funds.

PLUSES

Less time involvement

Professional management

Broader diversification

MINUSES

Taxes on annual capital gains, whether received or not

Less flexibility in identifying shares for sale.

Higher interest rates immediately reduce value of bond-type funds.

Mutual Fund Costs

You don't get the professional management and the buying and selling of investments through mutual funds for no cost. Mutual funds charge LOADS a variety of seemingly confusing fees. The fees are also referred to as "loads."

The fees charged by mutual funds can be grouped into three types: (1) fees charged when you buy mutual fund shares (so-called "front end" fees), (2) fees charged when you sell mutual fund shares (so-called "back-end" fees), and (3) fees charged each year (called marketing and management fees). So mutual funds can get you coming, going, and in-between.

"NO-LOAD" FUNDS Don't be misled by advertisements for "no-load" funds. A no-load fund is a fund which does not charge a front-end fee. However, the fund can still charge a back-end fee and annual fees.

A problem for the mutual fund investor is how to compare fund fees and decide which fund has the lowest set of fees. For example, suppose PROFIT PLUS Fund has a front-end fee of 8 percent, a back-end fee of 2 percent, and no annual fees, whereas UNLIMITED Fund has a 1 percent front-end fee, but has a back-end fee of 5 percent and an annual fee of 4 percent. It's not obvious which fee structure is cheaper.

READING THE FINANCIAL PAGES

At first glance, the financial pages of any local newspaper or of the *Wall Street Journal* may appear to be overwhelming. However, if you will make a small investment of time in learning how to read the financial pages, the rewards in understanding the financial markets and national economy can be great.

The financial pages are arranged into several sections representing the different financial markets and types of investments: the New York Stock Exchange (NYSE), the American Stock Exchange (AMEX), the over-the-counter market (OTG), bonds, mutual funds (MUTUALS), and earnings reports.

In the New York Stock Exchange listing, for example, stocks are listed by their abbreviated name. However, since the listings are alphabetized by the actual company name, the abbreviations may not be in alphabetical order.

For each stock listed on the NYSE, six pieces of information are listed:

- P-E is the price-earnings ratio. This is determined by dividing the price per share by the annual earnings per share, Many investors use the P-E ratio as an investment guide, purchasing stocks with low P-E's and selling those with high P-E's.
- Three prices are then shown—the high and the low price per share paid for the stock in the previous 12 months, and the closing price for the stock on the previous trading day.
- Finally, the change in the price of the stock over the previous trading day is shown. Note that price is shown in dollars and fractions of dollars. To convert these fractions, use 1/8 = 12.5 cents; 1/4 = 25 cents; 3/8 = 37.5 cents; 1/2 = 50 cents; 3/4 = 75 cents and 7/8 = 87.5 cents.

Sometimes the stock abbreviation will have a symbol next to it. Symbols are explained at the bottom of the page listing the NYSE stocks. There are similar listings for the other stock exchanges.

Typical information for bonds includes the following:

- Rate is the stated interested rate specified when the bond was issued.
- Mat. Date is the date when the bond matures.
- Bid is the dollars per $100 of the bond's face value that a broker will pay to buy the bond. The numbers to the right of the decimal point are fractions of 32nds. So, .23 means 23/32 or .72, 99.23 means a $100 bond can be sold for $99.72.
- Asked is the percent of the bond's face value that you have to pay to buy the bond from a broker. The asked price will always be higher than the bid price to account for the broker's commission.
- Yield is yield to maturity.

C O N S U M E R   T O P I C

C
O
N
S
U
M
E
R

T
O
P
I
C

Mutual fund information is grouped under the fund's "family name." The "family name" is just the investment group which offers the fund. For each fund is listed its net asset value (NAV), which is the share price received when the fund is sold, the offer price, which is the share price, paid when the fund is bought, and the change in the NAV from the previous day. The difference between the offer price and the NAV is the broker's take. If the fund is "N.L.," then the NAV and offer price are the same.

Earnings reports show how a company has done over both the recent quarter and the year to date, The most important information listed here is the net income (or profit) per share.

References: Wurman, R. S., Alan Siegel, and Kenneth M. Morris, *The Wall Street Journal Guide to Understanding Money and Markets,* N.Y Access Press Ltd.

Greenleaf, James, Ruth Foster, and Robert Prinsky. *Understanding Financial Data in The Wall Street Journal,* Princeton, NJ. Dow Jones & Company, Inc.

The solution is simple. Just convert all fees to an annual fee, and then just compare two numbers! How do you do this? Again, our future value and present value factor tables come to the rescue. To turn a front-end fee into an annual fee, *divide* the front end fee by the *present value factor sum* associated with the number of years you expect to be invested in the fund and the expected annual interest rate earned on the fund (Why does this work? You're doing the same thing you did to calculate mortgage payments for a home loan.) To turn a back-end fee into an annual fee, *divide* the back-end fee by the *future value facter sum* associated with the number of years you expect to be invested in the fund and the expected annual interest rate earned on the fund. In implementing this procedure, you'll generally want to use the same interest rate and same holding period for the funds being compared. Here then, are five steps to follow in comparing the fee structures of mutual funds.

STEPS	EXAMPLE		
1. Identify the fees of the two funds.	PROFITPLUS FUND		UNLIMITED FUND
	Front-end	8%	1%
	Back-end	3%	5%
	Annual	0%	4%
2. Select an interest rate and holding period.	Use a 6% interest rate and 6 year holding period.		

Continued on next page

STEPS	EXAMPLE
3. Convert the front-end fee to an annual fee.	
(a) Calculate the present value factor sum associated with interest rate and holding period	From Appendix Table A-4, the sum of the PV factors for 6% and years 1 to 6 is: 0.943 + 0.890 + 0.840 + 0.792 + 0.747 + 0.705 = 4.917

(b) Divide the front-end fee by the present value factor sum.

PROFITPLUS FUND
8%/4.917 = 1.63%

UNLIMITED FUND
1%/4.917 = 0.20%

4. Convert the back-end fee to an annual fee.

(a) Calculate the future value factor sum associated with interest rate and holding period.

From Appendix Table A-1, the sum of the FV factors for 6% and years 1 to 6 is: 1.060 + 1.124 + 1.191 + 1.262 + 1.338 + 1.419 = 7.394

(b) Divide the back-end fee, by the future value factor sum.

PROFITPLUS FUND
3%/7.394 = 0.41%

UNLIMITED FUND
5%/7.394 = 0.68%

5. Add the annualized front-end fee, the annualized back-end fee, and the annual fee to get a total annualized fee.

1.63 + 0.41% + 0% = 2.04%.

0.20%+ 0.68%+ 4% = 4.88%.

The fund with the lowest total annualized fee has the cheaper fee structure.

PROFITPLUS FUND has the cheaper fee structure.

The holding period has a very important effect on the total annualized cost of a fund's fee structure. The longer the holding period, the relatively more important becomes the fund's annual fee in the total annualized cost. EXAMPLE 9-16 illustrates this by reworking the comparison between PROFITPLUS FUND and UNLIMITED FUND for a 12 year holding period.

EXAMPLE 9-16: Recalculate the total annualized costs of the fee structures of PROFITPLUS FUND and UNLIMITED FUND using a 12-year holding period.

ANSWER: Present value factor sum for 6% and 12 years (from Appendix Table A-4) :

9.943 + 0.890 + 0.840 + 0.792 + 0.747 + 0.705 + 0.665 + 0.627 + 0.592 + 0.558 + 0.527 + 0.497 = 8.383

Annualized front end fee

PROFITPLUS FUND: 8%/8.383 = 0.95%
UNLIMITED FUND: 1%/8.383 = 0.12%

Future value factor sum for 6% and 12 years (from Appendix Table A-l) :

1.060 + 1.124 + 1.191 + 1.262 + 1.338 + 1.419 + 1.504 + 1.594 + 1.689 + 1.791 + 1.898 + 2.012 = 17.882

Annualized back-end fee   PROFITPLUS FUND: 3%/17.882 = 0.17%

UNLIMITED FUND: 5%/17.882 = 0.28%

Total annualized fee   PROFITPLUS FUND: 0.95% + 0.17% +

0% = 1.12%

UNLIMITED FUND: 0.12% + 0.28% +

4 = 4.40%

The PROFITPLUS FUND is still cheaper, but now the UNLIMITED FUND is almost four times as costly.

Evaluating Mutual Funds

Like other investments, mutual funds should be evaluated on the basis of their returns and risk. Fortunately, we can apply the same measure of risk and return to mutual funds as to other investments.

Returns to stock mutual funds are best measured by the dividends and capital gains earned per share, just as with an individual stock. Returns to bond mutual funds are best measured by the fund's "yield to maturity," and fortunately new federal laws require bond funds to use this measure in their advertising. Returns to money market mutual funds, which invest in short-term CDs and Treasury bills, are measured simply by the average interest rate earned.

The risk of any mutual fund can be measured by the standard deviation in its return. For stock mutual funds, beta values can be calculated.

In evaluating the risks and returns of mutual funds, use calculations that are averaged over a number of years (5 to 10), and not just the most recent year. You should be interested in the long run performance of a fund. It shouldn't be surprising that risk and return move together for mutual funds just as for individual investments.

Dorf recommends calculating a "risk-adjusted return" for stock mutual funds.[14] The risk-adjusted return (AR) is:

$$AR = \frac{R - R_f}{b}, \text{ where}$$

R   = fund's actual return

R_f = a risk-free return, such as the interest earned on a Treasury bill.

b   = fund's beta.

Dorf recommends choosing funds with higher AR values.

---

[14]Dorf, Richard C. *The New Mutual Fund Investment Advisor,* Probus, Chicago, 1986, p. 88.

EXAMPLE 9-17: Use the following data for PROFITPLUS FUND and UNLIMITED FUND to calculate the funds' AR values and to choose between the funds.

	Return	Beta
PROFITPLUS	25.6%	1.4
UNLIMITED	16.7%	0.7
Treasury bill	7.0%	—

ANSWER:

$$\text{PROFITPLUS AR} = \frac{25.6 - 7.0}{1.4} = 13.3\%$$

$$\text{UNLIMITED AR} = \frac{16.7 - 7.0}{0.7} = 13.9\%$$

By the AR measure, the UNLIMITED FUND gives a slightly higher risk-adjusted return.

A problem with the risk-adjusted return measure is that it assumes the tradeoff between risk and return is always the same whatever the level of risk. However, it's likely that as risk increases, investors require increasing amounts of return as compensation.

Some Specific Funds

Money market mutual funds (MMMFs) have been mentioned several times. MMMFs are short-term, liquid investments which earn a floating interest rate and which can be used as a checking account.

MMMFs invest funds in safe, short-term investments, such as T-bills, commercial paper (short-term corporate debt), and bank CDs. MMMFs operate on a mutual fund principle: the money of investors is pooled to purchase a set of investments; each investor owns shares of all the investments rather than a specific investment security. The pooling of money allows many individuals to invest in securities which would effectively be closed to them due to their high minimum deposits (for example, the minimum deposit for a Treasury bill is $ 10,000).

LIQUID
INVESTMENTS

The short term nature (e.g., 30 to 60 day average term to maturity) of the MMMFs investments allows MMMFs to permit investors to add and withdraw funds at will. Therefore, MMMFs are perfectly liquid investments. In fact, most MMMFs provide checks to investors which can be used to withdraw money subject to minimal withdrawal

FLOATING RATE

amounts (e.g., $250, $500). The short maturity of MMMF investments also means that the rate of return paid on MMMFs is a floating rate. MMMFs are constantly buying new investments as existing investments mature. In general, the rate of return on MMMFs follows market rates with a lag equal to the MMMFs average term to maturity. For most MMMFs this lag is 30 to 60 days. Thus, if market interest rates are rising, MMMF rates will correspondingly rise with a 30 to 60 day lag; conversely, if market interest rates are falling, MMMF rates will correspondingly fall with a 30 to 60 day lag.

The required minimum deposit on MMMFs varies from $1 to $10,000. Most MMMFs require an initial deposit in the $250 to $5,000 range. However, the initial deposit is generally higher than the balance required to be on deposit anytime after opening the account.

DEFAULT RISK Since the rate of return earned on MMMFs is a floating rate, MMMFs are not subject to inflation risk. However, *default* risk is a consideration for MMMFs. In general, MMMFs have low default risk. Specifically though, MMMFs are as safe as their purchased securities. With respect to the purchased securities, T-bills are riskless; hence, MMMFs which have a greater percentage of their investments in T-bills are relatively safer. Commercial paper is a relatively safe investment, although the potential investor in MMMFs may wish to examine the names of the corporate issuers of the commercial paper bought by the MMMF. Similarly bank CDs are relatively safe investments, although such CDs are generally in amounts greater than $100,000 and therefore do not carry federal insurance. Again, the potential investor in MMMFs may want to examine the names of the banks issuing the CDs bought by the MMMF.

Why might an MMMF fail? The most likely reason has to do with the comparison of the rate of return earned on the MMMF and the market rate of return. MMMFs can "get into trouble" if they extend their term to maturity to such a point that their rate of return changes far less rapidly than the rate of return on competing funds. Such a circumstance could occur if a particular MMMF thought that interest rates were going to fall in the future and the MMMF wanted to "lock-in" a higher rate of return for a longer period of lime. However, if in fact market interest rates rose, then the MMMF would be at a competitive disadvantage. As a result, investors would have an incentive to withdraw funds from the MMMF and invest in competing MMMFs, thereby creating a "run" on the MMMF. Such a "run" could force the MMMF into an insolvent position.

MONEY MARKET DEPOSIT ACCOUNTS MMMFs should not be confused with money market deposit accounts (MMDAs) offered at banks, S&Ls, and credit unions. The two investments are similar in that they're both short-term, variable rate accounts whose interest rates rise and fall with market conditions. However, MMDAs are usually federally insured whereas MMMFs aren't. Consequently, MMMFs usually pay higher interest rates than money market deposit accounts.

CONSUMER TOPIC

HOW MUCH EMERGENCY CASH SHOULD YOU KEEP?

You should always keep some cash in a safe, liquid investment for emergencies. This investment might be a bank savings account, a bank money market deposit account, or a broker's money market mutual fund.

But how much cash should you set aside for emergencies? A typical "rule of thumb" says to keep an emergency fund equal to three to six months of your take-home pay. But financial planner, Michael Leonetti, says this rule of thumb may not be adequate. Like most rules of thumb, it's simple, but it may result in too much or not enough emergency cash.

Leonetti recommends a more complicated, yet more adequate, way of determining your emergency cash needs. First, recognize that your need for emergency cash comes from four unpleasant and unforeseen situations:

1. You become disabled and you must live off your emergency cash until your disability policy benefits begin;
2. You lose your job, and you need emergency cash to supplement money you receive from unemployment compensation until a new job is found;
3. You have a major medical or property loss and you need emergency cash to pay the deductible and coinsurance rate on your policy, or;
4. A major household appliance or piece of equipment not covered by a warranty needs replacing, or a major repair to your home is necessary, and emergency cash must cover the expense.

Leonetti recommends that you evaluate the "worst case" for each of these four situations and determine how much emergency cash would be needed. In the case of disability, the emergency cash needed will be directly related to the waiting period of the disability insurance policy. In the case of unemployment, Leonetti says to plan for a year of unemployment. Recognize that unemployment compensation benefits from the state will usually last only 20 weeks and return 36 percent of your income. To find your emergency cash needs, take the highest of the cash needed for disability or unemployment and add to it the cash needed to pay medical deductibles and co-insurance and household equipment disasters. The table illustrates these calculations with an example.

1. *Disability*—Joe's policy begins 6 months after disability. Joe's expenses are 70% of his salary, Joe's monthly salary is \$3000. He needs 70% of this for 6 months = \$3000 × .7 × 6 = \$12,600.
2. *Unemployment*—If unemployed for a year, Joe's expenses are 70% of his salary (\$36,000 × .70 = \$25,200). Unemployment benefits will pay 36% of Joe's salary for 20 weeks (5 months). \$3,000 ×.36 × 5 =\$5,400.

   Joe needs \$25,200 − \$5,400 = \$19,800 to cover unemployment for a year.

C O N S U M E R   T O P I C

3. Joe has a $500 medical deductible and a 10% co-insurance rate with a $1000 cap.

   Joe needs $1,500.

   Joe has a $500 deductible on his auto insurance.

   Joe needs $500.

   Joe has a $250 deductible on his house insurance.

   Joe needs $250.

4. The "worst-case" household appliance/equipment to need replacement would be the heating/cooling system at $5,000.

   Joe needs $5000.

   Total emergency cash needs:

Unemployment (since it is more than disability)	$19,800
Insurance	2,250
Heating/cooling system	5,000
	$27,050

   (75% of annual income of $36,000)

Reference: Leonetti, Michael. "Liquidity: How Much Cash Should You Have on Hand." *American Association of Individual Investors Journal*, Vol. 10, No. 9, October 1988, pp. 22–24.

In short, MMMFs are an excellent way to provide the investor with a relatively safe, liquid, floating rate investment. Such investments are preferred when the inflation rate is rising. Currently, stock brokerage houses are the main marketers of MMMFs, although some insurance companies and banks (via their trust departments) have also gotten into the field.

OPEN-END FUND, CLOSED-END FUND

When examining mutual funds, you may run into a comparison between *open-end funds* and *closed-end funds*. Open-end funds are funds which stand ready to always issue new shares. That is, the fund can expand beyond its initial offering. Also, the value of a share in an open-end fund always equals the net assets value of the fund. That is, the value of a share in an open-end fund is totally dependent on the fund's investments.

In contrast, a closed-end mutual fund is a fund which will sell no additional new shares after the initial offering. Of course, existing shares can still be traded between investors. However, unlike an open-end fund, a closed-end fund can take on a life of its own. That is, the value of a share of a closed-end fund will not necessarily equal the net assets value of the fund. Why? If investors think the closed-end fund's investments will perform very well in the future, higher demand for the fund's shares will push the share's value up in anticipation of the investments' good performance. Conversely, if investors think the closed-end fund's investments will perform poorly in the future, lower demand for the fund's shares will push the fund's shares down in anticipation of the investments' bad performance. Closed-end funds therefore have an extra element of risk as compared to open-end funds.

INDEX FUNDS

Stock index mutual funds are favorites of investors who believe the stock market is efficient (meaning stocks can't be consistently selected that give above average risk-adjusted returns). Stock index funds hold a representative sample of the entire stock market. Stock index funds are therefore designed to give the investor the average return yielded by the stock market, no more and no less!

UNIT INVESTMENT TRUSTS

Unit investment trusts are offered by brokerage houses as a way to avoid the relatively high required minimum deposits of some investments (e.g., Treasury bills, Ginnie Mae's, some bonds). Essentially the brokerage house subdivides the Treasury bill, bond, or Ginnie Mae's into smaller units and sells those units to investors.

So far unit investment trusts sound very much like mutual funds. But there's one big difference. Unit investment trusts don't have to be "marked to market." This is very important for bond unit investment trusts. A unit investment trust will always hold its investments to maturity. For unit investment trusts investing in bonds, this means you're guaranteed getting $1000 back at maturity for every $1000 invested. Bond mutual funds can't make this guarantee because they are constantly "marked to market."

EXCHANGE-TRADED FUNDS (ETFS)

An exchange-traded fund, commonly referred to as an ETF, is an investment fund traded on stock exchanges. An ETF combines the valuation feature of a mutual fund or unit investment trust with tradability feature of a closed-end fund. Like a mutual fund, ETFs hold many assets such as stocks and bonds, but unlike mutual funds, shares of ETFs are not bought from the company, but are bought and sold like stocks in the secondary markets. ETFs have become extremely popular over the years because they generally provide the easy diversification, low expense ratios, and tax efficiency of mutual funds, while still maintaining all the features of ordinary stock trading such as different types of orders and options.

How Mutual Funds Measure Up

Wow! That was a lot of information about mutual funds. How can we sum up? We can't really put up a summary "risk and return" table as we did for other investments because mutual funds are so varied and diverse.

Probably the best point to address is whether an investor should invest directly or via mutual funds. The biggest "plus" for mutual funds is the built-in management and built-in diversity. For example, $1000 put in a stock mutual fund will be spread into many more stocks than $1000 invested directly in the stock market. If you think particular managers can make better choices than you can, then this is a bonus too. However, counterbalancing these pluses is the fact that the investor gives up control and loses some tax advantages regarding capital gains distributions. Also, the investor always faces inflation risk in bond-type mutual funds, whereas this risk can be "ridden out" with direct investing in bonds if the bonds are held to maturity.

The Bottom Line

Mutual funds are a way of investing, not a type of investment. Mutual funds pool your money with other investors' monies and use professional managers to make day-to-day investment decisions. Almost anything anywhere can be bought via a mutual fund, although each fund will put limits on its investments and operations.

If you want professional management and greater diversity than you can achieve on your own, then mutual funds are for you. However, mutual funds have their faults. You don't call the shots; the professional managers do, although you can always sell your shares in the fund. You don't have control over when you receive capital gains with a mutual fund as you do with direct investing. Bond mutual funds must be constantly "marked to market." With a bond mutual fund, you have no guarantee that you'll receive back the face values of the bonds when they mature as you do with direct investing.

10. How Can You Save for Your Child's Education?

In today's society, attending college is almost a necessity if the individual is to earn a high salary (remember the wage differentials based on education discussed in Chapter 1). Most parents plan to have their children attend college. According to the College Board, in 2012-2013, the average tuition and fees was $17,860 for 4-year public in-state colleges and $30,911 for out-of-state colleges. Tuition and fees at private colleges average about $40,000. Furthermore, college costs have been rising faster than the inflation rate. Of course, inflation will push these costs even higher in future years.

Given the substantial costs for college, most parents will want to begin saving for their children's college education far in advance of when the children will attend college. This gives rise to two important questions: (1) how much must be saved each year so that your child can attend the college of his/her choice in the future, and (2) what investments are best suited for this college saving?

How Much Must Be Saved: The Typical Approach

The typical approach followed by investment counselors and financial planners in calculating required educational savings is, first, calculate what college will cost in the future and, second, calculate how much must be saved each year to accumulate the required money for college. In making these calculations, assumptions must be made about the inflation rate for college costs and the interest rate earned on the money invested for college.

To implement this procedure, three steps are followed:

1. Using the assumed college cost inflation rate, calculate future college costs.
2. Calculate the present value of college costs at the point that the child will enter college. Use the assumed investment interest rate as the discount rate. This converts the college costs to a lump sum amount.
3. Using the lump sum amount of college costs from step (2), calculate the annual amounts needed to be saved in order to accumulate the lump sum amount. This is done by dividing the lump sum amount by the sum of annual future value factors associated with the interest rate earned and the number of years over which saving will be done. EXAMPLE 9-18 illustrates this approach.

EXAMPLE 9-18: Marjorie and Jim eventually want to send their newborn daughter, Beth, to Excelsior College. Today Excelsior College costs $18,000 annually. Marjorie and Jim expect Excelsior College's costs to increase 6 percent annually. How much must Marjorie and Jim save each year for 18 years in order to fund four years of college at Excelsior if they can earn 8 percent (after-taxes) on their savings?

ANSWER:
1. Calculate future college costs:
   In year 19: $18,000 × future value factor, 6%,
   19 yrs. = $18,000 × 3.026 = $54,468.
   In year 20: $18,000 × future value factor, 6%,
   20 yrs. = $18,000 × 3.207 = $57,726.
   In year 21: $18,000 × future value factor, 6%,
   21 yrs. = $18,000 × 3.400 = $61,200.
   In year 22: $18,000 × future value factor, 6%,
   22 yrs. = $18,000 × 3.604 = $64,872.

2. Calculate the present value of college costs at the beginning of year 19 using the investment rate of 8 percent as the discount rate. We'll

assume the first year's amount will be needed immediately, so begin discounting with year 2.

$54,208 × 1.00		=	$ 54,468
57,726 × 0.926 (PV factor, 8%, yr 1)		=	53,454
61,200 × 0.857 (PV factor, 8%, yr 2)		=	52,448
64,872 × 0.794 (PV factor, 8%, yr 3)		=	51,508
		TOTAL =	$211,878

3. Calculate the annual amounts to save in order to accumulate $211,878 in 18 years. To do this, divide $211,878 by the sum of the future value factors associated with 8 percent (the interest rate earned on the savings) and years 1 to 18.

Future value factor sum = 1.080 + 1.166 + 1.260 + 1.360 + 1.469 + 1.587 + 1.714 + 1.851 + 1.999 + 2.159 + 2.332 + 2.518 + 2.720 + 2.937 + 3.172 + 3.426 + 3.700 + 3.996 = 40.446

$$\text{Annual amount to save} = \frac{\$211,878}{40.446} = \$5,238.54$$

If Marjorie and Jim save $5,238.54 each year for 18 years and earn 8 percent (after taxes) on the savings, they will accumulate enough to fund four years at Excelsior College assuming college costs rise 6 percent annually.

PROBLEMS WITH TYPICAL APPROACH

There are three problems with this approach. First, parents must forecast the average inflation rate for college costs. As you've already learned, forecasting inflation rates for any product or service is difficult and hazardous. If the inflation rate for college costs is underestimated, too little savings will be done and college expenses won't be met. Second, parents must forecast the average interest rate earned on investments. Again, you've learned how difficult it is to forecast interest rates. Third, the approach results in the same dollar amount being saved each year. Since parents' income will likely rise over time with inflation, this means the burden of college saving will be highest in the early years of saving and then decline.

How Much Must Be Saved: An Alternative Approach

An alternative approach to calculating college savings overcomes each of these problems. The benefit of the approach is that parents don't have to project college cost inflation rates or investment interest rates; instead, only the difference between the two must be projected. Then, after an initial annual amount to save is calculated, that amount is increased each year by the *actual* inflation rate occurring in college costs.

The alternative approach has three steps.

1. Using current college costs, calculate the lump sum amount needed at the start of college in order to fund total college expenses. The lump sum amount is calculated as follows:

   (a) If the college cost inflation rate is assumed to equal the investment interest rate, then use the current annual cost of college multiplied by the number of years in college (e.g., 4).

   (b) If the investment interest rate is assumed to be greater than the college cost inflation rate, then use the current annual cost of college multiplied by the sum of the present value factors over the number of years of college and associated with the difference between the interest rate earned and the college cost inflation rate.

   (c) If the college cost inflation rate is assumed to be greater than the investment interest rate, then use the current annual cost of college multiplied by the sum of the future value factors over the number of years of college and associated with the difference between the college cost inflation rate and the investment interest rate.

Before moving on to the second step, let's quickly illustrate this first step with an example.

EXAMPLE 9-19: Consider Excelsior College again with its $18,000 current annual cost Calculate the lump sum amount needed to fund four years of college, assuming:

(a) the college cost inflation rate equals the investment interest rate,
(b) the investment interest rate exceeds the college cost inflation rate by 2 percentage points,
(c) the college cost inflation rate exceeds the investment interest rate by 2 percentage points.

ANSWER: (a) $18,000 × 4 = $72,000.

(b) Again assume the first year's expenses are needed at the beginning of the year, so begin discounting with the second year:

$18,000 × (1.000 + 0.980 + 0.961 + 0.942) = $69,894.

(c) $18,000 × (1.000 + 1.020 + 1.040 + 1.061) = $74,178.

2. Convert the lump sum amount to an initial annual amount to save. How this is done again depends on the relationship between the college cost inflation rate and the investment interest rate:

(a) If the college cost inflation rate equals the investment interest rate, simply divide the lump sum amount by the number of years before college begins.

(b) If the investment interest rate exceeds the college cost inflation rate, divide the lump sum amount by the future value factor sum associated with the difference between the two rates and the number of years before college. Future value factors are used because, with the investment rate exceeding the inflation rate, a dollar today will yield more than a dollar in purchasing power tomorrow.

(c) If the college cost inflation rate exceeds the investment interest rate, divide the lump sum amount by the present value factor sum associated with the difference between the two rates and the number of years before college. Present value factors are used because, with the inflation rate exceeding the investment rate, a dollar today will yield less than a dollar of purchasing power tomorrow.

Let's illustrate this step by continuing our example.

EXAMPLE 9-18 CONTINUED

(a) If the college cost inflation rate and investment interest rate are equal, then take the $72,000 from step 1 and divide by 18:

$$\frac{\$72,000}{18} = \$4,000. \text{ This is the amount to save in yr. 1}$$

(b) If the investment interest rate exceeds the college cost inflation rate by 2 percentage points, then sum the future value factors under 2 percent for years 1 to 18:

(1.020 + 1.040 + 1.061 + 1.082 + 1.104 + 1.126 + 1.149 + 1.172 + 1.195 + 1.219 + 1.243 + 1.268 + 1.294 + 1.319 + 1.346 + 1.373 + 1.400 + 1.428) = 21.839

$$\frac{\$69,894}{21.839} = \$3,200.42. \text{ This is the amount to save in yr. 1}$$

(c) If the college cost inflation rate exceeds the investment interest rate by 2 percentage points, then sum the present value factors under 2 percent for year 1 to 18:

(0.980 + 0.961 + 0.942 + 0.924 + 0.906 + 0.888 + 0.871 + 0.853 + 0.837 + 0.820 + 0.804 + 0.788 + 0.773 + 0.758 + 0.743 + 0.728 + 0.714 + 0.700) = 14.99.

$$\frac{\$74,178}{14.99} = \$4,948.50. \text{ This is the amount to save in yr. 1}$$

Step 3 is to simply increase the annual amount to save by the actual percentage increase in college costs each year. For example, if college costs actually increase by *6 percent* annually, then the amounts to save are:

	(a) College cost inflation rate = investment interest rate	(b) Investment interest rate — college inflation rate = 2% pts.	(c) College cost cost inflation rate — investment int. rate = 2% pts.
Year 1	$ 4,000.00	$3,200.42	$ 4,948.50
2	4,240.00	3,992.45	5,245.41
3	4,494.40	3,595.99	5,560.13
4	4,764.06	3,811.75	5,893.74
5	5,049.91	4,040.46	6,247.37
6	5,352.90	4,282.88	6,622.21
7	5,674.08	4,539.86	7,019.54
8	6,014.52	4,812.25	7,440.71
9	6,375.39	5,100.98	7,887.16
10	6,757.92	5,407.04	8,360.39
11	7,163.39	5,731.46	8,862.01
12	7,593.19	6,075.35	9393.73
13	8,048.79	6,439.87	9,957.35
14	8,531.71	6,826.27	10,554.79
15	9,043.62	7,235.84	11,188.08
16	9,586.23	7,669.99	11,859.36
17	10,161.41	8,130.19	12,570.93
18	10,771.09	8,618.01	13325.18

Notice the difference in the amounts to save among the three possibilities compared. This illustrates how very important it is to consider the relationship between the inflation rate in college costs and the investment rate. Compare also the results for situation (b) to the result for EXAMPLE 9-18, where a constant $5,238.54 is saved each year. In situation (b) a constant percentage of income will be saved as long as income rises at the same rate as college costs rise.

How to Save for a College Education

SAVING FOR COLLEGE

Savings and investing for a college education can be implemented just like any other investment program. Any type of investment can be used. The parent-investor faces all the same investment decisions and trade-offs, such as how much risk to take to get a higher rate of return, how to allocate money among the different types of investments, and whether to try to "beat" the business cycle or just stay and hold.

One of the best ways to increase the affordability of your child's education is to take advantage of federal tax breaks aimed at families saving and paying for college. These include the following:

1. Qualified Tuition Programs (529 plans). 529 plans are sponsored by states, state agencies, or educational institutions, and are authorized by Section 529 of the Internal Revenue Code. Earnings in 529 plans grow tax-deferred and distributions are tax-free when used for qualified post-secondary education costs. In addition to state-tax benefits, some states offer state tax breaks as well.

2. Coverdell Education Savings Accounts (ESAs)—Earnings grow tax-deferred and distributions are tax-free when used for qualified post-secondary education cots. ESAs may also be withdrawn tax-free for primary and secondary school expenses. The annual contribution limit for a beneficiary is $2,000 per year. The limit is gradually phased out with incomes between $190,000 and $220,000 in 2013.

4. Individual Retirement Accounts—Early withdrawal penalties are waived when Roth IRAs and traditional IRAs are used to pay the qualified post-secondary education costs of yourself, your spouse, your children, or your grandchildren. (Taxes may still be due on the withdrawals, however.)

5. You can put investments in the child's name. Tax law allows children under certain age to earn investment interest tax-free up to a certain limit. The limit may change over time and the rules are somewhat complicated. In any event, it might make sense to put college investment money in the child's name so the child will have some investment income for college expenses tax-free.

6. American Opportunity tax credit—Through 2017, a parent may claim a tax credit for 100% of the first $2,000 and 25% of the next $2,000, of a dependent child's college tuition and mandatory fees, for a maximum of $2,500 annual tax credit per child. Students may claim the credit only if they are not claimed as a dependent on another person's tax return. The credit is phased out for higher income consumers. The credit is allowed only for students who are attending a degree program at least half-time and who have not completed their first four years of academic study before the beginning of the taxable year. It cannot be claimed in more than four tax years for any one student.

7. Lifetime Learning credit—A consumer may claim a tax credit for 20% of up to $10,000 in combined tuition and fees for himself, his spouse, and his dependent children. This equates to a $2,000 tax credit. This credit is phased out for higher income consumers. Claiming the American Opportunity credit described above means that you may not claim a Lifetime Learning credit for any of that student's expenses in the same tax year. There is no requirement that the student be

studying towards a degree or be enrolled at least half-time, and there is no limit on the number of years the credit may be taken.

8. If your income is below certain level (the amount varies over time), tuition and fees and student loan interest may be tax deductible. Most scholarships are tax-free if the recipient does not have to provide services in exchange for the award. In addition, tax-free educational assistance plans allow employers to pay and deduct college and graduate school costs for their employees up to a certain limit.

The Bottom Line

The major problem in saving for college is to save enough to keep up with rising college costs. A procedure was outlined for determining how much to save which doesn't require that future college costs be predicted. The only factor that must be assumed is the relationship between the college cost inflation rate and the investment interest rate. 529 plans, Coverdell Education Savings Accounts, U.S. Savings Bonds, Individual Retirement Accounts, and investment in the child's name are all special ways to save for college.

11. Now That You've Read All This, What Do You Do?

You've learned a lot about various types of investments. However, unlike many "popular" investment books and TV programs, you've learned that there's no major formula to get rich quick (or even to get rich slowly). You can make above average rates of return on your money only by taking more risk or by being lucky. Luck, though, can't be predetermined.

Nevertheless, most investors try to outguess and "beat the market" by being "in" investments which are performing best at any point in time. You've learned how difficult and next to impossible this is. Not only must you identify economic and investment trends correctly, but you must have incredible skill at timing. Sharpe's research (see CONSUMER TOPIC) is sobering. For a market timing approach to outperform a buy and hold approach, the investor must be correct 70 percent of the time in identifying trends.

Where does this leave you as an investor? We recommend that you consider these three points before you invest.

1. PICK A GOAL FOR YOUR INVESTMENT.

GOALS

For what purpose are you investing? Are you investing for retirement, for your child's education, for a new car? How far away is the goal? Knowing the goal and the number of years before the investment will be used will help determine how much should be saved and invested each year to meet the goal.

CAN MARKET TIMING WORK?

C O N S U M E R   T O P I C

Market timing means moving your money out of investments which will do poorly and moving your money into investments which will do best in a given time period. Most investors strive to be "market-timers," but you've learned in the text how difficult a task market timing can be. The alternative to market timing is a "buy and hold" strategy in which you buy a set of investments and hold them until you need the cash.

Clearly if you can successfully "time the market," you can earn a much higher return than with a "buy and hold" strategy. For example, William Sharpe calculated that a perfect market timing strategy implemented from 1929 to 1972, in which the investor always invested in the stock market during the market's "good" years but invested in cash (e.g., money market funds) when the stock market did poorly, resulted in an average rate of return of almost 14 percent annually compared to an 8 percent annual return from a "buy stocks and hold them" strategy.*

Of course, no one is able to perfectly time the stock market and always know when the market will do well and when it will do poorly. But how right does an investor have to be for market-timing to beat buy and hold? Again, taking into account brokerage fees, Sharpe found that the market timer must be right 70 percent of the time to beat the buy and hold investor. The market timer must accurately predict good stock years from bad stock years in 7 out of 10 years to beat the investor who buys stocks and stands pat.

In a similar study Jeffrey found that the market timer who was right 67 percent of the time could increase returns 8-fold if everything worked perfectly, but at a risk of losing 95 percent of the return earned by the "buy and hold" investor in the worst-case scenario. These studies give sobering conclusions about market timing and suggest that most investors should throw away their newsletters and crystal balls and just ride the market!

*These rates of return were calculated net of brokerage fees of 2 percent of each trade.

Reference: Sharpe, William F. "Likely Gains from Market Tinting." *Financial Analysts Journal*, Vol. 31, No. 2, March-April 1975, pp. 60–69.

Jeffrey, Robert H. "The Folly of Stock Market Timing." *Harvard Business Review* Vol. 84, No. 4, July/August, 1984, pp. 102–110.

2. PICK A RISK LEVEL FOR YOUR INVESTMENTS.
   In general, the farther away your investment goal and the more income you have, the more you can take greater risk in your investments. A greater ability to take risk means putting more money into stocks, real estate, and gold, while a lesser ability to take risk means putting more money in Treasury securities, CDs, money market funds, and low risk bonds.

**C
O
N
S
U
M
E
R**

**T
O
P
I
C**

SHOULD YOU BUY THE SERVICES OF A FINANCIAL PLANNER?

Financial planning is a relatively new profession. A financial planner is supposed to be a one-stop financial adviser. A financial planner will give advice on all personal financial decisions, including credit, insurance, investing, and retirement planning. The advantage of a financial planner over a stock broker, insurance agent, or banker is that the financial planner can look at your entire financial picture and see how the individual pieces fit together. The other financial advisers generally only look at one part of your personal finances.

There are two things that a financial planner can do. One is to offer advice—that is, to provide a financial plan to meet your goals. This financial plan might tell you how much insurance coverage to have, how much to save for your children's education, how much to save for your retirement, and where to invest your savings. You pay a fee to the financial planner for this advice.

The second thing that financial planners can do is to implement the financial plan. Here the financial planner will buy the insurance and buy the investments which were recommended in the financial plan. The planner is compensated by the commissions earned on the purchase of financial products.

Planners who offer only advice on financial plans are called "fee-only" planners. Planners who offer both advice and implementation of the plan are called "fee and commission" planners. Fee-only planners often claim they are more objective than "fee and commission" planners because they're not tempted to certain investments by high commissions and they're not tempted to make frequent trades just to generate more commissions. Fee and commission planners reply that someone must implement the plan, so why not the person who designed the plan.

In selecting a financial planner look first at the planner's credentials. In most states, anyone can call himself a financial planner regardless of his training. So in shopping for a planner, it's "buyer beware." You'd prefer a planner who has a college degree in economics, business, finance, or accounting. Also, there are training programs which individuals can take in order to be designated a "certified financial planners (CFPs). These programs are quite rigorous.

However, after grinding through this text, hopefully, you won't need the services of a financial planner. You can act as your own personal financial adviser!

3. PICK AN INVESTMENT APPROACH.

There are three parts to this step.

CAN YOU BEAT THE
BUSINESS CYCLE OR
MARKET?

(a) Will you try to "beat the business cycle" by attempting to anticipate trends in the economic roller coaster and shifting your investments according to your perceived trends? Or do you think that attempting to beat the business cycle is fruitless (remember Sharpe's study)? If this is the case, you want to follow an "asset allocation" approach—having money in all major kinds of investments at all times.

(b) Within each major investment category, will you try to "beat the market" or merely accept the average return of the market? This is best considered with the stock market. Will you try to pick stocks that outperform other stocks on a risk-adjusted basis? Or are you willing to take the stock market's average rate of return, in which case you want to pick about 15 diversified stocks or a stock index fund.

(c) Will you invest directly in investments or invest through a mutual fund? If you are knowledgeable about investments and you have decided on an approach to investing, then direct investing is probably best for you. If you want to put your investments in someone else's hands, then mutual funds are a way of doing that. However, remember the disadvantages of mutual funds, particularly with respect to taxes.

The Bottom Line

There's no "free lunch" in investing. There's little opportunity to make above average returns without extraordinary luck or knowledge or, of course, without taking on greater risk. The realistic investor will consider, first, his investment goals, second, the level of acceptable risk and, third, his approach to investing.

WORDS AND CONCEPTS YOU SHOULD KNOW

Treasury securities
Treasury bills
Treasury bonds
Buying at discount
Series I savings bonds
Series EE savings bonds
Certificates of deposit
Federal deposit insurance
Variable rate CD
Bonds
Inflation risk with bonds
Call feature of bonds
Capital gains and capital losses with bonds
Premium bonds
Discount bonds
Current yield
Yield to maturity
Zero coupon bond
Municipal bond
"Junk" bond
Mortgage-back securities
Collateralized Mortgage Obligations (CMOs)
Mortgage pass-through securities
Ginnie-Mae's
Stock dividends
Stock appreciation
Growth stock
Stock market and inflation
Dow Jones Industrial Average
Standard and Poor's 500 Stock Composite Index
Wilshire 5000 Index

"Beat the Market" strategy
Fundamental analysis
Intrinsic stock value
Technical analysis
Moving average
Efficient markets approach
P/E ratio
"Neglected" stocks
Gold
Real estate deductions
Depreciation
"Paper losses"
Capitalization approach to valuing real estate
Zoning
Real estate investment rust
Master limited partnership
Mutual fund
Undistributed capital gains
Mark-to-market
Front-end fee or load
Back-end fee or load
Annual fee or load
"No-load" fund
Risk-adjusted return
Money market mutual fund
Open-end fund
Closed-end fund
Unit investment trust
Exchange Traded Funds (ETFs)
Stock index mutual fund
College savings in child's name
529 plans

Coverdell Education Savings Accounts
American Opportunity tax credit

Lifetime Learning credit

TYPES OF INVESTMENTS—A SUMMARY

1. Investments issued by the Federal government have the advantage of having the lowest default risk. If you want to sleep perfectly soundly at night, loan your money to the federal government. This can be done in two ways:

   A. *Treasury securities* come with fixed interest rates and various terms. Inflation risk is present especially for the long term securities (Treasury bonds). Interest earnings are exempt from state and local taxes. The short term securities (T-bills) have minimums of $10,000.

   B. There are two types of U.S. Savings bonds currently offered, Series EE bonds and Series I bonds. In addition, there is a Series HH bonds that were discounted in August 2004. However, because HH bonds earn interest for up to 20 years, some investors may still have HH bonds that earn interest. The interest earned on U.S. saving bonds is subject to federal income tax, but not state or local income tax. EE bonds earn a fixed rate of interest for up to 30 years, whereas I bonds earn interest based on combining a fixed rate and an inflation rate the usually changes every six months.

2. A CD (certificate of deposit) usually pays a fixed interest rate for a specific term. Some CDs pay variable rates tied to the stock market, gold, or the prime interest rate. Most CDs are backed by federal insurance. CDs sold by stockbrokers frequently pay a higher rate, but sometimes the entire CD isn't insured and brokers often charge fees.

   Buy short-term CDs if interest rates are expected to rise, and buy long-term CDs if interest rates are expected to fall. If you don't know where rates are going, buy a mix of short and long term CDs.

3. Bonds are long term investments which pay a fixed annual return and which can be sold anytime. Default risk for bonds varies from very low to very high (junk bonds). Check a bond's rating for its default risk.

   A. The "true" return from a bond is measured by its "yield to maturity," which accounts for the annual return and the capital gain or loss which occurs when the bond is cashed in.

   B. The value (price) of a bond moves opposite to current interest rates. Big money can be made with bonds when interest rates are falling, but big losses occur when interest rates rise.

   C. Bonds have very high inflation risk.

D. Zero-coupon bonds pay no annual interest, but pay all the accumulated interest when the bond matures.

E. The interest earnings of municipal bonds are not taxable by the federal government and sometimes not by state and local governments.

F. "Junk" bonds are high (default) risk bonds which in turn pay a high rate of interest.

4. Investors can invest in mortgages by buying "mortgage-backed securities," including mortgage pass-through's and collateralized mortgage obligations (CMOs). The most popular mortgage pass-through is the Ginnie Mae. With the Ginnie Mae, the investor receives monthly payments of part interest and part return of the principal. Retired investors may especially like this kind of payment structure. The monthly payments made by Ginnie Mae's are backed by the federal government, but the interest rate earned is not guaranteed. A collateralized mortgage obligation (CMO) is a type of mortgage-backed security backed by a trust that holds Ginnie Mae and other federal government-supported mortgages. When a CMO is created, it is subdivided into classes called "tranches." The principal repayments received by the CMO are initially paid to the first tranche until it has been entirely retired. Once the first tranche is retired payments are directed to the second tranche, then third tranche, so on and so forth until all the tranches have been repaid. Each tranche may have different principal balances, coupon rates, risks, and maturity dates. CMOs are highly sensitive to changes in interest rates.

5. Stocks can earn two kinds of return—annual dividends, and appreciation in value. The stock market is measured by a number of indices, including the Dow Jones Industrial Average, the S&P 500 Composite Index, and the Wilshire 5000.

The major reason for investing in stocks is that total stock returns have consistently beaten the inflation rate over long periods of time. However, stocks perform poorly when the inflation rate unexpectedly rises.

There are a number of risks in stock market investing, including default risk, liquidity risk and rate risk. Default risk can be reduced through diversification. Stocks enjoy a tax advantage in that value appreciation is not taxed until the stock is sold.

There are four approaches to stock market investing:

A. Try to "beat the business cycle" and "beat the market."

B. Try to "beat the business cycle" but accept the average return of the stock market.

C. Stay invested in the stock market throughout the business cycle, but try to select stocks to "beat the market."

D. Stay invested in the stock market throughout the business cycle and accept the average return of the stock market.

6. The three major approaches to picking stocks are fundamental analysis, technical analysis, and the efficient markets approach.

Followers of the fundamental approach buy stocks whose prices are less than their intrinsic value. A stock's intrinsic value equals the present value of its expected future earnings. The problem with the fundamental approach is estimating future earnings.

Technical analysis picks stocks by trying to detect patterns in stock prices. Technical analysts frequently use stock charts and graphs. A problem with technical analysis is that stock patterns can't be detected until after they've occurred.

The efficient markets approach says that no stock bargains can be found. The current stock price already reflects all information and expectations about the stock and the company. High stock returns can only be achieved by taking high risk. Followers of the efficient markets approach concentrate on buying a diversified set of stocks.

Studies of the stock market support the efficient markets approach with these exceptions:
A. Stocks with low price/earnings ratios give high returns, even after adjusting for risk.
B. Stocks not followed by the large brokerage houses, so-called "neglected stocks" give high risk-adjusted rates of return.
C. Superior returns can be earned by buying stocks of firms which are being merged with other firms. However, the superior returns are only earned for the period between the announcement of the merger bid and the actual merger.

7. Gold is the premiere inflation hedge. When the inflation rate unexpectedly rises, gold prices soar. However, when the inflation rate falls, gold prices fall.

Investing in gold can be done with gold coins, gold certificates, gold mutual funds, bullion accounts, and stock shares of mining companies.

8. Real estate is also an inflation hedge. In most years real estate returns, from rent and value appreciation, exceed the inflation rate.

There are major tax benefits to investing in real estate. Mortgage interest, real estate taxes, operating expenses, repairs, insurance, and depreciation can be deducted from rental income. If these deductions exceed rental income, they can result in "paper losses." In some cases, up to $25,000 of paper losses can be used to offset other wage and salary income.

A piece of real estate is valued by the present value sum of its future annual net incomes. When the annual net incomes are the same, value equals (net income/discount rate).

9. Mutual funds are not a kind of investment but a way of investing. Mutual funds pool the money of many investors and use professional managers to buy and sell individual investments. Mutual funds can invest in anything, although each fund will limit the specific kinds of investments.

The advantages of mutual funds are less time involvement, professional management, and broader diversification than the individual could achieve. But there are three disadvantages to mutual funds:
A. Taxes must be paid each year on capital gains earned by the fund, even if investors don't receive the gains.
B. When mutual fund shares are sold, the investor doesn't control which shares are sold. This affects the tax on value appreciation.
C. Mutual funds must be marked-to-market every day. This is particularly important for bond funds because it means that increases in interest rates will result in an immediate drop in the value of the bond fund shares.

There can be three different costs of mutual funds: front-end fees, back-end fees, and annual fees. To compare fees, convert all fees to an annual fee.

Money market funds invest in short-term financial securities and can be used like checking accounts. Unit investment trusts offer parts of financial securities, like bonds, but don't have the disadvantage of being "marked-to-market" as long as the trust is held to maturity Stock index mutual funds are funds which attempt to replicate the entire stock market. They're great for investors who simply want the average return of the market.

Exchange Traded Funds (ETFs) are investment funds traded on the stock exchanges. An ETF combines the valuation features of a mutual funds or unit investment trust with tradability feature of a closed-end fund.

10. There are two questions to address in savings for a child's education: how much to save each year, and where to invest the savings.

Calculating the annual amount to save for college involves three steps:
  A. Using current college costs, calculate the lump sum amount needed at the start of college to fund total college expenses.
  B. Using an assumed difference between the investment interest rate and the college cost inflation rate, and using the number of years until college, calculate the initial amount to save for college.
  C. Increase the amount to save each year by the actual college inflation rate in the previous year.

One of the best ways to increase the affordability of your child's education is to take advantage of federal tax breaks aimed at families saving and paying for college. These include the following: qualified Tuition Programs (529 plans), Coverdell Education Savings Accounts, U.S. Savings Bonds , Individual Retirement Accounts, putting investments in the child's name, American Opportunity tax credit, and Lifetime Learning credit.

DISCUSSION QUESTIONS

1. Why do investments issued by the federal government have the lowest default risk?

2. What does it mean to purchase a Treasury bill at discount?

3. If you follow the idealistic strategy when should you buy Treasury securities?

4. What are some disadvantages of buying CDs from stockbrokers?

5. What factors should you consider in choosing between short-term CDs and long-term CDs?

6. What is the biggest risk associated with investing in bonds?

7. How can you earn large capital gains on a bond?

8. How is reinvestment risk avoided with a zero-coupon bond?

9. What kind of investors should consider buying junk bonds?

10. Discuss what can go wrong with a Ginnie Mae investment.

11. Historically, what has been the advantage of investing in the stock market for the long run?

12. How is the stock market affected by an increase in the inflation rate which is a surprise to everyone?

13. Your stockbroker calls you with a "hot tip" about a stock. How will your approach to the stock market determine how you will respond?

14. It's been said that the efficient markets approach only works because investors believe in fundamental and technical analyses. Please comment.

15. When does gold glitter?

16. How can real estate generate "paper losses," and how can these losses become gains?

657

17. You own some rental property in the Happy Acres neighborhood. How will the value of your rental property likely be affected if a landfill is established nearby?

18. "Pop" investment advisors often mention investing in mutual funds in the same breath as investing in stocks, bonds, and real estate. What's wrong with calling mutual funds a "type" of investment?

19. A bond mutual fund advertises a rate of return of 15 percent. What will happen to this rate of return if interest rates rise, and why?

20. How is investing in a unit investment bond trust less risky than investing in a bond mutual fund?

21. Discuss the advantages and disadvantages various ways of saving for a child's college education.

PROBLEMS

1. Melanie buys a $ 10,000 Treasury bill for $9800. The bill matures in 13 weeks. If Melanie's alternative investment is a 7 percent money market account, what's the total effective annual yield from the Treasury bill?

2. George has a CD in his name for $50,000, a CD in a joint account with his wife for $40,000, a joint account CD with his son for $30,000, and a joint account CD with his daughter for $25,000, all at the same S&L. How much of George's accounts are insured by federal depository insurance?

3. A five year CD pays 9 percent interest, and a five year Treasury note pays 8 percent interest. If the investor's state and local income tax bracket is 8 percent, which has the higher after-tax rate of return?

4. John buys a bond today for $750. The bond will mature in seven years and pay a face value of $1000. The bond pays $80 in annual interest. What is the bond's (a) current yield and (b) yield to maturity?

5. Susan buys a bond today for $1150. The bond matures in nine years and will pay a face value of $1000. The bond pays $110 in annual interest. What is the bond's (a) current yield and (b) yield to maturity?

6. Jerry bought a $3000, 20-year, 10 percent zero coupon bond five years ago. The bond will be worth $32,000 when it is cashed in. Jerry wants to sell the bond today. Interest rates on comparable zero-coupon bonds are now 8 percent. How much would Jerry get for his zero?

7. A municipal bond pays $7\frac{1}{2}$ percent interest and a corporate bond pays $8\frac{1}{2}$ percent interest. The municipal bond is exempt from all taxes. Which bond is better if the investor's total tax bracket is 35 percent?

8. KITTYCO stock will pay a dividend of $8/share next year. KITTYCO dividends are expected to increase 5 percent annually. Calculate the intrinsic value of KITTYCO stock using a discount rate of 10 percent.

9. Jack and Jane buy a rental house for $135,000. The land is valued at $40,000. How much can Jack and Jane deduct for depreciation each year?

10. Use the following data for a rental house to calculate the after-tax rate of return to the investor. Assume the investor's tax bracket is 28 percent.

Investor's equity:	$30,000
Rental Income:	$20,000
Appreciation:	$2,000
Mortgage Interest:	$5,000
Real Estate Taxes:	$3,000
Operating Expenses:	$1,500
Repairs:	$750
Insurance:	$500
Depreciation:	$2,750

11. Using the capitalization approach, calculate a property's value if the property has net income of $5000 annually and the discount rate is 6 percent.

12. The SUPERDUPER mutual fund has a front-end fee of 2 percent, a back-end fee of 5 percent, and an annual fee of 3 percent. Convert this fee structure to a single annual fee using a 7 percent interest rate and a four year holding period.

13. Calculate the risk-adjusted return for the **SUPERDUPER** fund using the following information:

Rate of Return:	32%
Beta:	1.8
Treasury bill rate:	8%

14. The Watsons want to send son David to State College in 12 years. Currently tuition and room and board at State costs $8,000 annually. The Watsons want to save an initial amount this year and then increase that amount in future years by the actual increase in college costs. How much must the Watsons save this year in order to begin funding four years of college for David at State. Assume the Watsons can invest funds at a rate exceeding the college inflation rate by 3 percentage points, how then will this annual amount saved change in the future?

CHAPTER 10

Retirement Planning

Introduction

Retirement planning, or more specifically, financial retirement planning, is really an extension of investing. The idea of financial retirement planning is simple. At retirement you'll stop working and therefore you won't be earning wages or a salary (or, at the least, you'll substantially reduce your work and wages and salary). However, you'll still have living expenses during retirement. How will you meet those living expenses? You answer this question by undertaking *retirement planning*.

There's nothing magical about retirement planning. Retirement planning is simply saving. You'll save money while you're working and transfer those funds to the future for use in your retirement. Some of this saving is automatic because it is forced on you. Social Security and private pensions are examples of forced retirement savings. The rest of the savings, if needed, is voluntary. A major question answered by retirement planning is how much voluntary saving is required to supplement the forced savings of Social Security and company pensions. That is, how much must you save each year for your retirement?

Since retirement planning involves transferring money that you earn while working to the future when you retire, a major concern is preserving the purchasing power of this money, that is, making sure this money keeps pace with inflation. How can you do this (actually, you should already have the answer!)? This question will be addressed in retirement planning.

There are two other questions which we'll address in the retirement planning topics. First, how should money which you save and target for retirement be invested? Are there any special investment vehicles specifically designed for retirement planning? Secondly, once you've accumulated your retirement nest egg and you are retired, how can you draw down on that nest egg in meeting living expenses? Is there any way to insure that you won't outlive your retirement nest egg?

Many of you reading these words are very young, and are very far from retirement. You're probably thinking—why worry about retirement now; that's light-years away? There are two reasons to worry about retirement planning while you're young. Number one, the earlier you begin financially planning for retirement, the easier it will be to accumulate that retirement nest egg. Number two, waiting until you're near retirement to financially plan for retirement can be an instant recipe for financial disaster in your retirement years.

So, now that you're properly motivated, let's plan for retirement!

1. How Much Should You Save for Retirement?

If you understood (and hopefully you did!) the topic on education savings (see *How Can You Save for Your Child's Education?*), then this topic should be a breeze. The procedure outlined here exactly follows the procedure outlined for educational savings.

Let's first briefly outline what the retirement saving procedure will do. We're concerned if there will be a gap between our living expenses in retirement and our income from social security, pensions, and other funds. So we'll first estimate this gap and convert it to a lump sum amount at the point of retirement. Of course, if there is no gap then we can stop—no additional saving will be needed. If there is a gap, then we'll want to figure out how much to save each year in order to accumulate that lump sum amount. When we do this we're done!

REAL DOLLARS   As with educational saving, it's easiest to work with "real dollars." In this way we can avoid predicting an average future inflation rate. Instead, the key assumption will be the difference between the investment interest rate and the average inflation rate. Here, unlike educational saving, it's safe to assume that the investment interest rate will exceed the average inflation rate. A difference of two percentage points is a good estimate.

There is one exception where we'll need to assume an inflation rate. This will occur when the consumer receives a private pension which does *not* increase with the cost of living. In this case the private pension payments will have to be converted to real purchasing power dollars.

Figure 10-1. Calculating retirement saving.

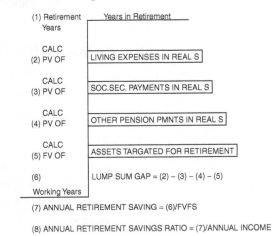

The Procedure in Detail

This section describes the retirement savings procedure in detail. Figure 10-1 is a schematic of the procedure. Each step of the procedure is briefly described, an example is given, and then more details are provided about components of the procedure.

Step 1: Pick a retirement age and the number of years planned for in retirement. A common retirement age is 65, and twenty or thirty years are usually enough years to plan for in retirement.

Step 2: In current dollars, estimate the amount of expenses each year in retirement, and then calculate the lump sum present value of these expenses using a real interest rate (.02 is recommended).

Step 3: In current dollars, estimate the amount of Social Security payment received each year. The Social Security payment will be based on your current income and your age at retirement (more on this later). Calculate a lump sum present value of these Social Security payments using the real interest rate.

Step 4: In current dollars, estimate the amount of other annual pension payments received from *defined benefit plans* and calculate the lump sum present value amount.

If these pension payments are adjusted each year in retirement for increases in the cost of living, then the present value amount is calculated in the same way as in STEPS 2 and 3. However, most private pensions are not adjusted for inflation. If this is the case, then each pension payments must first be deflated to purchasing power terms before the present value is calculated.

Step 5: Calculate the future value of assets which you own today that will be cashed in and added to the retirement nest egg at retirement. Include the current value of defined contribution pension plans here. Other assets which you *may* want to include are your house, rental property, and a stock portfolio. Calculate the future value using the assumed real interest rate.

Step 6: Calculate your financial retirement gap as: Lump sum retirement expenses minus Lump sum Social Security payments, Lump sum of other pension payments, and Lump sum of targeted assets.

If this result is zero or less than zero, then you can stop. You have no need to save more for retirement. If this result is greater than zero, then you have a financial retirement gap and you should complete STEPS 7 and 8.

Step 7: Calculate the initial additional amount to save for retirement by dividing the lump sum gap (from STEP 6) by the future value factor sum associated with the number of working years left until you retire and the assumed real interest rate (investment interest rate minus the inflation rate). Why divide by a future value factor sum? If the investment interest rate and inflation rate were assumed to be equal (to cancel each other), then you'd just divide by the number of years until retirement. But if the investment interest rate exceeds the inflation rate, then less is needed to be saved.

Step 8:   Calculate the additional retirement savings ratio as the result of STEP 7 divided by your current income. Then, assuming your income rises with the average inflation rate, your retirement savings will also rise at the rate of inflation.

Let's quickly go to an example to clear up any questions you might have about using the procedure. In order to make the calculations easy (for demonstration purposes), the example will be unrealistic regarding both the time until retirement and the time planned for in retirement.

EXAMPLE 10-1:   Doris and Dick Donaldson plan to retire in five years and they want to plan for five years in retirement. They want $25,000 real dollars annually for expenses in retirement. They expect to receive $10,000 annually (real $) in Social Security payments and $3000 annually (real $) in other pension payments, both of which are annually adjusted for increases in the cost of living. The Donaldsons have property worth $30,000 today which they plan to cash in at retirement to help fund retirement expenses. The Donaldsons' current income is $35,000. What percent of their current income, if any, do they need to save for retirement? Assume the Donaldsons can invest money at 2 percentage points above the inflation rate.

Step 1:   The Donaldsons have five years until they retire and they are planning for five years in retirement.

Step 2:   Lump sum present value amount of retirement expenses (using a 2 percent real interest rate):

$25,000 × PVFS (r = 2%, n = 5 years)

= $25,000 × [1.000 + 0.980 + 0.961 + 0.942 + 0.924]

= $25,000 × 4.807

= $120,175.

Note that we started discounting with Year 2 so that funds are available at the beginning of each year. This is a safer approach than assuming funds are only available at the end of the year. In reality, the Donaldsons will need the funds monthly, so having all the funds available at the beginning of each year is a stiffer requirement than necessary.

Step 3: Lump sum present value amount of Social Security payments: $10,000 × PVFS (r = 2%, n = 5 years) (begin discounting in Year 2 to be comparable with the discounting of expenses)

= $10,000 × 4.807

= $48,070.

Step 4: Lump sum present value amount of other pension payments:

= $3,000 × 4.807

= $14,421.

Step 5: Future value of current assets targeted for retirement:

$30,000 × FVF (r = 2%, n = 5 years)

= $30,000 × 1.104

= $33,120.

Step 6: Financial Retirement Gap = $120,175 – $48,070 – $14,421 – $33,120 = $24,564.

Step 7: Initial amount to save: If we assume funds are saved at the end of each year, make the first future value factor 1.000 (since the last year's savings will not earn interest for the last year). If funds are assumed to be saved at the beginning of each year, then use the regular future value factors.

To be conservative, let's assume funds are saved at the end of each year. Then the future value factor sum for 2 percent and 5 years is:

$$1.000 + 1.020 + 1.040 + 1.061 + 1.082 = 5.203$$

(If funds were assumed to be invested at the beginning of each year, the future value factor sum would be 1.020 + 1.040 + 1.061 + 1.082 + 1.104, or 5.307. Notice that using this future value factor sum in the next calculation would give a smaller amount to save.)

$$\text{Initial Amount To Save:} \quad \frac{\$24,564}{5.203} = \$4,721.12$$

DO RETIREES LIVE OFF THEIR SAVINGS?

C O N S U M E R

T O P I C

Does empirical research support the idea that retirees draw down on their savings to meet retirement expenses? Some research does and some research doesn't! Research which looks at the savings rates of different aged households at the same point in time (called "cross-section" analysis) doesn't support the idea that retirees at least partially live off their savings. But a flaw in this research is that the same households are not followed over their life span. Instead, the "cross-section" analysis is based on the assumption that a retiree today will adequately predict the behavior of a younger working household in the future.

A better way to address the question is to look at the same households as they move from working to retirement (this is called "panel" analysis). This is exactly what Michael Hurd did in his study of the savings behavior of retirees. His results strongly support the notion that retirees do draw down on their savings to help meet retirement expenses. Hurd found that retirees withdraw from their savings at the average rate of 3.2 percent per year. This withdrawal rate increases as the retiree ages and life expectancy decreases. Furthermore, Hurd found no difference between the withdrawal rate of retirees with children and retirees without children. Rather than accumulating savings in retirement to pass along to their children, Hurd found that parents transfer wealth to their children before retirement.

Source: Hurd, Michael P. "Savings of the Elderly and Desired Bequests," *American Economic Review*, Vol. 77, No. 3, June 1987, pp. 298–312.

Step 8:   The savings percentage is:

$$\frac{\$4,721.12}{\$35,000} = 13.5\%$$

Assuming the Donaldson's income rises with the inflation rate, they should target $13\frac{1}{2}$ percent of it for supplemental retirement savings.

Figure 10-2 schematically illustrates the procedure in the Donaldsons' case.

At this point you may be a little confused and uneasy about the use of real dollars and a real investment interest rate. What would the retirement gap and required savings look like in an "actual" situation where an inflation rate is incorporated? To alleviate your concerns, let's look at the Donaldson's situation if the inflation rate is 5 percent annually. Figure 10-3 shows what happens.

"ACTUAL DOLLARS"

With a 5 percent annual inflation rate, the shortfall between retirement expenses and income (which was $25,000 minus $10,000 minus $3000, or $12,000 annually in real dollars) is $15,315 in Year 1 of retirement,

Figure 10-2. The Donaldson's situation in "Real" dollars.

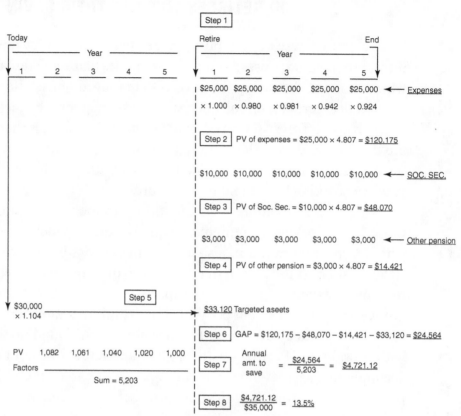

$16,081 in Year 2, $16,885 in Year 3, $17,729 in Year 4, and $18,616 in Year 5. The initial "real" amount to save was derived to be $4,721.12. However, we assumed all saving occurs at the end of the year. So with a 5 percent inflation rate the first working year, the initial amount to save is $4,721.12 × 1.05 or $4,957.18. Then in each subsequent working year (years 2, 3, 4, and 5), the amount to save is increased by 5 percent per year.

Recall from Chapter 1 that with a 5 percent inflation rate and 2 percent "real" interest rate, the nominal (or actual) interest rate is 1.05 × 1.02, or 1.071. Because we want the numbers to come out "just right" we'll use 1.071 rather than 1.07. Figure 10-3 shows how the annual amounts saved during the five working years and the targeted assets grow to a retirement nest egg of $73,630.39 at the time of retirement. Figure 10-3 shows how the nest egg is drawn from to meet the retirement gap during the retirement years. Remaining balances in the nest egg earn 7.1 percent interest annually. Notice that at the end of year 5 in retirement the nest egg balance is within a few dollars of zero.

So the procedure does work in an actual situation. Simply remember to increase the initial calculated amount to save by the inflation rate if saving is assumed to be done at the end of each year.

What happens to our calculations if the other private pension payments are not indexed to the cost of living, as is the case for the majority of private pensions? In this situation the *real* value of the private

Figure 10-3.   What the Donaldsons actually save assuming five percent inflation.

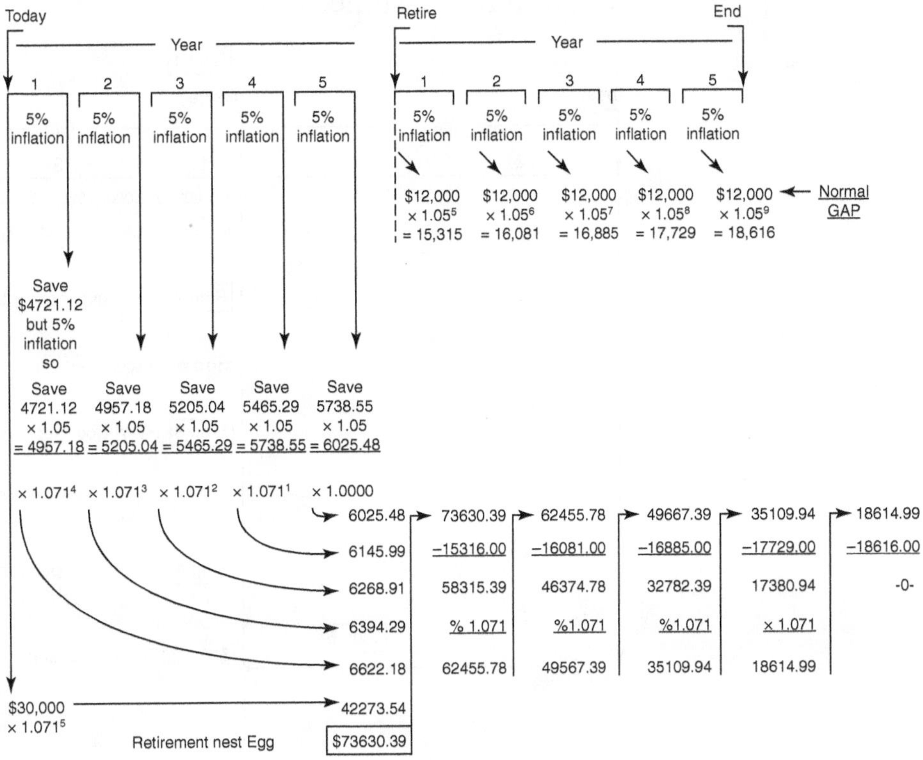

PRIVATE PENSION
NOT INDEXED

pension payments must be discounted by the real interest rate and an assumed inflation rate; that is, the private pension payments must be discounted by a nominal interest rate. So for this part of the procedure you must forecast a future inflation rate—there's no way around it. It's wise if you err to the high side and project a high inflation rate.

Figure 10-4 redoes the Donaldson's calculations assuming that the $3000 private pension payment is not indexed to the cost of living and assuming that the future inflation rate averages 7 percent annually. With a real interest rate of 2 percent, this means the private pension payments are discounted using 9 percent. Notice that the resulting amount and percent to save are higher than in Figure 10-2.

Now you understand the procedure for calculating retirement savings. The following sections give more details about the components of the procedure. However, discussion of Social Security benefits and private pensions are left to later topics.

Years Planned for in Retirement

If you're doing your financial planning in the early part of your work career (which is when you should), it's hard to know how long to plan for in retirement. When you're 20 or 30, it's difficult, if not impossible, to know how long you will live, or what medical technology will be like when you retire.

Figure 10-4. The Donaldsons' calculations assuming the private pension is not indexed to the Cost of Living (7 percent inflation rate assumed).

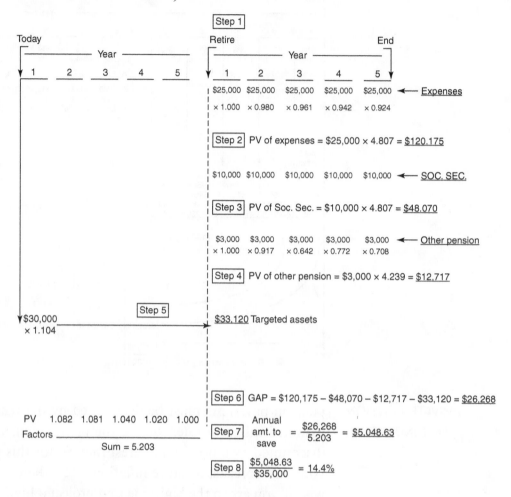

The best recommendation is to plan for a long period in retirement. Plan to build a retirement nest egg which will last 25, 30, or 35 years in retirement.

PLAN LONG

Retirement Expenses

The easiest way to estimate retirement expenses is to calculate them as some percentage of your current real income. Research shows that most consumers will not need as much real income in retirement in order to maintain the same standard of living as they had during their working years. Housing expenses and clothing and transportation costs will likely be lower (in real terms), and the retired consumer will not have to save for retirement, either privately or through Social Security. On the other hand, medical expenses may be higher.

REPLACEMENT RATE

The percentage of pre-retirement income needed in retirement to meet retirement expenses is called the *replacement rate*. Common financial planning advice suggests target replacement rates should be between 0.70 to 0.85 of preretirement income. Low income households are thought to need higher replacement rates than high income households. One sophisticated study[1] concluded that while many factors affect optimal replacement rate, median optimal target replacement rate was 0.75 for married couples and 0.55 for singles.

Of course, a consumer's real income changes during his working career. Typically, real income will peak in the 45 to 55 year age range. What if you begin saving for retirement when your real income is low (meaning your retirement expenses are low because they're based on the low real income), but then your real income rises, and you want your retirement expenses to be based on the higher real income? How do you calculate the necessary adjustment in your retirement savings percentage?

RECALCULATING RETIREMENT SAVING

The adjustment is simple. Merely find the current value of what you have saved for retirement to date. Treat this current value as an asset which you will target for retirement and calculate the future real value of this asset at the time of retirement. Then recalculate your retirement savings requirement based on today's current income and the remaining years until retirement. EXAMPLE 10-2 is an illustration.

EXAMPLE 10-2: Cosmo and Morticia Adams plan to retire in fifteen years. They have already saved $100,000 for their retirement. They want to base their retirement expenses on their current income of $50,000. The Adams family will receive $20,000 annually in Social Security payments (real $) during retirement. The Adams family has $30,000 of property which they will cash in for use in retirement. If the Adams family wants a retirement nest egg that will fund 60 percent of their current income in retirement, how much must they save to fund 25 years in retirement? Use a two percent real interest rate.

Step 1:   The Adams family has 15 years until they retire and they are planning for 25 years in retirement.

Step 2:   Lump sum present value of retirement expenses, using a 2 percent real interest rate:

$.60 \times \$50,000 \times$ PVFS (r = 2%, n = 25 years) =

$.60 \times \$50,000 \times$ [1.000 + 0.980 + 0.961 + 0.942 + 0.924 + 0.906 + 0.888 + 0.871 + 0.853 + 0.837 + 0.820 + 0.804 +

---

[1]Scholz, JK and Seshadri, A. What Replacement Rates Should Households Use? University of Michigan Retirement Research Center Working Paper WP2009-214. Retrieved 4/30/2013 online at http://www.mrrc.isr.umich.edu/publications/papers/pdf/wp214.pdf

0.788 + 0.773 + 0.758 + 0.743 + 0.728 + 0.714 + 0.700 + 0.686 + 0.673 + 0.660 + 0.647 + 0.634 + 0.622] = \$30,000 × 19.912 = \$597,360

Step 3: Lump sum present value amount of Social Security payments = \$20,000 × 19.912 = \$398,240.

Step 4: Lump sum present amount of other pension payments:

None.

Step 5: Future value of current assets targeted for retirement:

Here is where the \$100,000 already saved for retirement comes into play. Simply treat them like other targeted assets:

$$(\$100,000 + \$30,000) \times \text{FVF} \ (r = 2\%, n = 15 \text{ years}) =$$

$$\$130,000 \times 1.346 = \$174,980$$

Step 6: Financial Retirement Gap: \$597,360 − \$398,240 − \$174,980 = \$24,140.

Step 7: Initial amount to save, assuming end of year saving: \$24,140 / FVFS (r = 2%, n = 15 years) =

$$\frac{\$24,140}{[1.000 + 1.020 + 1.040 + 1.061 + 1.082 + 1.104 + 1.126 + 1.149 + 1.172 + 1.195 + 1.219 + 1.243 + 1.268 + 1.294 + 1.319]}$$

$$= \frac{\$24,140}{17.292} = \$1,396.02$$

Step 8: The savings percentage is

$$\frac{\$1,396.02}{\$50,000} = 2.8\%$$

Planning Together or Separately

A final issue to consider is whether to plan for a husband and wife together or whether to plan for each separately. The issue is important because Social Security and pension payments likely will be different for husband and wife.

The safest tactic is to plan separately. That is, calculate a retirement gap separately for the husband and for the wife and then combine the savings to get total savings for the family. Use the Social Security and pension payments that pertain to each person and allocate assets targeted for retirement to one person. Table 10-1 illustrates an example of individual retirement planning for each spouse. Ozzie should save 18 percent of his income for retirement and Harriet should save about 1 percent.

What if, in Table 10-2, Harriet doesn't work, so that all the retirement saving is done by Ozzie? This is fine, except that if Ozzie dies there will be no one to save for her retirement unless Harriet goes to work. The solution is life insurance bought on Ozzie with Harriet as the beneficiary. Calculate the amount of life insurance needed as:

**LIFE INSURANCE
AGAIN**

Life Insurance: Needed	Present value of annual savings desired for retirement	−	Current value of assets targeted for retirement

In Ozzie and Harriet's case, if Harriet doesn't work and she wants to insure that $7,291 can be saved for each of 25 years in the case of Ozzie's death, then the required life insurance amount is:

$7,291 × 22.813 PVFS (r = 2%, n = 30 years) – $75,000 = <u>$91,330</u>.

Some Answers

What are some typical required savings rates for retirement? Tables 10-2 and 10-3 give some answers. Both tables assume a higher replacement rate for lower income consumers and a lower replacement rate for higher income consumers and on the consumer only receiving Social Security in retirement. The tables assume retirement at age 65 and 25 years in retirement. No current assets are targeted for retirement. Table 10-2 is for a retired worker only and Table 10-3 is for a retired worker and a non-working spouse (Social Security payments are higher in this case). The calculations assume a 2 percent real interest rate.

Some interesting patterns emerge from the tables. Looking down any column, notice that required savings rates increase the later that retirement saving is begun. For example, in Table 10-2, a worker earning $35,000 needs to save only 5.7 percent annually if saving is begun at age 25, but the same worker must save 20.6 percent annually if saving is begun at age 45. The message is clear: the burden of saving for retirement is smaller the earlier the saving begins.

Looking across any row, notice that required savings rates generally increase with income. This is because Social Security replaces a smaller percentage of the worker's income as income increases (more on this in the next topic). So the greater your income, the relatively more you must save for your retirement.

Table 10-1   Separate retirement planning for Ozzie and Harriet.

Ozzie	Harriet
Age 40, retire in 25 yrs. Plan for 30 yrs. in retirement.	Age 35, retire in 30 yrs. Plan for 30 yrs. in retirement.
Current income: $40,000	Current income: $25,000
Retirement Expenses = .66 × $40,000 = $26,400	Retirement Expenses = .71 × $25,000 = $17,750
Social Security payments = $15,000	Social Security payments = $12,000.
Other pension = $2,000, unadjusted for inflation.	Other pension = 0.
Targeted assets = $0	Targeted assets = $75,000
STEP 1: Retire in 25 yrs; 30 yrs. in retirement.	**STEP 1:** Retire in 30 yrs; 30 yrs. in retirement.
STEP 2: PV of expenses: $26,400 × 22.813 [PVFS (r = 2%, n = 30 years)] = $602,263.	**STEP 2:** PV of expenses: $17,750 × 22.813 [PVFS (r = 2%, n = 30 years)] = $404,931.
STEP 3: PV of Social Security = $15,000 × 22.813 = $342,195.	**STEP 3:** PV of Social Security = $12,000 × 22.813 = $273,756.
STEP 4: PV of other pension = $2,000 × 13.278 [PVFS (r = 7%, n = 30 years). assume 5% inflation rate] = $26,556.	**STEP 4:** PV of other pension = 0.
STEP 5: Future value of targeted assets = 0.	**STEP 5:** Future value of targeted assets = $75,000 × 1.641 [FVF(n = 2%, n = 25 years)] =$123,075.
STEP 6: GAP = $602,263 – $342,195 – $26,556 = $233,512.	**STEP 6:** GAP = $404,931 - $273,756 -$123,075 = $8,100.
STEP 7: Initial amount to save:	**STEP 7:** Initial amount to save:
$$\frac{\$233,512}{32.029} = \$7,291$$	$$\frac{\$8,100}{40.567} = \$200$$
STEP 8:	**STEP 8:**
$$\% = \frac{\$7,291}{\$40,000} = 18.2\%$$	$$\% = \frac{\$200}{\$25,000} = 0.8\%$$

The Bottom Line

Don't rely only on Social Security payments for your retirement income. In most cases additional retirement savings will be necessary to provide an adequate standard of living in retirement. Use an eight-step procedure to calculate what additional saving is necessary. The earlier you begin saving for retirement, the less you will have to save each year.

Table 10-2 Required retirement savings rates for worker only.*

	Income				
	$20,000	**$40,000**	**$50,000**	**$60,000**	**$120,000**
Replacement Rate	86%	71%	66%	60%	55%
Age When Savings Begin:					
25	1.9%	3.9%	5.7%	5.7%	10.2%
35	5.5%	8.0%	10.3%	10.3%	16.2%
45	14.4%	17.1%	20.6%	20.5%	28.9%
55	43.4%	47.1%	55.7%	55.2%	69.7%

*Assumes worker receives only Social Security payments (no pension and no assets targeted for retirement), retirement age 65, 25 years in retirement, 2 percent real interest rate, end of year saving and beginning of year expenditures.

Table 10-3 Required retirement savings rates for worker and a non-working spouse.*

	Income				
	$20,000	**$40,000**	**$50,000**	**$60,000**	**$120,000**
Replacement Rate	86%	71%	66%	60%	55%
Age When Savings Begin:					
25	0%	0%	0%.	0%	6.2%
35	0%	0%	0%	0.7%	10.8%
45	0%	0%	4.1%	6.1%	20.9%
55	0%	6.1%	22.9%	28.3%	54.6%

*Assumes worker and spouse receive only Social Security payments (no pension and no assets targeted for retirement), retirement age 65, 25 years in retirement, 2 percent real interest rate, end of year saving and beginning of year expenditures.

2. How Much Will You Get from Social Security?

Ninety percent of American workers are in the Social Security system and will receive Social Security benefits when they retire. Recall from the previous topic *(How Much Should You Save for Retirement?)* that Social Security benefits received at retirement are a major part of the procedure for calculating how much you should save for retirement.

How much you will get from Social Security depends on your income during your working years, the average inflation rate in wages and salaries while you worked, and whether you have a spouse who didn't work. Table 10-4 shows annual Social Security benefits in 2013 dollars for a 22 year old person who plans to retire at age 67. Since these nominal dollar amounts will change over time due to inflation, perhaps better information is given in Table 10-5. Table 10-5 shows the percentage of 2013 incomes that Social Security will pay. Notice in particular that the replacement percentage falls as income rises. In other words, Social Security replaces a higher percentage of pre-retirement income for low income consumers.

A very important feature of Social Security benefits is that they are indexed to the inflation rate. Specifically, Social Security benefits in any year are increased by the previous year's inflation rate (measured from the third quarter to the third quarter). So, if for example, the annual inflation rate from Third Quarter 2011 to Third Quarter 2012 is 1.7%, then Social Security benefits in *2013* will increase 1.7 percent over 2012.

How Benefits Are Calculated

The numbers in Table 10-4 are averages. The Social Security benefit you will receive is based on your own earnings history. How is this

Table 10.4. Future Social Security benefits of a worker born on 1/1/1992 and plans to retire at age 67 (in 2013$)

Today's income	Monthly SS Benefits	Annual SS benefits	% Income replacement
$ 30,000	$1,258	$15,096	50.3%
$ 40,000	$1,525	$18,300	45.8%
$ 50,000	$1,791	$21,492	43.0%
$ 60,000	$2,019	$24,228	40.4%
$ 70,000	$2,144	$25,728	36.8%
$ 80,000	$2,269	$27,228	34.0%
$ 90,000	$2,394	$28,728	31.9%
$100,000	$2,519	$30,228	30.2%
$110,000	$2,644	$31,728	28.8%
$120,000	$2,690	$32,280	26.9%
$130,000	$2,690	$32,280	24.8%

Estimates obtained using Social Security Administration's online calculator at http://www.ssa.gov/retire2/AnypiaApplet.html. Benefit formula updated December 2012.

WILL SOCIAL SECURITY SURVIVE?

Surveys of young Americans show that most of them think that Social Security won't be around when they retire. They think the system will go bankrupt before they collect a penny of benefits.

Is this worry warranted? Yes and no. Yes if no policy changes are made between now and then. No if the Congress takes actions soon to either reduce Social Security benefits or increase Social Security revenue, or both. Under current policies, the Social Security Administration's Board of Trustees reported that the annual cost has exceeded and will continue to exceed non-interest income starting from 2010. The Social Security trust fund will be exhausted in 2035. At that point, Social Security will not have enough income or any assets to draw from to pay the promised benefits.

Projected Social Security cost generally increases more rapidly than projected non-interest income because the retirement of the baby-boom generation will increase the number of beneficiaries much faster than the increase of the number of workers. In addition, because of the advances in medical technology, Social Security beneficiaries live longer, thus drawing more total benefits per person.

For Social Security to remain financially sound in the long run, the Trustees recommend several policy changes: (1) to increase the payroll tax rate, (2) to reduce scheduled benefits, (3) to draw on alternative sources of revenue, and (4) to adopt some combinations of the above approaches. The Trustees recommend that the lawmakers address this issue in a timely way in order to phase in necessary changes and give workers and beneficiaries time to adjust to them. The sooner changes happen, the less drastic the measures need to be. Unfortunately, policy changes are difficult to put through, especially if the change will lead to higher taxes or lower benefits or both. As such, although the problem with the financial future of our Social Security program has been well known for many years, so far no policy changes alleviating these problems have been agreed upon.

Source: Social Security Administration, 2012 Annual Report of the Board of Trustees, available at http://www.ssa.gov/oact/tr/2012/tr2012.pdf.

benefit calculated? This section answers this question. Although you may never want to do these calculations, it's still good to know what's going on!

In a nutshell, your Social Security benefit is based on the average of your real monthly earnings. Social Security calls this average "the average indexed monthly earnings," or AIME. Up to 35 years of earnings are needed to compute the AIME. These earnings are first adjusted or "indexed" to reflect the change in general wage levels that occurred during the worker's years of employment. After Social Security Administration determine the number of years, they choose those years with the highest indexed earnings, sum such indexed earnings, and divide the

IS THE SOCIAL SECURITY TAX REGRESSIVE?

**C
O
N
S
U
M
E
R**

**T
O
P
I
C**

It has been said that the Social Security tax is a regressive tax. This is because after a worker earns $113,700 (in 2013 and changes every year), no additional tax is paid for Social Security (there is, however, still a payroll tax paid for Medicare). This means, for example, that a worker earning $30,000 pays 6.2% in Social Security taxes, but a worker earning $200,000 pays only 3.5% in Social Security Taxes (($113,700 × 0.62)/$200,000). Thus, Social Security tax is indeed regressive over the full range of incomes.

But there is a very logical reason for this structure of the Social Security tax. Workers earning more than $113,700 in 2013 don't pay more Social Security tax because their Social Security benefits don't increase for income beyond this amount. In other words, a person retiring with a final income of $200,000 receives the same Social Security benefit as the person retiring with a final income of $113,700 (assuming similar work histories).

Furthermore, as shown in the text, the calculation of Social Security monthly benefits gives more weight to earnings of at lower income levels. The monthly benefit formula for 2013 replaces 90¢ of every dollar of average indexed monthly earnings (AIME) under $791, but replaces only 32¢ of every dollar of AIME between $791 and $4,768, and only 15¢ of every dollar of AIME above $4,768. This means that lower income consumers receive a Social Security benefit which is a higher percentage of their work income than higher income consumers. Therefore, Social Security redistributes what it collects in favor of lower income consumers.

Figure 10-4 gives an example of the Social Security benefit calculation for a worker born on 1/1/1992 and plans to retire at age 67, with various level of AIME converted annual earnings for simplicity. The computation is done using Social Security Administrations' online calculator.

total amount by the total number of months in those years. The result is the AIME. The monthly Social Security benefit is then calculated using the following formula in 2013:

2013 Monthly Benefit = 90% of first $791 of AIME
+ 32% of AIME between $791 and $4,768
+ 15% of AIME between $4,768 and $113,700

BEND POINTS   The dollar amounts in the monthly benefit equation are called "bend points." Each year these bend points are increased by the previous year's increase in average wages.

However, the marginal rates (90%, 32%, and 15%) have not been changed for many years. As you can see the procedure does make economic sense because most past earnings are inflated to current (when you retire) values. Also note that the monthly benefit equation puts more weight on lower incomes, which results in lower income retirees receiving a high percentage of their pre-retirement income than higher income retirees.

Starting from May 2012, you can obtain a copy of your Social Security statement online at www.socialsecurity.gov. If you are an eligible worker, the statement provides you with secure and convenient access to your Social Security earnings and benefit information. You can use the information on this statement to help with your retirement planning. If you are interested in doing the calculation yourself, there is a worksheet on Social Security Administration's website at http://www.ssa.gov/pubs/EN-05-10070.pdf.

The Effect of Early or Late Retirement

As early as you reach 62 you can receive Social Security benefits. However, full benefits are received if you retired at the age of 65 to 67, depending on your birth year. Table 10-6 shows the normal retirement age to receive full Social Security benefits under the current law (in 2013).

Table 10-5.   Normal retirement age to receive full Social Security benefits

Birth year	Full (normal) retirement age
1937 or earlier	65
1938	65 and 2 months
1939	65 and 4 months
1940	65 and 6 months
1941	65 and 8 months
1942	65 and 10 months
1943–1954	66
1955	66 and 2 months
1956	66 and 4 months
1957	66 and 6 months
1958	66 and 8 months
1959	66 and 10 months
1960 and later	67

If a worker decides to retire after the age of 62 but before his or her normal retirement age, reduced benefits are paid. In the case of a person retiring at exactly age 62 in 2013, the benefit will be 25% less than the person's full benefit amount. On the other hand, if the person decides to retire later than his or her normal retirement age, a credit is given so benefits can be higher than the normal Social Security benefit amount. No delayed retirement credit is given after age 69.

IS SOCIAL SECURITY BEING SQUANDERED?

C O N S U M E R   T O P I C

As the result of the 1983 Amendments to Social Security, Social Security has been taking in more money each year than it is paying out until 2010 when expenditures exceeded non-interest income. This means that between 1983 and 2009, Social Security had surpluses each year that went into a Social Security Trust Fund.

What happens to the Social Security Trust Fund? By law (a law which, incidentally, goes back to the 1930s) the funds in Social Security Trust Fund must be used to buy Treasury securities. This means that the surpluses in the Trust Fund are loaned back to the federal government and used to fund government operation, including various programs.

The fact that the Social Security Trust Fund is holding Treasury IOU's rather than cash has alarmed some people. Some think that this means the surpluses are gone forever, having been spent on various federal programs.

Are the Social Security surpluses being squandered by being used to by Treasury securities? Not really, as long as the federal government will honor its debt. As you learned in Chapter 9, Treasury securities are considered the safest domestic investment. The federal government has never defaulted on a Treasury security and it likely never will. This is precisely why the originators of the Social Security system required that any surpluses be invested in Treasury IOU's rather than other investments like stocks and corporate bonds.

However, with the drastic increase of national debt especially in recent years, the worry that the federal government may default on its loan has increased. In 2011, credit rating agency Stand & Poor's (S&P) downgraded its credit rating of the U.S. federal government from AAA (outstanding) to AA+ (excellent), leading to criticisms by the U.S. Treasury Department and many businessmen and economists. All things considered, while it is unlikely that the U.S. federal government will default on its debt obligations, it is likely that tax rates will increase in the future to pay for these debt obligations.

Taxation of Benefits

Social Security benefits can be taxed by the Federal government. To find out if a tax is owed, follow these two steps:

1. First, add one-half of your annual Social Security benefits and any non-taxable interest income (like interest from municipal bonds) to your adjusted gross income. If the sum is greater than $32,000 for a married couple filing jointly or greater than $25,000 for a single person, then tax is owed. If not, no tax is owed.
2. If tax is owed, then the amount subject to tax is the smaller of (a) one-half of the Social Security benefits or, (b) one-half of the amount of income in excess of $25,000 for a single person or $32,000 for a married couple.

EXAMPLE 10-3: Harry and Martha receive $14,000 annually in Social Security benefits and have other income (adjusted gross) of $30,000 (including municipal bond interest). What part of their Social Security benefits is subject to federal tax?

ANSWER: .5 × $14,000 + $30,000 = $37,000

One-half of excess = ($37,000 − $32,000) = $2,500

One-half of Social Security benefits = $7,000.

The amount of Social Security benefits subject to tax is $2,500.

There is another way that Social Security benefits can be "taxed." This can possibly happen if the recipient works and earns money from that work. If you retire before reaching the full retirement age, Social Security Administration deducts $1 from annual benefit payment for every $2 you earn above the annual limit, which is $15,120 in 2013. During the year you reach full retirement age, Social Security Administration deducts $1 for every $3 you earn above a different limit, which is $40,080 for 2013. However, earnings are counted against the $40,080 limit only for months before your full retirement age is reached. Starting with the month you reach your full retirement age, you can get your full benefits with no limit on your earnings.

Harry, age 63, has a part-time job for which he earned $20,000 in 2013. Did he lose any Social Security benefits and, if so, how much?

"Excess earning" = $20,000-$15,120 = $4,880.

$4,880/2 = $2,440 of Social Security benefits lost.

C O N S U M E R   T O P I C

SHOULD SOCIAL SECURITY BE REVAMPED?

Because of the aging of the baby-boom generation and the increasing life expectancy, Social Security is facing long-term financial challenges. Under current policies, the Social Security Administration's Board of Trustees reported that the annual cost has exceeded and will continue to exceed non-interest income starting from 2010. The Social Security Trust Fund will be exhausted in 2035. At that point, Social Security will not have enough income or any assets to draw from to pay the promised benefits.

Because of these financial challenges, reform proposals continue to circulate with some urgency. One of the changes proposed is to let workers directly invest part of their Social Security taxes in their own accounts with their names on the accounts. For example, maybe the workers could take 2% of the 6.2% Social Security tax and put the money in their own investments targeted for their retirement. This reform scheme is referred to as partial privatization of Social Security and these accounts are referred to as "personal accounts" or "private accounts."

How would this help the future solvency of Social Security? It could help because the 2% work-controlled Social Security money could be invested in stocks, bonds, and other investments that might yield higher returns than the Treasury securities that Social Security surpluses are restricted to. Workers could get "more bang" for their Social Security buck.

But such a revamping of Social Security raises several concerns as well. Could workers squander their Social Security money in high risk investments? What happens if a worker's investment goes bad and there is no money left in his portion of Social Security investment when he retires? Would the government just pick up the tab and put this person on welfare? Would the cost of managing individual portfolios be too high to cancel out any potential benefit?

But perhaps the biggest question, and problem, is this. As current workers withdraw some of their Social Security taxes for their own investments, less money would be available for current and near-term retirees. This problem arises because much of the Social Security taxes paid by today's worker's taxes goes to the Social Security fund, current retirees can be left "high and dry."

This is called the "transition problem" of Social Security reform. One proposed remedy is a temporary tax to continue funding current retirees until everyone is on the new system. The transition problem makes Social Security reform all the more difficult.

Other proposals of Social Security reform include further raising retirement age, raising the annual maximum amount of compensation that is subject to the Social Security payroll tax to help fund the program, reducing overall benefits by using a different Consumer Price Index to account for consumer behavior of using substitutes with changes in relative prices, and cutting benefits to higher income consumers while not changing benefits to lower income consumers. In general, ideology plays a major part of framing the Social Security reform debate. While status quo is not sustainable in the long run, lawmakers have not been able to reach any agreement on a particular form of reform.

The Bottom Line

Social Security retirement benefits will replace some of your pre-retirement income, but not all of it. Social Security benefits will replace more of a low income person's pre-retirement income than of a high income person's pre-retirement income.

You can obtain an estimate of your retirement benefits online at www.socialsecurity.org. This estimate can be used directly in the retirement savings procedure.

3. What Will You Get from Your Pension?

A pension is a retirement benefit you receive from your company or place of work. Pensions are an important source of consumers' retirement income.

IMPORTANCE OF PENSIONS

Pensions are more important as a source of retirement income for higher income retirees than for lower income retirees. You can already guess the reason why: Social Security benefits replace a higher percentage of a low-income person's pre-retirement income than a high-income person's pre-retirement income.

Types of Pensions

There are two major kinds of pension plans, the defined benefit plan (DB) and the defined contribution plan (DC). Each plan has particular advantages and disadvantages. In recent years there has been a shift away from defined benefit plans to defined contribution plans (see CONSUMER TOPIC).

DEFINED BENEFIT PLAN

In a defined benefit plan your company or employer promises to pay you a specified pension benefit when you retire. In amassing the funds for this pension, the company contributes money and you, the employee, may contribute money also. However, the company takes the risk of guaranteeing the pension benefit. That is, the company promises and "defines" the benefit.

What are the rules specifying what pension you will get under a defined benefit plan? Most defined benefit plans will follow one of these three formulas:

PENSION FORMULAS

1. Pension benefit equals some fixed dollar amount per month multiplied by the years of service at the company.
   EXAMPLE: The fixed dollar amount per month is $20 and Jane worked 10 years at ABC Company, so Jane's monthly pension from ABC Company is $20 × 10 or $200/month or $2400/year.
2. Pension benefit equals your average salary at the job multiplied by some fixed percentage and then further multiplied by years of service at the company.

WHY DEFINED BENEFIT PENSION PLANS HAVE SLIPPED

Defined benefit (DB) pension used to be the dominant type of pension plan in the old days. But they have slipped in their dominance. According to the Bureau of Labor Statistics, from 1980 through 2008, the proportion of private wage and salary workers participating in DB pension plans fell from 38% to 20%. In contract, the percentage of workers covered by a defined contribution (DC) plan only has increased from 8% in 1980 to 31% in 2008. More recently, many employers have frozen their DB benefit plans.

Butrica et al (2009) gave a good summary of factors contributing to this trend. First, government regulations have tended to favor DC plans over DB plans. This began in the early 1980s after IRS regulations implemented a provision of the 1978 Revenue Act, which allowed employees to make voluntary contributions to employer-sponsored retirement plans with pretax dollars. Subsequent tax legislation enacted in the 1980s reduced incentives for employers to maintain their DB plans. Since then, the adoption of DB pension plans by new businesses has virtually halted and has been replaced by DC plans. Second, the employment-sector shift away from manufacturing toward service and information technology decreased the availability of DB plans, as new firms in growing sectors of the economy adopted DC plans instead. These structural changes in the economy are estimated to explain from 20 to 50 percent of the decline in DB pension plans. Finally, some analysts suggest that worker demand has partly contributed to the popularity of DC plans over DB plans. They assert that employees prefer DC plans because these plans are portable across jobs, balances are more transparent, and assets are managed by employees themselves.

Reference: Butrica, B.A., Iams, H.M, Smith, K.E., and Toder, E. "The Disappearing Defined Benefit Pension and Its Potential Impact on the Retirement Incomes of Baby Boomers." Social Security Bulletin, 69(3). 2009. Available on line at http://www.ssa.gov/policy/docs/ssb/v69n3/v69n3p1.html

(Margin text: CONSUMER TOPIC)

EXAMPLE: Jane's average salary while working at ABC Company was $20,000, and she worked 10 years there. The fixed pension percentage per year is 1 percent. Jane's annual pension from ABC Company is $20,000 × .01 × 10, or $2,000.

3. Pension benefit equals your final average salary at the job multiplied by some fixed percentage and then further multiplied by years of service at the company. The "final average salary" may be the final salary or the average over the last 3 or 5 years.

EXAMPLE: In the last three years of work at ABC Company Jane earned $30,000, $32,000, and $35,000, or an average of $32,333. Jane worked 10 years at ABC Company. The fixed pension percentage per year is 1 percent. Jane's annual pension from ABC Company is $32,333 × .01 × 10, or $3,233.[2]

Are any of the three methods better than the others? A big advantage of the third method is that the pension is based on your final salaries. If your final salaries have kept up with inflation, then your initial pension will be based on the current purchasing power of dollars. In contrast, the average in method (2) is an average of dollars with different purchasing powers. In other words, it will take many more dollars today to equal the purchasing power of your early salaries, but if those actual salaries are used in the average, this will pull the average down. Some pension plans following method (2) to solve this problem by adjusting earlier salaries for inflation (e.g., inflating them to current dollars). This is very desirable.

DEFINED CONTRIBUTION PLAN

The second major kind of pension plan, the defined contribution plan, is much simpler than the defined benefit plan. With this type of plan you, and maybe your employer, contribute to an investment account. The account is sheltered from taxes. What you receive in a pension depends on how much you and your employer contribute and the investment performance of the investment fund. No specific pension amount is guaranteed. That is, what is defined is the amount of your contribution, not the amount of your ultimate benefit—hence the term "defined contribution."

TARGET BENEFIT PLAN

There is a type of defined contribution plan called a "target benefit plan" which some call a cross between a defined benefit plan and a defined contribution plan. However, a target benefit plan is really a defined contribution plan. A target benefit plan simply provides contribution guidelines which are to be followed if a certain pension amount is desired. However, unlike a defined benefit plan, the pension amount in a target benefit plan is not guaranteed.

DB VS. DC PLANS

Which is better, a defined benefit or defined contribution plan? Each has advantages and disadvantages (see summary in Table 10-6). The big plus on the side of defined benefit plans is that you know exactly what pension you'll receive, and you can leave it in the company's hands to worry about meeting that pension. Disadvantages of defined benefit plans include the fact that the plans aren't portable, meaning that you don't take possession of the plan's money if you move to another job, federal insurance premiums must be paid (see CONSUMER TOPIC), and the fund may not always be fully funded.

---

[2]The federal government puts limits on the annual pension from a defined benefit plan. In 2013 the limit is the lesser of (a) $205,000 or (b) 100 percent of the retiree's average compensation during the three consecutive calendar years of highest compensation. The amount in (a) is adjusted for inflation each year.

Table 10-6 DB vs. DC pensions.

DB (Defined Benefit) Plans

Advantages	Disadvantages
• Predictable benefits	• Not portable.
• Company assumes investment risk	• Federal pension insurance premiums must be paid.
	• May not always be fully funded.

DC (Defined Contribution) Plans

Advantages	Disadvantages
• Portable	• Benefits less predictable.
• No Federal pension insurance premiums paid	• Employee assumes investment risk.
• Always fully funded.	
• Employee can select investments.	
• Easy to calculate value at any time.	

The big pluses of defined contribution plans are that they're easier to understand, the money always goes with you if you change jobs, and you (the employee) have more control over how the money is invested. On the negative side, no specific pension benefits are guaranteed with a defined contribution plan, and you (the employee) assume the risk of meeting specific pension goals.

Vesting and Integration

VESTING

You are not entitled to receive any benefits from a company's pension plan until you have been *vested* with the company. If you're vested, it simply means you are entitled to receive those pension benefits. Most companies now allow vesting after you've been on the job for five years.

INTEGRATION

Companies sometimes "integrate" their pension with Social Security benefits, and this can work to the disadvantage of the employee. Benefit integration means the company will take into account what you will receive in Social Security benefits in calculating your pension, and often your pension will be reduced if you also receive Social Security. For example, the company could reduce your pension by the dollar amount you receive from Social Security. Or, the company may pay a pension based only on your wage or salary above the Social Security maximum.

C
O
N
S
U
M
E
R

T
O
P
I
C

FEDERAL PENSION INSURANCE

In 1974 Congress established the Pension Benefit Guaranty Corporation, or PBGC for short. PBGC is a government insurance plan for private pensions. In exchange for a private pension plan paying insurance premiums and following certain rules, PBGC promises to pay the benefits of the plan in the event that the plan goes bankrupt.

PBGC insurance is limited to defined benefit pension plans. Defined contribution plans are not insured because no benefits are guaranteed in these plans. PBGC insurance premiums are a combination of a flat fee and a risk-related fee. In 2013, the annual premium for single employers is $42 per employee participant. Underfunded pension plans pay an additional variable-rate charge of $9 per $1,000 of unfunded vested benefits. The flat rate premium for multiemployer pension plans is $12 per participant per year.

Pension plans participating in PBGC insurance must also follow certain financial rules and regulations which are designed to limit the risk and increase the solvency of the plans. The PBGC has the authority to audit participating pension plans.

Will Changing Jobs Hurt Your Pension?

Changing jobs can hurt your pension, particularly if you have a defined benefit pension based on your highest salary. Look at Table 10-7. Mary and Nancy both follow the same salary career. Both begin with a salary of $15,000 and receive three percent raises each year. At the end of 40 years both end their work career with a salary of $48,931. However, Mary worked at four different jobs and Nancy only worked at one job.

Both Mary and Nancy have annual pensions defined to be the final salary multiplied by 1 percent and then multiplied by the years of service at the company. For Nancy the calculation is easy: $48,931 × .01 × 40, or $19,572. However, Mary will receive four separate pensions, each based on her final salary at each company she worked for and her years of service there. The calculations are shown in Table 10-7. Mary's total pension from all four companies comes to $13,259, only two-thirds of Nancy's pension. The difference is due to the fact that Nancy's pension is entirely based on her last salary of $48,931, whereas only part of Mary's pension is based on that final salary. So clearly frequent job changes will hurt your pension when you have a defined pension plan based on your final salary or final highest 3 or 5 year salaries.

Table 10-7 Mary and Nancy's pensions—Defined Benefit based on final salary.

Mary*	Yrs. of Service	Formula		Highest Pay		Annual Pension
Job 1	10	10 × 1%	×	$20,159	=	$ 2,016
Job 2	10	10 × 1%	×	27,092	=	2,709
Job 3	10	10 × 1%	×	36,409	=	3,641
Job 4	10	10 × 1%	×	48,931	=	4,893
				TOTAL		$13,259
Nancy*	**Yrs. of Service**	**Formula**		**Highest Pay**		**Annual Pension**
Job 1	40	40 × 1%	×	$48,931	=	$19,572

*Assumes starting salary of $15,000 and pay increases of 3% annually.

Job changes will not hurt defined benefit pension plans based on the average of your salary over all years of service at each job. Table 10-8 shows this for the Mary and Nancy example. Likewise, job changes won't hurt pension plans based on a fixed dollar amount multiplied by years of service, as long as the fixed dollar amount at the new job at least equals the fixed dollar amount at the old job. And, of course, job changes don't hurt defined contribution plans since they are entirely portable.

The Bottom Line

The higher your salary, the more interested you should be in your company pension because it will be a more important source of your retirement income than for a person with a lower income. With a defined benefit pension plan, the company guarantees you a specific pension. With a defined contribution plan, your pension depends on how much you contribute and the investment returns that money earns. If you have a defined pension plan based on your final salary with the company, then frequent job changes will likely reduce your ultimate pension. ___

4. How Can You Receive Your Retirement Income?

Once you've saved for retirement and then reached retirement, another question you'll face is how to draw down on your retirement nest egg. One worry that you'll have is that you draw down on your retirement nest egg in such a way that you won't outlive your nest egg.

Table 10-8   Mary and Nancy's pensions—Defined Benefit based on average salary.

Mary	Years of Service	End of Year Salary		Annual Pension
Job 1	10	$15,450.00	$17,910.78	
		15,913.50	18,448.11	
		16,390.91	19,001.55	
		16,882.63	19,571.60	Average = $17,711.69 × .01
		17,389.11	20,158.75	× yrs. service = $ 1,771.17
Job 2	10	$20,763.51	$24,070.60	
		21,386.41	24,792.71	
		22,028.01	25,536.50	
		22,688.85	26,302.59	Average = $23,803.04 × .01
		23,369.51	27,091.67	× yrs. service = $ 2,380.30
Job 3	10	$27,904.42	$32,348.87	
		28,741.55	33,319.34	
		29,603.80	34,318.92	
		30,491.91	35,348.48	Average = $31,989.29 × .01
		31,406.67	36,408.94	× yrs. service = $ 3,198.93
Job 4	10	$37,501.21	$43,474.18	
		38,626.24	44,778.40	
		39,785.03	46,121.75	
		40,978.58	47,505.41	Average = $42,990.93 × .01
		42,207.94	48,930.57	× yrs. service = $ 4,299.09
			TOTAL	$11,649.49

Nancy	Years of Service	40-Year Average of End of Year Salaries		Annual Pension
Job 1	40	$29,123.74 × .01 × 40 (yrs. of service)	=	$11,649.49

ANNUITY

There's a particular kind of financial product which solves this problem, and it's called an annuity. Most private pensions are paid as an *annuity*. Annuities give you the assurance of receiving an annual benefit yet never running out of money. The annuity pays you a monthly or annual amount as long as you live. When you die, it stops paying. Let's see how this works.

Calculation of Annuity Benefits

You've already run into the term "annuity." Mortgage payments are an annuity. An annual amount of money which is paid or received on a regular basis for a number of periods, and which is based on an initial lump sum amount, is called an annuity. Usually each annuity payment is the same nominal dollar amount although, as you'll see, this isn't necessary. Mortgage payments are an annuity which usually runs for 360 months. The unique feature of a retirement annuity is that it can run indefinitely.

To understand how a retirement annuity is calculated, let's first review how a mortgage payment is calculated. We start with the loan amount. We add the present value factors associated with the mortgage's interest rate and the term of the mortgage. The periodic (e.g., monthly) mortgage payment then equals the loan amount divided by the present value factor sum.

PROBABILITY WEIGHTED PRESENT VALUE FACTORS

A lifetime retirement annuity is calculated in the same way with one major difference. Before the present value factors are added, each factor is multiplied by the probability that the individual will be alive that period to receive the payment. These factors are called "probability-weighted" present value factors. The probability-weighted present value factors are then summed and divided into the retirement nest egg existing at the date of retirement. The result is the periodic annuity payment.

Mortality tables are used to provide the "probability of living" factors that are multiplied by the present value factors. However, the same mortality table as is used for calculating life insurance premiums is not used for annuity calculations because companies have found that people buying annuities tend to live longer.[3] Table 10-9 shows how a retirement annuity for a male age 65 is calculated. Notice that the denominator on the "probability weights" is always the number of people alive at the beginning of the annuity—in this case, 8,577,575, the number alive at age 65.

The calculations in Table 10-9 result in an annual annuity benefit of $22,657.24. However, if you took the same amount of money ($250,000) and wanted to spread it over 51 years (age 65 to 115), you would sum the present value factors (*not* probability-weighted) and divide that sum into $250,000. In this case the result is an annual payment of $14,912.91 ($250,000/16.764). Why is the payment smaller than in the annuity case? Because you're guaranteed of receiving the $14,912.91 for each of 51 years. In the case of the annuity of $22,657.24, you're only guaranteed of receiving this until you die.

---

[3]The fact that they buy annuities doesn't make them live longer; the causation goes the other way. People who live longer are more likely to buy annuities so they don't outlive their income.

Table 10-9   Calculations of a retirement annuity for a male, age 65.

Assumptions: Retirement lump sum amount at age 65 is $250,000; interest rate is 6 percent; first payment begins immediately.

Age	PV Factor, 6% beginning with 1.000		Probability of Living Rate		Probability-weighted PV Factor
65	1.000	×	$\frac{8,577,575}{8,577,575}$	=	1.000
66	0.943	×	$\frac{8,467,345}{8,577,575}$	=	0.931
67	0.890	×	$\frac{8,347,117}{8,577,575}$	=	0.866
68	0.840	×	$\frac{8,215,925}{8,577,575}$	=	0.805
69	0.792	×	$\frac{8,072,853}{8,577,575}$	=	0.745
70	0.747	×	$\frac{7,917,079}{8,577,575}$	=	0.689
71	0.705	×	$\frac{7,747,883}{8,577,575}$	=	0.637
72	0.665	×	$\frac{7,564,669}{8,577,575}$	=	0.586
73	0.627	×	$\frac{7,366,997}{8,577,575}$	=	0.539
74	0.592	×	$\frac{7,154,570}{8,577,575}$	=	0.494
75	0.558	×	$\frac{6,927,098}{8,577,575}$	=	0.451
76	0.527	×	$\frac{6,684,331}{8,577,575}$	=	0.411

(*continued on next page*)

Table 10-9 Calculations of a retirement annuity for a male, age 65 (Continued)

Age	PV Factor, 6% beginning with 1.000		Probability of Living Rate		Probability-weighted PV Factor
77	0.497	×	$\dfrac{6,426,109}{8,511,575}$	=	0.372
78	0.469	×	$\dfrac{6,152,440}{8,577,575}$	=	0.336
79	0.442	×	$\dfrac{5,863,577}{8,577,575}$	=	0.302
80	0.417	×	$\dfrac{5,560,108}{8,577,575}$	=	0.270
81	0.394	×	$\dfrac{5,243,037}{8,577,575}$	=	0.241
82	0.371	×	$\dfrac{4,913,821}{8,577,575}$	=	0.213
83	0.350	×	$\dfrac{4,574,369}{8,577,575}$	=	0.187
84	0.331	×	$\dfrac{4,227,138}{8,577,575}$	=	0.163
85	0.312	×	$\dfrac{3,875,313}{8,577,575}$	=	0.141
86	0.294	×	$\dfrac{3,522,710}{8,577,575}$	=	0.121
87	0.278	×	$\dfrac{3,173,532}{8,577,575}$	=	0.103
88	0.262	×	$\dfrac{2,832,133}{8,577,575}$	=	0.087
89	0.247	×	$\dfrac{2,502,711}{8,577,575}$	=	0.072

90	0.233	×	$\dfrac{2{,}188{,}886}{8{,}577{,}575}$	=	0.059
91	0.220	×	$\dfrac{1{,}893{,}634}{8{,}577{,}575}$	=	0.049
92	0.207	×	$\dfrac{1{,}619{,}298}{8{,}577{,}575}$	=	0.039
93	0.196	×	$\dfrac{1{,}367{,}612}{8{,}577{,}575}$	=	0.031
94	0.185	×	$\dfrac{1{,}139{,}728}{8{,}577{,}575}$	=	0.025
95	0.174	×	$\dfrac{936{,}244}{8{,}577{,}575}$	=	0.019
96	0.164	×	$\dfrac{757{,}221}{8{,}577{,}575}$	=	0.014
97	0.155	×	$\dfrac{602{,}202}{8{,}577{,}575}$	=	0.011
98	0.146	×	$\dfrac{470{,}247}{9{,}577{,}575}$	=	0.008
99	0.138	×	$\dfrac{359{,}864}{8{,}577{,}575}$	=	0.006
100	0.130	×	$\dfrac{269{,}218}{8{,}577{,}575}$	=	0.004
101	0.123	×	$\dfrac{196{,}285}{8{,}577{,}575}$	=	0.003
102	0.116	×	$\dfrac{138{,}948}{8{,}577{,}575}$	=	0.002
103	0.109	×	$\dfrac{95{,}065}{8{,}577{,}575}$	=	0.001
104	0.103	×	$\dfrac{62{,}517}{8{,}577{,}575}$	=	0.001

(continued on next page)

Table 10-9 Calculations of a retirement annuity for a male, age 65 (Continued)

Age	PV Factor, 6% beginning with 1.000		Probability of Living Rate		Probability-weighted PV Factor
105	0.097	×	$\dfrac{39,255}{8,577,575}$	=	0.000
106	0.092	×	$\dfrac{23,346}{8,577,575}$	=	0.000
107	0.087	×	$\dfrac{13,021}{8,577,575}$	=	0.000
108	0.082	×	$\dfrac{6,727}{8,577,575}$	=	0.000
109	0.077	×	$\dfrac{3,168}{8,577,575}$	=	0.000
110	0.073	×	$\dfrac{1,333}{8,577,575}$	=	0.000
111	0.069	×	$\dfrac{487}{8,577,575}$	=	0.000
112	0.065	×	$\dfrac{148}{8,577,575}$	=	0.000
113	0.061	×	$\dfrac{35}{8,577,575}$	=	0.000
114	0.058	×	$\dfrac{6}{8,577,575}$	=	0.000
115	0.054	×	$\dfrac{1}{8,577,575}$	=	0.000
				SUM	11.034

$$\text{Annual Annuity} = \frac{\$250,000}{11.034} = \$22,657.24$$

How can an annuity promise to pay someone a fixed annual amount for the lifetime of that person? Won't the annuity company run out of money? For example, in the annuity calculated in Table 10-9, if the annuity recipient did indeed live to be 115, he would receive $1,155,519.20 (51 years × $22,657.24) in total payments. However, $250,000 invested at 6 percent would only generate total payments of $760,558.41.[4] Where would extra money come from?

WHY ANNUITY COMPANIES DON'T LOSE MONEY

The extra money would come from payments that aren't made to people who die very early. Annuities work like life insurance (in fact, they're usually handled by life insurance companies). For every person that the annuity company loses money on because that person lives a long time, they make money on a person who dies early. Why do retirees use annuities if they know they can lose? Because they don't know exactly when they'll die! Any retiree who knows he will die soon shouldn't buy an annuity.

Types of Annuities

STRAIGHT LIFE ANNUITY

The annuity described in the previous section is called the *"straight life annuity."* It is the basic kind of annuity. Benefits are only paid while the retiree lives. Once the retiree dies, the benefits stop.

As you might expect, many retirees don't like the straight life annuity because they don't like the idea of a large part of their retirement nest egg going to the annuity company if they die early. For this reason annuity companies have developed other kinds of annuities which guarantee that at least part of the remaining retirement nest egg will be passed on to the retiree's spouse or beneficiaries in the case that the retiree dies early. Of course, there's a price for this guarantee. The annuity benefit on all the alternatives will be less than the benefit on the straight life annuity.

Annuity with a Refund: This annuity guarantees that if the retiree dies before the initial investment value (retirement nest egg; $250,000 in Table 10-9) of the annuity is received, then the unpaid balance will be received by the retiree's beneficiaries. The unpaid balance can be received in a series of payments (installment refund) or in a lump sum (cash refund).

Annuity with a Guaranteed Payment Period: This annuity guarantees that if the retiree dies before the end of a specified period, then the payments will continue to the retiree's designated beneficiary for the remainder of the period. Typical specified periods are 5, 10, and 20 years.

---

[4]Divide $250,000 by the present value factor sum (*not* probability weighted) associated with 6 percent and 51 years. This results in an annual payment of $14,912.91. Multiply by 51 to get $760,558.41.

Joint Life and Survivorship Annuity: This is an annuity based on the life span of two people. If the retiree receiving the annuity dies, then the payment continues to a designated beneficiary for the life of that beneficiary. Joint life and survivorship annuities are usually bought with the retiree's spouse as the beneficiary.

The annuity with a refund, the annuity with a guaranteed payment period, and the joint life and survivorship annuity will each result in periodic benefits lower than the straight life annuity. This is because they all guarantee some additional benefit in the case that the retiree dies early.

A "REAL" Annuity

A major problem with the vast majority of annuities is that they are fixed in nominal dollar amount. A very small percentage of private pension annuities have automatic cost-of-living indexing. Going back to Table 10-9, the retiree receives $22,657.24 each year. This may sound like a lot, but the problem is that the amount doesn't rise with the cost of living. The retiree receives $22,657.24 in the first year of the annuity and in every subsequent year. Obviously, therefore, the purchasing power of the annuity falls over time.

A solution to this problem is the *real annuity*.[5] With a real annuity, the initial benefit is calculated based on a real interest rate. Each year, the annuity benefit is increased by a percentage equal to the difference between the nominal interest rate and the real interest rate. If this difference is a close approximation to the inflation rate (which it should be), then the annuity benefit will increase with the cost of living each year.

Table 10-10 takes the same information as used in Table 10-9 and calculates a real annuity based on a real interest rate of 2 percent. Notice that the initial payment is much lower as calculated in Table 10-9. If, then, the nominal interest rate is 7 percent annually, then the annuity benefits would increase 5 percent each year. Figure 10-5 shows how the real annuity benefits would look over time compared to the fixed (in nominal terms) benefits.

At first glance it may look like the real annuity wins hands-down. At age 115, the real annuity would pay over $180,000 whereas the nominal annuity would still pay only $22,657. But remember, your "personal rate of time preference" principle. The disadvantage of the real annuity is that the benefits are lower in the early years of the annuity than with the nominal annuity. In this example, the real annuity pays lower

---

[5]A technical discussion of the real annuity is in King, Francis P. "An Increasing Annuity Based on Nominal Interest Rates and Debt Instruments." *The Journal of Risk and Insurance.* Vol. 51, No. 4, Dec. 1984, pp. 624–637.

benefits until age 72. For a person age 65, the value of the higher benefits with the nominal annuity in the first seven years of retirement may be more important than the potential higher benefits with the real annuity later.

Figure 10-5. Real annuity vs. nominal annuity.

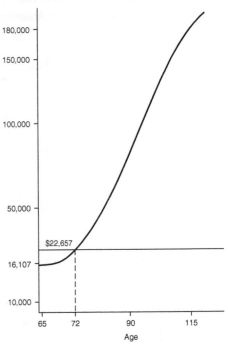

VARIABLE ANNUITY   Don't confuse a *variable annuity* with a real annuity. A variable annuity is an annuity in which the money is invested in securities and financial instruments that earn a variable rate of return, rather than a fixed rate of return. An example is a variable annuity in which the money is invested in stocks, as compared to a fixed annuity in which the money is invested in long term bonds paying a fixed interest rate.

VARIABLE ANNUITY DOESN'T PROVIDE FULL INFLATION PROTECTION

It's sometimes claimed that variable annuities provide inflation protection. If by "inflation protection" it is meant that the benefits paid by an annuity increase at a rate equal to the inflation rate, then variable annuities *do not* provide inflation protection. The payment from a variable annuity will vary. However, if the variable annuity's investments provide a perfect hedge against inflation (meaning their rate of return increases by the increase in the inflation rate), then the benefit payments from a variable annuity will increase only by the *increase in the inflation rate, not by the full inflation rate.* Likewise, if the inflation rate falls (there's still inflation, but at a lower rate), the benefit payment from a variable annuity falls.

For example, suppose a variable annuity initially pays an annual benefit of $20,000. Suppose this benefit is based on a current nominal interest rate of 8 percent, which includes a real rate component of 3 percent and an inflation rate of 5 percent. Now let's assume that next year the inflation rate increases to 6 percent, which also increases the nominal interest rate earned to 9 percent. The annual annuity benefit would increase by only 1 percent (the increase in the inflation rate) to $20,200. The annuity benefit would not increase by the full inflation rate of 6 percent. However, if in the third year the inflation rate fell from 6 percent to 4 percent, thereby reducing the nominal interest rate earned from 9 percent to 7 percent, the annual annuity payment would actually fall by 2 percent. So again, to emphasize, variable annuities do not provide full inflation protection.

Table 10-10 Calculations of a real retirement annuity for a male, age 65.

Assumptions: Retirement lump sum amount at age 65 is $250,000; interest rate is 2 percent; first payment begins immediately.

Age	PV Factor, 2% beginning with 1.000		Probability of Living Rate		Probability-weighted PV Factor
65	1.000	×	$\dfrac{8,577,575}{8,577,575}$	=	1.000
66	0.980	×	$\dfrac{8,467,345}{8,577,575}$	=	0.967
67	0.961	×	$\dfrac{8,347,117}{8,577,575}$	=	0.935
68	0.942	×	$\dfrac{8,215,925}{8,577,575}$	=	0.902
69	0.924	×	$\dfrac{8,072,853}{8,577,575}$	=	0.870
70	0.906	×	$\dfrac{7,917,079}{8,577,575}$	=	0.836
71	0.888	×	$\dfrac{7,747,883}{8,577,575}$	=	0.802
72	0.871	×	$\dfrac{7,564,669}{8,577,575}$	=	0.768
73	0.853	×	$\dfrac{7,366,997}{8,577,575}$	=	0.733
74	0.837	×	$\dfrac{7,154,570}{8,577,575}$	=	0.698
75	0.820	×	$\dfrac{6,927,098}{8,577,575}$	=	0.662
76	0.804	×	$\dfrac{6,684,331}{8,577,575}$	=	0.627

77	0.788	×	$\dfrac{6{,}426{,}109}{8{,}577{,}575}$	=	0.590
78	0.773	×	$\dfrac{6{,}152{,}440}{8{,}577{,}575}$	=	0.554
79	0.758	×	$\dfrac{5{,}863{,}577}{8{,}577{,}575}$	=	0.518
80	0.743	×	$\dfrac{5{,}560{,}108}{8{,}577{,}575}$	=	0.482
81	0.728	×	$\dfrac{5{,}243{,}037}{8{,}577{,}575}$	=	0.445
82	0.714	×	$\dfrac{4{,}913{,}821}{8{,}577{,}575}$	=	0.409
83	0.700	×	$\dfrac{4{,}574{,}369}{8{,}577{,}575}$	=	0.373
84	0.686	×	$\dfrac{4{,}227{,}138}{8{,}577{,}575}$	=	0.338
85	0.673	×	$\dfrac{3{,}875{,}313}{8{,}577{,}575}$	=	0.304
86	0.660	×	$\dfrac{3{,}522{,}710}{8{,}577{,}575}$	=	0.271
87	0.647	×	$\dfrac{3{,}173{,}532}{8{,}577{,}575}$	=	0.239
88	0.634	×	$\dfrac{2{,}832{,}133}{8{,}577{,}575}$	=	0.209
89	0.622	×	$\dfrac{2{,}502{,}711}{8{,}577{,}575}$	=	0.181
90	0.610	×	$\dfrac{2{,}188{,}886}{8{,}577{,}575}$	=	0.156

(*continued on next page*)

Table 10-10 Calculations of a real retirement annuity for a male, age 65 (Continued)

Age	PV Factor, 2% beginning with 1.000		Probability of Living Rate		Probability-weighted PV Factor
91	0.598	×	$\dfrac{1,893,634}{8,577,575}$	=	0.132
92	0.586	×	$\dfrac{1,619,298}{8,577,575}$	=	0.111
93	0.574	×	$\dfrac{1,367,612}{8,577,575}$	=	0.092
94	0.563	×	$\dfrac{1,139,728}{8,577,575}$	=	0.075
95	0.552	×	$\dfrac{936,244}{8,577,575}$	=	0.060
96	0.541	×	$\dfrac{757,221}{8,577,575}$	=	0.048
97	0.531	×	$\dfrac{602,202}{8,577,575}$	=	0.037
98	0.520	×	$\dfrac{470,247}{9,577,575}$	=	0.029
99	0.510	×	$\dfrac{359,864}{8,577,575}$	=	0.021
100	0.500	×	$\dfrac{269,218}{8,577,575}$	=	0.016
101	0.490	×	$\dfrac{196,285}{8,577,575}$	=	0.011
102	0.481	×	$\dfrac{138,948}{8,577,575}$	=	0.008
103	0.471	×	$\dfrac{95,065}{8,577,575}$	=	0.005

104	0.462	×	$\dfrac{62,517}{8,577,575}$	=	0.003
105	0.453	×	$\dfrac{39,255}{8,577,575}$	=	0.002
106	0.444	×	$\dfrac{23,346}{8,577,575}$	=	0.001
107	0.435	×	$\dfrac{13,021}{8,577,575}$	=	0.001
108	0.427	×	$\dfrac{6,727}{8,577,575}$	=	0.000
109	0.418	×	$\dfrac{3,168}{8,577,575}$	=	0.000
110	0.410	×	$\dfrac{1,333}{8,577,575}$	=	0.000
111	0.402	×	$\dfrac{487}{8,577,575}$	=	0.000
112	0.394	×	$\dfrac{148}{8,577,575}$	=	0.000
113	0.387	×	$\dfrac{35}{8,577,575}$	=	0.000
114	0.379	×	$\dfrac{6}{8,577,575}$	=	0.000
115	0.371	×	$\dfrac{1}{8,577,575}$	=	0.000

SUM   11.034

$$\text{Annual Annuity} = \frac{\$250,000}{15.521} = \$16,107,21$$

Taxation of Pension Benefits

Not all of your pension benefits will be taxed. Only that part of your pension which either your employer contributed or which you contributed with before-tax dollars (dollars which weren't taxed) is taxed.

As you now know, most pensions are received as an annuity. How much of each annuity is taxable and how much is not taxable? To answer this question, the IRS has developed a formula for dividing each annuity benefit into a taxable part and non-taxable part. The formula follows these steps:

WHAT PART OF AN ANNUITY IS TAXED?

1. Find out how much you contributed to the pension using after-tax dollars (dollars that you were already taxed on). Your company should be able to tell you this. Take the simple sum of these contributions and call them your *cost*. If your cost is zero, then all of your annuity benefit is taxable, and you can stop here. Don't do any more of the steps.
2. Enter your annual annuity payment, that is, what you will receive.
3. Divide your annuity *cost* (step 1) by a factor provided by the IRS (Publication 575). The factor is based on your age and serves to spread your annuity cost (step 1) over your life of receiving annuity payments.
4. Take the result from step 3, multiply it by 12, and then subtract it from your annual annuity payment. The remainder is the taxable amount of the annuity.

EXAMPLE 10-5: Harold contributed $50,000 in after-tax dollars to his pension. Harold has now retired, and his pension plan will pay him an annual straight life annuity of $8,000. Harold is 65. What part of Harold's pension is taxable?

ANSWER: **Step 1:** Harold's cost is $50,000.

Step 2: Harold's annual annuity payment is $8,000.

Step 3: The appropriate factor from IRS Publication 575 is 260.

$$\frac{\$50,000}{260} = \$192.30$$

Step 4: $192.30 × 12 = $2,307.60
$8,000 − $2,307.60 = $5,692.40.

This is the taxable portion of Harold's annuity. The exclusion is calculated the same way for a real annuity. Notice that in this case, an increasing amount of the real annuity is taxed each year.

Lump Sum Distribution

Some pension plans allow you to receive your pension nest egg in one "lump sum" amount. There are three reasons why some retirees may want to consider this. First, retirees who want to make a large expenditure can use some or all of the lump sum distribution to finance the expenditure. Examples may be retirees who want to finance a home, boat, or "round-the-world" trip. Of course, before making such a large expenditure from their pension nest egg, such retirees should make sure **TAX CONSEQUENCES** they will have an adequate retirement income from other sources.

Retirees who have found that they can purchase a better annuity than the one provided by their company pension may want to take the lump sum distribution and purchase the better annuity. Lastly, retirees who want to have a "real annuity," but find that their company pension doesn't offer it, may want to use the lump sum distribution to buy a "real" annuity or construct their own "real" annuity.

There are, however, important tax consequences of taking a pension nest egg in a lump sum distribution. That amount of the lump sum dis-**ROLLOVER** tribution in excess of the retiree's after-tax contributions to the pension and in excess of any unrealized capital gains will be taxed in the year of the distribution.[6]

If you receive a lump-sum distribution from a qualified employee plan or qualified employee annuity and the plan participant was born before 1936, you may be able to elect optional methods of figuring the tax on the distribution such as the 20% capital gain tax or the 10-year tax option, which is a special formula used to figure a separate tax on ordinary income part of a lump sum distribution.

Another way to reduce the tax on a lump-sum distribution is to "rollover" the taxable part of the distribution into an Individual Retirement Account (Individual Retirement Accounts are discussed in a later topic). While the distribution is in the Individual Retirement Account, it is not taxed. When the money is withdrawn from the Individual Retirement Account it is taxed.

The Bottom Line

Most pensions paid in equal annual installments called annuities. The advantage of an annuity is that you'll never outlive the money—payments will continue as long as you live.

The big disadvantage of most annuities is that they are constant in dollar amount—that is, they don't increase with the cost-of-living. "Real" annuities solve this problem, but you must search far and wide to find them.___

---

[6]An example of unrealized capital gains is the appreciated value of stocks in the retirement nest egg. These gains are taxed when the stock shares are sold.

5. Should You Retire Early?

Should I retire early—what a question! Why not—let's retire as early as possible.

The disadvantage of retiring early is that, in most cases, you'll lose money. You'll lose money in two ways. First, during the years that you're retired instead of working, your retirement income will likely be less than your work income. Second, your retirement income from retiring early will usually be less than the retirement income you'd receive if you retired at the normal time. Figure 10-6 illustrates this.

In this topic you'll learn a framework which can be used to evaluate early retirement. Before the framework is developed, let's first review how much you could lose by retiring early.

Figure 10-6. The cost of retiring early.

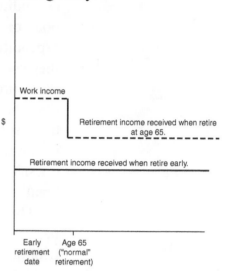

Losses from Early Retirement

You can lose money in several ways by retiring early:

♦ Your retirement income during the early retirement years will be lower than your work income.

♦ Social Security payments will be lower if you retire early. Recall from the topic on Social Security that monthly Social Security benefits are reduced if you retire before your normal retirement age of 65 to 67 depending on your birth year.

♦ If you have a defined pension plan, your annual pensions will be lower for two reasons: (1) your years of service will be lower, and (2) your final salary will be lower.

♦ If you have a defined contribution plan, your annual pension will be lower because you will have contributed to the plan for a fewer number of years.

Sometimes companies encourage employees to retire early by compensating the employee for some of the losses he suffers by retiring early. This compensation can be in the form of a lump sum payment at retirement or supplemental annual payments.

A Decision Framework

In order to decide if early retirement is in your best interest, first collect the necessary information which will allow you to put numbers into the framework shown in Figure 10-6. First, find out what your retirement income will be, from both Social Security and pensions if you retire early. If you receive a lump sum payment for retiring early, convert the payment to an annuity. Second, find out what your work income will be if you continue working until normal retirement age. Last, find out what your retirement income will be if you retire at the normal time.

If the retirement income you will receive upon early retirement is not adequate to meet your retirement expenses, then you can stop here—you can't afford to retire early. But if your early retirement income is adequate, how do you decide whether or not to retire early?

BENEFIT/COST ANALYSIS

You must do a benefit/cost analysis. The costs of retiring early are the reductions in income, both during the early retirement years and during the normal retirement years. These costs can be converted to a single number at the decision date (the early retirement date) by calculating their present value. But what are the benefits of early retirement? The major benefit of early retirement is the increase in leisure time during the early retirement years. This increase in leisure time equals the hours you won't work if you take early retirement.

So you now have the costs of early retirement (present value of reduction in income) and the benefits (increase in leisure time during the early retirement period). To see what each hour of leisure costs you, simply divide the costs of early retirement by the benefits (the increase in leisure time). If your leisure is worth more than this, then you should retire early. If your leisure is worth less than this dollar amount, then you shouldn't retire early.

Application of the Framework

John is trying to decide whether to retire early at age 62 or at age 65. If he retires at age 62 his pension will be based on a final salary of $43,000. If he works until age 65 his pension will be based on a final expected salary of $50,000. Annual Social Security benefits if John retires at age 62 will be $8,640, and the benefits will be $11,000 if he retires at age 65. John's company is offering him a lump sum payment (severance pay) of $30,000 if he retires at age 62. John can convert this into an annual annuity payment of $2,700.

Figure 10-7 shows the calculations that John should make to evaluate the costs and benefits of retiring early. Notice that a 2 percent (real) discount rate is used for dollars which are indexed to inflation, and a 6 percent nominal discount rate (assuming a 4 percent inflation rate) is

Figure 10-7. John's early retirement decision.

```
                  Age      Age      Age
                  62       63       64
─────────────────────────────────────────
Normal            $45,000  $47,000  $50,000    Social Security = $11,000 (indexed)
Retirement                                     Pension = $50,000 × .01 × 35 =
                                                              $17,500 (not indexed)_____



Early        S.S. = $8,640 (indexed)
Retirement   Pension = $43,000 × .01 × 32 = $13,760 (not indexed)_____
             $30,000 = $2,700 annuity (not indexed)

─────────────────────────────────────────────────────────────────────────────────────────────────
             Age                        Age                              Age
             62                         65                               90
```

Retire at Age 65
PV of Work Income (use 6% discount rate) = $45,000×0.943+$47,000×0.890+$50,000×0.840=$126,265
PV of Soc. Sec.   (use 2% discount rate) = $11,000 × PVFS (2%, yrs.4-29) of 18.037 = $198,403
PV of pension   (use 6% discount rate) = $17,500 × PVFS (6%, yrs.4-29) of 10.126 = $177,198
                                  TOTAL = $126,265 + $198,403 + $177,198 = $501,866

Retire at Age 62
PV of Soc. Sec. (use 2% discount rate) = $8,640 × PVFS (2%, yrs.1-29) of 21.844 = $188,735
PV of pension   (use 6% discount rate) = ($13,760 + $2,700) × PVFS (6%, yrs.1-29) of 13.591 = $223,703
plus severance pay annuity
                          TOTAL = $188,735 + $223,703 = $412,438

Cost of Retiring Early: $501,866 - $412,438 = $89,428

Benefit of Retiring Early: Gain 6000 Leisure hours

Cost per Hour of Leisure = $89,428/6000 = $14.90

used for dollars which are not indexed to inflation. The calculations are done through age 90.

It will cost John $89,428 in present value dollars to retire at age 62. If John gains 6000 hours (40 hrs/wk × 50 weeks × 3 years) of leisure by retiring early, then the cost per hour of additional leisure is $14.90. If John's leisure time is worth more than $14.90, then retiring early is, on net, beneficial. If John's leisure time is not worth $14.90, then he should not retire at age 62.

The Bottom Line

Retiring early will usually cost you money. What you gain is leisure time. To decide if retiring early is worthwhile, calculate the cost of each leisure hour gained by retiring early. If your leisure time is worth more than this cost, then retiring early is beneficial.

6. Should You Use Annuities to Save for Retirement?

We've already discussed annuities as a way to receive your retirement income. But annuities can also be used as a way to build up your retirement nest egg. Let's see how they work as an investment.

The Benefit of Annuities

NON-QUALIFIED ANNUITY

INTEREST EARNINGS NOT TAXED UNTIL LATER

There are two ways that annuities can be favored by the tax law. One way is when money which you invest in an annuity is not taxed until a later date. The second way is when interest which your annuity money earns is not taxed until a later date. Annuities purchased through a qualified retirement plan have both advantages. However, we'll talk about these in the next topic with Individual Retirement Accounts (IRAs). In this topic we'll focus on annuities which have only the second tax advantage. With these annuities (so-called "non-qualified" annuities), the money you invest is taxed, but the interest earned by that money is not taxed until it is withdrawn from the annuity account.

You might say—"How do I benefit? I pay taxes now or I pay taxes later. How do I gain by simply delaying taxes?" The answer is simple, but very important. Money which you would have paid in taxes continues to work for you and earn interest. This means that when the money is taxed, there will be a larger pot of money to be taxed (meaning that you'll be left with more even after taxes), than if the money had been taxed away in the first place and couldn't earn interest for you. Only if the delayed tax rate is much higher than the tax rate today could you possibly lose money by investing in an annuity.

BENEFITS OF DELAYED TAXATION

How big are the benefits from this delayed taxation? Table 10-11 shows how much more money you'll have on a percentage basis, *after-taxes* from the annuity investment than from a comparable investment in which interest is taxed in the year it's earned. The calculations use a .33 percent tax rate and assume the same before-tax interest rate earned by the annuity and the alternative investment. Notice that the gain from the annuity is greater the higher the interest rate and the longer the term. Also, there's no limit on how much you can invest in a "nonqualified" annuity, so there's no limit to the gains. Annuities offer no tax advantages over directly investing in individual growth stocks (stocks whose return is all appreciation) because the price appreciation in growth stocks isn't taxed until the stocks are cashed in. Annuities do offer tax advantages over directly investing in mutual funds because, as you've learned, capital gains due to stock trading earned by mutual funds are passed on to the investor and taxed.

How Annuity Money Is Invested

Annuities are a way of investing; they are not a specific investment like a CD, Treasury security, or stock. The money you put in an annuity ultimately is invested in a specific kind of investment.

FIXED ANNUITY

VARIABLE ANNUITY

The investor in annuities has two general options about how the money in the annuity is ultimately invested. The options are fixed annuities and variable annuities. Money in fixed annuities is invested in financial securities which pay a fixed interest rate, like CDs, Treasury securities, and bonds. The interest rate earned by the annuity will change as the interest rates earned on the underlying investments change. However, there is no risk related to potential capital losses on the underlying investment.

Table 10-11   Percentage increase in after-tax investment in an annuity (dollars invested in annuity are taxed but interest earnings are taxed at end of term).

Before-tax interest rate: (after-tax rate):	5% (3.35%)	7% (4.69%)	9% (6.03%)	11% (7.37%)	15% (10.05%)
Term— 5 years	10.5%	1.0%	1.5%	2.3%	4.0%
10	2.2	4.2	9.1	9.5	16.5
15	4.9	9.6	14.9	21.5	37.5
20	9.2	16.8	26.3	38.1	66.4
25	14.0	26.1	41.4	59.3	104.3
30	20.0	37.1	59.2	85.7	152.6

Tax rate of 33% used for both annuity and alternative investment. Assumes no early withdrawal penalty. Entries calculated as:

$$\frac{\{[(1+R)^N - 1] \times .67\} + 1}{[1+.67R]^N} - 1$$

where R is the before-tax interest rate and N is the term.

Money in variable annuities is put in investments which earn variable rates of return. These investments are typically mutual funds, especially stock mutual funds. The annuity shelters the capital gains earned by the stock mutual fund from taxes.

Fixed and variable annuities each have their advantages and disadvantages. Investors in fixed annuities are assured of earning a guaranteed interest rate for a specified period of time. Investors in variable annuities give up this assurance for the chance of "big returns" if their underlying mutual fund skyrockets in value. The risk-averse investor should probably divide his money between fixed and variable annuities.

Disadvantages of Annuities

One big disadvantage of annuities is their illiquidity. If you withdraw any money from an annuity before age 59½, two things will happen. First, you will be taxed on the withdrawal, and all withdrawals will be considered interest and will therefore be fully taxable until all interest has been withdrawn. Second, you will pay a penalty equal to 10 percent of the amount withdrawn. The penalty is not paid, however, if you are disabled. To top this off, some companies may impose an additional withdrawal penalty (called a surrender charge) if you make withdrawals before a specified period (say within 10 years).

EARLY WITHDRAWAL
PENALTY

SURRENDER
CHARGE

In addition, if the capital gain tax rate is lower than the tax rate on ordinary income, non-qualified annuity could be at a disadvantage if investment is held in stocks or stock mutual funds where a large portion of the gain is capital gain. As discussed in the investment chapter, capital gain tax rate has changed frequently in the past. As of 2013 long-term capital gain tax rate is lower than tax rate on ordinary income. Therefore, if you are considering annuity for retirement purpose, you need to weigh the cost and benefit of paying a lower capital gain tax now vs. paying a higher ordinary income tax rate later.

ANNUITY FEES

Another disadvantage of annuities is fees. Annuities can have three types of fees: an up-front fee of 3½ to 5 percent, which means all of the dollars you put into the annuity are not invested; an annual fee of 1½ to 2½ percent; and a fee, or surrender charge of 4 to 10 percent, when you withdraw money. However, the surrender charge is usually eliminated after you've kept the annuity for ten years.

If the annuity fees are high enough, they can wipe out the advantages of annuities. Look at Table 10-12. You can invest $10,000 in an annuity paying 8 percent in which the interest is accumulated tax-free until withdrawal. However, there's a 4 percent up-front fee, which means only $9,600 is actually invested. There's also an annual fee of 1.5 percent, which means the effective interest rate earned is 6.5 percent. The calculations in Table 10-12 show that the after-tax value of

Table 10-12 How fees can eat up the benefits of an annuity.

Annuity	CD
Invest $10,000 in an annuity paying 8%.	Invest $10,000 in a series of CDs paying 8%.
Up-front fee = 4%, so only $9,600 is invested.	No up-front or annual fee.
Annual fee of 1.5% so effective interest rate earned is 6.5%.	After-fax interest rate = 5.36%. (33% tax bracket)
Accumulation after 30 yrs. is $9600 $\times (1.065)^{30} =$ $63,497.92.	Accumulation after 30 yrs. = $10,000 $\times$ $(1.0536)^{30} = \underline{$47,893.09}$.
33% tax on ($63,497.92 – $10,000) = tax of $17,654.31.	
After tax accumulation = $63,497.92 –$17,654.31 = $\underline{$45,843.61}$.	

the annuity after 30 years is $45,843.61. In contrast, investing $10,000 in a series of taxable CDs paying 8 percent gives a total value after 30 years of $47,893.09. In this case the CD wins.

The moral of the story is that you should take into account fees when evaluating the relative benefits of annuities. Fees reduce some of the luster of annuities.

A final disadvantage of some annuities is that lower interest rates are earned by "old money" than by "new money." "Old money" is money that you contributed to the annuity in earlier years, and "new money" is money that you contributed in more recent years. Obviously, this practice reduces the overall benefit of the annuity.

"OLD MON'EY"
"NEW MONEY"

Safety

The companies offering annuities are insurance companies. Insurance companies can financially fail. Many states have insurance programs which provide some protection for annuities in case of failure of the company, but the coverage is usually limited to $100,000 per account. Your "best" bet is to check the A. M. Best Company rating of the insurance company and only do business with companies having an A or A+ rating.

BEST RATING

The Bottom Line

Buying annuities is a way to save for retirement which provides potential tax benefits. However, these benefits can be reduced if withdrawal is made before age 59½ or by fees charged by annuities. You should check the fee structure before investing and compare the benefits after deducting the fees. Also, annuities should be bought as a long-run investment.

7. Should You Use IRAs and Similar Plans to Save for Retirement?

Traditional individual Retirement Accounts (IRAs), Keogh plans, Simplified Employee Pension (SEP) plans, and deferred compensation plans (401k and 403b) are all ways to save for your retirement which give big tax advantages. Like annuities, these plans have the advantage that interest earned by money in the plans is not taxed until the money is withdrawn. You've already seen the benefit of this with annuities (see Table 10-11). But, in addition, these plans have the further advantage that money invested in the plans is tax-deferred as well. That is, you're able to use pre-tax dollars when you invest in these plans, so that for income tax purposes, it's like you never received the money (you do, however, pay Social Security tax on the money). The money you originally invested in the plans is, like its earnings, taxed when you withdraw it.

DOUBLE-BARRELED TAX ADVANTAGE

Size of Tax Advantages

The double-barreled tax advantages of traditional IRAs and similar plans mean that the gains to saving for retirement via one of these plans will be even greater than with an annuity. Look at the simple example in Table 10-13. Three investments are compared: a traditional IRA, an annuity, and a fully taxable investment. Each investment earns a before-tax interest rate of 7 percent, and your tax bracket is 33 percent. You have $100 in pre-tax dollars to put in either of the investments.

In the traditional IRA the full $100 is invested and the before-tax interest rate of 7 percent is earned each year. At the end of the five year term, the total accumulation is taxed, leaving a balance of $93.97. In the annuity the $100 is first taxed before it is invested leaving $67 to be put into the annuity. The before-tax interest rate of 7 percent is earned each year. At the end of the five years the interest earned is taxed (the original $67 is not taxed), leaving a balance of $85.07. In the fully taxable investment, $67 is invested but it only earns an after-tax interest rate of 4.69 percent ($7\% - .33 \times 7\%$) annually. The accumulation at the end of five years is $84.26. So the IRA investment wins over both the annuity and the fully taxable investment.

Table 10-14 shows how much more money you'll have, on a percentage basis, *after-taxes* from the traditional IRA or similar investment. As with the annuity, notice that the advantage of the traditional IRA increases with the interest rate and with the term.

Like an annuity, Congress gave tax advantages to traditional IRAs and similar investments to encourage consumers to save for their own retirement. Therefore, if money is pulled out of an IRA or like investment before age 59½, not only is the withdrawal fully taxed, but a

Table 10-13   Traditional IRA vs. annuity vs. fully taxable investment

	Before-tax interest rate = 7%.
	Tax rate = 33%.
Traditional IRA:	Begin with $100.
	End of yr. 1: × 1.07 = $107.00
	End of yr. 2: × 1.07 = 114.49
	End of yr. 3: × 1.07 = 122.50
	End of yr. 4: × 1.07 = 131.08
	End of yr. 5: × 1.07 = 140.26

After tax of 33% = $140.26 - .33 × $140.26 = <u>$93.97</u>.

Annuity:	Begin with $67.
	End of yr. 1: × 1.07 = $71.69
	End of yr. 2: × 1.07 = 76.71
	End of yr. 3: × 1.07= 82.08
	End of yr. 4: × 1.07= 87.82
	End of yr. 5: × 1.07= 93.97

After tax of 33% on earnings = $93.97 - .33 × ($93.97 - $67) = $<u>85.07.</u>

Fully Taxable Investment:	Begin with $67.
	End of yr. 1: × 1.0469 = $70.14
	End of yr. 2: × 1.0469= 73.43
	End of yr. 3: × 1.0469= 76.88
	End of yr. 4: × 1.0469 = 80.48
	End of yr. 5: × 1.0469 = <u>$84.26</u>

10 percent penalty is also imposed (there are some circumstances in which the penalty isn't imposed; these are discussed later).

Specifics in Traditional IRAs

Traditional IRAs have big tax advantages, but there are a number of restrictions about who can use traditional IRAs and how much they can put in each year. In 2013, eligible workers can invest a maximum of $5,500 annually in an IRA. If you are age 50 and over, the contribution limit is raised to $6,500. Eligible married workers can each contribute to the limit annually. These limits are for the year 2013, and may change from time to time.

Table 10-14   Percentage increase in after-tax investment in a traditional IRA (or similar investment) compared to a fully taxable investment.

Before-tax interest rate: (after-tax rate):	5% (3.35%)	7% (4.69%)	9% (6.03%)	11% (7.37%)	15% (10.05%)
Term—5 years	8.2%	11.9%	14.4%	17.7%	24.6%
10	17.2	24.5	32.5	39.7	55.3
15	26.6	39.1	51.6	64.6	93.3
20	37.5	55.1	73.6	94.2	104.9
25	48.4	72.3	99.3	129.8	201.1
30	61.1	92.5	129.1	170.3	274.3

Tax rate of 33% used for both annuity and alternative investment. Assumes no early withdrawal penalty. Entries calculated as:

$$\frac{1 \times (1 + R)^N \times .67}{.67 \times (1 + .67R)^N} - 1$$

where R is the before-tax interest rate and N is the term.

Who is eligible to make these traditional IRA investments? First, any worker who is not covered by a private pension plan at work can contribute to a traditional IRA. For two working spouses, if one spouse is covered by a private pension plan, then the family is ineligible to contribute if its adjusted gross income exceeds $188,000 in 2013.

Second, even if you are covered by a private pension plan, if you earn less than $59,000 (adjusted gross income) in 2013 as a single person or less than $95,000 in 2013 as a married couple filing jointly, you can make a full IRA contribution. However, if you are covered by a private pension and earn more than $69,000 (adjusted gross income) in 2013 as a single person or more than $115,000 in 2013 as a married couple, then you cannot contribute to an IRA. For single persons earning between $59,000 and $69,000 and for married couples earning between $95,000 and $115,000, a partial IRA contribution is allowed. If your income falls within one of these ranges, then your maximum allowable traditional IRA is proportionately reduced. The income limits are increased each year.

EXAMPLE 10-6: Tom is 52 and Theresa is 48. They both work, and their adjusted gross income is $110,000 in 2013. Sally is 48, single, and earns $62,000. All are covered by a company pension plan. What IRA deduction can each make?

ANSWER: Tom and Theresa:

Step 1. Excess income: $110,000 – $95,000 = $15,000

Step 2. Find the difference between the partial contribution limit and the full contribution limit for married filing jointly: $115,000 – $95,000 = $20,000

Step 3. Divide excess income by that difference in limits: $15,000/$20,000 = 0.75

Step 4. Multiply your maximum contribution for each person by (1- the number found in Step 4):

Allowable contribution for Tom (over 50 so the contribution limit is $6,500): $6,500 × (1 – 0.75) = $1,625

Allowable contribution for Theresa (contribution limit is $5,500): $5,500 × (1 – 0.75) = $1,375

Sally:

Step 1. Excess income: $62,000 – $59,000 = $3,000

Step 2. Find the difference between the partial contribution limit and the full contribution limit for singles: $69,000 – $59,000 = $10,000

Step 3. Divide excess income by that difference in limits: $3,000/$10,000 = 0.3

Step 4. Multiply her maximum contribution by (1- the number found in Step 4):

Allowable contribution for Sally (contribution limit is $5,500): $5,500 × (1-0.3) = $3,850

Non-Deductible IRAs

If you can't make a deductible traditional IRA contribution, you can still make a non-deductible traditional IRA of up to the contribution limit. This means that the contribution is taxed (meaning you use after-tax dollars) but the earnings are accumulated tax-free until they are withdrawn. Therefore, non-deductible traditional IRAs are just like annuities, except that there are limits to the IRA contribution.

Where to Invest IRA Money

IRA money can be invested anywhere—stocks, bonds, CDs, mutual funds, gold coins, etc.—except in collectibles like artwork. Where you invest your IRA money depends on your investment strategy.

IRA money can be moved from investment to investment with no penalty, although there may be a penalty from the individual investment for early withdrawal (e.g., if money from a CD is withdrawn early). The best way to move IRA money is to have the investing institution (e.g., bank, stock brokerage firm) directly move the money. However, you can take possession of the IRA money in its transfer with no penalty as long as you hold the funds for no more than 60 days.

Traditional IRA Payouts

AVOIDING EARLY WITHDRAWAL PENALTY

As mentioned earlier, if you withdraw traditional IRA money before age 59½ you must pay a 10 percent penalty in addition to taxes. There are a couple of ways to avoid the penalty. You don't have to pay the 10 percent penalty on early IRA withdrawals if you receive the withdrawal amount as an annuity based on your life expectancy. For example, if you were age 55 and you withdrew $10,000 from your IRA account, you'd be slapped with a 10 percent penalty in addition to taxes. But if you withdrew the $10,000 as, say, an equivalent annuity of $400 per year, you would not pay the 10 percent penalty (but you'd still pay taxes). You can also avoid the penalty if you withdraw the IRA money and use it for disability or certain medical problems, educational purposes, or certain first-time homeowner expenses.

THE AGE 70½ REQUIREMENT

There are also restrictions on how late you can wait to withdraw your traditional IRA money (this is because the IRS wants a chance to tax it all!). Once you reach age 70½ you must begin withdrawing your IRA money based on minimum required amount. The minimum required payout each year after you reach age 70½ is your IRA account balance divided by your life expectancy or the joint life expectancy of you and your beneficiary.

Roth IRAs

In 1997, lawmakers created the Roth IRA, named after its sponsor, Senator Roth from Delaware. Like the traditional IRA, the Roth IRA is designed to encourage saving for retirement with tax benefits. However, unlike the traditional IRA, contributions to the Roth IRA are not tax deductible. However, withdrawals from the Roth IRA are not taxed, which means interest earnings are not taxed.

In any given year, your combined contribution to traditional IRA and Roth IRA is subject to contribution limits, which are $5,500 for those under age 50 and $6,500 for those 50 and older in 2013. In 2013, maximum contribution is allowed if your adjusted gross income is less than $112,000 for single filing status and $178,000 for married filing jointly. No contribution is allowed if your adjusted gross income is more than $127,000 for single filing status and $188,000 for married filing jointly. These income limits are higher than income limits for traditional IRAs.

Which is better, the traditional IRA or the Roth IRA? That will depend on your current tax bracket and your anticipated tax bracket when you start your withdrawals. It is possible that there may be no difference between these two alternatives. However, if your income is higher than the traditional deductible IRA income limits but lower than the Roth IRA income limits, then Roth IRA provides you with a better retirement tax shelter than traditional IRA.

Keogh Accounts

Keogh Accounts are IRAs for self-employed people. Therefore, in order to have a Keogh account, you must have income from work which you do for yourself.

HIGH CONTRIBUTION LIMITS

One advantage of Keogh Accounts over IRAs is that the contribution limits for Keogh Accounts are much more generous. If you set up a defined contribution Keogh plan, your annual contribution is limited to the lesser of 25 percent of your self-employed income or $51,000 for 2013. However, if you set up a defined benefit Keogh plan, your annual contribution can be the lesser of $205,000 (for 2013; this amount is adjusted for inflation each year) or the average of your highest three consecutive year earnings. Investment, early withdrawal, and other withdrawal features are similar for a Keogh as for an IRA.

Simplified Employee Pensions

With a Simplified Employee Pension, or SEP, the employer can contribute each year up to 25 percent of the worker's salary or $51,000 in 2013, whichever is less, to a pension account for the employee. Earnings are not taxed while they're in the plan. If the employee leaves the company, the employee can take the SEP money with him and transfer it to another SEP or an IRA. SEPs can also be set up by self-employed workers.

401-k Plans

401-k retirement plans have the same double-barreled tax advantages of IRAs, but they have the advantage of bigger contribution limits. The annual limit in 2013 is $17,500 and $23,000 if you are 50 or older and each year the limit is increased by the inflation rate. Both the employee and company can contribute to the 401-k. There's usually a choice of where the 401-k money can be invested, including stock and bond mutual funds and fixed rate investments.

Money can be withdrawn before age 59½ if the use is for medical bills, tuition, or down payment on a house you'll live in and if you have exhausted all other assets and can't borrow from a bank or finance company. However, even after meeting all these requirements you'll still have to pay taxes and maybe the 10 percent penalty on the withdrawal.

BORROWING FROM 401-K PLANS

A unique feature of 401-k plans is that you can borrow against them with no penalty, taxes, or restrictions. The money must be repaid within five years (a longer repayment time is allowed if the money is used to buy a house) with interest. The interest is not tax deductible.

403-B Plans

403-B plans are similar to 401-k plans but are limited to employees of nonprofit institutions. Annual employee contributions are limited to $17,500 in 2013 and $23,000 if you are 50 or older. However, the 403-B annual contribution limit will increase with the rate of inflation. The total of your elective salary deferral plus employer matching contributions is limited to $51,000 for 2013. Withdrawal and loan provisions are the same as for 401-k plans. Roth 401-k and 403-B plans are also available.

The Bottom Line

IRA accounts, Keogh plans, 401-k, 403-B, and SEP accounts are all excellent ways to save for retirement. The double-barreled tax advantages of these plans (pre-tax dollars are invested and interest is earned tax fee) mean that your money grows faster than in a fully taxed investment. However, the plans have penalties for any withdrawal of money before retirement age (59½), so the plans should be considered long-term investments.

8. Should You Use Life Insurance as a Source of Retirement Income?

Many retirees face decisions about what kind of annuity to choose for their retirement pension. A big decision concerns whether to select a straight life annuity or a joint and survivorship annuity. A straight life annuity has the advantage of providing the maximum amount of income per year from the pension nest egg, but at the cost of providing no money to a surviving spouse if the retiree dies first. A joint and survivorship annuity has the advantage of providing money to a surviving spouse if the retiree dies first, but at the cost of lower payments to the retiree while he or she lives.

An alternative which has been suggested by the life insurance industry proposes this solution. Select the straight life annuity which provides maximum income while the retiree is alive but no income to a surviving spouse or other beneficiary. Then, with some of the money saved by buying the straight life annuity rather than the joint and survivorship annuity, buy a life insurance policy with the retiree as the insured and with the spouse (or other family member) as the beneficiary. If the retiree dies before the spouse, the spouse can use the life insurance policy to provide income for the remainder of the spouse's life.

Is this life insurance alternative a good option? Figure 10-8 illustrates the decision. With the joint and survivorship annuity option, the retiree gets A_{JS} each year and the beneficiary gets $B if the retiree dies. With the life annuity/life insurance option, the retiree gets A_L-$Prem.

Figure 10-8. The joint and survivorship annuity option vs. the life annuity/life insurance options.

Joint and Survivorship Annuity option	Life Annuity/Life insurance option
Retiree gets after-tax annuity A_{JS}	Retiree gets after-tax annuity A_L - $Prem.
Beneficiary gets after-tax annuity $B	Beneficiary gets after-tax annuity $B

Question: Is A_L - $Prem. bigger than A_{JS}

symbols:

A_{JS}:   after-tax annuity to retiree from joint and survivorship annuity.

A_L: after-tax annuity to retiree from life annuity.

$Prem: life insurance premium necessary to buy annuity of $B.

each year and the beneficiary gets $B if the retiree dies. $Prem. is the annual life insurance premium necessary to provide a life insurance policy big enough to be converted into a life annuity giving $B each year. If A_L -$Prem. is bigger than A_{JS}, then the life annuity/life insurance option is better. If A_{JS} is bigger than A_L-$Prem., then the joint and survivorship annuity option is better.

An Example

Figure 10-9 gives a hypothetical example of the decision for Fred and Sarah. Fred can take a joint and survivorship annuity from his pension which will pay him $20,000 annually and will pay Sarah $20,000 annually if Fred dies first. Alternatively, Fred can take a straight life annuity paying $32,000. He can also buy a $250,000 life insurance policy which can be converted to a life annuity providing $20,000 annually. The $250,000 life insurance policy will cost Fred $10,000 annually in premiums.

Which way should Fred and Sarah go? In this example the life annuity/life insurance option is the clear favorite. After subtracting the annual life insurance premium ($10,000) from the life annuity ($32,000), Fred will have $22,000 each year, which is more than the $20,000 under the joint and survivorship annuity option.

Some Cautions

There is no clear reason why the life annuity/life insurance option will be better than the joint and survivorship annuity option, or vice-versa.

You'll have to gather the numbers and do a comparison as is done in Figure 10-9.

However, one study by Gustavson and Trieschmann did find the life annuity/life insurance option generally superior to the joint and survivorship annuity option.[7] Gustavson and Trieschmann used data from the Teachers' Insurance and Annuity Association.

Figure 10-9. Fred and Sarah's decision.

Joint and Survivorship Annuity option	Life Annuity/Life insurance option
Retiree gets annual after-tax benefit of $20,000.	Retiree gets annual after-tax benefit of $32,000.
Beneficiary (spouse) gets annual after-tax benefit of $20,000 if retiree dies.	Annual cost of $250,000 life insurance policy is $10,000.
	Life insurance policy of $250,000 will buy a life annuity paying $20,000 annually after-taxes.

You should, of course, be very careful in examining the life insurance policy involved with the life annuity/life insurance option. Particularly if the policy is a universal life policy, make sure the premiums are not "artificially low" because very optimistic investment interest rates were assumed.

The Bottom Line

Taking a straight life annuity and buying a life insurance policy to provide income to a surviving spouse or beneficiary can be a viable alternative to a joint and survivorship annuity. Work through the numbers to see which is best. Carefully examine the life insurance policy for overly optimistic investment rates of return.

9. How Can You Use Your House for Retirement Income?

Three-fourths of people over age 65 own their homes. This is a lot of wealth which retired consumers can tap for their retirement income.

One way to tap this equity is for the retired person to sell the home, use part of the proceeds to buy a smaller home or to rent, and use the DOWNSIZING remainder of the proceeds for retirement income. This is called "downsizing." For retired homeowners who want to leave the old homestead and move somewhere else, it's an excellent option.

But what if the retired homeowners don't want to sell their current homes, and in fact, they want to spend their remaining years in their

---

[7] Gustavson, Sandra G. and James S. Trieschmann. "Universal Life Insurance as an Alternative to the Joint and Survivor Annuity." *Journal of Risk and Insurance,* Vol. 55, No. 3, Sept. 1988, pp. 529–538.

current homes? Is there a way they can stay in their homes yet tap some of the home equity for retirement income?

REVERSE MORTGAGE   There is a way to do this and it's called a *reverse mortgage.* The reverse mortgage requires that the retired homeowner own the house free of a mortgage (that is, the mortgage has been fully paid). The retired homeowner uses the house's value to obtain a loan. The loan is invested and used to generate periodic payments to the retired homeowner. The loan is repaid through sale of the house at some future date. The lender makes money by charging a loan interest rate higher than the investment interest rate. Thus, the advantage of the reverse mortgage is that the retired homeowner makes use of equity in his/her home for periodic income while remaining in the home. The disadvantage of the reverse mortgage is that the retired homeowner will not have the house to pass on to descendants.

This is a general description of the reverse mortgage. In reality there are several types of reverse mortgages, distinguished by: (1) whether income to the homeowner is also generated by appreciation in the house's value; and (2) whether payments to the homeowner are for a specific term or for the remaining life of the homeowner.

Reverse Mortgage with a Specified Term and No Shared Appreciation

This is the most conservative of the reverse mortgages. The current value of the house (or some percentage of the current value) is used to obtain a loan from which periodic payments for a specified term are generated. However, out of the payments interest must be paid on the loan. At the end of the specified term, the house is sold. From the sale, the original house value is repaid to the lender, and the retired homeowner keeps any appreciation. Schematically, this reverse mortgage is represented in Figure 10-10. Now let's work an example.

EXAMPLE 10-7:   Fred and Sarah's house is valued at $80,000. For simplicity, assume they can obtain a reverse mortgage loan for $80,000 with an annual interest rate charge of 10 percent and a term of 8 years. The $80,000 can be invested at 8 percent.

How much can $80,000 invested at 8 percent generate in annual benefits of both principal and interest?

ANSWER: This is an annuity problem. The answer is found by dividing $80,000 by the present value factor sum associated with 8 percent and 8 years. If payments are to begin immediately, the first present value factor is 1.000. The following calculations show how much Fred and Sarah would net annually.

$$\text{Gross annual benefit} = \frac{\$80,000}{\text{PVFS } (r = 8\%, n = 8 \text{ years, BOM})}$$

$$= \frac{\$80,000}{6.206} = \$12,890.75$$

$$\text{Annual interest due} = \$80,000 \times .10 = \underline{8,000.00}$$

$$\text{NET ANNUAL BENEFIT} = \$ 4,890.75$$

At the end of the eight years Fred and Sarah would owe the $80,000 to the lender. The $80,000 would be repaid by selling the house. Fred and Sarah would keep any difference between the house's sale value and the $80,000.

Reverse Mortgage with a Specified Term and Shared Appreciation

The difference between this reverse mortgage and the previous one is that interest on the loan is not paid periodically by the retired homeowner. Instead, the interest is accumulated and paid out of the appreciation of the house's value. The advantage to the homeowner is that periodic payments are higher. Figure 10-11 illustrates this type of reverse mortgage. Using our previous example, the reverse mortgage with 100 percent shared appreciation would generate annual payments to the elderly homeowner of $14,998 for each of the eight years. For the sale of the house after the eighth year to fully repay this loan, the house would obviously have to appreciate at 10 percent or more per year.

The fact that the appreciation rate of the house is unknown is a problem for lenders with this type of reverse mortgage. One way to address this problem is to loan less than 100 percent of the initial value of the house. When this is done, then the required rate of appreciation of the house will be lower.

Figure 10-10. Reverse mortgage with specified term and no shared appreciation.

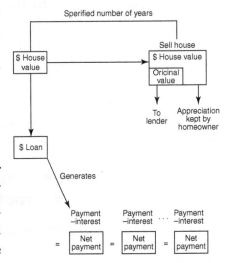

EXAMPLE 10-8: Fred and Sarah now want to consider a shared appreciation mortgage with a specified term. They can get a loan of $50,000 on their $80,000 house

for a term of eight years. The loan interest rate is 10 percent and the $50,000 earns 8 percent annually. Fred and Sarah want three questions answered:

Figure 10-11. Reverse mortgage with specified term and shared appreciation.

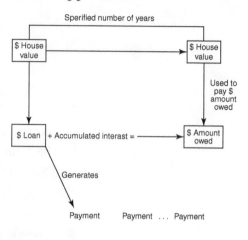

1. How much money can they receive each year?
2. How much will they owe at the end of the eight years? and
3. What is the house's minimum required appreciation rate each year necessary to generate enough money to repay the loan and its accumulated interest?

ANSWER:

1. Fred and Sarah's gross annual benefit is $50,000 divided by the present value factor sum associated with 8 percent and 8 years

$$= \frac{\$50,000}{6.206} = \$8,056.72$$

(assuming first factor is 1.000).

Since no interest payments are made by Fred and Sarah each year, $8,056.72 is the net benefit they will receive each year.

2. At the end of eight years Fred and Sarah will owe a sum equal to $50,000 multiplied by the future value factor associated with 10 percent and 8 years:

$$\$50,000 \times 2.144 = \$107,200.$$

3. The current house value, $80,000, must appreciate to at least $107,200 by the end of eight years. To find the required annual appreciation rate, divide $107,200 by $80,000, and find this future value factor in Appendix Table A-1 for eight years.

$$\frac{\$107,200}{\$80,000} = 1.34.$$

The closest associated interest rate is *4 percent.*

Reverse Mortgage with Unlimited Term and No Shared Appreciation

One disadvantage, from the retired homeowner's perspective, of the aforementioned reverse mortgages is that the term of the mortgage is limited. When the term is up, the elderly homeowner will most likely have to sell the house and move.

An alternative is to specify an unlimited term. That is, the retired homeowner will receive benefits until he/she dies. In this case, the loan is used to purchase an annuity. These types of reverse mortgages are called reverse annuity mortgages. The retired homeowner receives the annuity benefits until death. In the case of a reverse annuity mortgage with no shared appreciation, the net annuity benefit to the homeowner equals the gross annuity benefit minus the interest payment.

EXAMPLE 10-9: Re-work EXAMPLE 10-7 using a reverse annuity mortgage instead of the reverse term mortgage. Use a life annuity for Fred, who is age 65.

ANSWER: To convert the $80,000 loan to a life annuity payment, $80,000 must be divided by the probability-weighted present value factor sum associated with 8 percent (the investment interest rate) and a male age 65. Using the survival rates (probability of living rates) from Table 10-9, this probability-weighted present value factor sum is 9.589 (see Table 10-15 for the calculations).

$$\text{Gross annual benefit: } \frac{\$80,000}{9.589} = \$8,342.89$$

$$\text{Annual interest due} = \$80,000 \times .10 = 8,000.00$$
$$\text{Net annual benefit} = \$ 342.89$$

The reverse annuity mortgage would only net Fred and Sarah $342.89 annually. The $80,000 is repaid after Fred dies from the proceeds of the house sale. Any appreciation would be kept by Sarah or other beneficiaries.

Reverse Mortgage with Unlimited Term and Shared Appreciation

A way to increase the net annual benefit to retired homeowners of a reverse annuity mortgage is to not have interest payments each year, but instead have the accumulated interest ultimately paid from the proceeds of the final house sale. This is a reverse annuity mortgage with shared appreciation. The lender, of course, will be concerned about the ability of the house to appreciate and pay-off the loan.

The next example illustrates the workings of this type of reverse annuity mortgage.

Table 10-15 Probability-weighted present value sum for Fred and Sarah's Reverse Annuity Mortgage.

Age	PV factor 8% beg. with 1	Survival Rate	Prob-wgt PV Factor	Age	PV factor 8% beg. with 1	Survival Rate	Prob-wgt PV factor
65	1.000 ×	1.000 =	1.000	91	0.135 ×	0.221 =	0.030
66	0.926 ×	0.987 =	0.914	92	0.125 ×	0.189 =	0.024
67	0.857 ×	0.973 =	0.834	93	0.116 ×	0.159 =	0.018
68	0.794 ×	0.958 =	0.761	94	0.107 ×	0.133 =	0.014
69	0.735 ×	0.941 =	0.692	95	0.099 ×	0.109 =	0.011
70	0.681 ×	0.923 =	0.629	96	0.092 ×	0.088 =	0.008
71	0.630 ×	0.903 =	0.569	97	0.085 ×	0.070 =	0.006
72	0.583 ×	0.882 =	0.514	98	0.079 ×	0.055 =	0.004
73	0.540 ×	0.859 =	0.464	99	0.073 ×	0.042 =	0.003
74	0.500 ×	0.834 =	0.417	100	0.068 ×	0.031 =	0.002
75	0.463 ×	0.808 =	0.374	101	0.063 ×	0.023 =	0.001
76	0.429 ×	0.779 =	0.334	102	0.058 ×	0.016 =	0.001
77	0.397 ×	0.749 =	0.297	103	0.054 ×	0.011 =	0.001
78	0.368 ×	0.717 =	0.264	104	0.050 ×	0.007 =	0.000
79	0.340 ×	0.684 =	0.233	105	0.046 ×	0.005 =	0.000
80	0.315 ×	0.648 =	0.204	106	0.043 ×	0.003 =	0.000
81	0.292 ×	0.611 =	0.178	107	0.039 ×	0.002 =	0.000
82	0.270 ×	0.573 =	0.155	108	0.037 ×	0.001 =	0.000
83	0.250 ×	0.533 =	0.133	109	0.034 ×	0.000 =	0.000
84	0.232 ×	0.493 =	0.114	110	0.031 ×	0.000 =	0.000
85	0.215 ×	0.452 =	0.097	111	0.029 ×	0.000 =	0.000
86	0.199 ×	0.411 =	0.082	112	0.027 ×	0.000 =	0.000
87	0.184 ×	0.370 =	0.058	113	0.025 ×	0.000 =	0.000
88	0.170 ×	0.330 =	0.056	114	0.023 ×	0.000 =	0.000
89	0.158 ×	0.292 =	0.046	115	0.021 ×	0.000 =	0.000
90	0.146 ×	0.255 =	0.037				
						SUM =	9,589

EXAMPLE 10-10: Re-work EXAMPLE 10-8 using a reverse annuity mortgage instead of the reverse term mortgage. Again, use a life annuity for Fred at age 65.

1. Using the probability-weighted present-value factor from EXAMPLE 10-9 (9.589), Fred and Sarah's gross annual benefit is:

$$\frac{\$50,000}{9.589} = \$5,214.31.$$

Since no interest payments are made by Fred and Sarah each year, this is what they pocket annually.

2. The lender now doesn't know how long the loan will last, Here's what Fred and Sarah will owe at the end of certain years:

    End of 5 yrs: $50,000 × FVF (10%, 5 yrs.) =
    $50,000 × 1.611 = $80,550.

    End of 10 yrs: $50,000 × FVF (10%, 10 yrs.) =
    $50,000 × 2.594 = $129,700.

    End of 20 yrs: $50,000 × FVF (10%, 20 yrs.) =
    $50,000 × 6.727 = $336,350.

    End of 30 yrs: $50,000 × FVF (10%, 30 yrs.) =
    $50,000 × 17.449 = $872,450.

3. The current house value is $80,000. To meet the loan payment at the end of each period noted above, the required appreciation rates are:

    For 5 yrs: $\dfrac{\$80,550}{\$80,000} = 1.007$

    Associated with annual rate of under 1 percent.

    For 10 yrs: $\dfrac{\$129,700}{\$80,000} = 1.621$

    Associated with annual rate of 5 percent.

    For 20 yrs: $\dfrac{\$336,350}{\$80,000} = 4.204$

    Associated with annual rate of 7.5 percent.

    For 30 yrs: $\dfrac{\$872,450}{\$80,000} = 10.906$

    Associated with annual rate of about 8 percent.

Why Reverse Mortgages Haven't Taken Off

Reverse mortgages have been available for decades, but they've never become very popular. There are at least two reasons for their unpopularity—one on the demand side and one on the supply side.

BEQUEST MOTIVE   On the demand side, many retired homeowners like to leave their house as a bequest to children or other beneficiaries. The existence of a loan against some or all of the house's value obviously reduces the value of this bequest. Many retired homeowners don't like term reverse mortgages because it means there's a good chance they'll need to sell the house before their death in order to meet the loan payment.

On the supply side, the lenders supplying reverse annuity mortgages must have a large number of homeowners participating in order that the life spans balance out (those living a long time and collecting a large amount of money are balanced by those dying early and collecting little money). Frequently, the necessary number of homeowners interested in reverse annuity mortgages haven't been there to make the program viable.

Sale Leaseback

There's one other way for a retired homeowner to get money out of his home without leaving it. The technique is called a *sale leaseback*. Under a sale leaseback, the retired homeowner sells the house to an investor. However, the sales contract stipulates that the seller can remain in the house until death. The retired seller uses the proceeds from the sale of the house to purchase a life annuity. The retired seller must pay rent to the investor-owner, so the net annuity benefit equals the gross benefit minus the rent payment. So this plan is similar to the reverse mortgage where the retired homeowner pays annual interest to the lender.

The sale leaseback can generate larger net benefits to retired person than the reverse mortgage because the retiree can use 100 percent of the house value to purchase an annuity. Also, the greater the investor expects the house to appreciate in value, the lower the rent payment will be and the larger the net benefit to the retiree.

The investor-owner gets the depreciation advantage associated with a rental house and, of course, benefits from all future appreciation in the house's value. The owner-investor is liable for all repairs, maintenance, and taxes on the house.

The Bottom Line

Reverse mortgages and sale leasebacks tap the equity in a retired person's home for retirement income without forcing the retiree to move. One of the costs of these techniques is that the retired homeowner loses the ability to pass the house and property on to descendants. _____

10. Do You Need an Estate Plan?

You've heard the old phrase, "you can't take it with you." You've also heard the phrase, "there's nothing certain except death and taxes." In this topic we'll examine not whether you can take your assets with you, but whether your descendants can take your assets with them. We'll also examine if taxes, in this case estate taxes, are the government's final grab at your money. Questions about transferring assets to your descendants and taxes due on those transfers are generally classified under the heading "estate planning."

ESTATE PLANNING

An estate plan directs how your assets will be distributed when you die. An estate plan can be important for two reasons. First, an estate plan will allow you to specify who gets your assets when you die. Second, an estate plan can be used to reduce the taxes that must be paid on your assets when you die.

You might say, "What assets will I have left, especially if I live a full life?" You may very well plan to "use up your assets" in retirement, in which case estate planning is less of an issue. But many individuals like to leave assets to children or descendants. For these individuals, estate planning can be very important.

Who Gets Your Assets

A *will* is a document which you can prepare (in consultation with an attorney) to specify who gets your assets when you die. Thus, a will gives you control over the disposition of your assets.

If you don't have a will, then when you die the state in which you live will specify who gets your assets. In most states your assets are divided between your spouse and your children; for example, on a 50–50 basis. If you have no children, then usually your assets are divided between your spouse and parents. If you have no spouse and no children, then usually your parents get everything, and if you have no spouse, children, or surviving parents, then your other relatives (e.g., brothers and sisters) will receive your assets.

Wills can also be used to establish management of assets for your young children in the case that both parents die. Wills can establish a guardian for the children and a manager for your assets in the event that young children are orphaned when they are young.

Since the value of your assets will change over time, it's usually better to specify inheritors' shares as a percentage of total assets or as a specific asset (e.g., your spouse receives the stock portfolio) rather than as a dollar amount.

Wills can be changed. Major changes in your family (e.g., birth of a new child, divorce) or major changes in your assets are reasons for changing a will.

Reducing Estate Taxes

When you die and your net worth is positive (your assets are greater than your debts), then taxes must be paid on this net worth when it is transferred to those you have designated as inheriting the net worth. At

FEDERAL ESTATE
TAXES

the federal level these taxes are called estate taxes, and at the state level they are called inheritance taxes. Federal estate taxes are much greater than state inheritance taxes. This section will concentrate on federal estate taxes and ways to reduce them.

The federal estate tax has changed almost every year since 2001 as the effective exclusion climbed from $675,000 in 2001 to $3.5 million in 2009, and the maximum rate fell from 55% to 45%. In 2010, the tax disappeared entirely, only to return in 2011 with a $5 million exemption indexed for inflation and a 35% tax rate. Under the American Taxpayer Relief Act, signed into law in January 2013, the federal estate tax exemption has been indexed for inflation and therefore increased from $5.12 million in 2012 to $5.25 million in 2013. Estate tax rate for estates over this exemption amount has increased from 35% in 2012 to 40% in 2013.

In addition, portability of the federal estate tax exemption between married couples has become permanent for 2013 and beyond. Portability of the estate tax exemption means married couples could add any unused portion of the estate tax exemption of the first spouse to die to the surviving spouse's estate tax exemption. This means that in 2013 married couples can pass on $10.5 million to their heirs free from federal estate taxes without any special planning tools.

If you are lucky enough to have an estate larger than the exemption, there are still ways of reducing estate taxes, but most of these methods have disadvantages.

One method that does not have disadvantages is to deduct any outstanding debts and costs of settling the estate (legal fees, etc.) from the gross estate before paying taxes. That is, only the *net* worth of the estate (the gross value of the estate minus outstanding debts and minus estate settlement costs) are subject to estate taxes.

GIVING AWAY YOUR
ESTATE

Another way to reduce taxes on your estate is to give your estate away either before you die or when you die! You can give $14,000 (in 2013) to an individual per year to as many individuals as you desire without paying estate tax on the money (and the recipient doesn't pay tax either!). This amount doubles for a married couple. Also, when you die, any money you leave to charities will not be taxed.

The obvious disadvantage of giving your estate away before you die is that you can't use the money. If you need the money in your estate to help pay for expenses during retirement, then giving the money away just to avoid estate taxes isn't a viable option.

TRUSTS

Estate taxes can also be reduced through the use of *trusts.* A trust is a legal entity which is granted control of assets you give it. The assets are therefore no longer considered part of your estate. A trustee manages the assets. When you die, the assets in the trust can be passed on to designated beneficiaries without estate taxes being due.

There are two disadvantages of trust: (1) They cost money to set up and to maintain. The annual cost may be as much as 1 percent of the assets in the trust; (2) You lose some use of the assets you put into a trust. Some trusts allow you to receive and use the *income* generated each year by the trust's assets, but usually you can't touch the principal (the original asset value put into the trust). Therefore, if you need both the principal and interest of your assets in order to meet living expenses, then trusts aren't a good idea.

The Bottom Line

Have a will written so that your assets are given to those you want to receive them in the case of your death. If your net worth is substantial then estate taxes must eventually be paid unless: (a) you give your estate away before you die or to a charity at death or; (b) you put some of your estate in a trust. However, only do these things if you don't need the assets for living expenses.

WORDS AND CONCEPTS YOU SHOULD KNOW

Assets targeted for retirement
Lump sum gap
Replacement rate
Social Security benefits
Averaged indexed monthly earnings
Defined contribution pension
Defined benefit pension
Target benefit pension
Vesting
Integration
Annuity
Probability-weighted present value factors
Straight life annuity
Annuity with a refund
Annuity with a guaranteed payment period
Joint life and survivorship annuity
Real annuity
Fixed annuity

Variable annuity
Exclusion proportion
Lump sum distribution
Rollover
Traditional individual retirement account
Non-deductible IRA
Roth IRA
Keogh accounts
Simplified employee pensions
401-k plan
403-B plan
Life annuity/life insurance option
Reverse mortgage
Reverse annuity mortgage
Sale leaseback
Estate tax
Portability of estate tax exemption

RETIREMENT PLANNING—A SUMMARY

1. Follow an eight step procedure to calculate your required savings rate for retirement:
   - **A** (1) Determine your years in retirement.
   - **B** (2) Calculate the present value at the retirement date of retirement living expenses in real dollars.
   - **C** (3) Calculate the present value at the retirement date of Social Security payments in real dollars.
   - **D** (4) Calculate the present value at the retirement date of other pension payments in real dollars.
   - **E** (5) Calculate the future value at the retirement date of assets targeted for retirement in real dollars.
   - **F** (6) Calculate the lump sum gap as (2) - (3) - (4) - (5).
   - **G** (7) Calculate the initial dollar amount to save for retirement by dividing the lump sum gap by the future value factor sum associated with the number of working years remaining and the real interest rate.
   - **H** (8) Calculate the savings ratio as (7) divided by current income.

2. You'll need to replace approximately 55 to 85 percent of your pre-retirement income to meet retirement expenses. The replacement rate is lower for higher incomes.

3. Required retirement savings rates increase with the age that savings begin and with income.

4. A benefit of Social Security benefits is that they are indexed for inflation. Social Security replaces a higher percentage of low income retiree's pre-retirement income. Social Security benefits are based on an inflation-adjusted average of the worker's income history, with greater weight given to lower income dollars.

5. Defined benefit plans guarantee a certain dollar amount of pension at retirement. A typical defined benefit pension is one percent of your final salary multiplied by years at the job. Your pension from a defined contribution plan is not guaranteed, but is based on how much is saved and what interest is earned by the contributions. A target benefit plan is a defined contribution plan with contributions specified to yield a certain dollar-valued pension.

    A. Defined benefit plans have the advantage that benefits are predictable and the company assumes the investment risks. Defined benefit plans are disadvantageous because they are not portable and they may not always be fully funded.

    B. Defined contribution plans are portable, always fully funded, and the worker can select the specific investments. Disadvantages of defined contribution plans include the fact that benefits are less predictable and the worker assumes the investment risk.

6. Changing jobs frequently will reduce your pension if you have a defined benefit plan based on your final salary.

7. Most pensions are received as an annuity. The periodic annuity payment equals the retirement investment sum divided by the probability-weighted present value factor sum.

    A. A straight life annuity pays a constant dollar amount for life.

    B. An annuity with a refund guarantees that the balance of a specified sum will be paid to a beneficiary if the retiree dies before the sum is received.

    C. An annuity with a guaranteed payment period guarantees that if the retiree dies before the end of a specified period, then payments will continue to a beneficiary for the remainder of the guaranteed period.

    D. A joint life and survivorship annuity makes payments for the combined life of the retiree and beneficiary (usually a spouse).

8. A disadvantage of most annuities is that benefits are not adjusted for inflation. A "real" annuity is calculated using a real interest rate. Benefits increase each year by a percentage equal to the difference between the earned interest rate and real rate. Variable annuities are not the same as real annuities. Variable annuity payments are not directly linked to the inflation rate.

9. Lump sum distributions of pensions have tax implications. They can be "rolled over" into IRAs for tax deferral.

10. Retiring early will usually result in less income for you, both less work income and less pension income. You must decide if the lost income is worth the gain in leisure. To do this, calculate the lost income per additional hour of leisure gained.

11. Annuities can be bought while you're working as a way to save for retirement. Interest is earned tax free until money is withdrawn. Taxes, a 10 percent penalty, and possibly surrender charges must be paid if money is withdrawn before age 59½. Fees charged by annuities can substantially reduce the investment benefits of annuities.

12. Traditional and Roth individual Retirement Accounts (IRAs), Keogh plans, Simplified Employee Pension (SEP) plans, 401-k plans, and 403-B plans are all ways to save for retirement which enjoy big tax benefits. Contributions to Roth plans are after-tax but withdrawals will be tax-free. Contributions to other traditional retirement plans are typically pre-tax. All money will be taxed when funds are withdrawn. You can earn as much as 100 or 200 percent more in these plans as compared to fully taxed investments. There's tax and a 10 percent penalty on withdrawals before age 59½ (unless withdrawn as an annuity on an IRA or Keogh plan), and withdrawals must begin by age 70½.

13. A life annuity on a retiree with life insurance on a dependent spouse is a viable option to a joint and survivorship annuity.

14. Reverse mortgages allow a retired homeowner with no mortgage to convert the house's value to periodic income. The reverse mortgage can be established for a specific term or for the lifetime of the owner (called a reverse annuity mortgage). Higher periodic income can be received if interest payments are delayed and paid out of the house's value appreciation. The homeowner loses the ability to use all of the house as a bequest.

15. With a sale leaseback, the retired homeowner sells the house to an investor but receives a guarantee to rent the house for life. Proceeds from sale of the house are used to buy a straight life annuity, and net benefits to the retired renter equal the periodic annuity benefit minus rent.

DISCUSSION QUESTIONS

1. Why is it important for a person to plan for retirement early in their work career? Why not just worry about retirement when it comes?

2. Why do higher income consumers have to worry more about retirement planning than lower income consumers?

3. Is it "fair" that workers stop contributing to Social Security after a certain income level is reached each year?

4. Which kind of pension would you prefer, a defined benefit pension or a defined contribution pension?

5. What are the advantages and disadvantages of the three common methods of calculating a defined benefit pension?

6. How does the type of pension affect the costs and benefits of changing jobs?

7. How is an annuity benefit calculated?

8. How can a straight life annuity promise to pay benefits for the life of the retiree?

9. What's a major disadvantage of typical annuities which are constant in nominal dollars? Are there any ways to overcome this disadvantage?

10. Are annuities with a refund, annuities with a guaranteed payment, and joint life and survivorship annuities naturally better than straight life annuities, where payments stop once the retiree dies?

11. Why don't variable annuity benefits fully adjust to inflation?

12. Briefly describe how you would decide if retiring early is worthwhile.

13. If you're eventually taxed on annuities and IRAs anyway, why are they better investment vehicles than regular fully taxed investments?

14. Why do you think that very few retired homeowners use reverse mortgages?

PROBLEMS

1. Jack and Jill are age 40, and they plan to retire at age 65. Jack's income is $40,000 and Jill's income is $45,000. They will receive Social Security and they have $50,000 of assets targeted for use in retirement. They will each receive $8,000 (real $) annually in a company pension, which isn't indexed for inflation. Jack and Jill want to replace 70 percent of their pre-retirement income in retirement, and they want to plan for 35 years in retirement. What percent of their income should Jack and Jill save for retirement, assuming a 2 percent real interest rate and 5 percent inflation rate?

2. What percentage must Jack and Jill save if the company pension is indexed for inflation?

3. What percentage must Jack and Jill save if they reduce their replacement rate for pre-retirement income to 55 percent?

4. Larry works for 30 years at the same job and ends with a salary of $50,000. Curly works for 10 years at each of three jobs. Curly left job 1 earning $20,000; he left job 2 earning $48,000; and he retired from job 3 earning $50,000. If both Larry's and Curly's pensions are calculated as 1 percent of final salary multiplied by years of service, what will be the pensions of both retirees?

5. Betty contributed $75,000 in after-tax dollars to her pension. Betty has now retired and her pension pays her an annual straight life annuity of $10,000. If the IRS says that Betty's life expectancy is 25 years, what part of Betty's pension is taxable?

6. Pete started work at his current job at age 30. Pete would like to retire at age 62 instead of 65. If he retires at 62 his pension will be based on his final salary of $47,000. If he works until age 65 his pension will be based on a final expected salary of $55,000. If Pete retires at age 65, his salary schedule from age 62 to 64 is: Age 62, $47,000; Age 63, $50,000; Age 64, $55,000. Pensions are one percent of final salary multiplied by years of service, and are not indexed. Social Security benefits for Pete at age 62 will be $9,000; at 65 his benefits will be $11,000. If Pete retires at age 62 his company will give him a check for one-year's pay ($47,000), which Pete can convert to an annual annuity payment of $4,500. What's the cost to Pete of retiring early if he uses a life span of Age 90? Use a 6 percent discount rate for nominal dollars and 2 percent for real dollars.

7. You have $10,000 on which you haven't yet paid taxes. Your tax bracket is 33 percent. How much money will you have in twenty years after taxes in each of these three types of investments?
   (a) A fully taxable investment paying a 6½ percent after-tax interest rate,
   (b) An annuity paying a 9½ percent before-tax interest rate,
   (c) A traditional IRA paying a 9½ percent before-tax interest rate.

   NOTE: When the annuity and IRA money are withdrawn after 10 years, no penalty is paid.

8. Lucy and Ricky's house is valued at $120,000. They can obtain a 75 percent loan for a reverse mortgage. They can invest the loan at 10 percent, and they will be charged 12 percent interest. If they pay interest on the loan each year, how much can they net with a reverse mortgage with a term of ten years?

Shopping and Information Gathering

Introduction

This chapter addresses a number of issues, which you probably don't think about, related to shopping and information gathering. Shopping and information gathering are economic issues because they take time and money resources which you can use in other ways. This chapter will address such questions as:

♦ how many stores should you visit for comparison shopping before you buy?

♦ what is the best shopping strategy for getting the lowest price and minimizing shopping costs?

♦ when you pay a higher price, will you get better quality?

♦ should you buy only during sales?

♦ can you buy something cheaper by classifying yourself in the right way?

♦ will buying in bulk always save you money?

♦ are warranties and service contracts worth their cost?

You can think of the marketplace as an organized jungle. Where do you start to find the best deal? How long should you take in searching for the best deal? (Remember, you time is valuable.) Are there any "deals" available anyway? Should you just "shop until you drop"? You may be surprised when you learn that there are limits to the benefits of shopping for the lowest price, that higher prices don't always bring higher quality, and that bulk buying isn't always cheaper.

In some topics of this chapter you'll be put in the place of the seller. You'll learn the tactics that sellers use to maximize profit. Once you know the tactics of the opponent (the seller), you'll be better able to combat those tactics to get a better deal. You'll learn about the very common tactic of "price discrimination" and the lesser, but important, tactics of loss-leaders, rain-checks, and bait and switch.

The final two topics of this chapter deal with protection—the kind you can buy (no, not from Uncle Vito) in the form of warranties and service contracts, and the kind provided by the government in the form of laws (either in restricting seller behavior or mandating seller behavior). Are these forms of protection worth their cost?

And now, on to becoming a wiser shopper!

1. Does "Shopping Around" Pay?

One of the favorite slogans of television consumer reporters is to "shop around for the best price." The reporters imply that smart shoppers take time to visit many stores to compare products and prices.

You should immediately be suspicious of this advice because you now know that shopping takes time and money (for transportation), and these are both valuable resources. So the more "shopping around" you do, the more you spend in time and money. Where should you stop?

In general you want to shop and collect more information about products and prices as long as the benefits of shopping exceed the costs. The benefits of shopping are:

reduction in price   quantity of
of product due to   × product bought;
shopping; call this   call this Q
δP

The costs of shopping are the time and transportation costs (gas and wear and tear on car) in traveling from store to store. (Call these costs C. So shopping is beneficial as long as:

$$\delta P \times Q > C.[1]$$

For example, suppose you are shopping for four automobile tires. Table 11-1 shows the benefits and costs of shopping at one, two, three, or four stores.

In each case, a lower price can be found by shopping at more stores. However, the extra transportation and time costs of going to the fourth store exceed the reduction in the tire price. Therefore, in this example, shopping at three stores is optimal.

How Much Price Dispersion Is There?

Can you really expect to get lower prices by shopping at more stores? How much does the price of the same product vary among stores in a local market?

There's more price variation than you might expect. Research shows that some products' prices vary by as much as 400%, with 50% (meaning

Table 11-1   Costs and benefits of tire shopping.

	Lowest Tire Price (4 tires)	**Savings by Shopping One More Store**	**Shopping Costs**	**Extra Costs by Shopping One More Store**
At 1 store	$400		$ 5	
At 2 stores	$360	$40	$ 8	$3
At 3 stores	$350	$10	$12	$4
At 4 stores	$349	$ 1	$15	$3

[1]Of course, if a consumer gets pleasure from shopping (that is, shopping is a form of recreation), then this pleasure will offset some of the costs of shopping. Such consumers will obviously shop more than consumers who get no pleasure from shopping.

the highest price is 50% greater than the lowest price) being a common price variation.[2]

Why is there such great price dispersion? Quality differences in the same product between different stores could be an answer, but the studies cited in footnote 2 have only looked at products with the same quality, or have accounted for quality differences in other ways.

One answer is that characteristics of sellers (stores) differ, and these differences are reflected in the price of products. For example, sellers which are more conveniently located, with wider selection and more knowledgeable salespersons, with a better inventory and a more favorable return policy should be able to sell their products for a higher price. Rosemary Key and Loren Geistfeld have found some support for this explanation.[3] Using data from Columbus, Ohio, they found seller characteristics such as those cited above affecting the prices of products.

However, even after they accounted for seller characteristics, Key and Geistfeld still found considerable price variation. There are two reasons why you should expect price variation to remain for the same product in a local market. First, as we've emphasized, information is costly for consumers to collect. Therefore, the average consumer won't visit all sellers and make all possible price comparisons. This will allow the average seller to sell products at a price higher than if consumers made all price comparisons. Second, price comparison information becomes obsolete as sellers change. Consumers acting on outdated information about price comparisons can allow some sellers to charge higher prices.

Research on Shopping

This section summarizes the findings of three research papers which examined costs and benefits of shopping strategies.

Bruce Hall calculated the benefits of shopping at more than one food store.[4] Using data from stores in New York state, Hall estimated that consumers could save 4 percent on food costs by shopping at two stores rather than one, consumers could save 6 percent by shopping at three stores rather than one, and consumers could save 7 percent on food costs by shopping at four stores rather than one. Notice that the savings

---

[2]Maynes, E. Scott, Robin A. Douthitt, Greg J. Duncan, and Loren V. Geistfeld. "Informationally Imperfect Markets: Implications for Consumers," in *The Collection and Analysis of Economic and Consumer Behavior Data: In Memory of Robert Ferber.* Bureau of Economic and Business Research and Survey Research Lab, University of Illinois 1984, pp. 185–197.

[3]Key, Rosemary and Loren Geistfeld, "Product Price, A Reflection of Seller Characteristics," *Proceedings of the 35th Annual Conference of the American Council on Consumer interests,* Baltimore, Maryland, 1989, pp. 250–256.

[4]Hall, Bruce F. "Price Dispersion and the Gains from Search in Local Food Markets." *Journal of Consumer Affairs,* Vol. 17, No. 2, Winter 1983, pp. 388–401.

increase with more stores visited, but at a decreasing rate. Hall's results varied slightly depending on the size of the city or town where the stores were located. The savings are not net of transportation and time costs of shopping. Hall's results imply that consumers with higher food bills and lower values of time are better-off shopping at more stores.

Hawkins and McCain investigated the benefits and costs of alternative shopping strategies.[5] Say you want to buy a vacuum cleaner. How would you go about finding the lowest priced vacuum cleaner if you wanted to minimize your shopping costs? Hawkins and McCain calculated that telephone shopping, where you call stores to find the lowest price before visiting them, was the lowest cost strategy as long as sellers would quote prices over the phone. The next cheapest strategy was

CONSUMER TOPIC

WHO SHOPS 'TIL THEY DROP?

For many consumers, shopping is not a chore but is an enjoyable activity. Many consumers find browsing in stores and comparing information about selection and prices a relaxing and enjoyable experience. We might, expect such consumers to shop more than consumers for whom shopping is just a disguised form of work. The impact of "enjoyment of shopping" on time spent shopping was the focus of a study by Jane Kolodinsky of the University of Vermont. Professor Kolodinsky used data on shopping for groceries from a sample of consumers in Onondago County, New York in 1986. The consumers in the survey were asked if they considered time spent on grocery shopping, clipping coupons, or reading food ads, as work, enjoyment, or a combination of both. Those saying at least one of the activities was considered enjoyment were classified as "enjoying shopping." Professor Kolodinsky found that those consumers classified as "enjoying shopping" spent more minutes per week shopping than other consumers with similar characteristics.

Professor Kolodinsky's research produced other interesting results, Older consumers were found to spend less time shopping. If age is a measure of experience in shopping, then this result means that more experienced shoppers spend less time shopping.

Consumers with children were found to shop less than similar consumers without children. Since children demand much time and attention from parents, it makes sense that parents with children at home will economize on shopping time.

Finally consumers whose value of time was higher shopped less than similar consumers with lower time values.

Source: Kolodinsky Jane. "Time as a Direct Source of Utility: The Case of Price information Search for Groceries," *The. Journal of Consumer Affairs*, Vol. 24, No. 1, Summer 1990, pp. 89–109.

---

[5]Hawkins, Del and Gary McCain, "An Investigation of Returns to Different Shopping Strategies," *Journal of Consumer Affairs*, Vol. 13, No. 1, Summer 1979, pp. 64–74.

one where the consumer first visited the store with the lowest advertised price, then visited the other stores in such a way as to minimize transportation costs. Of course, these days the cheapest way of gathering information is probably using the Internet. However, many local stores do not have price information on the Internet for all their products. Therefore, calling the stores is still a good idea, at least for now.

Walker and Cude examined the benefits and costs of alternative shopping strategies within food stores.[6] You can spend much time comparing prices in a food stores and probably save money, or at the other extreme, you can shop very quickly and save time, but spend more money. In order to evaluate these trade-offs, Walker and Cude evaluated benefits and costs of seven different in-store shopping strategies. Buying the product with the lowest unit price resulted in the lowest money expenditure, but this strategy required over 200 price comparisons in order to purchase the 19 standard products. Buying generic products was only slightly more expensive in money costs, but required only 20 price comparisons. Obviously, consumers with a high value of time would be better-off buying generic, sale, or large size items than shopping using unit prices.

Some Guidelines

It's now time to summarize our discussion about shopping and develop some rules of thumb you can use in your shopping expeditions.

Rule 1

The Greater the Consumer's Expenditure on a Product, the Greater the Benefits from Search. Remember our formula saying that the benefits from search are the reduction in the product's price multiplied by the quantity of the product purchased. This implies that the greater the expenditure on the product (price multiplied by quantity), the greater the benefits from search.

This means, for example, that it's more beneficial to shop for a house, a car, or furniture than for the weekly groceries or socks. In some cases the benefits of shopping are so great that it's worthwhile to pay brokers (for example, real estate brokers) to help you shop or to purchase information (e.g., *Consumer Reports*) which will reduce your shopping time.

Rule 2

The Greater the Variation of Price of a Product in a Market, the Greater the Benefits from Search.

---

[6]Walker, Rosemary and Brenda Cude. "In-Store Shopping Strategies: Time and Money Costs in the Supermarket," *Journal of Consumer Affairs*, Vol. 17, No. 2, Winter 1983, pp. 356–369.

This rule of thumb should be obvious. Where prices for the same product vary more, you're more likely to find a much lower price by searching more.

For example, the pay-off to searching more for cameras, bicycles, and stereos is greater than the pay-off to searching for milk, eggs, and heating oil.

Rule 3

The More Frequently a Consumer Buys a Product, the Greater the Benefits from Search.

Joe buys gasoline twice weekly, and Pat buys gasoline only every other week. Searching for the lowest gasoline price is more valuable to Joe than to Pat.

There is an important new addition to this discussion. In the past decade, the emergence and explosive growth of e-commerce have ushered in a new era of retail business. Online retailing promises the potentials of low barrier of entry, easy access of information, and low transactions costs. Since customers can obtain price information in online markets easily and inexpensively, it might be expected that online price dispersion should be small. However, empirical studies have found significant price differences and persistent price dispersions in the Internet markets.[7]

The Bottom Line

"Shop until you drop" usually isn't worth the cost. Shopping is costly in terms of time and transportation costs (gasoline). Shop more for expensive products, for products which you buy frequently, and for products whose prices vary widely in your local market._____

2. Do Higher Prices Indicate Higher Quality?

You've now learned that information is costly to collect. Therefore, you should be interested in finding short-cuts which could reduce your shopping costs.

One possible short-cut to judging the quality of a product is price. For example, say you're looking for a vacuum cleaner (again!). Is it safe to assume that higher-priced vacuum cleaners are better quality vacuum cleaners? If the answer is "yes," then you could use price as a "signal" of quality. That is, instead of taking the time to examine a product in order to judge its quality, you could simply assume that higher-priced models of a product have better quality.

---

[7]Tang F.F. & Xing X.L. "Price Dispersion on the Internet: A Further Review and Discussion." In the Encyclopedia of E-Business Development and Management in the Global Economy. IGI Global. 2010.

Price Does Not Signal Quality

Unfortunately, existing research indicates that price is not a reliable signal of quality. Higher priced models of a product are not necessarily better quality models. Professor Loren Geistfeld observed that numerous studies over 35 years of research have found the association between price of a product and its quality to be "generally weak."[8]

Gerstner however, found that price-quality associations are higher for some products than for other products.[9] Gerstner found that higher priced products that are purchased infrequently (for example, appliances, auto-visual equipment) have higher price-quality associations than lower priced products that are purchased often (e.g., food). The reason is based on the benefits of search. Consumers take more time in shopping and comparing prices of higher priced products because the benefits of finding a lower price for a given quality product are greater. The greater amount of searching by consumers forces prices to more accurately reflect quality.

Other Reasons for the Price/Quality Puzzle

There are three reasons why the association between price and quality is low for many products.

First, quality of a product is a difficult and multi-faceted characteristic to assess. In many cases quality is in the eye of the beholder. Many of the studies referenced earlier use quality measures developed by Consumers Union. Although these quality measures are based on extensive testing and evaluation, there may still be enough error in the measures so as to affect the price-quality associations.

A second reason for low price-quality relationships of products may be the fact already mentioned, that a product's price also reflects characteristics of the seller. A vacuum cleaner sold in a store conveniently located, with more knowledgeable salespersons, longer hours, and a better return policy will likely sell for more than the exact same vacuum cleaner sold in an inaccessible store with short hours, inexperienced

---

[8]Geistfeld, Loren V. and Rosemary J. Key. "Price-Quality Research: Implications for Consumer Decision-Making." *Cornell Consumer Close-ups,* No. 3, 1988–89, Dept. of Consumer Economics and Housing, Cornell University. Some of the more prominent price-quality studies are: Geistfeld, Loren, "The Price-Quality Relationship—Revisited, *Journal of Consumer Affairs,* Vol. 16, 1982, pp. 334–346;

[9]Gerstner, Eitan, "Do Higher Prices Signal Higher Quality?" *Journal of Marketing Research,* Vol. 22, 1985, pp. 209–215; Ginter, James L., Murray A. Yang, and Peter R. Dickson. "A Market Efficiency Study of Used Car Reliability and Prices," Journal of Consumer Affairs, Winter 1987, Vol. 21, No.2, pp. 258–276; Riesz, Peter "Price-Quality Correlations for Packaged Food Products." *Journal of Consumer Affairs,* Vol. 13, 1979, pp. 236–247: Sproles, George B. "New Evidence on Price and Product Quality." *Journal of Consumer Affairs,* Vol. 11, 1979, pp. 63–77.

salespersons, and no returns. Yet the price-quality studies don't account for seller characteristics. Key and Geistfeld have presented evidence that seller characteristics do influence product prices and do affect price-quality associations.

BRAND NAME   Lastly, price-quality relationships may be low because consumers are willing to pay more for brand name products. Consumers may use brand as a short-cut signal for quality. If this is the case, then studies which use objective measures of quality (not including brand) may find low price-quality associations. A study by Lesser and Masson lends support to this reason. Lesser and Masson found that consumers are willing to pay 5 to 32 percent more for brand name products than for similar non-branded products.[10]

The Bottom Line

Research to date shows that the association between price and quality is weak. However, price is a better "signal" of quality for more expensive, infrequently purchased products. The association between price and quality may be weak, in part, because consumers pay for seller characteristics through product price and because consumers are willing to pay more for brand-names.

3. Why Do Sellers Charge Different Prices for the Same Product?

Recall our discussion of the consumer's *demand curve* from Chapter 1 (see Figure 11-1). The demand curve for a specific consumer product shows the price *per unit* that the consumer is *willing* to pay for various quantities of the product. Typically, consumers are willing to pay a higher price per unit for initial units of a product, and the price per unit that the consumer is willing to pay drops as more units are bought (this is directly related to the fact that consumers' marginal value of an additional unit of a product usually falls as more units are consumed). For example, in Figure 11-1 (a) the consumer is willing to pay P_1 for the first unit (Q_1) of the product, but the consumer is only willing to pay P_5 for the fifth unit (Q_5) of the product.

Now let's look at consumer demand from the seller's point of view. Suppose a seller faces a consumer demand curve like that in Figure 11-1 (a). If the seller sells Q^1 units to the consumer, P_1 per unit is paid and the seller's revenues are equal to the area P_1EQ_1O. If the seller sells five units (Q_1, Q_2, Q_3, Q_4, Q_5) to the consumer and sells all units at the same

[10]Lesser, W H. and R. T. Masson. "Price, Quality, and the Brand Image: Evidence from Consumer's Union." Cornell Agricultural Economics Staff Paper 80-15, June 1980, Cornell University.

unit price, then P_5 is charged for each unit and total revenues are P_5FQ_5O. However, the consumer gets a "deal," or bonus, with this pricing scheme because for units Q_1, Q_2, Q_3, and Q_4 he is willing to pay a higher unit price for them than for Q_5.

Sellers, of course, recognize this and would like to charge the maximum price per unit that the consumer is willing to pay for each unit. For example, consider Figure 11-1 (b) where, again, five units of the product are sold to the consumer. The seller would obtain maximum revenue if he could charge P_1 for the first unit (Q_1), P_2 for the second unit (Q_2), P_3 for the third unit (Q_3), P_4 for the fourth unit (Q_4), and P_5 for the fifth unit (Q_5). The total revenues to the seller from this pricing scheme would be the hatched area in Figure 11-1 (b). Obviously, these total revenues are greater than the revenues represented in area P_5FQ_5O in Figure 11-1(a).

Figure 11-1. A consumer's typical demand curve.

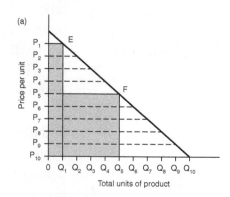

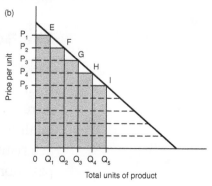

Sellers would like to sell different units of a product to consumers at different unit prices as in Figure 11-1(b) because they make more money this way. In most cases competition between sellers prevents this. However, sellers have devised some strategies to price their products more like the pricing strategy in Figure 11-1(b) than in Figure 11-1 (a).

Market Segmentation

PRICE
DISCRIMINATION

A very common pricing strategy by sellers that uses the consumer's demand curve is *market segmentation*. Another name for market segmentation is price discrimination. Market segmentation is based on the idea that not all consumers have the same demand curve. As you know, the demand curve looks at the relationship between the money price of a unit of a product and the number of units of that product that the consumer buys. Consumers buy more units of the product as the money price of the product falls, and consumers buy fewer units of the product as the money price of the product rises.

But how fast the consumer changes the number of units of a product purchased, when the money price changes, differs between consumers and depends on a number of factors. Important among these factors are the individual consumer's tastes and preferences for the product, the availability of substitutes for the product, and the consumer's value of time. Differences in these consumer characteristics result in different demand curves.

The idea of market segmentation by sellers is to recognize different demand curves by consumers for the same product and to *charge different consumers a different price for the same product*. Going back to Figure 11-1, this means that not all consumers are charged, say, P_5 for a unit of the product. Instead, some consumers may be charged P_1, some may be charged P_3, and some may be charged P_5. Sellers attempt to charge a higher price to consumers who have a strong demand for the product and who are willing to purchase the product even at a relatively higher price, while charging a lower price to consumers who have a low demand for the product and who would substitute to another product if charged a high price.

Market Segmentation at Work

GROUPING OF
CONSUMERS

Market segmentation works easiest for sellers when consumers can be identified and separated into groups according to their demand curve. A good example is airline travel. Business travelers tend to have a strong demand for air travel and are willing to pay a higher price for a ticket than are vacation travelers. This is because business travelers have schedules to meet which often can't be changed, whereas vacation travelers have more flexible planning. In order to separate business travelers and vacation travelers and charge the two types of travelers different prices, airlines charge higher fares during weekday travel, when most business travel is undertaken, and charge lower fares if travel spans a weekend. Since few business trips span a weekend, the lower fares will primarily attract vacation travelers.

SENIOR CITIZEN
DISCOUNTS

Many forms of market segmentation are based on differences in the value of time between consumers. Price discounts for senior citizens are a form of market segmentation by sellers rather than altruism. Senior citizens, who are usually retired from work, have more time to shop and compare prices. Senior citizens, therefore, as a group tend to be more sensitive to price changes and to high prices than non-senior citizens. Sellers separate senior citizens into a separate group (or market) by granting senior citizen discounts. This enables sellers to charge higher prices to non-senior citizens.

COUPONS

Another common technique of market segmentation by sellers employs the use of *coupons*. Coupons allow the consumer to purchase a product at a lower *money price*. But using coupons is a time intensive activity—it takes time to search for coupons, clip coupons, and use coupons at the checkout lane. Therefore, consumers who have a lower value of time are more likely to use coupons, whereas consumers who have a higher value of time are more likely not to use coupons. Issuing coupons is therefore a way for sellers to separate consumers into one group which has a higher value of time and a higher willingness to pay for the product and another group which has a lower value of time and a lower willingness to pay for the product. The first group is charged a higher money price for the product than would have prevailed in the absence of coupons, while the second group gets a lower money price for the product after using coupons.

AUTO SALES

Perhaps the ultimate form of market segmentation is auto sales. Here each individual consumer becomes a group. Through various techniques (see CONSUMER TOPIC: The Art of the Car Deal) auto dealers try to "extract" the maximum price that each consumer is willing to pay for a car. Rarely is the same car sold to two different buyers at the same price. "Knowledgeable" buyers, who know more about the wholesale value of the new car, who know about the costs of options, and who know the true market value of their trade-in, are able to purchase autos at lower prices. "Ignorant" buyers, who haven't done their homework, get taken to the cleaners!

Other forms of market segmentation, or price discrimination, are listed in Table 11-2. As you can see, market segmentation is quite common. Market segmentation allows sellers to capture more of a consumer's total willingness to pay for a product. However, for market segmentation to work, sellers need an easy way to subdivide consumers by their different "demands," and the product should not be able to be resold between consumers.

Market Segmentation and Product Differentiation

Market segmentation and product differentiation go hand-in-hand. Product differentiation means taking a standard product and adding numerous alternative features to it in order to turn it into many "different" products. Autos are a good example. Autos come in different colors and with almost unlimited features: auto vs. manual shift, GPS or no GPS, radio or radio and CD player, sunroof or no sunroof, etc. Product differentiation can also be practiced with claims about service and "caring for the customer." How many times have you heard sellers claim that they are your "friend," that they put "service first," or that they're the seller with the "hometown touch"? These are all techniques used to differentiate the seller and her products from other sellers selling the same product. They're popular among sellers because they're hard for consumers to evaluate!

Sellers claim that product differentiation allows them to cater to different consumer tastes. This may be true, but product differentiation serves another purpose. Product differentiation allows sellers to more

**C
O
N
S
U
M
E
R**

**T
O
P
I
C**

THE ART OF THE CAR DEAL

In his highly informative and often humorous book, *The Car Buyers Art: How to Beat the Salesman At His Own Game,* Darrell Parrish reports that dealers often earn profits of 20% on new car sales, when the profit on the trade-in and on financing are included. Parrish suggests that the car buyer's goal should be to reduce this profit rate to about 7 percent.

How can dealers make such large profits? As we've discussed, "dealing" is the ultimate form of market segmentation because the dealer attempts to sell a car to each buyer at the maximum price that buyer is willing to pay. Parrish reports that dealers use a number of standard techniques to accomplish this. First, dealers attempt to classify each buyer into a category: "real" buyer, "looker," "gullible and nervous" buyer or "tough" customer. The classification will dictate the tactics and time the dealer will use with the buyer.

Dealers will show you the car you request, but they'll also try to steer you to other models with higher profit margins. Dealers also play a game between salesmen and the buyer. The first salesman you work with will try to become your "friend" and excite you by offering a "sweet" deal and "special consideration." Then, just as your deal is to be closed, another salesman, typically the manager, will veto the deal and say that certain costs must be included. Of course, the original "sweet" deal and its veto were all worked out in advance by the salesmen. The dealer's expectation is that, the buyer is so excited about getting the car that he will agree to the added costs.

Another tactic used by dealers is to add costs at the last moment after a verbal agreement to a deal has been made. Typically these will be transportation, installation, or other preparation costs. The dealer will try to make the buyer feel "dumb" by saying something like, "Well, of course you realize we have to charge you for installation."

How can a buyer counter the dealers' tactics. Parrish offers a number of suggestions:

1. Know what you want in a car before you shop, including options. Read publications such as *Consumer Reports* and *Motor Trend Magazine* and visit website such as *Edmund.com* and *Kelley Blue Book* (*website kbb.com*) for ideas and information.
2. Become informed about prices and financing. Check ads for current retail prices. Find out where you qualify for financing. Research online websites such as Edmund.com and kbb.com for dealer invoice price, manufacture recommended price (MSRP) and market price of new cars and also for the value of your trade-in.
3. Visit a minimum of three dealerships.
4. Try to deal with a young, inexperienced salesman who is not as "seasoned" in using the dealer tactics.
5. Record all monetary offers made by the salesman on the back of his card.

(*continued on next page*)

C
O
N
S
U
M
E
R

T
O
P
I
C

(continued from previous page)

6. Test drive only the cars you are considering buying or identical lot cars. "Demo" cars may be manipulated to drive and ride better.

7. Don't be in a rush to buy. Make the dealer work for the sale.

8. Dealers make money on financing. Have the contract drawn up and the price of the car established as if you are taking the dealer financing. The dealer will be more likely to reduce the price of the car in this case. At the last minute, say you will pay cash or finance elsewhere.

9. Begin asking $500 more for your trade-in than you're willing to take. Also, gradually increase your down payment offer at periodic points in the negotiation.

10. Aim to purchase the car for its invoice price plus 7 percent.

11. Keep the salesman "off-balance" by giving hint conflicting signals that you're a "buyer" or a "looker." Also, don't buy alone. Bring along someone who can create uncertainty in the salesman's mind about your intentions.

12. Recognize that the real "dealing" goes on in the salesman's office. All promises made on the showroom floor by the salesman are not binding.

13. Take a calculator and check all figures on the contract. Beware of added amounts. Question anything that hasn't been discussed.

14. The best times to buy a car are:
   - the middle of the week when sales are low,
   - the end of the month when salesmen are trying to reach their quota,
   - the end of the model year when inventories are being reduced,
   - during the Christmas season when sales are low, and
   - during dinnertime when the tough and experienced salesmen are gone.

15. Sign the contract before you leave the lot with the car.

16. Don't expect to get a good deal for high-demand, low-availability cars.

Source: Parrish, Darrell. *The Car Buyer's Art: How to Beat the Salesman At His Own Game.* Bellflower, California, Book Express, 1989.

effectively practice market segmentation. Product differentiation allows sellers to more effectively target particular versions of the same standard product to different consumers. Product differentiation prevents consumers from paying separately for particular features and forces consumers to face an "all or nothing" purchase decision. In this way, sellers can more easily categorize buyers and charge the highest possible price to each consumer group.

Lessons for Consumers

This discussion has probably been very sobering and has reinforced your belief that sellers are crooks who are out to "cheat" the consumer. This belief isn't correct.

Table 11-2   Market segmentation tactics.

Higher Price Paid by:	Lower Price Paid by:
consumers without coupons,	consumers with coupons,
consumers under age 65,	consumers over age 65,
business travellers,	pleasure travellers,
patrons of evening movie,	patrons of matinee movie,
existing buyers of magazines,	new buyers of magazines,
non-frequent fliers,	frequent fliers,
renters of resorts during the "on-season,"	renters of resorts during the "off-season,"
"ignorant" buyer of a new car,	"knowledgeable" buyer of a new car,
long-distance caller during day time.	long-distance caller during evening.

Sellers use market segmentation and product differentiation to charge the highest price that a consumer is *willing* to pay for a product. The consumer's task is to try to convince the seller that his willingness to pay is really lower than it actually is.

How can consumers do this? Consumers can use three techniques to try to "heat the game" of market segmentation.

Technique 1

Put yourself in a market segment that is charged a lower price. For example, go to matinee movies rather than evening movies, vacation in the "off-season" rather than the "in-season," fly over weekends rather than over weekdays, and make long-distance calls at night rather than the day. Of course, in some cases this advice can't be followed. For example, if you work during the day, then you can't go to matinee movies. Also, if your vacation is in the summer, then you'll have to go to the beach during the "on-season" period.

Technique 2

Recognize that sellers use product differentiation to implement market segmentation. Only pay for options or features on products that you really want. If you want the feature, try to determine its individual price and only offer the seller this additional price.

For example, suppose you want a built-in GPS unit in your new car. Find out what it would cost to have such a GPS unit installed by an independent dealer (not the auto dealer), and only offer the auto dealer this additional price to have the GPS unit installed on the new car.

TAKING THE HASSLE OUT OF CAR BUYING

C O N S U M E R   T O P I C

Trying to "outdeal" the car dealer can be a time-consuming and stressful process, If you don't have the personality or time for battling the dealer one-on-one, there is an alternative. It's a car-buying program.

Car-buying programs are organized by banks, credit unions, and other consumer membership organizations such as warehouse clubs. The organization contracts with the auto dealership for a special "fleet-price" for members. Members of the organization simply contact the sales representative at the dealership who handles the program and prove membership in the organization. Once this is done the consumer gets the special price without going through the grind of haggling with a salesman.

Why would an auto dealership provide such a great deal to any organization? The answer is in one word—*volume*. In order to attract the large number of buyers which the organization can deliver, the dealer offers the organization a lower unit price. Think back to the traditional downward-sloping consumer demand curve. Remember that in order to motivate consumers to buy more units the seller typically reduces the unit price. That's what is going on here. The large volume buyer gets a lower unit price.

Why do organizations like banks, credit unions, and warehouse clubs sponsor car-buying programs? There are two reasons. First, it's a good way to encourage membership in the organization. Second, the organization usually receives a small commission from the dealer for each sale.

Car-buying programs appear to be good deals for buyers in terms of price. Dealers typically charge 6 percent over their invoice costs to car program buyers, as compared to 10 to 20 percent over invoice for individual buyers. However dealers participating in car buying programs may restrict the cars available to be purchased on the program.

Source: Schwanhausser, Mark. "Buying Programs Offer Alternative to Price-Haggling," *The Raleigh News and Observer.* May 17, 1900, p. 1D.

Technique 3

Use "bargaining" techniques to reduce the price on large ticket items where individual market segmentation is practiced. Arm yourself with as much information about the price of the product to the dealer as you can. Sellers will settle for a lower price to consumers who appear knowledgeable, who know exactly what they want, and who are willing to take their business elsewhere.

The Bottom Line

Sellers sell the same product to different consumers at different prices to take advantage of different consumer "demands" and to charge each consumer the maximum amount she's willing to pay for the product. To practice this "market segmentation," sellers must be able to subdivide consumers into groups and prevent consumers from reselling the product.

A consumer can retaliate against market segmentation by putting himself into the "low-price" group where possible, by being informed about the actual price of the product and its features to the seller, and by practicing successful bargaining techniques. _____

4. Are "Sales" Ever for Real?

"Sale," you say "Sales are only gimmicks. A seller only puts a product on sale after jacking the price way up. Nothing is ever really on sale."

Your attitude is probably representative of most consumers. Most consumers think sales are gimmicks. However, you may be surprised to learn in this topic that there are "real" sales, and there are legitimate reasons why sellers put products on sale. This means there are times when consumers can take advantage of "real sales."

Alternative Theories of Sales

In the economics literature, there are four theories of sales: the inventory cost theory, the advertising theory, the loyalty theory, and the market segmentation theory.[11]

INVENTORY COST THEORY

The inventory cost theory recognizes that holding a product in storage is costly for a seller. Usually, consumers want a product as soon as they purchase it. If there is a long waiting time to obtain the product after purchase, the consumer may very well take her business elsewhere. Sellers know this, so they keep some of the product "in stock" in order to meet consumer demands quickly.

But holding inventories is costly in terms of storage space, property taxes, utility costs, and workers to operate the warehouses. Therefore, at certain times sellers may want to reduce their inventories in order to save money. To do this, sellers put products "on sale." Although the sale reduces the price the seller receives for the product, the seller benefits because his reduction in inventory costs more than makes up the

---

Table 11-3 Theories of "Sales."

Inventory Cost Theory

Advertising Theory

Loyalty Theory

Market Segmentation Theory

---

[11]See Liebowitz, S. J. "Sales Promotions, Deals, and Price Discrimination," mimeograph, North Carolina State University, April 1990.

difference. Typically inventory reduction sales occur after holidays when stocking of inventories has been high to meet expected high consumer demand.

ADVERTISING THEORY   The advertising theory of sales says that sales are a form of promotion designed to "excite" and attract new customers. This theory suggests that new customers must be given a reduction in the product's price in order to try the new product. The seller obviously hopes that once the new customer tries the product, he will like the product and be willing to pay the full price in the future.

LOYALTY THEORY   The loyalty theory of sales is the opposite of the advertising theory. The loyalty theory says that products are periodically put "on sale" in order to reward existing customers for their loyalty and to keep them. Sales are a form of "thank you" to existing customers for their patronage.

MARKET SEGMENTATION THEORY   Finally, the market segmentation theory says that sales can be used to sell the same product to different consumers at different prices. The theory goes like this. First, sellers sell their product at the "regular" price. Consumers who place a high value on the product and who want to buy the product as soon as possible will purchase at the regular price. Later the seller will reduce the price of the product in order to sell to consumers who have a lower value of the product and who do not mind waiting for the product. In this case, "time" is the factor segmenting the market. Consumers who want the product soon pay the higher price, and consumers who are willing to wait for the product, and risk that the product will be "sold out," pay the lower price.

Implications for Consumers

The inventory cost theory and market segmentation theory of sales have the most implications for consumers. The inventory cost theory suggests that you can buy a product on a "real" sale if you wait until after a holiday period or seasonal selling period. For example, you can get good bargains if you buy a leftover new 2013 car at the beginning of the 2014 model year, or if you buy summer clothing in August or September. You get a "deal" because sellers don't want to store the old models or out-of-season clothes.

The market segmentation theory suggests that you get a product on sale if you're willing to wait until the luster of its newness has worn off. Don't be the first to buy a newly published bestseller or to buy the new season's fashions. If you wait until new becomes old, you'll get a lower price.

COST OF WAITING FOR SALE   However, a potential cost of both of these strategies of waiting to buy a product on sale is that the product may be sold out before it can go on sale, or it may become quickly sold out after going on sale. So you must weigh your intensity of desire for the product against the potential bargain you could get by waiting.

The Bottom Line

Some sales are "real." In particular, if you can afford to wait until after the peak selling season or model year for the product, you can frequently purchase it on sale. However, the risk you run by waiting is that the product will be sold out or the selection drastically reduced. _____

5. Will Buying in Bulk Save You Money?

Your mother probably told you to buy in bulk in order to save money. What she meant was that by buying in bulk the price per unit will be lower and you'll save money as compared to buying a number of smaller sizes. In other words, the large "economy-size" is the wise buy. But as you will see below, this isn't always true! The "economy-size" doesn't always have the lowest unit price. This chapter will explore why and the implications for consumers.

The Existence of Quantity Price Surcharges

QUANTITY PRICE DISCOUNT

If a product's price per unit falls as the product's package size increases, then we say that there is a *quantity price discount* for the product. For example, if the price of a 10 ounce can of corn is 80¢, then the price per unit is 8¢ per ounce for the 10 ounce can. If the price of a 20 ounce can of corn is $1.20, then the price per unit is 6¢ per ounce for the 20 ounce can. In this case there is a quantity price discount because the price per ounce is lower for the larger can.

QUANTITY PRICE SURCHARGE

In contrast, if a product's price per unit rises as the product's package size increases, then we say there is a *quantity price surcharge* for the product. In our corn example, if the 20 ounce can had cost $2.00, then its price per unit would have been 10¢ per ounce and there would have been a quantity price surcharge from the 10 ounce can to the 20 ounce can.

Research on food products shows there is a significant percentage of quantity price surcharges. Glide and Walker found quantity price surcharges in 10 percent of price comparisons.[12] Widrick found quantity price surcharges in 34 percent of his price comparisons.[13]

The economic expectation is that quantity price discounts should prevail. The reason relates to the consumer's downward sloping demand curve (see Figure 11-2). To entice consumers to buy more units of a product, the price per unit must drop. Therefore, consumers who buy larger

---

[12]Cude, Brenda and Rosemary Walker. "Quantity Price Surcharges: Are They Important in Choosing a Shopping Strategy?" *Journal of Consumer Affairs,* Vol. 18, No. 2, Winter 1984, pp. 287–295.

[13]Widrick, S.M. "Quantity Surcharges: A Pricing Practice Among Grocery Store Items—Validation and Extension" *Journal of Relating,* Vol. 55, Summer 1979, pp. 99–107.

package sizes get the advantage of a lower unit price because they are "farther-out" on the demand curve, and the consumers who buy smaller package sizes pay higher unit prices because they are at the "early part" of the demand curve.

Figure 11-2. Unit price and consumer demand.

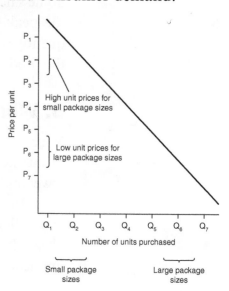

ECONOMIES OF SCALE IN PACKAGING

We might also expect sellers to be able to sell larger packages at lower unit prices as a result of economies-of-scale in packaging. That is, in many cases it takes less packaging per unit for a large package than for a small package. But the savings in packaging material certainly varies with the type of material. Also, for some packaging material, it may actually take more material per unit for larger packages than for smaller packages. For example, for some products packaged in bags and cardboard boxes, it may actually take more material per unit for large packages in order to support the added weight and stress of the large package. In this case, sellers would incur greater costs per unit of large packages, and they would pass these costs on to consumers. *Therefore, one explanation for the existence of quantity price surcharges is that for some packaging materials, the cost per unit of packaging actually increases for larger package sizes.*

STORAGE REQUIREMENTS

Another potential explanation for quantity price surcharges is based on storage requirements in the supermarket. You know that many products in the supermarket can be stored on shelves at "room temperature," but other products must be kept refrigerated and some products must be kept frozen. It is a physical fact that it takes less time, and is therefore cheaper, to cool or freeze individual packages of a given size than one big package. That is, it takes less time to cool two five ounce orange juice concentrates to a given temperature than it does to cool one 10 ounce orange juice concentrate to that same temperature. Therefore, the costs of storage per unit for refrigerated and frozen products are greater for larger packages than for smaller packages. If the additional unit costs are great enough, quantity price surcharges to consumers could result.

Research by Walden found support for the ideas that differences in packaging material and storage requirements are related to the existence of quantity price surcharges among supermarket products.[14] Walden

[14]Walden, Michael L. "Why Unit Prices of Supermarket Products Vary." *Journal of Consumer Affairs,* Vol. 22, No. 1, Summer 1988, pp. 74–84.

found there was a greater chance of finding quantity price surcharges for products packaged in boxes, bags, and bottles rather than for those packaged in jars and cans. This makes sense since cardboard and bag material more likely needs reinforcing in large package sizes. Walden also found that refrigerated products had smaller quantity price discounts than shelf stored products, and that the frequency of quantity price surcharges was greatest for frozen products.

Is Bulk Buying Always Cheaper?

You now know that the answer to this question is "no," since quantity price surcharges exist for a significant number of products. So don't automatically assume that larger is cheaper per unit, particularly for frozen products and products packaged in boxes, bags, and bottles.

But even if you can buy a large package size of a product at a lower unit price, the total costs to you may not be cheaper. You must have the space to store the larger package. Do you want to turn your basement into a food warehouse? Obviously this eliminates use of the basement for some other purpose.

Home storage space becomes especially critical for spoilable items. It's usually cheaper per pound to buy a side of beef than to buy individual beef cuts, but men you must have a large freezer to store the beef, and you must pay the electricity bill to keep it cool (also, you have to eat all parts of the side of beef).

You should also not forget the difference in *handling costs* between small packages and large packages. Large packages are bulkier and more time consuming to move and handle. As you use down from a large package, frequently you want to repackage the remaining contents into a smaller package. With some large packages, repackaging may not be possible, so you may have to use more of the product at one time than you desire. Although these handling costs aren't "out-of-pocket" money costs, they are a cost in terms of time and convenience.

The Bottom Line

Larger packages of a product do not always have a lower unit price. In fact, among supermarket products, studies have shown that unit price rises in 10 to 30 percent of the package size comparisons. Such "quantity price surcharges" are more prevalent for products packaged in boxes, bags, and bottles and for refrigerated and frozen products. Even if larger sizes are cheaper per unit, their total cost to the consumer may not be lower when home storage costs and handling costs are considered.

6. Should You Avoid "Loss-Leaders," "Rain Checks," and "Bait and Switch" Tactics?

LOSS LEADER

Loss-leaders are products which sellers sell at very low prices, sometimes below cost, in order to attract consumers to their stores. Sellers expect that while consumers are in their store, they will also purchase other products that generate much higher profits. If the sellers runs out of the loss-leader, consumers are given a *rain check.* The rain check is a promise to sell the product to the consumer later at the advertised low price.

RAIN CHECK

BAIT AND SWITCH

Bait and switch occurs when a seller advertises a product at a low price (the "bait"), then tries to switch the customer to a more profitable product once the consumer is in the store. Under current law, bait and switch tactics are illegal if the seller refuses to show the consumer the advertised low price product (the bait). However, sellers can still show consumers the bait and then try to persuade them to buy another product.

What's Wrong?

What's wrong with loss-leaders and bait and switch? A problem with loss-leaders is the high chance that the loss-leader will be out of stock when the consumer visits the store. For example, Hess and Gerstner estimate that loss leaders are three to seven times more likely to be out-of-stock than other "non-leader" products.[15] In fact, Hess and Gerstner show that sellers will purposefully run out of the loss-leader and issue rain checks in order to make consumers return to the store a second time. In this way, sellers have two chances to sell other "non-leader" products to consumers at higher profits.

Bait and switch isn't illegal as long as the consumer has the opportunity to evaluate both the bait and the alternative products. The concern is that the seller will attempt to "steer" the consumer away from the bait to the alternative products. In this case, the consumer must be informed enough to be able to evaluate the bait and its alternatives.

Can Consumers Benefit?

Although loss-leaders and bait and switch seem like devious strategies, they can be beneficial to consumers. Gerstner and Hess argue that consumers can benefit from loss-leaders and bait and switch by the lower prices of the loss-leader and the bait.[16] Gerstner and Hess show that sell-

---

[15]Hess, James P., Eitan Gerstner, "Loss Leader Pricing and Rain Check Policy," *Marketing Science,* Vol. 6, No. 4, Fall 1987, pp. 358–374.

[16]Gerstner, Eitan and James D. Hess. "Can Bait and Switch Benefit Consumers?" Faculty Working Paper No. 153, Dept. of Economics and Business, North Carolina State University, November 1989.

DOES ADVERTISING HELP OR HURT CONSUMERS?

C O N S U M E R   T O P I C

Economists are divided over the issue of whether advertising helps or hurts consumers. One view says that advertising hurts consumers because it leads to less competition among firms and higher prices. Here advertising is used as a barrier to keep out new competitors. The existing firms spend so much on advertising and generate so much brand loyalty that new firms can't break into the market and can't hope to win over consumers.

The other view of advertising takes the exact opposite position. This view says that advertising informs consumers of the name and location of alternative sellers and thereby leads to more competition and lower prices. Advertising extends the range of consumer choice and allows consumers to shop and compare sellers more efficiently.

Which view is correct? Unfortunately, there's no consensus answer to this question. Some studies have found a positive relationship between advertising and industry concentration and between advertising and profit rates. On the other hand, other studies have found that advertising leads to lower prices for consumers. For example, Lee Benham's study of advertising and eyeglass prices found that the introduction of advertising cut 50 percent from the price of eyeglasses.

One explanation for these seemingly contradictory results is that the impact of advertising varies by type of product. For products that consumers can easily examine and evaluate for quality, advertising will promote competition and lower prices. This is because sellers know that consumers can easily evaluate the accuracy of the advertising. But for products whose quality cannot be easily evaluated by consumers, advertising may lead to less competition and higher prices. In this case consumers may use advertising as a "signal" for quality. Since it's hard for consumers to judge quality, consumers may assume (as a short-cut) that the more heavily advertised products are the better products.

This distinction in the impact of advertising also has implications for the accuracy of advertising. For products which consumers can easily evaluate, accuracy of the information in the advertisement is not a major issue because consumers can readily evaluate the product. But for products which are hard for consumers to evaluate, especially expensive products, truthfulness of the advertisement's information is an issue. Unfortunately, in these cases it's also most difficult to judge the advertisement's accuracy.

Sources: Comanor, William S. and Thomas A. Wilson, "The Effect of Advertising on Competition: A Survey." *The Journal of Economic Literature*, Vol. 17, No. 2, June 1979, pp. 453–476.

Benham, Lee "The Effect of Advertising on the Price of Eyeglasses." *Journal of Law and Economics*, Vol. 15, No. 2, October, 1972, pp. 337–352.

ers won't offer products at below cost (loss leaders and bait products) unless they have some chance of enticing some consumers to return to the store a second time (via rain checks) or of getting consumers to switch to a more expensive product. Therefore, consumers who resist sellers' tactics and purchase the loss leader or bait can, in fact, benefit.

The Bottom Line

Loss leaders and bait and switch are tactics used by sellers to attract consumers to stores with low priced products and then sell them higher priced products. Consumers can benefit by buying the lower priced advertised products.

7. Are Warranties and Service Contracts "Good Deals"?

Warranties and service contracts are ways that you can buy protection against defects and malfunctions of durable goods, such as vehicles, appliances, and even houses. Warranties and service contracts are like insurance. By purchasing warranties and service contracts you're buying protection against the risk of loss from a defect or faulty operation of the durable good. The responsibility for fixing the durable good then rests with the seller or manufacturer.

In this topic we'll explore the details of warranties and service contracts. We'll also evaluate whether they're "good deals" in terms of costs and benefits to the consumer.

Types of Warranties and Service Contracts

FULL WARRANTY

There are three kinds of warranties: full, limited, and implied (see Table 11-4). A *full warranty* means that:

♦ a defective product will be fixed or replaced free of charge,
♦ the product will be fixed or replaced within a reasonable time,
♦ you won't have to do anything unreasonable to have the product fixed or replaced,
♦ the warranty is valid for anyone who owns the product during the warranty period, and
♦ if the product can't be fixed, you have your choice of a new one or your money back.

A full warranty doesn't necessarily cover the entire product. It may only cover part of the product. For example, a full warranty on a TV may only cover the picture tube. If something happens to another part of the TV the full warranty doesn't provide coverage.

Table 11-4   Types of warranties.

FULL WARRANTY:

—replaces or repairs defective products free of charge,

—fixes product within reasonable time,

—owner not required to send product anywhere,

—valid for all owners,

—if product can't be fixed, owner can get money back.

LIMTTED WARRANTY:

—pays for parts but not labor,

—owner may be required to return product for servicing,

—valid only for first owner,

—if product can't be fixed, owner receives only partial refund.

IMPLIED WARRANTY:

—says product must do what it's designed for,

—says product must do what seller says it will do,

—if the product can't be fixed, you have your choice of a new one or your money back.

LIMITED WARRANTY   A *limited warranty* is any warranty that doesn't provide all the coverage of a full warranty. For example, a limited warranty may:

♦ cover parts, but not labor,
♦ require you to return a product to the seller for service,
♦ cover only the first purchaser,
♦ charge for handling expenses,
♦ give you only a partial refund of your money based on how long you've owned the product.

IMPLIED WARRANTY   Implied warranties are warranties created by the state and not by the company. Implied warranties come with every product unless the seller states in writing that he gives no warranty. There are two common kinds of implied warranties, the "warranty of merchantability," and the "warranty of fitness for a particular purpose." The "warranty of merchantability" means that the product must do the normal functions it is designed for. For example, a car must run, an oven must bake, and a radio must play. The "warranty of fitness for a particular purpose" means that if a seller states that a product will perform in a certain way, then the product must in fact perform in this way. For example, if a seller tells you a coat will keep you warm in zero degree weather, then the seller has created an implied warranty guaranteeing that claim.

Warranties often come with a new product at no extra explicit charge. However, since the warranty coverage does create costs for the seller, you should expect that a product with a warranty will cost more than the same product without a warranty. Warranties are usually for a specific time period, although some warranty coverage can last the lifetime of the product.

Warranties are most common on vehicles and appliances. However, there are also home warranties. Home warranties come in two varieties. One type provides protection for structural defects of the house, such as a sinking foundation or a leaking roof. The other type provides protection for the home's built-in appliances and the home's mechanical systems, such as the heating/cooling, electrical, and plumbing systems.

SERVICE CONTRACTS   *Service contracts* are not warranties. Service contracts are sold to provide protection instead of a warranty or to provide protection after the warranty has lapsed. Service contracts are priced separately from the price of a product. Service contracts pay for specified repairs, parts, and labor for the product.

Are They Worth the Cost?

Warranties and service contracts do cost the consumer money. Either the consumer pays an explicit fee, or the cost of the contract is imbedded in the price of the product. Is paying for a warranty or service contract worth the cost?

If you had all the available information, how would you answer this question? In this case you would pull out our old present value analysis! To evaluate if a warranty or service contract is worthwhile, you'd want to compare the price of the warranty or service contract to the present value of future repair costs which the warranty or service contract would pay (see Figure 11-3). If the price of the warranty or service contract is less than the present value of future repair costs, then the warranty or service contract is a "good deal;" if not, then the warranty or service contract is not a "good deal."

Figure 11-3. Evaluating warranties and service contracts.

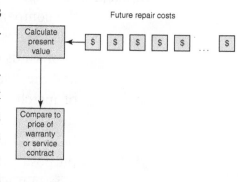

Bryant and Gerner employed this methodology to calculate the benefits and costs of warranties and service contracts for refrigerators.[17] Since warranties weren't priced separately, Bryant and Gerner first had to determine the implicit price of a refrigerator warranty. They did this by comparing the prices of the same refrigerators with and without a warranty.

WARRANTIES AND SERVICE CONTRACTS DON'T PAY

Bryant and Gerner's results showed that both warranties and service contracts on refrigerators don't pay for consumers. They found the implicit price of the warranty to be four times the present value of expected repair costs, and the price of the service contract to be twice the present value of expected repair costs. In a study of homeowner warranties, Brewster, Crespi, Kalvzny, Ohls, and Thomas also round that the cost of warranties exceeds their benefits.[18]

The research findings showing that warranties and service contracts don't pay for themselves shouldn't be surprising. As you've already learned, consumers on average don't make money from insurance (and warranties and service contracts are forms of insurance). Instead, insurance is bought to guard against high losses—in this case, to guard against very high repair bills.

However, in the studies of warranties and service contracts the researchers did not include the time costs of repairing products using warranties and service contracts versus shopping for repair services on your own. If having a warranty or service contract saves the owner time in repairing a product, then the value of the time savings can partially narrow the difference between the costs of warranties and service contracts and their benefits.

So which consumers should consider purchasing warranties and service contracts? Bryant and Gerner's research suggests that warranties and service contracts are best suited for three types of consumers: (1) consumers who don't want to take the chance of having big repair bills, (2) consumers who aren't good at doing their own repairs, and (3) consumers who have a very high value of time and don't want to take the time to find and compare repair shops—instead, they'd rather rely on the repair shop provided by the warranty or service contract.

The Bottom Line

Warranties and service contracts are forms of insurance which pay for repair costs on consumer durables. Research shows that the costs of warranties and service contracts to the consumer are greater than the benefits as measured by expected future repair costs.

---

[17]Bryant, W. Keith and Jennifer Gerner, "The Price of a Warranty; The Case for Refrigerators," *Journal of Consumer Affairs,* Vol." 12, No. 1, Summer 1978, pp. 30–47.

[18]Brewster, J. Allan, Irving Crespi, Richard Kalvzny, James Ohls, and Cynthia Thomas. "Homeowner Warranties: A Study of the Need and Demand for Protection Against Unanticipated Repair Expenses," *Journal of the American Real Estate and Urban Economics Association,* Vol. 8, No. 2, Summer 1980, pp. 207–217.

Warranties and service contracts are best suited for consumers who want to guard against very high repair bills, who can't do repairs themselves, and who have a high value of time. _____

8. Should Consumers Be Protected?

This topic is different from the others in that it is directed at public policy decisions and not at individual decisions. Two issues are addressed in this topic: does the consumer need protection by the government in the economic marketplace and, if so, what kind of protection should be provided.

You might be thinking, why are we talking about consumer protection in the shopping and information chapter? The answer is that the argument for protection arises from the lack of perfect information by the consumer. If the consumer had perfect information about products, there would be no need for protection. Consumers could make their decisions with full knowledge of the safety, quality, and operation of products. No one could say that consumers were taken advantage of, or "hoodwinked," if consumers had complete knowledge of the products they were buying.

LACK OF FULL INFORMATION

But, in reality, sellers are in the driver's seat and consumers are at a disadvantage in the marketplace. Sellers usually know much more about the product they're selling than do consumers. This means consumers frequently buy products with less than full information. This is the major argument for consumer protection.

Protecting Consumers from Risk

The most common kind of consumer protection is protection against risks which consumers can't easily (that is, without considerable expense) detect and predict. In particular, if the hard-to-detect risks involve health and safety, then there is justification for consumer protection. Examples are risks involving food and medicine.

LABELS AND WARNINGS

There are two ways to protect consumers from risk. One way identifies the level of risk for the consumer, but still allows the consumer to choose how much risk to take. Examples are expiration dates on foods, warnings about cigarettes, warnings on medicines about how and when to take the medicine, and warnings about the safe use of products. In all these cases the consumer can choose to ignore the information and accept a greater risk. Consumers may do this if they think the benefits from taking the risk are greater than the cost of the risk. For example, you may decide to take your medicine earlier than indicated if you're in a hurry. Or, you may decide to ignore warnings about not using your lawn mower on a slope if you think you can be careful enough not to have an accident.

PROHIBITION

The other way of protecting consumers against risk is prohibition. Here the government simply prohibits sale of certain risky products or prohibits certain kinds of risky behavior. For example, the U. S. Food and Drug Administration prohibits sale of certain drugs, and the U. S. Department of Agriculture requires that foods meet certain handling and processing conditions before they are sold. Most state governments prohibit transporting a small child without use of a child safety seat.

HAS THE CONSUMER PRODUCT SAFETY COMMISSION WORKED?

Congress created the Consumer Product Safety Commission (CPSC) in 1972 and gave it four tasks: (1) to conduct research on potential product hazards; (2) to work with industry in developing voluntary safety standards; (3) to set mandatory standards if needed; and (4) to recall hazardous products from the marketplace. In reaching its decisions, the CPSC analyzes the costs and benefits of possible actions both in terms of dollar costs and benefits and in terms of lives saved.

The CPSC has supporters and critics. Supporters say the CPSC is needed to make technical evaluations about safety which consumers are not competent to make. The CPSC provides safety information to consumers in much the same way that the Food and Drug Administration provides health information.

Critics argue that the CPSC can "force too much safety down consumers' throats." If this motivates consumers to simply substitute one form of risk for another, then the CPSC's actions may not end up saving lives and reducing injuries. For example, if CPSC regulations mandate special safety guards on lawn mowers, some consumers may react by being more careless with lawn mowers. The injuries resulting from the added carelessness may counterbalance the reduction in injuries resulting from the added safety guards.

Cathleen Zick, Robert Mayer, and Laverne Snow examined one aspect of the CPSC debate by trying to determine if the CPSC's actions have resulted in fewer accidental home deaths, Zick, Mayer, and Snow examined state data on accidental home deaths for the period 1960-1982. This time period includes twelve years before the establishment of the CPSC and ten years after its establishment. The researchers recognized that many factors other than the CPSC affects accidental home deaths, including consumer income and demographic factors, like the proportion of the population under 14 or over 65 years of age. The probable impact of consumer income on accidental home deaths is that higher income consumers will buy safer products, and this will lead to fewer accidents. Children are generally more careless, so states with more children should have more accidental home deaths. Also, the physical condition of the elderly may make them more accident-prone.

After accounting for the impact of these other factors on accidental home deaths, Zick, Mayer, and Snow did find that accidental home deaths were lower after the institution of the CPSC. The researchers estimated the CPSC to be responsible for saving 17,941 lives in home accidents.

Source: Zick, Cathleen D., Robert M Mayer, and Laverne Snow. "Does the U.S. Consumer Product Safety Commission Make a Difference: An Assessment of Its First Decade." *Journal of Consumer Policy.* Vol. 6, 1986, pp. 25–40.

The philosophy behind prohibition is that there are some risks which are simply too great to allow consumers to consider taking.

There are two issues which are constantly debated in protecting consumers from risk. One issue is why not simply prohibit all risky products and risky behavior? In other words, why not eliminate the first method of protection (identification and labeling of the risk) and use the second method (prohibition) exclusively?

The answer is that risky products and behavior provide benefits, and that many consumers are willing to accept the risk for the benefits. For example, the government could require that all cars be built with regulators that wouldn't allow the car to travel more than 65 mph. Yet many consumers are quite willing to accept the dangers of traveling above that speed in order to reap the benefits of shorter travel time. Or, the government could require that all lawn mowers be built with special apparatus that prevents them from tipping over on hills. However, such lawn mowers would be much more expensive, and many consumers are probably willing to accept the risk of tipping over their lawn mower on a hill in exchange for the benefit of a lower price.

This issue has perhaps been most hotly debated with respect to the U.S. Food and Drug Administration (FDA). The FDA has the reputation of being very slow in its approval of new drugs, particularly those drugs designed to fight AIDS and cancer. It has been argued that many consumers afflicted with these dreaded diseases would be more than willing to accept the risk associated with the drugs in exchange for having some hope of surviving the disease. So the issue is whether the FDA should choose the level of risk that consumers can take or should individual consumers make that choice as long as they are informed.

The second issue relates directly to this last point. Will consumers use information about risk or will they ignore it? If they will ignore it, then this is an argument in favor of prohibition. If consumers will use the information, then this is an argument in favor of identification of risk but letting consumers choose.

The answer to this second issue is an empirical one. However, evidence from the declining consumption of cigarettes indicates that consumers do respond to health warnings.[19]

It's important to emphasize that this section has dealt with risks that are difficult and expensive for the average consumer to predict. For risks that are known and predictable, there's no need for protection because the consumer can evaluate the risks and take them into account in their decisions. For example, if it's widely known and understood that gasoline is harmful if swallowed, then there's no need for consumer protection from gasoline.

---

[19]Schneider, L., B. Klein, and K. Murphy. "Government Regulation of Cigarette Health Information. "*Journal of Law and Economics,* Vol. 24, No. 3, 1981, pp. 575–612.

Who Should Be Liable?

BUYER BEWARE? Another aspect of consumer protection is liability assignment. The question is who should be held at fault if a consumer is injured by a product? Should the consumer be held at fault for improper use, or should the SELLER BEWARE? producer or seller be held at fault? That is, should the "buyer beware" (caveat emptor), or should the "seller beware" (caveat venditor)?

CONSUMER "PROTECTION" CAN BACKFIRE: THE CASE OF AUTO DEALERSHIPS

A large number of states regulate auto dealerships. The regulation is in the form of restricting the number of auto dealerships operating in a given territory. To be granted approval for opening, a new auto dealership must show that enough consumers live in the market area to support both the existing dealerships and the new dealership. Usually a state board or commission rules on the application of a new auto dealership.

These restrictions on auto dealerships have been justified as protection for the auto-buying consumer. "The consumer is alleged to benefit in three ways. First, with fewer auto dealerships, each dealer sells more cars and, it is argued, can take advantage of "economies of scale." "Economies of scale" means that costs per product fall as sales increase because the dealer can be more efficient in his operation. These lower costs can then be passed on to the consumer in the form of lower prices for autos.

With fewer auto dealers competing against each other it's also claimed that competition for scarce resources, such as skilled mechanics, will be reduced, and these scarce resources won't be able to command high prices. This also saves money for the auto buying consumer. Last, the control over the number of auto dealerships is supposed to reduce the possibility of "cut-throat" competition between dealers and to promote long-lasting stability in dealers. Consumers are supposed to prefer doing business with an auto dealer who they know will be in business for a long time.

Although these reasons sound good, there's another viewpoint which claims just the opposite—that restrictions on the number of auto dealerships actually hurt consumers by driving up the price of autos. This viewpoint says that restrictions on entry simply keep out competitors and help to preserve a degree of "monopoly" power by existing dealerships. By keeping out new dealerships, existing dealerships can maintain a "captive market" and can sell autos at higher prices.

In an exhaustive study, Richard L Smith II found support for the viewpoint that, restrictions on the number of auto dealerships in a local market actually hurts consumers by making them pay higher prices for autos, Professor Smith found that the restrictions increase auto prices an average of 7.5 to 10 percent. In 1972 he estimated that this resulted in a transfer of $6.7 billion in wealth from auto buying consumers to auto dealers.

Source: Smith, Richard L, II, "Franchise Regulation: An Economic Analysis of State Restrictions on Automobile," *Journal of Law and Economics,* Vol. 25, April 1982, pp. 125–157.

FULL PRICE

Most of you would probably say that the producer or seller should be held at fault, and compensation should be given to the injured consumer. But let's think about this a minute. Will the assignment of liability affect the "full price" of the product, where the full price includes the price of the product and the cost of any injuries? If consumers are assigned liability, then the full price to consumers will be the price paid for the product plus the average cost of injuries. If producers are assigned liability, then producers will purchase insurance to cover expected liability losses. The insurance cost per product will equal the average cost of injuries. The insurance cost will be "wrapped into" the price of the product, so the money price (here the full price) to the consumer will be higher.

ARE USED VEHICLES ALL LEMONS?

C O N S U M E R

T O P I C

What happens when consumer lack total information about products? In a famous article in the *Quarterly Journal of Economics,* George Akerlof speculated that there were two possible outcomes. One outcome is that bad products will drive out the good products. Since consumers can't judge which are the good quality products, they won't be willing to offer a premium for any of the products. No producer will therefore be willing to produce good quality products. The market will be composed totally of bad quality products, or lemons.

The other possible outcome is that consumers will hire experts to judge the quality of products. If the experts can separate good and bad quality products, both types of products will be offered in the marketplace. Consumers will pay a premium for the good quality products.

Which outcomes occur in the real world? Eric Bond attempted to answer this question for the used truck market. Is the used truck market only a market of bad quality trucks; that is—lemons, or are there both good quality and bad quality used trucks?

Professor Bond speculated that if the used truck market is a market composed only of lemons, then average maintenance costs of used trucks, controlling for age and mileage, will be greater than average maintenance costs for new trucks. On the other hand, if consumers are able to hire experts or buy expert information that allows them to ascertain the quality of trucks, then average maintenance costs of used trucks and new trucks will be the same for trucks of the same age and mileage.

Professor Bond found no difference in average maintenance costs, after controlling for vehicle age and mileage. Thus the market for used trucks seems not to be a market of lemons.

Sources: Akerlof, George A. "The Market for 'Lemons': Quality Uncertainty and the Market Mechanism, *Quarterly Journal of Economics,* August 1970, 1984, pp. 488–500.

Bond, Eric W. "A Direct Test of the 'Lemons' Model: The Market for Used Pickup Trucks," *American Economic Review,* Vol. 72, No. 4, September 1982, pp, 836–845.

So if the "full price" of the product, on average, is the same however liability is assigned, should we just flip a coin to determine liability assignment? No—liability should be assigned to the side for whom it's cheaper to prevent accidents and injuries. If it's cheaper for producers to add equipment to make products safer than it is for consumers to take actions to avoid accidents, then liability should be assigned to producers. But if it's cheaper for consumers to safely use products, then liability should be assigned to consumers.

Again consider a lawn mower. If liability for all lawn mower accidents was put on the producer, producers would likely add much safety equipment and apparatus to the lawn mower and substantially increase its cost. But if liability for lawn mower accidents is put on consumers, much of this safety equipment and apparatus won't be added, and consumers will have to exercise caution in using a lawn mower to avoid accidents. If it's cheaper for consumers to safely use lawn mowers than it is for producers to add enough apparatus to prevent accidents, then society's costs are minimized by assigning liability to consumers.

Providing Consumers with Information

When consumers cannot easily evaluate the health and safety features of products, we've argued that consumers should be protected with mandatory labeling, standards, or prohibition. But what about other situations where health and safety aren't involved? Should producers and sellers be required to provide certain kinds of information to consumers before consumers purchase a product?

EXPERIENCE GOODS   For inexpensive, frequently purchased products (so-called "experience" goods) the answer to the question is no. For experience goods consumers can quickly judge products and decide whether to make further purchases. Furthermore, if consumers do make a mistake in buying an experience good, the monetary loss is not great. For example, consumers can rely on their frequent purchase of cereal to judge which cereal they prefer.

For infrequently purchased, expensive products, such as autos and appliances, more than looking at the product is required in order to judge the product's quality. In this case, consumers require additional information in order to make a sound decision. There are many options for sources of this information. Consumers can rely on what the seller tells them about the product. Consumers can use their own knowledge and self inspection of the product. Or, consumers can purchase information about a product. For example, in inspecting a car, consumers can read about the car's expected performance in *Consumer Reports,* or consumers can hire mechanics to inspect the car.

At first glance, you might immediately throw out one of these information options—information from the seller. You might say, "Why trust the seller? She just wants to sell the product, and will tell me anything to get me to buy!"

This may be true for some sellers. Some sellers do indeed misrepresent products in order to make sales. But there are some voluntary restraints on sellers which prevent all of them from practicing fraud.

REPEAT BUSINESS

The restraint is the impact of fraud on reputation and repeat business. If you get a "raw deal" from an auto dealer, it's unlikely you will buy again from that dealer, and you'll also tell your friends not to buy from the dealer. If the dealer's bad reputation becomes widespread, he won't be able to stay in business. So reputation or length of time in business can be used, in part, as signals for the reliability of the seller's information.

There are other ways that sellers can "signal" the reliability of their product to consumers. Warranties and money-back guarantees are two of the most common signals. They are meant to convey to the consumer the seller's trust and confidence in the producer.

But beyond these "market" approaches to information, where sellers voluntarily supply information or signal reliability, should sellers be required to supply some minimum level of information? If the answer is yes, the next question becomes, how much and what kind of information? The answer to this question is particularly difficult since all consumers do not value information to the same degree, and we know that sellers will pass on to consumers any costs of providing information.

The best answer seems to be to require provision of information that meets three criteria: (1) the information is highly valued by most consumers, (2) The information is based on objective rather than subjective evaluation; and (3) the information is less costly for the seller to provide than for the consumer to collect.

Information about complex financial contracts is a good example of information meeting these three characteristics. Indeed, there are legal requirements for information provision for most loan contracts. For example, the federal Truth-in-Lending law requires that the lender provide the consumer the APR (annual percentage rate) of the loan as well as other loan terms. There is also federal legislation requiring disclosure of information on mortgages and home equity loans. The Securities and Exchange Commission regulates the information that brokers and other financial intermediaries provide to consumers when investments are made. An issue currently debated by consumer economists is whether there should be laws regulating how banks, stock brokers, and other financial intermediaries calculate and quote investment interest rates to consumers.

TRUTH-IN-LENDING

Where the information provision doesn't meet the three criteria, the benefits of requiring sellers to provide information are less clear.

Consider a car for example. Much of the evaluation of a car and its performance is subjective. How can it be objectively decided, where everyone agrees with the decision, that a car is reliable, will have low repair bills, is comfortable, and has a smooth ride? These characteristics are subjective and are best left to individual equation. However, it is reasonable to require disclosure of characteristics which are objective, such as the odometer readings.

Protection from "Externalities"

An externality is an impact on a consumer caused when another consumer or a producer uses a product. Externalities can be good or bad. An example of a good externality is the pleasure you receive when your neighbor landscapes his lawn. An example of a bad externality if the displeasure you receive when your neighbor's teenage son blasts his stereo at one o'clock in the morning.

BAD EXTERNALITY

The existence of bad externalities is a reason for consumer protection. The protection usually is in the form of restrictions on the behavior of consumers or producers who produce the bad externality. For example, most localities have restrictions on the playing of loud music in residential areas during the "wee" hours of the morning. Water and air pollution are examples of bad externalities caused by producers and consumers. There are federal and state regulations which attempt to limit such pollution.

The bad externality argument can be used to justify many kinds of restrictions on consumer and producer behavior, and many of these restrictions are hotly debated. The issue of secondary smoke is an excellent example. Some medical studies have found that secondary smoke is harmful to non-smokers. Therefore, secondary smoke is a bad externality to non-smokers. This logic has been used to justify restrictions on smoking in public areas.

SPEED LIMITS

The bad externality argument has been frequently used to restrict consumer behavior where health and safety are at stake. Speed limits are a good example. Drunk drivers and drivers who text while driving risk not only their lives, but also risk the lives of other motorists. A different twist to the argument has been used to justify mandatory seat belts and motorcycle helmets. The logic here is that motorists not using seat belts and motorcyclists not wearing helmets are more likely to sustain severe injuries in accidents. If some of these injured motorists and cyclists don't have health insurance, then the public will pick up the bill for their injuries. Thus, the public bears a bad "financial" externality from drivers not using seat belts and motorcyclists not using helmets. Opponents of such restrictions argue that the injured should bear the full financial responsibility for their actions.

Price Regulation

The last form of consumer protection that we'll discuss is price regulation. Supporters of price regulation think it's a simple solution. If prices are too high, simply pass a law which lowers them. The same can be done with interest rates. To prevent interest rates from going too high, simply pass a law putting a ceiling (a usury ceiling) on interest rates.

USURY CEILING

CONSUMER TOPIC

RENT CONTROL: YOU CAN'T HAVE YOUR CAKE AND EAT IT TOO!

Most consumers who have not been educated in the realities of economics probably think rent control is a great example of consumer protection. If rents are controlled at affordable levels, then consumers will be better off and wealthy landlords will be prevented from making excess profits. But this is a short-sighted and unrealistic view of rent control. While rent control may reduce the rents paid by consumers, it imposes other costs on consumers.

A good example of the impacts of rent control can be seen from the rent control program introduced by the province of Ontario, Canada, in 1975. On the surface it seemed like a reasonable program. Rents were not even strictly controlled. Rents were allowed to be increased by increases in costs faced by the landlord. However, the landlord's net rent or profit (rent, minus costs) was held at a constant dollar level.

However, if the dollar value of net rents is held constant, then real (inflation-adjusted) net rents will fall over time. Indeed, in Toronto (the capital of Ontario), real net monthly rent for a one bedroom apartment fell from $111 in 1975 to $85 in 1980 (1975 dollars). Also, since the value of real estate is equal to the capitalized value of its net returns, falling real net rents should result in falling apartment values. True to form, the real value of apartments in Toronto fell 39 percent from 1975 to 1980.

But the impacts of rent control go further. With rent control reducing the real value of apartments, fewer developers will want to build apartments. In Toronto, construction of rental units fell from 36,846 in the year before rent control (1974) to an average of 14,509 during the first five years of rent control. The ultimate result of rent control is to reduce vacancies and to make it harder to find a rental unit. In Toronto, rising real incomes and falling real rents made the vacancy rate fall from 3.1 percent in 1974 to under 1 percent in 1980. In 1980, it was virtually impossible to find a vacant apartment in Toronto.

One final result concerns the impact of rent control on maintenance and repair of rental units. If landlord profits fall as a result of rent control, then landlords don't have as much incentive to upkeep their units. In Toronto, the ratio of maintenance expenditures to total expenditures fell an estimated 9 percent between 1975 and 1980. Not only did rent control make apartments hard to find, it made good-quality apartments almost extinct!

Source: Smith, Lawrence B. and Peter Tomlinson, "Rent Controls in Ontario: Roofs or Ceilings? *Journal of the American Real Estate and Urban Economics Association*, Vol. 9, No. 2, Summer 1981, pp. 93–114.

Price (and interest rate) regulations backfire. If the price of a product is held below its market level, shortages arise and non-price mechanisms, such as waiting lines and bribery, will be used to equate supply and demand. The same result follows from interest rate ceilings. If the ceiling holds interest rates below their market level, lenders will reduce the number of borrowers by tightening characteristics for loan qualification.

The Bottom Line

Consumer protection is best used in situations where consumers' health and safety is at stake and consumers lack information to easily judge the risk to their health and safety. Consumer protection is also warranted to regulate "bad" externalities. However, protection of consumers from high prices and interest rates via regulation of prices and interest rates is counterproductive.

WORDS AND CONCEPTS YOU SHOULD KNOW

Benefits of shopping
Costs of shopping
Price as a signal
Brand name
Price per unit
Market segmentation
Price discrimination
Grouping of consumers
Senior citizen discounts
Coupons
Product differentiation
Inventory cost theory of sales
Advertising cost theory of sales
Loyalty theory of sales
Market segmentation theory of sales
Quantity price discount
Quantity price surcharge
Economies of scale in packaging
Handling costs

Loss-leaders
Rain checks
Bait and switch
Full warranty
Limited warranty
Implied warranty
Warranty of fitness for a particular purpose
Warranty of merchantability
Service contract
Ways to protect consumers
Buyer beware
Seller beware
Full price
Experience goods
Truth-in-lending
Bad externality
Good externality
Usury ceiling

SHOPPING AND INFORMATION GATHERING—A SUMMARY

1. The benefits of shopping equal the reduction in the unit price of the product due to shopping multiplied by the quantity bought of the product. The costs of shopping are the time and transportation costs in traveling from store to store. Continue to shop as long as the benefits of visiting one more store exceed the costs.

   A. Considerable price dispersion exists for a product in a local market, although some of this dispersion is due to differences in selling characteristics.

   B. Research on food shopping shows that most of the benefits of shopping can be achieved by shopping at three stores. When shopping for one item, the most efficient strategy is telephone shopping.

   C. Research on shopping within a food store shows that comparing unit prices is cheapest in money costs but most expensive in time costs.

   D. Use three rules to guide your shopping:
      1. The greater your expenditure on a product, the greater the benefits from shopping.
      2. The greater the variation in the price of a product in a market, the greater the benefits from shopping.
      3. The more frequently a product is purchased, the greater the benefits from shopping.

2. Products with higher prices are not necessarily better quality products. Research shows that the relationship between product price and product quality is generally weak. However, the price-quality relationship is strongest for infrequently purchased, expensive products.

   The relationship between product price and product quality is weak for three reasons:

   A. Quality is a multi-faceted characteristic which is difficult to assess,

   B. Price of a product is also affected by seller characteristics, and

   C. Consumers seem to be willing to pay more for brand name products.

3. Sellers attempt to divide consumers into separate markets, and charge each market a different price for the product, in order to increase profits. This practice is called market segmentation, or price discrimination. It's based on the idea that consumers with different characteristics are willing to pay different prices for the same product.

A. For market segmentation to be successful, sellers must be able to easily separate consumers into different groups. Examples of market segmentation are:

Higher Price Paid by:	Lower Price Paid by:
consumers without coupons,	consumers with coupons,
consumers under age 65,	consumers over age 65,
business travelers,	pleasure travelers,
long-distance caller during daytime.	long-distance caller during evening.

B. Sellers also use product differentiation to sell the same (or similar) product to different consumers at different prices. Product differentiation means taking a standard product and adding numerous alternative features to it in order to turn it into many "different" products. Sellers also practice product differentiation by claims of "exceptional service" or "friendly attitudes."

C. You can battle the high prices often associated with market segmentation by:
1. putting yourself in the market segment that is charged the lower price,
2. only paying for options or features that are really desired, and
3. arming yourself with information about the product before buying.

4. Sales can be for real. There are four theories of sales:
   A. Inventory cost theory—sellers put products on sale in order to reduce inventory stocks,
   B. Advertising cost theory—sales are used as promotions to attract new customers,
   C. Loyalty theory—sales are used as rewards to existing customers in order to keep their business,
   D. Market segmentation theory—consumers who place a high value on purchasing the product as soon as possible buy at the regular price. Consumers who are willing to wait for the product buy at the "sale" price.

5. Quantity price discounts occur when a product's unit price falls as the product's package size increases. Quantity price surcharges occur when a product's unit price rises as the product's package size increases.
   A. For supermarket products, quantity price discounts prevail, but quantity price surcharges are found in 10 to 34 percent of the price comparisons.
   B. Quantity price discounts should dominate because the typical consumer demand curve shows that consumers will only buy more quantity if the unit price is lower.
   C. There are two explanations for the existence of quantity price surcharges. One is that the cost per unit of packaging actually increases for larger package sizes for some packaging materials. The second explanation is that the cost of storage per unit increases with larger package sizes for some types of storage. Research has found that quantity price surcharges are more likely for products packaged in boxes, bags, and bottles and for refrigerated and frozen products.
   D. Even if the money costs per unit are cheaper for larger packages, greater time handling and storage costs may offset some of these savings.

6. Loss leaders are products which sellers sell at very low prices (sometimes below cost) in order to attract consumers to their stores. If the seller runs out of the loss leader, consumers are given a rain check which promises them the loss leader at the same low price at a later date.

Bait and switch occurs when a seller advertises a product at a low price and then tries to switch the customer to a more profitable product once the consumer is in the store.

Consumers can benefit from loss leaders by purchasing the loss leader at the low price. Consumers can benefit from bait and switch tactics by buying the "bait" and ignoring the "switch."

7. A full warranty means:
   - a defective product will be fixed or replaced free,
   - the product will be fixed or replaced within a reasonable time,
   - the consumer won't have to do anything unreasonable to have the product fixed or replaced,
   - the warranty is valid for anyone who owns the product during the warranty period,
   - if the product can't be fixed, the consumer can have the choice of a new product or her money back.

A limited warranty may:
- cover parts but not labor,
- require the consumer to return the product to the seller for service,
- cover only the first purchaser,
- charge for handling expenses,
- give only a partial refund of money based on how long the product has been owned.

Implied warranties have two components:
- the "warranty of merchantability" means the product must do the normal functions it is designed for,
- the "warranty of fitness for a particular purpose" means that if a seller states a product will perform in a certain way, then the product must perform in this way.

Service contracts pay for specified repairs, parts, and labor for a product.

Research shows that warranties and service contracts are not worth their cost. Research on warranties and service contracts for refrigerators has shown that warranties cost four times the present value of expected repair expenses and service contracts cost twice the present value of expected repair expenses.

Warranties and service contracts are best suited for three types of consumers:
   A. Consumers who don't want to take the chance of having big repair bills;
   B. Consumers who aren't good at doing their own repairs; and
   C. Consumers who have a very high value of time and don't want to take the time to find and compare repair shops.

8. Consumer protection is an issue of information. If consumers had perfect information about all products, there would be no need for consumer protection.
   A. Consumer protection can most easily be justified in the cases of consumer health and safety. Where there are risks which are very hard or expensive for consumers to detect, there is justification for consumer protection.
   B. Consumer protection can be in two forms:
      1. identification of risks but still allowing consumers to choose how much risk to take, or
      2. prohibition of certain risky products or behavior.

C. Liability for injuries from use of a product can be assigned either to consumers (buyer beware) or to sellers (seller beware). If it's cheaper for sellers to take actions to reduce injuries then liability should be assigned to sellers. If it's cheaper for consumers to safely use products, then liability should be assigned to consumers.

D. The fear of losing repeat business or of getting a bad reputation will restrain sellers from misleading consumers. However government requirements about seller provision of information make most sense when:

1. the information is highly valued by many consumers,
2. the information is based on objective rather than subjective evaluation, and
3. the information is less costly for the seller to provide than for the consumer to collect.

E. "Bad externalities" occur when the actions of a consumer or producer have a negative impact on another consumer or producer. Bad externalities can be controlled by restrictions on consumer and producer behavior.

DISCUSSION QUESTIONS

1. In high income neighborhoods, why is there a market for individuals hired to shop and do errands for households?

2. Consumer "experts" often recommend shopping by comparing unit prices. Why might this be bad advice for some consumers?

3. Why do higher prices not always indicate higher product quality?

4. Are stores that offer senior citizens special discounts doing so to be nice to senior citizens? Why or why not?

5. How many examples of market segmentation can you name in your community? Should market segmentation tactics used by sellers be outlawed?

6. How can you counter market segmentation tactics? Are there any costs to you of doing so?

7. Now that you know that real sales do occur, will you always wait to buy products "on sale?" Are there any costs to you of doing this?

8. Assume you live in a house with a basement. Evaluate the wisdom of turning the basement into a storage room for canned and other non-perishable foods.

9. How are warranties and service contracts like insurance?

10. What would be wrong with requiring all products to be risk-free?

11. As society's real income rises, why might consumers lobby for more protection from risky products and behavior?

PROBLEMS

1. Determine whether the following data indicate a quantity price discount or quantity price surcharge for bread, detergent, and frozen orange juice.

Products:	Bread	Detergent	Frozen O.J.
	30¢ for 24 oz.	75¢ for 16 oz.	$1.20 for 8 oz.
	55¢ for 50 oz.	$1.30 for 30 oz.	$2.70 for 16 oz.

2. A service contract on your new window air conditioner costs $100. The unit has an average life of ten years. Repair costs average $12/year (real dollars). If the real discount rate is 3 percent, will the service contract pay for itself?

CHAPTER 12

Summing Up

This is the final chapter, and it's the shortest one (at last, a short chapter you say)! In fact, we won't even do an introduction and separate topics—we'll just say it all here.

Hopefully, you've learned a lot. You've learned much useful information and techniques that will guide you to making the best consumer decisions for yourself and your family. Hopefully, you can now be your own financial planner and consumer advisor. This is important because you are best able to make decisions and judgements for yourself.

You will encounter decisions not covered in the text, or you will encounter new financial products that were not addressed. Don't panic. You now have the skills necessary to address any consumer decision or financial product. Just keep in mind these key points:

1. Always use present value or future value techniques to convert dollars paid or received at different points in time to the same value.
2. Always convert to after-tax dollars.
3. Remember that nothing is free. For resources that aren't explicitly priced, always include the opportunity cost of those resources.
4. Remember that time is a resource. For those decisions in which time use is important, remember to value that time.

Finally, remember the importance of planning in consumer decisions. Take a tip from businesses. Successful businesses are those that plan. Don't just let things happen in your financial life. Decide on your goals (make sure they're reasonable) and plan for them. Know where you are and where you're going. However, recognize that you can't control everything. In particular, you can't control the economy. The economy, and your financial fortunes, will always ride a roller coaster. However, if you have a plan and realize a roller coaster exists, you'll be better able to ride it.

Luck is also important. In fact, many fortunes were made on luck. So, realizing this, we will wish you good reasoning, good planning, and good luck!

APPENDIX

Table A-1 Annual future value factors (FVF).

ANNUAL INTEREST RATE

Years	1 FVF	1.5 FVF	2 FVF	2.5 FVF	3 FVF	3.5 FVF	4 FVF	4.5 FVF	5 FVF	5.5 FVF	6 FVF	6.5 FVF	7 FVF	7.5 FVF	8 FVF	8.5 FVF	9 FVF	9.5 FVF	10 FVF	10.5 FVF
1	1.010	1.015	1.020	1.025	1.030	1.035	1.040	1.045	1.050	1.055	1.060	1.065	1.070	1.075	1.080	1.085	1.090	1.095	1.100	1.105
2	1.020	1.030	1.040	1.051	1.061	1.071	1.082	1.092	1.102	1.113	1.124	1.134	1.145	1.156	1.166	1.177	1.188	1.199	1.210	1.221
3	1.030	1.046	1.061	1.077	1.093	1.109	1.125	1.141	1.158	1.174	1.191	1.208	1.225	1.242	1.260	1.277	1.295	1.313	1.331	1.349
4	1.041	1.061	1.082	1.104	1.126	1.148	1.170	1.193	1.216	1.239	1.262	1.286	1.311	1.335	1.360	1.386	1.412	1.438	1.464	1.491
5	1.051	1.077	1.104	1.131	1.159	1.188	1.217	1.246	1.276	1.307	1.338	1.370	1.403	1.436	1.469	1.504	1.539	1.574	1.611	1.647
6	1.062	1.093	1.126	1.160	1.194	1.229	1.265	1.302	1.340	1.379	1.419	1.459	1.501	1.543	1.587	1.631	1.677	1.724	1.772	1.820
7	1.072	1.110	1.149	1.189	1.230	1.272	1.316	1.361	1.407	1.455	1.504	1.554	1.606	1.659	1.714	1.770	1.828	1.888	1.949	2.012
8	1.083	1.126	1.172	1.218	1.267	1.317	1.369	1.422	1.477	1.535	1.594	1.655	1.718	1.783	1.851	1.921	1.993	2.067	2.144	2.223
9	1.094	1.143	1.195	1.249	1.305	1.363	1.423	1.486	1.551	1.619	1.689	1.763	1.838	1.917	1.999	2.084	2.172	2.263	2.358	2.456
10	1.105	1.161	1.219	1.280	1.344	1.411	1.480	1.553	1.629	1.708	1.791	1.877	1.967	2.061	2.159	2.261	2.367	2.478	2.594	2.714
11	1.116	1.178	1.243	1.312	1.384	1.460	1.539	1.623	1.710	1.802	1.898	1.999	2.105	2.216	2.332	2.453	2.580	2.714	2.853	2.999
12	1.127	1.196	1.268	1.345	1.426	1.511	1.601	1.696	1.796	1.901	2.012	2.129	2.252	2.382	2.518	2.662	2.813	2.971	3.138	3.314
13	1.138	1.214	1.294	1.379	1.469	1.564	1.665	1.772	1.886	2.006	2.133	2.267	2.410	2.560	2.720	2.888	3.066	3.254	3.452	3.662
14	1.149	1.232	1.319	1.413	1.513	1.619	1.732	1.852	1.980	2.116	2.261	2.415	2.579	2.752	2.937	3.133	3.342	3.563	3.797	4.046
15	1.161	1.250	1.346	1.448	1.558	1.675	1.801	1.935	2.079	2.232	2.397	2.572	2.759	2.959	3.172	3.400	3.642	3.901	4.177	4.471
16	1.173	1.269	1.373	1.485	1.605	1.734	1.873	2.022	2.183	2.355	2.540	2.739	2.952	3.181	3.426	3.689	3.970	4.272	4.595	4.941
17	1.184	1.288	1.400	1.522	1.653	1.795	1.948	2.113	2.292	2.485	2.693	2.917	3.159	3.419	3.700	4.002	4.328	4.678	5.054	5.460
18	1.196	1.307	1.428	1.560	1.702	1.857	2.026	2.208	2.407	2.621	2.854	3.107	3.380	3.676	3.996	4.342	4.717	5.122	5.560	6.033
19	1.208	1.327	1.457	1.599	1.754	1.923	2.107	2.308	2.527	2.766	3.026	3.309	3.617	3.951	4.316	4.712	5.142	5.609	6.116	6.666
20	1.220	1.347	1.486	1.639	1.806	1.990	2.191	2.412	2.653	2.918	3.207	3.524	3.870	4.248	4.661	5.112	5.604	6.142	6.727	7.366
21	1.232	1.367	1.516	1.680	1.860	2.059	2.279	2.520	2.786	3.078	3.400	3.753	4.141	4.566	5.034	5.547	6.109	6.725	7.400	8.140

22	1.245	1.388	1.546	1.722	1.916	2.132	2.370	2.634	2.925	3.248	3.604	3.997	4.430	4.909	5.437	6.018	6.659	7.364	8.140	8.994
23	1.257	1.408	1.577	1.765	1.974	2.206	2.465	2.752	3.072	3.426	3.820	4.256	4.741	5.277	5.871	6.530	7.258	8.064	8.954	9.939
24	1.270	1.430	1.608	1.809	2.033	2.283	2.563	2.876	3.225	3.615	4.049	4.533	5.072	5.673	6.341	7.085	7.911	8.830	9.850	10.982
25	1.282	1.451	1.641	1.854	2.094	2.363	2.666	3.005	3.386	3.813	4.292	4.828	5.427	6.098	6.848	7.687	8.623	9.668	10.835	12.135
26	1.295	1.473	1.673	1.900	2.157	2.446	2.772	3.141	3.556	4.023	4.549	5.141	5.807	6.556	7.396	8.340	9.399	10.587	11.918	13.410
27	1.308	1.495	1.707	1.948	2.221	2.532	2.883	3.282	3.733	4.244	4.822	5.476	6.214	7.047	7.988	9.049	10.245	11.593	13.110	14.818
28	1.321	1.517	1.741	1.996	2.288	2.620	2.999	3.430	3.920	4.478	5.112	5.832	6.649	7.576	8.627	9.818	11.167	12.694	14.421	16.374
29	1.335	1.540	1.776	2.046	2.357	2.712	3.119	3.584	4.116	4.724	5.418	6.211	7.114	8.144	9.317	10.653	12.172	13.900	15.863	18.093
30	1.348	1.563	1.811	2.098	2.427	2.807	3.243	3.745	4.322	4.984	5.743	6.614	7.612	8.755	10.063	14.558	13.268	15.220	17.449	19.993
31	1.361	1.587	1.848	2.150	2.500	2.905	3.373	3.914	4.538	5.258	6.088	7.044	8.145	9.412	10.868	12.541	14.462	16.666	19.194	22.092
32	1.375	1.610	1.885	2.204	2.575	3.007	3.508	4.090	4.765	5.547	6.453	7.502	8.715	10.117	11.737	13.607	15.763	18.250	21.114	21.411
33	1.389	1.634	1.922	2.259	2.652	3.112	3.648	4.274	5.003	5.852	6.841	7.990	9.325	10.876	12.676	14.763	17.182	19.983	23.225	26.975
34	1.403	1.659	1.961	2.315	2.732	3.221	3.794	4.466	5.253	6.174	7.251	8.509	9.978	11.692	13.690	16.018	18.728	21.882	25.548	29.807
35	1.417	1.684	2.000	2.373	2.814	3.334	3.946	4.667	5.516	6.514	7.686	9.062	10.677	12.569	14.785	17.380	20.414	23.960	28.102	32.937
36	1.431	1.709	2.040	2.433	2.898	3.450	4.104	4.877	5.792	6.872	8.147	9.651	11.424	13.512	15.968	18.857	22.251	26.237	30.913	36.395
37	1.445	1.735	2.081	2.493	2.985	3.571	4.268	5.097	6.081	7.250	8.636	10.279	12.224	14.525	17.246	20.460	24.254	28.729	34.004	40.217
38	1.460	1.761	2.122	2.556	3.075	3.696	4.439	5.326	6.385	7.649	9.154	10.947	13.079	15.614	18.625	22.199	26.437	31.458	37.404	44.439
39	1.474	1.787	2.165	2.620	3.167	3.825	4.616	5.566	6.705	8.060	9.704	11.658	13.995	16.785	20.115	24.086	28.816	34.447	41.145	49.105
40	1.489	1.814	2.208	2.685	3.262	3.959	4.801	5.816	7.040	8.513	10.286	12.416	14.974	18.044	21.725	26.133	31.409	37.719	45.259	54.261

(continued on next page)

Table A-1 Annual future value factors (FVF) (Continued).

	Annual Interest Rate																		
Years	**11**	**11.5**	**12**	**12.5**	**13**	**13.5**	**14**	**14.5**	**15**	**15.5**	**16**	**16.5**	**17**	**17.5**	**18**	**18.5**	**19**	**19.5**	**20**
	FVF	FVF	FVF	FVF	FVF	FVF	FVF	FVF	FVF	FVF	FVF	FVF	FVF	FVF	FVF	FVF	FVF	FVF	FVF
1	1.110	1.115	1.120	1.125	1.130	1.135	1.140	1.145	1.150	1.155	1.160	1.165	1.170	1.175	1.180	1.185	1.190	1.195	1.200
2	1.232	1.243	1.254	1.266	1.277	1.288	1.300	1.311	1.322	1.334	1.346	1.357	1.369	1.381	1.392	1.404	1.416	1.428	1.440
3	1.368	1.386	1.405	1.424	1.443	1.462	1.482	1.501	1.521	1.541	1.561	1.581	1.602	1.622	1.643	1.664	1.685	1.706	1.728
4	1.518	1.546	1.574	1.602	1.630	1.660	1.689	1.719	1.749	1.780	1.811	1.842	1.874	1.906	1.939	1.972	2.005	2.039	2.074
5	1.685	1.723	1.762	1.802	1.842	1.884	1.925	1.968	2.011	2.055	2.100	2.146	2.192	2.240	2.288	2.337	2.386	2.437	2.488
6	1.870	1.922	1.974	2.027	2.082	2.138	2.195	2.253	2.313	2.374	2.436	2.500	2.565	2.632	2.700	2.769	2.840	2.912	2.986
7	2.076	2.143	2.211	2.281	2.353	2.426	2.502	2.580	2.660	2.742	2.826	2.913	3.001	3.092	3.185	3.281	3.379	3.480	3.583
8	2.305	2.389	2.476	2.566	2.658	2.754	2.853	2.954	3.059	3.167	3.278	3.393	3.511	3.633	3.759	3.888	4.021	4.159	4.300
9	2.558	2.664	2.773	2.887	3.004	3.126	3.252	3.383	3.518	3.658	3.803	3.953	4.108	4.269	4.435	4.607	4.785	4.969	5.160
10	2.839	2.970	3.106	3.247	3.395	3.548	3.707	3.873	4.046	4.225	4.411	4.605	4.807	5.016	5.234	5.460	5.695	5.939	6.192
11	3.152	3.311	3.479	3.653	3.836	4.027	4.226	4.435	4.652	4.880	5.117	5.365	5.624	5.894	6.176	6.470	6.777	7.097	7.430
12	3.498	3.692	3.896	4.110	4.335	4.570	4.818	5.078	5.350	5.636	5.936	6.250	6.580	6.926	7.288	7.667	8.064	8.480	8.916
13	3.883	4.117	4.363	4.624	4.898	5.187	5.492	5.814	6.153	6.510	6.886	7.282	7.699	8.138	8.599	9.085	9.596	10.134	10.699
14	4.310	4.590	4.887	5.202	5.535	5.888	6.261	6.657	7.076	7.519	7.988	8.483	9.007	9.562	10.147	10.766	11.420	12.110	12.839
15	4.785	5.118	5.474	5.852	6.254	6.682	7.138	7.622	8.137	8.684	9.266	9.883	10.539	11.235	11.974	12.758	13.590	14.472	15.407
16	5.311	5.707	6.130	6.583	7.067	7.585	8.137	8.727	9.358	10.030	10.748	11.514	12.330	13.201	14.129	15.118	16.172	17.294	18.488
17	5.895	6.363	6.866	7.406	7.986	8.609	9.276	9.993	10.761	11.585	12.468	13.413	14.426	15.511	16.672	17.915	19.244	20.666	22.186
18	6.544	7.095	7.690	8.332	9.024	9.771	10.575	11.442	12.375	13.381	14.463	15.627	16.879	18.226	19.673	21.229	22.901	24.696	26.623
19	7.263	7.911	8.613	9.373	10.197	11.090	12.056	13.101	14.232	15.455	16.777	18.205	19.748	21.415	23.214	25.156	27.252	29.511	31.948
20	8.062	8.821	9.646	10.545	11.523	12.587	13.743	15.001	16.367	17.850	19.461	21.209	23.106	25.163	27.393	29.810	32.429	35.266	38.338
21	8.949	9.835	10.804	11.863	13.021	14.286	15.668	17.176	18.822	20.617	22.574	24.708	27.034	29.566	32.324	35.325	38.591	42.143	46.005
22	9.934	10.966	12.100	13.346	14.714	16.215	17.861	19.666	21.645	23.812	26.186	28.785	31.629	34.740	38.142	41.860	45.923	50.361	55.206

n																		
23	11.026	12.227	13.522	15.014	16.627	18.404	20.362	22.518	24.891	27.503	30.376	33.535	37.006	40.820	45.008	49.605	54.649	60.181	66.247
24	12.239	13.633	15.179	16.891	18.788	20.888	23.212	25.783	28.625	31.766	35.236	39.068	43.297	47.963	53.109	58.781	65.032	71.917	79.497
25	13.585	15.179	17.000	19.003	21.231	23.708	26.462	29.521	32.919	36.690	40.874	45.514	50.658	56.357	62.669	69.656	77.388	85.940	95.396
26	15.080	16.949	19.040	21.378	23.991	26.909	30.167	33.802	37.857	42.577	47.414	53.024	59.270	66.219	73.949	82.542	92.092	102.699	114.475
27	16.739	18.898	21.325	24.050	27.109	30.541	34.390	38.703	43.535	48.946	55.000	61.773	60.345	77.808	87.260	97.813	109.589	122.725	137.371
28	18.580	21.072	23.884	27.056	30.633	34.664	39.204	11.315	50.066	56.532	63.800	71.966	81.134	91.424	102.967	115.908	130.411	146.657	164.845
29	20.624	23.495	26.750	30.438	34.616	39.344	44.603	50.741	57.575	65.295	74.009	85.840	94.927	107.423	121.501	137.351	155.189	175.255	197.814
30	22.892	26.197	29.960	34.243	39.116	44.656	50.950	58.098	66.212	75.415	85.850	97.674	111.065	126.222	143.371	162.761	184.675	209.429	237.376
31	25.410	29.209	33.555	38.524	44.201	50.684	58.083	66.523	76.144	87.105	99.586	113.790	129.946	148.311	169.177	192.872	219.764	250.268	284.852
32	28.206	32.568	37.582	43.339	49.947	57.526	66.215	76.169	87.565	100.606	115.520	132.565	152.036	174.266	199.629	228.553	261.519	299.070	341.822
33	31.308	36.314	42.092	48.757	56.440	65.293	75.485	87.213	100.700	116.200	134.003	154.438	177.883	204.762	235.563	270.835	311.207	357.389	410.186
34	34.752	40.490	47.113	54.851	63.777	74.107	86.053	99.859	115.805	134.211	155.443	179.921	208.123	240.595	277.964	320.940	370.337	427.080	492.224
35	38.575	45.146	52.800	61.708	72.069	84.111	98.100	114.338	133.176	155.013	180.314	209.608	243.503	282.700	327.997	380.314	440.701	510.360	590.668
36	42.818	50.338	59.136	69.421	81.437	95.457	111.834	130.917	153.152	179.041	209.164	244.193	284.899	332.172	387.037	450.672	524.434	609.880	708.802
37	47.528	56.127	66.232	78.099	92.024	108.354	127.491	149.900	176.125	206.792	242.631	284.485	333.332	390.302	456.703	534.046	624.076	728.807	850.562
38	52.756	62.581	74.180	87.861	103.987	122.982	145.340	171.636	202.543	238.845	281.452	331.425	389.998	458.605	538.910	632.845	742.651	870.924	1020.675
39	58.559	69.778	83.081	98.844	117.506	139.585	165.687	196.523	232.925	275.865	326.484	386.110	456.298	538.861	635.914	749.921	883.754	1040.755	1224.810
40	65.001	77.803	93.051	111.199	132.782	158.429	188.884	225.019	267.864	318.625	378.721	449.818	533.869	633.162	750.378	888.657	1051.668	1243.702	1469.772

Table A-2 Monthly future value factors (FVF).

Months	Annual Interest Rate																			
	1	1.5	2	2.5	3	3.5	4	4.5	5	5.5	6	6.5	7	7.5	8	8.5	9	9.5	10	10.5
	FVF	FVF	FVF	FVF	FVF	FVF	FVF	FVF	FVF	FVF	FVF	FVF	FVF	FVF	FVF	FVF	FVF	FVF	FVF	FVF
1	1.001	1.001	1.002	1.002	1.002	1.003	1.003	1.004	1.004	1.005	1.005	1.005	1.006	1.006	1.007	1.007	1.007	1.008	1.008	1.009
2	1.002	1.003	1.003	1.004	1.005	1.006	1.007	1.008	1.008	1.009	1.010	1.011	1.012	1.013	1.013	1.014	1.015	1.016	1.017	1.018
3	1.003	1.004	1.005	1.006	1.008	1.009	1.010	1.011	1.013	1.014	1.015	1.016	1.018	1.019	1.020	1.021	1.023	1.024	1.025	1.026
4	1.003	1.005	1.007	1.008	1.010	1.012	1.013	1.015	1.017	1.018	1.020	1.022	1.024	1.025	1.027	1.029	1.030	1.032	1.034	1.035
5	1.004	1.006	1.008	1.010	1.013	1.015	1.017	1.019	1.021	1.023	1.025	1.027	1.030	1.032	1.034	1.036	1.038	1.040	1.042	1.045
6	1.005	1.008	1.010	1.013	1.015	1.018	1.020	1.023	1.025	1.028	1.030	1.033	1.036	1.038	1.041	1.043	1.046	1.048	1.051	1.054
7	1.006	1.009	1.012	1.015	1.018	1.021	1.024	1.027	1.030	1.033	1.036	1.039	1.042	1.045	1.048	1.051	1.054	1.057	1.060	1.063
8	1.007	1.010	1.013	1.017	1.020	1.024	1.027	1.030	1.034	1.037	1.041	1.044	1.048	1.051	1.055	1.058	1.062	1.065	1.069	1.072
9	1.008	1.011	1.015	1.019	1.023	1.027	1.030	1.034	1.038	1.042	1.046	1.050	1.054	1.058	1.062	1.066	1.070	1.074	1.078	1.082
10	1.008	1.013	1.017	1.021	1.025	1.030	1.034	1.038	1.042	1.047	1.051	1.056	1.060	1.064	1.069	1.073	1.078	1.082	1.087	1.091
11	1.009	1.014	1.018	1.023	1.028	1.033	1.037	1.042	1.047	1.052	1.056	1.061	1.066	1.071	1.076	1.081	1.086	1.091	1.096	1.101
12	1.010	1.015	1.120	1.025	1.030	1.036	1.041	1.046	1.051	1.056	1.062	1.067	1.072	1.078	1.083	1.088	1.094	1.099	1.105	1.110
13	1.011	1.016	1.022	1.027	1.033	1.039	1.044	1.050	1.056	1.061	1.067	1.073	1.079	1.084	1.090	1.096	1.102	1.108	1.114	1.120
14	1.012	1.018	1.024	1.030	1.036	1.042	1.048	1.054	1.060	1.066	1.072	1.079	1.085	1.091	1.097	1.104	1.110	1.117	1.123	1.130
15	1.013	1.019	1.025	1.032	1.038	1.045	1.051	1.058	1.064	1.071	1.078	1.084	1.091	1.098	1.105	1.112	1.119	1.126	1.133	1.140
16	1.013	1.020	1.027	1.034	1.041	1.048	1.055	1.062	1.0.69	1.076	1.083	1.090	1.098	1.105	1.112	1.120	1.127	1.134	1.142	1.150
17	1.014	1.021	1.029	1.036	1.043	1.051	1.058	1.066	1.073	1.081	1.088	1.096	1.104	1.112	1.120	1.127	1.135	1.143	1.152	1.160
18	1.015	1.023	1.030	1.038	1.046	1.054	1.062	1.070	1.078	1.086	1.094	1.102	1.110	1.119	1.127	1.135	1.144	1.153	1.161	1.170
19	1.016	1.024	1.032	1.040	1.049	1.057	1.065	1.074	1.082	1.091	1.099	1.108	1.117	1.126	1.135	1.144	1.53	1.162	1.171	1.180
20	1.017	1.025	1.034	1.043	1.051	1.060	1.069	1.078	1.087	1.096	1.105	1.114	1.123	1.113	1.142	1.152	1.161	1.171	1.181	1.190
21	1.018	1.027	1.036	1.045	1.054	1.063	1.072	1.082	1.091	1.101	1.110	1.120	1.130	1.140	1.150	1.160	1.170	1.180	1.190	1.201
22	1.018	1.028	1.037	1.047	1.056	1.066	1.076	1.086	1.096	1.106	1.116	1.126	1.137	1.147	1.157	1.168	1.179	1.189	1.200	1.211
23	1.019	1.029	1.039	1.049	1.059	1.069	1.080	1.090	1.100	1.111	1.122	1.132	1.143	1.154	1.165	1.176	1.188	1.199	1.210	1.222
24	1.020	1.030	1.041	1.051	1.062	1.072	1.083	1.094	1.105	1.116	1.127	1.138	1.150	1.161	1.173	1.185	1.196	1.208	1.220	1.233
25	1.021	1.032	1.043	1.053	1.064	1.076	1.087	1.098	1.110	1.121	1.133	1.145	1.157	1.169	1.181	1.193	1.205	1.218	1.231	1.243

26	1.022	1.033	1.044	1.056	1.067	1.079	1.090	1.102	1.114	1.126	1.138	1.151	1.163	1.176	1.189	1.201	1.214	1.228	1.241	1.254
27	1.023	1.034	1.046	1.058	1.070	1.082	1.094	1.106	1.119	1.131	1.144	1.157	1.170	1.183	1.197	1.210	1.224	1.237	1.251	1.265
28	1.024	1.036	1.048	1.060	1.072	1.085	1.098	1.110	1.123	1.137	1.150	1.163	1.177	1.191	1.204	1.219	1.233	1.247	1.262	1.276
29	1.024	1.037	1.049	1.062	1.075	1.088	1.101	1.115	1.128	1.142	1.156	1.170	1.184	1.198	1.213	1.227	1.242	1.257	1.272	1.287
30	1.025	1.038	1.051	1.064	1.078	1.091	1.105	1.119	1.133	1.147	1.161	1.176	1.191	1.206	1.221	1.236	1.251	1.267	1.283	1.299
31	1.026	1.039	1.053	1.067	1.080	1.094	1.109	1.123	1.138	1.152	1.167	1.182	1.198	1.213	1.229	1.245	1.261	1.277	1.293	1.310
32	1.027	1.041	1.055	1.069	1.083	1.098	1.112	1.127	1.142	1.158	1.173	1.189	1.205	1.221	1.237	1.253	1.270	1.287	1.304	1.322
33	1.028	1.042	1.056	1.071	1.086	1.101	1.116	1.131	1.147	1.163	1.179	1.195	1.212	1.228	1.245	1.262	1.280	1.297	1.315	1.333
34	1.029	1.043	1.058	1.073	1.089	1.104	1.120	1.136	1.152	1.168	1.185	1.202	1.219	1.236	1.253	1.271	1.289	1.307	1.326	1.345
35	1.030	1.045	1.060	1.076	1.091	1.107	1.124	1.140	1.157	1.174	1.191	1.208	1.226	1.244	1.262	1.280	1.299	1.318	1.337	1.357
36	1.030	1.046	1.062	1.078	1.094	1.111	1.127	1.144	1.161	1.179	1.197	1.215	1.233	1.251	1.270	1.289	1.309	1.328	1.348	1.368
48	1.041	1.062	1.083	1.105	1.127	1.150	1.173	1.197	1.221	1.245	1.270	1.296	1.322	1.349	1.376	1.403	1.431	1.460	1.489	1.519
60	1.051	1.078	1.105	1.133	1.162	1.191	1.221	1.252	1.283	1.316	1.349	1.383	1.418	1.453	1.490	1.527	1.566	1.605	1.645	1.687
72	1.062	1.094	1.127	1.162	1.197	1.233	1.271	1.309	1.349	1.390	1.432	1.475	1.520	1.566	1.614	1.622	1.713	1.764	1.818	1.872
84	1.072	1.111	1.150	1.191	1.233	1.277	1.323	1.369	1.418	1.468	1.520	1.574	1.630	1.688	1.747	1.809	1.873	1.939	2.008	2.079
96	1.083	1.127	1.173	1.221	1.271	1.323	1.376	1.432	1.491	1.551	1.614	1.680	1.748	1.819	1.892	1.969	2.049	2.132	2.218	2.308
108	1.094	1.144	1.197	1.252	1.310	1.370	1.432	1.498	1.567	1.639	1.714	1.792	1.874	1.960	2.050	2.143	2.241	2.343	2.450	2.256
120	1.105	1.162	1.221	1.284	1.349	1.418	1.491	1.567	1.647	1.731	1.819	1.912	2.010	2.112	2.220	2.333	2.451	2.576	2.707	2.845
132	1.116	1.179	1.246	1.316	1.390	1.469	1.552	1.639	1.731	1.829	1.932	2.040	2.155	2.276	2.404	2.539	2.681	2.832	2.991	3.158
144	1.127	1.197	1.271	1.349	1.433	1.521	1.615	1.714	1.820	1.932	2.051	2.177	2.311	2.453	2.603	2.763	2.933	3.113	3.304	3.506
156	1.139	1.215	1.297	1.384	1.476	1.575	1.681	1.793	1.913	2.041	2.177	2.323	2.478	2.643	2.819	3.007	3.208	3.422	3.650	3.893
168	1.150	1.234	1.323	1.419	1.521	1.631	1.749	1.875	2.011	2.156	2.312	2.478	2.657	2.848	3.053	3.273	3.509	3.761	4.032	4.322
180	1.162	1.252	1.350	1.454	1.567	1.689	1.820	1.962	2.114	2.278	2.454	2.644	2.849	3.069	3.307	3.563	3.838	4.135	4.454	4.798
192	1.173	1.271	1.377	1.491	1.615	1.749	1.894	2.052	2.222	2.406	2.605	2.821	3.055	3.308	3.581	3.878	4.198	4.545	4.920	5.326
204	1.185	1.290	1.405	1.529	1.664	1.811	1.972	2.146	2.336	2.542	2.766	3.010	3.276	3.565	3.879	4.220	4.592	4.996	5.436	5.913
216	1.197	1.310	1.433	1.568	1.715	1.876	2.052	2.245	2.455	2.685	2.937	3.212	3.513	3.841	4.201	4.593	5.023	5.492	6.005	6.565
228	1.209	1.330	1.462	1.607	1.767	1.943	2.136	2.348	2.581	2.837	3.118	3.427	3.766	4.139	4.549	4.999	5.494	6.037	6.633	7.289
240	1.221	1.350	1.491	1.648	1.821	2.012	2.223	2.455	2.713	2.997	3.310	3.656	4.039	4.461	4.927	5.441	6.009	6.636	7.328	8.092
300	1.281	1.455	1.648	1.867	2.115	2.396	2.714	3.074	3.481	3.943	4.465	5.056	5.725	6.483	7.340	8.310	9.408	10.651	12.057	13.648
360	1.350	1.568	1.821	2.115	2.457	2.853	3.313	3.848	4.468	5.187	6.023	6.992	8.116	9.422	10.936	12.692	14.731	17.095	19.837	23.019

(continued on next page)

799

Table A-2 Monthly future value factors (FVF) (Continued).

Months	11 FVF	11.5 FVF	12 FVF	12.5 FVF	13 FVF	13.5 FVF	14 FVF	14.5 FVF	15 FVF	15.5 FVF	16 FVF	16.5 FVF	17 FVF	17.5 FVF	18 FVF	18.5 FVF	19 FVF	19.5 FVF	20 FVF
1	1.009	1.010	1.010	1.010	1.011	1.011	1.012	1.012	1.012	1.013	1.013	1.014	1.014	1.015	1.015	1.015	1.016	1.016	1.017
2	1.018	1.019	1.020	1.021	1.022	1.023	1.023	1.024	1.025	1.026	1.027	1.028	1.029	1.029	1.030	1.031	1.032	1.033	1.034
3	1.028	1.029	1.030	1.032	1.033	1.034	1.035	1.037	1.038	1.039	1.041	1.042	1.043	1.044	1.046	1.047	1.048	1.050	1.051
4	1.037	1.039	1.041	1.042	1.044	1.046	1.047	1.049	1.051	1.053	1.054	1.056	1.058	1.060	1.061	1.063	1.065	1.067	1.068
5	1.047	1.049	1.051	1.053	1.055	1.058	1.060	1.062	1.064	1.066	1.068	1.071	1.073	1.075	1.077	1.079	1.082	1.084	1.086
6	1.056	1.059	1.062	1.064	1.067	1.069	1.072	1.075	1.077	1.080	1.083	1.085	1.088	1.091	1.093	1.096	1.099	1.102	1.104
7	1.066	1.069	1.072	1.075	1.078	1.081	1.085	1.088	1.091	1.094	1.097	1.100	1.103	1.107	1.110	1.113	1.116	1.119	1.123
8	1.076	1.079	1.083	1.086	1.090	1.094	1.097	1.101	1.104	1.108	1.112	1.115	1.119	1.123	1.126	1.130	1.134	1.138	1.141
9	1.086	1.090	1.094	1.098	1.102	1.106	1.110	1.114	1.118	1.122	1.127	1.131	1.135	1.139	1.143	1.148	1.152	1.156	1.160
10	1.096	1.100	1.105	1.109	1.114	1.118	1.123	1.128	1.132	1.137	1.142	1.146	1.151	1.156	1.161	1.165	1.170	1.175	1.180
11	1.106	1.111	1.116	1.121	1.126	1.131	1.136	1.141	1.146	1.152	1.157	1.162	1.167	1.173	1.178	1.183	1.189	1.194	1.199
12	1.116	1.121	1.127	1.132	1.138	1.144	1.149	1.155	1.161	1.166	1.172	1.178	1.184	1.190	1.196	1.202	1.207	1.213	1.219
13	1.126	1.132	1.138	1.144	1.150	1.157	1.163	1.169	1.175	1.182	1.188	1.194	1.201	1.207	1.214	1.220	1.227	1.233	1.240
14	1.136	1.143	1.149	1.156	1.163	1.170	1.176	1.183	1.190	1.197	1.204	1.211	1.218	1.225	1.232	1.239	1.246	1.253	1.260
15	1.147	1.154	1.161	1.168	1.175	1.183	1.190	1.197	1.205	1.212	1.220	1.227	1.235	1.243	1.250	1.258	1.266	1.274	1.281
16	1.157	1.165	1.173	1.180	1.118	1.196	1.204	1.212	1.220	1.228	1.236	1.244	1.252	1.261	1.269	1.277	1.286	1.294	1.303
17	1.168	1.176	1.184	1.193	1.201	1.209	1.218	1.227	1.235	1.244	1.253	1.261	1.270	1.279	1.288	1.297	1.306	1.315	1.324
18	1.179	1.187	1.196	1.205	1.214	1.223	1.232	1.241	1.251	1.260	1.269	1.279	1.288	1.298	1.307	1.317	1.327	1.337	1.347
19	1.189	1.199	1.208	1.218	1.227	1.237	1.247	1.256	1.266	1.276	1.286	1.296	1.306	1.317	1.327	1.337	1.348	1.358	1.369
20	1.200	1.210	1.220	1.230	1.240	1.251	1.261	1.272	1.282	1.293	1.303	1.314	1.325	1.336	1.347	1.358	1.369	1.380	1.392
21	1.211	1.222	1.232	1.243	1.254	1.265	1.276	1.287	1.298	1.309	1.321	1.332	1.344	1.355	1.367	1.379	1.391	1.403	1.415
22	1.222	1.233	1.245	1.256	1.28	1.279	1.291	1.302	1.314	1.326	1.338	1.350	1.363	1.375	1.388	1.400	1.413	1.426	1.439
23	1.234	1.245	1.257	1.269	1.281	1.293	1.306	1.318	1.331	1.343	1.356	1.369	1.382	1.395	1.408	1.422	1.435	1.449	1.463
24	1.245	1.257	1.270	1.282	1.295	1.308	1.321	1.334	1.347	1.361	1.374	1.388	1.402	1.415	1.430	1.444	1.458	1.472	1.487
25	1.256	1.269	1.282	1.296	1.309	1.323	1.336	1.350	1.364	1.378	1.393	1.407	1.421	1.436	1.451	1.466	1.481	1.496	1.512

Annual Interest Rate

26	27	28	29	30	31	32	33	34	35	36	48	60	72	84	96	108	120	132	144	156	168	180	192	204	216	228	240	300	360
1.537	1.563	1.589	1.615	1.642	1.669	1.697	1.725	1.754	1.783	1.813	2.211	2.696	3.287	4.009	4.888	5.961	7.268	8.863	10.807	13.178	16.069	19.595	23.894	29.136	35.528	43.323	52.828	142.421	383.964
1.521	1.545	1.570	1.596	1.622	1.648	1.675	1.702	1.730	1.758	1.787	2.168	2.630	3.192	3.873	4.700	5.702	6.919	8.396	10.188	12.362	15.000	18.201	22.086	26.799	32.518	39.457	47.878	125.941	331.284
1.504	1.528	1.552	1.577	1.602	1.627	1.653	1.679	1.706	1.733	1.760	2.126	2.567	3.099	3.742	4.518	5.455	6.587	7.954	9.604	11.596	14.001	16.906	20.413	24.648	29.761	35.935	43.390	111.362	285.815
1.489	1.511	1.535	1.558	1.582	1.607	1.632	1.657	1.682	1.708	1.735	2.084	2.504	3.009	3.615	4.344	5.219	6.271	7.534	9.053	10.877	13.069	15.703	18.867	22.669	27.237	32.726	39.321	98.466	246.572
1.473	1.495	1.517	1.540	1.563	1.587	1.610	1.634	1.659	1.684	1.709	2.043	2.443	2.921	3.493	4.176	4.993	5.969	7.137	8.533	10.202	12.198	14.584	17.437	20.848	24.927	29.803	35.633	87.059	212.704
1.457	1.478	1.500	1.522	1.544	1.566	1.589	1.612	1.636	1.660	1.684	2.004	2.384	2.836	3.374	4.014	4.776	5.682	6.761	8.043	9.569	11.385	13.545	16.115	19.173	22.811	27.139	32.289	76.969	183.477
1.442	1.462	1.483	1.504	1.525	1.547	1.569	1.591	1.613	1.636	1.659	1.964	2.326	2.753	3.260	3.859	4.569	5.409	6.404	7.581	8.975	10.626	12.580	14.893	17.632	20.874	24.713	29.258	68.046	158.256
1.426	1.446	1.466	1.486	1.506	1.527	1.548	1.569	1.591	1.613	1.635	1.926	2.269	2.673	3.149	3.710	4.371	5.149	6.066	7.146	8.418	9.917	11.683	13.763	16.214	19.101	22.503	26.510	60.153	136.494
1.411	1.430	1.449	1.468	1.488	1.508	1.528	1.548	1.569	1.590	1.611	1.888	2.214	2.595	3.042	3.566	4.181	4.901	5.745	6.735	7.895	9.255	10.850	12.719	14.910	17.478	20.489	24.019	53.174	117.717
1.396	1.414	1.432	1.451	1.470	1.489	1.508	1.527	1.547	1.567	1.587	1.852	2.160	2.519	2.939	3.428	3.999	4.665	5.442	6.348	7.405	8.637	10.076	11.753	13.710	15.993	18.656	21.762	47.002	101.517
1.381	1.399	1.416	1.434	1.452	1.470	1.488	1.507	1.526	1.545	1.564	1.815	2.107	2.446	2.839	3.296	3.825	4.440	5.154	5.983	6.944	8.061	9.356	10.860	12.606	14.633	16.985	19.715	41.544	87.541
1.367	1.383	1.400	1.417	1.434	1.451	1.469	1.486	1.504	1.523	1.541	1.780	2.056	2.374	2.743	3.168	3.659	4.226	4.881	5.638	6.512	7.522	8.688	10.035	11.591	13.388	15.464	17.861	36.718	75.485
1.352	1.368	1.384	1.400	1.416	1.433	1.449	1.466	1.483	1.501	1.518	1.745	2.006	2.305	2.649	3.045	3.500	4.022	4.623	5.314	6.107	7.019	8.068	9.272	10.657	12.249	14.078	16.180	32.451	65.085
1.338	1.353	1.368	1.383	1.399	1.415	1.430	1.447	1.463	1.479	1.496	1.711	1.957	2.238	2.559	2.927	3.348	3.828	4.379	5.008	5.727	6.550	7.491	8.567	9.798	11.206	12.816	14.657	28.679	56.114
1.323	1.338	1.352	1.367	1.382	1.397	1.412	1.427	1.442	1.458	1.474	1.677	1.909	2.172	2.472	2.813	3.202	3.644	4.147	4.719	5.370	6.112	6.955	7.915	9.008	10.251	11.666	13.277	25.343	48.377
1.309	1.323	1.337	1.351	1.365	1.379	1.393	1.408	1.422	1.437	1.452	1.644	1.862	2.109	2.388	2.704	3.062	3.468	3.927	4.447	5.036	5.703	6.458	7.313	8.281	9.378	10.620	12.026	22.395	41.704
1.295	1.308	1.321	1.335	1.348	1.361	1.375	1.389	1.403	1.417	1.431	1.612	1.817	2.047	2.307	2.599	2.929	3.300	3.719	4.191	4.722	5.321	5.996	6.756	7.613	8.579	9.667	10.893	19.788	35.950
1.281	1.294	1.306	1.319	1.331	1.344	1.357	1.370	1.383	1.396	1.410	1.581	1.772	1.987	2.228	2.498	2.801	3.141	3.522	3.949	4.428	4.965	5.567	6.242	6.998	7.847	8.799	9.866	17.484	30.987
1.268	1.279	1.291	1.303	1.315	1.327	1.339	1.351	1.364	1.376	1.389	1.550	1.729	1.929	2.152	2.401	2.679	2.989	3.335	3.721	4.152	4.632	5.168	5.766	6.433	7.178	8.008	8.935	15.448	26.708

Table A-3 Monthly future value factor sums (FVFS).

Annual Interest Rate

Months	1	1.5	2	2.5	3	3.5	4	4.5	5	5.5	6	6.5	7	7.5	8	8.5	9	9.5	10	10.5
	FVFS	FVFS	FVFS	FVFS	FVFS	FVFS	FVFS	FVFS	FVFS	FVFS	FVFS	FVFS	FVFS	FVFS	FVFS	FVFS	FVFS	FVFS	FVFS	FVFS
12	12.055	12.083	12.111	12.138	12.166	12.194	12.222	12.251	12.279	12.307	12.336	12.364	12.393	12.421	12.450	12.479	12.508	12.537	12.556	12.595
18	18.128	18.195	18.257	18.322	18.388	18.453	18.519	18.585	18.652	18.719	18.786	18.853	18.921	18.989	19.057	19.126	19.195	19.264	19.333	19.403
24	24.231	24.348	24.466	24.584	24.703	24.822	24.943	25.064	25.186	25.309	25.432	25.556	25.681	25.807	25.933	26.060	26.188	26.317	26.447	26.577
36	36.530	36.790	37.070	37.344	37.621	37.900	38.182	38.466	38.753	39.043	39.336	39.632	39.930	40.231	40.536	40.843	41.153	41.466	41.782	42.101
48	48.952	49.437	49.929	50.427	50.931	51.442	51.960	52.484	53.015	53.553	54.098	54.650	55.209	55.776	56.350	56.931	57.521	58.118	58.722	59.335
60	61.499	62.267	63.047	63.841	64.647	65.466	66.299	67.146	68.006	68.881	69.770	70.674	71.593	72.527	73.477	74.442	75.424	76.422	77.437	78.469
72	74.172	75.290	76.431	77.593	78.779	79.989	81.223	82.481	83.764	85.073	86.409	87.771	89.161	90.579	92.025	93.501	95.007	96.544	98.111	99.711
84	86.972	88.510	90.084	91.694	93.342	95.028	96.754	98.521	100.329	102.179	104.074	106.013	107.999	110.032	112.113	114.245	116.427	118.662	120.950	123.294
96	99.901	101.930	104.013	106.151	108.347	110.603	112.919	115.297	117.741	120.250	122.829	125.477	128.199	130.995	133.869	136.821	139.856	142.975	146.181	149.476
108	112.960	115.552	118.223	120.974	123.809	126.731	129.741	132.845	136.043	139.341	142.740	146.245	149.859	153.586	157.430	161.394	165.483	169.702	174.051	178.544
120	126.150	129.380	132.597	136.172	139.741	143.433	147.250	151.198	155.282	159.508	163.879	168.403	173.085	177.930	182.946	188.138	193.514	199.081	204.845	210.815
132	139.472	143.417	147.509	151.754	156.158	160.728	165.471	170.395	175.506	180.812	186.323	192.045	197.990	204.165	210.580	217.247	224.175	231.375	238.860	246.642
144	152.929	157.666	162.597	167.730	173.074	178.639	184.435	190.473	196.764	203.319	210.150	217.271	224.695	232.436	240.508	248.928	257.712	266.875	276.438	286.417
156	166.520	172.130	177.990	184.110	190.505	197.187	201.172	211.474	219.109	227.095	235.447	241.186	253.331	262.902	272.920	283.410	294.394	305.899	317.950	330.576
168	180.248	186.813	193.639	200.904	208.466	216.395	224.713	233.440	242.598	252.212	262.305	272.904	284.037	295.733	308.023	320.940	334.518	348.795	363.809	379.602
180	194.114	201.717	209.713	218.123	226.973	236.286	246.090	256.415	267.289	278.746	290.819	303.545	316.962	331.112	346.038	361.786	378.406	395.949	414.470	434.030
192	208.119	216.847	226.057	236.051	246.043	256.884	268.339	280.445	293.243	306.776	321.091	336.238	352.268	369.239	387.209	406.244	426.410	447.782	470.436	494.456
204	222.265	232.205	242.730	253.879	265.693	278.215	291.494	305.579	320.525	336.388	353.231	371.120	390.126	410.325	431.797	454.631	478.918	504.760	532.263	561.542
216	236.553	247.795	259.740	272.438	285.940	300.305	315.592	331.868	349.202	367.670	387.353	408.339	430.721	454.601	480.086	507.295	536.352	567.393	600.563	630.020
228	250.985	263.620	277.093	291.466	306.804	323.180	340.673	359.365	379.347	400.717	423.580	448.050	474.250	502.314	532.383	564.614	599.173	636.242	676.016	718.706
240	265.561	279.685	294.797	310.975	328.302	346.869	366.775	388.124	411.034	435.627	462.041	490.421	520.927	553.731	589.020	626.999	667.887	711.924	759.369	810.505
300	340.670	363.721	388.821	416.175	446.008	478.568	514.130	552.998	595.510	642.037	692.994	748.837	810.072	877.261	951.026	1032.058	1121.122	1219.066	1326.833	1445.469
360	419.628	454.297	492.725	535.368	582.737	635.413	694.049	759.386	832.259	913.612	1004.515	1106.178	1219.971	1347.445	1490.359	1650.706	1830.743	2033.035	2260.488	2516.401

Annual Interest Rate

Months	11	11.5	12	12.5	13	13.5	14	14.5	15	15.5	16	16.5	17	17.5	18	18.5	19	19.5	20
	FVFS	FVFS	FVFS	FVFS	FVFS	FVFS	FVFS	FVFS	FVFS	FVFS	FVFS	FVFS	FVFS	FVFS	FVFS	FVFS	FVFS	FVFS	FVFS
12	12.624	12.653	12.683	12.712	12.741	12.771	12.801	12.831	12.860	12.890	12.920	12.950	12.981	13.011	13.041	13.072	13.102	13.133	13.163
18	19.473	19.544	19.615	19.686	19.757	19.829	19.901	19.973	20.046	20.119	20.193	20.266	20.340	20.415	20.489	20.564	20.640	20.715	20.792
24	26.709	26.841	26.973	27.107	27.242	27.377	27.513	27.650	27.788	27.927	28.066	28.207	28.348	28.490	28.634	28.778	28.922	29.068	29.215
36	42.423	42.748	43.077	43.409	43.743	44.083	44.423	44.767	45.116	45.467	45.822	46.180	46.542	46.907	47.276	47.648	48.025	48.404	48.788
48	59.956	60.585	61.223	61.868	62.523	63.186	63.838	64.539	65.228	65.927	66.636	67.354	68.081	68.818	69.565	70.322	71.089	71.867	72.655
60	79.518	80.585	81.670	82.773	83.894	85.035	86.195	87.375	88.575	89.795	91.036	92.298	93.581	94.887	96.215	97.565	98.939	100.337	101.758
72	101.344	103.010	104.710	106.445	108.216	110.024	111.868	113.751	115.674	117.636	119.639	121.583	123.771	125.902	128.077	130.298	132.566	134.882	137.247
84	125.695	128.154	130.672	133.252	135.895	138.602	141.376	144.218	147.129	150.112	153.169	156.302	159.512	162.801	166.173	169.628	173.170	176.800	180.521
96	152.864	156.347	159.927	163.609	167.394	171.287	175.290	179.407	183.641	187.996	192.476	197.084	201.825	206.702	211.720	216.883	222.196	227.663	233.289
108	183.177	187.958	192.893	197.985	203.242	208.667	214.269	220.052	226.023	232.188	238.554	245.129	251.920	258.933	266.178	273.662	281.393	289.381	297.634
120	216.998	223.403	230.039	236.913	244.037	251.419	259.069	266.998	275.217	283.737	292.571	301.729	311.226	321.074	331.288	341.882	352.870	364.269	376.095
132	254.733	263.146	271.896	280.997	290.463	300.312	310.560	321.223	332.320	343.870	355.892	368.408	381.439	395.006	409.135	423.850	439.176	455.140	471.771
144	296.834	307.708	319.062	330.917	343.298	356.230	369.740	383.854	398.602	414.014	430.122	446.960	464.563	482.967	502.211	522.336	543.385	565.403	588.436
156	343.807	357.674	372.209	387.448	403.426	420.183	437.758	456.196	475.540	495.838	517.140	539.500	562.972	587.616	613.494	640.670	669.213	699.197	730.698
168	396.216	413.698	432.097	451.464	471.853	493.323	515.935	539.753	564.845	591.285	619.149	648.518	679.479	712.123	746.545	782.850	821.145	861.544	904.170
180	454.690	476.516	499.580	523.957	549.726	576.972	605.786	636.264	668.507	702.624	738.730	776.949	817.410	860.253	905.625	953.683	1004.594	1058.537	1115.700
192	519.930	546.951	575.622	606.049	638.347	672.640	709.056	747.738	788.833	832.501	878.912	928.249	980.706	1036.489	1095.822	1158.942	1226.100	1297.569	1373.638
204	592.719	625.927	661.308	699.012	739.202	782.052	827.749	876.494	928.501	984.002	1043.243	1106.491	1174.030	1246.165	1323.226	1405.564	1493.558	1587.613	1688.165
216	673.932	714.480	757.861	804.284	853.977	907.184	964.167	1025.212	1090.623	1160.728	1235.884	1316.472	1402.905	1495.626	1595.115	1701.887	1816.500	1939.555	2071.697
228	764.542	813.771	866.659	923.496	984.595	1050.294	1120.959	1196.987	1278.805	1366.879	1461.711	1563.844	1673.868	1792.419	1920.189	2057.925	2206.437	2366.603	2539.373
240	865.638	925.101	989.255	1058.494	1133.242	1213.965	1301.166	1395.392	1497.239	1607.355	1726.442	1855.266	1994.659	2145.527	2308.854	2485.713	2677.267	2884.787	3109.652
300	1576.133	1720.115	1878.847	2053.917	2247.092	2460.334	2695.826	2955.993	3243.530	3561.435	3913.014	4302.065	4732.626	5209.319	5737.253	6322.118	6970.245	7688.685	8485.287
360	2804.520	3129.097	3494.964	3907.609	4373.270	4899.036	5492.971	6164.242	6923.280	7781.950	8753.759	9854.078	11100.408	12512.678	14113.585	15928.985	17988.334	20325.199	22977.838

Table A-4 Annual present value factors (PVF).

									Annual Interest Rate											
	1	1.5	2	2.5	3	3.5	4	4.5	5	5.5	6	6.5	7	7.5	8	8.5	9	9.5	10	10.5
Years	PVF	PVF	PVF	PVF	PVF	PVF	PVF	PVF	PVF	PVF	PVF	PVF	PVF	PVF	PVF	PVF	PVF	PVF	PVF	PVF
1	0.990	0.985	0.980	0.976	0.971	0.966	0.962	0.957	0.952	0.948	0.943	0.939	0.935	0.930	0.926	0.922	0.917	0.913	0.909	0.905
2	0.980	0.971	0.961	0.952	0.943	0.934	0.925	0.916	0.907	0.898	0.890	0.882	0.873	0.865	0.857	0.849	0.842	0.834	0.826	0.819
3	0.971	0.956	0.942	0.929	0.915	0.902	0.889	0.876	0.864	0.852	0.840	0.828	0.816	0.805	0.794	0.783	0.772	0.762	0.751	0.741
4	0.961	0.942	0.924	0.906	0.888	0.871	0.855	0.839	0.823	0.807	0.792	0.777	0.763	0.749	0.735	0.722	0.708	0.696	0.683	0.671
5	0.951	0.928	0.906	0.884	0.863	0.842	0.822	0.802	0.784	0.765	0.747	0.730	0.713	0.697	0.681	0.665	0.650	0.635	0.621	0.607
6	0.942	0.915	0.888	0.862	0.837	0.814	0.790	0.768	0.746	0.725	0.705	0.685	0.666	0.648	0.630	0.613	0.596	0.580	0.564	0.549
7	0.933	0.901	0.871	0.841	0.813	0.786	0.760	0.735	0.711	0.687	0.665	0.644	0.623	0.603	0.583	0.565	0.547	0.530	0.513	0.497
8	0.923	0.888	0.853	0.821	0.789	0.759	0.731	0.703	0.677	0.652	0.627	0.604	0.582	0.561	0.540	0.521	0.502	0.484	0.467	0.450
9	0.914	0.875	0.837	0.801	0.766	0.734	0.703	0.673	0.645	0.618	0.592	0.567	0.544	0.522	0.500	0.480	0.460	0.442	0.424	0.407
10	0.905	0.862	0.820	0.781	0.744	0.709	0.676	0.644	0.614	0.585	0.558	0.533	0.508	0.485	0.463	0.442	0.422	0.404	0.386	0.368
11	0.896	0.849	0.804	0.762	0.722	0.685	0.650	0.616	0.585	0.555	0.527	0.500	0.475	0.451	0.429	0.408	0.388	0.369	0.350	0.333
12	0.887	0.836	0.788	0.744	0.701	0.662	0.625	0.590	0.557	0.526	0.497	0.470	0.444	0.420	0.397	0.376	0.356	0.337	0.319	0.302
13	0.879	0.824	0.773	0.725	0.681	0.639	0.601	0.564	0.530	0.499	0.469	0.441	0.415	0.391	0.368	0.346	0.326	0.307	0.290	0.273
14	0.870	0.812	0.758	0.708	0.661	0.618	0.577	0.540	0.505	0.473	0.442	0.414	0.388	0.363	0.340	0.319	0.299	0.281	0.263	0.247
15	0.861	0.800	0.743	0.690	0.642	0.597	0.555	0.517	0.481	0.448	0.417	0.389	0.362	0.338	0.315	0.294	0.275	0.256	0.239	0.224
16	0.853	0.788	0.728	0.674	0.623	0.577	0.534	0.494	0.458	0.425	0.394	0.365	0.339	0.314	0.292	0.271	0.252	0.234	0.218	0.202
17	0.844	0.776	0.714	0.657	0.605	0.557	0.513	0.473	0.436	0.402	0.371	0.343	0.317	0.292	0.270	0.250	0.231	0.214	0.198	0.183
18	0.836	0.765	0.700	0.641	0.587	0.538	0.494	0.453	0.416	0.381	0.350	0.322	0.296	0.272	0.250	0.230	0.212	0.195	0.180	0.166
19	0.828	0.754	0.686	0.626	0.570	0.520	0.475	0.433	0.396	0.362	0.331	0.302	0.277	0.253	0.232	0.212	0.194	0.178	0.164	0.150
20	0.820	0.742	0.673	0.610	0.554	0.503	0.456	0.415	0.377	0.343	0.312	0.284	0.258	0.235	0.215	0.196	0.178	0.163	0.149	0.136
21	0.811	0.731	0.660	0.595	0.538	0.486	0.439	0.397	0.359	0.325	0.294	0.266	0.242	0.219	0.199	0.180	0.164	0.149	0.135	0.123

22	0.803	0.721	0.647	0.581	0.522	0.469	0.422	0.380	0.342	0.308	0.278	0.250	0.226	0.204	0.184	0.166	0.150	0.136	0.123	0.111
23	0.795	0.710	0.634	0.567	0.507	0.453	0.406	0.363	0.326	0.292	0.262	0.235	0.211	0.189	0.170	0.153	0.138	0.124	0.112	0.101
24	0.788	0.700	0.622	0.553	0.492	0.438	0.390	0.348	0.310	0.277	0.247	0.221	0.197	0.176	0.158	0.141	0.126	0.113	0.102	0.091
25	0.780	0.689	0.610	0.539	0.478	0.423	0.375	0.333	0.295	0.262	0.233	0.207	0.184	0.164	0.146	0.130	0.116	0.103	0.092	0.082
26	0.772	0.679	0.598	0.526	0.464	0.409	0.361	0.318	0.281	0.249	0.220	0.194	0.172	0.153	0.135	0.120	0.106	0.094	0.084	0.075
27	0.764	0.669	0.586	0.513	0.450	0.395	0.347	0.305	0.268	0.236	0.207	0.183	0.161	0.142	0.125	0.111	0.098	0.086	0.076	0.067
28	0.757	0.659	0.574	0.501	0.437	0.382	0.333	0.292	0.255	0.223	0.196	0.171	0.150	0.132	0.116	0.102	0.090	0.079	0.069	0.061
29	0.749	0.649	0.563	0.489	0.424	0.369	0.321	0.279	0.243	0.212	0.185	0.161	0.141	0.123	0.107	0.094	0.082	0.072	0.063	0.055
30	0.742	0.640	0.552	0.477	0.412	0.356	0.308	0.267	0.231	0.201	0.174	0.151	0.131	0.114	0.099	0.087	0.075	0.066	0.057	0.050
31	0.735	0.630	0.541	0.465	0.400	0.344	0.296	0.256	0.220	0.190	0.164	0.142	0.123	0.106	0.092	0.080	0.069	0.060	0.052	0.045
32	0.727	0.621	0.531	0.454	0.388	0.333	0.285	0.244	0.210	0.180	0.155	0.133	0.115	0.099	0.085	0.073	0.063	0.055	0.047	0.041
33	0.720	0.612	0.520	0.443	0.377	0.321	0.274	0.234	0.200	0.171	0.146	0.125	0.107	0.092	0.079	0.068	0.058	0.050	0.043	0.037
34	0.713	0.603	0.510	0.432	0.366	0.310	0.264	0.224	0.190	0.162	0.138	0.118	0.100	0.086	0.073	0.062	0.053	0.046	0.039	0.034
35	0.706	0.594	0.500	0.421	0.355	0.300	0.253	0.214	0.181	0.154	0.130	0.110	0.094	0.080	0.068	0.058	0.049	0.042	0.036	0.030
36	0.699	0.585	0.490	0.411	0.345	0.290	0.244	0.205	0.173	0.146	0.123	0.104	0.088	0.074	0.063	0.0.53	0.045	0.038	0.032	0.027
37	0.692	0.576	0.481	0.401	0.335	0.280	0.234	0.196	0.164	0.138	0.116	0.097	0.082	0.069	0.058	0.049	0.041	0.035	0.029	0.025
38	0.685	0.568	0.471	0.391	0.325	0.271	0.225	0.188	0.157	0.131	0.109	0.091	0.076	0.064	0.054	0.045	0.038	0.032	0.027	0.023
39	0.678	0.560	0.462	0.382	0.316	0.261	0.217	0.180	0.149	0.124	0.103	0.086	0.071	0.060	0.050	0.042	0.035	0.029	0.024	0.020
40	0.672	0.551	0.453	0.372	0.307	0.253	0.208	0.172	0.142	0.117	0.097	0.081	0.067	0.055	0.046	0.038	0.032	0.027	0.022	0.018

(continued on next page)

Table A-4 Annual present value factors (PVF) (Continued).

Annual Interest Rate

Years	11 PVF	11.5 PVF	12 PVF	12.5 PVF	13 PVF	13.5 PVF	14 PVF	14.5 PVF	15 PVF	15.5 PVF	16 PVF	16.5 PVF	17 PVF	17.5 PVF	18 PVF	18.5 PVF	19 PVF	19.5 PVF	20 PVF
1	0.901	0.897	0.893	0.889	0.885	0.881	0.877	0.873	0.870	0.866	0.862	0.858	0.855	0.851	0.847	0.844	0.840	0.837	0.833
2	0.812	0.804	0.797	0.790	0.783	0.776	0.769	0.763	0.756	0.750	0.743	0.737	0.731	0.724	0.718	0.712	0.706	0.700	0.694
3	0.731	0.721	0.712	0.702	0.693	0.684	0.675	0.666	0.658	0.649	0.641	0.632	0.624	0.616	0.609	0.601	0.593	0.586	0.579
4	0.659	0.647	0.636	0.624	0.613	0.603	0.592	0.582	0.572	0.562	0.552	0.543	0.534	0.525	0.516	0.507	0.499	0.490	0.482
5	0.593	0.580	0.567	0.555	0.543	0.531	0.519	0.502	0.497	0.487	0.476	0.466	0.456	0.446	0.437	0.428	0.419	0.410	0.402
6	0.535	0.520	0.507	0.493	0.480	0.468	0.456	0.444	0.432	0.421	0.410	0.400	0.390	0.380	0.370	0.361	0.352	0.343	0.335
7	0.482	0.467	0.452	0.438	0.425	0.412	0.400	0.388	0.376	0.365	0.354	0.343	0.333	0.323	0.314	0.305	0.296	0.287	0.279
8	0.434	0.419	0.404	0.390	0.376	0.363	0.351	0.338	0.327	0.316	0.305	0.295	0.285	0.275	0.266	0.257	0.249	0.240	0.233
9	0.391	0.375	0.361	0.346	0.333	0.320	0.308	0.296	0.284	0.273	0.263	0.253	0.243	0.234	0.225	0.217	0.209	0.201	0.194
10	0.352	0.337	0.322	0.308	0.295	0.282	0.270	0.258	0.247	0.237	0.227	0.217	0.208	0.199	0.191	0.183	0.176	0.168	0.162
11	0.317	0.302	0.287	0.274	0.261	0.248	0.237	0.225	0.215	0.205	0.195	0.186	0.178	0.170	0.162	0.155	0.148	0.141	0.135
12	0.286	0.271	0.257	0.243	0.231	0.219	0.208	0.197	0.187	0.177	0.168	0.160	0.152	0.144	0.137	0.130	0.124	0.118	0.112
13	0.258	0.243	0.229	0.216	0.204	0.193	0.182	0.172	0.163	0.154	0.145	0.137	0.130	0.123	0.116	0.110	0.104	0.099	0.093
14	0.232	0.218	0.205	0.192	0.181	0.170	0.160	0.150	0.141	0.133	0.125	0.118	0.111	0.105	0.099	0.093	0.088	0.083	0.078
15	0.209	0.195	0.183	0.171	0.160	0.150	0.140	0.131	0.123	0.115	0.108	0.101	0.095	0.089	0.084	0.078	0.074	0.069	0.065
16	0.188	0.175	0.163	0.152	0.141	0.132	0.123	0.115	0.107	0.100	0.093	0.087	0.081	0.076	0.071	0.066	0.062	0.058	0.054
17	0.170	0.157	0.146	0.135	0.125	0.116	0.108	0.100	0.093	0.086	0.080	0.075	0.069	0.064	0.060	0.056	0.052	0.048	0.045
18	0.153	0.141	0.130	0.120	0.111	0.102	0.095	0.087	0.081	0.075	0.069	0.064	0.059	0.055	0.051	0.047	0.044	0.040	0.038
19	0.138	0.126	0.116	0.107	0.098	0.090	0.083	0.076	0.070	0.065	0.060	0.055	0.051	0.047	0.043	0.040	0.037	0.034	0.031
20	0.124	0.113	0.104	0.095	0.087	0.079	0.073	0.067	0.061	0.056	0.051	0.047	0.043	0.040	0.037	0.034	0.031	0.028	0.026
21	0.112	0.102	0.093	0.084	0.077	0.070	0.064	0.058	0.053	0.049	0.044	0.040	0.037	0.034	0.031	0.028	0.026	0.024	0.022
22	0.101	0.091	0.083	0.075	0.068	0.062	0.056	0.051	0.046	0.042	0.038	0.035	0.032	0.029	0.026	0.024	0.022	0.020	0.018
23	0.091	0.082	0.074	0.067	0.060	0.054	0.049	0.044	0.040	0.036	0.033	0.030	0.027	0.024	0.022	0.020	0.018	0.017	0.015

24	0.082	0.073	0.066	0.059	0.053	0.048	0.043	0.039	0.035	0.031	0.028	0.026	0.023	0.021	0.019	0.017	0.015	0.014	0.013
25	0.074	0.066	0.059	0.053	0.047	0.042	0.038	0.034	0.030	0.027	0.024	0.022	0.020	0.018	0.016	0.014	0.013	0.012	0.010
26	0.066	0.059	0.053	0.047	0.042	0.037	0.033	0.030	0.026	0.024	0.021	0.019	0.017	0.015	0.014	0.012	0.011	0.010	0.009
27	0.060	0.053	0.047	0.042	0.037	0.033	0.029	0.026	0.023	0.020	0.018	0.016	0.014	0.013	0.011	0.010	0.009	0.008	0.007
28	0.054	0.047	0.042	0.037	0.033	0.029	0.026	0.023	0.020	0.018	0.016	0.014	0.012	0.011	0.010	0.009	0.008	0.007	0.006
29	0.048	0.043	0.037	0.033	0.029	0.025	0.022	0.020	0.017	0.015	0.014	0.012	0.011	0.009	0.008	0.007	0.006	0.006	0.005
30	0.044	0.038	0.033	0.029	0.026	0.022	0.020	0.017	0.015	0.013	0.012	0.010	0.009	0.008	0.007	0.006	0.005	0.005	0.004
31	0.039	0.034	0.030	0.026	0.023	0.020	0.017	0.015	0.013	0.011	0.010	0.009	0.008	0.007	0.006	0.005	0.005	0.004	0.004
32	0.035	0.031	0.027	0.023	0.020	0.017	0.015	0.013	0.011	0.010	0.009	0.008	0.007	0.006	0.005	0.004	0.004	0.003	0.003
33	0.032	0.028	0.024	0.021	0.018	0.015	0.013	0.011	0.010	0.009	0.007	0.006	0.006	0.005	0.004	0.004	0.003	0.003	0.002
34	0.029	0.025	0.021	0.018	0.016	0.013	0.012	0.010	0.009	0.007	0.006	0.006	0.005	0.004	0.004	0.003	0.003	0.002	0.002
35	0.026	0.022	0.019	0.016	0.014	0.012	0.010	0.009	0.008	0.006	0.006	0.005	0.004	0.004	0.003	0.003	0.002	0.002	0.002
36	0.023	0.020	0.017	0.014	0.012	0.010	0.009	0.008	0.007	0.006	0.005	0.004	0.004	0.003	0.003	0.002	0.002	0.002	0.001
37	0.021	0.018	0.015	0.013	0.011	0.009	0.008	0.007	0.006	0.005	0.004	0.004	0.003	0.003	0.002	0.002	0.002	0.001	0.001
38	0.019	0.016	0.013	0.011	0.010	0.008	0.007	0.006	0.005	0.004	0.004	0.003	0.003	0.002	0.002	0.002	0.001	0.001	0.001
39	0.017	0.014	0.012	0.010	0.009	0.007	0.006	0.005	0.004	0.004	0.003	0.003	0.002	0.002	0.002	0.001	0.001	0.001	0.001
40	0.015	0.013	0.011	0.009	0.008	0.006	0.005	0.004	0.004	0.003	0.003	0.002	0.002	0.002	0.001	0.001	0.001	0.001	0.001

Table A-5 Monthly present value factors (PVF).

												Annual Interest Rate								
	1	2	3	4	5	6	7	7.25	7.5	7.75	8	8.25	8.5	8.75	9	9.25	9.5	9.75	10	10.25
Months	PVF	PVF	PVF	PVF	PVF	PVF	PVF	PVF	PVF	PVF	PVF	PVF	PVF	PVF	PVF	PVF	PVF	PVF	PVF	PVF
1	0.999	0.998	0.998	9.997	0.996	0.995	0.994	0.994	0.994	0.994	0.993	0.993	0.993	0.993	0.993	0.992	0.992	0.992	0.992	0.992
2	0.998	0.997	0.995	0.993	0.992	0.990	0.988	0.988	0.988	0.987	0.987	0.986	0.986	0.986	0.985	0.985	0.984	0.984	0.984	0.983
3	0.998	0.995	0.993	0.990	0.988	0.985	0.983	0.982	0.981	0.981	0.980	0.980	0.979	0.978	0.978	0.977	0.977	0.976	0.975	0.975
4	0.997	0.993	0.990	0.987	0.984	0.980	0.977	0.976	0.975	0.975	0.974	0.973	0.972	0.971	0.971	0.970	0.969	0.968	0.967	0.967
5	0.996	0.992	0.988	0.983	0.979	0.975	0.971	0.970	0.969	0.968	0.967	0.966	0.965	0.964	0.963	0.962	0.961	0.960	0.959	0.958
6	0.995	0.990	0.985	0.980	0.975	0.971	0.966	0.965	0.963	0.962	0.961	0.960	0.959	0.957	0.956	0.955	0.954	0.953	0.951	0.950
7	0.994	9.988	0.983	0.977	0.971	0.966	0.960	0.959	0.957	0.956	0.955	0.953	0.952	0.950	0.949	0.948	0.946	0.945	0.944	0.942
8	0.993	0.987	0.980	0.974	0.967	0.961	0.955	0.953	0.951	0.950	0.948	0.947	0.945	0.944	0.942	0.940	0.939	0.937	0.936	0.934
9	0.993	0.985	0.978	0.970	0.963	0.956	0.949	0.947	0.945	0.944	0.942	0.940	0.938	0.937	0.935	0.933	0.931	0.930	0.928	0.926
10	0.992	0.983	0.975	0.967	0.959	0.951	0.943	0.942	0.940	0.938	0.936	0.934	0.932	0.930	0.928	0.926	0.924	0.922	0.920	0.918
11	0.991	0.982	0.973	0.064	0.955	0.947	0.938	0.936	0.934	0.932	0.930	0.927	0.925	0.923	0.921	0.919	0.917	0.915	0.913	0.911
12	0.990	0.980	0.970	0.961	0.951	0.942	0.933	0.930	0.928	0.926	0.923	0.921	0.919	0.917	0.914	0.912	0.910	0.907	0.905	0.903
13	0.989	0.979	0.968	0.958	0.947	0.937	0.927	0.925	0.922	0.920	0.917	0.915	0.912	0.910	0.907	0.905	0.903	0.900	0.898	0.895
14	0.988	0.977	0.966	0.954	0.943	0.933	0.922	0.919	0.916	0.914	0.911	0.909	0.906	0.903	0.901	0.898	0.895	0.893	0.890	0.888
15	0.988	0.975	0.963	0.951	0.940	0.928	0.916	0.914	0.911	0.908	0.905	0.902	0.900	0.897	0.894	0.891	0.888	0.886	0.883	0.880
16	0.987	0.974	0.961	0.948	0.936	0.923	0.911	0.908	0.905	0.902	0.899	0.896	0.893	0.890	0.887	0.884	0.881	0.879	0.876	0.873
17	0.986	0.972	0.958	0.945	0.932	0.919	0.906	0.903	0.899	0.896	0.893	0.890	0.887	0.884	0.881	0.878	0.875	0.871	0.868	0.865
18	0.985	0.970	0.956	0.942	0.928	0.914	0.901	0.897	0.894	0.891	0.887	0.884	0.881	0.877	0.874	0.871	0.868	0.864	0.861	0.858
19	0.984	0.969	0.954	0.939	0.924	0.910	0.895	0.892	0.888	0.885	0.881	0.878	0.874	0.871	0.868	0.864	0.861	0.857	0.854	0.851
20	0.983	0.967	0.951	0.936	0.920	0.905	0.890	0.887	0.883	0.879	0.876	0.872	0.868	0.865	0.861	0.858	0.854	0.851	0.847	0.844
21	0.983	0.966	0.949	0.933	0.916	0.901	0.885	0.881	0.877	0.874	0.870	0.866	0.862	0.858	0.855	0.851	0.847	0.844	0.840	0.836
22	0.982	0.964	0.947	0.929	0.913	0.896	0.880	0.876	0.872	0.868	0.864	0.860	0.856	0.852	0.848	0.845	0.841	0.837	0.833	0.829
23	0.981	0.962	0.944	0.926	0.909	0.892	0.875	0.871	0.866	0.862	8.58	0.854	0.850	0.846	0.842	0.838	0.834	0.830	0.826	0.829
24	0.980	0.961	0.942	0.923	0.905	0.887	0.870	0.865	0.861	0.857	0.853	0.848	0.844	0.840	0.836	0.832	0.828	0.823	0.819	0.815
25	0.979	0.959	0.939	0.920	0.901	0.883	0.865	0.860	0.856	0.851	0.847	0.843	0.838	0.834	0.830	0.825	0.821	0.817	0.813	0.808
26	0.979	0.958	0.937	0.917	0.898	0.878	0.860	0.855	0.850	0.846	0.841	0.837	0.832	0.828	0.823	0.819	0.815	0.810	0.806	0.802
27	0.978	0.956	0.935	0.914	0.894	0.874	0.855	0.850	0.845	0.840	0.836	0.831	0.826	0.822	0.817	0.813	0.808	0.804	0.799	0.795

28	0.977	0.954	0.932	0.911	0.890	0.870	0.850	0.845	0.840	0.835	0.830	0.825	0.821	0.816	0.811	0.807	0.802	0.797	0.793	0.788
29	0.976	0.953	0.930	0.908	0.886	0.865	0.845	0.840	0.835	0.830	0.825	0.820	0.815	0.810	0.805	0.800	0.796	0.791	0.786	0.781
30	0.975	0.951	0.928	0.905	0.883	0.861	0.840	0.835	0.830	0.824	0.819	0.814	0.809	0.804	0.799	0.794	0.789	0.784	0.780	0.775
31	0.975	0.950	0.926	0.902	0.879	0.857	0.835	0.830	0.824	0.819	0.814	0.809	0.803	0.798	0.793	0.788	0.783	0.778	0.773	0.768
32	0.974	0.948	0.923	0.899	0.875	0.852	0.830	0.825	0.819	0.814	0.808	0.803	0.798	0.793	0.787	0.782	0.777	0.772	0.767	0.762
33	0.973	0.947	0.921	0.896	0.872	0.848	0.825	0.820	0.814	0.809	0.803	0.798	0.792	0.787	0.781	0.776	0.771	0.766	0.760	0.755
34	0.972	0.945	0.919	0.893	0.868	0.844	0.821	0.815	0.809	0.803	0.798	0.792	0.787	0.781	0.776	0.770	0.765	0.759	0.754	0.749
35	0.971	0.943	0.916	0.890	0.865	0.840	0.816	0.810	0.804	0.798	0.793	0.787	0.781	0.775	0.770	0.764	0.759	0.753	0.748	0.743
36	0.970	0.942	0.914	0.887	0.861	0.836	0.811	0.805	0.799	0.793	0.787	0.781	0.776	0.770	0.764	0.758	0.753	0.747	0.742	0.736
48	0.961	0.923	0.887	0.852	0.819	0.787	0.756	0.749	0.742	0.734	0.727	0.720	0.713	0.706	0.699	0.692	0.685	0.678	0.671	0.665
60	0.951	0.905	0.861	0.819	0.779	0.741	0.705	0.697	0.688	0.680	0.671	0.663	0.655	0.647	0.639	0.631	0.023	0.615	0.608	0.600
72	0.942	0.887	0.835	0.787	0.741	0.698	0.658	0.648	0.639	0.629	0.620	0.611	0.602	0.593	0.584	0.575	0.567	0.558	0.550	0.542
84	0.932	0.869	0.811	0.756	0.705	0.658	0.613	0.603	0.593	0.582	0.572	0.562	0.553	0.543	0.534	0.525	0.516	0.507	0.498	0.489
96	0.923	0.852	0.787	0.727	0.671	0.620	0.572	0.561	0.550	0.539	0.528	0.518	0.508	0.498	0.488	0.478	0.469	0.460	0.451	0.442
108	0.914	0.835	0.764	0.698	0.638	0.584	0.534	0.522	0.510	0.499	0.488	0.477	0.467	0.456	0.446	0.436	0.427	0.417	0.408	0.399
120	0.905	0.819	0.741	0.671	0.607	0.550	0.498	0.485	0.473	0.462	0.451	0.439	0.429	0.418	0.408	0.398	0.388	0.379	0.369	0.360
132	0.896	0.803	0.719	0.645	0.578	0.518	0.464	0.452	0.439	0.428	0.416	0.405	0.394	0.383	0.373	0.363	0.353	0.344	0.334	0.325
144	0.887	0.787	0.698	0.619	0.549	0.488	0.433	0.420	0.408	0.396	0.384	0.373	0.362	0.351	0.341	0.331	0.321	0.312	0.303	0.294
156	0.878	0.771	0.677	0.595	0.523	0.459	0.404	0.391	0.378	0.366	0.355	0.343	0.333	0.322	0.312	0.302	0.292	0.283	0.274	0.265
168	0.869	0.756	0.657	0.572	0.497	0.433	0.376	0.364	0.351	0.339	0.327	0.316	0.306	0.295	0.285	0.275	0.266	0.257	0.249	0.240
180	0.861	0.741	0.638	0.549	0.473	0.407	0.351	0.338	0.326	0.314	0.302	0.291	0.281	0.270	0.261	0.251	0.242	0.233	0.225	0.216
192	0.852	0.726	0.619	0.528	0.450	0.384	0.327	0.315	0.302	0.291	0.279	0.268	0.258	0.248	0.238	0.229	0.220	0.211	0.203	0.195
204	0.844	0.712	0.601	0.507	0.428	0.362	0.305	0.293	0.281	0.269	0.258	0.247	0.237	0.227	0.218	0.209	0.200	0.192	0.184	0.176
216	0.835	0.698	0.583	0.487	0.407	0.341	0.285	0.272	0.260	0.249	0.238	0.228	0.218	0.208	0.199	0.190	0.182	0.171	0.167	0.159
228	0.827	0.684	0.566	0.468	0.388	0.321	0.266	0.253	0.242	0.230	0.220	0.210	0.200	0.191	0.182	0.174	0.166	0.158	0.151	0.144
240	0.819	0.671	0.549	0.450	0.369	0.302	0.248	0.236	0.224	0.213	0.203	0.193	0.184	0.175	0.166	0.158	0.151	0.143	0.136	0.130
300	0.779	0.607	0.473	0.368	0.287	0.224	0.175	0.164	0.154	0.145	0.136	0.128	0.120	0.113	0.106	0.100	0.094	0.088	0.083	0.078
360	0.741	0.549	0.407	0.302	0.224	0.166	0.123	0.114	0.106	0.099	0.091	0.085	0.079	0.073	0.068	0.063	0.058	0.054	0.050	0.047

(continued on next page)

Table A-5 Monthly present value factors (PVF) (Continued).

Months	10.5 PVF	10.75 PVF	11 PVF	11.25 PVF	11.5 PVF	11.75 PVF	12 PVF	12.25 PVF	12.5 PVF	12.75 PVF	13 PVF	13.25 PVF	13.5 PVF	13.75 PVF	14 PVF	14.25 PVF	14.5 PVF	14.75 PVF	15 PVF	15.25 PVF
1	0.991	0.991	0.991	0.991	0.991	0.990	0.990	0.990	0.990	0.989	0.989	0.989	0.989	0.989	0.988	0.988	0.988	0.988	0.988	0.987
2	0.983	0.982	0.982	0.982	0.981	0.981	0.980	0.980	0.979	0.979	0.979	0.978	0.978	0.977	0.977	0.977	0.976	0.976	0.975	0.975
3	0.974	0.974	0.973	0.972	0.972	0.971	0.971	0.970	0.969	0.969	0.968	0.968	0.967	0.966	0.966	0.965	0.965	0.964	0.963	0.963
4	0.966	0.965	0.964	0.963	0.963	0.962	0.961	0.960	0.959	0.959	0.958	0.957	0.956	0.955	0.955	0.954	0.953	0.952	0.952	0.951
5	0.957	0.956	0.955	0.954	0.953	0.952	0.951	0.950	0.950	0.949	0.948	0.947	0.946	0.945	0.944	0.943	0.942	0.941	0.940	0.939
6	0.949	0.948	0.947	0.946	0.944	0.943	0.942	0.941	0.940	0.939	0.937	0.936	0.935	0.934	0.933	0.932	0.930	0.929	0.928	0.927
7	0.941	0.939	0.938	0.937	0.935	0.934	0.933	0.931	0.930	0.929	0.927	0.926	0.925	0.923	0.922	0.921	0.919	0.918	0.917	0.915
8	0.933	0.931	0.930	0.928	0.927	0.925	0.923	0.922	0.920	0.919	0.917	0.916	0.914	0.913	0.911	0.910	0.908	0.907	0.905	0.904
9	0.925	0.923	0.921	0.919	0.918	0.916	0.914	0.913	0.911	0.909	0.908	0.906	0.904	0.903	0.901	0.899	0.898	0.896	0.894	0.893
10	0.917	0.915	0.913	0.911	0.909	0.907	0.905	0.903	0.902	0.900	0.898	0.896	0.894	0.892	0.890	0.889	0.887	0.885	0.883	0.881
11	0.909	0.907	0.904	0.902	0.900	0.898	0.896	0.894	0.892	0.890	0.888	0.886	0.884	0.882	0.880	0.878	0.876	0.874	0.872	0.870
12	0.901	0.899	0.896	0.894	0.892	0.890	0.887	0.885	0.883	0.881	0.879	0.877	0.874	0.872	0.870	0.868	0.866	0.864	0.862	0.859
13	0.893	0.891	0.888	0.886	0.883	0.881	0.879	0.876	0.874	0.872	0.869	0.867	0.865	0.862	0.860	0.858	0.855	0.853	0.851	0.849
14	0.885	0.883	0.880	0.878	0.875	0.872	0.870	0.867	0.865	0.862	0.860	0.857	0.855	0.853	0.850	0.848	0.845	0.843	0.840	0.838
15	0.877	0.875	0.872	0.869	0.867	0.864	0.861	0.859	0.856	0.853	0.851	0.848	0.846	0.843	0.840	0.838	0.835	0.833	0.830	0.827
16	0.870	0.867	0.864	0.861	0.858	0.856	0.853	0.850	0.847	0.844	0.842	0.839	0.836	0.833	0.831	0.828	0.825	0.822	0.820	0.817
17	0.862	0.859	0.856	0.853	0.850	0.847	0.844	0.841	0.838	0.836	0.833	0.830	0.827	0.824	0.821	0.818	0.815	0.812	0.810	0.807
18	0.855	0.852	0.849	0.845	0.842	0.839	0.836	0.833	0.830	0.827	0.824	0.821	0.818	0.815	0.812	0.809	0.806	0.803	0.800	0.797
19	0.847	0.844	0.841	0.838	0.834	0.831	0.828	0.825	0.821	0.818	0.815	0.812	0.809	0.805	0.802	0.799	0.796	0.793	0.790	0.787
20	0.840	0.837	0.833	0.830	0.826	0.823	0.820	0.816	0.813	0.809	0.806	0.803	0.800	0.796	0.793	0.790	0.786	0.783	0.780	0.777
21	0.833	0.829	0.826	0.822	0.818	0.815	0.811	0.808	0.804	0.801	0.797	0.794	0.791	0.787	0.784	0.780	0.777	0.774	0.770	0.767
22	0.826	0.822	0.818	0.814	0.811	0.807	0.803	0.800	0.796	0.793	0.789	0.785	0.782	0.778	0.775	0.771	0.768	0.764	0.761	0.757
23	0.818	0.815	0.811	0.807	0.803	0.799	0.795	0.792	0.788	0.784	0.780	0.777	0.773	0.769	0.766	0.762	0.759	0.755	0.751	0.748
24	0.811	0.807	0.803	0.799	0.795	0.791	0.788	0.784	0.780	0.776	0.772	0.768	0.765	0.761	0.757	0.753	0.750	0.746	0.742	0.739
25	0.804	0.800	0.796	0.792	0.788	0.784	0.780	0.776	0.772	0.768	0.764	0.760	0.756	0.752	0.748	0.744	0.741	0.737	0.733	0.729

Annual Interest Rate

26	0.720	0.724	0.728	0.732	0.736	0.740	0.744	0.748	0.752	0.756	0.760	0.764	0.768	0.772	0.776	0.780	0.785	0.789	0.793	0.797
27	0.711	0.715	0.719	0.723	0.727	0.731	0.735	0.739	0.743	0.748	0.752	0.756	0.760	0.764	0.769	0.773	0.777	0.782	0.786	0.790
28	0.702	0.706	0.710	0.714	0.719	0.723	0.727	0.731	0.735	0.740	0.744	0.748	0.752	0.757	0.761	0.766	0.770	0.775	0.779	0.784
29	0.693	0.697	0.702	0.706	0.710	0.714	0.719	0.723	0.727	0.732	0.736	0.740	0.745	0.749	0.754	0.758	0.763	0.767	0.772	0.777
30	0.685	0.689	0.693	0.697	0.702	0.706	0.710	0.715	0.719	0.724	0.728	0.733	0.737	0.742	0.747	0.751	0.756	0.761	0.765	0.770
31	0.676	0.680	0.685	0.689	0.694	0.698	0.702	0.707	0.711	0.716	0.721	0.725	0.730	0.735	0.739	0.744	0.749	0.754	0.758	0.763
32	0.668	0.672	0.676	0.681	0.685	0.690	0.694	0.699	0.704	0.708	0.713	0.718	0.723	0.727	0.732	0.737	0.742	0.747	0.752	0.757
33	0.659	0.664	0.668	0.673	0.677	0.682	0.687	0.691	0.696	0.701	0.706	0.710	0.715	0.720	0.725	0.730	0.735	0.740	0.745	0.750
34	0.651	0.655	0.660	0.665	0.669	0.674	0.679	0.684	0.688	0.693	0.698	0.703	0.708	0.713	0.718	0.723	0.728	0.733	0.738	0.744
35	0.643	0.647	0.652	0.657	0.662	0.666	0.671	0.676	0.681	0.686	0.691	0.696	0.701	0.706	0.711	0.716	0.721	0.727	0.732	0.737
36	0.635	0.639	0.644	0.649	0.654	0.659	0.664	0.668	0.673	0.678	0.684	0.689	0.694	0.699	0.704	0.709	0.715	0.720	0.725	0.731
48	0.545	0.551	0.556	0.562	0.567	0.573	0.579	0.585	0.590	0.596	0.602	0.608	0.614	0.620	0.626	0.633	0.639	0.645	0.652	0.658
60	0.469	0.475	0.480	0.486	0.492	0.499	0.505	0.511	0.517	0.524	0.530	0.537	0.544	0.550	0.557	0.564	0.571	0.578	0.586	0.593
72	0.403	0.409	0.415	0.421	0.427	0.434	0.440	0.447	0.454	0.460	0.467	0.474	0.481	0.488	0.496	0.503	0.511	0.518	0.526	0.534
84	0.346	0.352	0.358	0.365	0.371	0.377	0.384	0.391	0.398	0.404	0.412	0.419	0.426	0.434	0.441	0.449	0.457	0.465	0.473	0.481
96	0.298	0.303	0.309	0.316	0.322	0.328	0.335	0.342	0.348	0.355	0.363	0.370	0.377	0.385	0.392	0.400	0.408	0.416	0.425	0.433
108	0.256	0.261	0.267	0.273	0.279	0.286	0.292	0.299	0.305	0.312	0.319	0.327	0.334	0.341	0.349	0.357	0.365	0.373	0.382	0.390
120	0.220	0.225	0.231	0.237	0.243	0.249	0.255	0.261	0.268	0.274	0.281	0.288	0.296	0.303	0.311	0.318	0.326	0.335	0.343	0.352
132	0.189	0.194	0.199	0.205	0.211	0.216	0.222	0.228	0.235	0.241	0.248	0.255	0.262	0.269	0.276	0.284	0.292	0.300	0.308	0.317
144	0.162	0.167	0.172	0.177	0.183	0.188	0.194	0.200	0.206	0.212	0.218	0.225	0.232	0.239	0.246	0.253	0.261	0.269	0.277	0.285
156	0.139	0.144	0.149	0.154	0.159	0.164	0.169	0.175	0.180	0.186	0.192	0.199	0.205	0.212	0.219	0.226	0.233	0.241	0.249	0.257
168	0.120	0.124	0.128	0.133	0.138	0.142	0.147	0.153	0.158	0.164	0.169	0.175	0.182	0.188	0.195	0.201	0.209	0.216	0.224	0.231
180	0.103	0.107	0.111	0.115	0.119	0.124	0.129	0.133	0.139	0.144	0.149	0.155	0.161	0.167	0.173	0.180	0.186	0.193	0.201	0.208
192	0.089	0.092	0.096	0.100	0.104	0.108	0.112	0.117	0.121	0.126	0.131	0.137	0.142	0.148	0.154	0.160	0.167	0.173	0.180	0.188
204	0.076	0.079	0.083	0.086	0.090	0.094	0.098	0.102	0.106	0.111	0.116	0.121	0.126	0.131	0.137	0.143	0.149	0.155	0.162	0.169
216	0.065	0.068	0.071	0.075	0.078	0.082	0.085	0.089	0.093	0.098	0.102	0.107	0.111	0.117	0.122	0.127	0.133	0.139	0.146	0.152
228	0.056	0.059	0.062	0.065	0.068	0.071	0.074	0.078	0.082	0.086	0.090	0.094	0.099	0.103	0.108	0.114	0.119	0.125	0.131	0.137
240	0.048	0.051	0.053	0.056	0.059	0.062	0.065	0.068	0.072	0.075	0.079	0.083	0.087	0.092	0.096	0.101	0.107	0.112	0.118	0.124
300	0.023	0.024	0.026	0.027	0.029	0.031	0.033	0.035	0.037	0.039	0.042	0.045	0.048	0.051	0.054	0.057	0.061	0.065	0.069	0.073
360	0.011	0.011	0.012	0.013	0.014	0.015	0.017	0.018	0.019	0.021	0.022	0.024	0.026	0.028	0.030	0.032	0.035	0.037	0.040	0.043

(continued on next page)

Table A-5 Monthly present value factors (PVF) (Continued).

Annual Interest Rate

Months	15.5 PVF	15.75 PVF	16 PVF	16.25 PVF	16.5 PVF	16.75 PVF	17 PVF	17.25 PVF	17.5 PVF	17.75 PVF	18 PVF	18.25 PVF	18.5 PVF	18.75 PVF	19 PVF	19.25 PVF	19.5 PVF	19.75 PVF	20 PVF
1	0.987	0.987	0.987	0.987	0.986	0.986	0.986	0.986	0.986	0.985	0.985	0.985	0.985	0.985	0.984	0.984	0.984	0.984	0.984
2	0.975	0.974	0.974	0.973	0.973	0.973	0.972	0.972	0.971	0.971	0.971	0.970	0.970	0.969	0.969	0.969	0.968	0.968	0.967
3	0.962	0.962	0.961	0.960	0.960	0.959	0.959	0.958	0.957	0.957	0.956	0.956	0.955	0.955	0.954	0.953	0.953	0.952	0.952
4	0.950	0.949	0.948	0.948	0.947	0.946	0.945	0.945	0.944	0.943	0.942	0.941	0.941	0.940	0.939	0.938	0.938	0.937	0.936
5	0.938	0.937	0.936	0.935	0.934	0.933	0.932	0.931	0.930	0.929	0.928	0.927	0.926	0.925	0.924	0.924	0.923	0.922	0.921
6	0.926	0.925	0.924	0.922	0.921	0.920	0.919	0.918	0.917	0.916	0.915	0.913	0.912	0.911	0.910	0.909	0.908	0.907	0.906
7	0.914	0.913	0.911	0.910	0.909	0.908	0.906	0.905	0.904	0.902	0.901	0.900	0.898	0.897	0.896	0.895	0.893	0.892	0.891
8	0.902	0.901	0.899	0.898	0.897	0.895	0.894	0.892	0.891	0.889	0.888	0.886	0.885	0.883	0.882	0.880	0.879	0.878	0.876
9	0.891	0.889	0.888	0.886	0.884	0.883	0.881	0.879	0.878	0.876	0.875	0.873	0.871	0.870	0.868	0.867	0.865	0.863	0.862
10	0.880	0.878	0.876	0.874	0.872	0.871	0.869	0.867	0.865	0.863	0.862	0.860	0.858	0.856	0.855	0.853	0.851	0.849	0.848
11	0.868	0.866	0.864	0.862	0.861	0.859	0.857	0.855	0.853	0.851	0.849	0.847	0.845	0.843	0.841	0.839	0.838	0.836	0.834
12	0.857	0.855	0.853	0.851	0.849	0.847	0.845	0.843	0.841	0.838	0.836	0.834	0.832	0.830	0.828	0.826	0.824	0.822	0.820
13	0.846	0.844	0.842	0.840	0.837	0.835	0.833	0.831	0.828	0.826	0.824	0.822	0.820	0.817	0.815	0.813	0.811	0.809	0.807
14	0.836	0.833	0.831	0.828	0.826	0.824	0.821	0.819	0.817	0.814	0.812	0.810	0.807	0.805	0.803	0.800	0.798	0.796	0.793
15	0.825	0.822	0.820	0.817	0.815	0.812	0.810	0.807	0.805	0.802	0.800	0.797	0.795	0.792	0.790	0.788	0.785	0.783	0.780
16	0.814	0.812	0.809	0.806	0.804	0.801	0.798	0.796	0.793	0.791	0.788	0.785	0.783	0.780	0.778	0.775	0.773	0.770	0.768
17	0.804	0.801	0.798	0.796	0.793	0.790	0.787	0.785	0.782	0.779	0.776	0.774	0.771	0.768	0.766	0.763	0.760	0.758	0.755
18	0.794	0.791	0.788	0.785	0.782	0.779	0.776	0.773	0.771	0.768	0.765	0.762	0.759	0.756	0.754	0.751	0.748	0.745	0.743
19	0.784	0.781	0.778	0.774	0.771	0.768	0.765	0.762	0.760	0.757	0.754	0.751	0.748	0.745	0.742	0.739	0.736	0.733	0.730
20	0.774	0.770	0.767	0.764	0.761	0.758	0.755	0.752	0.749	0.746	0.742	0.739	0.736	0.733	0.730	0.727	0.724	0.721	0.719
21	0.764	0.760	0.757	0.754	0.751	0.747	0.744	0.741	0.738	0.735	0.731	0.728	0.725	0.722	0.719	0.716	0.713	0.710	0.707
22	0.754	0.751	0.747	0.744	0.740	0.737	0.734	0.731	0.727	0.724	0.721	0.717	0.714	0.711	0.708	0.705	0.701	0.698	0.695
23	0.744	0.741	0.737	0.734	0.730	0.727	0.724	0.720	0.717	0.713	0.710	0.707	0.703	0.700	0.697	0.693	0.690	0.687	0.684
24	0.735	0.731	0.728	0.724	0.721	0.717	0.713	0.710	0.706	0.703	0.700	0.696	0.693	0.689	0.686	0.683	0.679	0.676	0.673
25	0.726	0.722	0.718	0.714	0.711	0.707	0.704	0.700	0.696	0.693	0.689	0.686	0.682	0.679	0.675	0.672	0.668	0.665	0.662
26	0.716	0.712	0.709	0.705	0.701	0.697	0.694	0.690	0.686	0.683	0.679	0.675	0.672	0.668	0.665	0.661	0.658	0.654	0.651
27	0.707	0.703	0.699	0.695	0.692	0.688	0.684	0.680	0.676	0.673	0.669	0.665	0.662	0.658	0.654	0.651	0.647	0.644	0.640

28	0.630	0.633	0.637	0.640	0.644	0.648	0.652	0.655	0.659	0.663	0.667	0.671	0.674	0.678	0.682	0.686	0.690	0.694	0.698
29	0.619	0.623	0.627	0.630	0.634	0.638	0.642	0.646	0.649	0.653	0.657	0.661	0.665	0.669	0.673	0.677	0.681	0.685	0.689
30	0.609	0.613	0.617	0.620	0.624	0.628	0.632	0.636	0.640	0.644	0.648	0.652	0.656	0.660	0.664	0.668	0.672	0.676	0.680
31	0.599	0.603	0.607	0.611	0.614	0.618	0.622	0.626	0.630	0.634	0.638	0.642	0.647	0.651	0.655	0.659	0.663	0.667	0.672
32	0.589	0.593	0.597	0.601	0.605	0.609	0.613	0.617	0.621	0.625	0.629	0.633	0.638	0.642	0.646	0.650	0.655	0.659	0.663
33	0.580	0.584	0.587	0.591	0.595	0.600	0.604	0.608	0.612	0.616	0.620	0.624	0.629	0.633	0.637	0.642	0.646	0.650	0.655
34	0.570	0.574	0.578	0.582	0.586	0.590	0.594	0.599	0.603	0.607	0.611	0.616	0.620	0.624	0.629	0.633	0.637	0.642	0.646
35	0.561	0.565	0.569	0.573	0.577	0.581	0.585	0.590	0.594	0.598	0.602	0.607	0.611	0.616	0.620	0.625	0.629	0.634	0.638
36	0.552	0.556	0.560	0.564	0.568	0.572	0.577	0.581	0.585	0.589	0.594	0.598	0.603	0.607	0.612	0.616	0.621	0.625	0.630
48	0.452	0.457	0.461	0.466	0.470	0.475	0.480	0.485	0.489	0.494	0.499	0.504	0.509	0.514	0.519	0.524	0.530	0.535	0.540
60	0.371	0.376	0.380	0.385	0.390	0.394	0.399	0.404	0.409	0.414	0.420	0.425	0.430	0.435	0.441	0.446	0.452	0.457	0.463
72	0.304	0.309	0.313	0.318	0.323	0.327	0.332	0.337	0.342	0.347	0.353	0.358	0.363	0.369	0.374	0.380	0.385	0.391	0.397
84	0.249	0.254	0.258	0.263	0.267	0.272	0.277	0.281	0.286	0.291	0.296	0.302	0.307	0.312	0.318	0.323	0.329	0.334	0.340
96	0.205	0.209	0.213	0.217	0.221	0.226	0.230	0.235	0.239	0.244	0.249	0.254	0.259	0.264	0.270	0.275	0.280	0.286	0.292
108	0.168	0.172	0.175	0.179	0.183	0.187	0.192	0.196	0.200	0.205	0.209	0.214	0.219	0.224	0.229	0.234	0.239	0.245	0.250
120	0.138	0.141	0.145	0.148	0.152	0.156	0.159	0.163	0.168	0.172	0.176	0.180	0.185	0.189	0.194	0.199	0.204	0.209	0.214
132	0.113	0.116	0.119	0.122	0.126	0.129	0.133	0.136	0.140	0.144	0.148	0.152	0.156	0.160	0.165	0.169	0.174	0.179	0.184
144	0.093	0.095	0.098	0.101	0.104	0.107	0.110	0.114	0.117	0.121	0.124	0.128	0.132	0.136	0.140	0.144	0.148	0.153	0.158
156	0.076	0.078	0.081	0.084	0.086	0.089	0.092	0.095	0.098	0.101	0.104	0.108	0.111	0.115	0.119	0.123	0.127	0.131	0.135
168	0.062	0.064	0.067	0.069	0.071	0.074	0.077	0.079	0.082	0.085	0.088	0.091	0.094	0.097	0.101	0.104	0.108	0.112	0.116
180	0.051	0.053	0.055	0.057	0.059	0.061	0.064	0.066	0.069	0.071	0.074	0.077	0.079	0.082	0.086	0.089	0.092	0.096	0.099
192	0.042	0.044	0.045	0.047	0.049	0.051	0.053	0.055	0.057	0.060	0.062	0.065	0.067	0.070	0.073	0.076	0.079	0.082	0.085
204	0.034	0.036	0.037	0.039	0.041	0.042	0.044	0.046	0.048	0.050	0.052	0.054	0.057	0.059	0.062	0.064	0.067	0.070	0.073
216	0.028	0.029	0.031	0.032	0.034	0.035	0.037	0.038	0.040	0.042	0.044	0.046	0.048	0.050	0.052	0.055	0.057	0.060	0.063
228	0.023	0.024	0.025	0.027	0.028	0.029	0.031	0.032	0.034	0.035	0.037	0.039	0.040	0.042	0.044	0.047	0.049	0.051	0.054
240	0.019	0.020	0.021	0.022	0.023	0.024	0.025	0.027	0.028	0.029	0.031	0.033	0.034	0.036	0.038	0.040	0.042	0.044	0.046
300	0.007	0.007	0.008	0.008	0.009	0.010	0.010	0.011	0.011	0.012	0.013	0.014	0.015	0.016	0.017	0.018	0.019	0.020	0.021
360	0.003	0.003	0.003	0.003	0.003	0.004	0.004	0.004	0.005	0.005	0.005	0.006	0.006	0.007	0.007	0.008	0.008	0.009	0.010

Table A-6 Monthly present value factor sums (PVFS).

Months	Annual Interest Rate																			
	1	2	3	4	5	6	7	7.25	7.5	7.75	8	8.25	8.5	8.75	9	9.25	9.5	9.75	10	10.25
	PVFS	PVFS	PVFS	PVFS	PVFS	PVFS	PVFS	PVFS	PVFS	PVFS	PVFS	PVFS	PVFS	PVFS	PVFS	PVFS	PVFS	PVFS	PVFS	PVFS
12	11.935	11.871	11.807	11.744	11.681	11.619	11.557	11.542	11.526	11.511	11.496	11.481	11.465	11.450	11.435	11.420	11.405	11.390	11.375	11.359
18	17.858	17.718	17.580	17.442	17.307	17.173	17.040	17.007	16.974	16.942	16.909	16.876	16.844	16.811	16.779	16.747	16.715	16.683	16.651	16.619
24	23.752	23.507	23.266	23.028	22.794	22.563	22.335	22.279	22.222	22.166	22.111	22.055	21.999	21.944	21.889	21.834	21.780	21.725	21.671	21.617
36	35.451	34.913	34.386	33.871	33.366	32.871	32.386	32.267	32.148	32.030	31.912	31.795	31.678	31.562	31.447	31.332	31.218	31.104	30.991	30.879
48	47.033	46.093	45.179	44.289	43.423	42.580	41.760	41.559	41.358	41.159	40.962	40.766	40.571	40.377	40.185	39.994	39.804	39.615	39.428	39.242
60	58.501	57.052	55.652	54.299	52.991	51.726	50.502	50.202	49.905	49.611	49.318	49.029	48.741	48.456	48.173	47.893	47.615	47.339	47.065	46.794
72	69.854	67.795	65.817	63.917	62.093	60.340	58.654	58.243	57.837	57.434	57.035	56.639	56.248	55.861	55.477	55.097	54.720	54.348	53.979	53.613
84	81.095	78.324	75.681	73.159	70.752	68.453	66.257	65.724	65.196	64.675	64.159	63.649	63.145	62.647	62.154	61.667	61.185	60.708	60.237	59.771
96	92.223	88.646	85.255	82.039	78.989	76.095	73.348	72.683	72.026	71.378	70.738	70.106	69.482	68.867	68.258	67.658	67.065	66.480	65.901	65.331
108	103.241	98.763	94.345	90.572	86.826	83.293	79.960	79.156	78.364	77.583	76.812	76.053	75.305	74.567	73.839	73.122	72.415	71.717	71.029	70.351
120	114.150	108.680	103.562	98.770	94.281	90.073	86.126	85.178	84.245	83.326	82.421	81.531	80.654	79.791	78.942	78.105	77.281	76.470	75.671	74.884
132	124.950	118.401	112.312	106.648	101.374	96.460	91.877	90.780	89.702	88.642	87.601	86.576	85.570	84.580	83.606	82.649	81.708	80.783	79.873	78.978
144	135.642	127.929	120.804	114.217	108.121	102.475	97.240	95.992	94.766	93.564	92.383	91.224	90.086	88.968	87.871	86.794	85.736	84.697	83.677	82.674
156	146.228	137.269	129.045	121.490	114.540	108.140	102.242	100.840	99.466	98.119	96.798	95.504	94.235	92.990	91.770	90.573	89.400	88.249	87.120	86.012
168	156.709	146.424	137.043	128.478	120.646	113.477	106.906	105.350	103.827	102.336	100.876	99.447	98.047	96.677	95.335	94.020	92.733	91.472	90.236	89.026
180	167.086	155.398	144.805	135.192	126.455	118.504	111.256	109.545	107.873	106.239	104.641	103.078	101.550	100.055	98.593	97.164	95.765	94.396	93.057	91.747
192	177.359	164.195	152.338	141.644	131.982	123.238	115.313	113.448	111.629	109.852	108.117	106.423	104.768	103.152	101.573	100.030	98.523	97.050	95.611	94.205
204	187.531	172.817	159.649	147.843	137.239	127.697	119.096	117.079	115.113	113.196	111.327	109.503	107.725	105.990	104.297	102.645	101.032	99.459	97.923	96.424
216	197.601	181.269	166.744	153.799	142.241	131.898	122.624	120.457	118.347	116.292	114.291	112.341	110.441	108.591	106.787	105.029	103.315	101.645	100.016	98.427

228	207.571	189.553	173.629	159.523	146.999	135.854	125.914	123.599	121.348	119.158	117.027	114.955	112.937	110.974	109.064	107.203	105.392	103.628	101.910	100.236
240	217.441	197.674	180.311	165.022	151.525	139.581	128.983	126.522	124.132	121.810	119.554	117.362	115.231	113.159	111.145	109.186	107.281	105.428	103.625	101.870
252	227.214	205.634	186.796	170.306	155.832	143.091	131.844	129.241	126.716	124.266	121.888	119.579	117.338	115.162	113.048	110.995	109.000	107.061	105.177	103.345
264	236.889	213.437	193.089	175.383	159.928	146.397	134.513	131.771	129.114	126.539	124.042	121.621	119.274	116.997	114.788	112.644	110.563	108.543	106.582	104.677
276	246.468	221.085	199.197	180.261	163.825	149.511	137.001	134.124	131.339	128.642	126.031	123.503	121.053	118.679	116.378	114.148	111.985	109.888	107.854	105.880
288	255.952	228.582	205.124	184.949	167.533	152.444	139.322	136.313	133.404	130.590	127.868	125.235	122.687	120.220	117.832	115.519	113.279	111.109	109.005	106.966
300	265.342	235.930	210.876	189.452	171.060	155.207	141.487	138.350	135.320	132.393	129.565	126.831	124.189	121.633	119.162	116.770	114.456	112.216	110.047	107.947
312	274.638	243.133	216.459	193.780	174.415	157.809	143.505	140.244	137.098	134.061	131.131	128.301	125.568	122.928	120.377	117.911	115.527	113.221	110.991	108.832
324	283.842	250.194	221.877	197.938	177.608	160.260	145.388	142.006	138.747	135.606	132.577	129.655	126.836	124.115	121.488	118.951	116.501	114.133	111.845	109.632
336	292.954	257.115	227.135	201.934	180.644	162.569	147.144	143.646	140.279	137.036	133.912	130.902	128.000	125.203	122.504	119.900	117.387	114.961	112.618	110.354
348	301.975	263.899	232.237	205.773	183.533	164.743	148.781	145.171	141.699	138.359	135.145	132.051	129.070	126.200	123.433	120.766	118.193	115.712	113.317	111.006
360	310.907	270.549	237.189	209.461	186.282	166.792	150.308	146.590	143.018	139.584	136.283	133.109	130.054	127.113	124.282	121.555	118.927	116.394	113.951	111.595

(continued on next page)

Table A-6 Monthly present value factor sums (PVFS) (Continued).

Annual Interest Rate

Months	10.5 PVFS	10.75 PVFS	11 PVFS	11.25 PVFS	11.5 PVFS	11.75 PVFS	12 PVFS	12.25 PVFS	12.5 PVFS	12.75 PVFS	13 PVFS	13.25 PVFS	13.5 PVFS	13.75 PVFS	14 PVFS	14.25 PVFS	14.5 PVFS	14.75 PVFS	15 PVFS	15.25 PVFS
12	11.344	11.330	11.315	11.300	11.285	11.270	11.255	11.240	11.226	11.211	11.196	11.181	11.167	11.152	11.137	11.123	11.108	11.094	11.079	11.065
18	16.587	16.555	16.524	16.492	16.461	16.430	16.398	16.367	16.336	16.305	16.274	16.243	16.212	16.182	16.151	16.121	16.090	16.060	16.030	15.999
24	21.563	21.509	21.456	21.402	21.349	21.296	21.243	21.191	21.138	21.086	21.034	20.982	20.931	20.879	20.828	20.777	20.726	20.675	20.624	20.574
36	30.767	30.656	30.545	30.435	30.325	30.216	30.108	30.000	29.892	29.785	29.679	29.573	29.468	29.363	29.259	29.155	29.052	28.949	28.847	28.746
48	39.057	38.874	38.691	38.510	38.330	38.152	37.974	37.798	37.622	37.448	37.275	37.103	36.933	36.763	36.595	36.427	36.261	36.096	35.931	35.768
60	46.525	46.258	45.993	45.730	45.470	45.211	44.955	44.701	44.449	44.198	43.950	43.704	43.460	43.217	42.977	42.739	42.502	42.267	42.035	41.804
72	53.251	52.892	52.537	52.186	51.837	51.492	51.150	50.812	50.477	50.144	49.815	49.490	49.167	48.847	48.530	48.216	47.906	47.598	47.292	46.990
84	59.310	58.854	58.403	57.957	57.516	57.080	56.648	56.222	55.800	55.382	54.969	54.561	54.157	53.757	53.362	52.971	52.584	52.201	51.822	51.448
96	64.767	64.210	63.660	63.117	62.581	62.051	61.528	61.011	60.500	59.996	59.498	59.006	58.520	58.040	57.566	57.097	56.634	56.177	55.725	55.278
108	69.682	69.023	68.372	67.730	67.098	66.473	65.858	65.251	64.651	64.061	63.478	62.903	62.335	61.775	61.223	60.678	60.141	59.610	59.087	58.570
120	74.110	73.347	72.595	71.855	71.126	70.408	69.701	69.004	68.317	67.641	66.974	66.318	65.671	65.034	64.405	63.786	63.176	62.575	61.983	61.399
132	78.098	77.232	76.380	75.543	74.719	73.908	73.111	72.326	71.554	70.795	70.047	69.312	68.588	67.875	67.174	66.484	65.805	65.136	64.478	63.830
144	81.690	80.723	79.773	78.840	77.923	77.022	76.137	75.267	74.413	73.573	72.747	71.936	71.138	70.354	69.583	68.826	68.081	67.348	66.628	65.919
156	84.926	83.860	82.814	81.788	80.781	79.793	78.823	77.871	76.937	76.020	75.120	74.236	73.368	72.516	71.679	70.858	70.051	69.258	68.480	67.715
168	87.840	86.678	85.539	84.423	83.329	82.257	81.206	80.176	79.166	78.176	77.204	76.252	75.318	74.402	73.503	72.621	71.756	70.908	70.075	69.258
180	90.465	89.210	87.982	86.780	85.603	84.450	83.322	82.217	81.134	80.075	79.036	78.019	77.023	76.046	75.090	74.152	73.233	72.333	71.450	70.584
192	92.830	91.485	90.171	88.886	87.630	86.401	85.199	84.023	82.873	81.747	80.646	79.568	78.513	77.481	76.470	75.481	74.512	73.563	72.634	71.724
204	94.959	93.530	92.134	90.770	89.438	88.136	86.865	85.622	84.408	83.221	82.060	80.926	79.817	78.732	77.671	76.634	75.619	74.626	73.654	72.703
216	96.878	95.367	93.892	92.454	91.050	89.680	88.343	87.038	85.763	84.519	83.303	82.116	80.956	79.824	78.716	77.635	76.577	75.543	74.533	73.545
228	98.606	97.017	95.469	93.960	92.488	91.054	89.655	88.291	86.960	85.662	84.395	83.159	81.953	80.775	79.626	78.503	77.407	76.336	75.290	74.268
240	100.162	98.500	96.882	95.306	93.771	92.276	90.819	89.400	88.017	86.669	85.355	84.074	82.824	81.606	80.417	79.257	78.125	77.021	75.942	74.890

252	101.564	99.832	98.148	96.509	94.915	93.363	91.853	90.382	88.951	87.556	86.198	84.875	83.586	82.330	81.105	79.911	78.747	77.612	76.504	75.424
264	102.827	101.030	99.283	97.585	95.935	94.330	92.770	91.252	89.775	88.338	86.939	85.578	84.252	82.961	81.704	80.479	79.286	78.122	76.988	75.883
276	103.964	102.105	100.300	98.547	96.845	95.191	93.583	92.021	90.503	89.026	87.591	86.194	84.835	83.512	82.225	80.972	79.752	78.563	77.405	76.277
288	104.989	103.072	101.212	99.407	97.656	95.956	94.306	92.703	91.146	89.633	88.163	86.734	85.344	83.993	82.679	81.400	80.155	78.944	77.765	76.616
300	105.912	103.940	102.029	100.176	98.380	96.637	94.947	93.306	91.713	90.167	88.665	87.207	85.789	84.412	83.073	81.771	80.505	79.273	78.074	76.908
312	106.743	104.720	102.761	100.864	99.025	97.243	95.515	93.840	92.215	90.638	89.107	87.621	86.179	84.778	83.416	82.093	80.807	79.557	78.341	77.158
324	107.492	105.421	103.418	101.479	99.601	97.782	96.020	94.312	92.657	91.052	89.495	87.985	86.519	85.096	83.715	82.373	81.069	79.802	78.571	77.373
336	108.166	106.051	104.006	102.028	100.114	98.262	96.468	94.731	93.048	91.417	89.836	88.304	86.817	85.374	83.975	82.616	81.296	80.014	78.769	77.558
348	108.774	106.617	104.534	102.520	100.572	98.688	96.866	95.101	93.393	91.739	90.136	88.583	87.077	85.617	84.201	82.826	81.492	80.197	78.939	77.717
360	109.321	107.126	105.006	102.959	100.980	99.068	97.218	95.429	93.698	92.022	90.400	88.828	87.305	85.829	84.397	83.009	81.662	80.355	79.086	77.854

(continued on next page)

Table A-6   Monthly present value factor sums (PVFS) (Continued).

Annual Interest Rate

Months	15.5	15.75	16	16.25	16.5	16.75	17	17.25	17.5	17.75	18	18.25	18.5	18.75	19	19.25	19.5	19.75	20	20.25
	PVFS	PVFS	PVFS	PVFS	PVFS	PVFS	PVFS	PVFS	PVFS	PVFS	PVFS	PVFS	PVFS	PVFS	PVFS	PVFS	PVFS	PVFS	PVFS	PVFS
12	11.050	11.036	11.022	11.007	10.993	10.979	10.964	10.950	10.936	10.922	10.908	10.893	10.879	10.865	10.851	10.837	10.823	10.809	10.795	10.781
18	15.969	15.939	15.909	15.879	15.850	15.820	15.790	15.761	15.731	15.702	15.673	15.643	15.614	15.585	15.556	15.527	15.498	15.470	15.411	15.412
24	20.524	20.473	20.424	20.374	20.324	20.275	20.226	20.177	20.128	20.079	20.030	19.982	19.934	19.886	19.838	19.790	19.743	19.695	19.648	19.601
36	28.645	28.544	28.444	28.344	28.245	28.146	28.048	27.951	27.854	27.757	27.661	27.565	27.470	27.375	27.281	27.187	27.093	27.001	26.908	26.816
48	35.606	35.445	35.285	35.127	34.969	34.812	34.636	34.501	34.347	34.194	34.043	33.892	33.742	33.593	33.445	33.298	33.151	33.006	32.862	32.719
60	41.575	41.347	41.122	40.898	40.676	40.456	40.237	40.020	39.805	39.592	39.380	39.170	38.962	38.755	38.550	38.346	38.144	37.944	37.745	37.547
72	46.691	46.394	46.100	45.809	45.521	45.235	44.952	44.671	44.393	44.118	43.845	43.574	43.306	43.041	42.778	42.517	42.258	42.002	41.749	41.497
84	51.077	50.710	50.347	49.988	49.633	49.282	48.934	48.590	48.249	47.912	47.579	47.249	46.922	46.599	46.279	45.963	45.649	45.339	45.032	44.729
96	54.837	54.401	53.970	53.544	53.124	52.708	52.297	51.891	51.490	51.094	50.702	50.314	49.931	49.553	49.179	48.809	48.444	48.083	47.725	47.372
108	58.060	57.557	57.061	56.571	56.087	55.610	55.138	54.673	54.214	53.761	53.314	52.872	52.436	52.006	51.581	51.161	50.747	50.338	49.934	49.535
120	60.823	60.256	59.697	59.146	58.602	58.066	57.538	57.017	56.504	55.998	55.498	55.006	54.521	54.042	53.570	53.104	52.645	52.192	51.745	51.304
132	63.192	62.564	61.946	61.337	60.737	60.147	59.565	58.993	58.428	57.873	57.326	56.787	56.256	55.733	55.217	54.709	54.209	53.716	53.230	52.751
144	65.223	64.538	63.864	63.201	62.550	61.908	61.277	60.657	60.046	59.445	58.854	58.272	57.700	57.136	56.581	56.035	55.498	54.969	54.448	53.935
156	66.964	66.226	65.501	64.788	64.088	63.400	62.724	62.059	61.406	60.764	60.132	59.512	58.901	58.301	57.711	57.131	56.560	55.999	55.447	54.904
168	68.456	67.669	66.897	66.138	65.394	64.663	63.945	63.241	62.549	61.869	61.201	60.546	59.902	59.269	58.647	58.036	57.436	56.846	56.266	55.696
180	69.735	68.903	68.087	67.287	66.502	65.732	64.977	64.236	63.509	62.796	62.096	61.408	60.734	60.072	59.422	58.784	58.157	57.542	56.938	56.345
192	70.832	69.959	69.103	68.265	67.443	66.638	65.849	65.075	64.316	63.573	62.843	62.128	61.427	60.739	60.064	59.402	58.752	58.115	57.489	56.875
204	71.772	70.862	69.970	69.097	68.242	67.405	66.585	65.782	64.995	64.224	63.469	62.729	62.003	61.592	60.596	59.912	59.242	58.585	57.941	57.309
216	72.578	71.633	70.709	69.805	68.920	68.054	67.207	66.377	65.565	64.770	63.992	63.230	62.483	61.752	61.036	60.334	59.646	58.972	58.311	57.664
228	73.269	72.293	71.340	70.407	69.495	68.604	67.732	66.879	66.045	65.229	64.430	63.648	62.883	62.134	61.400	60.682	59.979	59.290	58.613	57.954
240	73.862	72.858	71.878	70.920	69.984	69.069	68.176	67.302	66.448	65.613	64.796	63.997	63.215	62.451	61.702	60.970	60.253	59.551	58.864	58.191
252	74.370	73.341	72.336	71.356	70.399	69.464	68.550	67.658	66.786	65.935	65.102	64.288	63.492	62.714	61.952	61.208	60.479	59.766	59.069	58.386
264	74.805	73.753	72.728	71.727	70.751	69.797	68.867	67.958	67.071	66.204	65.358	64.531	63.722	62.932	62.160	61.404	60.665	59.743	59.236	58.545
276	75.178	74.106	73.062	72.043	71.049	70.080	69.134	68.211	67.310	66.431	65.572	64.733	63.914	63.113	62.331	61.566	60.819	60.088	59.374	58.675
288	75.498	74.408	73.347	72.312	71.303	70.319	69.360	68.424	67.511	66.621	65.751	64.902	64.073	63.264	62.473	61.701	60.946	60.208	59.486	58.781
300	75.772	74.666	73.590	72.540	71.518	70.522	69.551	68.604	67.681	66.780	65.901	65.043	64.206	63.389	62.591	61.811	61.050	60.306	59.579	58.868
312	76.007	74.887	73.797	72.735	71.701	70.694	69.712	68.755	67.823	66.913	66.026	65.161	64.317	63.493	62.688	61.903	61.136	60.387	59.655	58.939
324	76.209	75.076	73.974	72.901	71.856	70.839	69.848	68.883	67.942	67.025	66.131	65.259	64.409	63.579	62.769	61.978	61.207	60.453	59.717	58.997
336	76.382	75.237	74.124	73.042	71.988	70.962	69.963	68.990	68.042	67.119	66.219	65.341	64.485	63.650	62.836	62.041	61.265	60.507	59.768	59.045
348	76.530	75.375	74.253	73.162	72.100	71.066	70.060	69.081	68.127	67.197	66.292	65.409	64.549	63.710	62.891	62.092	61.313	60.552	59.809	59.084
360	76.657	75.494	74.363	73.264	72.194	71.154	70.142	69.157	68.198	67.263	66.333	65.466	64.602	63.759	62.937	62.135	61.353	60.389	59.844	59.116

Annual Interest Rate

Months	20.5 PVFS	20.75 PVFS	21 PVFS	21.25 PVFS	21.5 PVFS	21.75 PVFS	22 PVFS	22.25 PVFS	22.5 PVFS	22.75 PVFS	23 PVFS	23.25 PVFS	23.5 PVFS	23.75 PVFS	24 PVFS	24.25 PVFS	24.5 PVFS	24.75 PVFS	25 PVFS	25.25 PVFS
12	10.767	10.753	10.740	10.726	10.712	10.698	10.684	10.671	10.657	10.643	10.630	10.616	10.602	10.589	10.575	10.562	10.548	10.535	10.521	10.508
18	15.384	15.355	15.327	15.299	15.270	15.242	15.214	15.186	15.158	15.130	15.102	15.075	15.047	15.020	14.992	14.965	14.937	14.910	14.883	14.856
24	19.554	19.507	19.461	19.414	19.368	19.322	19.276	19.230	19.185	19.139	19.094	19.049	19.004	18.959	18.914	18.869	18.825	18.781	18.737	18.693
36	26.725	26.633	26.543	26.453	26.363	26.273	26.185	26.096	26.008	25.920	25.833	25.747	25.660	25.574	25.489	25.404	25.319	25.235	25.151	25.068
48	32.576	32.434	32.294	32.154	32.015	31.877	31.740	31.604	31.468	31.334	31.200	31.067	30.935	30.804	30.673	30.543	30.415	30.287	30.159	30.033
60	37.351	37.157	36.964	36.773	36.583	36.394	36.207	36.021	35.837	35.654	35.473	35.293	35.114	34.937	34.761	34.586	34.413	34.241	34.070	33.901
72	41.248	41.001	40.756	40.514	40.274	40.035	39.799	39.565	39.333	39.103	38.876	38.650	38.426	38.204	37.984	37.766	37.550	37.336	37.123	36.913
84	44.428	44.131	43.836	43.545	43.256	42.970	42.688	42.408	42.131	41.856	41.585	41.316	41.050	40.786	40.526	40.267	40.011	39.758	39.508	39.259
96	47.023	46.678	46.337	46.000	45.666	45.336	45.010	44.688	44.369	44.054	43.742	43.434	43.129	42.828	42.529	42.235	41.943	41.654	41.369	41.087
108	49.141	48.752	48.368	47.989	47.614	47.244	46.878	46.517	46.160	45.808	45.460	45.116	44.777	44.441	44.110	43.782	43.458	43.139	42.823	42.510
120	50.869	50.440	50.017	49.600	49.188	48.781	48.380	47.984	47.594	47.208	46.828	46.453	46.082	45.716	45.355	44.999	44.647	44.300	43.957	43.619
132	52.280	51.815	51.356	50.905	50.459	50.020	49.588	49.161	48.741	48.326	47.917	47.514	47.116	46.724	46.338	45.956	45.580	45.209	44.844	44.483
144	53.431	52.933	52.444	51.962	51.487	51.019	50.559	50.105	49.658	49.218	48.784	48.357	47.936	47.521	47.112	46.709	46.312	45.921	45.535	45.155
156	54.370	53.844	53.327	52.818	52.317	51.825	51.340	50.862	50.393	49.930	49.475	49.027	48.585	48.151	47.723	47.302	46.887	46.478	46.076	45.679
168	55.136	54.586	54.044	53.512	52.988	52.474	51.968	51.470	50.980	50.499	50.025	49.559	49.100	48.649	48.205	47.768	47.338	46.914	46.497	46.087
180	55.762	55.189	54.627	54.074	53.531	52.997	52.473	51.957	51.450	50.952	50.463	49.981	49.508	49.042	48.584	48.134	47.691	47.255	46.827	46.405
192	56.272	55.680	55.099	54.529	53.969	53.419	52.879	52.348	51.827	51.315	50.811	50.317	49.831	49.353	48.884	48.422	47.969	47.523	47.084	46.653
204	56.689	56.080	55.483	54.898	54.323	53.759	53.205	52.661	52.128	51.604	51.089	50.583	50.087	49.599	49.120	48.649	48.186	47.732	47.285	46.845
216	57.029	56.406	55.795	55.197	54.609	54.033	53.468	52.913	52.369	51.834	51.310	50.795	50.290	49.793	49.306	48.827	48.357	47.895	47.442	46.996
228	57.306	56.671	56.049	55.439	54.840	54.254	53.679	53.115	52.561	52.019	51.486	50.963	50.450	49.947	49.453	48.968	48.491	48.023	47.564	47.113
240	57.532	56.887	56.254	55.635	55.027	54.432	53.849	53.277	52.716	52.166	51.626	51.097	50.578	50.068	49.569	49.078	48.596	48.124	47.660	47.204
252	57.717	57.062	56.421	55.793	55.178	54.576	53.985	53.406	52.839	52.283	51.738	51.203	50.679	50.164	49.660	49.165	48.679	48.202	47.734	47.275
264	57.868	57.205	56.557	55.922	55.300	54.691	54.095	53.510	52.938	52.377	51.827	51.287	50.759	50.240	49.732	49.233	48.744	48.264	47.792	46.876
276	57.991	57.322	56.667	56.026	35.399	54.785	54.183	53.594	53.017	52.451	51.897	51.354	50.822	50.300	49.788	49.287	48.794	48.312	47.838	47.373
288	58.091	57.417	56.756	56.111	55.479	54.860	54.254	53.661	53.080	52.511	51.954	51.408	50.872	50.348	49.833	49.329	48.834	48.349	47.873	47.407
300	58.173	57.494	56.829	56.179	55.543	54.920	54.311	53.715	53.131	52.559	51.999	51.450	50.912	50.385	49.869	49.362	48.866	48.379	47.901	47.433
312	58.240	57.556	56.888	56.234	55.595	54.969	54.357	53.738	53.171	52.597	52.034	51.483	50.944	50.415	49.896	49.388	48.890	48.402	47.923	47.453
324	58.295	57.608	56.936	56.279	55.637	55.009	54.394	53.792	53.204	52.627	52.063	51.510	50.969	50.438	49.918	49.409	48.909	48.420	47.940	47.469
336	58.339	57.649	56.975	56.316	55.671	55.040	54.424	53.820	53.230	52.651	52.085	51.531	50.988	50.457	49.936	49.425	48.925	48.434	47.953	47.481
348	58.375	57.683	57.006	56.345	55.698	55.066	54.447	53.842	53.250	52.671	52.103	51.548	51.004	50.471	49.949	49.438	48.936	48.445	47.963	47.491
360	58.405	57.711	57.032	56.369	55.721	55.087	54.467	53.860	53.267	52.686	52.118	51.561	51.016	50.483	49.960	49.448	48.946	48.454	47.971	47.498

(continued on next page)

Table A-6 Monthly present value factor sums (PVFS) (Continued).

Annual Interest Rate

Months	25.5 PVFS	25.75 PVFS	26 PVFS	26.25 PVFS	26.5 PVFS	26.75 PVFS	27 PVFS	27.25 PVFS	27.5 PVFS	27.75 PVFS	28 PVFS	28.25 PVFS	28.5 PVFS	28.75 PVFS	29 PVFS	29.25 PVFS	29.5 PVFS	29.75 PVFS	30 PVFS	30.25 PVFS
12	10.495	10.481	10.468	10.455	10.441	10.428	10.415	10.402	10.388	10.375	10.362	10.349	10.336	10.323	10.310	10.297	10.284	10.271	10.258	10.245
18	14.829	14.802	14.775	14.748	14.721	14.694	14.668	14.641	14.615	14.588	14.562	14.536	14.509	14.483	14.457	14.431	14.405	14.379	14.353	14.328
24	18.649	18.605	18.562	18.518	18.475	18.432	18.389	18.346	18.304	18.261	18.219	18.177	18.134	18.093	18.051	18.009	17.968	17.926	17.885	17.844
36	24.985	24.902	24.820	24.738	24.656	24.575	24.495	24.414	24.334	24.255	24.176	24.097	24.019	23.941	23.863	23.786	23.709	23.632	23.556	23.480
48	29.907	29.782	29.658	29.535	29.412	29.291	29.170	29.049	28.930	28.811	28.693	28.575	28.459	28.343	28.227	28.113	27.999	27.886	27.773	27.661
60	33.732	33.565	33.400	33.235	33.072	32.910	32.749	32.589	32.431	32.274	32.117	31.962	31.808	31.656	31.504	31.354	31.204	31.056	30.909	30.762
72	36.704	36.497	36.292	36.089	35.887	35.688	35.490	35.293	35.098	34.905	34.714	34.524	34.336	34.150	33.965	33.781	33.599	33.419	33.240	33.063
84	39.013	38.770	38.529	38.290	38.054	37.820	37.588	37.358	37.131	36.906	36.683	36.462	36.243	36.027	35.812	35.599	35.389	35.180	34.974	34.769
96	40.808	40.531	40.258	39.988	39.721	39.456	39.195	38.936	38.680	38.426	38.176	37.928	37.682	37.439	37.199	36.961	36.726	36.493	36.263	36.035
108	42.202	41.897	41.595	41.298	41.003	40.712	40.425	40.141	39.860	39.582	39.308	39.036	38.768	38.503	38.241	37.981	37.725	37.472	37.221	36.973
120	43.285	42.955	42.629	42.308	41.990	41.677	41.367	41.061	40.759	40.460	40.166	39.875	39.587	39.303	39.023	38.745	38.472	38.201	37.934	37.670
132	44.127	43.775	43.429	43.087	42.749	42.416	42.088	41.764	41.444	41.128	40.817	40.509	40.205	39.906	39.610	39.318	39.029	38.745	38.458	38.186
144	44.780	44.411	44.047	43.688	43.334	42.984	42.640	42.301	41.966	41.636	41.310	40.989	40.672	40.359	40.051	39.746	39.446	39.150	38.858	38.569
156	45.289	44.904	44.525	44.151	43.783	43.420	43.063	42.711	42.364	42.021	41.684	41.351	41.024	40.700	40.382	40.067	39.758	39.452	39.151	38.853
168	45.683	45.286	44.894	44.509	44.129	43.755	43.387	43.024	42.667	42.314	41.968	41.626	41.289	40.957	40.630	40.308	39.990	39.677	39.368	39.064
180	45.990	45.582	45.180	44.784	44.395	44.012	43.635	43.263	42.897	42.537	42.183	41.833	41.489	41.151	40.817	40.488	40.164	39.845	39.530	39.220
192	46.228	45.811	45.401	44.997	44.600	44.209	43.824	43.446	43.073	42.707	42.346	41.990	41.641	41.296	40.957	40.623	40.294	39.970	39.651	39.336
204	46.414	45.989	45.572	45.161	44.757	44.360	43.970	43.585	43.207	42.835	42.469	42.109	41.755	41.406	41.062	40.724	40.391	40.063	39.740	39.422
216	46.558	46.127	45.704	45.288	44.879	44.476	44.081	43.692	43.310	42.933	42.563	42.199	41.841	41.488	41.141	40.800	40.464	40.133	39.807	39.486
228	46.669	46.234	45.806	45.385	44.972	44.566	44.166	43.773	43.387	43.008	42.634	42.267	41.906	41.550	41.201	40.856	40.518	40.185	39.856	39.533
240	46.756	46.317	45.885	45.460	45.044	44.634	44.231	43.836	43.447	43.064	42.688	42.318	41.955	41.597	41.245	40.899	40.558	40.223	39.893	39.569
252	46.824	46.381	45.946	45.518	45.099	44.686	44.281	43.883	43.492	43.107	42.729	42.357	41.992	41.632	41.279	40.931	40.589	40.252	39.921	39.595
264	46.876	46.430	45.993	45.563	45.141	44.727	44.320	43.919	43.526	43.140	42.760	42.387	42.020	41.659	41.304	40.955	40.611	40.273	39.941	39.614
276	46.917	46.469	46.029	45.598	45.174	44.758	44.349	43.947	43.552	43.165	42.783	42.409	42.041	41.679	41.322	40.972	40.628	40.289	39.956	39.628
288	46.949	46.499	46.058	45.624	45.199	44.781	44.371	43.968	43.572	43.183	42.801	42.426	42.056	41.694	41.337	40.986	40.641	40.301	39.967	39.639
300	46.973	46.522	46.079	45.645	45.218	44.800	44.388	43.984	43.588	43.198	42.815	42.438	42.068	41.705	41.347	40.996	40.650	40.310	39.976	39.647
312	46.992	46.540	46.096	45.661	45.233	44.814	44.402	43.997	43.599	43.209	42.825	42.448	42.077	41.713	41.355	41.003	40.657	40.317	39.982	39.653
324	47.007	46.554	46.109	45.673	45.245	44.824	44.412	44.006	43.608	43.217	42.833	42.455	42.084	41.720	41.361	41.009	40.662	40.322	39.987	39.657
336	47.019	46.565	46.119	45.682	45.254	44.833	44.419	44.013	43.615	43.223	42.839	42.461	42.089	41.724	41.366	41.013	40.666	40.325	39.990	39.660
348	47.028	46.573	46.127	45.690	45.260	44.839	44.425	44.019	43.620	43.228	42.843	42.465	42.093	41.728	41.369	41.016	40.669	40.328	39.993	39.663
360	47.035	46.580	46.133	45.695	4.566	44.844	44.430	44.023	43.624	43.232	42.847	42.468	42.096	41.731	41.372	41.019	40.671	40.330	39.994	39.664

Annual Interest Rate

Months	30.5 PVFS	30.75 PVFS	31 PVFS	31.25 PVFS	31.5 PVFS	31.75 PVFS	32 PVFS	32.25 PVFS	32.5 PVFS	32.75 PVFS	33 PVFS	33.25 PVFS	33.5 PVFS	33.75 PVFS	34 PVFS	34.25 PVFS	34.5 PVFS	34.75 PVFS	35 PVFS	35.25 PVFS
12	10.232	10.219	10.206	10.193	10.181	10.168	10.155	10.142	10.130	10.117	10.104	10.092	10.079	10.066	10.054	10.041	10.029	10.016	10.004	9.991
18	14.302	14.276	14.251	14.225	14.200	14.175	14.149	14.124	14.099	14.074	14.049	14.024	13.999	13.974	13.949	13.925	13.900	13.875	13.851	13.826
24	17.803	17.762	17.721	17.681	17.640	17.600	17.560	17.520	17.480	17.440	17.401	17.361	17.322	17.283	17.244	17.205	17.166	17.127	17.089	17.050
36	23.405	23.330	23.255	23.181	23.107	23.033	22.960	22.887	22.814	22.742	22.670	22.598	22.527	22.456	22.385	22.315	22.245	22.176	22.106	22.037
48	27.550	27.440	27.330	27.221	27.112	27.004	26.897	26.791	26.685	26.580	26.475	26.371	26.268	26.165	26.063	25.961	25.860	25.760	25.660	25.561
60	30.617	30.473	30.330	30.188	30.047	29.907	29.769	29.631	29.494	29.358	29.223	29.089	28.956	28.823	28.692	28.562	28.433	28.304	28.177	28.050
72	32.887	32.713	32.540	32.368	32.198	32.029	31.862	31.696	31.532	31.369	31.207	31.046	30.887	30.729	30.573	30.418	30.263	30.111	29.959	29.809
84	34.566	34.365	34.166	33.969	33.774	33.581	33.389	33.199	33.011	32.824	32.640	32.457	32.275	32.096	31.918	31.741	31.566	31.393	31.222	31.051
96	35.809	35.585	35.364	35.145	34.929	34.714	34.502	34.292	34.084	33.878	33.675	33.473	33.273	33.075	32.880	32.686	32.494	32.304	32.116	31.929
108	36.728	36.486	36.246	36.009	35.775	35.543	35.314	35.087	34.863	34.641	34.422	34.205	33.990	33.777	33.567	33.359	33.154	32.950	32.749	32.550
120	37.409	37.151	36.896	36.644	36.395	36.149	35.906	35.666	35.428	35.193	34.961	34.732	34.505	34.281	34.059	33.840	33.623	33.409	33.197	32.988
132	37.912	37.641	37.374	37.110	36.849	36.592	36.338	36.086	35.838	35.593	35.351	35.112	34.875	34.642	34.411	34.183	33.958	33.735	33.515	33.297
144	38.284	38.004	37.726	37.453	37.182	36.916	36.652	36.392	36.136	35.883	35.632	35.385	35.141	34.900	34.663	34.428	34.195	33.966	33.740	33.516
156	38.560	38.271	37.986	37.704	37.426	37.152	36.882	36.615	36.352	36.092	35.836	35.582	35.333	35.086	34.842	34.602	34.365	34.130	33.899	33.671
168	38.764	38.468	38.176	37.889	37.605	37.325	37.049	36.777	36.509	36.244	35.982	35.724	35.470	35.219	34.971	34.727	34.485	34.247	34.012	33.780
180	38.915	38.614	38.317	38.024	37.736	37.452	37.171	36.895	36.622	36.353	36.088	35.827	35.569	35.314	35.063	34.815	34.571	34.330	34.092	33.857
192	39.027	38.721	38.421	38.124	37.832	37.544	37.260	36.981	36.705	36.433	36.165	35.900	35.640	35.383	35.129	34.879	34.632	34.389	34.148	33.911
204	39.109	38.801	38.497	38.197	37.902	37.612	37.325	37.043	36.765	36.490	36.220	35.953	35.691	35.432	35.176	34.924	34.675	34.430	34.188	33.950
216	39.170	38.859	38.553	38.251	37.954	37.661	37.373	37.088	36.808	36.532	36.260	35.992	35.727	35.467	35.210	34.956	34.706	34.460	34.217	33.977
228	39.216	38.903	38.594	38.291	37.992	37.697	37.407	37.121	36.840	36.562	36.289	36.019	35.754	35.492	35.234	34.979	34.728	34.481	34.237	33.996
240	39.249	38.934	38.625	38.320	38.019	37.724	37.432	37.145	36.863	36.584	36.310	36.039	35.773	35.510	35.251	34.996	34.744	34.496	34.251	34.010
252	39.274	38.958	38.647	38.341	38.040	37.743	37.451	37.163	36.879	36.600	36.325	36.053	35.786	35.523	35.263	35.007	34.755	34.506	34.261	34.019
264	39.292	38.975	38.664	38.357	38.054	37.757	37.464	37.175	36.891	36.611	36.335	36.064	35.796	35.532	35.272	35.016	34.763	34.514	34.268	34.026
276	39.306	38.988	38.676	38.368	38.065	37.767	37.474	37.185	36.900	36.620	36.343	36.071	35.803	35.539	35.278	35.022	34.769	34.519	34.273	34.031
288	39.316	38.998	38.685	38.377	38.073	37.775	37.481	37.191	36.906	36.626	36.349	36.076	35.808	35.543	35.283	35.026	34.773	34.523	34.277	34.034
300	39.323	39.005	38.691	38.383	38.079	37.780	37.486	37.196	36.911	36.630	36.353	36.080	35.812	35.547	35.286	35.029	34.776	34.526	34.280	34.037
312	39.329	39.010	38.696	38.387	38.083	37.784	37.490	37.200	36.914	36.633	36.356	36.083	35.814	35.549	35.288	35.031	34.778	34.528	34.281	34.038
324	39.333	39.014	38.700	38.391	38.087	37.787	37.493	37.202	36.917	36.635	36.358	36.085	35.816	35.551	35.290	35.033	34.779	34.529	34.283	34.040
336	39.336	39.016	38.702	38.393	38.089	37.789	37.495	37.204	36.918	36.637	36.360	36.087	35.817	35.552	35.291	35.034	34.780	34.530	34.284	34.041
348	39.338	39.019	38.704	38.395	38.091	37.791	37.496	37.206	36.920	36.638	36.361	36.088	35.818	35.553	35.292	35.035	34.781	34.531	34.284	34.041
360	39.340	39.020	38.706	38.396	38.092	37.792	37.497	37.207	36.921	36.639	36.362	36.088	35.819	35.554	35.293	35.035	34.781	34.531	34.285	34.042

(continued on next page)

Table A-6 Monthly present value factor sums (PVFS) (Continued).

Annual Interest Rate

Months	35.5	35.75	36	36.25	36.5	36.75	37	37.25	37.5	37.75	38	38.25	38.5	38.75	39	39.25	39.5	39.75	40	40.25
	PVFS	PVFS	PVFS	PVFS	PVFS	PVFS	PVFS	PVFS	PVFS	PVFS	PVFS	PVFS	PVFS	PVFS	PVFS	PVFS	PVFS	PVFS	PVFS	PVFS
12	9.979	9.966	9.954	9.942	9.929	9.917	9.905	9.892	9.880	9.868	9.856	9.844	9.831	9.819	9.807	9.795	9.783	9.771	9.759	9.747
18	13.802	13.778	13.754	13.729	13.705	13.681	13.657	13.633	13.609	13.585	13.562	13.538	13.514	13.491	13.467	13.444	13.420	13.397	13.374	13.351
24	17.012	16.974	16.936	16.898	16.860	16.822	16.785	16.747	16.710	16.673	16.635	16.598	16.562	16.525	16.488	16.452	16.416	16.379	16.343	16.307
36	21.969	21.900	21.832	21.765	21.697	21.630	21.563	21.497	21.431	21.365	21.299	21.234	21.169	21.104	21.040	20.976	20.912	20.849	20.786	20.723
48	25.462	25.364	25.267	25.170	25.074	24.978	24.883	24.788	24.694	24.600	24.508	24.415	24.323	24.232	24.141	24.051	23.961	23.872	23.783	23.695
60	27.924	27.800	27.676	27.552	27.430	27.309	27.188	27.069	26.950	26.832	26.714	26.598	26.482	26.368	26.254	26.140	26.028	25.916	25.805	25.695
72	29.660	29.512	29.365	29.220	29.075	28.932	28.790	28.649	28.509	28.370	28.233	28.096	27.961	27.826	27.693	27.561	27.429	27.299	27.170	27.042
84	30.883	30.716	30.550	30.386	30.223	30.062	29.902	29.744	29.587	29.431	29.277	29.124	28.973	28.822	28.673	28.526	28.379	28.234	28.090	27.948
96	31.745	31.562	31.381	31.202	31.025	30.849	30.675	30.503	30.332	30.163	29.995	29.830	29.665	29.503	29.341	29.182	29.024	28.867	28.712	28.558
108	32.352	32.157	31.964	31.773	31.584	31.397	31.212	31.028	30.847	30.667	30.490	30.314	30.140	29.967	29.797	29.628	29.460	29.295	29.131	28.968
120	32.781	32.576	32.373	32.173	31.974	31.778	31.584	31.393	31.203	31.015	30.830	30.646	30.464	30.284	30.107	29.931	29.756	29.584	29.413	29.245
132	33.082	32.870	32.660	32.452	32.247	32.044	31.843	31.645	31.449	31.255	31.063	30.874	30.686	30.501	30.318	30.136	29.957	29.780	29.604	29.431
144	33.295	33.077	32.861	32.648	32.437	32.229	32.023	31.820	31.619	31.421	31.224	31.030	30.839	30.649	30.462	30.276	30.093	29.912	29.733	29.556
156	33.445	33.222	33.002	32.785	32.570	32.358	32.148	31.941	31.737	31.535	31.335	31.138	30.943	30.750	30.560	30.371	30.185	30.002	29.820	29.640
168	33.551	33.324	33.101	32.880	32.663	32.447	32.235	32.025	31.818	31.613	31.411	31.211	31.014	30.819	30.626	30.436	30.248	30.062	29.878	29.697
180	33.625	33.396	33.170	32.947	32.727	32.510	32.295	32.083	31.874	31.668	31.464	31.262	31.063	30.866	30.672	30.480	30.290	30.103	29.918	29.735
192	33.678	33.447	33.219	32.994	32.772	32.553	32.337	32.124	31.913	31.705	31.500	31.297	31.096	30.898	30.703	30.510	30.319	30.131	29.945	29.761
204	33.715	33.482	33.253	33.027	32.804	32.584	32.366	32.152	31.940	31.731	31.524	31.320	31.119	30.920	30.724	30.530	30.339	30.150	29.963	29.778
216	33.741	33.507	33.277	33.050	32.826	32.605	32.386	32.171	31.958	31.749	31.541	31.337	31.135	30.935	30.738	30.544	30.352	30.162	29.975	29.790
228	33.759	33.525	33.294	33.066	32.841	32.619	32.401	32.184	31.971	31.761	31.553	31.348	31.146	30.946	30.748	30.553	30.361	30.171	29.983	29.798
240	33.772	33.537	33.306	33.077	32.852	32.630	32.410	32.194	31.980	31.769	31.561	31.356	31.153	30.953	30.755	30.560	30.367	30.177	29.989	29.803
252	33.781	33.546	33.314	33.085	32.859	32.637	32.417	32.200	31.986	31.775	31.567	31.361	31.158	30.957	30.760	30.564	30.371	30.180	29.992	29.806
264	33.787	33.552	33.320	33.091	32.865	32.642	32.422	32.205	31.991	31.779	31.571	31.365	31.161	30.961	30.763	30.567	30.374	30.183	29.995	29.809
276	33.792	33.556	33.324	33.094	32.868	32.645	32.425	32.208	31.993	31.782	31.573	31.367	31.164	30.963	30.765	30.569	30.376	30.185	29.996	29.810
288	33.795	33.559	33.327	33.097	32.871	32.648	32.427	32.210	31.995	31.784	31.575	31.369	31.165	30.964	30.766	30.570	30.377	30.186	29.998	29.811
300	33.797	33.561	33.329	33.099	32.873	32.649	32.429	32.211	31.997	31.785	31.576	31.370	31.166	30.966	30.767	30.571	30.378	30.187	29.998	29.812
312	33.799	33.563	33.330	33.100	32.874	32.650	32.430	32.212	31.998	31.786	31.577	31.371	31.167	30.967	30.768	30.572	30.379	30.188	29.999	29.813
324	33.800	33.564	33.331	33.101	32.875	32.651	32.431	32.213	31.999	31.787	31.578	31.371	31.168	30.967	30.768	30.572	30.379	30.188	29.999	29.813
336	33.801	33.565	33.332	33.102	32.875	32.652	32.431	32.214	31.999	31.787	31.578	31.372	31.168	30.967	30.769	30.573	30.379	30.188	30.000	29.813
348	33.801	33.565	33.332	33.102	32.876	32.652	32.432	32.214	31.999	31.787	31.578	31.372	31.168	30.967	30.769	30.573	30.379	30.188	30.000	29.813
360	33.802	33.566	33.333	33.103	32.876	32.652	32.432	32.214	32.000	31.788	31.579	31.372	31.168	30.967	30.769	30.573	30.379	30.188	30.000	29.813

Annual Interest Rate

Months	40.5 PVFS	40.75 PVFS	41 PVFS	41.25 PVFS	41.5 PVFS	41.75 PVFS	42 PVFS	42.25 PVFS	42.5 PVFS	42.75 PVFS	43 PVFS	43.25 PVFS	43.5 PVFS	43.75 PVFS	44 PVFS	44.25 PVFS	44.5 PVFS	44.75 PVFS	45 PVFS	45.25 PVFS
12	9.735	9.723	9.711	9.699	9.687	9.675	9.663	9.651	9.640	9.628	9.616	9.604	9.593	9.581	9.569	9.558	9.546	9.534	9.523	9.511
18	13.327	13.304	13.281	13.258	13.235	13.212	13.190	13.167	13.144	13.122	13.099	13.077	13.054	13.032	13.009	12.987	12.965	12.943	12.920	12.898
24	16.271	16.235	16.200	16.164	16.129	16.094	16.058	16.023	15.988	15.953	15.919	15.884	15.850	15.815	15.781	15.747	15.713	15.679	15.645	15.611
36	20.660	20.598	20.536	20.474	20.413	20.351	20.290	20.230	20.170	20.109	20.050	19.990	19.931	19.872	19.813	19.755	19.696	19.638	19.581	19.523
48	23.607	23.520	23.433	23.347	23.261	23.176	23.091	23.007	22.923	22.840	22.757	22.675	22.593	22.511	22.430	22.350	22.270	22.190	22.111	22.032
60	25.586	25.477	25.369	25.262	25.156	25.050	24.945	24.840	24.737	24.634	24.532	24.430	24.329	24.229	24.129	24.031	23.932	23.835	23.738	23.642
72	26.914	26.788	26.663	26.539	26.415	26.293	26.171	26.051	25.931	25.812	25.695	25.578	25.462	25.347	25.232	25.119	25.006	24.895	24.784	24.674
84	27.806	27.666	27.527	27.390	27.253	27.117	26.983	26.850	26.718	26.587	26.457	26.328	26.201	26.074	25.948	25.824	25.700	25.578	25.456	25.336
96	28.405	28.255	28.105	27.957	27.810	27.664	27.520	27.377	27.236	27.096	26.957	26.819	26.682	26.547	26.413	26.280	26.148	26.018	25.888	25.760
108	28.808	28.649	28.491	28.335	28.180	28.027	27.876	27.726	27.577	27.430	27.284	27.140	26.997	26.855	26.715	26.576	26.438	26.301	26.166	26.032
120	29.078	28.912	28.749	28.587	28.427	28.268	28.111	27.956	27.802	27.650	27.499	27.349	27.202	27.055	26.910	26.767	26.625	26.484	26.345	26.207
132	29.259	29.089	28.921	28.755	28.591	28.428	28.267	28.107	27.950	27.794	27.639	27.487	27.335	27.186	27.038	26.891	26.746	26.602	26.460	26.319
144	29.381	29.208	29.036	28.867	28.699	28.534	28.370	28.208	28.047	27.889	27.732	27.576	27.423	27.271	27.120	26.971	26.824	26.678	26.534	26.391
156	29.463	29.287	29.113	28.942	28.772	28.604	28.438	28.274	28.111	27.951	27.792	27.635	27.479	27.326	27.174	27.023	26.874	26.727	26.581	26.437
168	29.517	29.340	29.165	28.991	28.820	28.651	28.483	28.318	28.154	27.992	27.832	27.673	27.517	27.362	27.208	27.057	26.907	26.758	26.612	26.467
180	29.554	29.376	29.199	29.025	28.852	28.682	28.513	28.346	28.182	28.019	27.858	27.698	27.541	27.385	27.231	27.079	26.928	26.779	26.631	26.485
192	29.579	29.399	29.222	29.047	28.873	28.702	28.533	28.365	28.200	28.036	27.875	27.715	27.557	27.400	27.246	27.093	26.941	26.792	26.644	26.498
204	29.596	29.415	29.237	29.061	28.888	28.716	28.546	28.378	28.212	28.048	27.886	27.725	27.567	27.410	27.255	27.102	26.950	26.800	26.652	26.505
216	29.607	29.426	29.248	29.071	28.897	28.725	28.554	28.386	28.220	28.056	27.893	27.732	27.574	27.417	27.261	27.108	26.956	26.806	26.657	26.510
228	29.614	29.433	29.254	29.078	28.903	28.731	28.560	28.392	28.225	28.061	27.898	27.737	27.578	27.421	27.265	27.112	26.960	26.809	26.661	26.514
240	29.619	29.438	29.259	29.082	28.907	28.735	28.564	28.395	28.229	28.064	27.901	27.740	27.581	27.423	27.268	27.114	26.962	26.812	26.663	26.516
252	29.623	29.441	29.262	29.085	28.910	28.737	28.567	28.398	28.231	28.066	27.903	27.742	27.583	27.425	27.270	27.116	26.964	26.813	26.664	26.517
264	29.625	29.443	29.264	29.087	28.912	28.739	28.568	28.399	28.232	28.067	27.904	27.743	27.584	27.426	27.271	27.117	26.964	26.814	26.665	26.518
276	29.627	29.445	29.266	29.088	28.913	28.740	28.569	28.400	28.233	28.068	27.905	27.744	27.585	27.427	27.271	27.117	26.965	26.815	26.666	26.518
288	29.628	29.446	29.266	29.089	28.914	28.741	28.570	28.401	28.234	28.069	27.906	27.745	27.585	27.428	27.272	27.118	26.966	26.815	26.666	26.519
300	29.628	29.447	29.267	29.090	28.915	28.742	28.570	28.401	28.234	28.069	27.906	27.745	27.586	27.428	27.272	27.118	26.966	26.815	26.666	26.519
312	29.629	29.447	29.267	29.090	28.915	28.742	28.571	28.402	28.235	28.070	27.907	27.745	27.586	27.428	27.272	27.118	26.966	26.815	26.666	26.519
324	29.629	29.447	29.268	29.090	28.915	28.742	28.571	28.402	28.235	28.070	27.907	27.745	27.586	27.428	27.272	27.118	26.966	26.815	26.666	26.519
336	29.629	29.447	29.268	29.091	28.915	28.742	28.571	28.402	28.235	28.070	27.907	27.745	27.586	27.428	21.273	27.119	26.966	26.816	26.667	26.519
348	29.629	29.448	29.268	29.091	28.915	28.742	28.571	28.402	28.235	28.070	27.907	27.746	27.586	27.428	27.273	27.119	26.966	26.816	26.667	26.519
360	29.629	29.448	29.268	29.091	28.916	28.742	28.571	28.402	28.235	28.070	27.907	27.746	27.586	27.429	27.273	27.119	26.966	26.816	26.667	26.519

(continued on next page)

Table A-6 Monthly present value factor sums (PVFS) (Continued).

Annual Interest Rate

Months	45.5 PVFS	45.75 PVFS	46 PVFS	46.25 PVFS	46.5 PVFS	46.75 PVFS	47 PVFS	47.25 PVFS	47.5 PVFS	47.75 PVFS	48 PVFS	48.25 PVFS	48.5 PVFS	48.75 PVFS	49 PVFS	49.25 PVFS	49.5 PVFS	49.75 PVFS	50 PVFS	50.25 PVFS
12	9.500	9.488	9.476	9.465	9.454	9.442	9.431	9.419	9.408	9.396	9.385	9.374	9.362	9.351	9.340	9.329	9.317	9.306	9.295	9.284
18	12.876	12.854	12.833	12.811	12.789	12.767	12.745	12.724	12.702	12.681	12.659	12.638	12.617	12.595	12.574	12.553	12.532	12.511	12.490	12.469
24	15.577	15.544	15.510	15.477	15.444	15.411	15.378	15.345	15.312	15.280	15.247	15.214	15.182	15.150	15.118	15.086	15.054	15.022	14.990	14.958
36	19.466	19.409	19.353	19.296	19.240	19.184	19.128	19.073	19.018	18.963	18.908	18.854	18.800	18.746	18.692	18.639	18.585	18.532	18.480	18.427
48	21.954	21.876	21.799	21.722	21.645	21.569	21.494	21.418	21.344	21.269	21.195	21.122	21.048	20.976	20.903	20.831	20.760	20.688	20.618	20.547
60	23.546	23.451	23.357	23.263	23.170	23.077	22.985	22.894	22.803	22.713	22.623	22.535	22.446	22.358	22.271	22.184	22.098	22.013	21.928	21.843
72	24.564	24.456	24.348	24.242	24.136	24.030	23.926	23.822	23.719	23.617	23.516	23.415	23.315	23.216	23.117	23.019	22.922	22.826	22.730	22.635
84	25.216	25.098	24.980	24.863	24.748	24.633	24.519	24.406	24.294	24.183	24.073	23.964	23.855	23.747	23.641	23.535	23.430	23.325	23.222	23.119
96	25.633	25.507	25.382	25.258	25.136	25.014	24.893	24.774	24.655	24.537	24.421	24.305	24.191	24.077	23.965	23.853	23.742	23.632	23.523	23.415
108	25.900	25.768	25.638	25.509	25.381	25.255	25.129	25.005	24.881	24.759	24.638	24.518	24.399	24.282	24.165	24.049	23.934	23.821	23.708	23.596
120	26.070	25.935	25.801	25.668	25.537	25.407	25.278	25.150	25.024	24.898	24.774	24.651	24.529	24.408	24.289	24.170	24.053	23.936	23.821	23.707
132	26.180	26.042	25.905	25.770	25.636	25.503	25.372	25.242	25.113	24.985	24.859	24.734	24.610	24.487	24.365	24.245	24.126	24.007	23.890	23.774
144	26.250	26.110	25.971	25.834	25.698	25.564	25.431	25.299	25.169	25.040	24.912	24.785	24.660	24.536	24.413	24.291	24.171	24.051	23.933	23.816
156	26.294	26.153	26.013	25.875	25.738	25.602	25.468	25.335	25.204	2.5.074	24.945	24.817	24.691	24.566	24.442	24.320	24.198	24.078	23.959	23.841
168	26.323	26.181	26.040	25.901	25.763	25.627	25.492	25.358	25.226	25.095	24.966	24.837	24.710	24.585	24.460	24.337	24.215	24.094	23.975	23.856
180	26.341	26.198	26.057	25.917	25.779	25.642	25.507	25.373	25.240	25.109	24.979	24.850	24.722	24.596	24.472	24.348	24.226	24.105	23.985	23.866
192	26.353	26.210	26.068	25.928	25.789	25.652	25.516	25.382	25.249	25.117	24.987	24.858	24.730	24.604	24.479	24.355	24.232	24.111	23.991	23.872
204	26.360	26.217	26.075	25.934	25.795	25.658	25.522	25.387	25.254	25.122	24.992	24.862	24.735	24.608	24.483	24.359	24.236	24.115	23.994	23.875
216	26.365	26.221	26.079	25.939	25.799	25.662	25.526	25.391	25.257	25.125	24.995	24.865	24.738	24.611	24.485	24.361	24.239	24.117	23.996	23.877
228	26.368	26.224	26.082	25.941	25.802	25.664	25.528	25.393	25.260	25.127	24.997	24.867	24.739	24.613	24.487	24.363	24.240	24.118	23.998	23.879
240	26.370	26.226	26.084	25.943	25.804	25.666	25.529	25.394	25.261	25.129	24.998	24.869	24.740	24.614	24.488	24.364	24.241	24.119	23.999	23.879
252	26.371	26.227	26.085	25.944	25.805	25.667	25.530	25.395	25.262	25.130	24.999	24.869	24.741	24.614	24.489	24.365	24.242	24.120	23.999	23.880
264	26.372	26.228	26.086	25.945	25.805	25.667	25.531	25.396	25.262	25.130	24.999	24.870	24.742	24.615	24.489	24.365	24.242	24.120	23.999	23.880
276	26.373	26.229	26.086	25.945	25.806	25.668	25.531	25.396	25.263	25.130	25.000	24.870	24.742	24.615	24.489	24.365	24.242	24.120	24.000	23.880
288	26.373	26.229	26.086	25.945	25.806	25.668	25.532	25.396	25.263	25.131	25.000	24.870	24.742	24.615	24.490	24.365	24.242	24.120	24.000	23.880
300	26.373	26.229	26.087	25.946	25.806	25.668	25.532	25.397	25.263	25.131	25.000	24.870	24.742	24.615	24.490	24.365	24.242	24.120	24.000	23.880
312	26.373	26.229	26.087	25.946	25.806	25.668	25.532	25.397	25.263	25.131	25.000	24.870	24.742	24.615	24.490	24.365	24.242	24.121	24.000	23.881
324	26.373	26.229	26.087	25.946	25.806	25.668	25.532	25.397	25.263	25.131	25.000	24.870	24.742	24.615	24.490	24.365	24.242	24.121	24.000	23.881
336	26.374	26.229	26.087	25.946	25.806	25.668	25.532	25.397	25.263	25.131	25.000	24.870	24.742	24.615	24.490	24.365	24.242	24.121	24.000	23.881
348	26.374	26.229	26.087	25.946	25.806	25.668	25.532	25.397	25.263	25.131	25.000	24.870	24.742	24.615	24.490	24.365	24.242	24.121	24.000	23.881
360	26.374	26.229	26.087	25.946	25.806	25.668	25.532	25.397	25.263	25.131	25.000	24.870	24.742	24.615	24.490	24.365	24.242	24.121	24.000	23.881

Annual Interest Rate

Months	50.5 PVFS	50.75 PVFS	51 PVFS	51.25 PVFS	51.5 PVFS	51.75 PVFS	52 PVFS	52.25 PVFS	52.5 PVFS	52.75 PVFS	53 PVFS	53.25 PVFS	53.5 PVFS	53.75 PVFS	54 PVFS	54.25 PVFS	54.5 PVFS	54.75 PVFS	55 PVFS	55.25 PVFS
12	9.273	9.262	9.250	9.239	9.228	9.217	9.206	9.195	9.184	9.173	9.162	9.151	9.140	9.129	9.119	9.108	9.097	9.086	9.075	9.064
18	12.448	12.427	12.406	12.385	12.364	12.344	12.323	12.303	12.282	12.262	12.241	12.221	12.200	12.180	12.160	12.140	12.120	12.100	12.080	12.060
24	14.927	14.895	14.864	14.833	14.802	14.771	14.740	14.709	14.678	14.647	14.617	14.586	14.556	14.526	14.495	14.465	14.435	14.405	14.376	14.346
36	18.375	18.323	18.271	18.219	18.168	18.117	18.066	18.015	17.964	17.914	17.864	17.814	17.765	17.715	17.666	17.617	17.568	17.520	17.471	17.423
48	20.477	20.407	20.338	20.269	20.201	20.133	20.065	19.997	19.930	19.864	19.797	19.731	19.666	19.601	19.536	19.471	19.407	19.343	19.279	19.216
60	21.759	21.676	21.593	21.510	21.429	21.347	21.266	21.186	21.106	21.027	20.948	20.870	20.792	20.715	20.638	20.562	20.486	20.410	20.335	20.261
72	22.541	22.447	22.354	22.262	22.170	22.079	21.989	21.899	21.810	21.721	21.633	21.546	21.460	21.374	21.288	21.203	21.119	21.035	20.952	20.870
84	23.018	22.916	22.816	22.717	22.618	22.520	22.423	22.326	22.231	22.136	22.041	21.948	21.855	21.763	21.671	21.581	21.491	21.401	21.312	21.224
96	23.308	23.202	23.097	22.992	22.888	22.786	22.684	22.583	22.482	22.383	22.284	22.186	22.089	21.993	21.897	21.803	21.709	21.615	21.523	21.431
108	23.485	23.376	23.267	23.159	23.052	22.946	22.841	22.736	22.633	22.530	22.429	22.328	22.228	22.129	22.031	21.933	21.837	21.741	21.646	21.551
120	23.593	23.481	23.370	23.260	23.151	23.042	22.935	22.828	22.723	22.619	22.515	22.412	22.310	22.209	22.109	22.010	21.912	21.814	21.717	21.622
132	23.659	23.546	23.433	23.321	23.210	23.100	22.992	22.884	22.777	22.671	22.566	22.462	22.359	22.257	22.156	22.055	21.956	21.857	21.759	21.662
144	23.700	23.585	23.471	23.358	23.246	23.135	23.026	22.917	22.809	22.702	22.597	22.492	22.388	22.285	22.183	22.082	21.982	21.882	21.784	21.686
156	23.724	23.608	23.494	23.380	23.268	23.156	23.046	22.937	22.828	22.721	22.615	22.509	22.405	22.302	22.199	22.097	21.997	21.897	21.798	21.700
168	23.739	23.623	23.508	23.394	23.281	23.169	23.058	22.949	22.840	22.732	22.626	22.520	22.415	22.311	22.209	22.107	22.006	21.906	21.806	21.708
180	23.748	23.632	23.516	23.402	23.289	23.177	23.066	22.956	22.847	22.739	22.632	22.526	22.421	22.317	22.214	22.112	22.011	21.911	21.811	21.713
192	23.754	23.637	23.521	23.407	23.294	23.181	23.070	22.960	22.851	22.743	22.636	22.530	22.425	22.321	22.217	22.115	22.014	21.914	21.814	21.716
204	23.757	23.640	23.525	23.410	23.297	23.184	23.073	22.963	22.853	22.745	22.638	22.532	22.427	22.323	22.219	22.117	22.016	21.915	21.816	21.717
216	23.759	23.642	23.526	23.412	23.298	2.3.186	23.075	22.964	22.855	22.747	22.640	22.533	22.428	22.324	22.221	22.118	22.017	21.916	21.817	21.718
228	23.760	23.643	23.528	23.413	23.299	2.3.187	23.075	22.965	22.856	22.748	22.640	22.534	22.429	22.325	22.221	22.119	22.017	21.917	21.817	21.719
240	23.761	23.644	23.528	23.414	23.300	2.3.187	2.3.076	22.966	22.856	22.748	22.641	22.535	22.429	22.325	22.222	22.119	22.018	21.917	21.818	21.719
252	23.762	23.645	23.529	23.414	23.300	23.188	23.076	22.966	22.857	22.748	22.641	22.535	22.430	22.325	22.222	22.119	22.018	21.918	21.818	21.719
264	23.762	23.645	23.529	23.414	23.301	23.188	23.077	22.966	22.857	22.749	22.641	22.535	22.430	22.325	22.222	22.120	22.018	21.918	21.818	21.719
276	23.762	23.645	23.529	23.414	23.301	23.188	23.077	22.966	22.857	22.749	22.641	22.535	22.430	22.325	22.222	22.120	22.018	21.918	21.818	21.719
288	23.762	23.645	23.529	23.414	23.301	23.188	23.077	22.966	22.857	22.749	22.641	22.535	22.430	22.326	22.222	22.120	22.018	21.918	21.818	21.719
300	23.762	23.645	23.529	23.415	23.301	23.188	23.077	22.966	22.857	22.749	22.641	22.535	22.430	22.326	22.222	22.120	22.018	21.918	21.818	21.719
312	23.762	23.645	23.529	23.415	23.301	23.188	23.077	22.966	22.857	22.749	22.641	22.535	22.430	22.326	22.222	22.120	22.018	21.918	21.818	21.719
324	23.762	23.645	23.529	23.415	23.301	23.188	23.077	22.966	22.857	22.749	22.641	22.535	22.430	22.326	22.222	22.120	22.018	21.918	21.818	21.719
336	23.762	23.645	23.529	23.415	23.301	23.188	23.077	22.966	22.857	22.749	22.641	22.535	22.430	22.326	22.222	22.120	22.018	21.918	21.818	21.719
348	23.762	23.645	23.529	23.415	23.301	23.188	23.077	22.966	22.857	22.749	22.642	22.535	22.430	22.326	22.222	22.120	22.018	21.918	21.818	21.719
360	23.762	23.645	23.529	23.415	23.301	23.188	23.077	22.967	22.857	22.749	22.642	22.535	22.430	22.326	22.222	22.120	22.018	21.918	21.818	21.719

(continued on next page)

Table A-6 Monthly present value factor sums (PVFS) (Continued).

Months	55.5 PVFS	55.75 PVFS	56 PVFS	56.25 PVFS	56.5 PVFS	56.75 PVFS	57 PVFS	57.25 PVFS	57.5 PVFS	57.75 PVFS	58 PVFS	58.25 PVFS	58.5 PVFS	58.75 PVFS	59 PVFS	59.25 PVFS	59.5 PVFS	59.75 PVFS	60 PVFS	70 PVFS
12	9.054	9.043	9.032	9.022	9.011	9.000	8.990	8.979	8.968	8.958	8.947	8.937	8.926	8.916	8.905	8.895	8.884	8.874	8.863	8.461
18	12.040	12.020	12.000	11.980	11.961	11.941	11.921	11.902	11.882	11.863	11.843	11.824	11.805	11.785	11.766	11.747	11.728	11.709	11.690	10.964
24	14.316	14.287	14.257	14.228	14.199	14.170	14.141	14.112	14.083	14.054	14.025	13.997	13.968	13.940	13.911	13.883	13.855	13.827	13.799	12.746
36	17.375	17.328	17.280	17.233	17.186	17.139	17.092	17.046	16.999	16.953	16.907	16.861	16.816	16.771	16.725	16.681	16.636	16.591	16.547	14.916
48	19.153	19.091	19.029	18.967	18.905	18.844	18.783	18.723	18.662	18.603	18.543	18.484	18.425	18.366	18.308	18.250	18.192	18.134	18.077	16.015
60	20.187	20.113	20.040	19.968	19.895	19.821	19.752	19.681	19.611	19.541	19.471	19.402	19.333	19.265	19.197	19.129	19.062	18.996	18.929	16.572
72	20.788	20.706	20.625	20.545	20.465	20.386	20.308	20.229	20.152	20.075	19.998	19.922	19.847	19.772	19.697	19.623	19.549	19.476	19.404	16.854
84	21.137	21.050	20.964	20.878	20.794	20.709	20.626	20.543	20.460	20.378	20.297	20.217	20.136	20.057	19.978	19.900	19.822	19.745	19.668	16.996
96	21.340	21.249	21.160	21.071	20.983	20.895	20.808	20.722	20.636	20.551	20.467	20.383	20.300	20.218	20.136	20.055	19.974	19.894	19.815	17.069
108	21.458	21.365	21.273	21.182	21.091	21.002	20.912	20.824	20.736	20.649	20.563	20.478	20.393	20.309	20.225	20.142	20.060	19.978	19.897	17.105
120	21.526	21.432	21.339	21.246	21.154	21.063	20.972	20.883	20.794	20.705	20.618	20.531	20.445	20.360	20.275	20.191	20.107	20.025	19.943	17.124
132	21.566	21.471	21.377	21.283	21.190	21.098	21.007	20.916	20.826	20.737	20.649	20.561	20.475	20.388	20.303	20.218	20.134	20.051	19.968	17.133
144	21.589	21.494	21.398	21.304	21.211	21.118	21.026	20.935	20.845	20.755	20.667	20.578	20.491	20.405	20.319	20.234	20.149	20.065	19.982	17.138
156	21.603	21.507	21.411	21.317	21.223	21.130	21.038	20.946	20.855	20.766	20.677	20.588	20.501	20.411	20.328	20.242	20.157	20.073	19.990	17.140
168	21.611	21.514	21.418	21.324	21.230	21.136	21.044	20.952	20.862	20.771	20.682	20.594	20.506	20.419	20.333	20.247	20.162	20.078	19.994	17.142
180	21.615	21.519	21.423	21.328	21.234	21.140	21.048	20.956	20.865	20.775	20.685	20.597	20.509	20.422	20.335	20.250	20.165	20.080	19.997	17.142
192	21.618	21.521	21.425	21.330	21.236	21.142	21.050	20.958	20.867	20.777	20.687	20.599	20.511	20.423	20.337	20.251	20.166	20.082	19.998	17.143
204	21.619	21.523	21.427	21.331	21.237	21.144	21.051	20.959	20.868	20.778	20.688	20.600	20.512	20.424	20.338	20.252	20.167	20.083	19.999	17.143
216	21.620	21.523	21.427	21.332	21.238	21.144	21.052	20.960	20.869	20.778	20.689	20.600	20.512	20.425	20.338	20.253	20.167	20.083	19.999	17.143
228	21.621	21.524	21.428	21.333	21.238	21.145	21.052	20.960	20.869	20.779	20.689	20.600	20.512	20.425	20.339	20.253	20.168	20.083	20.000	17.143
240	21.621	21.524	21.428	21.333	21.239	21.145	21.052	20.960	20.869	20.779	20.689	20.601	20.513	20.425	20.339	20.253	20.168	20.084	20.000	17.143
252	21.621	21.524	21.428	21.333	21.239	21.145	21.052	20.961	20.869	20.779	20.690	20.601	20.513	20.425	20.339	20.253	20.168	20.084	20.000	17.143
264	21.621	21.525	21.428	21.333	21.239	21.145	21.053	20.961	20.869	20.779	20.690	20.601	20.513	20.425	20.339	20.253	20.168	20.084	20.000	17.143
276	21.622	21.525	21.428	21.333	21.239	21.145	21.053	20.961	20.870	20.779	20.690	20.601	20.513	20.425	20.339	20.253	20.168	20.084	20.000	17.143
288	21.622	21.525	21.429	21.333	21.239	21.145	21.053	20.961	20.870	20.779	20.690	20.601	20.513	20.426	20.339	20.253	20.168	20.084	20.000	17.143
300	21.622	21.525	21.429	21.333	21.239	21.145	21.053	20.961	20.870	20.779	20.690	20.601	20.513	20.426	20.339	20.253	20.168	20.084	20.000	17.143
312	21.622	21.525	21.429	21.333	21.239	21.145	21.053	20.961	20.870	20.779	20.690	20.601	20.513	20.426	20.339	20.253	20.168	20.084	20.000	17.143
324	21.622	21.525	21.429	21.333	21.239	21.145	21.053	20.961	20.870	20.779	20.690	20.601	20.513	20.426	20.339	20.253	20.168	20.084	20.000	17.143
336	21.622	21.525	21.429	21.333	21.239	21.145	21.053	20.961	20.870	20.779	20.690	20.601	20.513	20.426	20.339	20.253	20.168	20.084	20.000	17.143
348	21.622	21.525	21.429	21.333	21.239	21.145	21.053	20.961	20.870	20.779	20.690	20.601	20.513	20.426	20.339	20.253	20.168	20.084	20.000	17.143
360	21.622	21.525	21.429	21.333	21.239	21.145	21.053	20.961	20.870	20.779	20.690	20.601	20.513	20.426	20.339	20.253	20.168	20.084	20.000	17.143

Annual Interest Rate

Annual Interest Rate

Months	80 PVFS	90 PVFS	100 PVFS	125 PVFS	150 PVFS	175 PVFS	200 PVFS	250 PVFS	300 PVFS
12	8.086	7.735	7.408	6.677	6.053	5.518	5.056	4.305	3.725
18	10.306	9.706	9.159	7.987	7.040	6.266	5.626	4.641	3.928
24	11.813	10.983	10.243	8.710	7.526	6.596	5.852	4.749	3.981
36	13.531	12.347	11.327	9.329	7.885	6.806	5.977	4.795	3.999
48	14.323	12.919	11.743	9.517	7.972	6.847	5.996	4.799	4.000
60	14.323	13.159	11.901	9.575	7.993	6.855	5.999	4.800	4.000
72	14.856	13.260	11.962	9.592	7.998	6.857	6.000	4.800	4.000
84	14.934	13.303	11.986	9.598	8.000	6.857	6.000	4.800	4.000
96	14.969	13.320	11.994	9.599	8.000	6.857	6.000	4.800	4.000
108	14.986	13.328	11.998	9.600	8.000	6.857	6.000	4.800	4.000
120	14.994	13.331	11.999	9.600	8.000	6.857	6.000	4.800	4.000
132	14.997	13.332	12.000	9.600	8.000	6.857	6.000	4.800	4.000
144	14.999	13.333	12.000	9.600	8.000	6.857	6.000	4.800	4.000
156	14.999	13.333	12.000	9.600	8.000	6.857	6.000	4.800	4.000
168	15.000	13.333	12.000	9.600	8.000	6.857	6.000	4.800	4.000
180	15.000	13.333	12.000	9.600	8.000	6.857	6.000	4.800	4.000
192	15.000	13.333	12.000	9.600	8.000	6.857	6.000	4.800	4.000
204	15.000	13.333	12.000	9.600	8.000	6.857	6.000	4.800	4.000
216	15.000	13.333	12.000	9.600	8.000	6.857	6.000	4.800	4.000
228	15.000	13.333	12.000	9.600	8.000	6.857	6.000	4.800	4.000
240	15.000	13.333	12.000	9.600	8.000	6.857	6.000	4.800	4.000
252	15.000	13.333	12.000	9.600	8.000	6.857	6.000	4.800	4.000
264	15.000	13.333	12.000	9.600	8.000	6.857	6.000	4.800	4.000
276	15.000	13.333	12.000	9.600	8.000	6.8.57	6.000	4.800	4.000
288	15.000	13.333	12.000	9.600	8.000	6.857	6.000	4.800	4.000
300	15.000	13.333	12.000	9.600	8.000	6.857	6.000	4.800	4.000
312	15.000	13.333	12.000	9.600	8.000	6.857	6.000	4.800	4.000
324	15.000	13.333	12.000	9.600	8.000	6.857	6.000	4.800	4.000
336	15.000	13.333	12.000	9.600	8.000	6.857	6.000	4.800	4.000
348	15.000	13.333	12.000	9.600	8.000	6.857	6.000	4.800	4.000
360	15.000	13.333	12.000	9.600	8.000	6.857	6.000	4.800	4.000

(continued on next page)

Table A-7 Loan balance, 30 years.

Annual Interest Rate

Years Paid	6 MB	6.25 MB	6.5 MB	6.75 MB	7 MB	7.25 MB	7.5 MB	7.75 MB	8 MB	8.25 MB	8.5 MB	8.75 MB	9 MB	9.25 MB	9.5 MB	9.75 MB	10 MB	10.25 MB	10.5 MB	10.75 MB	11 MB
1	0.98772	0.98828	0.98882	0.98934	0.98984	0.99032	0.99078	0.99122	0.99165	0.99205	0.99244	0.99281	0.99317	0.99351	0.99383	0.99414	0.99444	0.99472	0.99499	0.99525	0.99550
2	0.97468	0.97581	0.97690	0.97794	0.97895	0.97992	0.98085	0.98174	0.98260	0.98342	0.98421	0.98497	0.98570	0.98639	0.98706	0.98769	0.98830	0.98888	0.98944	0.98997	0.99048
3	0.96084	0.96254	0.96417	0.96575	0.96727	0.96873	0.97014	0.97150	0.97280	0.97405	0.97526	0.97641	0.97752	0.97858	0.97960	0.98058	0.98152	0.98241	0.98327	0.98409	0.98487
4	0.94615	0.94841	0.95060	0.95271	0.95475	0.95671	0.95861	0.96043	0.96219	0.96388	0.96551	0.96708	0.96858	0.97003	0.97141	0.97274	0.97402	0.97525	0.97642	0.97754	0.97862
5	0.93054	0.93337	0.93611	0.93876	0.94132	0.94379	0.94617	0.94848	0.95070	0.95284	0.95490	0.95689	0.95880	0.96064	0.96241	0.96411	0.96574	0.96731	0.96882	0.97026	0.97165
6	0.91398	0.91737	0.92065	0.92384	0.92692	0.92990	0.93278	0.93556	0.93825	0.94085	0.94336	0.94577	0.94810	0.95035	0.95251	0.95459	0.95660	0.95852	0.96038	0.96215	0.96386
7	0.89639	0.90034	0.90416	0.90787	0.91147	0.91496	0.91834	0.92161	0.92477	0.92783	0.93079	0.93365	0.93640	0.93907	0.94163	0.94411	0.94649	0.94879	0.95100	0.95313	0.95518
8	0.87772	0.88221	0.88657	0.89080	0.89492	0.89891	0.90278	0.90654	0.91018	0.91370	0.91711	0.92041	0.92361	0.92669	0.92967	0.93255	0.93533	0.93801	0.94060	0.94309	0.94549
9	0.85790	0.86291	0.86779	0.87254	0.87716	0.88165	0.88602	0.89025	0.89437	0.89836	0.90223	0.90598	0.90961	0.91313	0.91653	0.91982	0.92300	0.92608	0.92905	0.93192	0.93468
10	0.83686	0.84238	0.84776	0.85301	0.85812	0.86310	0.86795	0.87266	0.87725	0.88170	0.88603	0.89022	0.89430	0.89825	0.90208	0.90579	0.90938	0.91286	0.91622	0.91948	0.92263
11	0.81451	0.82052	0.82639	0.83212	0.83771	0.84316	0.84848	0.85366	0.85870	0.86361	0.86839	0.87304	0.87755	0.88193	0.88619	0.89032	0.89433	0.89822	0.90199	0.90564	0.90917
12	0.79079	0.79726	0.80358	0.80977	0.81582	0.82173	0.82750	0.83313	0.83862	0.84398	0.84920	0.85428	0.85923	0.86405	0.86873	0.87328	0.87771	0.88201	0.88618	0.89023	0.89416
13	0.76561	0.77250	0.77925	0.78587	0.79235	0.79869	0.80489	0.81095	0.81688	0.82266	0.82831	0.83382	0.83919	0.84443	0.84954	0.85451	0.85934	0.86405	0.86863	0.87308	0.87741
14	0.73887	0.74615	0.75329	0.76030	0.76718	0.77392	0.78052	0.78699	0.79332	0.79952	0.80557	0.81149	0.81728	0.82292	0.82844	0.83381	0.83906	0.84417	0.84915	0.85400	0.85872
15	0.71049	0.71810	0.72559	0.73295	0.74019	0.74729	0.75427	0.76111	0.76782	0.77439	0.78083	0.78713	0.79330	0.79934	0.80524	0.81101	0.81665	0.82215	0.82752	0.83276	0.83787
16	0.68035	0.68825	0.69604	0.70370	0.71125	0.71867	0.72597	0.73314	0.74019	0.74711	0.75390	0.76056	0.76708	0.77348	0.77975	0.78588	0.79189	0.79776	0.80351	0.80912	0.81461
17	0.64836	0.65648	0.66450	0.67241	0.68022	0.68791	0.69548	0.70294	0.71027	0.71749	0.72458	0.73156	0.73840	0.74512	0.75172	0.75819	0.76454	0.77075	0.77685	0.78281	0.78866
18	0.61439	0.62267	0.63086	0.63895	0.64694	0.65483	0.66262	0.67030	0.67787	0.68533	0.69268	0.69991	0.70703	0.71403	0.72091	0.72768	0.73432	0.74085	0.74725	0.75353	0.75970
19	0.57832	0.58668	0.59496	0.60315	0.61126	0.61928	0.62721	0.63504	0.64278	0.65042	0.65796	0.66539	0.67272	0.67994	0.68705	0.69405	0.70094	0.70772	0.71439	0.72095	0.72739
20	0.54004	0.54838	0.55665	0.56486	0.57300	0.58106	0.58905	0.59696	0.60478	0.61252	0.62016	0.62772	0.63518	0.64255	0.64982	0.65700	0.66407	0.67104	0.67791	0.68468	0.69134
21	0.49939	0.50761	0.51578	0.52391	0.53197	0.53998	0.54793	0.55581	0.56362	0.57136	0.57903	0.58662	0.59413	0.60156	0.60890	0.61616	0.62333	0.63042	0.63741	0.64431	0.65112
22	0.45623	0.46422	0.47218	0.48010	0.48798	0.49582	0.50362	0.51136	0.51905	0.52668	0.53426	0.54177	0.54922	0.55661	0.56392	0.57116	0.57833	0.58543	0.59245	0.59939	0.60625
23	0.41041	0.41804	0.42565	0.43324	0.44081	0.44835	0.45586	0.46334	0.47078	0.47818	0.48553	0.49284	0.50010	0.50732	0.51447	0.52158	0.52862	0.53560	0.54253	0.54939	0.55618
24	0.36177	0.36889	0.37601	0.38312	0.39023	0.39732	0.40440	0.41146	0.41850	0.42551	0.43250	0.43946	0.44638	0.45327	0.46012	0.46693	0.47370	0.48043	0.48711	0.49374	0.50033
25	0.31012	0.31658	0.32304	0.32951	0.33599	0.34247	0.34895	0.35542	0.36188	0.36834	0.37478	0.38120	0.38761	0.39400	0.40037	0.40671	0.41303	0.41932	0.42558	0.43181	0.43800
26	0.25529	0.26090	0.26653	0.27217	0.27783	0.28350	0.28918	0.29487	0.30056	0.30626	0.31195	0.31765	0.32334	0.32902	0.33469	0.34036	0.34601	0.35165	0.35727	0.36288	0.36847
27	0.19708	0.20164	0.20623	0.21084	0.21547	0.22012	0.22478	0.22946	0.23416	0.23886	0.24358	0.24830	0.25303	0.25776	0.26250	0.26723	0.27197	0.27671	0.28144	0.28616	0.29089
28	0.13528	0.13857	0.14189	0.14523	0.14860	0.15198	0.15538	0.15880	0.16224	0.16569	0.16916	0.17264	0.17613	0.17963	0.18313	0.18665	0.19018	0.19371	0.19724	0.20078	0.20433
29	0.06966	0.07144	0.07324	0.07506	0.07689	0.07874	0.08059	0.08247	0.08435	0.08625	0.08816	0.09008	0.09201	0.09395	0.09590	0.09785	0.09982	0.10179	0.10377	0.10576	0.10775

Annual Interest Rate

Years Paid	11.25 MB	11.5 MB	11.75 MB	12 MB	12.25 MB	12.5 MB	12.75 MB	13 MB	13.25 MB	13.5 MB	13.75 MB	14 MB	14.25 MB	14.5 MB	14.75 MB	15 MB	15.25 MB	15.5 MB	15.75 MB	16 MB
1	0.99573	0.99596	0.99617	0.99637	0.99656	0.99675	0.99692	0.99709	0.99724	0.99739	0.99753	0.99767	0.99780	0.99792	0.99803	0.99814	0.99825	0.99834	0.99844	0.99852
2	0.99096	0.99142	0.99186	0.99228	0.99268	0.99306	0.99343	0.99377	0.99410	0.99441	0.99471	0.99499	0.99526	0.99551	0.99576	0.99599	0.99620	0.99641	0.99661	0.99679
3	0.98562	0.98634	0.98702	0.98767	0.98830	0.98889	0.98946	0.99000	0.99051	0.99100	0.99147	0.99191	0.99234	0.99274	0.99312	0.99348	0.99383	0.99416	0.99447	0.99477
4	0.97965	0.98064	0.98158	0.98248	0.98334	0.98417	0.98495	0.98570	0.98642	0.98710	0.98775	0.98837	0.98897	0.98953	0.99007	0.99058	0.99107	0.99153	0.99197	0.99239
5	0.97297	0.97425	0.97547	0.97663	0.97775	0.97882	0.97984	0.98082	0.98175	0.98264	0.98349	0.98431	0.98508	0.98583	0.98653	0.98721	0.98785	0.98846	0.98904	0.98960
6	0.96551	0.96708	0.96859	0.97004	0.97143	0.97276	0.97403	0.97526	0.97642	0.97754	0.97861	0.97963	0.98061	0.98155	0.98244	0.98329	0.98411	0.98488	0.98563	0.98633
7	0.95715	0.95904	0.96086	0.96261	0.96429	0.96590	0.96744	0.96893	0.97035	0.97171	0.97301	0.97426	0.97546	0.97660	0.97770	0.97875	0.97975	0.98071	0.98163	0.98250
8	0.94781	0.95003	0.95218	0.95424	0.95622	0.95813	0.95996	0.96172	0.96341	0.96504	0.96659	0.96809	0.96952	0.97090	0.97221	0.97347	0.97468	0.97584	0.97695	0.97801
9	0.93736	0.93993	0.94242	0.94481	0.94711	0.94933	0.95147	0.95353	0.95550	0.95741	0.95923	0.96099	0.96268	0.96430	0.96586	0.96735	0.96879	0.97016	0.97148	0.97275
10	0.92567	0.92860	0.93144	0.93418	0.93682	0.93937	0.94183	0.94420	0.94648	0.94868	0.95080	0.95284	0.95480	0.95669	0.95850	0.96025	0.96193	0.96354	0.96509	0.96658
11	0.91259	0.91590	0.91911	0.92220	0.92520	0.92809	0.93088	0.93358	0.93619	0.93870	0.94112	0.94346	0.94572	0.94789	0.94998	0.95200	0.95394	0.95581	0.95761	0.95934
12	0.89797	0.90166	0.90524	0.90871	0.91207	0.91531	0.91846	0.92150	0.92444	0.92729	0.93003	0.93269	0.93525	0.93773	0.94012	0.94243	0.94465	0.94680	0.94887	0.95086
13	0.88161	0.88569	0.88966	0.89350	0.89723	0.90085	0.90435	0.90775	0.91104	0.91423	0.91732	0.92031	0.92320	0.92599	0.92870	0.93131	0.93384	0.93628	0.93864	0.94092
14	0.86332	0.86779	0.87214	0.87637	0.88047	0.88447	0.88834	0.89211	0.89576	0.89930	0.90274	0.90607	0.90931	0.91244	0.91547	0.91841	0.92126	0.92402	0.92669	0.92927
15	0.84286	0.84771	0.85245	0.85706	0.86155	0.86591	0.87016	0.87430	0.87832	0.88223	0.88603	0.88972	0.89330	0.89678	0.90016	0.90344	0.90662	0.90971	0.91271	0.91561
16	0.81997	0.82520	0.83031	0.83530	0.84016	0.84491	0.84953	0.85403	0.85842	0.86270	0.86686	0.87092	0.87486	0.87870	0.88243	0.88606	0.88959	0.89302	0.89636	0.89960
17	0.79437	0.79997	0.80544	0.81078	0.81601	0.82112	0.82610	0.83097	0.83573	0.84037	0.84489	0.84931	0.85361	0.85781	0.86190	0.86589	0.86977	0.87355	0.87724	0.88082
18	0.76574	0.77167	0.77747	0.78316	0.78872	0.79417	0.79951	0.80473	0.80983	0.81482	0.81970	0.82447	0.82913	0.83368	0.83813	0.84247	0.84671	0.85084	0.85488	0.85882
19	0.73372	0.73993	0.74604	0.75203	0.75790	0.76367	0.76932	0.77486	0.78029	0.78561	0.79082	0.79593	0.80093	0.80582	0.81061	0.81529	0.81987	0.82435	0.82873	0.83302
20	0.69790	0.70436	0.71070	0.71695	0.72309	0.72912	0.73505	0.74087	0.74659	0.75220	0.75771	0.76312	0.76843	0.77363	0.77873	0.78374	0.78864	0.79345	0.79816	0.80278
21	0.65784	0.66446	0.67099	0.67742	0.68376	0.69000	0.69614	0.70219	0.70814	0.71399	0.71975	0.72542	0.73098	0.73645	0.74183	0.74712	0.75231	0.75740	0.76241	0.76733
22	0.61303	0.61973	0.62635	0.63288	0.63933	0.64570	0.65197	0.65817	0.66428	0.67030	0.67623	0.68208	0.68784	0.69351	0.69910	0.70461	0.71002	0.71536	0.72060	0.72577
23	0.56291	0.56958	0.57617	0.58269	0.58915	0.59553	0.60184	0.60807	0.61423	0.62032	0.62633	0.63227	0.63813	0.64392	0.64963	0.65526	0.66082	0.66631	0.67171	0.67705
24	0.50686	0.51334	0.51977	0.52614	0.53246	0.53871	0.54492	0.55106	0.55714	0.56316	0.56912	0.57502	0.58086	0.58663	0.59234	0.59799	0.60357	0.60909	0.61455	0.61994
25	0.44416	0.45028	0.45637	0.46241	0.46842	0.47438	0.48030	0.48618	0.49201	0.49779	0.50353	0.50922	0.51487	0.52046	0.52601	0.53150	0.53695	0.54235	0.54769	0.55299
26	0.37404	0.37958	0.38511	0.39060	0.39608	0.40153	0.40695	0.41234	0.41770	0.42303	0.42833	0.43360	0.43883	0.44403	0.44920	0.45433	0.45943	0.46449	0.46952	0.47450
27	0.29560	0.30031	0.30500	0.30969	0.31436	0.31903	0.32367	0.32831	0.33293	0.33753	0.34211	0.34668	0.35123	0.35576	0.36027	0.36476	0.36923	0.37367	0.37810	0.38250
28	0.20787	0.21142	0.21497	0.21851	0.22206	0.22560	0.22914	0.23268	0.23621	0.23974	0.24326	0.24678	0.25029	0.25380	0.25729	0.26078	0.26426	0.26773	0.27119	0.27465
29	0.10975	0.11175	0.11376	0.11577	0.11779	0.11981	0.12183	0.12385	0.12588	0.12790	0.12993	0.13196	0.13400	0.13603	0.13806	0.14009	0.14212	0.14415	0.14618	0.14821

Table A-8 Loan balance, 15 years.

Annual Interest Rate

Years Paid	6 MB	6.25 MB	6.5 MB	6.75 MB	7 MB	7.25 MB	7.5 MB	7.75 MB	8 MB	8.25 MB	8.5 MB	8.75 MB	9 MB	9.25 MB	9.5 MB	9.75 MB	10 MB	10.25 MB	10.5 MB	10.75 MB	11 MB
1	0.95758	0.95843	0.95927	0.96009	0.96090	0.96170	0.96249	0.96326	0.96402	0.96477	0.96551	0.96623	0.96695	0.96765	0.96834	0.96902	0.96968	0.97034	0.97098	0.97161	0.97224
2	0.91255	0.91419	0.91581	0.91740	0.91898	0.92053	0.92206	0.92357	0.92506	0.92652	0.92797	0.92939	0.93079	0.93217	0.93353	0.93487	0.93619	0.93749	0.93877	0.94002	0.94126
3	0.86474	0.86710	0.86944	0.87174	0.87402	0.87627	0.87850	0.88069	0.88286	0.88500	0.88711	0.88919	0.89125	0.89327	0.89527	0.89725	0.89919	0.90111	0.90300	0.90486	0.90670
4	0.81398	0.81699	0.81996	0.82290	0.82582	0.82870	0.83155	0.83437	0.83716	0.83991	0.84264	0.84533	0.84799	0.85062	0.85322	0.85579	0.85832	0.86082	0.86329	0.86573	0.86814
5	0.76009	0.76365	0.76717	0.77067	0.77413	0.77756	0.78096	0.78433	0.78766	0.79097	0.79424	0.79747	0.80068	0.80385	0.80699	0.81009	0.81317	0.81620	0.81921	0.82218	0.82512
6	0.70288	0.70688	0.71085	0.71479	0.71870	0.72259	0.72644	0.73027	0.73406	0.73782	0.74156	0.74526	0.74893	0.75257	0.75617	0.75974	0.76329	0.76679	0.77027	0.77371	0.77711
7	0.64213	0.64645	0.65075	0.65502	0.65927	0.66349	0.66769	0.67186	0.67601	0.68013	0.68422	0.68829	0.69232	0.69633	0.70031	0.70426	0.70818	0.71207	0.71593	0.71976	0.72356
8	0.57765	0.58214	0.58663	0.59109	0.59554	0.59997	0.60438	0.60877	0.61314	0.61749	0.62182	0.62612	0.63041	0.63467	0.63890	0.64312	0.64731	0.65147	0.65561	0.65972	0.66381
9	0.50918	0.51370	0.51821	0.52271	0.52720	0.53168	0.53615	0.54061	0.54505	0.54948	0.55390	0.55830	0.56268	0.56705	0.57140	0.57574	0.58006	0.58436	0.58864	0.59290	0.59714
10	0.43649	0.44085	0.44521	0.44957	0.45393	0.45828	0.46263	0.46697	0.47131	0.47565	0.47997	0.48429	0.48861	0.49291	0.49721	0.50149	0.50577	0.51003	0.51428	0.51853	0.52276
11	0.35932	0.36332	0.36732	0.37134	0.37535	0.37937	0.38340	0.38742	0.39145	0.39548	0.39952	0.40355	0.40758	0.41161	0.41564	0.41967	0.42370	0.42772	0.43174	0.43575	0.43977
12	0.27738	0.28080	0.28422	0.28765	0.29110	0.29455	0.29802	0.30149	0.30497	0.30845	0.31195	0.31545	0.31895	0.32247	0.32598	0.32951	0.33303	0.33656	0.34010	0.34363	0.34717
13	0.19040	0.19297	0.19555	0.19815	0.20075	0.20337	0.20600	0.20865	0.21130	0.21396	0.21664	0.21932	0.22201	0.22472	0.22743	0.23015	0.23288	0.23561	0.23836	0.24111	0.24386
14	0.09805	0.09949	0.10094	0.10241	0.10388	0.10536	0.10685	0.10835	0.10986	0.11138	0.11290	0.11444	0.11598	0.11753	0.11909	0.12066	0.12223	0.12381	0.12540	0.12700	0.12860

Annual Interest Rate

Years Paid	11.25 MB	11.5 MB	11.75 MB	12 MB	12.25 MB	12.5 MB	12.75 MB	13 MB	13.25 MB	13.5 MB	13.75 MB	14 MB	14.25 MB	14.5 MB	14.75 MB	15 MB	15.25 MB	15.5 MB	15.75 MB	16 MB
1	0.97285	0.97345	0.97404	0.97461	0.97518	0.97574	0.97629	0.97682	0.97735	0.97787	0.97837	0.97887	0.97936	0.97983	0.98030	0.98076	0.98121	0.98165	0.98209	0.98251
2	0.94248	0.94367	0.94485	0.94601	0.94715	0.94826	0.94936	0.95045	0.95151	0.95255	0.95358	0.95458	0.95557	0.95654	0.95750	0.95843	0.95935	0.96025	0.96114	0.96201
3	0.90851	0.91029	0.91205	0.91377	0.91548	0.91715	0.91880	0.92043	0.92203	0.92360	0.92515	0.92667	0.92817	0.92964	0.93109	0.93251	0.93391	0.93529	0.93664	0.93797
4	0.87051	0.87286	0.87517	0.87745	0.87970	0.88192	0.88411	0.88627	0.88839	0.89049	0.89255	0.89459	0.89659	0.89857	0.90051	0.90243	0.90431	0.90617	0.90800	0.90980
5	0.82802	0.83089	0.83372	0.83652	0.83929	0.84202	0.84472	0.84739	0.85002	0.85262	0.85518	0.85771	0.86021	0.86268	0.86511	0.86750	0.86987	0.87220	0.87450	0.87677
6	0.78049	0.78383	0.78713	0.79040	0.79364	0.79684	0.80001	0.80315	0.80624	0.80931	0.81234	0.81553	0.81829	0.82122	0.82411	0.82697	0.82979	0.83258	0.83533	0.83805
7	0.72733	0.73106	0.73476	0.73844	0.74207	0.74568	0.74925	0.75280	0.75630	0.75978	0.76322	0.76662	0.77000	0.77334	0.77664	0.77991	0.78315	0.78635	0.78952	0.79266
8	0.66786	0.67190	0.67590	0.67988	0.68382	0.68774	0.69163	0.69550	0.69933	0.70313	0.70690	0.71064	0.71435	0.71803	0.72168	0.72530	0.72888	0.73244	0.73596	0.73945
9	0.60136	0.60556	0.60973	0.61389	0.61802	0.62213	0.62622	0.63029	0.63433	0.63834	0.64233	0.64630	0.65024	0.65415	0.65804	0.66190	0.66573	0.66954	0.67332	0.67708
10	0.52697	0.53117	0.53536	0.53954	0.54369	0.54784	0.55196	0.55608	0.56017	0.56424	0.56830	0.57234	0.57636	0.58037	0.58435	0.58831	0.59225	0.59617	0.60008	0.60395
11	0.44377	0.44777	0.45176	0.45575	0.45973	0.46370	0.46767	0.47162	0.47557	0.47950	0.48343	0.48734	0.49125	0.49514	0.49902	0.50289	0.50675	0.51059	0.51442	0.51824
12	0.35071	0.35425	0.35780	0.36134	0.36488	0.36843	0.37197	0.37551	0.37905	0.38259	0.38612	0.38965	0.39318	0.39671	0.40023	0.40374	0.40725	0.41076	0.41426	0.41775
13	0.24663	0.24940	0.25217	0.25496	0.25774	0.26054	0.26333	0.26613	0.26894	0.27175	0.27456	0.27737	0.28019	0.28301	0.28583	0.28865	0.29148	0.29431	0.29713	0.29996
14	0.13021	0.13183	0.13345	0.13508	0.13672	0.13836	0.14000	0.14166	0.14332	0.14498	0.14665	0.14832	0.15000	0.15168	0.15337	0.15506	0.15676	0.15846	0.16017	0.16187

Table A-9 Loan balance, 5 years.

Annual Interest Rate

Years	6	6.25	6.5	6.75	7	7.25	7.5	7.75	8	8.25	8.5	8.75	9	9.25	9.5	9.75	10	10.25	10.5	10.75	11
Paid	MB	MB	MB	MB	MB	MB	MB	MB	MB	MB	MB	MB	MB	MB	MB	MB	MB	MB	MB	MB	MB
1	0.82320	0.82413	0.82506	0.82598	0.82690	0.82782	0.82874	0.82965	0.83056	0.83147	0.83237	0.83327	0.83417	0.83506	0.83596	0.83685	0.83773	0.83861	0.83949	0.84037	0.84125
2	0.63549	0.63694	0.63839	0.63984	0.64129	0.64274	0.64418	0.64562	0.64706	0.64849	0.64992	0.65136	0.65278	0.65421	0.65563	0.65705	0.65847	0.65989	0.66130	0.66271	0.66412
3	0.43620	0.43772	0.43923	0.44075	0.44226	0.44378	0.44529	0.44681	0.44832	0.44984	0.45135	0.45287	0.45438	0.45590	0.45741	0.45893	0.46044	0.46196	0.46347	0.46498	0.46650
4	0.22463	0.22568	0.22673	0.22779	0.22884	0.22990	0.23097	0.23203	0.23309	0.23416	0.23523	0.23630	0.23737	0.23844	0.23952	0.24060	0.24167	0.24276	0.24384	0.24492	0.24601

Annual Interest Rate

Years	11.25	11.5	11.75	12	12.25	12.5	12.75	13	13.25	13.5	13.75	14	14.25	14.5	14.75	15	15.25	15.5	15.75	16
Paid	MB	MB	MB	MB	MB	MB	MB	MB	MB	MB	MB	MB	MB	MB	MB	MB	MB	MB	MB	MB
1	0.84212	0.84298	0.84385	0.84471	0.84557	0.84642	0.84728	0.84813	0.84897	0.84981	0.85065	0.85149	0.85232	0.85316	0.85398	0.85481	0.85563	0.85645	0.85726	0.85807
2	0.66552	0.66693	0.66833	0.66972	0.67112	0.67251	0.67390	0.67529	0.67667	0.67805	0.67943	0.68080	0.68218	0.68354	0.68491	0.68627	0.68763	0.68899	0.69035	0.69170
3	0.46801	0.46952	0.47104	0.47255	0.47406	0.47557	0.47708	0.47859	0.48010	0.48161	0.48312	0.48463	0.48613	0.48764	0.48914	0.49065	0.49215	0.49366	0.49516	0.49666
4	0.24709	0.24818	0.24927	0.25036	0.25146	0.25255	0.25365	0.25474	0.25584	0.25694	0.25805	0.25915	0.26025	0.26136	0.26247	0.26358	0.26469	0.26580	0.26691	0.26802